Tensions of Empire

For Rena
with much
love Annie
1/26/97

Tensions of Empire

Colonial Cultures
in a Bourgeois World

Edited by
Frederick Cooper
Ann Laura Stoler

University of California Press
Berkeley / Los Angeles / London

University of California Press
Berkeley and Los Angeles, California

University of California Press
London, England

Copyright © 1997 by The Regents of
the University of California

Library of Congress Cataloging-in-Publication Data

Tensions of empire : colonial cultures in a bourgeois
    world / edited
    by Frederick Cooper, Ann Laura Stoler.
        p. cm.
    Includes bibliographical references and index.
    ISBN 0-520-20540-5 (alk. paper).—ISBN
0-520-20605-3 (pbk. : alk. paper)
    1. History, Modern—19th century. 2. History,
Modern—20th century. 3. Imperialism—History—
19th century. 4. Imperialism—History—20th
century. 5. Europe—History—1789–1900.
6. Europe—History—20th century. 7. Colonies.
I. Cooper, Frederick, 1947–. II. Stoler, Ann Laura.
D359.T4 1997
909.8—dc20
                                    96-32968
                                         CIP

Printed in the United States of America

1 2 3 4 5 6 7 8 9

The paper used in this publication meets the minimum
requirements of American National Standard for
Information Sciences—Permanence of Paper for
Printed Library Materials, ANSI Z39.48-1984

Contents

Preface

Collaborations are produced out of differences as much as synergy, and this one is no exception. Our work together began more than a decade ago when we—an anthropologist of Southeast Asia and a historian of Africa—realized that our research interests were following similar trajectories. We had both written books about the political economy of agricultural labor in two very different colonial settings, Dutch Sumatra and British East Africa. We were struck by how much our efforts at studying labor history from the bottom up pointed us, in different ways, toward looking more carefully at the conflicting agendas and shifting strategies of those who were looking from the top down. Both of us were moving toward analysis of colonial states and shared a sense that we knew far less than we should about their workings, their distinctive qualities, and the people who constituted them.

These concerns led us in several distinct directions: first, toward a recognition that systems of production did not just arise out of the impersonal workings of a world economy but out of shifting conceptual apparatuses that made certain kinds of action seem possible, logical, and even inevitable to state officials, entrepreneurs, missionaries, and other agents of colonization while others were excluded from the realm of possibility; second, toward a recognition that what was imaginable in terms of social policy reflected histories of distant metropoles as well as the immediate opportunities and constraints of conquest while the colonial experience shaped what it meant to be "metropolitan" and "European" as much as the other way around; third, toward a focus on the way colonial states sought knowledge and influence over the ways in which individuals, families, and institutions were reproduced. It was this stretch between the public institutions of the colonial state and the intimate reaches of people's lives that seemed to us to demand more attention. Seeing the differences in the colonial empires and the regions we studied, we wondered about the extent to which colonial histories were bound up in each individual encounter—with the way particular groups resisted, appropriated, refashioned, or adapted the social categories of colonizers—and the extent to which the colonizing projects of different states at different times influenced each other, giving rise to common colonial structures with distinct but related sequences of change. Meanwhile, we became increasingly concerned with the ways in which the very categories through which we learned about colonies—from archives, published accounts, and oral traditions—were constructed and what today's scholars as much as architects of colonial rule had invested in those particular sorts of classifications.

Out of our recognition of common ground came a series of discussions and eventually a conference, sponsored by the Wenner-Gren Foundation, "Tensions of Empire: Colonial Control and Visions of Rule." Selected papers from this conference were published as a special section of *American Ethnologist* in November 1989. Our undertaking coincided with a heightened interest in colonial questions within a variety of disciplines. The scholarship of the 1980s and early 1990s has witnessed a major shift in orientation: from one that focused primarily on the colonized and assumed that what it meant to be European, Western, and capitalist was one and the same to one that questioned the very dualism that divided colonizer from colonized, that sought to identify the processes by which they were mutually shaped in intimate engagement, attraction, and opposition. As our past and present title implies, our goal has been to focus on those tensions as a way of exploring how imperial projects were made possible and vulnerable at the same time. Our introduction to the 1989 collection was more a plea for research and analysis along these lines than an overview of where research stood.

Since then, colonial studies has attracted so much interest that it is time for a critical reassessment as well as additional entreaties to investigate the new possibilities that keep opening up. In the meantime, we have had the good fortune to be able to teach together and have twice offered a graduate course on the history and anthropology of colonialism, and we have worked with dissertation students who had already gravitated toward this topic. This volume includes the work of former students who worked with us to differing degrees (Nancy Hunt, Susan Thorne, and Lora Wildenthal) and other very recent scholarship, but it also includes articles from the 1970s and 1980s that we believe anticipated and helped to focus on the sorts of issues that we feel colonial studies should be engaging today. The present collection thus has very little overlap with what we published in 1989.

There are many things that this collection is not. It makes no attempt at a comprehensive treatment of colonization efforts across time and space, no effort to review the immense literatures within anthropology and history on this subject. We have tried to keep our focus firmly on a set of tensions particular to European imperialism in the nineteenth and twentieth centuries: between the universalizing claims of European ideology and the particularistic nature of conquest and rule, the limitations posed on rulers by the reproduction of difference as much as by the heightened degree of exploitation and domination that colonization entailed. To better focus on this question, we have narrowed our scope to areas of European colonial initiative during this period. This leaves out, most notably, Latin America, where the colonizing impulse occurred earlier and which was decolonizing itself during the nineteenth century. To be sure, many questions raised in this book would resonate among Latin Americanists, including the ways in which creole elites sought to distance themselves from Native Americans while claiming to "civilize them." We do look at the ways in which the practice of slavery in "old" (as well as "new") colonies both epitomizes and contradicts the colonial projects of the nineteenth century, but it is our goal to open discussion of the analytic categories that might be useful in exploring such questions rather than to compare how the dialectic of universal claims and particular power structures played themselves out in new, old, and former colonies. Similarly, we have tried to develop tools useful for the systematic comparison of the empires of different metropolitan states, as well as of different colonies of the same imperial state, without attempting such comparisons ourselves.

Our view of colonialism is that it was shaped in struggle—that thinking about empire as much as the daily efforts to manage it were deeply affected in every dimension by the actions of the "colonized." It is not our intention to make this a book about nationalism or anticolonial movements, nor does it attend especially to the extensive work done by anthropologists on populations that were colonized. Instead we hope the essays bring out the extent to which such collective action was part of a profound and varied encounter that called into question the conceptual frameworks and specific cultural logics of all sides.

Finally, although we think a careful analysis of colonialism has much to say about contemporary politics and culture in societies that experienced colonization—and we spell out some of those implications in our introduction—this is not a book about postcolonial situations.

We would like to acknowledge the sponsorship of the Wenner-Gren Foundation for funding the conference in 1989 that was the focus for our collaborative effort, and also for funding meetings between the two of us (before we both came to roost at Michigan) at which we planned the conference and reflected on its outcome. The University of Michigan—particularly the Departments of History and Anthropology and the programs in Comparative Studies of Social Transformations and the graduate program in History and Anthropology—has provided as stimulating and supportive an environment for teaching and research on this topic as one can reasonably hope for. We have learned much from our students and our colleagues at Michigan, as well as from colleagues elsewhere who attended the Mijas conference or various seminars at which one or the other of us tried out our ideas. We would also like to thank John Bowen, Jane Burbank, John Comaroff, Alice Conklin, Nicholas Dirks, Larry Hirschfeld, Benjamin Orlove, and Luise White for their comments on earlier drafts of the introduction. Our thanks to Javier Morillo-Alicea for preparing the index.

Acknowledgments

Chapter 1, "Liberal Strategies of Exclusion," appeared in *Politics and Society* 18, no. 4 (1990):427–454. Reprinted by permission of Sage Publications.

Chapter 2, "Imperialism and Motherhood," appeared in *History Workshop* 5 (1978):9–65. Reprinted by permission.

Chapter 3, "Of Mimicry and Man," appeared in *October* 28 (1984):125–133. © 1984 Institute for Architecture and Urban Studies and the Massachusetts Institute of Technology. Reprinted by permission.

Chapter 4, "Images of Empire, Contests of Conscience," reproduced by permission of the American Anthropological Association from *American Ethnologist* 16, no. 4 (1989):661–685. Not for further reproduction. Reprinted by permission.

Chapter 5, "Sexual Affronts and Racial Frontiers," appeared in *Comparative Studies in Society and History* 34, no. 3 (1992):514–551. Reprinted with the permission of Cambridge University Press.

Chapter 8, "Le bébé en brousse," appeared in *The International Journal of African Historical Studies* 21, no. 3 (1988):401–432. Reprinted by permission.

Chapter 9, "Tradition in the Service of Modernity," appeared in *Journal of Modern History* 59 (1987):291–316. © 1987 by The University of Chicago. All rights reserved. Reprinted by permission.

Chapter 10, "Educating Conformity in French Colonial Algeria," taken from Part 2, Chapter 3 and Part 3, Chapter 2 of *Instituteurs algériens, 1883–1839*, by Fanny Colonna, published in 1975 by Presses de la Fondation Nationale de Sciences Politiques, Paris. Reprinted by permission.

Chapter 11, "The Difference—Deferral of a Colonial Modernity," appeared in *Subaltern Studies VIII,* edited by David Arnold and David Hardiman, published in 1994 by Oxford University Press, New Delhi. Reprinted by permission.

Chapter 13, "Cars Out of Place," reprinted from *Representations* 43 (1993): 27–50. © 1993 by the Regents of the University of California. Reprinted by permission.

Between Metropole and Colony

Rethinking a Research Agenda

Ann Laura Stoler and Frederick Cooper

Europe's colonies were never empty spaces to be made over in Europe's image or fashioned in its interests; nor, indeed, were European states self-contained entities that at one point projected themselves overseas. Europe was made by its imperial projects, as much as colonial encounters were shaped by conflicts within Europe itself. How one goes about identifying the social and political reverberations between colony and metropole is a difficult task. This collection is built on extensive appraisals that are occurring within history, anthropology, and literary studies and contributes to efforts to revamp both our terrains of inquiry and the very questions that we need to pose. Our focus within the burgeoning scholarship on colonialism is on the contingency of metropolitan-colonial connections and its consequences for patterns of imperial rule.

Conquest, exploitation, and subjugation are old themes in world history. What was new in the Europe of the Enlightenment, of the development of liberalism, of the French Revolution, and of the classical economists was that such processes were set off against increasingly powerful claims in late eighteenth-century political discourse to universal principles as the basis for organizing a polity. Such claims—and competing visions of the universal public good—were bitterly contested within Europe, not least over questions of the social criteria (gender important among them) by which some groups would be included in the body politic while others would not. Ruling elites trying to claim power on the basis of generalized citizenship and inclusive social rights were forced to confront a basic question: whether those principles were applicable—and to whom—in old overseas empires and in newly conquered territory that were now becoming the dependencies of nation-states.

The French Revolution was still being fought in the streets of Paris when the "gens de couleur" of Saint Domingue—property-owning, slave-owning people descended from mixed unions of African slaves and French planters— asserted that the Rights of Man applied to them too. Shortly thereafter, many slaves—mostly first-generation Africans—began to challenge the white plantocracy and the gens de couleur, claiming the Rights of Man extended to them as well. Mobilizing African religious practices in a "revolution within the revolution," they rejected the very premise of French sovereignty and the notions of property that it entailed (James 1963; Fick 1990; Trouillot 1995). The escalating radicalism of the Saint Domingue revolution called into question the idea that slavery could remain a normal part of global commerce well before the antislavery movement in Europe had established its influence. It also raised doubts about the viability and legitimacy of colonization a century and a half before its demise as an accepted part of international politics. But the pioneer of free labor, Great Britain, the victor of a war for independence, the United States, and the country of the Rights of Man, France, did not hail the emergent nation of Haiti, with its newly freed peasantry, as the vanguard of liberation. Instead, their architects turned it into a symbol of backwardness and danger— not unlike what it remains today.

The image of Haiti would haunt French ruling elites even as they reasserted France's imperial aspirations under Napoleon, pushed for the conquest of Algeria in the 1830s, and extended French power to parts of Africa and Southeast Asia toward the end of the century. Haiti haunted British rulers too as they moved in the 1830s to transform the slave regime of its Caribbean islands while firmly maintaining a colonial relationship. The specter of Haiti remained vividly alive in Spain as well as it tried to keep Cuba a sugar-producing slave colony while its empire elsewhere in Latin America disintegrated. Most important, the danger that black Jacobins might demand to be included in an expanding version of citizenship in European empires—as well as the danger that African rebels or creole nationalists might seek to opt *out* of European civilization—raised profound questions about the universality of citizenship and civil rights within Europe. The colonial question was present from the start in such debates, and in transfigured form it remains resilient today.

The "new" colonialism of the nineteenth century certainly built on the experience of rule and the construction of cultural difference of the old empires. Its newness was part of the making of bourgeois Europe, with its contradictions and pretensions as much as its technological, organizational, and ideological accomplishments. The European bourgeoisie aspired to be, as Karl Marx called it, a "universal class," yet it marked its distinctiveness in particular cultural forms. The claims of property-owning classes to wealth and progress via free markets and entrepreneurship were mediated by the role of states in guaranteeing property, putting down the social disorders to which accumulation gave rise, and advancing the cause of specifically national classes.[1] European bourgeoisies valued technological advance, the growing capacity and rationality of European systems of government, and the very idea of social and economic progress and used those ideas to demarcate more clearly than in previous eras the distinctiveness of what it meant to be European. The European bourgeoisie fostered and embraced the idea of citizenship, but also a sense that citizenship was "a faculty to be learned and a privilege to be earned" (Eley 1991: 300; Mehta, this volume).

The colonies of France, England, and the Netherlands—more ambivalently, of Spain and Portugal—did more than reflect the bounded universality of metropolitan political culture: they constituted an imaginary and physical space in which the inclusions and exclusions built into the notions of citizenship, sovereignty, and participation were worked out. Reformist politics in the colonies, as with British or French antislavery, were more than the hypocritical ruses of bourgeois rhetoric. Efforts to define what a dominant class or a government could and could not do helped to create *Homo europeaus* and the social projects for which that entity stood, and thereby clarify who was most fit to rule, at home and abroad.

Eric Hobsbawm (1987: 81) argues that imperialism "dramatized the triumph" of the ruling and middle classes of Europe. But one could argue the other way around: colonial projects also showed up the fundamental contradictions inherent in bourgeois projects and the way universal claims were bound up in particularistic assertions. Joseph Schumpeter (1951) even asserted that modern imperialism represented a militaristic and aristocratic throwback to Europe's past: in the colonies conquest and command took pride of place over market and bureaucratic rationalities. It is more convincing, however, to suggest that the rationalizing, accumulating, and civilizing tendencies of European expansion both built on and could not escape the violence of militarism as that expansion blended coercive and persuasive strategies of racial rule.

Our subtitle, "Colonial Cultures in a Bourgeois World," is thus not meant to imply that the world indeed was remade in the image of European propertied classes or that bourgeois norms became the aspiration of the people of colonies. Our interest is more in how both colonies and metropoles shared in the dialectics of inclusion and exclusion, and in what ways the colonial domain was distinct from the metropolitan one. We hope to explore within the shared but differentiated space of empire the hierarchies of production, power, and knowledge that emerged in tension with the extension of the domain of universal reason, of market economics, and of citizenship.

This introductory essay begins with a consideration of different approaches to colonial studies, arguing that scholars need to attend more directly to the tendency of colonial regimes to draw a stark dichotomy of colonizer and colonized without themselves falling into such a Manichaean conception. Here we explore a most basic tension of empire: how a grammar of difference was continuously and vigilantly crafted as people in colonies refashioned and contested European claims to superiority. We turn next to examine the relationship of knowledge and rule, of how colonizers in the nineteenth and twentieth centuries tried to make the categories through which they classified and surveilled their subjects—from "tribe" or "caste" to the very idea of "India" or "Africa"—into organizing principles of daily life. We take it as well that the colonial contexts in which the disciplines of geography, anthropology, history, and literature developed are a part of the history we are examining. We then look to the tendency in recent scholarship—reversing trends two decades ago—to focus more on the culture of colonialism and its relationship to modernity than on political economy. We argue for a more dynamic relationship between the two approaches, and above all for careful interrogation of the relationship of colonial state to metropolitan state and of the making of nation to the making of empire. We ask as well how the ways in which colonial states organized knowledge constrain the scholar who returns to those archives (oral as well as written) in an attempt to analyze the colonial situation. The reproduction of colonial societies is our next topic, but it is a theme evident throughout the essay. We are concerned here not only with the ways—complicated as they are—in which colonial regimes regulated sexuality and biological reproduction but also with how categories of race, class, and gender helped to define moral superiority and maintain cultural differences that in turn justified different intensities of violence.

A central concern of this essay and one treated most directly in the section on the dynamics of empire questions how one studies empires over time, in relation to one another, and in relation to their component parts. With a founding premise that social transformations are a product of both global patterns and local struggles, we treat metropole and colony in a single analytic field, addressing the weight one gives to causal connections and the primacy of agency in its different parts. Finally, we wonder if our stress on contingency, contested categories, and engagement within colonial states and societies should not lead to a reexamination of recent scholarship on "postcolonial" situations. Even larger and more elusive is the question of how the dynamics of exclusion and inclusion in a bourgeois world continue to play themselves out today.

Colonial Studies and the Ambiguities of Difference

Over the past decades, students of colonialism have taken different issues to be at the heart of the colonial question. To some, colonies were a domain of exploitation where European powers could extract land, labor, and produce in ways that were becoming economically less feasible and politically impossible at home. In this view colonies were places where European merchants could find privileged markets sheltered from cross-national competition and stock those markets with goods produced by slaves, indentured laborers, and, selectively always, free workers (Barratt Brown 1974; Meillassoux 1975). To others, colonies have marked a place beyond the inhibitions of the increasingly bourgeois cultures of Europe (Hyam 1990). In this repressive model of history, the colonies were sites of unfettered economic and sexual opportunity where masculine self-indulgence could be given free vent (Stoler 1995a). Still other analyses have looked at colonies as laboratories of modernity, where missionaries, educators, and doctors could carry out experiments in social engineering without confronting the popular resistances and bourgeois rigidities of European society at home (Rabinow 1989; Wright 1991, this volume; Anderson 1995). Within this frame, the "measures of man" were rationality, technology, progress, and reason—carefully calibrated scales on which Africans and Asians rated low (Adas 1989). Finally, a flood of recent scholars has located in the colonies the Other against whom the very idea of Europeanness was expressed (Said 1978; Todorov 1993; Behdad 1994).

All of these approaches point to key aspects of empire in nineteenth- and twentieth-century Europe, but each can be misleading in specific ways. These "laboratories of modernity," as the authors cited above note, could never produce "controlled conditions" on colonial ground. What Europeans encountered in the colonies was not open terrain for economic domination, but people capable of circumventing and undermining the principles and practices on which extraction or capitalist development was based. The managing of a transition to wage labor in Africa and the West Indies, for example, ran up against the ability of former slaves to make themselves into something other than wage laborers (Cooper 1980; Holt 1990; Cooper et al. 1993; Harries 1994). In Africa and Southeast Asia, the inconsistent efforts of colonial regimes to encourage peasant production at one moment and to subordinate peasants to plantation regimes at another ran up against resiliencies that were neither anticipated nor controllable by French, British, and Dutch colonial states (Mintz 1974; Beinart 1982; Stoler 1985a; Beinart and Bundy 1987; Trouillot 1989; Atkins 1993).

While the colonies were marketed by colonial elites as a domain where colonizing men could indulge their sexual fantasies, those same elites were intent to mark the boundaries of a colonizing population, to prevent those men from "going native," to curb a proliferating mixed-race population that compromised their claims to superiority and thus the legitimacy of white rule (Ballhatchet 1980; Stoler 1991). In colonial societies as in Europe, "racial survival" was often seen to be precariously predicated on a strict adherence to cultural—and specifically gendered—prescriptions (Wildenthal, this volume; Stoler, this volume; Inglis 1975; van Onselen 1982; Knapman 1986).

Other approaches to the colonial encounter have come from anthropologists and historians concerned with the consequences of conquest for the colonized and the impact of physical and cultural violence on indigenous social and economic organization. Despite anthropology's successful efforts to move away from the isolated community studies of earlier generations, it has been harder than expected to get beyond treating colonialism as an abstract process, to take apart the shifts and tensions within colonial projects with the same precision devoted to analyzing the actions of those who were made their objects (Fabian 1983; Stoler 1989; Comaroff, this volume). For their part, historians of Africa and Asia have tried, since the 1960s, to counter the assumptions of an earlier tradition of imperial history by seeking to establish the complexity of non-Western reactions to European political and economic dominance (e.g., Boahen 1987; and for a review, Cooper 1994). Both disciplines have assumed more coherence to colonial enterprises than they warrant. Neither discipline has sufficiently explored how the rulers of empire reexamined their own hegemony and altered their visions when faced with cleavages within their own camp and challenges from the people they were trying to rule.

Colonial regimes were neither monolithic nor omnipotent. Closer investigation reveals competing agendas for using power, competing strategies for maintaining control, and doubts about the legitimacy of the venture. It is not clear that the idea of ruling an empire captivated European publics for more than brief periods or that a coherent set of agendas and strategies for rule was convincing to a broad metropolitan population, any more than the terms in which regimes articulated their power inspired awe or conviction among a broad range of the colonized.[2] Nor is it altogether clear how those we have assumed were reliable "agents of empire"—planters, low-level bureaucrats, and subordinate members of colonial armies—participated in those ventures (Heussler 1963, 1983, 1987; Arnold 1979, 1983; Kuklick 1979; Ballhatchet 1980; Ming 1983; Conklin forthcoming).

Identifying the competing agendas of colonizers and analyzing how cultural boundaries were maintained are not academic exercises in historical refinement. Social taxonomies allowed for specific forms of violence at specific times. How a person was labeled could determine that a certain category of persons could be killed or raped with impunity, but not others (Taussig 1984; Stoler 1985b; Breman 1989; Scully 1995). It could open or close down the possibilities for marriage, housing, education, or pensions. At the same time, the criteria used to determine who belonged where underscored the permeability of boundaries, opening possibilities for assertion among interstitial groups of "mixed-bloods" and "poor whites" as well as those more squarely identified as "the colonized." The idea of an indigenous "response" or "resistance" to an imperialist initiative—a favorite among scholars since the 1960s—does not capture the dynamics of either side of the encounter or how those sides were drawn (Ortner 1995; Stoler, forthcoming, b). The ambiguous lines that divided engagement from appropriation, deflection from denial, and desire from discipline not only confounded the colonial encounter, it positioned contestation over the very categories of ruler and ruled at the heart of colonial politics.

The most basic tension of empire lies in what has become a central, if now obvious, point of recent colonial scholarship: namely, that the otherness of colonized persons was neither inherent nor stable; his or her difference had to be defined and maintained. That analytic opening, however, has not focused as much as one might expect on what the quotidian repercussions of those moving categories were. Social boundaries that were at one point clear would not necessarily remain so. In pursuing a "civilizing mission" designed to make colonized populations into disciplined agriculturalists or workers and obedient subjects of a bureaucratic state, colonial states opened up a discourse on the question of just how much "civilizing" would promote their projects and what sorts of political consequences "too much civilizing" would have in store. As Fanny Colonna (this volume) has argued for French educational policy in colonial Algeria, the criterion of an "excellent" student was not to be "taken for a Frenchman" but was one's ability to function as a balanced intermediary, neither too removed from Kabyle society nor too close to French norms. Different approaches to such questions shaped the self-image of colonial regimes: British officials congratulated themselves and mocked the French by saying their own goal was to create better Africans while the French wanted to make Africans into Frenchmen. They were wrong on both counts: the Africans British officials wanted to make were of their own imagining, while French policy makers were highly ambivalent about how French their subjects could or should be (Cooper 1996). More curious still, Dutch officials in the Dutch East Indies made much the same argument, but in reference to a population that was not obviously "indigenous." They had in mind the children of European fathers and Asian mothers, for whom a carefully constructed educational curriculum and vocational environment would be devised to make them into what one Dutch official called "perfected natives, not imitation Europeans" (Stoler, forthcoming, a).

Colonial efforts at social engineering did not constitute the whole story. They do however provide entry points to question how people who lived inside those categories could turn them around. Luise White (this volume) shows that Africans took seriously European pretensions to technological and medical knowledge—and the new kinds of labor that imported technologies entailed—but interpreted them in idioms of power and danger that colonial officials could not grasp. In the Philippines as much as in Africa, people heard what Christian missionaries had to say but scrambled the message—sometimes finding in the mission community something valuable and meaningful to them, sometimes using their mission education to gain secular advantage, sometimes insisting that their conversion should entitle them to run the religious organizations themselves, and sometimes dismantling both doctrine and organization to build a religious edifice or even a revolutionary movement that was wholly new, neither the Christianity of Europe nor a recognizable variant of local religious practices. Vincent Rafael (1993) explores Tagalog "containment" of missionary discourse in the Philippines and Reynaldo Ileto (1979) examines the ways in which Spanish Christian passion plays and other devotional writings were reworked by those nonelite members of the population mobilizing against Spanish rule (see also Beidelman 1982; Comaroff 1985; Kipp 1990; Comaroff and Comaroff 1991; Keesing 1992; Chretien 1993; Mbembe 1993).

As Karen Fields (1985) shows, offshoots of Christian missionizing in Africa, notably Watchtower, were a direct affront to colonial officials' well-laid plans. Watchtower participants constructed religious networks and beliefs that stressed the utter irrelevance of the legitimizing structure that officials had attempted to put in place, one built around the idea of traditional authority that was negotiated with African chiefs under the system of indirect rule. Edward Said (1993) has made a related point about colonial intellectuals: they both used their own "civilized" participation in education and commerce to expose the hypocrisies of colonial rule and insisted that indigenous cultures offered viable alternatives to the norms of European bourgeois culture (see also Chakrabarty, this volume; Vaillant 1990; Appiah 1992). Colonial students, meanwhile, challenged representations of indigenous cultures as well as European claims to technological and scientific superiority: Vietnamese students in France, for instance, openly protested the idealized portrayal of their own society at the 1931 Colonial Exhibition in Paris (Lebovics 1992; Brocheux and Hémery 1995).

Paul Gilroy (1993) has shown that various expressions of popular culture as well as literary and philosophical productions coming out of the African diaspora—in Africa, the Americas, and Europe—evince a complex engagement with "Western" culture entailing more than either its repudiation or an attempt to build an "authentic" alternative. He argues that slavery, colonialism, and racism gave those who experienced them a vantage point on modernity that starkly revealed the limits to economic progress, political participation, and social inclusiveness. The "black Atlantic" became a critical transformative site of that modernity, not least because of the ambiguous encounter of the African diaspora with it.

The Manichaean world of high colonialism that we have etched so deeply in our historiographies was thus nothing of the sort. How to demarcate the boundaries of the "colonizers" and analyze how those boundaries were produced is proving as elusive a task as probing the multiple layers of oppositional discourse and politics. As we engage colonial archives further, we see how much protracted debate, how much political and cultural energy went into defining dichotomies and distinctions that did not have the predicted effects. Concubinary arrangements between European men and Asian women that were condoned by the Dutch East Indies state buttressed some of the hierarchies of rule but produced domestic milieus and cultural styles that subverted others (Taylor 1983). The point is that these colonial states were often in the business of defining an order of things according to untenable principles that themselves undermined their ability to rule.

This is not to suggest that our focus on the blurring of categories should reduce the discourse on racial fixities to a fiction alone. We are interested in understanding why Manichaean dichotomies had such sustaining power in the face of such obvious hybridity and variation. Why did so many people—contemporary actors, not just latter-day historians—subscribe to divisions out of sync with the quotidian experiences that they shared?

It would be misleading to think that the intellectual efforts that set indigenous cultures starkly against European ones were those of colonizing elites alone. John Pemberton (1995) points to the way in which a discourse on "Java" flourished in Javanese texts in spite of colonial conditions—as well as because of them. Nancy Florida (1995) similarly shows—via a very different set of texts and methodologies—how contemporary understandings of a "pure high Javanese culture" were produced out of the joint efforts of Dutch Javanologists and conservative native elites (see also Chatterjee 1989 on elite writing on British/Indian difference). In analyzing this distinction making, we need to find ways of attending to its force—understanding how this process arose within colonial situations—without being caught up in such dichotomies ourselves (see also Bhabha, this volume).

One thing is clear. It does us no service to reify a colonial moment of binary oppositions so that we can enjoy the postcolonial confidence that our world today is infinitely more complicated, more fragmented and more blurred. Hybridities of richly varied sorts existed not only in the French and Spanish Caribbean but in more starkly binary racial contexts. As early as 1848, Dutch authorities in the Indies worried openly that creole whites saw themselves more as part of a new "Indische fatherland," and sometimes even as "world citizens," rather than as partisans of a Netherlands homeland and Dutch rule. In South Africa in the 1930s, the Carnegie Commission openly tackled the fear that poor whites shared more of the habitus of their nonwhite co-workers than that of their middle-class European compatriots (Albertyn 1932). We need to think through not only a colonial history that appears as Manichaean but a historiography that has invested in that myth as well.

As we begin to look at the similarities and differences in social policy in Europe and the world it made colonial, it is clear that the resonance and reverberation between European class politics and colonial racial policies was far more complicated than we have imagined. Sidney Mintz (1985) has argued, for example, that the demand in Europe for sugar produced in the colonies was crucial to European working-class formation. If there were places where the European language of class provided a template for how the colonized racial "residuum" was conceived, sometimes the template worked the other way around. The language of class itself in Europe drew on a range of images and metaphors that were racialized to the core (Thorne, this volume; Comaroff, this volume; Comaroff and Comaroff 1992; Stoler 1995a). How the hierarchies of race and class played off one another had profound consequence: Edmund

Morgan (1975) shows that the desire of Virginia's planters in the eighteenth century to challenge British authority and build a republican ideology with appeal beyond their own class led them to break apart the ambiguous and overlapping connections among indentured white servants and black slaves. In this variant of liberalism, class—for whites—was being made into a relationship of co-optation and alliance while race became a line of exclusion far clearer than it had been before.

If at any one moment one could plausibly argue that the attitudes and policies of a metropolitan ruling class toward lower classes, local speech, and regional social practices in Europe were comparable to attitudes and policies toward colonized people, the exceptionalism of the colonial domain was more marked at specific times. The wave of nineteenth-century colonizations prompted Europe's ruling classes to reaffirm their own distinctiveness at the very moment when European states were emphasizing incorporation of parts of the popular classes into some form of citizenship and recognition of their accepted place in the polity (Brubaker 1992). But such incorporations were always bounded. What is striking is how much the consolidation of bourgeois power at home and abroad drew on a polyvalent discourse of civility that emphasized different criteria for its measure and at different moments could move state policy in opposite directions.

The inclusionary impulse was not confined to metropolitan Europe alone. Colonial projects were fundamentally predicated on a tension between notions of incorporation and differentiation that were weighted differently at different times (Sider 1987; Mehta, this volume; Stoler, this volume). This should not be construed as the difference between a liberal impulse, on the one hand, and a conservative reaction to it, on the other. Social reform policies were invariably derived from a tenuous balance between programs that would bind the interests of specific groups to the colonial state and policies that would maintain a range of cultural distinctions designed to contain and curtail the aspirations of those to be ruled (Fasseur 1993; Colonna, this volume).

Racial thinking was an organizing principle and a powerful rhetorical theme, but not always in the blatant ways that the common focus on scientific racism might lead us to expect. For the term ''race'' was shunned as often as it was applied. This is not to suggest that the criterion of race disappeared with an official rhetoric in which it was condemned. In the Netherlands Indies, for example, just when the ''criterion of race'' as a means to establish European equivalent status was to be removed from the Indies constitution in 1920, a subtle range of cultural distinctions (proficiency in Dutch by the age of seven, upbringing in a ''European milieu'') secured the same protections of privilege on which racial discrimination would continue to rest (Brugmans 1938; Stoler, this volume). Similarly, when French and British policy makers finally convinced themselves in the 1940s that Africans could come out of their ''tribal'' milieu and become disciplined workers, enterprising farmers, or responsible civil servants, their condemnation of the cultural backwardness of those Africans who had not made the transition took on a harshness not so evident in the days of "indirect rule" (Cooper 1996). That race underwrote the distinctions of rule long after racial equality and development were hailed as tenets of late colonial states is clear: the more interesting observation is how much what we now take to be the principles of "cultural racism" were honed as part of the intimate workings of empire in debates over domestic arrangements, the upbringing of small children, early pedagogy, and language use that are still seen as sites of subversion and threats to the "interior frontiers" of the United States and European nations today (Stoler, forthcoming, a).

Knowledge and Rule

While Michel Foucault's insistence on the inextricable relationship between knowledge and power has had a major impact on the last decade of colonial scholarship, such questions were not prompted by him alone.[3] Bernard Cohn's work (collected in 1987) has long emphasized the conscious way in which a model colonial regime—the Raj—went about creating the categories in which "British" and "Indian" were to define themselves. A large colonial bureaucracy occupied itself, especially from the 1860s, with classifying people and their attributes, with censuses, surveys, and ethnographies, with recording transactions, marking space, establishing routines, and standardizing practices. The total effect exceeded the sum of each appropriation of information: colonial regimes were trying to *define* the constituents of a certain kind of society, even as they embedded that act of creation within a notion that society was a natural occurrence and the state a nonpartisan regulator and neutral observer (see also Appadurai 1992). Self-conscious projects of collecting and organizing knowledge could be applied as a virtual package in different parts of different empires: the Dutch East Indies, Indochina, and less systematically in much of Africa. In the Philippines under American colonial rule, knowledge and surveillance of disease and of subversion went hand in hand (Ileto 1992). Regimes sought to tame the visual as well (Mitchell 1988; Wright, this volume; Bancel, Blanchard, and Gervereau 1993; Dirks 1994).

"Caste" in India and "tribe" in Africa were in part colonial constructs, efforts to render fluid and confusing social and political relationships into categories sufficiently static and reified and thereby useful to colonial understanding and control. But they could not be simply colonial categories: their elaboration required the knowledge of elders or pandits who were sought to manipulate the creation of knowledge for their own purposes (Dirks 1987; Hobsbawm and Ranger 1983; Chanock 1985). These competing visions did not necessarily create and naturalize the subunits of control: the very ideas of "India" and "Africa" were homogenizing and essentializing devices useful both for imperial definitions of what it was they ruled and for nationalists to claim a broad domain that their cultural knowledge qualified them to govern (Mudimbe 1988; Chatterjee 1993; Kaviraj 1993).

Visions of empire were created and clarified out of metropolitan discourses as well as by those fashioned in the colonies themselves. The relationship between Social Darwinism, ethnology, and colonial projects has been the most extensively and carefully explored (Rich 1984; Stocking 1987; Rich 1990). Other academic and popular discussions have received less attention. The class politics of Europe in the late nineteenth century gave rise to a profusion of debates by scientists, social reformers, and state agents over the biological and moral nature of the rapidly expanding European working-class populations (Stedman Jones 1971; Stepan 1982; Noordman 1989). As elites worried over the political mobilization of the underclasses, so did the bourgeoisie rivet their attention on the forms of child rearing, sexual standards, medical care, and moral instruction by which they would distinguish themselves and reproduce the social conditions for continued rule at "home" (Davin, this volume; Stuurman 1983; Regt 1984; Bock and Thane 1991; Koven and Michel 1993). One task is to analyze how (and when) the debates and terminologies of medicine, urban planning, social welfare, and industrial relations fed off one another and borrowed one another's idioms, without assuming that they were functionally compatible or that they reinforced imperial policy in all places and at all times (Arnold 1988; Adas 1989; Packard 1989; Rabinow 1989; Tolen 1991; Vaughan 1991).

Some metropolitan discourses resonated in the colonies; others did not. Debates over the reproductive advantages of miscegenation, for example, rarely surfaced in Asia and Africa as much as did the contrary theories arguing that racial mixing would result in the degeneration and disappearance of those whites who stayed in the colonies "too long" (Union Géographique Internationale 1938; Price 1939). The interesting question is how much the racist tendencies in medical science, eugenics in particular, received new credibility in the colonies and then reverberated at home.[4]

How European scientific knowledge—as well as political philosophy— would articulate with specific visions of empire is not self-evident. Leading French socialists justified the taking and holding of colonies in light of their vision of attaining a just, socialist society via a path that indigenous peoples, confined to their primitive or precapitalist worlds, could not by themselves follow (Liauzu 1982; Wall 1986).[5] Still, certain relativist social theories— arguments that each people has its own integrity, its own values, and its own path to the future—could be put to perhaps even more insidious uses. Cultural relativism provided the intellectual justification for segregated schools and housing, sexual sanctions, and ultimately, as in South Africa, for apartheid (Rich 1986; Gordon 1988; Ashforth 1990). Our questions are not directed at the intrinsic merits of universalizing or relativizing ideologies but at the ways in which they were harnessed and mobilized for particular political projects by colonial elites.

The struggle over whose knowledge was to prevail was unequal but not without its battles. Partha Chatterjee (1989) and Dipesh Chakrabarty (this volume) both argue that Indian (male) nationalist writers of the late nineteenth century conceded the realm of economics to British pandits but claimed knowledge of how to organize the domestic domain for Indian (middle-class) women and the spiritual domain for themselves. On the other hand, when colonial regimes were beginning to concede in the 1940s and 1950s that indigenous leaders were capable of running states and organizing economies, they did so in terms of "modernization" and "Westernization"—and a European-based concept of how states collected and used knowledge—that discredited the validity of African and Asian cultural epistemologies. Such struggles over what counts as knowledge are political ones, not just part of a wider battle, but a conflict over the nature of the battlefield itself.

The production of colonial knowledge occurred not only within the bounds of nation-states and in relationship to their subject colonized populations but also transnationally, across imperial centers. To what extent—and by what processes—did the knowledge of individual empires become a collective imperial knowledge, shared among colonizing powers? Was there ever a language of domination, crossing the distinct metropolitan politics and linguistic barriers of French, English, Spanish, German, and Dutch? Should we be looking toward a "modular" model of colonialisms as Benedict Anderson (1983) has suggested for the origins of nationalism? How much did the international congresses accompanying the world and colonial expositions that proliferated throughout Europe in the late nineteenth century provide a site not only to construct and affirm shared notions of race and civility but also to secure the relationship between the forging of a consensual notion of *Homo europeaus* and heightened feelings of national belonging at the same time?[6]

It has become widely accepted that imperial expansion was deeply implicated in the reconfiguration of European culture and science in the nineteenth and twentieth centuries: attention to the ways in which European literary forms have at once effaced empire and been shaped by it is at the charged political center of an important trend in contemporary literary criticism (Said 1978, 1993; Miller 1985; Spivak 1988; Ashcroft, Griffiths, and Tiffin 1989; Eagleton, Jameson, and Said 1990; Lowe 1991; Mills 1991; Ahmad 1992; Mellman 1992; Suleri 1992; Behdad 1994). Private collection of "primitive" art has long signaled the distinctions of a bourgeois home while museum collections continue to celebrate the preserving and ordering of the Others' cultural artifacts as part of the high culture of a European public sphere (Stocking 1985; Clifford 1988; Price 1989; Torgovnick 1990; Karp 1991). Others have argued that the modes of social discipline and discourses of sexuality that have defined the European bourgeois order derive from "models, inspirations and testing grounds" of imperial ventures (Pratt 1992: 36, Stoler 1995a).

While the disciplines of geography and anthropology helped to make the expanding world intelligible and manageable, the relationship of disciplinary knowledge and colonial rule was an ambiguous one. Geography brought the same conceit of science to domestic state building—making terrain, roads, sites of possible military conflicts, and resources knowable quantities—as to overseas ventures. But it would be more accurate to say that geographers' ways of looking at the world were shaped in the same historical process as state expansionism, rather than that the discipline grew up to serve the colonizing state (Pyenson 1993; Godlewska 1994).

Moreover, geographers and other social scientists disagreed among themselves. The turn-of-the-century debate among colonial geographers over whether the colonial world should be seen as a space to be categorized and analyzed or as a space to be remade for the benefit of the imperial economy had repeated manifestations among social scientists.[7] The question of whether the impoverished economies of Africa or Asia fell under the same universal laws as the rich economies of Western states or whether they should be condemned as "backward" or celebrated as "natural" appeared in a Dutch debate over "dualism" in the 1930s and manifested itself in a variety of ways from the 1940s until today (Hirschman 1981; Kahn 1993).

When confronted with the complexity of the task of rule, colonial elites called on the sort of knowledge anthropologists could supply, and that demand affected the growth of the profession (Stocking 1987, 1995). Yet anthropologists did not always supply the kind of knowledge that fit the neat administrative categories (Vincent 1990). For they also opened debates on the integrity or adaptability of particular indigenous societies that officials did not always welcome; sometimes their very presence revealed settler practices and government ineptitudes that regimes did not necessarily want discussed. Even if anthropologists often gave theoretical vigor and intellectual respectability to a world divided into colonized "tribes" and "traditional" cultures versus civilized nations, they often complicated the picture of which they were a part (Asad 1973; Brown 1979; Stocking 1991, 1995; Moore 1993).

Lest one imagine that decolonization always had a liberating effect on scholarship—and studies of the diversity and dynamism of African and Asian cultures have indeed flourished since the 1960s—one should remember that this new knowledge was often compartmentalized and confined even as it was produced. The 1950s witnessed a division of labor in the social sciences in which the universals of social theory were privileged. Sociology, political science, and economics most often took notice of Africa or Asia insofar as those regions conformed to the seemingly universal course of development and modernization. When modernization theory failed to stand the tests of empirical analysis, those disciplines largely pulled back from investigation of "exceptional" regions, leaving them to the allegedly particularistic disciplines of anthropology and history or to "area studies" in the era of decolonization and cold war.[8]

While the effort in this volume to underscore that metropole and colony, colonizer and colonized, need to be brought into one analytic field in some respects sets out a new agenda, in other ways it merely draws attention to a case that others have made earlier and well. Not least of all by George Balandier (1951), who cogently argued that the colonial situation had to be understood in its own right as the cultural and political construction of a particular moment and that those doing the colonizing were part of the story. Anthropologists, he insisted, could not assume that the "tribes" they studied had a pristine existence; they were part of a colonial system based on power, exploitation, and race. His argument owed something to the radical intellectuals Balandier had met in Dakar and the misery he had observed in Brazzaville; political mobilization against colonial authorities was making colonial realities hard to avoid. Yet his argument did not catch on at the time. Progressive social scientists of the 1950s were coming to share Balandier's belief that colonial rule in Africa or Asia was morally unacceptable, but they were generally more interested in showing that non-European peoples were capable of moving toward modernity than in analyzing a colonial system which they were ready to consign to the past. In the triumph of developmentalist social science in the 1950s, colonialism was at best a side issue. Anthropologists and, later, historians were willing to complicate the picture with a focus on the diversity of local contexts, but the framework often remained the same.[9] "Tradition" and "modernization" were the keywords of postwar scholarship and of the rulers of postcolonial states; the production and investments in those categories went largely unexamined while colonialism was reduced to a problematic "legacy" of racialism and hierarchy. Some anthropological research complicated that story, most notably Peter Worsley's (1957) study of cargo cults, which he understood not as a primitive and "irrational" curiosity but as a reasoned response to capitalist pressures and colonial demands.

For leftist scholars who began to critique the developmentalist framework in the 1970s, colonial issues were folded into the problem of global capitalism.[10] The sophisticated and subtle treatment that those such as Talal Asad and his colleagues (1973) offered concerning the connections between anthropology and colonial rule was taken up in some limited ways but not in others. While anthropology eagerly sought to show the effects of colonialism on contemporary populations, the ethnographic subject remained a specific Other—the colonized. Anthropologists rarely sought to examine the very making of that category itself (Stoler 1989). It was some years before Bernard Cohn's (1980) call to examine colonized and colonial within the same analytic field was reflected in the kind of topics scholars chose to investigate.

But the marginal treatment of the colonial situation had other roots that reflected the awkward divide in anthropology between those committed to a political economic analysis of colonialism and those who sought a cultural reading of it. Some such as Eric Wolf and Sidney Mintz as early as the 1950s had made concerted efforts to locate the specific ways in which colonialism affected the social relations in which people lived (Wolf 1959; Mintz 1974). What went under the rubric of Julian Steward's "cultural ecology" during this heyday of McCarthyism was in many ways the closest permissible thing to a culturally informed political economy of colonialism in which the state itself was conceived as an ethnographic unit of analysis (Steward 1956; Roseberry 1987; Vincent 1990). Still, even when colonialism was given considerable causal power, as in Clifford Geertz's *Agricultural Involution* (1968), its internal dynamics were rarely interrogated: in Geertz's case his very explanation of Java's poverty was strikingly reminiscent of "dualistic" notions of the economy devised by and so dear to Dutch colonial economists. It was only decades later that both Wolf and Mintz were in different ways to bring Europe and its colonized populations as well as working-class formation in Europe back into that story (Wolf 1982; Mintz 1985). But some argue that those later efforts skewed the balance between metropole and periphery precipitously in favor of the metropole again. According to Fernando Coronil (1995), both Mintz's and Wolf's accounts of the impact of capitalist production in the colonies leaves "all agency . . . located at one end." There is, however, the other case to make: namely, that European agency too often remains undifferentiated, assumed, and unexplored. Even in the wake of Edward Said's (1978) powerful critique of orientalism that prompted a wider impulse to examine the making of the ethnographic Other, anthropology still remained surprisingly silent about the plurality of competing visions by which Europeans in the colonies fashioned their distinctions, conjured up their "whiteness," and reinvented themselves.

Part of the problem is that the task is unwieldy and not easily carried out. For if we are to do an anthropology of empire, we can no longer confine ourselves to the units of analysis on which we have relied. We need to create, as Jean Comaroff and John Comaroff (1992) suggest, new archives of our own. We must carve out a new terrain of history writing that does more than match up shifts in the intellectual political history of Europe to their "expression" in local colonial projects that emanated from England, Holland, and France. We need to understand more fully how both these civilizing missions provided new sites for clarifying a bourgeois order, new definitions of social welfare, new ways in which the discourses and practices of inclusion and exclusion were contested and worked out.

What probably did more than anything else to open up the subject of colonialism again was growing disillusionment with the entire range of pro-gressivist ideologies. A critical reading of colonial texts gradually became a way of showing that cultural domination, racial exclusivity, and violence were written into modernizing, nationalist, and socialist projects. Anthropologists, among others, drew on their ethnographic expertise to document the economic inequities that the Green Revolution and other development initiatives exacerbated and produced (Gross 1970; Franke 1973). Much of the impetus for this critique came from intellectuals of former colonies: the Subaltern Studies group's simultaneous critique of Indian nationalism, Marxism, and the categories of colonial knowledge was one of the most astute and influential (Guha and Spivak 1988). In other ways, studies of colonialism provided one field among many in which to study how disciplines created their authority and their categories of knowledge. Feminist scholarship too challenged the facile premises that "everyone" had access to political inclusion and benefited from development initiatives.[11]

The opening of colonial studies in the 1980s has been prompted by other shifts as well. The historic turn in the social sciences coupled with the new weight given to cultural Marxism and discursive analysis have played no small part in making colonial studies one of the prime sites where the political nature of cultural projects could be minutely explored, where the colonial production of knowledge could be tracked, and where the cultural embeddedness of political economy could be worked out (Taussig 1980; Vincent 1982; Fagan 1984; Comaroff 1985; Kelly 1991; Gordon 1992).[12] If the colonial manipulation of space has been a central theme of analysis (White 1990a; Mitchell 1988; Wright, this volume), attention to the politics of temporality, historicity, and memory has been marked as well (Rosaldo 1980; Sahlins 1981, 1985; Fabian 1983; Price 1983a, 1983b; Ware 1992; Hoskins 1993). Feminist scholars in particular have challenged us to look at new domains in which colonial states intervened and where their projects were carried out (Gailey 1987; Silverblatt 1987; Linnekin 1990). More concerted attention to the "domesticating" impulse of European rule has prompted a rethinking of what we have taken to be the most salient representations of European authority and its key technologies (Chaudhuri 1988; White 1990a; Stoler 1991, 1995b; Summers 1991; Hansen 1992; Jolly 1993; McClintock 1995; Rafael forthcoming; Hunt, this volume).

Colonialism has come under new sorts of scrutiny as the production of what constitutes scientific, ethnographic, and colonial knowledge has been given more sustained consideration. Discrepancies in stories Europeans told themselves at different historical moments make it more difficult to posit a unified European point of view (Laffey 1977; Stoler 1985b; Guha and Spivak 1988; Thomas 1994). In examining these competing claims, it is clear that the colonial archives on which we are so dependent are themselves cultural artifacts, built on institutional structures that erased certain kinds of knowledge, secreted some, and valorized others (Gordon 1988; Kahn 1993; Trouillot 1995). We are confronted with the obvious fact that every document in a colonial archive—no matter how ignorant its author was of indigenous society or how unimportant his ideas were to future policy—is layered with the received account of earlier events and the cultural semantics of a political moment (Stoler, forthcoming, a). We cannot just *do* colonial history based on our given sources; what constitutes the archive itself, what is excluded from it, what nomenclatures signal at certain times are themselves internal to, and the very substance of, colonialism's cultural politics (Guha 1988; Rappaport 1994). Ethnographies of empire must find some balance between the universalizing idioms of rule and the cultural specificity of their content.

These impulses for rethinking colonial studies should in no way reverse the trends of the 1960s and 1970s toward a more intense and nuanced analysis of peoples whose histories are made up of more than the fact that they were colonized. The continuing challenge is to bring these scholarships together. Focus on the contingencies and contradictions of colonial rule emphasizes that political possibilities do not just lie in grand oppositions but in the interstices of power structures, in the intersection of particular agendas, in the political spaces opened by new and renewed discourses and by subtle shifts in ideological ground.

Colonial States: Political Economy and Imperial Culture

Twenty years ago, the colonial state and the imperial economy would have been the point of departure for most collections such as this one. Their importance has not diminished. Current academic fashions risk privileging the idea of nation over state institutions or of the power of Europe's claims to represent ''modernity'' over the tedious analysis of capital export, transnational corporations, and international commerce and banking.[13] Clearly this is not an either/or issue. The current focus on the cultural and representational features of colonial authority powerfully underscores that we can understand little about the political economy of colonialism without attending to culturally constructed and historically specific notions of ''labor,'' of ''trade,'' of ''freedom,'' and of the practices and perceptions in which relations of domination were lived (Holt 1990). But the cultural work in which states engage and the moralizing missions in which they invest are discursive fields both grounded in and constitutive of specific relations of production and exchange. While this may seem too obvious a point to belabor, the sharp discursive turn in colonial studies away from class analysis (induced in part by the reductionisms that it so frequently entailed) would suggest that it is not.

Those who have sought to single out the ''colonial economy'' as a distinct entity generally focus on two elements: a mercantilist concept of trade, through which the metropole assures privileged access to markets and raw materials by restricting the colony's ability to trade freely with all partners, and a conception of the colony as a domain in which a state can act in particular ways, especially by using coercion to obtain land for metropolitan settlers and labor for their enterprises. Within this functional frame, racial distinctions serve to channel different peoples into specific economic roles.[14]

World systems theory put the colonial economy in a wider context: colonization was one aspect of the development of a capitalist world system, through which the "core" allocated itself the more complex and lucrative productive processes—executed through the higher form of wage labor—and the "periphery" was allocated the task of producing primary commodities through slavery or coerced cash crop production (Amin 1974; Wallerstein 1974–1989; Aymard 1982). Its flaws have become familiar (Bose 1990; Cooper et al. 1993): inability to analyze agency, a functionalist mode of reasoning that in some formulations ends in tautology, inability to explain why some peripheral regions broke out of their status and others did not. The theory's assumption of passivity within colonial economies has been amply refuted by research in different parts of the world.

Particular interests certainly profited from the restrictions of colonial economies, such as less competitive metropolitan industries, banks, and settlers given below market labor costs. There is no question that economic *motivations* played a large part in colonization. But numerous efforts to calculate benefits to metropolitan capitalism do not suggest a strong case that colonial rule made a substantial long-term difference to accumulation in France or Great Britain; the "imperialism of free trade" may well have been the better bargain. In fact, the very ability of colonial firms to get help from the state in extracting cheap labor or low-cost commodities from indigenous communities led to what some metropolitan leaders themselves perceived (by the 1920s or 1930s at least) to be a colonial sclerosis, an inability to generate innovation, increase productivity, or build a more integrated and differentiated regional economy.[15]

A more fruitful line of inquiry may be to focus on the forms of power lodged in particular institutions and worked out in particular colonial projects, on the conflicting visions and practices of settlers, corporate leaders, and colonial officials, and on the struggles within plantations, mines, and factories in which economic and cultural power was deployed and deflected. The economic institutions of a colony—from trading depot to railway—were the sites of conflict found in other capitalist contexts, but also of conflict specific to the cultural configurations of a colonial situation. Colonial regimes oscillated between treating colonial labor situations as they did class conflict in Europe and invoking disciplinary procedures focused on racial and cultural distinctions specific to those colonial contexts (Chakrabarty 1989; Cooper, this volume).

Some of the more revealing discussions of the particular nature of the colonial state have analyzed it in relation to the contradictory and indeterminant structure of colonial economies. John Lonsdale and Bruce Berman (1979) took off from the idea of the "semiautonomous capitalist state" in vogue in the 1970s and showed that the colonial state had to cope with a configuration of problems distinct from those of metropolitan or autonomous states. In any capitalist society, this argument goes, the state had to referee disputes among different factions of capital and ensure that the process of capital accumulation did not get so out of hand that the stability of rule would be endangered. Colonial states had to mediate not only between factions of capital and classes but also between metropolitan and imperial interests and between capitalist and noncapitalist social relations of production and trade. Maintaining order—and indeed recruiting wage labor—required a colonial state, unable to work by coercion alone, that could forge alliances with preexisting authorities. That meant not only borrowing their legitimacy but also ensuring that indigenous elites had a chance to engage in their own accumulating ventures. The colonial state feared rebellion by Africans preyed on by both settlers and chiefs; it was dependent on revenue generated by the export of peasant crops; and it was caught between the conflicting interests of white settler farmers and Europe-based trading companies. Underlying the criticism that the government received—from missionaries for being too brutal and from settlers for not being brutal enough or from businessmen for not taking one approach or another to economic growth—was the inherently contradictory position of a colonial state.

This argument puts contradiction at the center of the colonial state's operative mode, rather than as an episodic manifestation of its reaction to crisis. Discourses about racial deference, about the virtues of maintaining "traditional" authority, about stamping out "barbarous practices," or about centralizing policing and decentralized "customary law" reveal the contradictory imperatives and criteria for measuring the state's effectiveness (Chanock 1985; Edwards 1989; Mann and Roberts 1991; Merry 1991). Lonsdale and Berman's argument encourages us to focus on the constant redeployment of different ideological mixes as subsequent colonial administrations sought different measures to alleviate the tension between economic profitability and political necessity (Stoler 1985b).

This call for complex engagement with colonial institutions and rhetorics did not resonate as much as might be expected. Many scholars preferred, it would seem, to take colonial states to be unambiguously determining or to analyze the relationship of colonization and modernity at a more abstract level.[16] So to a considerable extent what Paul Rabinow (1986: 259) noted some years ago remains true: "We need a more complex understanding of power in the colonies. The state is something we need to know a lot more about." While Lonsdale and Berman's insights open some possibilities, they leave others unattended (cf. Scott 1995). Their economic focus centers the "political" on the securing of profits and peace, and less on the cultural work that colonial states do in producing truth claims about racial categories, in establishing cultural criteria for citizenship, in "educating consent"—what Antonio Gramsci said all states do—by educating desire (Stoler 1995a, 1995b).

In assuming the colonial state's hegemonic operation, its unity and coherence, we also have assumed a neat fit between state power and the production of knowledge that precludes some basic questions. In archival perspective the omission is puzzling particularly because French officials in Indochina, Dutch colonial agents in the Netherlands Indies, and British administrations in India and Africa in fact continually debated the distinctiveness of their governing apparatus. In the Indies, for example, the moral scope of the colonial state was high on the agenda of successive generations of administrators. And with good reason. In thinking through the state's responsibility to provide public assistance to its "mixed-blood" and impoverished European populations, in debates over whether the state should provide formal elementary education versus the preparatory environment for it (in nurseries, kindergartens, and other forms of preschool), colonial authorities reflected openly about distinctions between church and state, about the similarities and differences between metropolitan states and colonial ones (Brugmans 1938; Stoler, forthcoming, b). Decisions on social reform raised questions about other categories: about what defined racial membership, what constituted poverty, and what the state took as its moral mission. In short, that in which states could not afford to invest in Holland (poor relief) was precisely that in which they could not afford *not* to intervene in the Indies; namely, in regulating the domestic environments in which several hundreds of thousands of people classified as European lived. What appeared as a similar semantics of social reform had disparate political meanings in these different contexts.

Our ignorance about the workings of the colonial state comes out in other ways as well. For in taking it as given that power breeds certain forms of knowledge, we have not questioned the basis of that knowledge, or how incomplete it often was. It is only when we focus on the production of the colonial archives and on the sorts of narratives contained within it that we find how much rumor, gossip, and fantasy pervaded the official field. Nor were all these narratives authored by colonizers themselves. On the contrary, those hierarchies of credibility that conferred facticity on some accounts and not others were continually breached by an indigenous population who turned European rumors about native insurrection and subversion against their authors and to other ends (Stoler 1992; White, this volume). The notion that there was an official hermetic discourse of the colonizer and a set of hidden scripts (Scott 1990) among the colonized flattens out a more complicated political and production process. We need to ask harder questions about how official accounts were produced, transmitted, classified, and stored. In attending to dissonant voices rather than assuming coherence, we may see beyond an omniscient colonial apparatus to one shot through with conflicts between plantation entrepreneurs and the state, between local officials and metropolitan policy makers, between colonial state agents who struggled—and often failed—to coordinate their efforts from top to bottom. At the very least such a perspective should allow us to explore how limited colonial authorities may have been in putting their policies into practice, how vulnerable—and decidedly nonhegemonic—their authority was to those who subverted or pushed it aside.[17]

Imperial states were also particular kinds of entities: nineteenth-century Great Britain or Holland was not Switzerland. Imperial states did not have a pristinely metropolitan existence that *then* got transported, in however complex a way, to the colonies. The "imagined community" that was, for example, England was imagined in relation to Ireland and Scotland, to Jamaica and the North American colonies, as well as in relation to Spain and France (Colley 1992).

The "nation-state" has become too centered in conceptions of European history since the late eighteenth century, and "empire" not centered enough.[18] It is not clear that simply considering empire as an extension of nation will get to the root of the problem. France—the most talked-about model of the nation-state—confronted even during its Revolution the fact that the territory it claimed was not coterminous with the boundaries of who was considered French. Shortly thereafter Napoleon set about both enlarging the space that—through a process of cultural homogenization—could be made into a French nation and extending military dominance over regions that could not be so integrated (Bourguet 1988; Woolf 1992; Godlewska 1994). Eric Hobsbawm's (1987: 56) observation should be kept in mind: the "age of empire" was called that not only because it heralded a new kind of imperialism but also because "the numbers of rulers officially calling themselves . . . 'emperors' was at a maximum."

We need to ask not only how nations were defined against empires—as Benedict Anderson has done—but also how empires were imagined in relation to contiguous as well as noncontiguous territory. Empire remained critical to France's ruling fictions: Louis Napoleon revived a range of imperial imageries and pretensions later in the century. When finally the Third Republic's effort to turn "peasants into Frenchmen"—to make state coterminous with society— within France's European territory was being realized (Weber 1976), France was already set on new imperial adventures in West Africa and Southeast Asia. France's ruling fictions were expressed as the France of one hundred million Frenchmen—less than half of whom lived in the "hexagon" or spoke French (Heffernan 1994). In Great Britain and Holland as well, "nation building" and "empire building" were mutually constitutive projects.

The relationship between empire and nation remained contested and problematic. France's assimilationist rhetoric had long been compromised by the need to maintain distinctions against a colonized population (Girardet 1972; Lebovics 1992). By the 1940s, the very idea of "citizenship" was being extended to French subjects and the "Union Française," not the French nation, was the supreme political entity (Thiam 1953). The rhetoric of supranationality was taken so seriously that one right-wing deputy remarked in 1946 that France risked becoming "the colony of its former colonies," a statement promptly challenged as racist and contrary to French principles by another deputy, the

Senegalese Léopold Sédar Senghor (France 1946: 3334). Much of the French Left was so captivated by the idea of bringing socialism and the French revolutionary tradition to the empire that it had a hard time coming to grips with what empire meant to those who lived within it (Liauzu 1982; Wall 1986). Although it is often argued that the European idea of a social democratic nation-state was a model for Asian or African nationalists, political movements in the colonies did as much to reshape the politics of metropolitan radicals.[19]

By the time the Paris elite could finally imagine that the end of empire was conceivable, they were already fixed on the possibility of other kinds of supranational unities. Jacques Marseille (1984) suggests that it was the growing interest in some kind of European Community that made colonies look relatively less important than before. France, in this sense, passed from an imperial mold to a partially European one without—in terms of self-representations as much as diplomatic conventions—fully securing what it would take to make it a national entity.

This volume does not address the meaning of empire in regard to contiguous territory, notably the conquests of Napoleon or the empires of the Hapsburgs or the tsars, situations in which the colonial pattern of reproducing difference might in theory be mitigated by the geographic possibility of absorption more readily than was the case overseas.[20] The extent to which models of rule passed back and forth across different kinds of imperial territory should be examined. French anxieties about their "internal enemies within" in the late nineteenth century were directed at German incursions into Alsace-Lorraine but also at Jewish, Italian, and Maltese naturalized Frenchmen in Algeria (Stoler, this volume). We can only make one point here: focus on the historical importance of nation-states should not diminish the longer history of empires and the patterns by which elites and subalterns moved about within them.

As Lora Wildenthal shows here, empire could complicate gender compromises at home: the intensity of debate over intermarriage in German colonies just after the turn of the century reflected German women's concerns that male sexual license in the colonies undermined women's claims to respectability within the unequal structure of class and gender in Germany, whereas certain men asserted that the very fact of their efforts to domesticate the wilds of Africa or Samoa entitled them to marry anyone they pleased. Both sides in effect demonstrated that a German "volk" was defined in colonies as much as at home, whether by masculine willfulness or by female efforts to contain and make respectable that very imperial trait. Indeed, a range of studies that explore the interplay of state authority and gender, between colony and metropole, is rapidly expanding the possibilities for approaching state building and empire building as familially generated social processes (Taylor 1983; White 1990a; Summers 1991; Manicom 1992; Adams 1994).

While some technologies of rule were honed in the colonies and then brought back to Europe, others were not. In some cases in which the apparatus of social engineering recently assembled in the metropole was applied to the colonies, the question of who, within the empire, should have what entitlements, what safety nets, and be subjects to what sort of surveillance became acute. In the 1950s, for example, British and French policy makers tried to separate out a working class acculturated to the workplace and urban residence from the rest of the African population. But the implication that these working men (as they were assumed to be) and their families would need social security provisions led to a drawing back from such plans. Thus the boundary of included/excluded within the concept of industrial society and the welfare state was no longer coterminous with the distinction between metropole and colony (Cooper, this volume).

In the end, metropolitan states with extensive colonial "holdings" shrank back before the implications of extending their universalistic social engineering theories overseas, but that very process unsettled the security of colonial rule itself. The problem came home to the metropole: former colonial subjects, now the citizens of sovereign countries within francophone or anglophone communities, migrated to their former metropoles—where they had for some time been an unsettling presence—rekindling forms of exclusion and racism and setting off political pressures for the narrowing of citizenship within Great Britain and France (Hall 1978; Miles 1982; Brubaker 1992; Tabili 1994).[21]

Locating the Tensions of Empire: The Problem of Reproduction

The weighty "ism" so often attached to "colonial" risks concealing the fact that the apparatuses by which conquering states ruled and by which they tried to impose their systems of order and knowledge were built by people who came from different classes and, as women and men, conceptualized their own participation and goals in distinct ways. One of the most basic forms of colonial control—by the military—depended on soldiers who were simultaneously coerced and coercing, who enforced the will of the elite yet made demands themselves. Similarly, the frontline troops of colonial commerce were in some contexts likely to establish close business and personal ties with local people, possibly creating still other interstitial and contradictory social categories (Priestley 1969). Those policies to control and condone certain kinds of domestic and sexual arrangements between European men and Asian women were based on prescriptions that could at once ensure the hierarchy of those relations while destabilizing those very categories. The progeny of such unions were more than the casualties of state-backed concubinary arrangements between subaltern European soldiers and Asian women. These children, whether thrown back into native villages or as adults situated at the lowest rung of a weighty colonial bureaucracy, were seen as a dangerous conduit of moral contamination and political subversion (Stoler 1991). Such constructions of danger had strategic consequences on domestic life: they compelled colonial regimes to ponder just who should be in the colonies, how long they might stay, where and with whom they might live.

Such concerns were historically contingent. In the eighteenth century, the slave plantations of the West Indies reproduced their labor force by massive importations from Africa. Yet it was this form of reproduction—the violence of slave raids and the horrors of transportation—that gave the antislavery movement in nineteenth-century Europe its most telling symbols of what was wrong with colonial slavery in a bourgeois world. Still later, the argument that forced labor prevented both demographic reproduction and the reproduction and extension of market relations became a key way in which European powers tried to distinguish the ''moral'' form of colonization that they practiced from unacceptable variants. And in the 1930s and 1940s, when British and French officials began to have doubts about the system of migrant labor that was by then widespread, they argued that migrancy reproduced the wrong kinds of laboring men. Employing men for short periods and keeping their families in villages meant that generations of workers could not be acculturated to industrial discipline and contemporary European ideas about nutrition and sanitation (Cooper, this volume; Manderson 1987; White 1990a).

Those charged with ruling the colonies were not the only ones trying to devise new ways of constituting marriages and families: educated and commercial African elites in a turn-of-the-century Nigerian city brought Christian and Yoruba practices into relation with one another, while in southern Africa male elders took advantage of colonial officials' quest for ''customary'' regulations of reproduction to entrench patriarchal power (Mann 1985; Chanock 1985). In the Indies in the same period, Javanese women troubled Dutch officials' notions of what native women would opt for if they had a choice: some women chose cohabitation over marriage with European men in the interests of protecting landed property they could no longer own once they became legally reclassified by conjugality as European (Stoler, this volume).

While students of colonial history have become increasingly confident in asserting that race, class, and gender are moving categories, we still have more work to do in accounting for how their political saliencies shift and which of those affiliations shape political choices in a specific place and time (Pedersen 1991). Feminist researchers have documented a wide range of fashions in which European women have been positioned—and have positioned themselves—both to fortify and undermine the tenets of white rule (Chaudhuri and Strobel 1992; Ferguson 1992; Ware 1992). In many colonial contexts, European women became the excuse for—and custodians of—racial distinctions that took the form of class-specific prescriptions for bourgeois respectability and sexual ''normalcy'' (Knapman 1986; Callaway 1987; Grimshaw 1989; Stoler 1991; Ware 1992). Medical discourse on the danger of physical contagion via colonized women slipped into a discourse on cultural and moral contamination and as such placed adherence to respectability and safeguards against racial degeneracy as imperatives of white rule. Sexuality was indeed "a dense transfer point of power" as Foucault held and as a wide range of scholars have insisted, but it was not the only medium of contagion (Ball-hatchet 1980; Hyam 1990; Kelly 1991; Stoler 1991; Young 1995). Colonial elites saw psychological dispositions and sentiments (toward work, consumption, children, nation, and authority) as contagious, dangerous, and identity defining as well.

If sexuality and sentiment could specify the contents of "Europeanness," it could also signal what was distinctly indigenous as defined by colonized people themselves. Partha Chatterjee (1993) describes a discussion among Indian men about Indian women that was one about culture and national identity. He argues that in compartmentalizing the domestic, nationalist intellectuals distanced themselves not only from British rulers but also from the large majority of Indians (see also Chakrabarty, this volume). But the discourses about sex were not only metaphoric of a wider set of power relations; sex was about control over bodies and selves—and also about their consequences. Colonial elites ran up against frequent boundary crossings that not only defied their received racial classifications but were turned in ways that went beyond the state's control. Colonial elites feared transgressions in both directions: that natives were surreptitiously entering the European ranks as "fabricated Europeans" and that "going native" was not confined to the destitute seaman and low-down bureaucrats that Somerset Maugham and George Orwell have caricatured so well.

The domestic arrangements both of colonized workers and of colonial agents were constantly subject to reexamination as those that made policies—and lived within them—thought out the relationship among subversion, domestic life, and sex (White 1990b; Nair 1990).[22] Policy makers alternately saw prostitution, concubinage, and "healthy conjugal sex" as the basis on which colonial authority might be secured or irreparably undermined. Sexuality was tied to politics in numerous ways: while the shuttling of men between workplace, male-only hostels, and rural villages was a means of cheaply reproducing a labor force, such migratory patterns could also be seen to foster social disorder and political dissonance. Stable family life was sometimes conceived as an antidote to subversion—as a way of depoliticizing the malcontent. Family ideology and political agendas were repeatedly linked by European administrators and "Mau Mau" rebels in Africa, and in Southeast Asia by Malay officials, Sumatra's Dutch planters, and subordinate whites. In the early 1930s, "extremist agitation" on Sumatra's estates was countered in part by the selective dismissal of what were perceived as cash-hungry bachelor elements and by the encouragement of "family formation" and "the semblance of rural village life" (Stoler 1985b; White 1990b; Allman 1994; Hunt, this volume). Tensions over what colonized people did by night were intimately tied to the daytime structures of colonial domination and to the psychological premises on which that authority was seen to rest.

If we can no longer explain how racial boundaries and class distinctions are secured without understanding how they are constituted in gender terms, then we can certainly not understand the construction of whiteness without exploring its class dimensions.[23] With the muting of political economy in recent colonial studies, class too has often been relegated to the sidelines, held constant, sometimes ignored. For the most part, students of imperialism have discussed class issues in two ways: by examining accumulation by metropolitan capitalist classes (sometimes in conflict with capitalist classes that had taken root in colonial societies) and by analyzing the process of class formation that capitalist penetration set off among indigenous peoples. But class impinged in the making of empire in other ways: constraining who came to the colonies, what visions they harbored, what features of European class culture were selectively reworked by French civil servants in Algeria, by British planters in Malaya, by the Dutch women whose husbands were civil servants in Java, by Dutch men who were underlings on Sumatra's estates (Butcher 1979; Prochaska 1990; Gouda 1995). Ultimately the class-specific privileges that colonialism guarded for some whites and bestowed on others were deeply implicated in the racial policies of rule.

In nineteenth-century South Africa or turn-of-the-century East Africa, the British used a vocabulary to describe Africans remarkably like that used at home to describe the lowest elements of the class order, "the residuum," the degraded class of criminals and casual laborers of Victorian cities (Stedman Jones 1971; Cooper 1980; Comaroff and Comaroff 1992). Only no respectable working class existed between the African residuum and the Arab, Indian, and European middle and upper classes. As John Comaroff shows here, the class baggage missionaries brought with them to South Africa in the mid-nineteenth century was more complex than the language with which the top described the bottom. The class positioning of missionaries on the "social margins" of bourgeois Britain led them to an idealization of rural peasant life. That in turn constrained their perceptions of the possibilities for African workers and put them in conflict with dominant factions of the colonial elite. Randall Packard (1989) has similarly shown how a medical discourse on native African reserves in South Africa rested on a bucolic vision, arising from a European class experience, not an African one. The point is that the industrial restructuring of class relations in Europe resonated in the social engineering of empire in subliminal visions as well as concrete policy.

But sometimes it worked the other way around. Susan Thorne's contribution to this volume seeks to reverse the analytical perspective by examining how that consciousness of class that the Victorians brought with them to the colonies was itself already constructed on the rhetorical basis of a "racial" nomenclature whose primary reference was the colonial encounter. In exploring how evangelical religions channeled imperial and racial imagery that permeated the metropolitan social imagination, she shows how tensions over whether missionaries should do their work in England or Africa raised further questions about where the "civilizing mission" should be located.

Looking at these various processes of reproduction, one is struck by the multiple circuits of persons, ideas, and institutions that were reproduced through them. While Benedict Anderson correctly points out that the pilgrimages in which colonial elites participated helped to forge an imagined community among certain men, we are taking a rather larger view of circuits than Anderson (1983) suggests, one that includes a broader spectrum of women and men.[24] Both colonizing and colonized elites were produced through imperial interconnections. The circuit of personnel around empires—as high- and low-ranking civil servants and military officers moved from Martinique to Chad, as cotton merchants went from Uganda to India, as French architects of educational reform in Indochina brought back models from Batavia to Hanoi, as prime ministers attended to crises from the Transvaal to Tasmania—grounded the idea of empire in global experience and produced alternative routes to class mobility (Rabinow 1989). Africans served in the Dutch militia in the Indies or in French wars in Asia or Europe itself; Indian soldiers participated in the British conquest of Africa; their officers spread a variety of stereotypes about the military "fitness" of various groups around the empires (Echenberg 1991). Through these circuits moved generations of families, tools of analysis, social policy, military doctrine, and architectural plans. Whole bodies of administrative strategy, ethnographic classification, and scientific knowledge were shared and compared in a consolidating imperial world. When, for example, the French colonial adviser for Indochina, Chailley-Bert, sought to devise a policy toward the métis population in Indochina, he traveled to Batavia to study what he saw as a successful policy toward the Indo-European population in the Dutch East Indies; he did not seek his advice from France.

The point is that colonial historiography has been so nationally bound that it has blinded us to those circuits of knowledge and communication that took other routes than those shaped by the metropole-colony axis alone. The colonial congresses of the late nineteenth century that tried to consolidate a formal, pan-European imperial moral and legal order (Gong 1984) represent only one kind of linkage. The racial dynamics of creole insurgence in Haiti resounded in the official debates about poor whites in the Indies and Anglo-Indians in India, just as educational policies used in British India were debated and assiduously avoided in the formulation of language policies in Indochina. Nor were the networks of communication shaped by the interests of colonizers alone. The negritude movement cut a horizontal swath across Africa; the Garveyite movement reverberated in African cities, Caribbean islands, and North American ghettos; Malay novelists took some of their anticolonial literary cues from Indonesia's native authors; and the Filipino revolution at the turn of the century resonated from the Indies to France. This is not a matter of refining imperial intellectual history but rather of locating the fields of force in which imperial culture was conceived as transnational and counterhistories were imagined and made.

The Dynamics of Empire

Any effort to compare different imperial systems—or even different parts of a single empire—raises questions about what it is we should be comparing: similar chronologies across different colonial contexts, or disparate chronologies but similar patterns and rhythms of rule?[25] Within the British empire, colonial officials were trying to turn slaves into wage laborers in Zanzibar and coastal Kenya around the same time they were giving up on a similar project in the West Indies and at last recognizing that peasant production might provide a more plausible colonial future. A related effort by Dutch officials to turn a directly coerced, indentured labor force into a self-reproducing workforce linked labor issues to family organization in ways that were to echo, in different rhythms, across colonial empires: the Dutch officials' focus on "family formation" as a strategy to stabilize reproduction and avert subversion in Deli, Sumatra's plantation belt, came in the 1920s at a time when French and British officials still considered the African family part of a naturalized world into which they could not delve—until the late 1940s when they began to intervene in earnest into the family life of African wage workers (Stoler 1985a; Cooper 1980, this volume; Trouillot 1989; Holt 1990). State interventions into labor and family point to further questions: whether other such incursions into the realm of the social—by medical doctors, by educators, by agricultural specialists—were chronologically linked to each other and whether the divisions of knowledge within which each intervention took place were subsets of a larger effort.

The disharmonies that emerge in comparing rhythms of rule underscore a central point: imperial elites may have *viewed* their domains from a metropolitan center, but their actions, let alone their consequences, were not necessarily *determined* there. But given the fact that empires were in competition as well as in contact, the question of conjunctures still arises. How can one link the specificity of contest within colonies to the periodicity of European history and global conflict? Approaching such a problem requires thinking seriously about global tendencies and connections without giving them deterministic weight. It requires being attentive to contingencies without assuming that they produce a random pattern.

We have focused on the tensions of empire in a bourgeois world not because we think the world in fact became bourgeois—the power of the bourgeoisie was contingent and constrained enough in Europe, let alone in its conquered territory—but because bourgeois projects laid claim to a kind of global universality in terms of which colonial projects were reconfigured. It was the issue of slavery that, in part, forced the question, first in the case of Haiti and then in the debates in Great Britain over slavery. Antislavery was not a purely bourgeois movement; it had working-class support as well, and many of its middle-class advocates saw the issue in religious terms. The question is why a particular way of critiquing slavery actually won out in Parliament. The morality of a form of labor practiced exclusively in colonies became a way to discuss the morality of the labor market in Europe at a time when capitalist consolidation was the focus of urban agitation and rural revolt (Davis 1975; Cooper 1980; Holt 1990).

It was in a broader transnational domain, not the nation, that British policy makers debated issues of moral economy, thought through the implications of property and labor, and sought to use the state to define a class structure. The move did not follow an automatic economic logic: the slave plantation was still the height of managerial and technological sophistication, but as David Brion Davis (1975) has shown, the ideological consequences of capitalist development in Great Britain itself were incompatible with the continuation of slave labor in its colonies. The bourgeois project soon became—by force of the British navy as much as the sweeping conception of political morality that free labor ideology entailed—a pan-European one, and colonial slavery was one of the major questions over which a cross-national class ideology was worked out: how the legitimate basis of bourgeois economy was made clear and the notion of a "civilized" nation was specified (Davis 1984; Gong 1984; Drescher 1987; Eltis 1989). Enslavement of non-European peoples was condemned in the name of a universal definition of free labor that transcended the moral vision of any one religion or any one state, raising the possibility of international standards for imperial behavior.

What went on in the colonies was far more complex than the transformation of a discourse on free labor from a radical idea into conventional bourgeois morality. Former slaves also brought their own visions into play; Saint Domingue—as well as other possibilities to abandon, overthrow, or transform plantation societies—reverberated among both slave owners and slaves. Capitalist expansion joined European powers in a common discourse and set of practices that were as strong as their interconnections (and rivalries) in world markets. But the same process forced each colonial regime into a series of encounters with the people who did the work, in ways that reconfigured the local hierarchies of race as well as the relationship of colony and metropole (Geertz 1970; Mintz 1974; Rodney 1981; Scott 1985; Holt 1990).

These encounters did not necessarily expand the domains included under principles of citizenship and market rationality. Indeed, Holt (1990) has shown that Jamaican former slaves' efforts to hold wage labor at arm's length led to a shift between two kinds of imperial conceptions: from an insistence that slaves be brought into the British model of wage labor and civilized behavior to a contention that their distinctiveness was racially based and required stern control. When slaves and former slaves in Cuba tried to insert their own claims into a struggle among creole elites over independence from Spain, they brought a "black peril" argument into the heart of a debate over how race and nation were to be imagined, in metropole and colony alike. Spanish liberals saw free labor and more open trading relationships as part of a pan-European bourgeois vision in which they wanted to share. Some colonial elites were prepared to abandon slavery because they wanted to "whiten" the colonial population, while some of Spain's most growth-minded capitalists saw slavery and colonial power as necessary to their own vision of economic progress (Ferrer 1995; Schmidt-Nowara 1995). Over the course of the nineteenth century, antislavery arguments defined slaves first as potentially civilizable—making European intervention a liberating phenomenon—and then as potentially resistant to the civilizing mission—making European intervention a necessity for global progress.[26]

The last quarter of the nineteenth century stands out as another moment when colonialisms became part of a pan-European debate on the practices of "civilized" states that consolidated an imperialist morality.[27] On the ground, this "new" imperialism was no less coercive and brutal than the old. Yet Europe's power elites were now taking pains (in congresses held in 1884–1885 and 1890–1891) to reassure each other that their coercion and brutality were no longer frank attempts at extraction but reasoned efforts to build structures capable of reproducing themselves: stable government replacing the violent, conflictual tyrannies of indigenous polities; orderly commerce and wage labor replacing the chaos of slaving and raiding; a complex structuring of group boundaries, racial identities, and permissible forms of sexual and social interaction replacing the disconcerting fluidities of an earlier age (Cooper forthcoming).[28]

The "embourgeoisement" of imperialism in the late nineteenth century enhanced expectations of hard work, managed sexuality, and racial distancing among the colonizing agents while opening a more intimate domain for condemnation and reform within societies being colonized. When other European polities condemned the atrocities in King Leopold's Congo, they signaled that colonizers could deviate only so far from the norms. A "culture of terror," in Michael Taussig's (1984) terms, did not disappear, but it expressed itself on a shifting terrain in which violence was condemned unless it could be linked to some kind of progressive reform.

Colonial violence took many forms. In some places the violence of conquest was becoming the violence of self-conscious and self-righteous interventions into the intimacies of social life, thereby defining what was the public and not the private domain. Elsewhere techniques of coercion existed as preserved possibilities, undergirding more persuasive techniques. It was precisely the intimacy of the domains in which colonial regimes intervened that prompted efforts within a wide range of communities to counter its totalizing impulse, to reassemble bits of the "civilizing mission" into something else. The intrusion of European models into "private" domains did not necessarily reproduce bourgeois civility but gave rise to diverse efforts—recounted here in the chapter by Chakrabarty—to find new and original ways for expressing ideals of a domestic domain, for demonstrating status, and indeed for showing that a man or a woman could be "modern" in a variety of ways. At a broader level, the idea—expressed in condescending terms by colonial apologists and in critical ones by some scholars of colonialism—that a bourgeoisie could exist among colonized people only in a stunted, even pathetic form was countered by the multiple ways people with education or wealth, or indeed those struggling to attain a modest measure of either, organized politically and expressed themselves culturally.[29] These efforts in turn forced regimes to redefine their means—and ultimately their goals. For this reason as well, a homogeneous periodization of colonial encounters misses the dynamics that shaped the edifices of colonial power and ultimately rendered them unsustainable.

The conventional break points of European history—the world wars, the depressions of the 1890s and the 1930s, the rise of a bipolar global politics after the 1940s—had a powerful impact in the colonies that deserves careful exploration, but these conjunctures did not necessarily produce the same effects. Governments were responding to a wide range of real and imagined threats: fears of pan-Arabism, of pan-Africanism, of the Red, Black, or Yellow Peril, of colonial students espousing liberal doctrines of self-determination. Elsewhere were challenges to the notion that the only political space for Africans and Asians was the bounded domain of ethnic groups or tribes. While the French policy of association and the British policy of indirect rule attempted to narrow the domain of politics, in India and parts of Southeast Asia, politics had already gone beyond any pretense of confinement to such a grid. Regimes had to acknowledge an Asian presence within the institutions of state while seeking to control who could enter that space and the kinds of arguments they could make. The sorts of debates about political and social policy that became acute in Africa in the late 1940s were already evident in India in the 1920s (Chakrabarty 1989; Cooper, this volume), but the inability of colonial institutions to confine those debates to "local" and "traditional" space made the 1930s and 1940s a moment when questions of social and economic entitlements were posed once again on empirewide scales.[30]

Colonial questions had resonance across a wide imperial field. What happened in one place had repercussions elsewhere. The conjunctural politics of different regions came together again in the post-1945 period not only because of the changing power structure and ideological climate that emerged from World War II but also because the modern colonial state, with its projects as well as its organizational instruments, was entering more domains of social life and turning conflicts over a variety of social issues into conflict over the state itself.

Beyond Empire

If our conception of the tensions of empire has validity, then there is something wrong with the way a domain of inquiry that has become quite popular in recent years has been carved out: "postcoloniality" or the "post-colonial moment." Some scholars have written as if people's historical experience of colonization—whether its formal phase ended in the 1820s as in much of Latin America or in the 1960s as in most of Africa—shapes a common concern, as if the culture of the imperial power still sets the standards against which diverse national cultures must measure themselves. Anne McClintock (1990) has rightly questioned the validity of generalizing so widely across time and space and wonders about the "post" in postcoloniality, suggesting that in many places cultural decolonization has yet to be accomplished. We question the "colonial" as well as the "-ity," the former because it homogenizes a power relationship whose limitations and contingencies need to be examined, the latter because it suggests an essential quality to the fact of having been colonized, implying that colonialism was the only thing of importance to people who live in what were once colonies.[31]

Thus our attention to the construction of colonial categories has much more contemporary salience than simply enhancing our understanding of colonial situations. For if we are to treat colonial studies as a history of the present, then we need a richer understanding of the colonial situation itself. The very ease with which we often use the term "colonial legacy" carries the suggestion that we already know very well what the oppressive coordinates of that legacy are and that this legacy constituted a recognizable, if not unchanging, bundle throughout the decades of postcolonial history. As we have shown, the colonial situation was characterized by alternative projects and by the displacement and failure of such projects in colonial encounters: such processes did not begin or end with decolonization. Meanings of institutions, bureaucratic habits, and cultural styles set up in the colonial era were continually being reshaped. Our intent here is not to design a postcolonial research agenda but to suggest the importance of analyzing the wide range of different engagements with colonial projects if we are to understand the equally varied engagements in postcolonial ones (see also Breckenridge and van der Veer 1992).

Today's world is often said to be one of global movement, of fractured social relations, implicitly or explicitly contrasted to a colonial world of spatial and cultural confinement. But it may be that we have taken the categories of colonial archives—organized around specific colonial powers, their territorial units, and their maps of subject cultures—too literally, and our colonial historiography has missed much of the dynamics of colonial history, including the circuits of ideas and people, colonizers and colonized, within and among empires.

Understanding the complexities of colonial history might prompt us to question other recent assessments of racism. We have already argued that the sharp demarcation of racial categories in the late nineteenth century needs to be seen in relation to the blurring of race and class in the eighteenth century and the sorts of conflicts that lie in between. We also might ask whether the notion of "cultural racism," often identified in current scholarship as the new racism of the late twentieth century, is a new one at all (Gilroy 1987). For as George Stocking (1991) and others have argued, the concepts of culture and race have long served to buttress one another in crucial ways. Racism has never been based on somatics alone, nor is a concern with physiology and biology its "pure" and originary form. It has long depended on hierarchies of civility, on cultural distinctions of breeding, character, and psychological disposition, on the relationship between the hidden essence of race and what were claimed to be its visual markers (Stoler 1995a; Hirschfeld 1996). As we pay more attention to the production of racial categories, not only within the ostensible public domain but also as categories that shaped the microdynamics of power, our attention is turned to learning of place and race outside the home and, as important, within it.

Similarly, the current emphasis on the hybridities and fractured identities of the postcolonial moment looks far less distinctive when the interstitiality of colonial lives is brought back into sharper relief (Taylor 1983; Stoler 1995a; Young 1995). Colonial dichotomies of ruler and ruled, white and black, colonizer and colonized only reflected part of the reality in which people lived. As we have stressed, these dichotomies took hard work to sustain, were precariously secured, and were repeatedly subverted. As Fanny Colonna's and Homi Bhabha's essays suggest, ambivalence was part of colonial encounters for colonizer and colonized. Attending to the dynamics of mimicry and mockery allows us to examine what rifts such ambiguities produced in the edifice of rule and in the subversive strategies toward it.

While it is a truism that it is the categories of colonialism, not colonialism itself, which are alive and well, we see still more work that can be done to identify how those categories have shaped postcolonial contexts and have been reworked in them. For example, the colonial "prose of counterinsurgency" that Ranajit Guha (1988) has so carefully described has shown up in antirevolutionary and postcolonial contexts in varied ways. During the Indonesian independence movement between 1945 and 1949, some Dutch officials grossly misconstrued the nature of popular support for the revolution by assuming, as had been done before, that anticolonial activists were largely made up of "nothing more" than the predatory robber bands that they had targeted in the colonial period (Stoler 1988). The word "terrorist" has an analogous significance in more recent times. The "prose of counterinsurgency" is not limited to warfare. Phrases like "target population" construct the objects of development initiatives in ways that position them as an obstructing force to global and national progress.

Just as colonial regimes let culture do much of the work of race in establishing distinctions, the notion of the civilizing mission gave way after World War II to the notion of development, embodying in a subtler way the hierarchy that civilizing entailed. At first glance, the concept of development serves as a kind of bridge across the period of decolonization, the last form in which colonial claims to hegemony were articulated and the first form through which independent regimes asserted the progressive nature of their rule. As James Ferguson (1990) has shown, the discourse of development agencies in southern Africa assumes its object to be aboriginal poverty—as a "normal" process of growth that poor people have somehow failed to attain rather than the product of a bitter history.

Development initiatives are often criticized not simply because they go wrong or because they are most often based on inadequate appreciation of the specifics of local situations, but because they inherently project a disempowering modernity onto backwardness (Sachs 1992; Escobar 1995). Yet there is more to the idea of development in its historical context: like other concepts, this one can be seized, turned around from a structure of depoliticization into a claim for entitlements. The colonial development project became the focus of claims by nationalist movements arguing that economic and social development required sovereignty. The "Third World" (deployed as a radical term at the Bandung Conference in the spirit of the "third estate") asserted itself around the idea that a decent standard of living was a fundamental human right. Within postcolonial states, governments legitimized their rule as leading the "battle for development," while opposition groups asserted that development had been hijacked and that only they provided a genuine commitment to it (Coquery-Vidrovitch, Hémery, and Piel 1988; Watts 1993; Diouf, forthcoming).

The volatility of the development question follows from the underlying instability of colonialism within a bourgeois world. Development is only a recent entry among a series of constructs that make ethnocentric claims in universalistic language, and colonial studies have accomplished much in exposing the centrality of this tension. Yet the very universalism of the language gives subordinated groups a handle, outside of the immediate power relations in which they are immersed, to single out local tyrannies and to claim global rights. The postmodern critique of development—or of bourgeois democracy—gives insufficient weight to the possibilities that universalistic notions of rights and participation can be deployed against the exclusions and inequities that have historically been associated with them.

The continuing study of colonial regimes should be more than a neoabolitionist denunciation of a form of power now safely consigned to history. Nor should one dismiss as inherently and unchangingly hypocritical all political philosophies that smack of "bourgeois equality" or invoke "universalist" claims. The most recent chapter in one of the longest histories of colonial domination—the dismantling of white rule in South Africa—was yet another reminder of the multiple levels of political action that together bring about change: the antiapartheid movements of the 1980s and 1990s drew on universalistic ideals of nonracialism, equality, Christian brotherhood, and citizenship—appealing as much to working-class South Africans as to sympathizers around the world. It depended too on an awareness of cultural distinctiveness and solidarity that grew up within particular communities and that drew on local traditions and the assertions of racial identity linked to pan-Africanism. The movement was torn by disagreements and violence, and the quest for economic betterment and social justice in the face of a power structure built under white domination is far from over. But the trade unions, civic organizations, and political parties that contributed to a democratic process in South Africa also have possibilities for injecting new meanings into the repertoire of rights and principles that are considered "universal." The success of the electoral revolution of 1994 reveals some of the same elements found in the "unsuccessful" political movements of the 1920s, if not the 1870s, where in rural areas and in cities, Africans simultaneously defended community, found possibilities for survival in the interstices of an oppressive system, and built on ideas of equality to bend a system when it could not be broken (Beinart and Bundy 1987; Bradford 1987). The history of colonies is not simply about implacable opposition against monolithic power; it is just as much a story of multifaceted engagements with cultures of rule as of efforts to negate them.

One should read the history of opposition to colonial domination neither as a victory won nor as an illusory moment in a protracted history of imperial domination. Struggles familiar to us from colonial history—over access to residential space, over children's education, over social welfare, over cultural conventions and who has the right to be a citizen—cut across Europe and its former colonial locations. One of the central themes of colonial history—elite efforts to reproduce distinction across lines of social and cultural connection and popular investment in those distinctions—is not limited to a remote past or to "somewhere else." The idea of Europe, starkly contrasted to its Others, is alive and well in a series of increasingly vocal right-wing movements across the continent (Asad 1990). Jean-Marie Le Pen, France's prophet of the National Front, among others, has harnessed strong political support around the sentiment that children born in France of parents from former French colonies should "go back where they belong" (see Taguieff 1989, 1991, 1995). The images on which Le Pen draws, like all traditions, are selectively recuperated and transformed as they are reproduced. The traditions of nonracialism and inclusive citizenship on which the principled opponents of anti-immigrant politics in Europe or the United States draw have histories locked into argument with the racialist categories these approaches denied, but they also have possibilities for being reworked and expanded. The tensions between the exclusionary practices and universalizing claims of bourgeois culture were crucial to shaping the age of empire, and—in different form—these tensions are still present today, as citizens of what were once called metropoles and colonies reinterpret their pasts to create their futures.

Notes

1. A bourgeoisie can be defined, in Marxist terms, as the owners of the means of production within a capitalist system, and the centrality of commodity exchange within such a system implies that such a class is "free" to accumulate wealth independent of any particular structure of status or power, as would be the case with an aristocracy or indeed a peasantry tied to the land. Hence the possibility of conceptualizing its economic and social role in universal terms and for identification with such a role to cross the borders of European states. But, as suggested above, there is no such entity as a pure bourgeoisie, and the growing importance and self-consciousness of such a class in the context of western Europe in the eighteenth and early nineteenth century is as much a story of cultural distinctions and of state power as it is of property and production. On the affinities between the bourgeoisie and liberalism and the cultural coordinates of both, see Blackburn 1991, Davidoff and Hall 1987, Mehta, this volume, Gay 1993.

2. Studies of imperial propaganda (Thorne, this volume; MacKenzie 1984; Schneider 1982; Rydell 1984; Kaplan and Pease 1993) certainly show that governments and colonial lobbies *tried* to convince a broad public of the value of empire. Ageron (1978) argues that the French public as a whole was not convinced, only a specific "party."

3. See Stoler 1995a for a discussion of some of the selective ways in which Foucauldian concepts have influenced colonial studies.

4. Note that the notion of a hybrid, mixed population underwrote nationalist discourse and the engendering of productive citizens in a number of Latin American contexts (Sommer 1991). This does not mean that eugenicist notions were absent from elite Latin American discourse. See Stepan 1991.

5. On leftist Zionists' belief in the validity of their own reformist project amid Arab backwardness in Palestine, see Atran 1989.

6. For examples of efforts by colonial administrators and scientists to think out "the colonial question" collectively, see Congrès Colonial International de Paris 1889, Union Géographique Internationale (1938). A subject much discussed at congresses was African slavery, giving the convening powers a chance to reaffirm their collective commitment to social progress and their representation of African societies as tyrannical and backward. See Cooper, forthcoming.

7. For debates among turn-of-the-century geographers, see Heffernan 1994. After the 1930s depression and widespread unemployment in Europe, the International Congress of Geography (Union Géographique Internationale 1938) convened in Amsterdam with colonial scientists, doctors, and administrators from throughout the imperial globe to debate "the possibilities of colonisation for the white race in the tropical zone"; the American Geographical Society pondered similar questions (Price 1939). Both volumes reflected a rethinking of what classes of whites could settle in the colonial tropics without

disrupting the balanced inequities of ruler and ruled (Stoler, forthcoming, b). Also see Winichakul 1994 for a discussion of French and British cartography in the making of the "geo-body" of nineteenth-century Siam and the Thai nation. Among the most prominent domains for knowledge-laden intervention—where European science was invoked to save backward peoples from their own ignorant practices—were agriculture, forestry, pedagogy, and medicine (Beinart 1984; Anderson and Grove 1987; Vaughan 1991; Packard 1989; Arnold 1993).

8. The cold war both fostered decolonization—for fear that unrequited nationalism would give rise to communism—and increased the uncertainty over political possibilities in former colonies. The discourse of colonial anti-insurgency gave birth to a discourse of anticommunist counterinsurgency, a process in which area studies as much as strategic studies figured in prominent but highly contested ways (Pletsch 1981; Wakin 1992).

9. The "Copperbelt anthropologists" (A. L. Epstein, J. C. Mitchell) of the 1950s and 1960s made a notable effort to show the effects of industrialization and urbanization on African life—and the originality and complexity of African responses to these forces—but they were reluctant to confront colonial rule as a specific system of power with the same depth as these forces of "modernization." For an interesting instance in which on-site investigations of urbanization and industrialization complicated a picture of movement toward modernity, see UNESCO 1956.

10. For an unusual study that examined the ways in which indigenous notions of respectability were shaped by colonial racism and European notions of breeding in the British Caribbean, see Wilson 1972.

11. Feminist critiques in anthropology galvanized in the 1970s and early 1980s around efforts to demonstrate the gender inequities built into the concept of development and the specific programs based on it. For some early examples, see Wellesley Editorial Committee 1977; Rogers 1980; Young, Wolkowitz, and McCullagh 1981; Beneria 1982; Buvinic, Lycette, and McGreevey 1983.

12. On the conceptual and political links that tied the anthropology of political economy in the late 1970s and early 1980s to the emergence of colonial studies, see Stoler 1995c.

13. Serious studies within this framework have not disappeared (Marseille 1984; Cain and Hopkins 1993) but are not being adequately integrated into other approaches to colonial studies.

14. An example of this genre is Brett 1973. A less critical reading of colonial economies asserts that British policy was more paternalistic than market oriented (Ehrlich 1973). On the other hand, a critical Dutch literature going back to the 1940s stressed how colonial rule created "dual" economies or "plural" societies (Boeke 1953; Furnivall 1948).

15. French journalists referred to the fact that Holland's economy boomed after it lost Indonesia in 1949 as the "Dutch phenomenon." On the profitability of colonies, see Marseille 1984, Huttenback and Davis 1986, and Cain and Hopkins (1993). A particularly telling study of what at first seems a highly successful instance of economic imperialism is Brocheux and Hémery 1995.

16. The latter is done with particular insight in Chatterjee 1993. For other approaches to the colonial state, see Vincent 1982; Cohn and Dirks 1988; Thomas 1990; Bayart 1993; Cribb 1994; Young 1994; Scott 1995.

17. A considerable debate has unfolded over whether colonial states should be considered hegemonic. What is clear is that colonial states pushed hegemonic *projects*— different modes of routinizing power and obtaining consent—but the consistency and plausibility, let alone success, of those projects remain very much in doubt. See Guha 1989; Engels and Marks 1994; Cooper 1994.

18. As Marks (1990: 114) notes, "It is extraordinary how quickly the enormous hold of empire over the British imagination has been forgotten." Giddens (1985: 269), presents a typology of nation-states in which the fact of having been colonized characterizes the state-building process, but the fact of having been a colonizer does not. What Giddens calls the "classical" model of state building completely elides the question of empire. Chatterjee (1986), in questioning whether politics in colonies was "derivative" from the European state model, may give that model too much credit.

19. On the slowness and difficulty of the British Left in coming to grips with the politics of people in the British empire, see Howe 1993.

20. Note that Kiernan (1969) pointed in that direction early on, while Ferro (1994: 25) explores the importance of contiguity and heterogeneity in shaping different modes of colonization. For a recent exploration of Russian history in imperial terms, see Burbank and Ransel, forthcoming.

21. Tabili (1994) shows that racism was neither an unambiguous sentiment among all or part of English society in the 1920s and 1930s nor an automatic response to job competition. Port employers tried to hire workers from the empire, particularly seamen, to reduce labor costs; unions hesitated between organizing these workers and trying to exclude them; the state worried about definitions of citizenship and claims being made on its resources. The emergence of a race-based definition of British nationality, Tabili concludes (p. 183), was "an effort to reinforce the inequalities that made the empire profitable."

22. On the relationship between politics and passion in nationalist and racist discourse, see Mosse 1985; Sommer 1991; Parker et al. 1992.

23. For a related argument set within the United States, see Roediger 1991.

24. See Julie Skurski's (1995) critique of Anderson's focus on fraternal community.

25. For recent comparative efforts that very differently pose the problem of what to compare, see Bayly and Kolff 1986; Daniel, Bernstein, and Brass 1992.

26. In other contexts the messiness of colonial encounters juxtaposed against the increasing confidence with which "Europe" defined itself as the locus of civilization led to increasingly invidious views toward people being colonized. The grudging admiration of ancient Egypt in the time of the Napoleonic conquest had become a totally negative conception of Arabs by the time of the Algerian conquest of the 1830s. See Woolf 1992; Conklin 1991.

27. On the relationship of one power's Republican ideology at home to its "civilizing mission" overseas, see Conklin forthcoming.

28. What is striking is how much students of colonialism have subscribed to a similar notion that colonial violence belongs to one earlier stage in the development of more sophisticated modes of suasion. In this evolutionary model force is replaced by compliance, if not consensus, in the technologies of rule. We prefer to view colonial violence not in opposition to cultural domination but as a preserved possibility that allowed for particular cultural strategies of rule. For students of comparative colonialisms, the claim of some Dutch historians that Dutch expansion did not fit the

characteristics of modern imperialism has always seemed somewhat belabored and surprising. For the most recent review of the literature, see Locher-Scholten (1994) who makes the strong case that the Netherlands' "high-minded goals" were subordinated to its imperialist priorities and projects.

29. Scholars of the Subaltern Studies school have taken varying positions on questions such as this. Guha (1989) emphasizes the political weakness of the Indian bourgeoisie; Chatterjee (1993) and Chakrabarty (1992, this volume)—while recognizing the structural constraints of a colonial situation and the power of seemingly inattainable colonial models of bourgeois behavior—attend rather to the different ways of demonstrating respectability in domestic and public spaces.

30. The effort at confinement had its effects, however, as colonial regimes helped to entrench notions of "communalism" in opposition to "national" politics. See Pandey 1990.

31. If "postcoloniality" has acquired a certain vogue among literary-minded scholars, "neocolonialism" did similar work at an earlier date for political economists. Here the implication is that the power relationships of colonialism were continued by other means—the structure of global markets, the power of transnational corporations, the enforcement power of the U.S. military—even after empires formally dissolved. The trouble with this reasoning is that it is a simple answer where some good questions are in order: How is power exercised in today's world? How do both "advanced" and "postcolonial" states function in the face of border-crossing multinational corporations and newly empowered international organizations, such as the International Monetary Fund? How do the political and social networks within former colonial states tap into transnational economic relations, and how do such networks reshape the bureaucratic structures of colonial states and cultures of domination (Mbembe 1992; *Radical History Review* 1993)?

References

Adams, Julia. 1994. "The Familial State: Elite Family Practices and State-making in the Early Modern Netherlands." *Theory and Society* 23: 505–539.

———. 1996. "Principals and Agents, Colonialists and Company Men: The Decay of Colonial Control in the Dutch East Indies." *American Sociological Review* 61(1): 12–28.

Adas, Michael. 1989. *Machines as the Measure of Man: Science, Technology, and Ideologies of Western Dominance.* Ithaca: Cornell University Press.

Ageron, Charles-Robert. 1978. *France coloniale ou parti colonial?* Paris: Presses Universitaires Françaises.

Ahmad, Aijaz. 1992. *In Theory: Classes, Nations, Literatures.* London: Verso.

Albertyn, R. R. 1932. *Die Armblanke ein Die Maatskappy: Verslag van die Carnegie-Kommissie.* Stellenbosch: Pro-ecclesia-drukkery.

Allman, Jean. 1994. "Making Mothers: Missionaries, Medical Officers and Women's Work in Colonial Asante, 1924–1945." *History Workshop Journal* 38: 23–47.

Amin, Samir. 1974. *Accumulation on a World Scale.* Trans. Brian Pearce. New York: Monthly Review Press.

Anderson, Benedict. 1983. *Imagined Communities: Reflections on the Origin and Spread of Nationalism.* London: Verso.

Anderson, David, and Richard Grove (eds.). 1987. *Conservation in Africa: Peoples, Policies and Practice.* Cambridge: Cambridge University Press.

Anderson, Warwick. 1995. "Excremental Colonialism: Public Health and the Poetics of Pollution." *Critical Inquiry* 21(3): 640–669.

Appadurai, Arjun. 1992. "Number in the Colonial Imagination." In *Orientalism and the Postcolonial Predicament: Perspectives on South Asia,* ed. Carol Breckenridge and Peter van der Veer, 314–339. Philadelphia: University of Pennsylvania Press.

Appiah, Anthony Kwame. 1992. *In My Father's House: Africa in the Philosophy of Culture.* New York: Oxford University Press.

Arnold, David. 1979. "European Orphans and Vagrants in India in the Nineteenth Century." *Journal of Imperial and Commonwealth History* 7: 104–127.

———. 1983. "White Colonization and Labour in Nineteenth-Century India." *Journal of Imperial and Commonwealth History* 11(2): 133–158.

———. 1988. "Touching the Body: Perspectives on the Indian Plague." In *Selected Subaltern Studies,* ed. Ranajit Guha and Gayatri Spivak, 391–426. New York: Oxford University Press.

———. 1993. *Colonizing the Body: State Medicine and Epidemic Disease in Nineteenth-Century India.* Berkeley: University of California Press.

Asad, Talal (ed.). 1973. *Anthropology and the Colonial Encounter.* London: Ithaca Press.

———. 1990. "Multiculturalism and British Identity in the Wake of the Rushdie Affair." *Politics and Society* 18(4): 455–480.

Ashcroft, Bill, Gareth Griffiths, and Helen Tiffin. 1989. *The Empire Strikes Back: Theory and Practice in Post-Colonial Literatures.* London: Routledge.

Ashforth, Adam. 1990. *The Politics of Official Discourse in Twentieth-Century South Africa.* Oxford: Clarendon Press.

Atkins, Keletso. 1993. *The Moon Is Dead! Give Us Our Money! The Cultural Origins of an African Work Ethic, Natal, South Africa, 1843–1900.* Portsmouth, N.H.: Heinemann.

Atran, Scott. 1989. "The Surrogate Colonisation of Palestine, 1917–1939." *American Ethnologist* 16: 719–744.

Aymard, Maurice (ed.). 1982. *Dutch Capitalism and World Capitalism.* London: Cambridge University Press.

Balandier, George. 1951. "La situation coloniale: Approche théorique." *Cahiers Internationaux de Sociologie* 11: 44–79.

Balibar, Etienne. 1994. "Racism as Universalism." In *Masses, Classes and Ideas.* London: Routledge.

Ballhatchet, Kenneth. 1980. *Race, Class and Sex under the Raj: Imperial Attitudes and Policies and Their Critics, 1793–1905.* New York: St. Martin's Press.

Bancel, Nicolas, Pascal Blanchard, and Laurent Gervereau (eds.). 1993. *Images et colonies: Iconographie et propagande coloniale sur l'Afrique française de 1880 à 1962.* Paris: BDIC-ACHAC.

Barratt Brown, Michael. 1974. *The Economics of Imperialism.* Harmondsworth, England: Penguin.

Bates, Robert H., V. Y. Mudimbe, and Jean O'Barr. 1993. *Africa and the Disciplines.* Chicago: University of Chicago Press.

Bayart, Jean-François. 1993. *The State in Africa: The Politics of the Belly.* London: Longman, 1993.

Bayly, C. A. 1989. *Imperial Meridian: The British Empire and the World, 1780–1830.* London: Longman.

Bayly, C. A., and D. H. A. Kolff (eds.). 1986. *Two Colonial Empires.* Dordrecht: Martinus Nijhoff.

Behdad, Ali. 1994. *Belated Travelers: Orientalism in the Age of Colonial Dissolution.* Durham: Duke University Press.

Beidelman, Thomas. 1982. *Colonialial Evangelism.* Bloomington: Indiana University Press.

Beinart, William. 1982. *The Political Economy of Pondoland, 1860–1930.* Cambridge: Cambridge University Press.

————. 1984. "Soil Erosion, Conservationism and Ideas about Development: A Southern African Exploration, 1900–1960." *Journal of Southern African Studies* 11: 52–83.

————. 1987. "*Amafelandawonye* (The Die-Hards): Popular Protest and Women's Movements in Herschel District in the 1920s." In *Hidden Struggles in Rural South Africa,* ed. William Beinart and Colin Bundy, 222–269. Berkeley: University of California Press.

Beinart, William, and Colin Bundy (eds.). 1987. *Hidden Struggles in Rural South Africa.* Berkeley: University of California Press.

Beneria, Lourdes. 1982. *Women and Development: The Sexual Division of Labor in Rural Societies.* New York: Praeger.

Berman, Bruce, and John Lonsdale. 1992. *Unhappy Valley: Conflict in Kenya and Africa.* London: James Currey.

Berreman, Gerald. 1981. *The Politics of Truth: Essays in Critical Anthropology.* Madras: South Asian Publishers.

Bhabha, Homi. 1994. *The Location of Culture.* New York: Routledge.

Blackburn, David. 1991. "The German Bourgeoisie: An Introduction." In *The German Bourgeoisie,* ed. David Blackbourn and Richard Evans, 1–45. London: Routledge.

Boahen, A. Adu. 1987. *African Perspectives on Colonialism.* Baltimore: Johns Hopkins University Press.

Bock, Gisela, and Pat Thane (eds.). 1991. *Maternity and Gender Policies: Women and the Rise of European Welfare States, 1880s–1950s.* London: Routledge.

Boeke, J. H. 1953. *Economics and Economic Policies of Dual Societies as Exemplified by Indonesia.* New York: Institute of Pacific Relations.

Bohannan, Paul. 1955. "Some Principles of Exchange and Investment among the Tiv." *American Anthropologist* 57: 60–70.

————. 1959. "The Impact of Money on an African Subsistence Economy." *Journal of Economic History* 19: 491–503.

Bose, Sugata (ed.). 1990. *South Asia and World Capitalism.* Delhi: Oxford University Press.

Bourguet, Marie-Noëlle. 1988. *Déchiffrer la France: La statistique départmentale à l'époque napoléonne.* Paris: Editions des archives contemporaines.

Bradford, Helen. 1987. *A Taste of Freedom: The ICU in Rural South Africa 1924–1930.* New Haven: Yale University Press.

Breckenridge, Carol, and Peter van der Veer (eds.). 1992. *Orientalism and the Post-colonial Predicament: Perspectives on South Asia*. Philadelphia: University of Pennsylvania Press.

Breman, Jan. 1989. *Taming the Coolie Beast: Plantation Society and the Colonial Order in Southeast Asia*. Delhi: Oxford University Press.

Brett, E. A. 1973. *Colonialism and Underdevelopment in East Africa: The Politics of Economic Change*. London: Heinemann.

Brocheux, Pierre, and Daniel Hémery. 1995. *Indochine: La colonisation ambiguë*. Paris: Editions la Découverte.

Brown, Richard. 1979. "Passages in the Life of a White Anthropologist: Max Gluckman in Northern Rhodesia." *Journal of African History* 20: 525–541.

Brubaker, Rogers. 1992. *Citizenship and Nationhood in France and Germany*. Cambridge, Mass.: Harvard University Press.

Brugmans, Dr. I. J. 1938. *Gescheidenis van het Onderwijs in Nederlandsch-Indie*. Groningen: J. B. Wolters.

Burbank, Jane, and David Rausel (eds.). Forthcoming. *Imperial Russia and Its Possibilities*.

Butcher, John G. 1979. *The British in Malaya, 1880–1941: The Social History of a European Community in South-East Asia*. Kuala Lumpur: Oxford University Press.

Buvinic, Mayra, Margaret Lycette, and William Paul McGreevey (eds.). 1983. *Women and Poverty in the Third World*. Baltimore: Johns Hopkins University Press.

Cain, P. J., and A. G. Hopkins. 1993. *British Imperialism*. 2 vols. London: Longman.

Callaway, Helen. 1987. *Gender, Culture and Empire: European Women in Colonial Nigeria*. London: Macmillan.

Chakrabarty, Dipesh. 1989. *Rethinking Working-Class History: Bengal 1890–1940*. Princeton: Princeton University Press.

———. 1992. "Postcoloniality and the Artifice of History: Who Speaks for 'Indian' Pasts?" *Representations* 37: 1–26.

Chanock, Martin. 1985. *Law, Custom and Social Order: The Colonial Experience in Malawi and Zambia*. Cambridge: Cambridge University Press.

Chatterjee, Partha. 1986. *Nationalist Thought and the Colonial World: A Derivative Discourse?* London: Zed Press.

———. 1989. "Colonialism, Nationalism, and Colonialized Women: The Contest in India." *American Ethnologist* 16(4): 622–633.

———. 1993. *The Nation and Its Fragments: Colonial and Postcolonial Histories*. Princeton: Princeton University Press.

Chaudhuri, Nupur. 1988. "Memsahibs and Motherhood in Nineteenth-Century Colonial India." *Victorian Studies* 13(4): 517–536.

Chaudhuri, Nupur, and Margaret Strobel (eds.). 1992. *Western Women and Imperialism: Complicity and Resistance*. Bloomington: Indiana University Press.

Chrétien, Jean-Pierre. 1993. *L'invention religieuse en Afrique: Histoire et religion en Afrique noire*. Paris: Karthala.

Clifford, James. 1988. *The Predicament of Culture: Twentieth-Century Ethnography, Literature and Art*. Cambridge, Mass.: Harvard University Press.

Clifford, James, and George Marcus (eds.). 1986. *Writing Culture: The Politics and Poetics of Ethnography*. Berkeley: University of California Press.

Cohen, David William, and E. S. Atieno-Odhiambo. 1992. *Burying SM: The Politics of Knowledge and the Sociology of Power in Africa*. Portsmouth, N.H.: Heinemann.

Cohn, Bernard. 1980. "History and Anthropology: The State of Play." *Comparative Studies in Society and History* 22 (April): 198–221.

———. 1987. *An Anthropologist among the Historians and Other Essays*. Delhi: Oxford University Press.

Cohn, Bernard, and Nicholas Dirks. 1988. "Beyond the Fringe: The Nation-State, Colonialism, and the Technologies of Power." *Journal of Historical Sociology* 1: 224–229.

Colley, Linda. 1992. "Britishness and Otherness: An Argument." *Journal of British Studies* 31 (October): 309–329.

Colonna, Fanny. 1975. *Instituteurs algériens: 1883–1939*. Paris: Presse de la Fondation nationale des sciences politiques.

Comaroff, Jean. 1985. *Body of Power, Spirit of Resistance: The Culture and History of a South African People*. Chicago: University of Chicago Press.

Comaroff, Jean, and John Comaroff. 1991. *Of Revelation and Revolution: Christianity, Colonialism, and Consciousness in South Africa*. Vol. 1. Chicago: University of Chicago Press.

———. 1992. "Homemade Hegemony." In *Ethnography and the Historical Imagination,* 265–295. Boulder, Colo.: Westview Press.

Congrés Colonial International de Paris. 1889. Paris: Challamel Augustin.

Conklin, Alice L. 1991. "Of Titians and Camels: The Origins of the *Mission Civilisatrice* in France." Paper for the Davis Seminar, Princeton University.

———. Forthcoming. *A Mission to Civilize: The Republican Idea of Empire in France and West Africa, 1895–1930*. Stanford: Stanford University Press.

Cooper, Frederick. 1980. *From Slaves to Squatters: Plantation Labor and Agriculture in Zanzibar and Coastal Kenya, 1890–1925*. New Haven: Yale University Press.

———. 1994. "Conflict and Connection: Rethinking Colonial African History." *American Historical Review* 99: 1516–1545.

———. 1996. *Decolonization and African Society: The Labor Question in French and British Africa*. Cambridge: Cambridge University Press.

———. Forthcoming. "'Conditions Analogous to Slavery': Imperialism and Free Labor Ideology in Africa." In *Beyond Slavery: Explorations of Race, Labor, and Citizenship in Postemancipation Societies,* ed. Frederick Cooper, Thomas Holt, and Rebecca Scott.

Cooper, Frederick, Allen Isaacman, Florencia Mallon, William Roseberry, and Steve Stern. 1993. *Confronting Historical Paradigms: Peasants, Labor, and the Capitalist World System in Africa and Latin America*. Madison: University of Wisconsin Press.

Cooper, Frederick, and Ann Stoler. 1989. *Tensions of Empire: Colonial Control and Visions of Rule*. Special Issue of *American Ethnologist* 16(4).

Coquery-Vidrovitch, Catherine, Daniel Hémery, and Jean Piel (eds.). 1988. *Pour une histoire du développement: Etats, sociétés, développement*. Paris: L'Harmattan.

Coronil, Fernando. 1995. "Beyond Occidentalism: Towards Non-Imperial Geohistorical Categories." *Cultural Anthropology* 11(1): 51–87.

Cribb, Robert (ed.). 1994. *The Late Colonial State in Indonesia: Political and Economic Foundations of the Netherlands Indies, 1880–1942.* Leiden: KITLV Press.

Curtin, Philip D. 1989. *Death by Migration: Europe's Encounter with the Tropical World in the Nineteenth Century.* New York: Cambridge University Press.

Daniel, Valentine, Henry Bernstein, and Tom Brass (eds.). 1992. *Plantations, Proletarians and Peasants in Colonial Asia.* London: Frank Cass.

Davidoff, Leonore, and Catherine Hall. 1987. *Family Fortunes: The Men and Women of the English Middle Class, 1780–1850.* Chicago: University of Chicago Press.

Davis, David Brion. 1975. *The Problem of Slavery in the Age of Revolution, 1770–1823.* Ithaca: Cornell University Press.

———. 1984. *Slavery and Human Progress.* New York: Oxford University Press.

Diouf, Mamadou. Forthcoming. "L'enterprise sénéglaise de développement: De la mobilisation de masse à l'élitisme technocratique." In *Development Knowledge and the Social Sciences,* ed. Frederick Cooper and Randall Packard.

Dirks, Nicholas. 1987. *The Hollow Crown: Ethnohistory of an Indian Kingdom.* Cambridge: Cambridge University Press.

———. 1994. "Guiltless Spoilations: Picturesque Beauty, Colonial Knowledge, and Colin McKenzie's Survey of India." In *Perceptions of South Asia's Visual Past,* ed. Catherine Asher and Thomas R. Metcalfe, 211–234. Delhi: Oxford University Press.

Dirks, Nicholas (ed.). 1992. *Colonialism and Culture.* Ann Arbor: University of Michigan Press.

Doorn, J. A. A. van. 1994. *De Laatste Eeuw van Indie: Ontwikkeling en ondergang van een koloniaal project.* Amsterdam: Bert Bakker.

Drescher, Seymour. 1987. *Capitalism and Antislavery: British Mobilization in Comparative Perspective.* New York: Oxford University Press.

Eagleton, Terry, Frederic Jameson, and Edward Said. 1990. *Nationalism, Colonialism and Literature.* Minneapolis: University of Minnesota Press.

Echenberg, Myron. 1991. *Colonial Conscripts: The Tirailleurs Sénégalais in French West Africa, 1857–1960.* Portsmouth, N.H.: Heinemann.

Edwards, David. 1989. "Mad Mullahs and Englishmen: Discourse in the Colonial Encounter." *Comparative Studies in Society and History* 31: 649–670.

Ehrlich, Cyril. 1973. "Building and Caretaking: Economic Policy in British Tropical Africa." *Economic History Review* 26: 649–667.

Eley, Geoffrey. 1991. "Liberalism, Europe and the Bourgeoisie." In *The German Bourgeoisie,* ed. David Blackburn and Richard Evans, 293–317. London: Routledge.

Eltis, David. 1987. *Economic Growth and the Ending of the Transatlantic Slave Trade.* New York: Oxford University Press.

Engels, Dagmar. 1989. "The Limits of Gender Ideology: Bengali Women, the Colonial State, and the Private Sphere, 1890–1930." *Women's Studies International Forum* 12(4): 425–438.

Engels, Dagmar, and Shula Marks (eds.). 1994. *Contesting Colonial Hegemony: State and Society in Africa and India.* London: I. B. Tauris.

Escobar, Arturo. 1995. *Encountering Development: The Making and Unmaking of the Third World.* Princeton: Princeton University Press.

Etienne, Mona, and Eleanor Leacock. 1980. *Women and Colonization: Anthropological Perspectives.* New York: Praeger.

Fabian, Johannes. 1983. *Time and the Other: How Anthropology Makes Its Object.* New York: Columbia University Press.

Fagan, Brian. 1984. *Clash of Cultures.* New York: W. H. Freeman.

Fanon, Frantz. 1966. *The Wretched of the Earth.* Trans. Constance Farrington. New York: Grove. Orig. publ. 1961.

Fasseur, C. 1993. *De Indologen: Ambtenaren voor de Oost, 1825–1950.* Amsterdam: Bert Bakker.

Ferguson, James. 1990. *The Anti-Politics Machine: "Development," Depoliticization, and Bureaucratic Power in Lesotho.* Cambridge: Cambridge University Press.

Ferguson, Moira. 1992. *Subject to Others: British Women Writers and Colonial Slavery, 1670–1834.* New York: Routledge.

Ferrer, Ada. 1995. "To Making a Free Nation: Race and the Struggle for Independence in Cuba, 1868–1898." Ph.D. dissertation, University of Michigan.

Ferro, Marc. 1994. *Histoire des colonisations: Des conquêtes aux indépendances XIIIe–XXe siècle.* Paris: Seuil.

Fick, Carolyn E. 1990. *The Making of Haiti: The Saint Domingue Revolution from Below.* Knoxville: University of Tennessee Press.

Fields, Karen. 1985. *Revival and Rebellion in Colonial Central Africa.* Princeton: Princeton University Press.

Florida, Nancy. 1995. *Writing the Past, Inscribing the Future: History as Prophecy in Colonial Java.* Durham, N.C.: Duke University Press.

France. 1946. *Débats de l'Assemblée Nationale Constituante* 2 (27 August).

Franke, Richard. 1973. "The Green Revolution in a Javanese Village." Ph.D. dissertation, Harvard University.

Furnivall, J. S. 1948. *Colonial Policy and Practice: A Comparative Study of Burma and the Netherlands Indies.* Cambridge: Cambridge University Press.

Gailey, Christine Ward. 1987. *Kinship to Kingship: Gender Hierarchy and State Formation in the Tongan Islands.* Austin: University of Texas Press.

Gay, Peter. 1993. *The Cultivation of Hatred: The Bourgeois Experience, Victoria to Freud.* New York: Norton.

Geertz, Clifford. 1968. *Agricultural Involution: The Processes of Ecological Change in Indonesia.* Berkeley: University of California Press.

Giddens, Anthony. 1985. *The Nation-State and Violence.* Berkeley: University of California Press.

Gilroy, Paul. 1987. *'There Ain't No Black in the Union Jack': The Cultural Politics of Race and Nation.* Chicago: University of Chicago Press.

———. 1993. *The Black Atlantic: Modernity and Double Consciousness.* Cambridge, Mass.: Harvard University Press.

Girardet, Raoul. 1972. *L'idée coloniale en France de 1871 à 1962.* Paris: Table Ronde.

Godlewska, Anne. 1994. "Napoleon's Geographers (1797–1815): Imperialists and Soldiers of Modernity." In *Geography and Empire,* ed. Anne Godlewska and Neil Smith, 31–55. Oxford: Blackwell.

Godlewska, Anne, and Neil Smith (eds.). 1994. *Geography and Empire.* Oxford: Blackwell.

Gong, Gerrit W. 1984. *The Standard of "Civilization" in International Society.* Oxford: Clarendon Press.

Gordon, Robert. 1988. "Apartheid's Anthropologists: The Genealogy of Afrikaner Anthropology." *American Ethnologist* 15(3): 535–553.

———. 1992. *The Bushmen Myth: The Making of a Namibian Underclass.* Boulder, Colo.: Westview Press.

Gouda, Frances. 1995. *Dutch Culture Overseas: Colonial Practices in the Netherlands Indies.* Amsterdam: Amsterdam University Press.

Grimshaw, Patricia. 1989. *Paths of Duty: American Missionary Wives in Nineteenth-Century Hawaii.* Honolulu: University of Hawaii Press.

Gross, Daniel. 1970. "Sisal and Social Structure in Northeastern Brazil." Ph.D. dissertation, Columbia University.

Guha, Ranajit. 1988. "The Prose of Counterinsurgency." In *Selected Subaltern Studies,* ed. Ranajit Guha and Gayatri Spivak, 45–86. New York: Oxford University Press.

———. 1989. "Dominance Without Hegemony and Its Historiography." In *Subaltern Studies VI,* ed. Ranajit Guha, 210–309. Delhi: Oxford University Press.

Guha, Ranajit, and Gayatri Spivak (eds.). 1988. *Selected Subaltern Studies.* New York: Oxford University Press.

Hall, Stuart. 1978. *Policing the Crisis: Mugging, the State, and Law and Order.* London: Macmillan.

———. 1980. "Race, Articulation and Societies Structured in Dominance." In UNESCO, *Sociological Theories: Race and Colonialism,* 305–345. Paris: UNESCO.

Hansen, Karen (ed.). 1992. *African Encounters with Domesticity.* New Brunswick, N.J.: Rutgers University Press.

Harries, Patrick. 1994. *Work, Culture, and Identity: Migrant Laborers in Mozambique and South Africa, c. 1860–1910.* Portsmouth, N.H.: Heinemann.

Heffernan, Michael J. 1994. "The French Geographical Movement and the Forms of French Imperialism, 1870–1920." In *Geography and Empire,* ed. Anne Godlewska and Neil Smith, 92–114. Oxford: Blackwell.

Heussler, Robert. 1963. *Yesterday's Rulers: The Making of the British Colonial Service.* Syracuse: Syracuse University Press.

———. 1983. *Completing a Stewardship: The Malayan Civil Service, 1942–57.* Westport, Conn.: Greenwood.

———. 1987. *British Rule in Malaya: The Malayan Civil Service and Its Predecessors, 1867–1942.* Westport, Conn.: Greenwood.

Heyningen, Elizabeth van. 1984. "The Social Evil in the Cape Colony, 1868–1902: Prostitution and the Contagious Disease Acts." *Journal of Southern African Studies* 10(2): 170–197.

Hirschfeld, Lawrence. 1996. *Race in the Making: Cognition, Culture and the Child's Construction of Human Kinds.* Cambridge: MIT Press.

Hirschman, Albert. 1981. "The Rise and Decline of Development Economics." In Hirschman, *Essays in Trespassing,* 1–24. Cambridge: Cambridge University Press.

Hobsbawm, Eric. 1987. *The Age of Empire: 1875–1914.* London: Weidenfeld and Nicolson.

Hobsbawm, Eric, and Terence Ranger (eds.). 1983. *The Invention of Tradition.* Cambridge: Cambridge University Press.

Holt, Thomas C. 1990. *The Problem of Freedom: Race, Labor and Politics in Jamaica and Britain, 1832–1938.* Baltimore: Johns Hopkins University Press.

Hoskins, Janet. 1993. *The Play of Time: Kodi Perspectives on Calendars, History, and Exchange.* Berkeley: University of California Press.

Howe, Stephen. 1993. *Anticolonialism in British Politics: The Left and the End of Empire, 1918–1964.* Oxford: Clarendon Press.

Huttenback, Robert, and Lance Davis. 1986. *Mannon and the Pursuit of Empire: The Political Economy of British Imperialism, 1860–1912.* New York: Cambridge University Press.

Hyam, Ronald. 1990. *Empire and Sexuality: The British Experience.* Manchester: Manchester University Press.

Ileto, Reynaldo. 1979. *Payson and Revolution: Popular Movements in the Philippines, 1840–1910.* Quezon City: Ateneo de Manila University Press.

———. 1992. "Cholera and the Origins of the American Sanitary Order in the Philippines." In *Imperial Medicine and Indigenous Societies,* ed. David Arnold, 125–148. Manchester: Manchester University Press.

Inglis, Amirah. 1975. *The White Women's Protection Ordinance: Sexual Anxiety and Politics in Papua.* London: Sussex University Press.

James, C. L. R. 1963. *The Black Jacobins: Toussaint L'Ouverture and the San Domingo Revolution.* New York: Vintage. Orig. publ. 1938.

Jolly, Margaret. 1993. "Colonizing Women: The Maternal Body and Empire." In *Feminism and the Politics of Difference,* ed. Senja Gunew and Anna Yeatman, 113–127. Boulder, Colo.: Westview Press.

Kahn, Joel S. 1993. *Constituting the Minangkabau: Peasants, Culture, and Modernity in Colonial Indonesia.* Providence, R.I.: Berg.

Kaplan, Amy, and Donald E. Pease (eds.). 1993. *Cultures of United States Imperialism.* Durham, N.C.: Duke University Press.

Karp, Ivan (ed.). 1991. *Exhibiting Cultures: The Poetics and Politics of Museum Display.* Washington, D.C.: Smithsonian Institution Press.

———. 1992. *Museums and Community: The Politics of Public Culture.* Washington, D.C.: Smithsonian Institution Press.

Kaviraj, Sudipta. 1993. "The Imaginary Institution of India." In *Subaltern Studies VII,* ed. Partha Chatterjee and Gyanendra Pandey, 1–39. Delhi: Oxford University Press.

Keesing, Roger. 1992. *Custom and Confrontation: The Kwaio Struggle for Cultural Autonomy.* Chicago: University of Chicago Press.

Kelly, Gail. 1975. "Franco-Vietnamese Schools, 1918–1938." Ph.D. dissertation, University of Wisconsin–Madison.

Kelly, John. 1991. *A Politics of Virtue: Hinduism, Sexuality and Countercolonial Discourse in Fiji.* Chicago: University of Chicago Press.

Kennedy, Dane. 1987. *Islands of White: Settler Society and Culture in Kenya and Southern Rhodesia, 1890–1939.* Durham, N.C.: Duke University Press.

Kiernan, Victor. 1969. *The Lords of Human Kind: European Attitudes Towards the Outside World in the Imperial Age.* London: Weidenfeld and Nicolson.

Kipp, Rita. 1990. *The Early Years of a Dutch Mission: The Karo Field.* Ann Arbor: University of Michigan Press.

Knapman, Claudia. 1986. *White Women in Fiji, 1835–1930: The Ruin of Empire?* London: Allen and Unwin.

Koven, Seth, and Sonya Michel. 1993. *Mothers of a New World: Maternalist Politics and the Origins of the Welfare State*. New York: Routledge.

Kuklick, Henrika. 1979. *The Imperial Bureaucrat: The Colonial Administrative Service in the Gold Coast, 1920–1939*. Stanford: Hoover Institution Press.

———. 1991. *The Savage Within: The Social History of British Anthropology, 1885–1945*. Cambridge: Cambridge University Press.

Laffey, John. 1975. "Education for Empire in Lyon during the Third Republic." *History of Education Quarterly* (Summer 1975): 169–184.

———. 1976. "Racism and Imperialism: French Views of the 'Yellow Peril,' 1894–1914." *Third Republic* 1: 1–52.

———. 1977. "Imperialists Divided: The Views of Tonkin's *Colons* before 1914." *Histoire Sociale* 10(19): 92–113.

Lebovics, Herman. 1992. *True France: The Wars over Cultural Identity, 1900–1945*. Ithaca: Cornell University Press.

Liauzu, Claude. 1982. *Aux origines des tiers-mondismes: Colonisés et anticolonialistes en France, 1919–1939*. Paris: L'Harmattan.

Linnekin, Jocelyn. 1990. *Sacred Queens and Women of Consequence: Rank, Gender and Colonialism in the Hawaiian Islands*. Ann Arbor: University of Michigan Press.

Locher-Scholten, Elsbeth. 1994. "Dutch Expansion in the Indonesian Archipelago around 1900 and the Imperialism Debate." *Journal of Southeast Asian Studies* 25(1): 91–111.

Lonsdale, John. 1981. "States and Social Processes in Africa: A Historiographical Survey." *African Studies Review* 24, nos. 2/3 (1981): 132–226.

Lonsdale, John, and Bruce Berman. 1979. "Coping with the Contradictions: The Development of the Colonial State in Kenya." *Journal of African History* 20: 487–506.

Lowe, Lisa. 1991. *Critical Terrains: French and British Orientalisms*. Ithaca: Cornell University Press.

MacKenzie, John M. 1984. *Propaganda and Empire: The Manipulation of British Public Opinion, 1880–1960*. Manchester: Manchester University Press.

MacKenzie, John (ed.). 1990. *Imperialism and the Natural World*. Manchester: Manchester University Press.

Majeed, Javed. 1992. *Ungoverned Imaginings: James Mill's "The History of British India and Orientalism."* Oxford: Clarendon Press.

Malkki, Liisa. 1992. "National Geographic: The Rooting of Peoples and the Territorialization of National Identity Among Scholars and Refugees." *Cultural Anthropology* 7 (1992): 24–44.

Manderson, Leonore. 1987. "Health Services and the Legitimation of the Colonial State: British Malaya, 1786–1941." *International Journal of Health Services* 17(1): 91–112.

Mangan, J. A. 1988. *"Benefits Bestowed"? Education and British Imperialism*. Manchester: Manchester University Press.

Mani, Lata. 1990. "Contentious Traditions: The Debate on *Sati* in Colonial India." In *Recasting Women: Essays in Indian Colonial History*, eds. Kumkum Sangari and Sudesh Vaid, 88–126. New Brunswick, N.J.: Rutgers University Press.

Manicom, Linzi. 1992. "Ruling Relations: Rethinking State and Gender in South African History." *Journal of African History* 33: 441–465.

Mann, Kristin. 1985. *Marrying Well: Marriage, Status, and Social Change among the Educated Elite in Colonial Lagos.* Cambridge: Cambridge University Press.

Mann, Kristin, and Richard Roberts (eds.). 1991. *Law in Colonial Africa.* Portsmouth, N.H.: Heinemann.

Marks, Shula. 1990. "History, the Nation and Empire: Sniping from the Periphery." *History Workshop Journal* 29: 111–119.

Marseille, Jacques. 1984. *Empire colonial et capitalisme français: Histoire d'un divorce.* Paris: Albin Michel.

Mbembe, Achille. 1992. "The Banality of Power and the Aesthetics of Vulgarity in the Postcolony." *Public Culture* 4, no. 2 (1992): 1–30.

———. 1993. *La naissance du maquis dans le Sud-Cameroun: Histoires d'indisciplines (1920–1960).* Paris: Karthala.

McClintock, Anne. 1990. "The Angel of Progress: Pitfalls of the Term 'Post-Colonialism.'" *Social Text,* no. 31/32: 84–98.

———. 1995. *Imperial Leather: Race, Gender and Sexuality in the Colonial Contest.* London: Routledge.

Meillassoux, Claude. 1975. *Femmes, greniers et capitaux.* Paris: Maspero.

Mellman, Billie. 1992. *Women's Orients: English Women and the Middle East, 1718–1918: Sexuality, Religion and Work.* Ann Arbor: University of Michigan Press.

Merry, Sally Engle. 1991. "Law and Colonialism." *Law and Society Review* 25: 889–922.

Miles, Robert. 1982. *Racism and Migrant Labor.* London: Routledge and Kegan Paul.

Miller, Christopher. 1985. *Blank Darkness: Africanist Discourse in French.* Chicago: University of Chicago Press.

Mills, Sara. 1991. *Discourses of Difference: An Analysis of Women's Travel Writing and Colonialism.* London: Routledge.

Ming, Hanneke. 1983. "Barracks-Concubinage in the Indies, 1887–1920." *Indonesia* 35: 65–93.

Mintz, Sidney. 1974. *Caribbean Transformations.* Chicago: Aldine.

———. 1985. *Sweetness and Power.* New York: Penguin.

Mitchell, Timothy. 1988. *Colonizing Egypt.* Berkeley: University of California Press.

Moore, Sally Falk. 1993. *Anthropology and Africa: Changing Perspectives on a Changing Scene.* Charlottesville: University Press of Virginia.

Morgan, Edmund S. 1975. *American Slavery, American Freedom: The Ordeal of Colonial Virginia.* New York: Norton.

Mosse, George. 1985. *Nationalism and Sexuality.* Madison: University of Wisconsin Press.

Mudimbe, V. Y. 1988. *The Invention of Africa: Gnosis, Philosophy, and the Order of Knowledge.* Bloomington: Indiana University Press.

Nair, Janaki. 1990. "Uncovering the Zenana: Visions of Indian Womanhood in Englishwomen's Writings, 1813–1940." *Journal of Women's History* 2(1): 8–34.

Nandy, Ashis. 1983. *The Intimate Enemy: Loss and Recovery of Self under Colonialism.* Delhi: Oxford University Press.

————. 1995. *The Savage Freud and Other Essays on Possible and Retrievable Selves.* Princeton: Princeton University Press.

Noordman, Jan. 1989. *Om de kwaliteit van het nageslacht: Eugenetica in Nederland, 1900–1950.* Nijmegen: SUN.

O'Hanlon, Rosalind. 1988. "Recovering the Subject: Subaltern Studies and Histories of Resistance in Colonial South Asia." *Modern Asian Studies* 22: 189–224.

Ong, Aihwa. 1987. *Spirits of Resistance and Capitalist Discipline: Factory Women in Malaysia.* Binghamton: State University of New York Press.

Ortner, Sherry. 1995. "Resistance and the Problem of Ethnographic Refusal." *Comparative Studies in Society and History* 37: 173–193.

Ott, Thomas O. 1973. *The Haitian Revolution, 1789–1804.* Knoxville: University of Tennessee Press.

Packard, Randall. 1989. "The 'Healthy Reserve' and the 'Dressed Native': Discourses on Black Health and the Language of Legitimation in South Africa." *American Ethnologist* 16: 686–703.

Pandey, Gyanendra. 1990. *The Construction of Communalism in Colonial North India.* Delhi: Oxford University Press.

Parker, Andrew, Mary Russo, Doris Sommer, and Patricia Yaeger. 1992. *Nationalisms and Sexualities.* New York: Routledge.

Pedersen, Susan. 1991. "National Bodies, Unspeakable Acts: The Sexual Politics of Colonial Policymaking." *Journal of Modern History* 63: 647–680.

Pemberton, John. 1994. *On the Subject of "Java."* Ithaca: Cornell University Press.

Phillips, Anne. 1989. *The Enigma of Colonialism: British Policy in West Africa.* London: James Currey.

Pletsch, Carl. 1981. "The Three Worlds and the Division of Social Scientific Labor circa 1950–1975." *Comparative Studies in Society and History* 34: 491–513.

Prakash, Gyan. 1992. "Writing Post-Orientalist Histories of the Third World: Perspectives from Indian Historiography." *Comparative Studies in Society and History* 32 (1990): 383–408.

Pratt, Mary Louise. 1992. *Imperial Eyes: Travel Writing and Transculturation.* London: Routledge.

Price, Grenfell. 1939. *White Settlers in the Tropics.* New York: American Geographical Society.

Price, Richard. 1983a. *Dutch Colonial Perspectives on the Saramka Wars.* Ann Arbor: Karoma Publishers.

————. 1983b. *First-time: The Historical Vision of an Afro-American People.* Baltimore: Johns Hopkins University Press.

Price, Sally. 1989. *Primitive Art in Civilized Places.* Chicago: University of Chicago Press.

Priestley, Margaret. 1969. *West African Trade and Coast Society: A Family Study.* London: Oxford University Press.

Prochaska, David. 1990. *Making Algeria French: Colonialism in Bône, 1870–1920.* Cambridge: Cambridge University Press.

Pyenson, Lewis. 1993. *Civilizing Mission: Exact Sciences and French Overseas Expansion, 1830–1940.* Baltimore: Johns Hopkins University Press.

Rabinow, Paul. 1986. "Representations are Social Facts: Modernity and Post-Modernity in Anthropology." In *Writing Culture: The Poetics and Politics of Ethnography,* ed. James Clifford and George Marcus, 234–261. Berkeley: University of California Press.

——. 1989. *French Modern: Norms and Forms of the Social Environment.* Cambridge, Mass.: MIT Press.

Radical History Review. 1990. Special issue. "Imperialism: A Useful Category of Historical Analysis?"

Rafael, Vincent. 1993. *Contracting Colonialism: Translation and Christian Conversion in Tagalog Society under Early Spanish Rule.* Durham, N.C.: Duke University Press.

——. Forthcoming. "Colonial Domesticity: White Women and United States Rule in the Philippines." *American Literature.*

Rappaport, Joanne. 1994. *Cumbre Reborn: An Andean Ethnography of History.* Chicago: University of Chicago Press.

Regt, Ali de. 1984. *Arbeidersgezinnen en beschavingsarbeid.* Amsterdam: Boom.

Rich, Paul. 1984. "The Long Victorian Sunset: Anthropology, Eugenics and Race in Britain, c. 1900–48." *Patterns of Prejudice* 18(3): 3–17.

——. 1986. *Race and Empire in British Politics.* Cambridge: Cambridge University Press.

——. 1989. *The Elixir of Empire: The English Public Schools, Ritualism, Freemasonry, and Imperialism.* London: Regency Press.

——. 1990. "Race, Science, and the Legitimization of White Supremacy in South Africa, 1902–1940." *International Journal of African Historical Studies* 23(4): 665–686.

Rodgers, Barbara. 1980. *The Domestication of Women: Discrimination in Developing Societies.* London: Tavistock.

Rodney, Walter. 1981. *A History of the Guyanese Working People, 1881–1905.* Baltimore: Johns Hopkins University Press.

Roediger, David. 1991. *The Wages of Whiteness: Race and the Making of the American Working Class.* London: Verso.

Rosaldo, Renato. 1980. *Ilongot Headhunting, 1883–1974: A Study in Society and History.* Stanford: Stanford University Press.

Roseberry, William. 1978. "Historical Materialism and the Peoples of Puerto Rico." *Revista/Review Interamericana* 8: 26–36.

——. 1987. "Political Economy." *Annual Review of Anthropology* 17: 161–185.

Ross, Robert (ed.). 1982. *Racism and Colonialism.* Leiden: Martinus Nijhoff.

Rushdie, Salman. 1991. "The New Empire within Britain." In Rushdie, *Imaginary Homelands: Essays of Criticism, 1981–1991.* New York: Granta Books.

Rydell, Robert. 1984. *All the World's a Fair.* Chicago: University of Chicago Press.

Sachs, Wolfgang (ed.). 1992. *The Development Dictionary: A Guide to Knowledge as Power.* London: Zed.

Sahlins, Marshall. 1981. *Historical Metaphors and Mythical Realities.* Ann Arbor: University of Michigan Press.

——. 1985. *Islands of History.* Chicago: University of Chicago Press.

Said, Edward. 1978. *Orientalism.* New York: Pantheon.

——. 1993. *Culture and Imperialism.* New York: Knopf.

Sangari, Kumkum, and Sudeh Vaid (eds.). 1989. *Recasting Women: Essays in Indian Colonial History*. New Brunswick, N.J.: Rutgers University Press.

Schmidt-Nowara, Christopher. 1995. "The Problem of Slavery in the Age of Capital: Abolitionism, Liberalism, and Counter-Hegemony in Spain, Cuba, and Puerto Rico, 1833–1886." Ph.D. dissertation, University of Michigan.

Schneider, William. 1982. *Empire for the Masses: The French Popular Image of Africa, 1870–1900*. Westport, Conn.: Greenwood.

———. 1990. *Quality and Quantity: The Quest for Biological Regeneration in Twentieth-Century France*. London: Cambridge University Press.

Schumpeter, Joseph. 1951. *Imperialism and Social Classes*. Trans. Heinz Norden. New York: Kelley.

Scott, David. 1995. "Colonial Governmentality." *Social Text* 43: 191–220.

Scott, James C. 1990. *Domination and the Arts of Resistance: Hidden Transcripts*. New Haven: Yale University Press.

Scott, Rebecca. 1985. *Slave Emancipation in Cuba: The Transition to Free Labor, 1860–1899*. Princeton: Princeton University Press.

Scully, Pamela. 1995. "Rape, Race, and Colonial Culture: The Sexual Politics of Identity in the Nineteenth-Century Cape Colony, South Africa." *American Historical Review* 100: 335–359.

Semmel, Bernard. 1993. *The Liberal Ideal and the Demons of Empire: Theories of Imperialism from Adam Smith to Lenin*. Baltimore: Johns Hopkins University Press.

Sider, Gerald. 1987. "When Parrots Learn to Talk, and Why They Can't: Domination, Deception and Self-Deception in Indian-White Relations." *Comparative Studies in Society and History* 29: 3–23.

Silverblatt, Irene. 1987. *Moon, Sun, and Witches: Gender Ideologies and Class in Inca and Colonial Peru*. Princeton: Princeton University Press.

Skurski, Julie. 1995. "The Ambiguities of Authenticity in Latin America: *Dona Barbara* and the Construction of National Identity." *Poetics Today* 15(4): 605–642.

Sommer, Doris. 1991. *Foundational Fictions: The National Romances of Latin America*. Berkeley: University of California Press.

Spivak, Gayatri Chakravorty. 1988a. *In Other Worlds*. London: Routledge.

———. 1988b. "Can the Subaltern Speak?" In *Marxism and the Interpretation of Culture*, ed. Cary Nelson and Larry Grossberg, 271–313. Urbana: University of Illinois Press.

Stedman Jones, Gareth. 1971. *Outcast London: A Study in the Relationship between Classes in Victorian Society*. Oxford: Oxford University Press.

Steedley, Mary Margaret. 1993. *Hanging without a Rope: Narrative Experience in Colonial and Postcolonial Karoland*. Princeton: Princeton University Press.

Stepan, Nancy. 1982. *The Idea of Race in Science: Great Britain, 1800–1960*. London: Macmillan.

———. 1991. *"The Hour of Eugenics": Race, Gender, and Nation in Latin America*. Ithaca: Cornell University Press.

Steward, Julian (ed.). 1956. *The Peoples of Puerto Rico*. Urbana: University of Illinois Press.

Stocking, George, Jr. 1987. *Victorian Anthropology*. New York: Free Press.

———. 1995. *After Tylor: British Social Anthropology 1888–1951*. Madison: University of Wisconsin Press.

Stocking, George, Jr. (ed.). 1985. *Objects and Others: Essays on Museums and Material Culture*. Madison: University of Wisconsin Press.

———. 1991. *Colonial Situations: Essays on the Contextualization of Ethnographic Knowledge*. Madison: University of Wisconsin Press.

Stoler, Ann Laura. 1985a. *Capitalism and Confrontation in Sumatra's Plantation Belt, 1870–1979*. New Haven: Yale University Press.

———. 1985b. "Perceptions of Protest: Defining the Dangerous in Colonial Sumatra." *American Ethnologist* 12(4): 642–658.

———. 1988. "Working the Revolution: Plantation Laborers and the People's Militia in North Sumatra." *Journal of Asian Studies* 47(2): 227–247.

———. 1989. "Rethinking Colonial Categories: European Communities and the Boundaries of Rule." *Comparative Studies in Society and History* 13(1): 134–161.

———. 1991. "Carnal Knowledge and Imperial Power: Gender, Race and Morality in Colonial Asia." In *Gender at the Crossroads of Knowledge: Feminist Anthropology in a Postmodern Era,* ed. Micaela di Leonardo, 55–101. Berkeley: University of California Press.

———. 1992. "'In Cold Blood': Hierarchies of Credibility and the Politics of Colonial Narratives." *Representations* 37: 151–189.

———. 1995a. *Race and the Education of Desire: Foucault's History of Sexuality and the Colonial Order of Things*. Durham, N.C.: Duke University Press.

———. 1995b. "A Sentimental Education: European Children and Native Servants in the Netherlands Indies." In *Fantasizing the Feminine: Sex and Death in Indonesia,* ed. Laurie Sears, 71–91. Durham, N.C.: Duke University Press.

———. 1995c. "[P]refacing *Capitalism and Confrontation* in 1995." In *Capitalism and Confrontation in Sumatra's Plantation Belt, 1870–1979*, vi–xxxiv. Ann Arbor: University of Michigan Press.

Stoler, Ann Laura. Forthcoming, a. *Ethnography in the Colonial Archives: Movements on the Historic Turn*. Princeton: Princeton University Press.

———. Forthcoming, b. *Carnal Knowledge and Imperial Power*. Berkeley: University of California Press.

Stuurman, Siep. 1983. *Verzuiling, Kapitalisme en Patriarchaat*. Nijmigen: SUN.

———. 1992. *Wacht op onze daden: Het liberalisme en de vernieuwing van de Nederlandse Staat*. Amsterdam: Bert Bakker.

Suleri, Sara. 1992. *The Rhetoric of English India*. Chicago: University of Chicago Press.

Summers, Carole. 1991. "Intimate Colonialism: The Imperial Production of Reproduction in Uganda, 1907–1925." *Signs* 16(4): 787–807.

Tabili, Laura. 1994. *"We Ask for British Justice": Workers and Racial Difference in Late Imperial Britain*. Ithaca: Cornell University Press.

Taguieff, Pierre-André. 1989. "The Doctrine of the National Front in France (1972–1989)." *New Political Science,* nos. 16/17: 29–70.

Taguieff, Pierre-André (ed.). 1991. *Face au racisme*. Paris: Editions La Découverte.

———. 1995. *Les fins de l'antiracisme*. Paris: Editions Michalon.

Taussig, Michael. 1980. *The Devil and Commodity Fetishism*. Chapel Hill: University of North Carolina Press.

———. 1984. "Culture of Terror—Space of Death: Roger Casement's Putumayo Report and the Explanation of Torture." *Comparative Studies in Society and History* 26: 467–497.

————. 1987. *Shamanism, Colonialism, and the Wild Man: A Study in Terror and Healing.* Chicago: University of Chicago Press.

Taylor, Jean. 1983. *The Social World of Batavia.* Madison: University of Wisconsin Press.

Thiam, Doudou. 1953. "La Portée de la citoyenneté Française dans les territoires d'outre-mer." Thèse pour le doctorat en droit, Université de Poitiers, 1951. Paris: Société d'éditions africaines.

Thomas, Nicholas. 1990. "Sanitation and Seeing: The Creation of State Power in Early Colonial Fiji." *Comparative Studies in Society and History* 32(1): 149–170.

————. 1991. *Entangled Objects: Exchange, Material Culture, and Colonialism in the Pacific.* Cambridge, Mass.: Harvard University Press.

————. 1994. *Colonialism's Culture: Anthropology, Travel and Government.* Princeton: Princeton University Press.

Todorov, Tzvetan. 1993. *On Human Diversity: Nationalism, Racism, and Exoticism in French Thought.* Cambridge: Harvard University Press.

Tolen, Rachel. 1991. "Colonizing and Transforming the Criminal Tribesman: The Salvation Army in British India." *American Ethnologist* 18: 106–125.

Torgovnick, Marianna. 1990. *Gone Primitive: Savage Intellects, Modern Lives.* Chicago: University of Chicago Press.

Trouillot, Michel Rolph. 1989. "Discourses of Rule and the Acknowledgment of the Peasantry in Dominica, W.I., 1838–1928." *American Ethnologist* 16: 703–718.

————. 1995. *Silencing the Past: Power and the Production of History.* Boston: Beacon Press.

UNESCO. 1956. *Social Implications of Industrialization and Urbanization in Africa South of the Sahara.* Paris: UNESCO.

Union Géographique Internationale. 1938. *Comptes Rendus du Congrès International de Géographie, Amsterdam.* Leiden: Brill.

Vaillant, Janet. 1990. *Black, French, and African: A Life of Léopold Sédar Senghor.* Cambridge, Mass.: Harvard University Press.

Valk, Loes van der. 1986. *Van Pauperzorg tot Bestaanszekerheid: Een onderzoek naar de ontwikkeling van de armenzorg in Nederland tegen de achtergrond van de overgang naar de Algemene Bijstandswet, 1912–1965.* Rotterdam: Erasmus.

Van Onselen, Charles. 1982. *Studies in the Social and Economic History of the Witwatersrand.* 2 vols. London: Longman.

Vaughan, Megan. 1991. *Curing Their Ills: Colonial Power and African Illness.* Cambridge: Polity Press.

Vincent, Joan. 1982. *Teso in Transformation: The Political Economy of Peasant and Class in Eastern Africa.* Berkeley: University of California Press.

————. 1990. *Anthropology and Politics: Visions, Traditions, and Trends.* Tucson: University of Arizona Press.

Viswanathan, Gauri. 1989. *Masks of Conquest: Literary Study and British Rule in India.* New York: Columbia University Press.

Wakin, Eric. 1992. *Anthropology Goes to War: Professional Ethics and Counterinsurgency in Thailand.* Madison: Center for Southeast Asian Studies.

Wall, Irwin. 1986. "Front Populaire, Front National: The Colonial Example." *International Labor and Working Class History* 30: 32–43.

Wallerstein, Immanuel. 1974–1989. *The Modern World System*. 3 vols. New York: Basic Books.

Ware, Vron. 1992. *Beyond the Pale: White Women, Racism and History*. London: Verso.

Warren, James Francis. 1990. "Prostitution and the Politics of Venereal Disease: Singapore, 1870–98." *Journal of Southeast Asian Studies* 21(2): 360–383.

Watts, Michael J. 1983. *Silent Violence: Food, Famine and Peasantry in Northern Nigeria*. Berkeley: University of California Press.

————. 1993. "Development I: Power, Knowledge, Discursive Practice." *Progress in Human Geography* 17, no. 2: 257–272.

Weber, Eugen. 1976. *Peasants into Frenchmen: The Modernization of Rural France, 1870–1914*. Stanford: Stanford University Press.

Wellesley Editorial Committee. 1977. *Women and National Development: The Complexities of Change*. Chicago: University of Chicago Press.

White, Luise. 1990a. *The Comforts of Home: Prostitution in Colonial Nairobi*. Chicago: University of Chicago Press.

————. 1990b. "Separating the Men from the Boys: Colonial Constructions of Gender in Central Kenya." *International Journal of African Historical Studies* 23: 1–26.

Williams, Patrick, and Laura Chrisman. 1994. *Colonial Discourse and Post-Colonial Theory: A Reader*. New York: Columbia University Press.

Wilson, Peter. 1972. *Crab Antics: The Social Anthropology of English-Speaking Negro Societies of the Caribbean*. New Haven: Yale University Press.

Winichakul, Thongchai. 1994. *Siam Mapped: A History of the Geo-Body of a Nation*. Honolulu: University of Hawaii Press.

Wolf, Eric. 1959. *Sons of the Shaking Earth*. Chicago: University of Chicago Press.

————. 1982. *Europe and the People without History*. Berkeley: University of California Press.

Woolf, Stuart. 1992. "The Construction of a European World-View in the Revolutionary-Napoleonic Years." *Past and Present* 137: 72–101.

Worsley, Peter. 1957. *The Trumpet Shall Sound*. London: MacGibbon and Kee.

Wright, Gwendolyn. 1991. *The Politics of Design in French Colonial Urbanism*. Chicago: University of Chicago Press.

Young, Crawford. 1994. *The African Colonial State in Comparative Perspective*. New Haven: Yale University Press.

Young, Kate, Carol Wolkowitz, and Roslyn McCullagh (eds.). 1981. *Of Marriage and the Market: Women's Subordination in International Perspective*. London: CSE Books.

Young, Robert. 1990. *White Mythologies: Writing Histories and the West*. London: Routledge.

————. 1995. *Colonial Desire: Hybridity in Theory, Culture and Race*. London: Routledge.

Part One

Framings

1

Liberal Strategies
of Exclusion

Uday S. Mehta

*Pure insight, however, is in the first instance without
any content; it is the sheer disappearance of content;
but by its negative attitude towards what it excludes
it will make itself real and give itself a content.*
Hegel, *Phenomenology of Mind*

In its theoretical vision, liberalism, from the seventeenth century to the present, has prided itself on its universality and politically inclusionary character. And yet, when it is viewed as a historical phenomenon, again extending from the seventeenth century, the period of liberal history is unmistakably marked by the systematic and sustained political exclusion of various groups and "types" of people. The universality of freedom and derivative political institutions identified with the provenance of liberalism is denied in the protracted history with which liberalism is similarly linked. Perhaps liberal theory and liberal history are ships passing in the night spurred on by unrelated imperatives and destinations. Perhaps reality and, as such, history always betrays the pristine motives of theory. Putting aside such possibilities, something about the inclusionary pretensions of liberal theory and the exclusionary effects of liberal practices needs to be explained.

One needs to account for how a set of ideas that professed, at a fundamental level, to include as their political referent a universal constituency nevertheless

59

spawned practices that were either predicated on or directed at the political marginalization of various people. More specifically, one must consider if the exclusionary thrust of liberal history stems from the misapprehension of the generative basis of liberal universalism or if in contrast liberal history projects with greater focus and onto a larger canvas the theoretically veiled and qualified truth of liberal universalism. Despite the enormous contrariety between the profession of political universality and the history of political exclusion, the latter may in fact elaborate the truth and ambivalence of the former.

In considering these issues, I am responding to two distinct though closely related questions. First, can one within the universalistic theoretical framework of liberalism identify a politically exclusionary impulse,[1] and if so, by what means is this effected? Second, does the work of theorists such as both the Mills evince a similar exclusionary impulse with specific reference to the articulation of colonial exclusions? It is by virtue of this latter question that I hope to suggest a way of linking the reading of liberal texts and the interpretation of liberal practices.

The argument of this article involves three related claims. The first concerns the articulation of liberal foundational and institutional principles to make clear the basis of liberal universalism. My purpose here is obviously not to present liberal foundations in all their complexity but rather with an eye to suggesting the anthropological capacities that are allegedly the basis of liberal universalism. This first claim is substantiated by reference to Locke's *Second Treatise of Government*. The second claim is motivated by the concern with exclusion; that is, with how liberal principles with their attending universal constituency get undermined in such a manner as to politically disenfranchise various people. The strategies involved in effecting this closure are crucial to the general argument. With Locke this involves the subtle invoking of politically exclusionary social conventions and manners. This is the first strategy I consider. It is the political role played by these exclusionary conventions that is ultimately most crucial in understanding the strategies by which universalistic theories, such as Locke's, issue in or at least allow for exclusionary practices. My point here and throughout this article is to underscore the exclusionary effect of the distinction between anthropological capacities and the necessary conditions for their political actualization. Third and finally, I shift my attention to nineteenth-century India to consider once again the strategies through which utilitarianism effected and sustained politically exclusionary practices. Here, in contrast to Locke, exclusion assumes a defiantly self-confident and explicit form. It is defended by reference to the "manifest" political incompetence of those to be excluded and justified by a plethora of anthropological descriptions that serve to buttress the claim of incompetence. With reference to this latter focus on the nineteenth century, I consider exclusionary strategies that involve (1) inscrutability and (2) civilizational infantilism.

In the course of moving from Locke to the nineteenth century, my focus shifts to theorists who are commonly identified as utilitarians. It may therefore be objected that the comparative argument I am making is vitiated by the obvious and important theoretical contrasts between Lockean liberalism and nineteenth-century utilitarianism. The force of this objection is considerable; indeed, it cannot be fully answered within the constraints of this article. Nevertheless, with respect to the issues being dealt with here, namely the anthropological basis of universalistic claims, it will, I hope, become evident that the two theoretical visions share important and relevant similarities.

Because this article makes the claim that liberalism has been exclusionary and that in this it manifests an aspect of its theoretical underpinnings and not merely an episodic compromise with the practical constraints of implementation, it is important to dispel some possible misapprehensions. I am not suggesting that liberalism's doctrinal commitment to freedom is merely a ruse. Nor am I denying that from its inception it has sought to limit the ambit of political authority by anchoring it in constitutional principles, in the process articulating a framework of rights that the state is not entitled to invade. My argument neither rests on the assumption of, nor encourages the denial of, the liberal commitment to respect the claims of conscience and tolerate the voices of dissension. Similarly in emphasizing its exclusionary character, I am not muffling its favorable disposition to representation, universal suffrage, or claims of self-determination, including those of minority groups. To deny these credentials as fundamental to liberalism, one would have to take a stand that is markedly at odds with common usage.[2]

And yet the exclusionary basis of liberalism does, I believe, derive from its theoretical core, and the litany of exclusionary historical instances is an elaboration of this core. It is so not because the ideals are theoretically disingenuous or concretely impractical,[3] but rather because behind the capacities ascribed to all human beings there exist a thicker set of social credentials that constitute the real bases of political inclusion. The universalistic reach of liberalism derives from the capacities that it identifies with human nature and from the presumption, which it encourages, that these capacities are sufficient and not merely necessary for an individual's political inclusion. It encourages this presumption by giving a specifically political significance to human *nature*. Being born equal, free, and rational, birth—notwithstanding its various uncertain potentialities—becomes the moment of an assured political identity. That long tutelage through which Plato's guardians acquired their political spurs and the revolutions through which in de Tocqueville's words nations and individuals "became equal" is in Locke's ostensible vision compressed into the moment of our birth. However, what is concealed behind the endorsement of these universal capacities are the specific cultural and psychological conditions woven in as preconditions for the actualization of these capacities.

Liberal exclusion works by modulating the distance between the interstices of human capacities and the conditions for their political effectivity. It is the content between these interstices that settles boundaries between who is included and who is not. Ironically culture in the broadest sense gets mobilized to compensate for the deficiencies of birth—deficiencies whose very existence allows for the qualification of the inclusionary vision associated with the naturalistic assumptions.

This formulation is meant, in part, to explain the use of the term "strategies" in the title of this article. Liberal exclusion is neither a theoretically dictated necessity nor merely an occasional happenstance of purely contingent significance. The distinction between universal capacities and the conditions for their actualization points to a space in which the liberal theorist can, as it were, raise the ante for political inclusion.[4] To the extent that such a distinction can be identified within the work of a particular theorist or more broadly within liberalism, it points to a theoretical space from within which liberal exclusion can be viewed as intrinsic to liberalism and in which exclusionary strategies become endemic. The distinction becomes, in effect, a gatekeeper to the particular form that liberal society takes and as such allows for the incorporation of a variety of strategic considerations. The considerations may amount to no more than having "a sense of justice" or being "reasonable" as with Rawls.[5] In contrast, they may require the significantly more exclusive benefits of a nineteenth-century, middle-class European mindset as with John Stuart Mill. The details structure the outcome without of necessity violating the presumed inclusionary vision.[6]

The significance of "strategies" can be further elaborated by contrasting it with the common exclusionary bases of eighteenth- and nineteenth-century conservative thought. For Edmund Burke, the most influential critic of liberal universalism or "abstract principles," exclusion is registered in the necessary partiality of inheritance: "It has been the uniform policy of our constitution to claim and assert our liberties, as an *entailed inheritance* derived to us from our forefathers, and to be transmitted to our posterity."[7] The idea of a shared and exclusive inheritance, which in the hands of a Disraeli becomes the grounds of an explicit preference for the "Rights of Englishmen" over the "rights of man" and which through various interpretive perversions comes to support nineteenth- and twentieth-century polygenics, circumvents the need for strategic exclusion.[8] For both Locke and Burke, birth has a special political significance. For the former, birth signals the universal potentialities requisite for consensual political society; for the latter, it designates the unique and specific tracks of a historical alignment. For Burke, exclusions define the norm; for Locke, a limiting point whose status requires special, even if veiled, theoretical intensity.[9] By way of contrast with both Locke and Burke, birth for Filmer designates a literal, precise and inescapable source of all obligations, including political ones.[10]

I

Liberal theoretical claims typically tend to be transhistorical, transcultural, and most certainly transracial. The declared and ostensible referent of liberal principles is quite literally a constituency with no delimiting boundary, namely, that of all humankind. The political rights it articulates and defends and the institutions such as laws, representation, and contract all have their justification in a characterization of human beings that eschews names, social status, ethnic background, gender, and race.

In the mere fact of its universality, liberalism is not unique. Indeed, the quest for universal principles and cognate institutions attends political philosophy from its Greek inception.[11] But whereas Plato grounds universal claims in a transcendent ontology, liberal universalism stems from almost the opposite, what one might call a philosophical anthropology.[12] What is meant by this is that the universal claims can be made because they derive from certain characteristics that are common to all human beings. Central among these anthropological characteristics or foundations for liberal theory are the claims that everyone is naturally free, that they are in the relevant moral respects equal, and finally that they are rational. One might therefore say that the starting point for the political and institutional prescriptions of liberal theory is an anthropological minimum or an anthropological common denominator. Precisely because it is a minimum and therefore common to all the normative claims that derive from this minimum are common to all and therefore universal in their applicability.[13]

It is to these common anthropological characteristics that Locke draws our attention at the outset of the state-of-nature chapter in the *Second Treatise:*

> To understand political power right, and derive it from its Original, we must consider what State *all* Men are naturally in, and that is, a *State of perfect Freedom* to order their Actions, and dispose of their Possessions, and Persons as they think fit, within the bounds of the Law of Nature, without asking leave, or depending upon the Will of any other Man.[14]

In this and in the following paragraph, Locke articulates the view that human beings are by their nature free, equal, and rational. It is this view of the individual that becomes the basis of Locke's justly famous opposition to political absolutism and for his endorsement of the sovereignty of the people and for limitations on the authority of government. Freedom, equality, and rationality evince what I earlier called an anthropological minimum. As natural attributes, they attend human beings irrespective of conventional norms. As Locke puts it, "there being nothing more evident, than that Creatures of the same species and rank promiscuously born to all the same advantages of Nature, and the use of the same faculties, should also be equal one amongst another without Subordination or Subjection."[15]

Locke's point, here and elsewhere, is not that human beings are devoid of all natural obligations but rather that these obligations do not include natural *political* obligations. Similarly, the view of natural equality is meant only to establish our moral equality with respect to natural rights and not as a denial of various social and economic inequalities whose existence he explicitly acknowledges.[16] With respect to political authority, the mere fact of our birth gives to all of us equally the natural right to freedom. The political centrality of birth and with it the attending identity of our faculties underscores the informational paucity of Lockean foundations. It eschews, at this foundational level, any reference to a sociological description of individuals. And similarly, in contrast to Filmer, it does not privilege any spatial or temporal context.

Locke's characterization of natural freedom is remarkable not merely for the universal constituency that it champions but also for the explicitly dramatic and expansive elaboration he gives to it. And not only are we told that *all* men are by their natures *perfectly free;* this condition itself allows us to give our *persons,* our *possessions,* and even our *actions* strikingly extreme expressions. It is this individual who becomes the subject of the contractual agreement from which liberal institutions derive. Locke's elaboration of the natural condition provokes an obvious question: What ensures that this condition of perfect freedom will not issue in a state of license and anarchical libertinage? Put differently, and only for illustrative purposes, how do the *Two Treatises* with such unrestrained foundations fortify themselves from being usurped by a variety of theorists who are commonly considered as anathema to liberalism, including not merely anarchists but also, for instance, the infamous French profligate the Marquis de Sade?

To this query, the obvious and immediate answer would be that the interpretation of the passage I have offered overlooks a crucial, even if textually brief, qualification.[17] That is, I have overlooked the point where Locke, having opened the expansive possibilities that issue from *perfect freedom,* immediately restricts them with the claim that they must remain "within the bounds of the Law of Nature." The qualification is indeed crucial not merely because its exclusion is likely from an anarchist's perspective but also because natural laws play an ostensibly critical role in Locke's political thought. As fundamental moral principles legislated for individuals and societies by God, natural laws are meant as preconventional limits on human actions. For Locke, they designate the plethora of obligations to which we are committed despite the fact of our natural freedom.

Natural laws may sufficiently distinguish the foundational claims Locke is making from those of an anarchist. Nevertheless since access to these laws is (by Locke) emphasized as being through natural human reason, they do not severely qualify the image of the individual I have presented. That is to say, the moral boundaries that natural laws set on the potential liberality of human action are themselves presented as part of the natural endowments of human beings.[18] Further along in this article, I will suggest how the access to natural law, which Locke in the *Two Treatises* presents as stemming from reason, in fact requires a highly conventionalistic regime of instruction and social manipulations. Such a conventionalistic molding vitiates the naturalistic and universalistic moral limits that natural law is meant to designate.

Aside from natural law, the anarchist challenge would most commonly be rebutted by pointing to the distinctly liberal institutions such as contract, rule of law, and representation that Locke endorses. Since all of these institutions are grounded in consent, it might furthermore be argued that they, no less than the expansive possibilities of freedom, are the distinctive features of liberalism. This claim is, I think, true, but only as true as any claim that treats what is really only a hope as a given fact. For although, no doubt, liberal institutions limit and give to the expressions of human freedom a measure of order, they are themselves never secure from the threat posed by the possibility that their authorizing consent will be withdrawn by anyone who thinks that the order is no longer just and therefore no longer binding. Given that it is natural for the Lockean individual to externalize his or her desires without depending on the will of any other person and furthermore given that we know from the *Essay Concerning Human Understanding* that this individual has no innate moral principles impressed on his or her nature, and finally, again from the *Essay,* given that this individual at a cognitive level freely associates and these associations can and do display a striking inconstancy, it can only be hoped that the particular manifestation that individuals give to their freedom will find in contract, representation, and so forth, an efficacious and adequately disciplined self-expression.[19]

My point is that Locke's minimalist anthropology, which serves as the foundation for his institutional claims, is indeed universalistic but in this it also exposes the vulnerability of the institutions it is meant to support. The potentialities of the Lockean individual, as it were, reside as a constant internal threat to the regularities requisite for Lockean institutions. John Dunn has rightly emphasized that the principal problem of Locke's politics was that of creating and ensuring a constancy and moderation in the expressions of desire of the citizens of his commonwealth.[20] It is in recognizing this and the centrality of its significance that one begins to appreciate the way in which Locke's texts, despite their foundational universality, have an effectively exclusionary thrust. It must be emphasized that this problem cannot be sufficiently assuaged at the foundational or anthropological level precisely because it is from this level that the inconstancy and extremity of desire derives its disturbing legitimacy.

Before considering the way in which Locke addresses this issue, it is worth distinguishing my own approach and emphasis to it from two interpretations that arrive at similar conclusions though from markedly different approaches. C. B. Macpherson in his justly famous *The Political Theory of Possessive Individualism* articulated what remains as a provocative interpretation of

Locke. Macpherson, in considering the issue of political exclusion, makes the claim that Locke "justifies, as natural, a class differential in rights and in rationality, and by doing so provides a moral basis for capitalist society."[21] In Macpherson's view Locke's political and economic partiality plainly commits him to a theoretical inconsistency. On the one hand, according to Macpherson, Locke appears to endorse universal rationality and with it supports a crucial condition for the possibility of universal political rights. On the other hand, Macpherson alleges that Locke in fact associates the difference between the propertyless and the propertied with a natural difference in their rationalities and thus justifies the political exclusion of the former. Locke's exclusions stem from this inconsistent commitment. While the broad strokes of this interpretation and the ingenuity with which it is presented are striking, the claim of differential rationality is at best weakly defended and its textual support unpersuasive.[22]

More recently, Carol Pateman has argued that Locke's naturalistic and uncritical conception of the "conjugal bond" serves to effectively eliminate women from Locke's understanding of the term "individual."[23] Despite this, she acknowledges that Locke, both in his polemic against Filmer and at various points in the *Second Treatise,* sharply distinguishes the power of a husband from that of a political ruler. It remains somewhat unclear in Pateman's analysis if the alleged exclusion from the category of "individual" trumps the possibility of being a citizen and as such excludes women through a disingenuous textual feint.[24] This possibility is made less likely by the fact that conjugal relationships are never presented as necessary to the designation of citizenship.

For both Macpherson and Pateman, the clue to understanding political exclusion in Locke, indeed the keystone that gives his argument a dubious coherence, is an implicit historical assumption—an assumption to which Locke's texts point through a revealing silence.[25] This is not to suggest that either one of these authors is methodologically committed to a notion in which at some fundamental level the boundaries between texts and contexts are irrepressibly porous. That is to say, their conclusions are not driven by methodological presumptions regarding the status of texts. Clearly, the understanding of texts may on occasion require them to be supplemented by historical considerations. My own divergence from Macpherson and Pateman on this general point is that, with regard to the issue of exclusion in Locke, one needs no such extratextual supplementing.

In contrast, my focus draws on some familiar insights from the sociological tradition to elaborate how Locke presumes on a complex constellation of social structures and social conventions to delimit, stabilize, and legitimize without explicitly restricting the universal referent of his foundational commitments. The exclusionary transformation of Locke's universalistic anthropology is effected by the implicit divisions and exclusions of the social world that Locke imagines. Sociologists since Durkheim have pointed to how the differentiations of a given society condition both its own reproduction and its various internal boundaries. The reliance on the semicodified social, linguistic, spatial, and so forth, oppositions of a society decisively reinforce what Durkheim called "logical conformity" by organizing the perception of the social world.[26] Classificatory schemes based on these implicit markings imply without explicitly stating a sense of limits. These limits are inscribed in the dense minutiae of social and cultural descriptions. Their elucidation turns on the perspective of an insider buffeted by particular circumstances. "Circumstances," as Burke suggested, "(which with some gentlemen pass for nothing) give in reality to every political principle its distinguishing color and discriminating effect."[27] I am suggesting that they also configure the boundary between the politically included and the politically excluded.

The efficacy of these structures and conventions in moderating the potentially exorbitant and unlimitable claims of an individual who is naturally free is proportional to the degree to which these structures and conventions are taken for granted. Their effectivity derives from a tacit allegiance to a particular ordering of society and through this to a particular set of distinctions that the society incorporates. Social structures and conventions function below the threshold of consciousness and theoretical discourse. As Pierre Bourdieu has suggested, "a 'sense of one's place' . . . leads one to exclude oneself from the goods, persons, places and so forth from which one is excluded."[28] Unlike universal anthropological injunctions, conventions and manners are the product of numberless, long-forgotten choices that anonymously buffer an individual's act of self-expression. Their anonymity stems in part from their embodying the collective sediment of a specific people, a religion, or a family. Conventions and manners are not, and seldom claim to be, universal.[29]

Locke was piercingly aware of the centrality of conventions in his own thought even though, for reasons I have touched on, he seldom fully admits this. He comes closest in the dedicatory epistle to his *Thoughts Concerning Education*[30] where, after stating that it is a work "fit" and "suited to our English gentry," he explicitly links the education of children with "the welfare and prosperity of the nation." It is, he goes on, a work that will produce "virtuous, useful, and able men in their distinct calling" though most crucially it is designed for a "gentleman's calling."[31]

In the context of studying exclusion there is an obvious reason for focusing on Locke's views on children and relatedly on his *Thoughts Concerning Education*. Along with "lunaticks" and "ideots," children are explicitly and unambiguously excluded from the consensual politics of the *Second Treatise*.[32] The status of the former two groups, although fascinating for various reasons and one that sustained with increasing emphasis Locke's interest throughout his life, is not directly relevant to the issue at hand.[33] In contrast, the exclusion of children—notwithstanding its presumed self-evidence—draws on a central argument of the *Second Treatise*. Stated simply, the argument involves consent as a fundamental ground for the legitimacy of political authority. For Locke, consent requires, inter alia, acting in view of certain constraints that can broadly be designated by the laws of nature. To know these laws requires reason.[34] Those who are either permanently (for example, madmen and idiots) or temporarily (that is, children) unable to exercise reason therefore do not meet a necessary requisite for the expression of consent. By implication, therefore, they can be excluded from the political constituency, or what amounts to the same thing, they can be governed without their consent. What the argument makes clear is that political inclusion is contingent on a qualified capacity to reason. [35] Clearly the precise effect of this claim turns on what, in Locke's view, is involved in developing these requisite capacities, credentials, and associations to be able to reason. The *Thoughts Concerning Education* are Locke's most elaborate response to this crucial issue.[36]

It is impossible to summarize the *Thoughts.* In fact, it is almost as difficult to pick out a few salient themes from the work. This lack of thematic and argumentary order is, however, revealing of Locke's conception of education and more specifically of what is involved in learning to reason. The *Thoughts* is replete with the most specific and precise details and instructions. The work reads like a manual with all the attending minutiae. It ranges over a concern with toilet-training; the imprudence of wearing tight-fitting bodices; the appropriate foods to be consumed at breakfast; the importance of knowing how to dance, fence, and ride; the appropriate comportment towards servants and others of "lower rank"; and the importance of being able to feign humility, anger, and concern.

The list could easily be extended. But even without that what is surely remarkable about such a bizarre and contextually detailed index is that it is, on the face of it, presented in support of a capacity that Locke acknowledges to be universal and natural: the capacity to reason. Even on a cursory review, this work suspends the very anthropological guarantees one would have expected Locke, given the claims of the *Treatises,* to have taken for granted.

Thus, for instance, Locke puts virtually no stock in the fact that human reason gives us a preconventional access to the precepts of natural law. Instead, the emphasis is wholly on the precise and detailed processes through which this rationality must get inculcated. The purpose of education, as Locke states, is to "[weave] habits into the very principles" of a child's nature even if the only means to ensure this result involves instilling "fear and awe," including that special fear of a father "who may perhaps disinherit" a child.[37] Similarly where the contractual logic of the *Treatises* is allegedly driven by the rationality of abstract individuals concerned with enhancing their self-interest, in the *Thoughts* Locke plainly states "the principle of all virtue and excellency lies in the power of denying ourselves the satisfaction of our desires . . . and this power is to be got and improved by custom, made easy and familiar by an early practice."[38] Where in the *Treatises* Locke with repeated emphasis reminds

Filmer and his readers that the fifth commandment refers both to Adam and Eve, in the *Thoughts* he speaks of the importance of "establish[ing] the Authority of a father."[39]

In the specific context of how to teach children "Reasoning," Locke concentrates at enormous length on the importance of the choice of an appropriate tutor or governor. Such a governor, he makes clear, is not to be had at "ordinary Rates."[40] Notwithstanding the considerable expense, when such a governor is found, this is how Locke characterizes his brief toward his pupil.

> To form a young Gentleman, as he should be, 'tis fit his *Governor* should himself be well-bred, understand the Ways of Carriage, and Measures of Civility in all the Variety of Persons, Times and Places; and keep his Pupil, as much as his age requires, constantly to the Observation of them. This is an Art not to be learnt, nor taught by books. Nothing can give it but good Company, and the Observation joyn'd together. . . . Breeding is that, which sets a Gloss upon all his other good qualities, and renders them useful to him, in procuring him the Esteem and Good Will of all that comes near.[41]

Breeding, which for Locke is clearly the most salient feature of education, requires an assimilation of the observed social distinctions of society. It cannot be taught through books, and it has no substitute in the thorough knowledge of Latin, Greek, and metaphysics. It is acquired simply through an immersion in "good Company" and a recognition of the "Measures of Civility" that structure such company. Further along, in the same section, Locke emphasizes the need to be "shocked by some, and caressed by others; warn'd who are like to oppose, who to mislead, who to undermine him, and who to serve him." In language that revealingly mirrors the terms used to describe laws in the *Second Treatise,* these social distinctions are presented as "the only fence against the World."[42] That education and more specifically reasoning involve understanding a world replete with social and hierarchical distinctions is unmistakable from even the most casual reading of the *Thoughts.* Far from giving expression to capacities that are universal because they presume on so little, education is an initiation into the enormously significant specifications of time, place, and social status. Locke is explicit in the narrow referent of his own work. In the concluding paragraph of *Thoughts* he states, "I think a Prince, a Nobleman and an ordinary Gentleman's son, should have different ways of breeding."[43]

The role of conventions is not restricted to the *Thoughts,* even though it is in that work that one gets a relatively unguarded glimpse into their significance. In the *Second Treatise,* after repeatedly emphasizing that a child be naturally free, Locke makes the claim that he only becomes really free when he understands the laws of England and that, Locke says, happens at the age of twenty-one. This is also the age when the young adult learns, as Locke says, "discretion."[44] There is reason to believe that Locke meant the use of this term in its precise etymological sense, namely, the age at which one learns to make *distinctions*—ones that are invisible in the universal claims. Similarly in the same chapter, Locke explicitly tells us that inheritance commits one to honor the conventions and conditions under which property was originally acquired. As he says, property is a "strong tie on a man's obedience."[45]

Finally, consider another example from the *Thoughts* which is significant because of its reference to the love of mastery, which, according to Locke, comes "almost as soon as [we] are born."

> I have told you before that Children love Liberty; and therefore they should be brought to do the things that are fit for them, without feeling any restraint laid upon them. Now I tell you, they love something more; and that is Dominion: And this is the first Original of most vicious habits, that are ordinary and natural.[46]

This love of power, Locke continues, takes two forms, an imperiousness toward others and a desire to have objects for themselves. Furthermore, it is these two forms that are the "roots of almost all the injustice and contention that so disturb human life."[47] The desire for mastery over others requires, for its modification, good manners and an appropriate set of attending feelings. Thus children must be accustomed from an early age to a careful deportment in "language . . . towards their inferiors and the meaner sort of people, particularly servants."[48] The child's "superiority" is to be erased by a feigned denial so as to make "Human Nature" appear equal. The vindication of a sense of our common humanity is thus to be meticulously cultivated in a child by a process that also reinforces the gentleman's scion's notion of superiority.

Terms such as "English gentry," "breeding," "gentleman," "honor," "discretion," "inheritance," and "servant" derive their meaning and significance from a specific set of cultural norms. They refer to a constellation of social practices riddled with a hierarchical and exclusionary density. They draw on and encourage conceptions of human beings that are far from abstract and universal and in which the anthropological minimum is buried under a thick set of social inscriptions and signals. They chart a terrain full of social credentials. It is a terrain that the natural individual equipped with universal capacities must negotiate before these capacities assume the form necessary for political inclusion. In this, they circumscribe and order the particular form that the universalistic foundations of Lockean liberalism assume. It is a form that can and historically has left an exclusionary imprint in the concrete instantiation of liberal practices.

II

In shifting my attention to nineteenth-century India, I must make clear that my purpose is not to chronicle the litany of colonial achievements or injustices.

Nor is it to assess the considerable impact that British liberal and utilitarian ideas had on virtually every aspect of public life in India. This shift is spurred by the narrower concern with trying to understand how universalistic doctrines sustained a status quo of unmistakable political exclusion. Given this concern, India's credentials as the site for this exploration are anything but unique. Clearly exclusion occurred elsewhere and could therefore be studied elsewhere. But if India's credentials for this exploration are not unique, its convenience is perhaps unusual.

It is of course well known that India was of crucial significance to the economic and political ambitions of imperial Britain. It retained this status even after it ceased to be a clear economic asset as was the case during much of the latter half of the nineteenth century. If for no other reason, its very size gave it the distinction of being the largest "jewel in the crown." What is often overlooked, however, is that, behind the exotic paraphernalia of empire and power, India played a sustained and extensive role in the theoretical imagination and exertion of most nineteenth-century British political thinkers. Almost without exception, all the important British political theorists from the late eighteenth century to the twentieth century dealt in an extensive and focused manner with India. Edmund Burke's writings on India exceed by a very considerable margin his written attention on any other issue.[49] Although James Mill never visited India, a fact that in his view rendered his understanding of it scientific, he wrote a monumental six-volume history of India. He also worked for several years as the chief examiner of Indian dispatches in the East India Company in London. This was a job that his son held for thirty-five years. Similarly, Bentham not only wrote with characteristic detail on issues of legislative design regarding India, but along with James Mill, he was the principle architect of the British-Indian judicial and penal systems. Lord Macaulay decisively recast the direction of Indian education, a fact that in Winston Churchill's view lay at the root of the proliferation of Indian nationalist leaders a century later. The list could be extended to include Sir Charles Grant, the Trevelyans, Thomas Carlyle, Walter Bagehot, and in the twentieth century the Fabians, Keynes, and of course George Orwell.

If the engagement with India was an active and biographically rich one, however, theoretically it was also a marginal one. The status of India oscillates between being outside the direct purview of the British imagination and being at its very center. Macaulay, for example, looked upon India as "the strangest of all political anomalies," while James Mill, despite years of association, thought of it as "no more than a mere accessory" to British commercial and legal concerns.[50] For John Stuart Mill, India was visibly outside the domain of his works *Representative Government* and *On Liberty* to which I will return. Ironically, it is this very status of being betwixt and between the liberal and utilitarian imagination that gives India the attributes of a laboratory from which to view the exertions of theoretical claims that were ostensibly universal.

Because my concern here is with the mediating strategies through which these universalistic doctrines issued in exclusionary practices, I will not address the broad framework either of utilitarianism or of nineteenth-century British liberalism. Instead, to highlight these strategies, the focus will be almost episodic, that is, on the theoretical maneuvers and descriptions by which India was barred from the very institutions these doctrines professed. The central institution, in this context, is obviously that of representative government.

From the standpoint of the foundational commitments of the theories being considered, the shift to the nineteenth century represents, in comparison with Locke, a significant change. The anthropological minimalism so conspicuous in Locke is, at best, dimly visible on the surface of nineteenth-century utilitarian theorists. Even in a theorist like Bentham, with his fixed conception of human nature, considerations of context and nationality are manifest and evident in the very title of his work, *Essay on the Influence of Time and Place in Matters of Legislation*. With the possible exception of James Mill, no theorist of this period evinces the unbridled theoretical neglect of historical and sociological details of Hobbes or Locke.[51] In John Stuart Mill, such considerations become the basis of a focused and sustained theoretical attention.

The presence of, and the theoretical role played by, contextual and sociological details raises the important question of what constitutes the precise basis of nineteenth-century universalism. It might, for instance, be suggested, and this suggestion carries particular force with John Stuart Mill, that his attention to matters of civilizational development, his theory of character development (ethology), his explicit commitment to competence criteria, and more generally his avowed indebtedness to the "Germano-Coleridgian doctrine" combine to vitiate any pretense to universalism. And that, as such, they stand outside, for the reasons Burke also does, the domain that defines the questions pursued in this article. The force of this suggestion cannot be fully addressed in this context because it requires in part delineating the theoretical motivations underlying these considerations. If for instance these contextual considerations could be identified as modifying responses to the issue of political universalism, then far from being outside, they would instead be central to the claims of this article. If instead such considerations are constitutive to the theoretical agenda, clearly they limit the relevance of my argument.[52] Notwithstanding the importance of these alternatives, in the present context, and again with particular reference to John Stuart Mill, there is, I believe, evidence of a substantially independent universalistic conception to which I will return underlying his view of human beings in *Utilitarianism* and *On Liberty*.

Descriptions are seldom neutral. They effect moral and political sensibilities and therefore carry, even when intended innocently, a normative valency.[53] This is particularly true in the context of liberalism because in presuming on so little, what I have called the anthropological minimum, it professes to accept so much. The putative perimeter of its sympathies is marked by the expansive range of the differences it tolerates. The limiting point of this perimeter is a form of alterity beyond which differences can no longer be accommodated. The alterity can take many forms. Consider the inaugural statement in James Mill's preface to his work on British India.

> In the course of reading and investigation, necessary for acquiring that measure of knowledge which I was anxious to possess, respecting my country, its people, its government, its interests, its policy, and its laws, I was met, and in some degree surprised, by extraordinary difficulties when I arrived at that part of my inquiries which related to India. On other subjects, of any magnitude and importance, I generally found, that there was some one book, or small number of books, containing the material part of the requisite information; and in which direction was obtained, by reference to other books, if, in any part, the reader found it necessary to extend his researches. In regard to India, the case was exceeding [*sic*] different. The knowledge, requisite for attaining an adequate conception of that great scene of British action, was collected no where. It was scattered in a great variety of repositories, sometimes in considerable portions, often in very minute ones; sometimes by itself, often mixed up with subjects of a very different nature; and, even where information relating to India stood disjoined from other subjects, a small portion of what was useful lay commonly embedded in a large mass of what was trifling and insignificant; and of a body of statements given indiscriminately as matters of fact, ascertained by the sense, the far greater part was in general only matter of opinion, borrowed, in succession, by one set of Indian gentlemen from another.[54]

Mill by his own admission is studying and investigating his own country where usually one book suffices to master subjects of any magnitude. The study of Britain, its people, its government, its interests, and its laws leads Mill without discontinuity to the study of India. But here India's "exceeding difference" sets in and confounds Mill's scholarly ease and equanimity. India, as it were, casts a dark epistemological shadow in which access is uncertain and in any case of apocryphal value. It subverts the otherwise solid distinctions between matters of fact and opinions, between the useful and the insignificant, and between the senses and reason.

The first couple of sentences of Mill's preface perform the double maneuver of the total inclusion of India as part of the study of Britain and of simultaneously sequestering it by a description that renders it all but inscrutable. The themes of inclusion and inscrutability mark strategies to which colonial discourse returns with unfailing regularity. Later in the same preface, Mill variously characterizes India as "impenetrable," "a chaotic mass" resistant to "all logical inquiry," and a sight where perceptual experience survives at the total expense of reflective judgment. India's exceeding difference does not occasion the need for an engagement with this alterity for a dialogic encounter between Mill's initial perspective and an alternative self-understanding that confronts him. Rather it serves to confirm Mill's perspective and indeed to expand its reach by placing the onus of elucidation on the very point of view from which India appears dense and impenetrable. India's status as an integral part of Britain's political ambit remains thoroughly unquestioned and yet, as a part, it is insistently characterized by its inscrutable and chaotic intransigence.

The significance of designating something as inscrutable can be illustrated by the distinction between something that resists comprehension and something that is inscrutable. The former description permits of a future change in which the object may, finally, become comprehensible. It also places the onus on the comprehending subject and not on the studied object. It suggests a limitation on our knowledge without predicating this on the essentiality of the object. In contrast, inscrutability designates an unfathomable limit to the object of inquiry without implicating either the process of inquiry or the inquirer. It is quite literally a description in which the object is made to appear, as it were, on its own reckoning as something that defies description and, hence, reception. Furthermore, inscrutability clearly places a limit on political possibilities by closing off the prospect that the object satisfies the (however minimal) conditions requisite for political inclusion. It renders mute the issue of whether this object can satisfy the condition of having reason for Locke or reasonableness for Rawls. Indeed, drawing on the connection that Hobbes suggests between the capacity to give authority to one's acts and the capacity to be "impersonated" and represented, one might suggest that those who are inscrutable correspond to those inanimate objects that Hobbes claims must be represented precisely because they cannot give authority on their own behalf.[55] Mill's opening sentence, therefore, not only designates India's inert insufficiency, but as part of the study of Britain, he designates Britain as the political compensator for this insufficiency. The textual simultaneity of these two claims recapitulates their political simultaneity in the practice of colonialism.

In the voluminous history of British writings on India, particularly in those that focus on the characters of Indians, the themes of opacity, mystery, and unfathomable inscrutability abound. Lord Macaulay's famous view, expressed early in the nineteenth century, of the Indian as "an enigma of mysterious origin and constitution" had a wide and popular currency. Even that great logician of human character, Sherlock Holmes, is humbled in the presence of "the second floor inhabit[ant] . . . Daulat Ras, the Indian. He is a quiet, inscrutable fellow; as most of those Indians are. He is well up in his work, though his Greek is his weak subject. He is steady and methodical."[56]

Clearly, Indian inscrutability trumps the access that could have been gleaned from the presence of those familiar Victorian virtues, the knowledge of Greek and a steady and methodical style. Premodern examples could similarly be added.[57] But this very lack of difference between liberalism and its premodern, nonliberal counterparts in the characterization of differences is revealing. Liberalism's alleged universality is impugned in its descriptive proximity to ideas that claim no such universality.

If the exclusionary effect of inscrutability is achieved by a crude descriptive fiat in refusing to engage in the particulars of India, the next strategy I will consider represents an almost total reversal. It involves delving into the arcane details of ancient theological, cultural, and historical particulars and through them exposing the deficiencies of India's political, although most often psychological, endowments. It presumes on the necessity of a complex set of individual and social indexes as the prerequisite of political inclusion. In this again it does not explicitly qualify the universalistic claims; rather it implicitly raises the ante and, by doing so, the conditions of inclusion. I shall refer to this as the strategy of civilizational infantilism. Despite what might be thought of as contradictory emphases of exclusion through inscrutability and exclusion through presumed infantilism, they are often, as in the case of James Mill, deployed in tandem.

In his essay *On Liberty,* John Stuart Mill defends the principle of liberty as a condition for the mental development of human beings. The application of the principle is limited by three restrictions. First, it applies only to mature adults, although interestingly like Locke he allows the law to fix the interpretation of this condition. Second and for the "same reason" as those required in the first, the principle of liberty has no application to backward societies. And finally, it requires that society not be in a state of war or severe internal turmoil.[58] In elaborating the second restriction, Mill states, "Liberty, as a principle, has no application to any state of things anterior to the time when mankind have become capable of being improved by free and equal discussion. Until then, there is nothing for them but implicit obedience to an Akbar or a Charlemagne, if they are so fortunate as to find one."[59]

Mill returns to this issue in greater detail in the chapter "The Government of Dependencies by a Free State" in his work *Representative Government.* The chapter is a striking instance of the embattled commitments of someone who was profoundly invested in liberty and representative government in the face of colonialism. It is also a revealing document on the increasing relevance of cultural, civilizational, linguistic, and racial categories in defining the constituency of Mill's liberalism.

At the outset of the chapter, Mill, having already expressed an indifference to small colonial outposts like Gibraltar and Aden, divides colonized countries into two classes. The first of these classes is composed of countries "of similar civilization to the ruling country; capable of and ripe for representative government: such as the British possessions in America and Australia."[60] The other class includes "others, like India, [who] are still at a great distance from that state."[61] Mill goes on to celebrate England's realization that countries in the first class must be the beneficiaries of "the true principle of government," namely, representative government. Indeed, Mill finds the practice of English colonialism toward those who "were of her [England's] own blood and language" variously "vicious," economically ill advised, and a betrayal of a "fixed principle . . . professed in theory" regarding free and democratic governance.[62] The populations of these countries are, as he says, ripe and "in a sufficiently advanced state to be fitted for representative government."[63]

Regarding the second class of countries, that is countries with a population whose civilization, culture, language, and race were different from the British, Mill's attitude is strikingly different and his recommendations correspondingly so. Not only is Mill opposed to dismembering colonialism, he is equally opposed to these countries being internally democratic. In fact, Mill strongly supports the colonizing country's internal posture within the colony remaining unmistakably authoritarian: "The ruling country ought to be able to do for its subjects all that could be done by a succession of absolute monarchs, guaranteed by irresistible force against the precariousness of tenure attendant on barbarous despotisms, and qualified by their genius to anticipate all that experience has taught to the more advanced nation.[64]

He goes on: "Such is the ideal rule of a free people over a barbarous or semi-barbarous one."[65] To govern a country with a people different from those of the rulers only allows for "a choice of despotisms";[66] it does not admit of the possibility of democratic representation.

Mill's conclusion is driven by a particular view of India's position in a time line of civilizational and individual development. Reminiscent of Locke's outlook toward children in the *Thoughts,* projected onto a civilizational scale, India is in need of despotism, just as her people are incapable of benefiting from free and equal discussion. The significance of this claim, from the standpoint of this essay, lies not with its truth or falsity. Similarly in the present context, the paucity of Mill's evidence in supporting these claims is of little relevance. Instead, their significance derives from the relevance of the anthropological, cultural, psychological, racial, and temporal categories that they evince. It is the sheer descriptive richness that Mill invokes to justify both his anticolonialism and his colonialism that is striking and most significant. There is not a hint of any minimalism.

All this might be taken to suggest that Mill lies outside the constraints defined in this article. If indeed there is not a hint of minimalism, then, for the reasons I have mentioned earlier, his commitment to a politically inclusionary universalism would be qualified from the outset in a manner akin to Burke. But such a notion is misguided for it overlooks Mill's real anthropological commitments and in the process the extent of his break with Bentham. Unlike the latter, Mill does espouse the "permanent interest of man as a progressive being."[67] Similarly in defending utilitarianism against the charge that it is a doctrine fit only for swine, he distinguishes "human beings [who] have faculties more elevated than the animal appetites . . . [and who] do not regard anything as happiness which does not include their gratification."[68] Again in contrast with Bentham for whom each unit of pain should "count for one and none for more than one," Mill believes that the interests of each should count for one and not more than one.[69] Similarly consider the language in which Mill introduces his doctrine of higher-order pleasures: "Of two pleasures, if there be one to which all or almost all who have experience of both give a decided preference, irrespective of any feeling of moral obligations to prefer it, that is the more desirable pleasure."[70] The distinction between the pleasures turns on the issue of experience and is as such consistent with Mill's more general commitment to the notion that people come to recognize in the course of their development that some pleasures are better than others. Further along in the same chapter, when Mill speaks of "a sense of dignity" as the "most appropriate appellation," it is one that "all human beings possess in one form or another."[71] Finally in considering that most critical capacity of "making a choice," Mill not only identifies it as "a distinctive endowment of a human being" but also links it, again in a manner reminiscent of Locke, with "the human faculties of perception, judgement, discriminative feeling, mental activity and even moral preference."[72] It is because he holds such a view of human nature and potentiality that Mill belongs squarely within the constraints of this article.

Mill's exclusion of India and other non-European colonies from representative institutions is not inconsistent with his ultimate commitments. Despite his break with Bentham, utility remains the unerring ground of Mill's "ultimate appeal." It is this ground that determines the appropriate institutional arrangements for a given situation. And it is by reference to utility that Mill comes to the view that representative institutions are appropriate for Europe and its predominantly white colonies and not for the rest. The bracketing of India and others is not therefore the mark of an embarrassing theoretical inconsistency precisely because at the theoretical level the commitment to representative institutions is subsequent and not prevenient to considerations of utility. My purpose here has been to uncover the specific descriptive grounds through which Mill arrived at the patronizing assessments of civilizational worth that led to India's exclusion.

Where Locke speaks of the identity of our faculties and the commonality of our birth, Mill speaks of the differences of people's cultures, social development, and races. Locke responds to the charge that his state of nature is a historical fiction by referring to "the inconveniences of that condition and the love, and want of Society no sooner brought any number of them [men] together, but they presently united and incorporated, if they designed to continue together," and that therefore the historical absence of such a state is to be understood by reference to the immediacy of its provenance. Civil government is, as he says, "everywhere antecedent to records."[73] In contrast, Mill makes representative government contingent on a precisely articulated and specific developmental trajectory. Far from being antecedent to records, it requires records of dense and exacting specifications. It should be reemphasized that in making this point I am not claiming that Mill fully shares the minimalist stipulations of Locke's foundational anthropology and that therefore the invoking of historical details is somehow in contradiction with Mill's foundational assumptions. My point is simply to highlight the theoretical modifications as a result of which Indians and others get politically excluded.

The theme of the genealogical specifications for representative government is a unifying thread in nineteenth-century British reflections on India. It is evident in the writings of the Evangelical tradition, in the work of figures such as Sir Charles Grant, William Wilberforce, and others from the Clapham Sect.[74] It is a conspicuous feature in Burke's writings on India; indeed, the lack of historical sensitivity is the basis of Burke's most vitriolic objections to Warren Hastings in the course of his celebrated trial.[75] But it is the elder Mill who deploys this theme with the greatest saliency and, it might be added, with the greatest antipathy toward Indians. Christopher Hutchins in his book, *The Illusion of Permanence: British Imperialism in India,* indeed argues that the principal substantive motive underlying James Mill's six-volume *History of India* was to provide the historical and developmental evidence for the permanent subjection of India.[76]

Consider as a final example of this theme:

> To ascertain the true state of the Hindus in the scale of civilization, is not only an object of curiosity in the history of human nature; but to the people of Great Britain, charged as they are with the government of that great portion of the human species, it is an object of the highest practical importance. No scheme of government can happily conduce to the ends of government, unless it is adapted to the state of the people for whose use it is intended. In those diversities in the state of civilization, which approach the extremes, this truth is universally acknowledged. Should anyone propose, for a band of roving Tartars, the regulations adapted to the happiness of a regular and polished society, he would meet with neglect or derision. The inconveniences are only more concealed, and more or less diminished, when the error relates to states of society which more nearly resemble one another. If the mistake in regard to Hindu society, committed by the British nation, and the British government, be very great; if they have conceived the Hindus to be a people of high civilization, while they have, in reality, made but a few of the earliest steps in the progress to civilization, it is impossible that in many of the measures pursued for the government of that people, the mark aimed at should not have been wrong.[77]

The political exclusion of India is clearly informed by the particulars in which it finds itself embedded, Burke also recognized the great variety and detail of India's historical particulars. But for him, this suggested the possibility and likelihood of a similarly different set of destinies. In contrast, James Mill, in speaking the language of civilizational progress, recognizes India's "exceeding difference" only to then husband it within a particular evolutionary path. India's strangeness marks it off from the present, but in the process it gets illuminated by its position on the primitive end of a civilizational schema. Elsewhere Mill, almost to ensure that India not be viewed as an utterly deviant anomaly with a corresponding potentiality, incorporates its present status as part of the prehistory of Britain itself: "The Druids among the ancient Britons . . . possessed many similar privileges and distinctions to those of the Brahmens."[78] Further along he remarks on the similarity and grossness of the written codes of present-day Indians with those of the early Anglo-Saxons.[79]

When this is viewed from a perspective that includes Locke's anthropological minimalism and both the Mills' detailed essentialistic characterizations of Indians, particularly Hindus, a revealing duality emerges. In Locke, the grounds on which the inclusionary vision is anchored is the universality of certain purported aspects of our nature. These aspects by being minimal extend their reach over a broad, indeed universal, constituency. Ironically, as both the Mills' descriptions make clear, the grounds on which, a century and a half after Locke, people get politically excluded are also aspects of their nature. Human nature, as it were, supports both the inclusionary and the exclusionary vision.

At the outset of this article, I referred to two questions that motivated it. The first involved the identification of an exclusionary impulse within the universalistic framework of Lockean liberalism and the specification of how this impulse gets expressed through the subtle incorporation of exclusionary social conventions. Locke's anthropological minimum is qualified, if not betrayed, by the density of the social norms that are required to support its apparent naturalism. If the education of Rousseau's Emile is an explicit and unmistakable support to the viability of the normative agenda of the *Social Contract,* the centrality of the *Thoughts Concerning Education* is no less to the *Two Treatises.* Although revealingly in the latter case, this centrality is hinted at with elliptical and truncated emphasis.

The second question was to explore the persistence of the exclusionary impulse in nineteenth-century British reflections on India and through this to suggest the mediating link between the theoretical claims and the concrete practices. In the absence of a clear recognition of such mediating links (strategies), the history of liberal theoretical pronouncements and of liberal practices are liable to pass each other on parallel planes. At a related, although in the present context secondary, level this essay is meant as a preliminary investigation into the puzzling fact that in the British case colonialism was never really justified by a theory commensurate with the political and economic significance of the phenomena. Barring John Stuart Mill, whose theoretical reflections on colonialism are systematic but far from sustained, there is, to my knowledge, no major British theorist in the eighteenth or nineteenth century whose work reflects the obvious cultural and political gravity that colonialism clearly had as a lived phenomenon. The facts of political exclusion—of colonial peoples, slaves, women, and those without sufficient property to exercise either suffrage or real political power—over the past three and a half centuries must be allowed to embarrass the universalistic claims of liberalism.

Finally and most tentatively, this article is meant as a preamble to considering whether the development and consolidation of nineteenth-century social science can be understood as a compensatory response to the anthropological neglect that seventeenth-century Lockean liberalism encouraged. One can imagine the immediate implications of Locke's anthropological minimalism could have been to devalue and slight the political importance of the study of cultural and historical datum. Clearly, by the eighteenth century, this neglect could not be sustained either because the exclusionary exigencies of colonialism required more than mere Lockean conventions or because the experience of colonialism exposed a richer variety of cultural and historical details. It is worth recalling that Haileybury College, where Malthus, Bentham, and so many other pioneers of social science got their start, was explicitly designed to facilitate the understanding and governing of colonial people by the East India Company.[80]

Notes

A number of friends and colleagues read and commented on earlier drafts of this chapter. I am grateful to Suzanne Berger, Bonnie Honig, Victoria Hattam, Ellen Immergut, Mary Katzenstein, Kostas Lavdas, Richard Locke, Jane Mansbridge, Gretchen Ritter, and Tejshree Thapa. Josh Cohen read and reread several drafts. With characteristic exactitude he helped me clarify, tighten, and understand the argument I was groping to make. I am deeply indebted and thankful to him for his help and encouragement.

1. The use of attitudinal terms such as "impulse" with reference to liberalism is not meant to imply an exclusionary *intention* on the part of the theories I discuss. Since this article considers exclusion from the vantage of the foundational commitments of liberalism, I do not deny that such intentions may in fact have existed. The argument I am making is simply indifferent to the issue of authorial intent.

2. To my knowledge, the best overview of the historical associations of liberalism is still Harold Laski's brief but remarkable *The Rise of European Liberalism* (London: Allen and Unwin, 1936).

3. My point is not to deny the significance of practicality. Indeed, a strong claim can probably be made for the "practical obstacles" that would have attended extending the franchise to women and to the propertyless in the seventeenth century and of colonial subjects in the eighteenth and nineteenth centuries. My point, in contrast (although not in necessary contradiction), is to suggest how, irrespective of such constraints, one can identify political exclusion by focusing exclusively on the relevant theoretical imperatives.

4. This is not a claim regarding the range of motives that could be at work here. They could, as in the case of Locke, include a commitment to a class-based view of the optimal social order or, as in the case of a host of colonial administrators, to the view

that the exigencies of governing large and distant colonies did not permit of broad representative institutions. On this latter point, see W. H. Morley, *The Administration of Justice in British India* (London, 1858); and Sir George Otto Trevelyan, *The Competition Wallah* (London, 1866).

5. John Rawls, "Kantian Constructivism in Moral Theory," *Journal of Philosophy* 77 (1980):525–528.

6. The distinction between universal capacities and the restrictive conditions for their actualization broadly corresponds to the distinction Robert Dahl makes between *categorical* and *contingent* principles in his very clear and thoughtful "Procedural Democracy" in *Democracy, Liberty, and Equality* (Oslo: Norwegian University Press, 1986), 210.

7. Edmund Burke, *Reflections on the French Revolution* (New York: Dutton, 1971), 3. For a characteristically insightful reflection on the political significance of birth, see Sheldon Wolin, "Contract and Birthright," *Political Theory* 15, no. 3 (1987); also Anne Norton, *Reflections on Political Identity* (Baltimore: Johns Hopkins University Press, 1988), pt. 1.

8. Benjamin Disraeli, *Lord George Bentinck: A Political Biography* (London: Allen & Co., 1852), 184; A. Carthill, *The Last Dominion* (London: William Blackwood and Sons, 1924). With particular reference to the significance of polygenics in America, see R. Horsman, *Race and Manifest Destiny* (Cambridge, Mass.: Harvard University Press, 1981), 132–160. Also Hannah Arendt, *The Origin of Totalitarianism* (New York: Meridian, 1966), 158–222.

9. Burke's deep doubts regarding the effect on Britain of including India within Britain's colonial domain remained acute even after he was reconciled to this fact. It is this concern that resurfaced with unmistakable sincerity and regularity in his long dispute with Warren Hastings. See Edmund Burke, *Works,* vol. 7 (Boston: Little, Brown, 1881).

10. The idea of birth as a significant political marker is an ancient one and has a rich lineage. Among the ancient Greeks, the Visigoths, and the Romans, birth along with place of birth was a precise political credential. Similarly in the Islamic tradition, it designated a specific political status. For instance, within some classificatory systems, slaves were defined as those not born of Muslim parentage and/or within a Muslim community. Regarding the Hindu classificatory system of caste, Louis Dumont (*Homo Hierarchicus,* trans. Mark Sainsbury [Chicago: University of Chicago Press, 1970]) makes the claim that caste "hierarchy in India certainly involves gradation, but is neither power nor authority" (p. 65). This would suggest that the caste system, while replete with social gradations, is indifferent to the relative political standing of different castes. Nevertheless, Dumont acknowledges that the caste system specifies precise privileges, many of which must be taken as politically significant. Thus, for instance, Dumont makes clear that "the learned Brahman (*srotriya*) is in theory exempt from taxes, and the Brahman is especially favoured by the law about lost objects" (pp. 69–70). I am grateful to Jane Mansbridge and Josh Cohen for drawing my attention to some of these additional examples regarding the political significance of birth.

11. See, among others, Charles Taylor, *Sources of the Self* (Cambridge, Mass.: Harvard University Press, 1989), chaps. 1, 5, 6; also A. H. Adkins, *From the Many to the One* (Ithaca: Cornell University Press, 1970).

12. Throughout this article, I use the term anthropology in its almost literal sense of referring to the study of human beings. This does not of necessity mean that my usage is in contrast with the more common disciplinary designation, although the associations triggered by the term *anthropology* as a discipline may be quite different.

13. It is worth pointing out here that the liberal theorist in the broad structure of his or her theoretical enterprise works in a way quite akin to the modern doctor. Presumably it is by virtue of an understanding of the minimally constitutive features of the human body that the doctor can make prescriptions for people of widely differing social, racial, economic, and other backgrounds. The image of the political theorist as the medic of the polity was one that Descartes, Hobbes, and Locke quite self-consciously endorsed. See Owsei Temkin, *The Double Face of Janus and Other Essays in the History of Medicine* (Baltimore: Johns Hopkins University Press, 1977); Kenneth Dewhurst, *John Locke (1632–1704) Physician and Philosopher* (London: Wellcome Historical Medical Library, 1963); Patrick Romanell, *John Locke and Medicine: A New Key to Locke* (Buffalo, N.Y.: Prometheus Books, 1984); and more recently, Richard Nelson, "Liberalism, Republicanism and the Politics of Therapy: John Locke's Legacy of Medicine and Reform," *Review of Politics* 51, no. 1 (Winter 1989).

14. John Locke, *Two Treatises of Government,* 2d ed., ed. P. Laslett (Cambridge: Cambridge University Press, 1967), II, par. 4.

15. Ibid.

16. Ibid., par. 54.

17. In II, paragraph 6, Locke entertains precisely this question by considering the distinction between the states of freedom and of license. The distinction for him turns on the limits in the former set by natural law also identified as "the Law of Reason."

18. Ibid., II, pars. 16, 57.

19. John Locke, *Essay Concerning Human Understanding,* ed. P. H. Nidditch (Oxford: Clarendon Press, 1975), chaps. 2, 3, 4. "Principles of action indeed there are lodged in men's appetite, but these are so far from being innate moral principles, that if they were left to their full swing, they would carry Men to the overturning of all Morality" (bk. 2, chap. 23, p. 75).

20. John Dunn, "The Concept of 'Trust' in the Politics of John Locke," in *Philosophy in History,* ed. R. Rorty, J. B. Schneewind, and Q. Skinner (Cambridge: Cambridge University Press, 1984), 279–301; also, "Trust and Political Agency," in the very thoughtful volume, Diego Gambetta, ed., *Trust: Making and Breaking Cooperative Relations* (Oxford: Basil Blackwell, 1990), 73–94.

21. C. B. Macpherson, *The Political Theory of Possessive Individualism: Hobbes to Locke* (Oxford: Oxford University Press, 1962), 221.

22. See Joshua Cohen, "Structure, Choice and Legitimacy: Locke's Theory of the State," *Philosophy and Public Affairs* 15 (1986): 301–324.

23. Carol Pateman, *The Sexual Contract* (Stanford: Stanford University Press, 1988), 52–55. During the past two decades at least, a number of feminist scholars, including Pateman, have addressed the problem of political exclusion by critically unpacking the exclusionary implications underlying the liberal distinction between the public sphere of political and commercial concerns and the private sphere of domestic life. Clearly, judging from the range of methodological and normative positions from which this distinction has been interrogated, it is a rich nexus for considering the

question of political exclusion. See, for example, Susan M. Okin, *Justice, Gender and the Family* (New York: Basic Books, 1989), chap. 6; Pateman, *The Sexual Contract,* chap. 4; Martha Minow, "We the Family: Constitutional Rights and American Families," *American Journal of History* 74, no. 3 (1987). My own somewhat orthogonal though by no means contradictory approach is partially motivated by a primary concern with colonial exclusions that do not usually turn on the public/private distinction.

24. Pateman, *The Social Contract.* Compare the remark "Women are excluded from the status of 'individual' in the natural condition" (p. 52) with "The subjection of woman (wives) to men (husbands) is not an example of political domination and subordination" (p. 53).

Mary Katzenstein has rightly pointed out to me that the argument being made in this essay is in a general sense akin to Pateman's historically anchored position. Both Pateman and I are pointing to the undermining of the presumed universality of Lockean principles. (Pateman's argument, of course, extends beyond Locke.) Her argument focuses on the implicit reliance of the historical inequality between men and women, an inequality that is embodied in the traditional understanding of the conjugal bond. My own approach is in this sense more textual because it locates the undermining of principles in the textually evident reliance on *social credentials.*

25. Macpherson is, of course, explicit in his reference to the centrality of hidden historical premises for understanding the tradition of possessive individualism. See Macpherson, *The Political Theory,* chap. 1.

26. E. Durkheim, *The Elementary Forms of Religious Life* (London: Allen and Unwin, 1915), 17.

27. Burke, *Works,* 6.

28. Pierre Bourdieu, *Distinction; A Social Critique of the Judgment of Taste,* trans. Richard Nice (Cambridge, Mass.: Harvard University Press, 1984), 471.

29. In concentrating on the link between political exclusion and social structures and conventions, I am obviously drawing on a rich and predominantly sociological tradition of scholarship. Because these works seldom refer to Locke and the British Utilitarian tradition and because they do not focus on political exclusion, their acknowledgment in this article is not adequately evident. I list some of them here to make this acknowledgment explicit: Durkheim, *The Elementary Forms of Religious Life;* Norbert Elias, *The Court Society* (New York: Pantheon, 1983); Norbert Elias, *The History of Manners* (Oxford: Basil Blackwell, 1978); Pierre Bourdieu, *Distinction: A Social Critique of the Judgement of Taste* (Cambridge, Mass.: Harvard University Press, 1984); Pierre Bourdieu, *Outline of a Theory of Practice* (Cambridge: Cambridge University Press, 1977); Stuart Hampshire, "Morality and Convention," in *Morality and Conflict* (Cambridge, Mass.: Harvard University Press, 1983).

30. John Locke, *Thoughts Concerning Education* (London: Spottiswoode and Co., 1880).

31. Ibid., 56–57.

32. Locke, *Second Treatise,* par. 60.

33. Locke's concern with madness and its ambivalent relationship to sobriety has been almost wholly overlooked by political commentators. This omission belies the frequency with which Locke returns to this issue and the political significance he gives it. For instance, the famous chapter "Of the Association of Ideas," which Locke

appended to the fourth edition of the *Essay,* is replete with politically charged suggestions regarding the troubling ubiquity of madness and its common root with reason. For an interesting discussion of some of the questions bearing on Locke's views on madness, see Ricardo Quintana, *Two Augustans* (Madison: University of Wisconsin Press, 1978).

34. Locke, *Second Treatise,* pars. 57, 59.

35. Dahl, *Democracy,* 208.

36. Apart from reason, there is of course, according to Locke, one other crucial means of access to natural laws—namely, the revealed scriptures of the New Testament. At various points, Locke refers to *reason* and *revelation* as the sources through which the precepts of these laws are comprehended (Locke, *Second Treatise,* pars. 6, 25, 56, 57; Locke, *The Reasonableness of Christianity,* ed. I. T. Ramsey [Stanford, Stanford University Press, 1989], secs. 231, 239, 242). The precise relationship between reason and revelation and natural laws is a complex one in Locke as it is in the long history of natural law theorizing. For instance, it is not entirely clear if Locke views revelation as a means to natural law or if he identifies it with the content of these laws. Hence despite his attempt to offer a rationalistic account of New Testament Christianity— which is designed to suggest its consistency with aspects of pre- and post-Christian ethics—in section 243 of *Reasonableness,* the understanding of the laws of nature is tied to the "knowledge and acknowledgment" of "our Savior." Similarly even though Locke presents faith in revelation as a more economical and broad-based venue to natural law by claiming that it obviates the need to carry out "a train of proofs" and "coherent deductions from the first principle" (sec. 243), he also denies that such laws could have been comprehended before "our Saviour's birth."

Clearly Locke places great stock in the significance of faith in revelation. As he says: "the greatest part cannot know and therefore they must believe" (sec. 243). My reason for focusing on reason rather than revelation is motivated by the concern with Locke's alleged universalism. To the extent that his argument is universalistic, he is committed to draw on reason rather than on revelation. The reason for this is that despite his attempts to incorporate Confucianism, Islam, Judaism, and other non-Christian ethical systems, the criterion for their exclusion remains particularistic precisely because it is tied to the extent to which these systems comport with the narrow and doctrinally exclusionary precepts of New Testament Christianity.

37. Locke, *Reasonableness,* 109.

38. Ibid., 103.

39. Quoted from Nathan Tarcov, *Locke's Education for Liberty* (Chicago: University of Chicago Press, 1984), 94.

40. Locke, *Thoughts,* sec. 94.

41. Ibid.

42. Ibid.

43. Ibid., sec. 217.

44. Locke, *Second Treatise,* sec. 59, par. 349.

45. Ibid., vol. 2, sec. 73, par. 358.

46. *Thoughts,* 102.

47. Ibid.

48. Ibid.

49. To my knowledge the best account of Burke's historical and theoretical involvement with India is Isaac Kramnick, *The Rage of Edmund Burke* (New York: Basic Books, 1977). See especially chapter 7.

50. Quoted in Eric Stokes, *The English Utilitarians and India* (Oxford: Clarendon Press, 1959), xi.

51. It is with respect to the lack of historical specification in James Mill's *Essay on Government* that Macaulay focused on in his famous and influential review of that work. Mill's universalistic commitment to representative democracy was grounded in the validity of a purely psychological deduction. And it is on this deduction that Macaulay centered his rebuke. The importance of this review and critique lies in the enormous influence it had on J. S. Mill: "In politics, though I had no longer accepted the doctrine of the *Essay on Government* as a scientific theory, though I ceased to consider representative democracy as an absolute principle, and regarded it as a *question of time, place and circumstance*" (John Stuart Mill, *Autobiography* [New York: Columbia University Press, 1924], 120; emphasis added).

52. There is of course a complex web of methodological considerations in making a distinction between what is constitutive to a theory and what is merely a modified part of it. Without getting into these methodological considerations, Section I of this article represents at least one instance where such a distinction is evinced as carrying credibility.

53. For a very thoughtful and synthetic essay that deals, among other things, with the political effects of the "starting points" from which differences are described, see Martha Minow, "Justice Engendered," *Harvard Law Review* 101, no. 1 (November (1987): 10–96.

54. James Mill, *The History of British India*, vol. 1 (New York: Chelsea House Publishers, 1968), xv.

55. Thomas Hobbes, *Leviathan* (New York: Viking Penguin, 1968), 217–222.

56. A. C. Doyle, "The Adventure of the Three Students," in *Sherlock Holmes: The Complete Novels and Stories*, vol. 1 (New York: Bantam Books, 1986), 832.

57. Louis Hartz, *The Liberal Tradition in America* (New York: Harcourt Brace Jovanovich, 1983), identifies a similar strategy in the domestic and international limits of American liberalism: "[The American] frame of mind has two axiomatic effects: it hampers creative action abroad by identifying the alien with the unintelligible, and it inspires hysteria at home by generating the anxiety that unintelligible things produce. The red scare, in other words, is not only our domestic problem: it is our international problem as well" (p. 285 passim).

Inscrutability as a mark of irredeemable alterity is clearly not unique to liberals. Tzvetan Todorov, *The Conquest of America* (New York: Harper & Row, 1984), makes repeated references to Columbus's unfamiliarity with Indian norms, including their languages, as the ground for characterizing them as devoid of distinct norms and languages.

58. J. S. Mill, "On Liberty," in *Three Essays* (Oxford: Oxford University Press, 1985), 15–16.

59. Ibid., 16.

60. Mill, "Representative Government," 402.

61. Ibid.

62. Ibid., 403.

63. Ibid., 408.

64. Ibid., 409.

65. Ibid.

66. Ibid., 410.

67. Mill, *On Liberty,* 16.

68. Ibid.

69. See Bikhu Parekh, "Bentham's Theory of Equality," *Political Studies* 18 (1970): 478–495. I am extremely thankful to Josh Cohen and Jane Mansbridge for helping in clearing up a number of confusions in my earlier discussion of Mill.

70. Ibid., 211.

71. Ibid., 212.

72. Mill, *On Liberty,* chap. 3, p. 72.

73. Locke, *Second Treatise,* par. 101, p. 378.

74. Charles Grant, "Observations on the State of Society among the Asiatic Subjects of Britain, Particularly with Respect to Morals: and on the Means of Improving It," *Parliamentary Papers* (HC); W. Wilberforce, *A Practical View of the Prevailing Religious System of Professed Christians* (London: Griffith, Farran, Okeden and Welsh, 1888); J. W. Kaye, *Christianity in India* (London, 1859).

75. Burke, "Speeches on the Impeachment of Warren Hastings," in *Works,* vol. VII.

76. Christopher Hutchins, *The Illusion of Permanence: British Imperialism in India* (Princeton, N.J.: Princeton University Press, 1967), chaps. 1, 3, 8.

77. Mill, *History of British India,* II:107.

78. Ibid., 188.

79. Ibid., 463.

80. There are a number of suggestions on this theme in Arendt, *The Origins of Totalitarianism.* Similarly, Ronald Meek, *Social Science and the Ignoble Savage* (Cambridge: Cambridge University Press, 1976), considers a closely related suggestion focusing on the role of native Americans in the development of French and British social science.

2

Imperialism and Motherhood

Anna Davin

Population and Power

Around the beginning of this century infant life and child health took on a new importance in public discussion, reinforced by emphasis on the value of a healthy and numerous population as a national resource. During the nineteenth century most political economists had tended to believe with Thomas Malthus that excessive population was dangerous, leading to the exhaustion of resources, and consequently to war, epidemic disease, and other natural checks on growth. This argument was strengthened by Darwinist notions of the struggle for existence as an essential part of the survival of the race.[1] In the last decades of the century it was used both by the radical neo-Malthusians, who recommended contraception as an artificial check on population and therefore a preventive of poverty (which they attributed to overpopulation, arguing for instance that wages were kept down by the competition for employment); and also by the advocates of what was coming to be known as eugenics, who wanted a selective limitation of population growth, to prevent the "deterioration of the race" and decline as an imperial nation through the proliferation of those they regarded as "unfit" (to breed).[2] There was, however, another view, early expressed by Charles Kingsley (in 1858), that overpopulation was impossible "in a country that has the greatest colonial empire that the world has ever seen." He believed that "since about four-fifths of the globe cannot be said to be as yet in any wise inhabited or cultivated," "it was a duty, one of the noblest of duties, to help the increase of the English race as much as possible," and he urged the members of the Ladies' Sanitary Association, whom he was addressing, to fight against infant mortality.[3]

Later enthusiasts for empire also tended to see population as crucial, especially after the publication of an influential work by J. R. Seeley, *The Expansion of England,* in 1883, and they were disturbed by the falling birthrate which each census after 1881 confirmed. The maintenance of empire, argued the prominent conservative journalist J. L. Garvin in 1905, "would be best based upon the power of a white population, proportionate in numbers, vigour and cohesion to the vast territories which the British democracies in the Mother Country and the Colonies control." If the British population did not increase fast enough to fill the empty spaces of the empire, others would. The threat was not from the indigenous populations, whom he does not mention, but from rival master races. The respective white populations of the United States, Germany, and the British Isles, he said, were 73 million, 61 million, and 54 million, and Britain's rate of increase was the slowest, as well as starting from the lowest base. And others protected their industry by tariffs, so that they could make the most of their larger labor forces.

> Germany and America absorb into their industrial system year by year a number of new workers twice and three times as large as we can find employment for. These states, therefore, gain upon us in man-power and money-power alike; in fighting-power and budget-power; and in strict consequence sea-power itself must ultimately be shared between them.[4]

The birthrate, then, was a matter of national importance: population was power. Children, it was said, belonged "not merely to the parents but to the community as a whole"; they were "a national asset," "the capital of a country"; on them depended "the future of the country and the Empire"; they were "the citizens of tomorrow."[5] This appreciation of their value was certainly strengthened by concern as to their supply. From the mid-seventies the birthrate had been declining, and this trend once recognized caused much anxiety, especially when it was realized that a substantial proportion of those born did not survive. The infant mortality rate for England and Wales in 1899 was 163—that is, out of every 1,000 children born, 163 died before reaching their first birthday. This was higher than the average for the decade (154), which in turn was higher than the average for the 1880s (142). Rates were highest in the poorest, most populous districts.[6] And as Alexander Blyth, Medical Officer of Health for Marylebone, pointed out in 1907,

> Over-production lessens, under-production enhances the value of commodities. Considering the life of an infant as a commodity its money value must be greater than 35 years ago. It is of concern to the nation that a sufficient number of children should annually be produced to more than make good the losses by death; hence the importance of preserving infant life is even greater now than it was before the decline of the birth rate.[7]

The influential author of the first comprehensive and authoritative treatise on infant mortality (*Infant Mortality: A Social Problem,* 1906), George Newman, who at this point was also a London medical officer of health (for Finsbury), expressed similar concern in its preface: "There is an annual loss to England and Wales of 120,000 lives by the death of infants. In past years there has been a similar drain upon the national resources of life. But it should not be forgotten that this loss of life is now operating in conjunction with a diminished income."[8] Similar statements (and metaphors) abounded at that time.

Infant mortality was not, of course, a new problem: Sir John Simon in his reports as medical officer to the Privy Council had already in midcentury identified it as an index of the general sanitary condition; and in the 1890s, when unlike other indices of health it seemed to be getting worse (although the new theories of bacteriology offered fresh hope of solution), medical officers of health were anxiously observing and analyzing it: As the new local monitors of public health they were in the best position to collate statistical information and to compare different factors and attempts at prevention.[9] Already in the 1890s some municipalities were distributing leaflets on infant care and providing instruction to mothers through visits to their homes. Such efforts were given new impetus not only by the epidemics of infant diarrhea during the hot summers of 1898–1900 but also by the climate of opinion in the 1900s, when in the wake of the disastrous Boer War fears for national standards of physique reached a peak.[10] Concern for the health of older children (which again had begun to preoccupy some doctors and teachers in the 1880s and 1890s) also greatly intensified, and the official investigations which resulted brought no reassurance.[11] Various measures followed, both at the national and the local levels. Laws designed to improve the conditions of infancy and childbirth were passed: midwives were required to have training (1902—though with delayed execution), local authorities were empowered to provide meals for needy children (1906), and obliged to organize medical inspection (though not treatment) in schools (1907), births had to be notified within six weeks so that health visitors could be sent round (1907), while the Children Act of 1908 made detailed provision across the spectrum of child welfare. Municipal authorities experimented with schemes to supply hygienic milk cheaply for weaned infants (at risk from the contaminated and adulterated milk normally on sale in working-class districts), and with prizes for healthy babies or for babies which survived their first year; they distributed endless leaflets and sent out battalions of health visitors. The Local Government Board organized two conferences on infant mortality, in 1906 and 1908, and conducted inquiries (through its medical department under Arthur Newsholme) into different aspects of infant mortality.[12]

Besides all this official activity, voluntary societies for the promotion of public health and domestic hygiene mushroomed in these years: the Institute of Hygiene (1903), the Infants' Health Society (1904), the National League for Physical Education and Improvement (1905), the Food Education Society (1908), the National League for Health, Maternity and Child Welfare (1905), the Eugenics Education Society (1908), the Women's League of Service for Motherhood (1910), and so on.[13] The officers and members of such societies were overwhelmingly ladies and gentlemen, sometimes of some prominence, who gave financial support, their names, and often their time and energy. Local branches would unite the socially conscious gentry of a neighborhood—doctors, clergymen, social workers, medical officers of health, councilors, teachers, nurses and health visitors, but most of all ladies whose work was voluntary and who would have no other job. Membership of such societies often overlapped with local authorities, and they would be called on to give evidence to official inquiries and also advice in the formation and execution of social policy. Their influence, in spite of their voluntary status, should not be underestimated. These new organizations, along with the older established societies of medical, social, statistical, and sanitary bent, were all in the 1900s eagerly taking up the issues of child welfare and domestic hygiene.

Their debates (reported in the national press, the medical press, and the journals of the societies) present immediate clues to all the interest and activity, in their constant references to national and imperial interest. The crucial factors seem to be that competition (both economic and political) from recently industrialized Germany and the United States appeared more and more threatening, and Japan too loomed as an impending rival. A poor military performance in the Boer War had dramatized fears of national inadequacy and exposed the poor health of the working class in Britain, from which were drawn both soldiers and sailors to defend the empire and workers to produce goods with which to dominate the world economically. At the same time the findings of the 1901 census confirmed that the birthrate was still falling, and medical statistics suggested that infant mortality was actually rising. The result was a surge of concern about the bearing and rearing of children—the next generation of soldiers and workers, the Imperial race.

Motherhood

Middle-class convention of the time took for granted that the proper context of childhood was the family, and the person most responsible the mother. So if the survival of infants and the health of children was in question, it must be the fault of the mothers; and if the nation needed healthy future citizens (and soldiers and workers), then mothers must improve. This emphasis was reinforced by the influential ideas of eugenists: good motherhood was an essential component in their ideology of racial health and purity. Thus the solution to a national problem of public health and of politics was looked for in terms of individuals, of a particular role—the mother—and a social institution—the family. This obscured to an extent which now seems astonishing the effects on child health of poverty and environment. It also contributed substantially to a shift in the dominant ideology. The family remained the basic institution of society, and woman's domestic role remained supreme, but gradually it was her function as mother that was being most stressed, rather than her function as wife. (Even the recommended reasons for marriage changed: in a manual of the 1860s the young woman was advised to seek as partner for life someone able to support her, willing to protect her, ready to help her, and qualified to guide and direct her—no mention of children—while a 1914 book on young women and marriage gave as the three main objects for marriage the reproduction of the race, the maintenance of social purity, and the mutual comfort and assistance of each married couple.)[14]

Moreover, the relationship between family and state was subtly changing. Since parents were bringing up the next generation of citizens, the state had an interest in how they did it.[15] Child rearing was becoming a national duty, not just a moral one: if it was done badly, the state could intervene; if parental intentions were good but there were difficulties, the state should give help; and if it was done well, parents should be rewarded at least by approval for their patriotic contribution. Arguments of this kind were gaining weight, overriding the old individualist protests about parental rights (already undermined by compulsory education) and the danger of "demoralizing" people by helping them. They were used to justify not only contemporary measures such as the power given to Poor Law guardians to remove children from unsuitable parents (Poor Law Act 1899) or the provision of school meals but also the campaigns for maternity insurance (benefit to help with the expenses of childbirth, which was included in Lloyd George's 1911 Health Insurance Act) and for "the endowment of motherhood," the forerunner of family allowances. State responsibility was, however, a generalized supervision, very much in the background as a safety net. The real everyday responsibilities belonged to the mother.

Because of the declining birthrate, motherhood had to be made to seem desirable; because high infant mortality was explained by maternal inadequacy, the standards of mothers must be improved. A powerful ideology of motherhood emerged in relation to these problems of the early twentieth century, though it was firmly rooted, of course, in nineteenth-century assumptions about women, domesticity, and individualism. Motherhood was to be given new dignity: it was the duty and destiny of women to be the "mothers of the race," but also their great reward. But just as it was the individual mother's duty and reward to rear healthy members of an imperial race, so it was her individual ignorance and neglect which must account for infant deaths or sick children. Thus moral blackmail, exploiting the real difficulties and insecurities of many mothers, underpinned their new lofty status. Nor did their elevation mean an end to subordination. To be good mothers they now needed instruction, organized through the various agencies of voluntary societies and local government, in the skills of what came to be known as mothercraft, as they were being defined by the medical profession. Doctors, district nurses, health visitors, were all asserting their superior knowledge and authority, establishing moral sanctions on grounds of health and the national interest, and denigrating traditional methods of child care—in particular, care by anyone except the mother: neighbors, grandmothers, and older children looking after babies were automatically assumed to be dirty, incompetent, and irresponsible. The authority of state over individual, of professional over amateur, of science over tradition, of male over female, of ruling class over working class, were all involved in the redefining of motherhood in this period, and in ensuring that the mothers of the race would be carefully guided, not carried away by self-importance.

The ideology of motherhood transcended class, even though its components had different class origins. Emphasis on the importance of women not "shirking" motherhood related to the belief that middle- and upper-class women were pursuing new opportunities in education and employment rather than marrying, or were marrying but restricting the number of their children, either tendency boding ill for the race. Emphasis on maternal ignorance related more to working-class women, who must by definition be ignorant, or at the very least irresponsible, since it was taken for granted that if you knew what you should be doing you would do it, and if in spite of that knowledge you didn't, it must be from fecklessness. It is perhaps significant that doctors were such prominent exponents of the ideology. On the one hand, their experience of normal working-class life was usually minimal, since doctors' fees were beyond the working-class budget except in case of emergency. On the other, as guardians of health they appeared to have some responsibility for such problems as the preservation of infant life, and mothers made useful scapegoats, relieving them of blame. Failure to breast feed, taking an infant to the minder in the cold early morning before clocking in at the mill, going out to work at all, were all signs of maternal irresponsibility, and infant sickness and death could always be explained in such terms. Even as careful a statistician as Arthur Newsholme, in his report on infant mortality for the medical department of the Local Government Board in 1910, ended up ignoring the evidence of his own tables as to regional variation and the excessive incidence of infant mortality wherever particular features of working-class urban life were concentrated (most of all overcrowding and the failure of local authorities to introduce a waterborne sewage system in place of middens and ash privies), and sounding off interminably about the "ignorance and fecklessness of mothers."[16]

This article, then, is an attempt to explore the context in which a new definition of woman's role developed in Britain in the early years of this century and to suggest some of the pressures which contributed to the formation of an ideology of motherhood whose influence still touches us today. The ramifications are many and complex, and to follow them all is impossible in this space, but in the final section I do try to draw some of them together. I hope readers will take this as a starting point for further debate, rather than any sort of final word.

A Matter of Imperial Importance

For many doctors and medical officers in the 1900s the saving of infant life seems to have become "a matter of Imperial importance."[17] At the very least, this became the normal rationalization for any discussion or concern in the area of infant mortality. Perhaps some went along with the rhetoric because it was catching, or thought their ideas would get more support if they could say the national interest was at stake. Some probably opposed it without getting much of a hearing, or kept quiet on any but strictly medical questions. But some were ardent propagandists for "the future of the race"; and some really shared the fears of Garvin, quoted above, as to depopulation both at home and in the Dominions, which "if not . . . occupied by people of British stock would sooner or later be occupied by other people." Such apprehensions, according to G. F. McCleary, in a book he wrote in the 1930s, were an important consideration with "those of us who over 36 years ago began to work for the preservation of infant life."[18] His testimony—on what appears to have been a lifelong obsession—might not carry much weight on its own, but it is continually confirmed by reading medical journals and discussion of the 1900s.

Short supply of the commodity was not the only problem: there was the question of quality as well as quantity. It was argued that the quality of survivors of infant disease was likely to be impaired: that "the conditions to which one in five or six of the children born are sacrificed, have a maiming effect upon the other four or five,"[19] and that this too should be of national concern. The outbreak of the Boer War in 1899 was the occasion for a wave of jingoistic propaganda and enthusiasm, which brought a great many young men to offer themselves as recruits. (Two further factors, then as now, affected their choice: namely, unemployment and the hope of travel and adventure—"a man's life.") Their eagerness was not, however, enough to qualify them: a great many of them were found to be physically unfit for service—too small, for instance, or too slight, or with heart troubles, weak lungs, rheumatic tendencies, flat feet, or bad teeth. In 1899, out of every 1,000, 330 were rejected on such grounds; in 1900, 280. (The apparent improvement is probably because the standard was lowered as the war went on.)[20] But it was later estimated, in an influential article by Maj. Gen. Sir Frederick Maurice KCB,[21] that if initial rejections and also subsequent losses through failure of health were both counted, only two out of every five volunteers remained as effective soldiers. Considering this "disproportion between the willing and the physically competent" appalling and disastrous, he argued that the crucial question was not how to improve the recruiting system (a subject much under debate just then), for

whatever steps are taken . . . to raise the standard of the Army either in numbers or physique seem to me to be only like more careful methods of extracting cream from milk. The more carefully you skim the milk the poorer is the residue of skimmed milk. I think it is safe to say that no nation was ever yet for any long time great and free when the army it put into the field no longer represented its own virility and manhood.

If, as it seemed, these puny young men were typical of their class ("the class which necessarily supplies the ranks of our army"), the problem was to discover why, and to change things. Proceeding to speculate on possible explanations, he accounted for the prevalence of bad teeth among recruits by unsuitable food in childhood ("the universal testimony that I have heard is that the parents give the children even in infancy the food from off their own plates"), and decided at once that "the great original cause" (of bad teeth at this point, but subsequently, and with as little evidence, of all the ill-health) was "ignorance on the part of the mothers of the necessary conditions for the bringing up of healthy children." He referred rather doubtfully to Rowntree's recent inquiry into poverty in York, but shied away from accepting general validity for its conclusions (though he quoted them), "that the wages paid for unskilled labour in York are insufficient to provide food, shelter and clothing adequate to maintain a family of moderate size in a state of bare physical efficiency," and that "in this land of abounding wealth, during a time of perhaps unexampled prosperity, probably more than one-fourth of the population are living in poverty." York, he felt, must be exceptional: "if this be true for the whole country, then the impediment to the rearing of healthy children is not the ignorance of the mothers so much as . . . that the conditions of modern life do not enable them to supply their children with sufficient sustenance." This conclusion was unacceptable; and he preferred to plump for "at least attackable causes such as the early marriages and the want of knowledge of the mothers." I quote his conclusions at length, and in spite of his repetition, because these themes recurred throughout the 1900s in the continuing and ramifying debate on "physical deterioration" set off by the unfit recruits.

> Whatever the primary cause . . . we are always brought back to the fact that . . . the young man of 16 to 18 years of age is what he is because of the training through which he has passed during his infancy and childhood. "Just as the twig is bent the tree's inclined." Therefore it is to the condition, mental, moral, and physical, of the women and children that we must look if we have regard to the future of our land. . . . Mr. Barnett in Whitechapel . . . found that the health and long life of the Jews, whose women did not go out to work, compared most favourably with that of the Christian population, the women of which worked without adequate regard to their function as mothers. It does not follow that a stereotyped copying of the habits of the Jews would be desirable, but it may explain and justify the view of the Emperor of Germany that for the raising of a virile race, either of soldiers or of citizens, it is essential that the attention of the mothers of a land should be mainly devoted to the three Ks—Kinder, Küche, Kirche [Children, Kitchen, and Church].

The General's call to arms found a ready audience. Alarmist cries of urban degeneration had been heard already, and invoked to explain city poverty, though as Gareth Stedman Jones points out they are better seen as "a mental landscape within which the middle class could recognize and articulate their own anxieties about urban existence."[22] And appeals for working-class girls to be taught the theory and practice of housekeeping were not new either: indeed, by the turn of the century such lessons were becoming more and more general.[23] "Physical Degeneration" (or "Race Degeneration" or "Deterioration") now became the order of the day, stimulating much debate, some research, and a parliamentary inquiry or two, most important the Physical Deterioration Committee, which reported in 1904. The problem was constantly linked with the question of childbearing and rearing, and with the "ignorance" of working-class mothers; and it was invoked to justify a wide variety of campaigns and reforms: on physical education, feeding of schoolchildren, pure food, clean milk, hygiene and cookery classes for schoolgirls, workgirls, and mothers, temperance, education for parenthood, refusal of marriage licenses to the "unfit" or "degenerate" or even their sterilization. (These included alcoholics, the tubercular, vagrants, and the chronically unemployed—and more or less anyone who counted as mentally sick or physically abnormal.)

In many cases the terms in which reforms were proposed also involved reference to the nation, the empire, or the race, and in this way measures might be rendered acceptable which otherwise would have smacked of socialism. So T. J. Macnamara (ex-schoolmaster and Liberal MP for North Camberwell, in London), writing in the *Contemporary Review* in 1905, after making a whole series of proposals, culminating in school canteens and free transport and baths for schoolchildren, concluded confidently,

> All this sounds terribly like rank Socialism. I'm afraid it is; but I am not in the least dismayed. Because I know it also to be first rate Imperialism. Because I know Empire cannot be built on rickety and flat-chested citizens. And because I know that it is "not out of the knitted gun or the smoothed rifle, but out of the mouths of babes and sucklings that the strength is ordained which shall still the Enemy and the Avenger."[24]

Comparisons could also be made with imperial rivals, who without accusations of socialism had successfully turned the attention of the state to national and particularly children's health. Japan (a very recent newcomer to the club of imperialist powers) was often quoted in this context, as at the annual congress of the Sanitary Institute in 1904, where members were told (apropos of the medical inspection of schoolchildren) that in Japan every schoolchild was under medical supervision and that first aid and hygiene were taught in school. Japan also was "in no danger of race-suicide," mothers there were not "shrinking from maternity as in other lands."[25] Germany was still more often compared, very directly in *The Improvement of the Dwellings and Surroundings of the People: The Example of Germany,* a book published by T. C. Horsfall in 1904. German provision of baths at school, and food and medical supervision, strongly influenced English reformers, sometimes simply as an example, sometimes as one explanation of Germany's success as the "country which has increased most rapidly in wealth and has become our most formidable industrial rival."[26]

Of course, socialists were indeed pushing for these reforms, though in the interests of the working class and the community, rather than the empire. In some cases, as with school meals, they had been demanding them for twenty years already.[27] But there were many views, even among those who called themselves socialists, as to what should be done and how. Some favored state or municipal action and collective solutions, some the one but not the other. They were not likely to work in the voluntary societies that were so active, because their tendency was too individualist. Much of their effort went into attempts to improve the conditions of children of school age, rather than infants, perhaps because local school boards (before their abolition) and local councils were the points at which they could most easily exert pressure, and were more receptive to projects that could be organized through the existing institutions of schools. Work of this kind was especially successful in Bradford. The socialist sisters Margaret and Rachel McMillan, both there in the 1890s and in London later, were very active in campaigning for more municipal and state concern for the health of children, but interestingly according to Margaret McMillan, they did not always have the support of their comrades.

> Even the Labour Party outside Bradford was cold. It was the old, old story that always brings a feeling of despair. "Mothers and fathers," it is said, "have a divine instinct out of which they produce everything that is needed." They have no such instinct. New help does not rise out of these dim underworlds. It comes always from another source. The infant death-rate was appalling.[28]

In the south both sisters made the health and happiness of children the main focus of their activity, putting into practice new ideas about nursery education, the benefits of open-air teaching (and even sleeping, in their Deptford "camp school"), and of school clinics. Margaret McMillan's writings on children, though suffused with a slightly cloying idealism, are notably free of reference to empire or race, or even to the next generation: children were important in themselves and as future citizens. Her main emphasis was humanist.[29]

But sometimes socialists too—or some kinds of Socialists—became infected with the rhetoric and even the assumptions of the empire builders and the eugenists. Ramsay MacDonald in his *Socialism and Government* (1909) tried to distinguish a socialist position on the problems, without abandoning the rhetoric. "Eugenics . . . is a matter of State concern—not the whole field of

Eugenics, but part of the field.'' He regarded race deterioration as a social phenomenon, the result of general ill-health, ''an organic disease undermining the system''; but saw a real conflict for socialists between their duty ''to protect the weak because our sentiments will not allow us to sacrifice them'' and the risk for society ''of their deteriorating the stock.'' He rejected the proposals of ''the individualist and the reformer'' for ''changed systems of Poor Law administration, segregation of the unfit, the lethal chamber and similar things as preventives'' without particularly discriminating between the first (presumably dismissed as tinkering with the system instead of transforming it), and the rest. His own rather vague solution lay in ''mutual aid'' and also in education ''to secure such personal tastes regarding beauty and strength as to guarantee that the race is being propagated by healthy and comely men and women.''[30]

MacDonald was one of those who resigned from the Fabian Society when it split over the question of support for imperialism, in 1900 during the Boer War. In this ''socialist'' organization a poll showed that 259 supported George Bernard Shaw and Sidney Webb's argument for ''a lofty and public-spirited Imperialism,'' and only 217 voted for the anti-imperialist position. The majority Fabian line thus became support for imperialism and the congenial doctrine of national efficiency, in alliance with the Liberal-Imperialists, Rosebery, Asquith, Grey, Haldane, and so on.[31] Webb quoted Asquith approvingly in his proclamation of the new position, an article in *The Nineteenth Century and After* published in September 1901. A program based on National Efficiency was needed.

> Here Mr Asquith is on the right track. What is the use of an Empire (he asks) if it does not breed and maintain in the truest and fullest sense of the word an Imperial race? What is the use of talking about Empire if here, at its very centre, there is always to be found a mass of people, stunted in education, a prey to intemperance, huddled and congested beyond the possibility of realizing in any true sense either social or domestic life?

And he called for a raising of standards of wages, education, and sanitation, because the Empire was ''rooted in the home.''[32] The Fabian imperialists, with their demands for greater state responsibility and planning, but their emphasis also on Britain's imperial role (which tended to go with ideas about the ''imperial race'' and the threat of its diminishing vitality), were easy prey to the racist ideology of eugenics.

Eugenics

The advocates of eugenics, whose influence in this period was pervasive, strongly believed in the importance of the family and especially the mother, because improving the racial stock was partly a question of breeding and partly of rearing, and in both her health and her role were essential. Although there was overlap between their ideas and those of other people concerned with infant mortality and child health, the priority they set on actually improving the race, and their assumptions about the importance of heredity, involved certain important differences. The more extreme of them argued that preventive medicine and injudicious state aid interfered with natural selection and would lead to "retrogression" and the multiplication of the unfit.

> Of far more importance to a people than a declining infantile mortality is the preservation of the national stamina. A multitude of weaklings is less to be preferred than a handful of virile men, and a healthy people pruned of its decadents by a high mortality amongst its children is better than a degenerate race weakened by the survival of its effete progeny.[33]

They mustered their evidence through a research group at the University of London, the Galton Laboratory, set up for "the study of agencies under social control that may improve or impair the racial qualities of future generations, either physically or mentally"; they believed that "to produce a nation healthy alike in mind and body must become a fixed idea—one of almost religious intensity— . . . in the minds of the intellectual oligarchy, which after all sways the masses and their leaders." Their command of genetic theory and the currency that their catchwords and indeed their ideas obtained, gave them a great sense of power or even mission: they were preparing for the approaching time when "we must consciously carry out that purification of the state and race which has hitherto been the work of the unconscious cosmic process."[34] The Darwinist and utilitarian origins of their arguments (and later their claims of statistical proofs) gave them an appearance of scientific and pragmatic authority. This no doubt strengthened their influence among those involved in theoretical or practical "social engineering"—Fabians, of course, social scientists (they founded the Sociological Association), administrators and social workers, and also doctors and Medical Officers of Health. Such influence was reinforced through their elitist and managerial attitude to politics. In their journal, *The Eugenics Review,* in the Sociological Society and its journal, through the meetings and publications of the Eugenics Society, and wherever else they could get a hearing, they zealously defended the cause of "nature against nurture": the influence of environment, they claimed, was "not one fifth that of heredity, and quite possibly not one tenth of it."[35]

Not surprisingly, they held strong views on marriage, in particular, that it should only be permitted where there was nothing nasty to be passed on. At a time of increasing anxiety about the spread of syphilis and other venereal diseases this demand would no doubt have had its attraction for doctors and medical workers, though they held heredity responsible also for a wide range of other ills. In an exposition of eugenics published in 1904 the eugenic marriage is explained as follows:

When a young man and a young woman, offering themselves for marriage, can produce certified records of their ancestry back for three or four generations, showing that their progenitors have been entirely, or largely, free from nervous prostration, sick headaches, neurasthenia, hysteria, melancholia, St Vitus' dance, epilepsy, syphilis, alcoholism, pauperism, criminality, prostitution and insanity—when they can further show that their ancestors have been free from all other inheritable forms of nervous disorders, including certain forms of deafness, colour blindness and other indications of defectiveness and degeneracy, then it may truly be said that such a union may be correctly styled a EUGENIC MARRIAGE.[36]

If alcoholism, pauperism, and criminality, which traditionally were blamed for poverty and the miseries of working-class life, could be attributed to heredity, by implication they could be ended if marriage and procreation by the poor were controlled. Conversely, failure to limit their multiplication would carry the risk of disaster: "the urban proletariat may cripple our civilization, as it destroyed that of ancient Rome."[37]

For those of "superior stock," whose marriages were not doom laden, there lay a great future. Motherhood was to be made in every way desirable: its status raised, its supremacy acknowledged, its economic security assured, for "the elevation of motherhood" was "the one fundamental method by which infantile mortality may be checked."[38] "Let us glorify, dignify and purify motherhood by every means in our power," demanded John Burns (once a militant socialist engineer, and by this time Liberal MP and president of the Local Government Board), in his presidential address at the Infant Mortality Conference in 1906,[39] and his words were often quoted by eugenists and other "maternalists." But it had to be informed and dedicated motherhood, and it was threatened by recent developments opening education and sports to middle-class girls. Karl Pearson, one of the eugenist founding fathers, was among those who believed with Herbert Spencer that individual intellectual development (especially in women) might impair the reproductive powers: in 1885 he wrote that "if child-bearing women must be intellectually handicapped, then the penalty to be paid for race predominance is the subjection of women," and such ideas continued to be held and voiced in the 1900s.[40]

The "new women" of the twentieth century, in spite of their "larger outlook on life," wrote a doctor in the *Eugenics Review* in 1911, were less fit than their predecessors "to become the mothers of a stronger and more virile race, able to keep Britain in its present proud position among the nations of the world."

There is no doubt that the new woman is a more interesting companion than her predecessors, and that she has made great progress in the arts and sciences, in trades and professions, but the question of questions is—is she a better mother of the race? Does, for instance, her knowledge of mathematics, or even her efficiency in athletics, make her intrinsically a better mother than the natural, bright, intelligent girl interested in frills, dances and flirtations? . . .

> Womanliness is disassociated in men's and also in most women's minds with either intellectual power or physical development, but is . . . rightly or wrongly associated with certain passive qualities, such as sympathy and tenderness . . . which best find their expression in the domestic sphere and more particularly in the roles of wife and mother. . . . [M]ay it not be that the manliness of men and the womanliness of women are . . . but the modern expression of Natural Selection?[41]

Others maintained that a woman's health and childbearing capacity would be damaged by excessive activity (physical or intellectual) in adolescence and advised against any but the most desultory occupations.[42] Mary Scharlieb, an influential eugenist doctor, would not go so far (perhaps because her professional status made her something of a "new woman" herself). She feared that excessive athletics and gymnastics would be harmful both to the individual and to the race, tending to produce what she called "the 'neuter' type of girl," whose boyish asexual figure was matched by disinclination for maternity. But she recommended general "physical culture" (especially dancing) for its moral and physical effects, and because

> ours is a people which has been commissioned to carry the lamp of light and learning to the uttermost ends of the earth, and it will neither fail as long as it is worthy, nor cease while aught remains to be done. That we may be worthy, it behoves us to perfect the spirit, mind and body of every man and every *woman* by our imperial race.[43]

Of course, the discussion of the value of exercise for adolescent girls was concerned only with the daughters of the well-to-do. Working-class girls at puberty worked in factories and laundries and in service with no reduction of the demands made on their strength.[44]

Woman must be taught how "to exercise her great natural function of choosing the fathers of the future" and to understand "the age at which she should marry, and the compatibility between the discharge of her incomparable functions of motherhood and the lesser functions which some women now assume."[45] Motherhood, though a destined and natural function, nevertheless needed to be taught; there were skills to be learned so that the eugenically conceived baby would also be reared to its best advantage. The responsible mother would study expert opinion and put herself and her family under the supervision of a doctor, preferably a specialist, whose instructions she would then execute. Teaching was desirable in "the subjects of food and dietetics, the physiology of nutrition, and the effects of proper sanitation," for in this way "by instruction leading to the improvement of the individual we shall aid in preserving women for their supreme purpose, the procreation and preservation of the race, and at the same time promote that race to a better standard, mentally and physically."[46] But this emphasis on the functions of motherhood was not to be thought belittling or confining: the thoughtful woman would realize that "upon womanhood largely depends the standard attained by the world's ethical code." Entrusted with the greatest of all human assets, the child, she would respond to the need for skillful care and guidance during "those impressionable years consecrated to character formation and physical development," for was it not "a trumpet call to awaken woman to her weighty obligations, as much imperial as domestic or social, and to arouse her to the imperative necessity of preparation, intelligent and sustained, for their fulfillment?"[47]

Eugenics propaganda was directed mainly at the middle and upper classes, partly because they tended to believe that even in an apparent democracy there was an elite who in fact were the only ones whose opinion counted, and also because in their analysis the poor were almost inevitably "dysgenic" (the opposite of eugenic), so there was little point in teaching them how to choose noble mates or rear little imperial assets. Indeed there was a class fear that the middle classes, who clearly were now beginning to limit their families, would limit themselves out of existence. The choice of abstinence from marriage was also more feasible for middle-class women, who were starting to have greater possibilities of economic independence without social stigma. So the reason for the trumpet call was partly to remind women that "the sacred duties of mother-hood must not be shirked,"[48] and the constant emphasis on the moral reward was perhaps necessary to offset the increasingly recognized advantages of the single life or the small family. Doctors too were seen to have a responsibility in this direction, presumably in discouraging their patients from restricting their families. (Bertrand Russell in his autobiography recorded the opposition of the family doctor to the decision he and his wife made to use contraception, though this was slightly earlier.)[49] At the inaugural meeting of the British Gynaeco-logical Society in 1904 the assembled gynecologists were warned that marriages among the better classes were now so sterile "that a quite undue and dangerous proportion of the rising generation was recruited from the lower, the more ignorant, the more vicious, and semi-criminal population." The speaker went on—invoking the full authority of his position as president—to adjure his audience in these words:

> I would like to sting my fellow countrymen into some proportionate sense of shame and duty. . . . [A]s the temporary head of a great British society which may well claim to be the greatest British authority on such questions, I am surely not overstepping my province if I ask for the grave interest of every fellow in this subject. . . . For with us lies a great responsibility, and ours will be to a very large extent the blame if in after years the lamp of the Anglo Saxons is found to be burning dimly.[50]

Fabians and the Endowment of Motherhood

In his pamphlet on the declining birthrate, published as a Fabian tract in 1907, Sidney Webb presented a more sophisticated argument, but with some of the same assumptions. He drew together various findings on the fall in the national birthrate over the previous two or three decades and suggested some likely consequences. His deductions were based not only on the clearly proved decline in births in all classes, but also on the assumption—for which statistical evidence of the same quality was not available—that the phenomenon was more marked among "the self-controlled and foreseeing members of each class" and was the result of intentional "regulation of the marriage state." He had no moral objections to such regulation, regarding it as rational and prudent under the prevailing social conditions, since in four-fifths of the nation's households the birth of children was "attended by almost penal consequences." (He meant the cost of rearing children.) But he regarded its implications for the nation with anxiety. In his view the argument that excessive population led to increased poverty no longer held, since collective bargaining and state control should between them make it possible to secure a national minimum standard of living. Population increase on the contrary must be encouraged, especially among those groups which were now limiting their families. Decline would be nationally disastrous, as the less provident, and therefore less desirable and fit, section of the population would go on breeding, which would lead to racial deterioration, and any vacuum would be filled by "freely-breeding alien immigrants," which would involve the country "gradually falling to the Irish and the Jews."

But he saw hope in the fact that the decline in births resulted from voluntary restriction rather than degeneracy of the national fertility. "A deliberately volitional interference, due chiefly to economic motives, can at any moment be influenced." The answer was to "alter the balance of considerations in favour of the child-producing family." This would involve a change of perspective, the realization, for instance, that "the most valuable of the year's crops, as it is the most costly, is not the wheat harvest or the lambing, but the year's quota of adolescent young men and women enlisted in the productive service of the community." The state would therefore have to recognize its responsibilities and encourage the rational choice to have children by "the systematic 'endowment of motherhood,' and place this most indispensable of all professions upon an honourable economic basis." He anticipated such measures being proposed as "the municipal supply of milk to all infants, and a free meal on demand to all mothers actually nursing their babies," the feeding of schoolchildren, and maintenance scholarships for secondary education to encourage middle-class parents.[51]

"Endowment of motherhood" was a demand for financial recognition by the state that mothers' work rearing children contributed to the good of society. Alys Russell was speaking on it in 1896 during a visit to the United States; it was a major demand in a French pamphlet published in translation by the Independent Labour Party in the 1890s as *Woman and the Suffrage;* and it was a common feature of socialist programs. Dr Alice Drysdale Vickery, balancing between socialism, feminism, and eugenics, argued in 1906 for its importance to women's economic independence, and feminists and socialists stressed this aspect. Eleanor Rathbone was to be its best-known and longest-persevering proponent, using every possible argument, including that it would give the state the power to "manipulate the birth rate."[52] As proposed in the 1900s by Webb and the Fabians it was effectively an economic version of the eugenists' "elevation of motherhood" (although not to be applied selectively, so not meeting their criteria); and indeed demands for improving the economic and the moral standing of motherhood often went together. A more moderate proposal, for maternity insurance, was also commonly put forward at this time, and was incorporated in the 1911 health insurance provisions: this was intended simply to help with the expenses of confinement, and in fact scarcely covered them. One doctor, C. T. Ewart, suggested in the *Empire Review* that such a scheme combined with "lactation premiums to those mothers who feed their own babies" would be "of greater vital importance to the race than old age pensions."[53]

Education for Motherhood

Emphasis on motherhood was by no means confined to the eugenists and their closer followers. It was the common feature in all the discussion of infant mortality and child welfare, whether the focus was on quality or quantity, on the encouragement and nurture of the fittest, or the preservation of all infant life. Eugenists talked also about education for parenthood; occasionally someone might recommend involving fathers in the upbringing of their children;[54] but overwhelmingly (and especially in the medical press) it was maternal ignorance that was blamed, not parental—"faulty maternal hygiene," or the mother's neglect, intemperance, employment, early marriage, and so on. From "the physiological law that infant life is dependant upon the mother from nine months before birth until nine months after birth,"[55] from the recognition that in pregnancy "the mother's well-being and the child's well-being are inseparable,"[56] from the discovery that mortality was lower among breast-fed babies,[57] came the argument "in dealing with infant mortality it is the mothers we must go for not the babies,"[58] and this was extended to mean far more than the mother's health. Biologically based reasoning was used to justify a social construct, motherhood. And the ideology was passed on to mothers along with practical advice in the newly proliferating manuals on child care, even those intended for the working class.

> If every woman who takes upon herself the sacred relationship of motherhood could be led to realize how she is responsible for the future of the baby-life, and how the true greatness of the individual constitutes the true grandeur of nations,

we should have healthier babies and happier homes, and the disintegration of family life would be a menace no more.[59]

Nineteenth-century criticism of mothers had dwelt most often on the iniquity of their going out to work.[60] Working mothers of the early twentieth century did not escape similar denunciation, but as ten years of legal restriction on the employment of mothers in the first month after childbirth had not lowered infant mortality, and as investigations showed that infant mortality rates were extremely high in some areas (Tyneside and South Wales particularly) where mothers rarely went out to work, it was increasingly recognized that other factors must be involved. Maternal ignorance provided an acceptable alternative explanation. It could include all the mother's failings, including going out to work, yet by stressing knowledge rather than necessity, it made the problems seem soluble. Mothers would want the best for the babies, therefore all that was necessary was to educate them in what they should be doing. So, for example, the British Medical Association in 1904, on the recommendation of its public health committee, launched a petition (for which they collected 1,400 signatures in the first week) representing to the Board of Education "that it is of urgent importance that elementary instruction in health subjects, including temperance, should be provided in all primary schools in order that the conditions which lead to deterioration of the national physique may be understood and as far as possible prevented."[61]

Special attention to the care and feeding of infants was to be taught to future mothers, which it was assumed meant all girls and young women. Mrs. Bosanquet, a well-known social worker and commentator on social problems, advocating what she called "a woman's remedy," in an article entitled "Physical Deterioration and the Poverty Line," enjoined,

> Begin with the girls in school, and give them systematic and compulsory instruction in the elementary laws of health and feeding, and care of children, and the wise spending of money. Go on with the young women in evening classes and girls' clubs; and continue with the mothers wherever you can get at them. . . . It has been possible to awaken an intelligent interest in window gardening in the very poorest quarters of our towns, and it ought not to be impossible to awaken a similar intelligent pride in the care of children. . . . What we want is a reform which will provide suitable food and care for the children from the first day of their lives, and continue to provide it throughout manhood and old age; and there is no way of securing that except through the mothers and wives.[62]

It is interesting in this passage that not only is all domestic instruction and responsibility relevant only to girls, but it is assumed that the babies are male: they are to be cared for as children and "throughout manhood" and old age. This was in fact quite often implied in the rhetoric of these discussions, and points to the very direct connection with concern about the "material of

Empire," as Masterman put it in his denunciation of conditions *At the Heart of the Empire* (1901)—"the future colonizers and soldiers, not to mention the traders, who hold the Empire together."[63] The word virile was constantly used, even when the issue was not specifically the health of recruits. "Future citizens," in those days when women did not vote, were men, of course; and the eugenist Karl Pearson defined the desirable characteristics of good English stock entirely in terms of the "typical English*man* of the past." ("A clean body, a sound if slow mind, a vigorous and healthy stock, a numerous progeny" were "the essentials of imperial race," the ideal of all "who have the welfare of the nation and our racial fitness for the world-struggle at heart.")[64] Mothers thus became responsible to the nation above all for the production and rearing of healthy sons; in spite of "the elevation of motherhood" the production of healthy future mothers was much less commonly demanded.

The focus on mothers provided an easy way out. It was cheaper to blame them and to organize a few classes than to expand social and medical services, and it avoided the political problem of provoking rate- and taxpayers by requiring extensive new finance.[65] And there seemed more chance of educating individuals, future or present mothers, than of banishing poverty. So even those who recognized—or paid lip service to—the importance of environment were liable to fall back on such measures as more domestic science in schools, and education for motherhood, and banning the employment of mothers. The parliamentary committee investigating physical deterioration in 1904, deciding that while actual deterioration remained unproven working-class health nevertheless left much to be desired, made fifty-three recommendations. Many of them dealt with the environment (overcrowding, open spaces, smoke, pollution, houses in bad repair, insanitary conditions, cooking facilities, milk supply, etc.), or with other aspects of working-class life (unemployment, the provision of creches, work conditions, overfatigue, the employment of young persons and of women in factories, adulterated food, insurance for sickness, for unemployment, and particularly for childbirth). Others dealt with the powers and organization of local and health authorities. But overwhelmingly, in the discussion which followed publication of the report, most of that range was ignored. The recommendations which were quoted and endorsed were those concerning the instruction of girls and women in cooking, hygiene, and child care. These were more acceptable than, for instance, the registration of landlords with a view to enforcing repairs and the provision of decent living conditions.

But there were in fact considerable problems in implementing the catchall solution of teaching future mothers. Provision for further education of girls who had left school (at 13 or 14 usually) was not widespread, was organized much more around commercial skills, and would not necessarily attract girls who had been at work all day and might well have their share of chores to do at home in the evening. (In fact it's likely that many of these "little mothers" who already had a great deal to do with child care would have felt they had little to learn.)

Girls' clubs, another of Mrs. Bosanquet's suggestions, were unevenly distributed and sometimes irregularly attended; in any case they reached only a few girls. In schools the syllabus of girls was already overloaded: to their original handicap of needlework had been added (in the big cities at least) classes in cookery, laundry, and housewifery, but with no very satisfactory results. It was expensive to provide the necessary equipment, and what was provided bore no relation to what they were used to, being too up-to-date and probably too large-scale. In cookery classes the dishes cooked were supposed to be paid for to cover their cost, but often the girls could not afford them and they might end up eaten by the teachers. Nor could the girls get much practice at home, even if any of the dishes they were taught were within the family's means: few mothers felt they could risk experiment with the carefully rationed supplies. There were complaints that laundry work was taught by giving the girls their teachers' washing to do; or that they were learning skills only relevant to domestic service, not to their family needs.[66] To set up classes in infant care was even more tricky—what could they practice on? Dolls were proposed, or borrowed babies, but one was too unrealistic, and the other was difficult to organize. Nevertheless, at the Board of Education, on the instigation of its president Walter Runciman, with the strong support of Robert Morant, its secretary, and of the chief medical officer, George Newman (all gentlemen without schoolteaching or presumably domestic experience), a circular was prepared by Janet Campbell urging on local education authorities and teachers "the great importance of increasing and improving the present inadequate provision in our schools for instructing the girls in the care and management of infants." The hope was that by teaching girls and women how to take care of infants both mortality and ill-health in infancy and childhood might be diminished.[67] All girls were to learn it, including the duller ones, who might well discover they could for once do something as well as the brighter ones and who would learn "with their brighter comrades" that "intellectual attainment is not the only issue of true education, and that in learning the art and practice of infant care they are helping to secure for themselves their true place in the future of the state."[68] They were, of course, "the mothers of the next generation."[69]

Maternalism

In 1906 the first National Conference for the Prevention of Infant Mortality took place, under the auspices of the Local Government Board.[70] The papers read at the conference explored some of the possible factors and ways of countering them. Like the recommendations of the Physical Deterioration Committee they went into possible administrative measures: the appointment of qualified women health visitors, public provision of pure milk, earlier notification of births, the regulation of child-minding, the amendment of the Infant

Life Protection Act, the powers of local authorities, the operation of the Mid-wives Act. But there was nothing on the environment, unless one counts the two papers on the milk supply. And the aspects of working-class life discussed had little to do with economics or work or poverty: there were two papers on infant life insurance, two on alcoholism,[71] and one on the employment of married women in factories. Only two examined health in childbirth (one on premature birth, one on ante-natal causes of infantile mortality, including alcoholism),[72] though one by Sykes touched on this area ("The Teaching of the Hygiene of the Expectant Mother"). The first paper was an address by the influential Dr. James Niven, medical officer of health for Manchester, on "The Teaching in Schools of Elementary Hygiene in Relation to the Rearing of Infants."

The presidential address was given by John Burns, in his capacity as president of the Local Government Board. He began by suggesting that "in equal parts the mother, society and industry" were to blame for high infant mortality. But his discussion of the problem was in fact couched entirely in terms of mothers. He blamed their delinquency in giving birth outside wedlock (the mortality rate was substantially higher for illegitimate children, probably because the economic situation of a woman on her own was so bad); their intemperance with alcohol; their employment (disastrous for moral training and discipline as well as health); even their alleged interest in physical exercise. (This is, of course, another example of the way that the rhetoric of motherhood ignored class difference.) He believed that "at the bottom of infant mortality, high or low, is good or bad motherhood. Give us good motherhood, and good pre-natal conditions, and I have no despair for the future of this or any other country." (This statement was to be quoted again and again.) The contributions of industry and society had disappeared: he attributed preventable death to "cruelty, over-feeding, under-feeding, ignorance, stupidity, or improper feeding."[73]

The next conference, in 1908, developed this emphasis on the mother still further: its program, as one of the participants (an enthusiastically eugenist doctor called Caleb Saleeby) later wrote, "proceeded upon a principle—the principle of the supremacy of motherhood."[74] Saleeby's subject, "The Human Mother," set the tone. Another eugenist, Alice Ravenhill (who in 1897–1898 had written three pamphlets for the Women's Co-operative Guild, and later a special report for the Board of Education on domestic science teaching in the United States),[75] spoke on "The Education of Girls and Women in the Functions and Duties of Motherhood." Alderman Broadbent of Huddersfield, where for several years a scheme had been operating to encourage breast feeding and provide support in child rearing through regular home visits (to which Broadbent's contribution during his year as mayor was a system of vouchers to the mothers of newborn babies which they could redeem for a sovereign if the infant survived its first year), spoke on "Education and Instruction for Mothers" (not on bribery).[76] There were two papers on the best way to help mothers below the poverty line, two on parental neglect, and one demanding controls on the sale of infant foods. The only other paper was "The Powers of Boards of Guardians in Relation to the Parents and the Need of Further Extension": this presumably dealt with the alternatives when mothers "failed."

Saleeby and Ravenhill, whose names crop up continually in these years, were ardent proponents of what Saleeby called "maternalism," as well as of eugenics. Saleeby saw himself as a follower of his "august master" Francis Galton, the father of eugenics, who apparently had said that "his disciples must instil these principles into the public mind like a new religion."[77] Both, however, were on the humane wing of eugenics; they were concerned with actual infant and child life as well as the eugenic ideal. Saleeby was against the so-called negative eugenic methods (sterilization or the lethal chamber, or opposition to preventive medicine): he argued that intervention to improve the race could only take place before conception: "from the moment of conception a new individual has been formed," and its destruction "except to save the life of the mother" would be murder.[78] He did not oppose preventive measures like creches and the provision of pure milk, though he regarded them as stopgaps and disliked them because they "infringed the maternalist principle," that is, they encouraged substitution for the mother. The hardline eugenist might believe "that in the present unorganized state of society, in the present dethroned state of motherhood, it were vastly better had many even of the healthy majority never been born," but in Saleeby's view since the children existed there was no choice but to do the best for them.[79]

Belief in preparation for parenthood, the strand in eugenic thinking that both Saleeby and Ravenhill most strongly propounded, and also concern for existing infants and children ("to stop this child slaughter and child damage"), led them to the mother. Woman was "Nature's supreme instrument of the Future," Saleeby wrote in the introduction to his book *Parenthood and Race Culture* (1909);[80] and he devoted a further volume entirely to *Woman and Womanhood* (1912), in which his ideas are set out at length. He seems to have been a popular speaker, certainly his turns of phrase in the books are often memorable; his criticism of municipal milk depots, for instance, ends up: "There is no State womb, there are no State breasts, there is no real substitute for the beauty of individual motherhood."[81] Marie Stopes, in the preface to *Married Love,* quoted him approvingly on the difference between the mother cat (instinctively expert) and the human mother (needing to be trained).[82] His flair for putting across the arguments is well illustrated in this passage: "The history of nations is determined not on the battlefield but in the nursery, and the battalions which give lasting victory are the battalions of babies. The politics of the future will be domestic."[83] But it was also no doubt important that what he was saying, especially on the subject of maternalism, was well within the mainstream of discussion.

Newman and Newsholme

Even those who were most expert in the field of infant mortality were liable to succumb to the rhetoric of maternalism. George Newman, for instance, in *Infant Mortality,* analyzed the causes of death and their variations and recognized environmental factors of all kinds, yet still gave them second place or expressed them in terms of motherhood: ''This book will have been written in vain if it does not lay the emphasis of this problem upon the vital importance to the nation of its motherhood.'' It becomes clear that he is including the physical state of the mother under this heading: deaths of premature infants are the result of the mothers' debility, and external conditions of poverty are mediated by the mother: their effects on her health as well as on how she manages to run the household all seem to count as motherhood.

> The problem of infant mortality is not one of sanitation alone, or housing, or indeed of poverty as such, *but is mainly a question of motherhood.* . . . Improved sanitation, better housing, cheap and good food, domestic education, a healthy life of body and mind—these are the conditions which lead to efficient motherhood from the point of view of child-bearing. They exert but an indirect effect on the child itself, who depends for its life in the first 12 months not upon the State or the municipality, not yet upon this or that system of creche or milk-feeding, but upon the health, the intelligence, the devotion and the maternal instinct of the mother. And if we would solve the great problem of infant mortality, it would appear that we must first obtain a higher standard of physical motherhood.[84]

This confusion between motherhood in the ideological sense and the health of the mother was presumably the result of overexposure to the endless mystification and rhetoric about motherhood, so that his actual observations of the role of maternal ill-health and the conditions of poverty got overlaid. Elsewhere, however, the contributions of poverty and ill-health were left out altogether, and the responsibility is once again placed on maternal ignorance and negligence.

> Death in infancy is probably more due to such ignorance and negligence than to almost any other cause, as becomes evident when we remember that epidemic diarrhoea, convulsive debility, and atrophy, which are among the most common causes of death, are brought about in large measure owing to improper feeding or ill-timed weaning; bronchitis and pneumonia are due not infrequently to careless exposure (indoor or outdoor); and death from measles and whooping cough is largely caused by mismanagement of nursing. To remedy this condition of things three measures need to be carried out: (a) instruction of mothers, (b) the appointment of lady health visitors, and (c) the education of girls in domestic hygiene.[85]

Newman was a lifelong Quaker whose career suggests a strong sense of public responsibility. After qualifying (in 1892) he specialized in public health, and with ten years' experience as a Medical Officer of Health (for Bedfordshire and for Finsbury) he became the first Chief Medical Officer of Health to the Board of Education in 1907 and organized the medical inspection of school-children, continually pressing in his annual reports that it should be extended to all areas. Perhaps his Quaker background and his own childless marriage made him particularly susceptible to the ideology of domesticity and moth-erhood; in any case he believed that homes were the vitals of a nation and that the British Empire depended "not upon dominions and territory alone, but upon men, not upon markets alone, but upon homes."[86] Certainly his position in the Board of Education and his close working relationship with its secretary, Sir Robert Morant, gave him the opportunity (as we have seen) to press his views on the usefulness of education for motherhood.

His older colleague, Arthur Newsholme, had also early turned his attention to infant mortality. In the tradition (as he pointed out in his autobiography many years later) of Simon and Farr, the mid-nineteenth-century pioneers of public health, Newsholme was a careful statistician and already in the 1880s was collecting data on the incidence of infant mortality in Brighton, where he was Medical Officer of Health. He saw the conditions of poverty as having a large influence and argued against simple generalizations about the incapacity of working-class mothers. He refused to associate himself with those who used the argument of race deterioration (as, for instance, in the British Medical Association's 1904 petition for hygiene lessons in school, which he would not sign though he partly agreed with the demand), on the grounds that urbanization and the current social arrangements had for some decades resulted in deplorable health for the working classes, and there was no evidence of recent changes for the worse, only a new awareness.[87] He almost never used the vocabulary of empire and nation: generally he took for granted that infant mortality deserved attention as a major health problem. Where he did introduce a political justification for health measures, in arguing the case for medical examination of schoolchildren, he talked of the "social value" of each scholar and of safeguarding their health "in the interests of the community."[88] He even countered eugenist allegations that the birthrate was declining fastest in the classes whose contribution to the race and the nation was most important, by arguing that "special fitness to replenish the world is not a monopoly of class, but occurs in stocks which are found in every social stratum"; or again that a distinction must be drawn between intrinsic inferiority and "inferiority associated with present social circumstances." While accepting that the chil-dren of the poor were handicapped in their potential achievement, he was "satisfied that no sufficient evidence has been produced to show that there is innate inferiority in a large proportion of the wage-earning class."[89] (On the question of race and empire, unfortunately, his views, though cautiously ex-pressed, seem more dubious: it could not be "a matter of indifference" what races peopled "the unfilled portions of the world," and every Briton would "wish that his race may have the preponderant share in shaping the future destinies of mankind.)"[90]

Newsholme's approach to the question of infant mortality (like Newman's) involved close examination of causes. Yet like Newman he sometimes let bias against mothers prevail, as in his 1910 report to the Local Government Board on infant and child mortality.[91] Nevertheless, his constant awareness of the context of poverty made him relatively realistic about working-class life, its problems, and its endless variation with region and community. In his auto-biography, written it is true in the 1930s, he largely escaped the influence of maternalism. Maternal ignorance, he tartly observed, provided a convenient explanation of excessive mortality, it was "a comfortable doctrine for the well-to-do person to adopt" since it led to "the notion that what is chiefly required is the distribution of leaflets of advice, or the giving of theoretical instruction in personal hygiene." Mothers in all classes, he pointed out, might be ignorant, but "the mother in comfortable circumstances" was able "to ensure for her infant certain advantages which the infant of the poorer mother often cannot obtain." These included relief from other household duties and help with the infant itself; access to the most hygienically obtained milk, and good conditions—a pantry or a cool place—in which to store it; alternative care for the child in case of the mother's illness ("if the working-class mother is ill the child must often suffer with its mother"); good nursing and medical attention for the child if sick; rest, so that her milk would be more plentiful and richer, and her relationship with the child under less stress than if she was overworked and suffering from chronic fatigue; a healthy environment as regards space, ventilation, sanitation, and so on. The ignorance of the working-class mother, he concluded, "is more dangerous, because associated with relative social helplessness."[92] Or again he stressed the need to foster the health of the mother, "aided by hygienic and medical help for her children."[93] He did, however, attach importance to education, though of the public mind and conscience in general as well as of mothers. In trying to explain the plummeting of infant deaths in the twentieth century (1900: 154 per 1,000 live births; 1920: 105 per 1,000; 1920: 80 per 1,000; 1930: 60) he suggested as one prime factor the influence of elementary schools, with their "constant stimulus of emulation towards tidiness and cleanliness," and pointed out that the girls in the first generation of compulsory schooling were the mothers of infants in the 1900s.[94] He also remarked that the declining birthrate (which in his view had affected the wage-earning classes as well as the better-off) meant smaller families and therefore "for the working-class mother, more time and an improved exchequer to devote to the care of each child," which would be likely to improve "each child's prospect of life and health." (This, however, like the improvement in living standards for most people over the last decades of the nineteenth century, could not, he argued, have been a chief factor in the decline of infant mortality, since both developments preceded it.)[95]

Working-Class Family Life

This is not the place for a detailed discussion of the causes of infant mortality, but it would perhaps be useful to give some idea of the conditions of working-class family life in the 1900s, and in that context to look at the explanations which were given for the "annual holocaust." The problem, as Newsholme remarked of infant diarrhea, was an urban one, and one mainly "of the artisan and still more of the lower labouring classes."[96] The working-class family at this time varied considerably, according to wage level, local employment opportunities and rents, and custom. As a general rule in the towns and cities, the better and more certain a wage a man could earn, the less likely his wife was to go out regularly to work, provided he remained in health and employment. Among artisans especially, where an adequate and regular wage was most usual, the way of life of the family would frequently approximate to the middle-class ideal: breadwinner, housekeeper, and dependent children. A better standard of living—more space, more furniture, more clothes, more food—tended also to mean more housework, so that the mother who could afford to stay at home would also be the one for whom the housewifely role was becoming more and more full-time. Her children would be regularly at school, so she would not have their help during the day; she would have higher standards as to their appearance and the state of the home, so there would be more washing and ironing and mending to do, and more cleaning and scrubbing and polishing. The care of infants and toddlers would be entirely in her hands. With money for food beyond bare essentials she would probably cook more. In short, she would be fulfilling the functions which she ought: she would be a proper housewife and mother by the definitions implicit in the exhortations to motherhood, though sometimes with quite a struggle.

At the other extreme of the working class would be families where the father was absent, dead, ill, or out of work, or where the wages that could be earned by him or other members of the family (including the mother) never quite stretched to meet their requirements. Rowntree's 1900 survey in York suggested that nearly 10 percent of the population were living in poverty with such causes, which he called primary causes, and another 18 percent in secondary poverty, where other reasons also operated: in short that over a quarter were living at a standard "insufficient to maintain mere physical efficiency." He regarded the overcrowding that resulted from high rents and low wages, and the poor nutrition that inadequate budgets made almost inevitable, as responsible for the generally poor level of health in the working class (with the exception of the artisan sector).[97] In these poorest families the woman's wage might be the only income, and certainly was essential. Space and possessions would be minimal, so that housework in the sense of daily maintenance was less, though a great deal of "transformation" work might be needed, making over old clothes to fit current needs, mending and washing frequently because there were no spares, and so on. Child care would be improvised—now a neighbor would help out, now an older child would stay home from school, now the baby would be taken along to the mother's cleaning job, or would crawl around the mother's feet as she sat pasteing paper bags or seaming trousers. Such a mother, however hardworking, would not appear as a model housewife, or as one properly dedicated to motherhood.

Between the very poor and the artisans was a shifting stratum where circumstances would determine everything—the number and ages of the children in particular, but also the husband's work and conditions in his trade, and of course his health. Here a mother with young children might not have to go out to work, but sometimes it might be necessary, or she might take in home work on a regular or an occasional basis. A mother whose children were older might well take casual or regular employment. (Most working-class children started full-time school at three, though in 1906 an adverse report by the inspectors on infant education led to attempts to end or at least limit school provision for children under five: one of the arguments was that they ought to be with their mothers anyway, but the economic strain put on the family by withdrawal of infant school provision was the main reason why it was not in fact abolished at this point.)[98] When times were difficult relatives or friends might take care of a child or two for a while, or even permanently; or it was not unusual for a family who was not in difficulties to take a girl cousin, say, perhaps from the country, to help the mother with children and housework, or for a local school leaver to come in regularly and give a hand, for a small wage, but often in a relationship closer to that of daughter than of servant.

In all of these groups breast feeding would be normal at least at first, if it was physically possible. It did not require a cash outlay, and it was thought to postpone conception. But of course, mothers who went out to work were unlikely to be able to suckle at work (though sometimes it was possible for the child to be brought in the dinner hour and put to the breast); and many mothers were not in good enough health to sustain the flow, their own nutrition being the worst in the family. Sometimes the better-off mothers may perhaps have succumbed to the claims of the patent baby food manufacturers (who were expanding fast and advertising heavily), and weaned their babies prematurely so as to give them these new ideal products. Eric Pritchard of the St. Marylebone Health Society, an influential figure in the infant mortality movement, had very strong views on the subject of infant feeding. Denouncing the wide popularity of "those infant exterminators known as infant foods," he emphasized that the ambition of maternity should be "not to make a fine fat baby, but to make a fine useful man," so that the starchy patent food preparations were useless; and what was needed was protein, or as he called it, nitrogenous food: "We have been taught in this country . . . to think imperially. *If our mothers could only be taught to think nitrogenously of infants, what an imperial asset this would be for the empire.*"[99] But many babies being "brought up by hand" would be bottle fed with the cheapest condensed milk, diluted with hot water. This was made from skimmed milk, so nutritionally it was almost useless, with less than a quarter of the fat content of breast milk, although it was often advertised with pictures of fine healthy babies. One kind had the brand name "Goat" and benefited from the common belief that goat's milk was the best substitute for breast milk. But it was skimmed cow's milk like the rest.[100] The bottles used were still occasionally the old-fashioned long-necked kind, whose long rubber tube was almost impossible to clean and which was always denounced by the health authorities. On bacteriological grounds this was clearly right, but they also criticized it because it was possible to leave it with the baby so that it would suck when it wanted (and so require less attention), whereas they advocated regular feeding even if the child had to be awakened. This was not popular: one doctor writing to the *British Medical Journal* complained that he had great difficulty in working-class families "persuading mother or nurse to take up the child every two or three hours in the daytime, when the baby is asleep. To these people it seems wrong to disturb a child out of its sleep."[101]

But the practice most commonly denounced was that of giving the baby a sup of whatever the other members of the family were having. On this point "expert" opinion since then has swerved more than once from opposition to tolerance: at present in baby clinics (or at least in the one I attend with my daughter) it is recommended from quite an early age to give them a little mashed-up adult food—potatoes and gravy, for instance—which is probably pretty much what was happening in the period under discussion, and what so much displeased the new professionals of child health. Babies in most working-class families were great pets, and a common expression of affection would be to take a child up during a meal and feed it tidbits. How far totally unsuitable foods were fed in a quantity sufficient to do damage is perhaps open to question.

The major killers for babies were, according to Newman, "prematurity, pneumonia, and diarrhea." Prematurity clearly had to do mainly with the mother's health: it might have been considered preventable but received relatively little attention. The other two were open to differing interpretations. Stomach ailments could be attributed to infection (as they had to be during the regular summer epidemics), or they could be blamed on unsuitable feeding and lack of cleanliness over the bottles and so on. It seems all too likely that inadequate sterilization would have been a real problem, especially in the earliest months, when it would matter most. Insufficient knowledge, badly designed bottles and teats, and lack of facilities in the kitchen would all have contributed. And condensed milk would have been particularly attractive to the numerous and lethal flies, because of the sugar in it, as well as being excellent ground for bacterial multiplication. Unsuitable feeding may be more dubious (apart from the skimmed milk problem), though where the baby shared food with the rest of the family it will of course have shared the inadequacies of that food, both hygienic and nutritional, and its resistance would be lower. Family food was designed simply to satisfy hunger at the least cost, and would often have fallen well below the optimum "nitrogenous" level. Babies who were not breast fed were very much more susceptible to infection; it was claimed especially of those fed on condensed milk that they had all the appearance of health but no resistance. But working-class mothers who could not breast feed, whether for physical reasons or because their wage was needed, had little choice: condensed milk was cheaper than fresh, and condensed skimmed milk cheapest of all; their budgets were already stretched beyond the possible, and if the baby appeared to flourish how could they know this was "unsuitable feeding"?

Chest infections too could be given different causes. The proponents of the maternal ignorance explanation would assume that they were caused by injudicious exposure: mothers were accused of not dressing the infants warmly enough (though in the context of older children and summer it was frequently said that they overdressed them), and of taking them out at all hours and in all weathers. Here the difference between middle-class and working-class attitudes to children has to be borne in mind. In the middle classes children were segregated and different, especially babies. They had special clothes, special food, special furniture, special rooms, sometimes special attendants. (The popular print of "His Majesty King Baby," the frilled infant in a regal perambulator with a uniformed nurse, conveys the image.) In the working class until very recently childhood had been a much briefer, less differentiated affair. Compulsory schooling over the previous two or three decades had extended children's period of dependence and reduced their economic role, but they were often still to middle-class outsiders "little adults" and "old before their time." Children—and babies—were much less excluded from adult life. Crowded homes and economies of fuel and light made separation at home impossible except perhaps for sleeping; many leisure activities would include children, and they were only to any extent excluded from the sphere of work. (And this would be less true of work in home workshops or kitchens.) It was shocking to the middle class to see this difference, and most of all when they saw a shawled infant in the street at night, on the way home from pub or music hall or other adult resort. (This gulf would also of course have affected their perception of the infant's being fed tidbits from the adult plate.) But bronchitis and pneumonia could as well be caused, and certainly would be much worsened in their impact, by cold damp homes, with leaking roofs, broken windows, ill-fitting doors, damp walls, cold floors, and insufficient heat. Such conditions—or not much better—would have been common among Rowntree's poverty-stricken 28 percent.

Instructing the Mothers

With hindsight, the conditions imposed by poverty seem likely to have been significant factors in infant mortality, to be ranked at least alongside "maternal ignorance'' perhaps.[102] A great deal of effort was nevertheless put into advice and instruction on motherhood—as we have seen these were measures very frequently proposed. The most general method was through leaflets on infant management handed out to mothers: this was sometimes organized by local authorities, sometimes by societies like the Ladies' Sanitary Association or the Infant Health Society, and was already an established method by the beginning of the century. How far they were read or followed is impossible to say. Dr. Sykes, in St. Pancras, received a shock when he tried to find out the impact of a leaflet he'd been circulating, which while recommending breast feeding if possible, also gave details on ''the best method of bottle feeding'': he found that the leaflet was being misinterpreted, and ''mothers were sedulously weaning their babes in order to follow the detailed advice of the medical officer of health in the method of hand feeding.''[103]

Lectures to mothers were also tried, especially by the National Health Society, whose Homely Talks included ''How to rear our little ones,''[104] but it was difficult to assemble the appropriate audience except where a mothers' meeting or a girls' club was prepared to listen, or perhaps a Women's Co-operative Guild group. In some cases, however, they were able to secure a captive audience. In Portsmouth Prison in 1904 women prisoners were being given a fortnightly series of lectures on sanitary subjects. The listeners were selected for good behavior; the prison was one ''to which many women are sent for various petty crimes which in the richer classes would be expiated by a small fine''; and the women, it was claimed, were ''responsive to teaching as to the dignity of housekeeping and the efficient discharge of the duties of wife and mother.'' (Or it might be more true that ''in a goal such lectures are attractive as a relief from the monotony of ordinary life.'')[105]

Infant consultations, the forerunners of today's baby clinics, were set up, on the pattern of those already existing in France. Another French initiative was also imitated, the ''hygienic milk depot'' whose aim was to provide sterile milk for bottle-fed babies. (The standard of hygiene in the sale of milk was not very high, in spite of inspection.) These were set up by various progressive local authorities, starting with St. Helen's in 1899.[106]

Many local authorities appointed lady health visitors. The Ladies' Health Society of Manchester and Salford started home instruction in domestic hygiene in the 1860s. In 1892, on the suggestion of Florence Nightingale, the Buckinghamshire County Council engaged full-time health visitors; Newsholme had one in Brighton in 1894; five ''lady health missioners'' were taken on in Worcestershire in 1897 to give instruction in child welfare; but in the beginning of the twentieth century the movement really got under way. Huddersfield had a well-organized system coordinating the efforts of two female assistant medical officers of health with a corps of about eighty involuntary visitors.[107] Birmingham appointed four lady health visitors in 1899. Their duties were to visit from house to house in such localities as the medical officer of health shall direct; to carry with them disinfectant powder and use it where required; to direct the attention of those they visit to the evils of bad smells, want of fresh air, and dirty conditions of all kinds; to give hints to mothers on the feeding and clothing of their children, and use their influence to induce them to send their children regularly to school; in case of sickness to assist in promoting the comfort of the invalid by advice and personal help; to urge, on all possible occasions, the importance of cleanliness, thrift and temperance.[108]

It is not perhaps surprising to find that their visits were not always welcome, or that George Newman urged that besides being trained they should above all "have insight and tact."[109] The reaction recorded by Somerset Maugham in his novel *Of Human Bondage* rings true. It will have been drawn from his experience as a medical student in Lambeth doing midwifery practice in people's homes in the 1890s.[110]

> The district visitor excited their bitter hatred. She came in without so much as a 'by your leave' or a 'with your leave.' . . . [S]he poked her nose into corners, and if she didn't say the place was dirty you could see what she thought right enough, 'an' it's all very well for them as 'as servants, but I'd like to see what she'd make of 'er room if she 'ad four children, and 'ad to see to the cooking, and mend their clothes, and wash 'em'.

But such intrusions were part of a general invasion of working-class life by the authorities and their well-intentioned supporters. Consider this complaint from a mother whose child's hair had been shorn after a school inspection for head lice:

> I should like to know how much more spite you intend to put upon my child, for it is nothing else. First you send the Sanitary Inspector and I have my home taken away, then my husband has to get rid of his few rabbits and chickens, and now you cut the few hairs my girl was just beginning to get so nice. . . . I know she had no need to have her hair off as it was washed with soft soap last night. The child is thoroughly heartbroken.[111]

School was of course an important component in the campaign to transform working-class life, teaching the ideology as well as the skills of domesticity and more generally instilling habits of regularity, obedience, punctuality, and discipline.[112] As we have seen, Newsholme rated highly the effects of school influence on domestic hygiene and therefore infant mortality. In some cases the exercise of power might go beyond intrusion: if there was any question of children being taken into the care of the local authority, then one criterion— contributory rather than basic—will no doubt have been whether the family, and the mother in particular, met requirements. The less housewifely activity, the more likely the family to be considered inadequate. The Poor Law authorities too had the power to make outdoor relief conditional on approval of the home: they wanted to be sure the mother fulfilled her functions, and felt it should not be necessary for her to go out to work.[113]

The St. Pancras School for Mothers

One attack on the problem of infant mortality, though it too was defined in terms of education, and though it did very much focus on the mother, was nevertheless based on a more comprehensive approach and firmly rooted in the realities of working-class life. It is, however, an illustration of the ideological basis of even humane and perceptive reformism. This was the St. Pancras School for Mothers.[114] Although it was simply one institution with a local impact that may well have been fairly limited, its influence in the growing infant welfare movement was considerable. This was partly because Dr. Sykes (the Medical Officer of Health for St. Pancras), one of its founders, was an admirable and articulate advocate of its merits, partly because of influential support, and partly because it appeared to succeed in diminishing infant mortality by going for the mothers. Thus in its practice as well as in the theory expounded by Sykes and others, it conformed with—and indeed strengthened—the ideology of motherhood. Sykes was quite explicit on the key role of the mother. She was to be made "the centre round which all the agencies revolved for the protection and preservation of the health of both mother and child."[115] She was also fundamental in his view of society. "Urbanization and subdivision of labour," he said, must if carried to the ultimate extremity,

> terminate in the subdivision of the family and the consequent destruction of family life and home, *which are the basis and incentive of labour itself.* The management of the home and the tending of the family, essentially women's work, if not maintained, must end in moral disaster. [He calls it moral: as so often in these pronouncements, political might be substituted.]

Labor-saving methods and appliances, he continued, "provided they do not destroy family life and the home, are worthy of serious consideration." Dr. Sykes is said to have invented the word *mothercraft.*[116]

After his unfortunate experiment with the leaflet on infant feeding, Dr. Sykes continued to study "social conditions and statistical facts" and concentrated on expanding a system of local weekly visiting of all infants, as far as they could be traced through midwives, baptisms, and so on, at the same time trying to direct people in need of help to the appropriate agency so as to treat some of the difficulties behind health problems.[117] His recognition that there were other difficulties made him receptive to ideas which went beyond instruction and advice, though he regarded milk depots as likely to be counterproductive (like his leaflet) because they might encourage early weaning.

In 1906–1907 reports came through of the success of experiments in the feeding of pregnant and nursing mothers. Alys Russell, after a visit with members of the Women's Co-operative Guild, described enthusiastically the working of such a scheme in Ghent, and a Mrs. Gordon gave an account of her own initiative in a poor West London district.[118] With the support of the St. Pancras Mothers' and Infants' Society a committee was formed; it received much publicity and support from members of the upper and middle classes who found it a worthy (and perhaps a fashionable) cause; and in June 1907 a center was opened in Chalton Street, Somers Town (behind St. Pancras station): the Babies' Welcome and School for Mothers. The official inauguration followed a few weeks later, with a conference on infant mortality organized by Sykes at St. Pancras Town Hall. Sir Robert Cecil was in the chair, and resolutions (on breast feeding, maternal instruction, and the new project) were moved and seconded by prominent speakers who included two doctors well known in the movement against national deterioration and infant mortality, Sir Thomas Barlow and Mary Scharlieb, the author and antisuffragist Mrs. Humphrey Ward, the Liberal temperance campaigner Lady Henry Somerset (founder of *Woman's Signal,* the temperance organ), Alys Russell (who through her marriage to Bertrand Russell was part of that aristocratic family, but whose own ideas and activities were radical), Countess Russell, George Alexander from the London County Council, and the Reverend C. Ensor Walters.

The new center provided:

1. Consultations and weighings (of babies and mothers)
2. Dinners for suckling mothers
3. Lessons on food and food values and prices (especially the feeding of suckling mothers)
4. Classes on simple cookery (for young wives and all mothers)
5. Lessons for mothers and young wives:
    —In the cutting out and making of babies' clothes
    —In the preparation for and care of babies
    —In housewifery and domestic health
6. Provident Maternity Club, for (1) doctor or midwife; (2) baby clothes; (3) extra help during confinement; (4) extra nourishment
7. Fathers' Evening Conferences on the duties of the father to the mother, the babe, the children, and the home. (Coffee handed round; smoking allowed.)

Outdoor—Visits to the homes of mothers attending the Welcome.

It was coordinated with municipal provisions, where Sykes, as local Medical Officer of Health, was of course also influential. These included notification of births, followed by advice cards on infant feeding (telling the mothers to breast feed or if they couldn't to consult their doctor or come to the Welcome); comparing registered deaths of infants with the notified births, for statistical purposes; and visiting "the most suitable cases," which were selected from the list of notified births on the basis of "the poorest houses in the poorest streets." Coordination with the local authority must certainly have helped the school workers to reach a wider range of people than was usually possible for a voluntary organization.

In spite of its name, one of the first priorities of the school was the very practical one of feeding the mothers. This blended interestingly into a rather different version of the argument that women needed to feel that motherhood was a noble and valuable function. The school's medical officer, Dora Bunting, started her account of the Welcome dinners by justifying the attempt to improve women's nutrition in terms of avoiding infant mortality and the deterioration of the race. She then suggested as a reason for their poor nutrition that working women didn't think themselves worth cooking for, and only cooked if husband or children would also be there to eat. From this she concluded that women "don't think enough of themselves."

> They never treat themselves, either in the home or in public affairs, as of any importance, and consequently no-one else thinks them important. One of the first steps needed to effect the political and social emancipation of women is a crusade on the part of man calling upon her to eat. And there never can be a really strong race of Britons until she does.[119]

Economy was of course a further reason why women stinted themselves, but this does not disprove her point, since it is clear that women did give themselves less of whatever the rest of the family was having, as though willpower would be enough for them to live on but others were weaker.[120] The dinners were well patronized, and the informal atmosphere of "the cheerful dining-room" gave "the greatest opportunities for unobtrusive teaching." They rightly recognized that didactic methods were far less effective than friendly conversations.

> During the dinner time we discuss things both great and small, from threatened strikes to baby's "comforters" (dummies), and the constant personal intercourse gives a privileged position which is also a great responsibility. We try not to forget that the Welcome is primarily a "school for mothers," and just as we know that the set lessons of school are the least, and the atmosphere the most important part of the education of the child, so we desire that our mothers may unknowingly breathe in more than they consciously learn.[121]

Another important factor in the success of the School for Mothers was probably that its workers did assume goodwill in the mothers. The accusations of maternal ignorance often carried with them implications of willful neglect, assertions that anyway poor parents would just as soon their infants died—it was one less mouth to feed and they might make something on the insurance.[122] Comments over a dead baby that it had gone to a better place, that maybe it was better off dead, which we might see as an attempt to make the loss less painful (and as a bitter reflection on how they saw their own lives), were quoted against mothers to illustrate their heartlessness. Advice and help from people with so little comprehension or sympathy can never have been easily accepted. At the school, however, it was considered that "mother-love is the greatest power in the world, and we may still reckon on it." True, from our point of view they were manipulating that love, towards concern over the infant's weight for instance.

> As we turned away last week from a girl-mother sobbing over her baby's loss of weight, we felt that even though the grief was probably shallow and transient, yet it was well it should be there. And when we go day by day and find her struggling with all the odds against her, to follow out the instructions given her to the very letter, and hear her earnest "Don't you think he looks a little fatter?" we begin to question the ephemeral nature of her affection, and to take fresh courage for our work. For she is only a rather "low" working girl, married just in time for her child to be born in wedlock. Not a high type—no, but capable of "growing up" nevertheless, because of her love for her child.[123]

This attitude, though still patronizing and class bound, was at least relatively sympathetic and tactful. The fact too that the Welcome existed, and was more a club than a school, with instruction almost incidental to other activities, and with an emphasis on practical help (like making a cheap cradle out of a banana box), immediately distinguished it from the intrusions of authority, or even from parish mothers' meetings. Visits to the home were acceptable because they developed out of an initiative originally the mother's and an actual relationship with the social worker, instead of having a bureaucratic origin and involving the arrival of a strange visitor, walking in "without so much as a 'by your leave.'" The individual approach of workers would be likely to have a considerable effect on the success of any project. Those who saw themselves too much as representatives of authority, supervising and directing, would surely get on less well than those who made some effort, however self-conscious and clumsy, to develop understanding and sympathy. This was the advice of Emilia Kanthack, a St. Pancras midwife and health visitor.

> You will not be a scrap of use to them or their babies unless you understand them and they understand you. So you must do your level best to make yourself acquainted with their habits of mind and modes of speech and their code of manners, as well as with their physical and economic conditions. . . . If they *like* you, and if you can succeed in impressing them with your air of experience, you can do anything with them.[124]

The St. Pancras School for Mothers seems to have had a success out of proportion with its scale. (Its local effectiveness either in terms of attendance or of changes in local attitudes and practice is difficult to measure, and of course no correlation can be proved with the actual decline in the birthrate.)[125] As McCleary pointed out in his history of the infant welfare movement, work on similar lines was going on elsewhere in 1906–1907, for instance, in Glasgow and in St. Marylebone; but it was always the example of the School for Mothers which was quoted, and that was the name which caught on. As the movement grew it was the work of "Schools for Mothers" that was praised and credited with influence even when many other kinds of centers were involved.

> The School gave a conspicuous example of a many-sided well-considered, co-ordinated, and effective body of preventive efforts. It was launched under distinguished auspices, had considerable social prestige, and was conducted with much enthusiasm and elan. And its position in the capital assisted in making it widely known and helped to expand the field over which the influence of the School was felt.[126]

Its reputation was certainly encouraged by the enthusiastic and detailed accounts of its work and its intentions which were published early on. *The School for Mothers* (1907), edited by Evelyn Bunting (joint Hon. Secretary with Sykes), gave both the history and ideology of the institution (mainly in the introduction by Sir Thomas Barlow and in Sykes's contribution) and a vivid account of its daily working. *The Pudding Lady* (1912) described an extension of their work: cooking lessons given both at the center and in women's own kitchens, with the aim of giving help and advice that was realistic under the actual living conditions of local women. And in other articles and books, as well as at conferences and meetings, the School became an example of what could be done. Similar initiatives multiplied and federated; and an Association of Infant Consultations and Schools for Mothers was set up, coordinating statistics, promoting new branches, encouraging competitions in mothercraft, spreading literature, and so on.[127]

From 1907 Schools for Mothers could qualify for official subsidy in respect of class teaching in domestic subjects.[128] Twenty-seven were receiving such grants in 1912, 150 in 1913, 290 in 1918.[129] But there were many more establishments, both Schools for Mothers and Infant Welfare Centers, which did not qualify. Probably they found class teaching less popular and less effective than informal methods such as the dinnertime conversations described by Dora Bunting, or remarks while a baby was being examined and weighed. Centers with and without grants numbered some four hundred by 1914, according to Eric Pritchard at the Liverpool Infant Mortality Conference that year.[130] (At the time of the Maternity and Child Welfare Act in 1918 there were well over 1,000, more than half of them voluntarily supported.)[131] From 1914 the Local Government Board cooperated with the Board of Education on grants, and their circular on the subject recognized other activities than class teaching, though the object of these "institutions of the nature of Schools for Mothers" was still expected to be "primarily educational."[132] But in the following year it was made clear that no grant was available for the provision of food ("except patent foods or milk for infants whose cost was incurred before 1 April 1915").[133] This explicit exclusion suggests that in official quarters it was above all the instruction of mothers that was thought useful, not attempts to improve their nutrition. The "Welcome" aspect of the St. Pancras School was not the one regarded as most important by the authorities, though one may suspect that it had considerable influence on its popularity with the mothers.

This educational focus presumably accounts for the way in which Schools for Mothers caught on. Just as maternal ignorance had most frequently been made the scapegoat for infant mortality by the expanding health profession, so education for mothers had been the universally demanded solution. A "School for Mothers" in its very name proclaimed itself the perfect answer. Of course, there were other tries—Babies' Welcomes, Infant Consultations, Schools of Mothercraft, Infant Health Societies—but in the lists of these organizations it is the School for Mothers which stands out as recurring most often;[134] and it was the title School for Mothers which stood for the others in official mention.

World War I and Cannon Fodder

It is significant that the number of these centers more than doubled during the war years. War gave new stimulus to the question of child welfare, especially perhaps as it became clear that the methods of modern warfare required cannon fodder in even vaster quantity.[135] In the preface to a new publication, *Child Welfare Annual,* its editor Dr. T. N. Kelynack held forth in familiar phrases:

> For long we have been accustomed to speak of the children as the most valuable of Imperial assets. Now it is for us to realize fully that the future of our existence is wrapt up in the well-being of the children of the present. . . . War has forced child welfare work into the forefront of national responsibilities. The problem of the conservation of child life is of paramount importance. The child of today . . . will be the citizen of the coming years and must take up and bear the duties of statesmanship, defence from foes, the conduct of labour, the direction of progress, the maintenance of a high level of thought and conduct, and all other necessities for the perpetuation of an imperial race.[136]

In the monthly *Maternity and Child Welfare,* which started to appear in 1917, the same themes recur, along with much detailed information on projects all over the country and correspondence. (A letter from a "materfamilias" proposed "motherships"—allowances for deserving widows of "our fallen fighting men,'' to be conditional on good mothercraft as approved by supervisors.)[137] Its advertisements also evoke the climate of concern: the Shaftesbury Society solicits money for its work with A GOOD PATRIOTIC INVESTMENT TO HELP MOTHERS AND SAVE BABIES; Glaxo, makers of a patent baby food, ask for the attention of welfare workers aware of the terrible obstacle of ignorant mothers (''perhaps the chief contributing cause of infant mortality''), point out how war work means more babies have to be artificially fed, and name some of ''the many Official Bodies continuously using Glaxo''; the British Commercial Gas Association recommends gas cookers (''Practise Thrift by using Gas Properly,'' and ''Simple Cookery for the People'' were free handouts that they offered) and gas washing coppers to schools for Mothers and Welfare Centers, for teaching mothers with; children's hospitals declare that ''The Children of Today are the Citizens of Tomorrow'' and ask ''Help us to Care for the Children and thus ensure a Healthy Race.'' There was a National Baby Week in 1917, with exhibitions, lectures, and competitions for the bonniest infant,[138] and the National Baby Week Council was founded, followed in 1918 by the Mothercraft Training Society.[139] Then the state took on altogether more extensive responsibility, with the 1918 Maternity and Child Welfare Act, which envisaged the provision of a network of infant welfare centers: the multifarious Schools for Mothers, Babies' Welcomes, and the rest were thus absorbed into the new comprehensive system. That official sanction was given under the name ''Infant Welfare Centre'' rather than School suggests that other factors than maternal ignorance were now being given more importance.

Maternity—Letters from Working Women

In spite of the mobilization of married women for war work and the temporary expansion of creches, motherhood remained a central preoccupation during the war. But behind the rhetoric was developing a deeper recognition of the handicaps of working-class motherhood, which strengthened the case for greater support for mothers from local and national authorities. A major part in this was played by the Women's Co-operative Guild and its secretary, Margaret Llewellyn Davies. After successfully campaigning for maternity benefit to be included in the 1911 National Insurance Act (and in 1913, for it to be paid to the woman, not the man), they brought pressure on the Local Government Board and its new president, the Fabian-influenced Liberal, Herbert Samuel, to adopt a series of proposals ''to insure effective care of Maternity and Infancy.'' Mothers with babies lobbied the offices of the Board, and Guild branches forcefully put the case to their local authorities.[140] Then in 1915 the Guild published a collection of letters from its officials (present and past) recounting briefly—even baldly—their experiences of pregnancy and childbirth. It had a short preface by Samuel, arguing that it was the duty of the state to act, both because unnecessary suffering should where possible be avoided and because numbers were indispensable to a strong state—"In the competition and conflict of numbers it is the mass of the nations that tells"—yet a large part of the possible population was being wasted. The excess of infant mortality in poor districts was due, he argued, "to ignorance, to malnutrition, to all the noxious influences that go with poverty." It was clearly the duty of the community and the state "to relieve motherhood of its burdens" through mothercraft teaching and medical aid. "The infant cannot indeed be saved by the State. It can only be saved by the mother. But the mother can be helped and can be taught by the State."[141]

Samuel's brief preface recapitulated and redefined some of the old arguments, perhaps stressing poverty more, but still ending up with the mother and motherhood in relation to the state. The letters themselves made a very different impact. Here for the first time were working women speaking out on the subject of maternity, and emerging as women, as people in their own right, not just mothers or suppliers of population, not even just wives. ("We must let the men know that we are human beings with ideals, and aspire to something higher than to be mere objects on which they can satisfy themselves," wrote a mother with seven children, three of them consumptive.)[142] The letters were vivid, convincing, and harrowing. They demonstrated how common were the experiences of miscarriages, stillbirths, and infant mortality: nearly half the writers had had stillbirths or miscarriages, and almost a quarter had lost children in their first year;[143] yet these women were not the most poverty-stricken and resourceless by any means. Time and again they describe pinching and scraping throughout pregnancy, stinting themselves to save up for attention at the birth and for help after it, struggling with heavy housework long before they were fit because they couldn't afford another week of help from someone who cost 10 shillings a week and who could not spin out the household budget as they did; "The strain to keep up to anything like a decent standard of housing, clothing, diet, and general appearance, is enough to upset the mental balance of a Chancellor of the Exchequer. How much more so a struggling pregnant mother," wrote a mother of five, and added that "preventives" (contraception) were largely used: "Race suicide, if you will, is the policy of the mothers of the future. Who shall blame us?"[144] Their health suffered, of course, and also their morale, even where the relationship with the husband was a source of strength. Too often it was not. One woman had seven children in ten years, during which time her husband was earning 30 shillings a week, of which he claimed a fifth "as pocket-money," leaving her to manage on the rest.

When at the end of 10 years I was almost a mental and physical wreck, I determined that this state of things should not go on any longer, and if there was no natural means of prevention, then, of course, artificial means must be employed, which were successful, and am happy to say that from that time I have been able to take pretty good care of myself, but I often shudder to think what might have been the result if things had been allowed to go on as they were.[145]

Women with considerate husbands eagerly give them credit; others were all too aware that "when you have got an unkind husband it is a terrible life,"[146] particularly of course if he drank, as a few husbands in this collection did, or if "he had not a bit of control over his passion." A writer who had seven children and two miscarriages, always getting pregnant too soon so that she was very weak and had much suffering from varicose veins, wrote,

> I do wish there could be some limit to the time when a woman is expected to have a child. . . . Practically within a few days of the birth, and as soon as the birth is over, she is tortured again. If the woman does not feel well she must not say so, as a man has such a lot of ways of punishing a woman if she does not give in to him.[147]

The women often talk of their own ignorance on marriage, but the knowledge that would have been of most use to them was obviously that of birth control, as some of them say. Knowledge that in pregnancy you need rest and good food was not enough to enable them to take proper care. "My husband was out of work during the greater part of the time, and I was not only obliged to work myself, but often went short of food and warm clothing when I was most in need of it."[148] Even without unemployment, how could you stretch a normally inadequate wage any further? The women's experiences often illustrate this dilemma, and some of them are very frank in their conclusions. "I feel sure it is not so much lack of knowledge as lack of means that entails so much suffering," wrote one woman. She argued for State Maternity Homes, because there was "no peace for the wife at home." She also advocated contraception.

> I know it is a delicate subject, but it is an urgent one. . . . All the beautiful in motherhood is very nice if one has plenty to bring up a family on, but what real mother is going to bring a life into the world to be pushed into the drudgery of the world at the earliest possible moment because of the strain on the family exchequer?

She went on to quote the recent comments of "Kitchener boys" billeted on her, who said her nine-year-old was as big as thirteen-year-olds where they came from, "But then, ma, you've only one to keep, which is different to seven or eight"; and ended with an appeal for the nation to wake up to the needs of the mothers of the future race.[149]

Margaret Llewellyn Davies, in her introduction, quoted from the letters and drew general conclusions. She noted that suffering and motherhood were commonly supposed to be inseparable and denounced the resultant fatalism, of doctors and others, which allowed "unnecessary and useless suffering." She saw "the roots of the evil" as lying in "the conditions of life which our industrial system forces upon the wage-earners"—irregular and low wages, insufficient medical care, poverty in pregnancy resulting in undernourishment and overwork.

> Writers on infant mortality and the decline of the birth-rate never tire of justly pointing to the evils which come from the strain of manual labour in factories for expectant mothers. Very little is ever said about the same evils which come from the incessant drudgery of domestic labour. People forget that the unpaid work of the working-woman at the stove, at scrubbing and cleaning, at the wash-tub, in lifting and carrying heavy weights, is just as severe manual labour as many industrial operations in factories. It is this labour which the mother performs often up to the very day on which the child is born, and she will be at it again perhaps six or eight days afterwards.

Although she dealt with the same problems as the infant welfare campaigners of the preceding decade, her starting point was different, as she remarked: they started with the infants and ended up at the mother, she started with the mothers and their actual experiences. This gave her a more realistic perspective. Familiarity with women's whole lives, instead of just the moment of childbirth and crises in the health of infants, enabled her to see more clearly the contribution of ante-natal factors. Her proposals were for the improvement of the economic position of the family, and for specific measures to "bring specialized knowledge, adequate rest, nourishment and care, medical supervision and treatment within reach." The Guild's scheme included more realistic maternity benefits, to be paid over the weeks before and after confinement, improved midwifery and nursing provision, more maternity beds in hospitals for difficult cases, maternity homes, milk depots, household helps, more participation of women in local government, and public health maternity subcommittees, to include representatives of women's and working-class organizations. Maternity and Infant Centres should be able to provide meals for mothers. It looked forward to the establishment of a Ministry of Health, with a maternity and infant life department, partly staffed by women. Its concluding paragraph stressed that government departments and public health committees should be in constant contact with working women: "It is by a partnership between the women who are themselves concerned, the medical profession, and the State that the best results of democratic government can be secured for the mothers and infants of the country."[150]

Between the Wars

The letters in *Maternity* and the campaigning of the Women's Co-operative Guild at every level must certainly have helped to turn attention more toward the mother's health and conditions of life. The cult of motherhood lost some of its force when confronted with the actuality, and maternal ignorance and neglect became increasingly insufficient explanations of infant mortality. (George Newman however continued to stress unenlightened motherhood as the all-pervading influence in the annual loss of 52,000 infants that impoverished the nation.)[151] Prospects improved with the establishment of the Ministry of Health in 1919 and greater awareness of the importance of maternal health,[152] but the cuts and restrictions on local spending between the wars were a brake on development; and the democratic partnership recommended by the Guild hardly developed. The most important influences on the experience of motherhood between the wars were probably not state attempts to improve the conditions of maternity but the spread of contraceptive information and the steady shrinking of the average family, and the rise—at least for a proportion of the working class—in the standard of living. In the distressed areas maternal health, infant mortality, and child health all remained major problems,[153] although in national terms the infant mortality rate continued to decline.

In the comparatively prosperous new estates of the midlands and the south motherhood was entering a new incarnation.[154] It was increasingly unusual for married women to go out to work, but their children were fewer, their health was likely to be better, and their housing conditions were much improved. This made room for a more intense and home-based family life, with much closer involvement of mother and even father with their children and home-centered activities like gardening, repairs, and improvements. Ideologically it was expressed through an emphasis on the interest and value of careful home management and the fulfillment to be found in efficient and loving care of husband, children, and house. It fitted nicely with the new orientation of British industry towards production for a home mass market and laid the foundation for the consumer housewife of postwar Britain. Homemaking and child care were a staple topic in the magazines that avidly reached out to the new market of housebound and literate women; experts expounded and exhorted, or answered queries; new products were recommended, tips collected on how to do this job or brighten up that corner.

The theoretical underpinning for much of the advice on child care was provided by Dr. Truby King, the Spock of that generation, though one may doubt how faithfully some of his precepts could be followed in working-class homes even on the new estates: they involved extreme separation of child from adult—the more a baby was left alone, the better—and rigorous adherence to a regular (four-hour) feeding schedule, with no indulgent picking up of a child howling for no good reason. This would require not only more housing space than most working-class families had but also more distant (or tolerant) neighbors, and no one in the family to whom undisturbed sleep was important. Truby King, like Marie Stopes, the evangelist of birth control whose influence in these years was of even greater importance, was much influenced by eugenic ideas. (His theories on infant rearing developed out of his experience as a stock breeder in New Zealand, which presumably made him particularly open to the notion of scientific management of breeding.) With mass unemployment the arguments in favor of boosting population might have been expected to weaken in favor of a eugenic emphasis on quality, but in fact both positions still had their followers. Eugenics was only gradually discredited by its abominable application in Nazi Germany; but the growing strength of the labor movement in Britain was a serious obstacle to extension of its influence. The plummeting birthrate led to doom-laden prophecies of national decline (in books like *The Twilight of Parenthood* and *The Menace of British Depopulation*),[155] and old imperialists like Leo Amery called for family allowances to encourage procreation.[156] In Germany similar fears combined with expansionist and racist ideology to stimulate a whole range of measures to encourage and support large families of Aryan stock and to develop an extreme cult of motherhood.[157] (Today John Tyndall of the National Front advocates similar policies: cutbacks in family planning, a ban on abortion, resources devoted to the prevention of infant mortality, and reorientation of state policy to favor large [white] families, to halt decline in the numbers and the racial quality of the "White world.")[158]

By the time of the Beveridge Report (1942), wartime labor and military requirements had reasserted the value of numbers. Moreover, Beveridge, in his comprehensive survey of social provision and his scheme "to abolish want" (without abolishing capitalism), was conscious that the falling birthrate combined with increasing life expectancy would mean an increasing imbalance between people of an age to be employed and productive and people who were too old to work and dependent on the state. His three main proposals were for a comprehensive health scheme, avoidance of mass unemployment, and family allowances. The first two were designed to minimize the waste of resources involved in bad health and unemployment. The third aimed to reduce the ill effects of low wages on the children of large families and to encourage parents to have more children, both aims relating to concern about labor power and population. Following the recently accepted doctrines of Keynes, Beveridge allowed that government intervention was permissible in the interests of fuller employment and other requirements of a healthy economy, but in relation to the family it had to be most cautious: the family must be strengthened, not replaced. So Beveridge's report, which was the basis for the "Welfare State" provisions brought in by the postwar Labour Government, was an extension of the old "national efficiency" arguments, still firmly limited by Liberal ideas of individual responsibility. No allowance was paid on the first child of a family, whose maintenance was to be wholly provided by the parents; and the payments on subsequent children were contributions, not full support. The state was admitting an interest rather than a responsibility. Nor was it paying a wage to the mother. The family allowance was a contribution to the family budget, designed to offset the effects of low wages on large families so that parents wouldn't be discouraged from having children, it was not an endowment of motherhood or a wage of housework.[159] Housewives and mothers had "vital work to do in ensuring the adequate continuance of the British race and of British ideals in the world,"[160] but that contribution would not be officially rewarded; they were to remain dependent on their husbands. Although many aspects of the experience of maternity had changed in the first half of the century, the mother's role was still essential, and the provisions of the Welfare State both expressed and reinforced the ideology of motherhood.[161]

Conclusion

How then do we explain the overriding importance of the mother—or of motherhood—in these developments of the early twentieth century? And what was the general context for the preoccupation with infant mortality and domestic management? Neither question is easily answered in a definitive way, though I have tried to sketch out some possibilities. It is much harder to prove connections than to suggest them, and these conclusions will be partly speculative.

The connection between "the health of the nation" and "the wealth of the nation" is nowadays comparatively easy to accept, since it has become a basic political tenet in contemporary Britain, so much taken for granted that it is seldom even articulated. But the timing of its emergence is significant, as is its particular focus. The recognition that population was power and that quality—the standard of physique of that population—was also important, is clearly part of that background. Speculative connections may indeed be made between, on the one hand, these two partly contradictory requirements and, on the other, different ruling-class views on empire and defense. Imperial domination (and/or exploitation) of a peopled country by a British military and administrative elite (India, Africa, China), perhaps with the aid of "native" soldiers from another territory (Ghurkas and Sepoys are the obvious example), would require officers and officials rather than men and would fit nicely with the emphasis on stimulating the middle-class birthrate. Conversely, preoccupation with settler territories like the white Dominions (McCleary's great interest) would favor an emphasis on saving the lives of "all" infants, that is, working-class ones. Anyone examining future roles for the Army, especially in the context of new imperial rivalry, would have been likely to think about not only the fitness of recruits but also the question of numbers. The much higher casualty rates of war conducted with machine guns (already starting to be used in the Boer War) would carry a double implication for the general health: the carefully skimmed cream of the nation's young men would be at great risk, and their inferiors who stayed at home unscathed would father the next generation, presumably to its detriment. Such considerations carried great weight in the context of general anxiety about national deterioration, particularly when economic competition from America and Germany and the addition of Japan to the imperialist powers were undermining Britain's world preeminence.

Healthier babies were required not only for the maintenance of empire but also for production under the changing conditions made necessary by imperialist competition. The old system of capitalist production (which itself had nourished imperial expansion), with its mobile superabundant workforce of people who were underpaid, underfed, untrained, and infinitely replaceable, was passing. In its place, with the introduction of capital-intensive methods, was needed a stable workforce of people trained to do particular jobs and reasonably likely to stay in them, neither moving on nor losing too much time through ill-health. This was the context of efforts to reduce casual labor (as in the docks) and to lessen the burden (on ratepayers at this point) of unemployment. It also involved a continuation of the separation of skilled and unskilled and progressive exclusion of women from any footholds in the skilled sectors. Attempts to force married women out of employed work through legislation had failed; but the limited opportunities and inadequate training of girls combined with increasing ideological pressures about the responsibilities of motherhood certainly operated as a brake on married women's work and helped to confirm women as the casual workers, the labor reserve to be summoned (as in wartime) or sacked (as in unemployment, when men are considered to have first right to whatever jobs are going), according to the convenience of employers and the state. Probably too the pressure on married women to stay at home, where it was combined with real economic need for their money as well as their labor contribution to the family's survival, helped to confirm outwork as an integral part of capitalist production, not a survival from a precapitalist past.

In the early twentieth century the doctrine of laissez-faire was losing credibility: state intervention was becoming more and more acceptable. Statistics were being collected on a whole range of social trends, administrative agencies were proliferating, and scientific planning of society was beginning to seem a possibility. This explains the Fabians' social engineering approach, and also eugenist ideas of selective breeding. It had been established through legislative measures like compulsory schooling (introduced in the 1870s) and the Prevention of Cruelty to Children Act (1889) that the state could intervene in relation to children, that parents' rights could be overridden; and it was even being said in some quarters that the rearing of children was "a co-operative undertaking, in which there are three parties—the father, the mother, and the State."[162] But effectively, in the matter of preserving infant life, only one of those parties, the mother, was considered, and the solutions attempted were not collectivist but individualist and based very much on the approach and structures of voluntary organizations. Although creches were well established and might have been much extended as a form of child care and for supervision of infant health, yet they and even kindergartens were objected to as "infringing the maternalist principle." Exceptional local authorities administering very poor districts did expand creche provision, recognizing that poor mothers did go out to work, but the prevailing idea among those in positions of power (medical, administrative, legislative, or whatever) was that mothers should be at home and children should be with their mothers. This is the assumption behind all the talk of motherhood. But it fitted well in other ways.

The association between woman and home was of course an old one, and it had already led to attempts by sanitary reformers to enlist her. "Long before the word sanitation was heard of, or any other word that conveyed the idea of a science of health, the good, trained, thrifty housewife was a practical sanitary reformer," wrote B. W. Richardson in 1880. Preventive medicine was to be her sphere (rather than curative, to be kept for the professional men), "not simply because women can carry it out, not simply because it pertains to . . . their special attributes, their watchfulness and their love, but because the whole work of prevention waits and waits until woman takes it up and makes it hers."[163] The Ladies' Sanitary Association (founded in 1857 and increasingly active in house visiting and leafleting) saw infant mortality as particularly a woman's concern; in their tracts of advice and moral stories the importance of being a good mother continually recurs. Sanitary progress showed that infant deaths were not necessary: not to learn and obey the laws of health was a sin; mothers were responsible to God for the lives of their children. This argument was combined with the middle-class ideal of a mother, home-keeping helpmeet as opposed to wage earner, which was also being imposed through the fact and the content of compulsory schooling. By the 1900s ignorance is stressed rather than sin, but woman's moral strength, an almost mystical power for good (which of course was easily identified with health), is invoked more than ever. This is perhaps surprising: the concern in the 1900s was a political and economic one and might therefore have been expected to produce solutions of the same kind rather than the moralistic "elevation of motherhood."

In parallel with the insistence on motherhood, complementing though apparently contradicting it, was the development of employment and even careers for single women in the expanding field of health. Saleeby in *Woman and Womanhood* is at pains to explain that while "racial motherhood" is essential, "individual motherhood" is not, and to expatiate on the potential usefulness of single women.

> Everyone knows maiden aunts who are better, more valuable, completer mothers in every non-physical way than the actual mothers of their nephews and nieces. This is woman's wonderful prerogative, that, in virtue of her *psyche,* she can realize herself, and serve others, on feminine lines, and without a pang of regret or a hint anywhere of failure, even though she forego physical motherhood. This book, therefore, is a plea not only for Motherhood but for Foster-Motherhood— that is Motherhood all but physical. In time to come the great professions of nursing and teaching will more and more engage and satisfy the lives and the powers of Virgin Mothers without number.[164]

Not only nursing and teaching, in which women were already well established, but all the new services arising out of greater official and voluntary preoccupation with childhood, family, and things domestic, provided work for women. This was justified ideologically by their greater suitability; it also made the new provisions less expensive. Women were even becoming increasingly acceptable in administration.[165] *The Times* in 1906 carried an article on "Home Economics as a Career for Women," which drew an analogy between administration and housekeeping ("all institutions are but homes on a large scale, and many philanthropic undertakings resolve themselves into a complicated form of housekeeping"), and argued that trained intelligent women would "prevent much waste of public money." By taking seats on boards of hospitals and of guardians, as well as on philanthropic committees, and by becoming paid officials in various institutions and organizations, women would "take their place not only as Empire-builders, but above all as Empire-conservers." At the same time they would "add immensely to the permanent stability of the country," since no nation could have surer foundations than that "in which the most capable women, those most highly trained, are the housekeepers and mothers."[166] Thus no woman was to escape motherhood: surrogate vocations of equal importance to the nation were to be found even for those who remained single. (An alternative sometimes argued was that they should emigrate to improve the balance between the sexes—among whites—in the colonies and also of course to breed there.)[167] But in the home or out of it, mothers and Foster-mothers would have male superiors to defer to: at a time when in some areas women seemed at last to be making gains, motherhood confirmed their subordination. A class difference may also be seen in the future postulated for these Foster-mothers: the professional "housekeepers" sitting on boards were no doubt to be from the middle and upper classes; womanly drudgery on the hospital floor and elsewhere would be the lot of poorer women.

Exhortation of working-class women on the duties of motherhood did not bear much relation to what was actually possible, at least for the majority, outside the artisan sector. In most cases if they went out to work their wage was indispensable; and the more flexible child-rearing arrangements (depending particularly on the help of older children), although they had been undermined by compulsory schooling, still had a function in enabling the family to cope with varying demands in the labor and time of its adults. Unless a mother could afford to stay at home it would be very difficult for her to continue breast feeding after the first few weeks, and in any case poor nutrition might well have made the milk inadequate. The great need "to bring home to the matrons of the nation the few homely truths which formed the basis of all true sanitation"[168] in fact involved the creation of a scapegoat. Of course, knowledge of basic sanitation was a good thing, though it is ironic that as health consciousness increased at the level of individual and family, so capitalist development (which had required the growth of that health consciousness) imposed new patterns of living that (insidiously perhaps) were more and more unhealthy—atmospheric pollution by industrial and household smoke, and later by exhaust fumes from innumerable motor vehicles, or overrefined, overpreserved, overprepared food. (Nineteenth-century food was often and notoriously adulterated by dilution or substitution for profit; today our food is adulterated by "additives" supposed to preserve it or make it more acceptable, again in the interests of profit, not health.) But the standards of hygiene set up by those who were calling for education of mothers often confused habit with hygiene: middle-class ritual and custom were advocated (with minor modifications perhaps) because they must be right. So, for instance, with the separation of adults and children: it must be wrong for children, especially infants, to be taken wherever adults went, because their place was in the nursery, eating childish food and keeping childish hours. If an infant died in its parents' bed it must have been "overlayed" because it was in the wrong place: it should sleep in a separate cot. (The "cot deaths" of today were still to be identified, let alone explained.) But space for a cot might be a problem; and in densely inhabited houses a baby crying would disturb everyone, so of course tired parents would prefer to let it snuggle in with them and would assume that they'd wake as usual if it was at risk.

The standards set up for motherhood were unrealistic in the context of much working-class accommodation. No amount of instruction and advice, whether from a medical officer of health's leaflets or a district visitor's calls at the house, could remove the basic handicaps of overcrowding, of damp, ill-drained, airless, bathless, tapless lodgings, of shared and filthy ash closets and middens.[169] No training for motherhood would ensure a supply of fresh uncontaminated milk, or provide food when there was no money. Edward Cadbury and his colleagues, in their inquiry into women's work and wages in Birmingham, remarked that "even where the mother is a good manager many children are enfeebled for life by recurrent periods of underfeeding."[170] Many of the mothers they visited took in home work (sewing hooks and eyes on to cards, for instance), and "apologized for their untidy rooms . . . cleaning and washing must be indefinitely postponed, for as they say, 'It's either wash the children or feed them, and it's better to earn the few pence for a bit of bread.'"[171] At best, education in thrift—tips in cooking and sewing and managing, perhaps how to budget—such as was advocated would enable housewives to spin out further the inadequate weekly income. (Presumably thrift was so often recommended by the employing classes because it meant wages could be kept lower.) But writers with a real and close acquaintance with working-class life, like Margaret Loane, for many years a district nurse, often commented on the amazing capacity of poor women.

> Would-be reformers of the culinary art among the poor coolly take for granted
> that the women who for countless generations have kept their men-kind more or
> less contented, have brought up to maturity a large proportion of their offspring,

and have done this on sums ranging from 10 shillings a week upwards, are, nevertheless, absolutely ignorant of their business. . . . The first thing that the instructors need to grasp is, how admirable are the results of a poor woman's cooking when compared with her means, and how much of value can be learnt from nearly every decent workman's wife.[172]

Those who were campaigning against infant mortality seem frequently to have been carried away by their own rhetoric. Motherhood was so powerful a symbol that often class differences disappeared, along with the realities of working-class life. All the individual real mothers were subsumed into one ideal figure, the Queen Bee, protected and fertile, producing the next generation for the good of the hive.[173] The home was "the cradle of the race . . . Empire's first line of defence,"[174] not a cramped cottage in Merthyr Tydfil or a squalid slum room. The family was such an accepted symbol for the state that its actual disparate identities were forgotten. Of course, many of the campaigners (doctors especially) came from families on the middle-class model and were likely to assume that anything else was all wrong, deviant rather than different. Fathers should be breadwinners, and "failed" if they were not—probably they must be good-for-nothing layabouts living off their wives; children should be dependent, so the "little adults" of the working class whose work might still provide a significant contribution to the family budget, even though it had to be combined with school, and whose responsibility for their younger brothers and sisters might still be extensive, were in their eyes tragic, neglected, and proof of dangerous inadequacies in the home life of the poor. They expected mothers to spend their days at home, so going out to work, whether full-time or for odd days at washing or cleaning, was immoral, even selfish—not provident, self-sacrificing, and necessary for the survival of the family as a group. Doctors and many of the other campaigners were also men, with their own interest in preserving the conventional family form. Although they may not have been much aware of this bias, it is likely to have colored their attitudes to the rearing of children and reinforced the idealization of motherhood. An unusually explicit expression of such bias is to be found in an article on the recruiting problem in 1903.

The tendency of the times is too much in favour of girls being educated in accomplishments in which only the few can excel. What is wanted for the comfort of their husbands and the proper rearing of their children is the knowledge of the duties of everyday life. To darn a pair of socks or to make an appetizing meal is far better than to strum the piano.[175]

His perspective is that of the well-to-do; from John Burns (once an engineer) we get a picture of the artisan ideal, the "kindly figure in a white apron" who should be there with "willing waiting hand" when her man comes home from work, "the mother at the head of the table, and her children around her, and the father coming home regularly to his meals.'' Married women's employment was to blame for their husband's drinking and for street gangs of ''anaemic, saucy, vulgar, ignorant, cigarette-smoking hooligans.''[176]

The inadequacy of individuals—mothers—and perhaps of the particular family, was a more acceptable explanation of infant mortality and ill-health than the shortcomings of society. It seemed more attackable. And it was the established response of the ruling class to poverty itself, reinforced by the Protestant ethic of the individual's power to prosper or to fall. There were the few ''deserving poor'' who had had bad luck but really tried to live right (that is, by middle-class standards) and be respectable; and there were the many ''undeserving'' poor, who were poor by their own fault. Small wonder if the attribution of personal fault continued: infant mortality was clearly connected to poverty, as the statistics showed; but poverty was the fault of the individuals, not an intrinsic part of a class society. And although in relation to poverty itself this attitude had been forcefully challenged by the 1900s, not least in the surveys of Booth and Rowntree, with their evidence of the structural character of poverty as well as its extent, nevertheless the frame of mind seems to have lingered strongly enough to support the doctrine of maternal fault. At the same time, for those who acknowledged state responsibility and interest even in territory (like the family) still largely considered to be the domain of individual right, emphasis on the individual—the mother—and on her education was a good way to reduce the opposition: it could justify intervention, and also through rhetoric obscure it. (The family as well as the mother could be used in this way.) School dinners, whose provision by local education authorities was resisted (before and after the 1907 Education Act legalized it at local discretion) by those who cried faulty motherhood and feared the ''demoralization'' of parents if their functions were fulfilled for them, were defended in one report as furnishing instruction and safety for the future, not just nutrition: ''As regards the children, who will be mothers and housekeepers of the future, the school dinner itself may be made to serve a valuable object lesson and used to reinforce practical instruction in hygiene, cookery and domestic economy.''[177] And they were also to provide an example of the civilized behavior that the mother ought to be inculcating— politeness, nice manners, using knives, forks, plates, and mugs correctly, and not spilling things.[178] For the mother's responsibility was moral as well as physical. Her offspring were not only to survive and be healthy, they had also to learn how to behave. This was partly a question of manners, but also of character building, that is, learning class and sex roles. Pritchard, in *Infant Education,* argues emphatically for the importance of maternal firmness in ''educational motherhood'' for the good of society.

> Many mothers seem to imagine that children should be coaxed and wheedled and cajoled into doing what is good for them, but there never was such a mistake. . . . When you find a mother of this invertebrate type you must in the first place impart

a little artificial stiffness to the moral backbone, if you wish the infant to be a credit to our society. If the child has to learn how to obey, the mother must know how to command. . . . If you find a child wilfully disobedient, dirty, untidy, slovenly or obstinate, and you wish to trace these results to their ultimate source, *cherchez la femme*—study the mother.[179]

It is not unusual to find references to the failure of working-class mothers to teach their children disciplined habits (as in their reluctance to wake a sleeping baby for "feeding-time"), but this passage suggests a particular interest in the connections between child rearing and society. It may reflect Pritchard's involvement with the Child Study Society, an organization of teachers, doctors, and some parents, whose field of study was mainly child development and psychology (without apparently any acquaintance with the work of Freud).[180] In their journal the importance of the mother to the character formation of the child not infrequently crops up, as in an article on "The Cultivation of the Mind in Children" by H. Davy (then president of the British Medical Association) in 1908. He advocated that for the good of the nation children should have implanted in them from the earliest age, by their mothers, the importance of self-control, of obedience, and of patriotism. (He cited the upbringing of Japanese children in devotion to family and country as a model.)[181]

Problems like infant mortality were defined, described, and "explained" by the new professionals of public health. By the turn of the century their numbers and their influence were fast expanding; they were in a position of power as regards both the development and the dissemination of ideology. Although increasing knowledge of, for instance, bacteriology was enabling them to understand such problems better, the contribution of infection was still underestimated or at least underblamed, as was the role of maternal health and malnutrition. It is significant that it was maternal, not medical, ignorance that always received the blame and that the minimal access of the poor to medical help in this period is never mentioned. Doctors and the rest created out of their own assumptions a set of explanations that overrode scientific observation and analysis. They knew at one level that 30 percent of infant deaths were related to the poor health of the pregnant and parturient mother; they knew that environmental factors and infection played a part in both stomach and respiratory infections; yet only the mothers' ignorance and neglect were stressed.

The vocabulary of concern also reflects their views of the world around them: the anxiety to build a race of strong *men,* to promote *virility,* and so on; and also the capitalist terminology of commodities, assets, and the rest. One striking example of this differentiates interestingly between women and men.

If men represent the income to be used and spent freely by each succeeding generation, women must be considered as capital to be spent sparingly in the present and to be husbanded carefully for the future and for the welfare of the race.[182]

The use of "husbanded" nicely fuses the ideologies of class and sex domination. Racist assumptions are also implicit or sometimes explicit throughout the discussion of racial stock: it is always clear that the only desirable stock is white, European, and preferably Anglo-Saxon. And of course imperialism itself was often presented in terms of the superiority (and therefore right to rule and mission to guide) of the British "imperial race" over the rest.

In the context, then, of racism and imperialism at one level and of class exploitation and sex prejudice at another, we come back to the mothers. The mothers' role in the creation of a healthier workforce, as of a virile army and navy, was crucial. In the fixing of the workforce, the development of a new kind of family, with head and housewife and pride in possessions, bound to one place and one job by a new level of emotional and financial investment in an increasingly substantial "home," was also to play a central part. The ideological approach to the question of infant mortality and domestic life can be seen therefore to have a close connection not only with the economic and political problems posed by falling birthrates but also with new developments in industrial capitalism, in Britain. The barrage of propaganda on the importance of child health, with its bias about motherhood, did provoke official action, inquiries, modest legislation, and various provisions by local authorities. It also helped to confirm or create attitudes about the relation between child and family and state, and most of all about the role of women; the influence of such changes was probably more far-reaching than any measures at the time. Where the solutions offered for improving national health were more concrete than the simple exaltation of motherhood, they were generally ones which tended to confirm the family in its bourgeois form and to consolidate the mother's role as child rearer and home keeper, as also did improvements in male wages—the family wage—and perhaps eventually family allowances.

This in turn served the interests of industry and of empire in a number of ways: by increasing the ties and the responsibilities of male workers and enabling them through the unpaid services of thrifty, conscientious, and hardworking wives to survive and keep better health without the need for industrial or state provision of maintenance; by ensuring that children—the next generation of workers and of soldiers—would be raised at minimum cost to the state and in serviceable condition; and by setting ideological barriers to married women's work outside the home, which where possible would keep women as a reserve labor force, available in emergency (as in two world wars) but not clogging the labor market in normal times, or requiring state subsidy when not employed. At the same time contradictions in the ideology have enabled it to be adapted to changing circumstances: whether married women's work is tolerated or denounced depends on whether it is needed. The unpaid housekeeper performing miracles on a low budget, the ideal housewife putting her energies (and her money) into careful shopping to make and maintain the ideal home for her family, the office cleaners or the twilight shift worker adding low-paid wage labor to her domestic shift because money is needed for the children's clothes, shoes, or food, or for holiday or toys, but she can't leave them in the daytime—all these are incarnations of motherhood.

Notes

This chapter originated in work with the Women against Population Control group in the early 1970s. Since then it has drawn so much on the reactions and suggestions of various people, both individually and in discussions when I have presented its earlier versions at History Workshop, Feminist History Group seminar, and on other occasions, that it is impossible to give credit wherever it is due. In drafting this latest version I am above all grateful to Walter Easey and to my comrades on the editorial collective of *History Workshop Journal.*

In the notes below, the following abbreviations are used:

BMJ—*British Medical Journal* (the authoritative weekly publication of the British Medical Association [BMA], voice of the medical establishment).

PP—Parliamentary Papers (printed government papers available in research libraries).

PRO—Public Record Office (now at Kew).

1. As, for instance, in T. H. Huxley, "The Struggle for Existence," *The Nineteenth Century,* February 1888.

2. The eugenists drew both on ideas of the survival of the fittest, as developed by Francis Galton and Karl Pearson, and on Mendel's theories of heredity as they came into currency at the turn of the century.

3. Charles Kingsley, *The Massacre of the Innocents,* address given at the first public meeting of the Ladies' National Association for the Diffusion of Sanitary Knowledge in 1858. Printed as a Ladies' Sanitary Association pamphlet.

4. J. L. Garvin, "The Maintenance of Empire," in *The Empire and the Century,* ed. C. S. Goldman, 1905, 72–81. Japan had also now established itself as a sea power by its skillful defeat of the much bigger Chinese navy in the 1894–1895 Sino-Japanese War. Compare J. Crichton Browne's presidential address to the Medical Section of the International Congress for the Welfare and Protection of Children, 1902, 6, 9.

5. E. Cadbury, M. C. Matheson, and G. Shann, *Women's Work and Wages,* 1906, 228–9; *BMJ* (30 July 1904); 231, address by Sir William Selby Church, president of the Royal College of Physicians, at annual meeting of BMA; T. J. Macnamara, Liberal MP, "In Corpore Sano," *Contemporary Review,* February 1905, 238; inaugural address by Earl Beauchamp to the International Congress for the Welfare and Protection of Children, 1902, 4.

6. G. F. McCleary, *The Early History of the Infant Welfare Movement,* 1933, 146.

7. Alexander Wynter Blyth, preface to Eric Pritchard, *Infant Education,* 1907. Pritchard was a prominent St. Marylebone doctor whose energies and powers of propaganda were devoted to saving infant lives for the nation through the mothers; he

believed that infants could "live and thrive in spite of poverty and bad sanitation" but would not "survive bad mothercraft." Eric Pritchard, "Schools for Mothers," *Proceedings of Infant Mortality Conference at Liverpool*, 1914, 54.

8. Newman, *Infant Mortality: A Social Problem*, 1906, p.v. George Newman (1870–1948) became first chief medical officer to the Board of Education, 1907; during World War I served on various important health committees; from 1919 was first chief medical officer at new Ministry of Health. Married but no children. See *Dictionary of National Biography* and text throughout.

9. Jeanne Brand, *Doctors and the State*, 1965, is a useful text for the history of medical officers of health.

10. See G. R. Searle, *The Quest for National Efficiency*, 1971.

11. For earlier concern see James Crichton Browne, "Education and the Nervous System," in *The Book of Health*, ed. Malcolm Morris, 1883; J C. Browne, "Report to Education Department upon Alleged Over-pressure of work in public elementary schools" (PP. 1884, lxi [293]); Francis Warner, "Physical and Mental Condition of 50,000 Children," *Journal of Royal Statistical Society* (1893) lvi: Childhood Society's report on the scientific study of the mental and physical conditions of childhood, 1895; and the campaign of the Women's Industrial Council against children's employment outside school, as in *Women's Industrial News*, April 1896, and Edith Hogg, "School Children as Wage-Earners," *The Nineteenth Century*, August 1897. Also J. C. Browne, *Physical Efficiency in Children*, 1902; Royal Commission on Physical Training (Scotland) PP. 1903, xxx; Interdepartmental Committee on Physical Deterioration PP. 1904, xxxii.

12. See McCleary, *Infant Welfare Movement*, and *Development of the British Maternity and Child Welfare Services*, 1945, and (less detailed) George Newman, *English Social Services*, 1941. For results attributed to the young infant welfare movement by John Burns and his assurance of the Local Government Board's "paternal interest in milk, the mothers and the babies," see *Proceedings of National Conference on Infant Mortality*, 1908, 12, and compare p. 28.

13. There is a useful list of voluntary societies "engaged in health propaganda of a public nature," with a few details in each, in Newman's *Public Education in Health*, 1924, 18–22.

14. J. W. Kirton, *Cheerful Homes: How to Get and Keep Them* (undated), 11–12; Mary Scharlieb, *What It Means to Marry or Young Women and Marriage*, 1914, 36–37. (Kirton devotes only 23 out of 288 pages to children—"Our Precious Darlings," Annie S. Swann in *Courtship and Marriage*, 1894, gives them 38 out of 144 pages; and Scharlieb, 60 out of 140, besides frequent mention.)

15. See Gertrude Tuckwell, *The State and Its Children*, 1894; John Gorst, *The Children of the Nation*, 1906; Reginald Bray, *The Town Child*, 1907; H. Llewellyn Heath, *The Infant, the Parent and the State*, 1907; Kelynack, *Infancy*, 1910, etc.

16. PP. 1910, xxxix (Cd. 5263), 71–73. Arthur Newsholme (1857–1943) was medical officer of health for Brighton from 1888; then from 1908 until he retired in 1919, principal medical officer to the Local Government Board, appointed by John Burns. He was an accepted authority on medical statistics and believed strongly in state medicine. Married but no children. See *Dictionary of National Biography* and text below throughout.

17. Newsholme, "Infantile Mortality, A Statistical Study," *Practitioner* (October 1905): 494.

18. G. F. McCleary, *The Menace of British Depopulation,* 1937, 9. McCleary was Battersea medical officer of health in the 1900s, with the support of John Burns, and an enthusiast for hygienic milk depots (see n. 106 below), quoting the experience of the pioneer one at Battersea. He wrote several Fabian pamphlets—"Municipal Bakeries" and "Municipal Hospitals" in 1900 and "Life in the Laundry" in 1902. Later he was chief medical officer to the National Insurance Commission, chairman of the National Council for Maternity and Child Welfare, and chairman of the National Association of Maternity and Child Welfare Centres and for the Prevention of Infant Mortality. His last book, *Peopling the British Commonwealth,* was published in 1955.

19. Report by Dr. James Kerr, medical officer for education, in *Medical Officer of Health for London's Annual Report,* 1904, Appendix III. The point was frequently made in discussion in the medical press: see, for instance, *Practitioner* (February 1905): p 217; and was generally accepted (except by eugenists) as confirming the need for action over infant health. See also Newsholme, 1910 report, pt. 1.

20. It should also be noted that urban recruits were particularly unfit. See Arnold White, *Efficiency and Empire,* 1901; *Annual Reports of Inspector General of Recruiting,* 1900–1903 (PP. 1901, Cd.519, ix; PP.1902, Cd.2175, xxii; PP.1903, Cd.1496, xxxviii; PP.1904, Cd.1778, viii), *Report of Interdepartmental Committee on Physical Deterioration.* For wider issues, see Anne Summers, "Militarism," *History Workshop* (1976) 2.

21. Frederick Maurice, "National Health: A Soldier's Study," *Contemporary Review,* January 1903. For earlier discussion in periodicals (though with less impact) see Pretorius, "The Army and Empire," and E. R. Dawson, "Britain's Duty to Britain's Labour," both in *Empire Review* (1901); and Henry Birchenough, "Our Last Effort for a Voluntary Army," and Arthur H. Lee, "The Recruiting Question," both in *The Nineteenth Century and After* (April 1901).

22. Gareth Stedman Jones, *Outcast London,* 1971, 151; and see chapter 6 for fears of urban degeneration in the second half of the nineteenth century. The prospect of "Deterioration of the Race" according to Samuel Sneade Brown in 1870 would bring the health of towns into the province of imperial care and control. "The Health of Towns," in his *Notes on Sanitary Reforms.*

23. See PP.1901, lvi, Statistics of Inspected Schools, 1889–1900, summary tables 52 and 54, for figures on the teaching of domestic economy and of cookery and laundry. See also two articles by Carol Dyhouse: "Social Darwinistic Ideas and the Development of Women's Education in England, 1880–1920," *History of Education,* 1976, and "Good Wives and Little Mothers: Social Anxieties and Schoolgirls' Curriculum, 1890–1920," *Oxford Review of Education,* 1977.

24. T. J. Macnamara, "In Corpore Sano," 248. (Macnamara was a lifelong supporter of Lloyd George, became parliamentary secretary to the Local Government Board in 1907, and in 1920 was first minister of labor under Lloyd George.) For the party politics of social reform in this period, see, for example, G. R. Searle, *The Quest for National Efficiency,* 1971; Bernard Semmel, *Imperialism and Social Reform* (which does not deal with the area discussed in this chapter); and Maurice Bruce, *The Coming*

of the Welfare State, 1961. A. Watt Smyth, *Physical Deterioration,* 1906, covers the range of provisions and reforms that were being considered by nonsocialists.

25. *BMJ* (30 July 1904); J. W. Taylor, "The Diminishing Birth-Rate and What Is Involved in It," Presidential Address to Inaugural Meeting of British Gynaecological Society, *BMJ* (20 February 1904): 427. (Taylor was quoting "a prominent Japanese" as reported in the *Daily Mail,* 23 December 1903.) See also "The Physique of the Japanese," *BMJ* (12 March 1904): 622.

26. Henry Birchenough, "Our Last Effort for a Voluntary Army," *The Nineteenth Century and After* (April 1901): 552. See also Arthur Shadwell, *Industrial Efficiency: A Comparative Study of Industrial Life in England, Germany and America,* 1906.

27. Already in 1885 the platform of Amie Hicks, SDF candidate in the Marylebone School Board election, included the demand for at least one free meal a day in every board school. *Justice* (3 October 1885): 1.

28. Margaret McMillan, *Life of Rachel McMillan,* 1927, 113.

29. See, for instance, *Early Childhood,* 1990, *Infant Mortality* and *Labour and Childhood,* both 1907, and even *The Child and the State,* 1911.

30. Ramsay MacDonald, *Socialism and Government,* 1909, 14–20.

31. See A. M. McBriar, *Fabian Socialism and English Politics,* 1962, chap. 5; Semmel, *Imperialism and Social Reform,* chap. 3.

32. Sidney Webb, "Lord Rosebery's Escape from Houndsditch," *The Nineteenth Century and After* (September 1901): 375–376.

33. William Butler, Presidential Address to Willesden and District Medical Society, read by request before Home Counties branch of Society of Medical Officers of Health, December 1899 and reprinted in *Public Health* (1899): 326. See also in same issue, J. Howard Jones (Medical Officer of Health for Newport and President of West of England and S. Wales branch of Society of Medical Officers of Health), "The Influence of Preventive Medicine upon the Evolution of the Race."

34. Karl Pearson, *The Scope and Importance to the State of the Science of National Eugenics* (lecture given in 1907), 1909, 10, 25.

35. Pearson, *Nature and Nurture: The Problem of the Future,* 1910, 27.

36. *The Science of Eugenics and Sex Life Regeneration of the Human Race,* ed. Charles H. Robinson, from the notes of W. J. Hadden, 1904, ii. This appears to be an American publication, but the statement would have been altogether acceptable to British eugenists. According to J. R. Rumsey (*Essays in State Medicine,* 1856), a legal ban had even then been proposed on the willful transmission of hereditary disease through marriage.

37. J. R. Inge (later Dean Inge), "Some Moral Aspects of Eugenics," *Eugenics Review* 1 (1909) 130, demanding "any legislation" that would reduce the slum dwellers' desire to breed. Comparisons were frequently made with past empires, whose fall was equated with degeneracy: Sir George Kekewich, former secretary to the Board of Education, when opening a conference on Diet, Cookery, and Hygiene in Schools, in 1913, actually quoted in Latin several lines of Horace on the way each generation is worse than the next, though he declared with optimism that he thought the opposite was going to be true. *Rearing an Imperial Race,* 1913, 7. Sparta was also occasionally quoted for its practice of exposing weakly infants to preserve national fitness.

38. C. W. Saleeby, *Parenthood and Race Culture,* 1909, 32.

39. Speech given in full as appendix to McCleary, *Infant Welfare Movement.*

40. Pearson, lecture, *"The Woman Question,"* 1885 (in *The Ethic of Free Thought,* 1901). Herbert Spencer in vol. 2 of his *Principles of Biology* had suggested that intellectual development of the individual—especially the female—impaired reproductive powers, and this seems to have been fairly commonly taken as a real possibility. See also Mrs. Arthur Philip, "Are Recent Developments in Women's Education in Favour of the Best Preparation for Wifehood and Motherhood?" *Parents Review* (1906) (the answer was no); and Dyhouse, "Social Darwinistic Ideas . . ."

41. R. Murray Leslie, "Woman's Progress in Relation to Eugenics," *Eugenics Review* (January 1991): 283. See also *Practitioner* (October 1905): 586.

42. For an extreme statement of this position, see R. R. Rentoul's pamphlet "for women and girl," *The Dignity of Woman's Health and the Nemesis of Its Neglect,* 1890, especially xxviii. (Rentoul was generally regarded as an extremist, and his views on sterilization provoked hostile reactions in the medical press.) See *BMJ* (12 March 1904) and subsequent correspondence (12 March, 19 March, 2 April, 9 April, 2 July, 30 July, 13 August), and his *Race Culture or Race Suicide,* 1906; and P. Z. Hebert, *The Killing of the Unfit and the Transmissibility of Acquired Characters,* 1907 (reprints from *Practitioner* attacking Rentoul).

43. Mary Scharlieb, "Recreational Activities of Girls During Adolescence," *Child Study* 4 (1911): 9, 14. Others were less cautious: "If we make our girls strong" (through athletics) "the mothers of future generations will be strong and the stronger will our nation become"—report of Tottenham Branch conference, *School Attendance Gazette,* December 1902.

44. For interesting recent work on the effect of social class on doctors' perceptions of their patients' health, see Karl Figlio, "The Social Structure of Disease" (typescript), and abstract in Society for the Social History of Medicine *Bulletin* (21 December 1977).

45. Saleeby, *Race Culture,* xii-iv.

46. J. E. Gemmell, Presidential Address N. of England Obstetrical and Gynecological Society, in *Journal of Obstetrics and Gynaecology of the British Empire* (December 1903): 590.

47. Alice Ravenhill, "Eugenic Ideals for Womanhood," *Eugenics Review* (1909): 267. C. T. Ewart in "Parenthood," *Empire Review* 19 (1910): 320, has a very similar phrase about a trumpet call, as well as a similar general argument. (For Ravenhill, see below notes 75 and 180.)

48. G. E. Shuttleworth, "Degeneracy: Physical, Mental and Moral," address to the Society for the Study of the Mental and Physical Conditions of Children, *BMJ* (21 May 1904): 1205.

49. Bertrand Russell, *Autobiography* 1872–1914, 84, referring to 1894.

50. Taylor, "The Diminishing Birth-rate."

51. Sidney Webb, *The Declining Birth-rate,* 1907 (Fabian Tract 131), esp. pp. 16–19. Fabian Tract 149 was *The Endowment of Motherhood,* 1910, by Henry D. Harben.

52. Russell, *Autobiography,* 132; Mrs Wibaut, "Working Women and the Vote," reprinted in *Women in Rebellion* 1900, intro Suzie Fleming, ILP Square One pamphlet, 1973. For Alice Drysdale Vickery's contribution to a discussion on restrictions in marriage and on studies in national eugenics; see *Sociological Studies* (1906) 21. For

the views of the Fabian Women's Group, see Mrs. Pember Reeves, *Round About a Pound a Week,* 1913, 1. And see *New Statesman,* 16 May 1914, supplement on Motherhood and the State; Eleanor Rathbone, *The Disinherited Family,* 1924 (and other publications); Mary Stocks, *The Case for Family Endowment,* 1927. D. V. Glass gives two chapters to the question in *The Struggle for Population,* 1936; see also his *Population Policies and Movements,* 1940, for international comparisons. There is a useful recent article on the later phase by Jane Lewis, "The Movement for Family Allowances, 1917–45" (typescript). And see note 161 below.

53. C. T. Ewart, "National Health," *Empire Review* (February–July 1910): 263.

54. See, for instance, *School for Mothers,* 51, 53; or Louise Creighton, "Women's Work for the Church and for the State," *Anglican Papers* (1908): 3.

55. Sykes introd. to *School for Mothers,* 8.

56. Emilia Kanthack, *The Preservation of Infant Life* (Lectures to Health Visitors), 1907, 10.

57. This had been observed for many years (see *The Lancet* in the 1870s for instance, or indeed the "great reputation" of Pip's sister in *Great Expectations* for her success in bringing him up "by hand"), but the statistics collected in the 1890s and 1900s brought dramatic proof. Newman summarized the state of information in the chapter on infant feeding in *Infant Mortality.* George Sims, in *The Cry of the Children,* 1905, 7, commented, "Back to the Land may be a good cry for the community, but Back to the Breast is a better cry for the race." Patent baby foods and condensed milk were much advertised at this time, and their use was thought to be increasing.

58. Kanthack, *Preservation of Infant Life,* 28.

59. Introduction, Cassell's *Penny Book for Mothers,* 1911; compare Edith L. Maynard, *Baby—Useful Hints for Busy Mothers,* 1906, esp. pp. 30–31. This was aimed at "busy women who have no time to read long books or attend lectures, and yet who are very anxious to do the best for their babies."

60. See Margaret Hewitt, *Wives and Mothers in Victorian Industry,* 1958, for the classic consideration of this question, and Carol Dyhouse, "Working-Class Mothers and Infant Mortality in England, 1895–1914," *Journal of Social History* 12 (1978): 248–281, for the slightly later history of the theory (as well as a useful discussion of the whole question of infant mortality).

61. *BMJ* (23 January 1904): 201, resolution of BMA Council; names of petition committee pp. 212–213; leader with information on 14,000 signatures (30 January): 261; presentation of petition (16 July), 129–130. By 1913, after some years of such teaching seemed to have made little difference, it was argued that the hours spent on domestic subjects were still insufficient, and at a National Food Reform Association conference Lady Meyer, chairman of the St. Pancras School for Mothers, even proposed that the school-leaving age should be raised to give more time "for the study of a subject of such consequence to the future mothers of the race." See *Rearing an Imperial Race,* xxxix, 180–181.

62. Helen Dendy Bosanquet, "Physical Degeneration and the Poverty Line," *Contemporary Review* (January 1904): 73.

63. C. E. G. Masterman, *The Heart of the Empire,* 1901, viii.

64. Pearson, *Scope,* 41.

65. The system of local option meant that measures sanctioned by Parliament were not necessarily compulsory, and whether they were put into practice depended on the local political and financial position and the attitude of the local authority. Gorst suggested that much more could be done than was. See review of his *Children of the Nation*, in *Progress*, 1907, 63.

66. Marion Phillips, a vigorous Australian socialist (Fabian and later Labor party) and historian voiced some of these criticisms at a meeting of the Association of Teachers in Domestic Subjects: reported in *The Times*, 29 January 1913.

67. R. Morant, Prefatory Note to Board of Education Circular 758 (1910), Memorandum on the Teaching of Infant Care and Management in Public Elementary Schools. For origins of circular, see PRO file, ED/11/51.

68. Janet Campbell, Circular 758, conclusion, 10.

69. Ibid., 1.

70. See Report of Proceedings of National Conference on Infantile Mortality with address by . . . John Burns MP, 1906, and PRO Home Office File HO 45 10335/138532/6 for list of resolutions. (This may also be the reference for an application for Royal Patronage of the conference made by John Burns on the grounds of the national interest being involved, but I have lost the relevant note.)

71. Drink was another widely quoted cause of infant mortality—parents drinking away the children's food money and mothers drinking away their health and crippling their infants were thought by some to be the chief cause of infant death. There was overlap between those involved in temperance and in infant welfare campaigns. See George Sims, *The Cry of the Children*, 1907, account of conference 25–36.

72. Ballantyne's paper on prenatal causes was a rare example of realism. He ignored problems of heredity, since he "did not regard them as solved to such an extent as to come within the range of the practical," described the problems of pregnancy, and urged greater care of the pregnant woman, including the provision of prematernity wards and hospitals (McCleary, *Infant Welfare Movement*, 109–10). Sykes of St. Pancras also saw that health in pregnancy was important, which led to the provision of meals for mothers at the St. Pancras School for mothers (see text below), but he fused such perceptions with rhetoric about motherhood. Ballantyne concentrated on the medical treatise.

73. Burns, Presidential Address to the Infant Mortality Conference, 1906; see McCleary, *Infant Welfare Movement*, appendix.

74. Saleeby, *Race Culture*, 132.

75. Ravenhill, *The Health of the Community and How to Promote It*, 1897, *How the Law Helps to Healthy Homes*, 1898, *Our Water Supply*, 1898; "The Teaching of Domestic Science in the United States of America," Board of Education Special Reports, PP. 1905, xxvi. Ravenhill was also active in the Child Study movement: see articles on children's hours of sleep, *Child Study* 2 (1909), and on play, *Child Study* 3 (1910); also expression of regret at her proposed emigration to Canada, *Child Study* 3 (1910): 84. (Also note 47 above.)

76. One hundred seven mothers claimed their sovereign; see Newman, *English Social Services*, 1941, 20; and McCleary, *Infant Welfare Movement*, 90–93. A similar scheme of vouchers was tried in Glasgow by the Anderston and District Health Association: *Progress* (April 1907): 113.

77. Saleeby, *Methods of Race Regeneration*, 1911, 8.

78. Others were prepared to go further: see Butler and Jones articles in *Public Health* (February 1899), Rentoul, "Dignity of Woman's Health," and *Proposed Sterilization of Certain Mental and Physical Degenerates: An Appeal to Asylum Managers and Others,* 1903; Chatterton Hill, "Race Progress and Race Degeneracy," *Sociological Review* (1909): 257; Arnold White, *Efficiency and Empire.* Pearson advocated "the expatriation of confirmed criminals" for eugenic reasons, as well as the exclusion of "undesirable aliens" and reduction in Poor Law assistance to paupers and the insane— *National Life from the Standpoint of Science* (lecture 1900), 1905, 104–105, and argued that racial and medical progress were incompatible in *Darwinism, Medical Progress and Eugenics,* 1912.

79. Saleeby, *Race Culture,* 29.

80. Ibid., 21, 19, xiv.

81. Saleeby, "The Human Mother," Infant Mortality Conference, 1908, 32.

82. Marie Stopes, preface, *Married Love,* 1920 ed., 16, 97.

83. Saleeby, *Race Culture,* 285.

84. Newman, *Infant Mortality,* 257.

85. Ibid., 262.

86. Newman, *The Health of the State,* 1907, 15, 183, 191.

87. Newsholme, *Fifty Years in Public Health,* 1935, 402–404.

88. *Fifty Years,* quoting editorial article he wrote for *BMJ* (14 November 1903), on the organization of medical inspection in schools.

89. Newsholme, *Declining Birth-rate,* and *Fifty Years,* 406–407 (quoting speech in 1904).

90. Newsholme, *Declining Birth-rate,* 57–58.

91. PP. 1910, xxxix (Cd. 5263), 70–73.

92. *Fifty Years,* 372–374.

93. Ibid., 321.

94. Ibid., 333.

95. Ibid., 330–331.

96. Newsholme, *Contribution to the Study of Epidemic Diarrhoea,* 1900, 13–15.

97. B. S. Rowntree, *Poverty: A Study of Town Life,* 1901, conclusions.

98. PP. 1906, xc(Cd. 2726), Reports on Children under Five in Public Elementary Schools (especially Miss Munday's and Miss Bathurst's reports); PP. 1908, lxxxii(Cd. 4259), Report of Board of Education Consultative Committee on School Attendance of Children below Five.

99. Pritchard, *Infant Education,* 19.

100. F. J. H. Coutts, *Condensed Milks,* 1911, Reports to Local Government Board on Public Health, n.s. 56.

101. F. G. Haworth, letter to *BMJ* (26 March 1904): 763. Compare Pritchard, *Infant Education,* 44–45; and A. Dingwall Fordyce, *The Care of Infants and Young Children,* 1911, 59–61, 98–99. Of course, nowadays "demand feeding" receives official sanction: see *Infant Feeding* 1975, Practice and Attitudes in England and Wales, HMSO, 1978.

102. Poverty was occasionally invoked. See *BMJ* (27 August 1904): 439, contribution by McCleary to discussion on Poverty and Public Health.

103. Sykes, *School for Mothers,* 7. For examples of earlier leafletting, *see Lancet* (7 February 1874): 212, (21 February 1874): 283; A. W. Jephson, *My Work in London,* 1910, 95.

104. *Progress* (April 1907): 117.

105. National Health Society lecturer was a pursuit recommended in J. E. Davidson, *What Our Daughters Can Do for Themselves,* 1893, 40; see also *BMJ* (12 March 1904): 629; (27 August 1904): 436; and for lectures by doctors, see (18 June 1904): 467 and (8 October 1904): 956. G. A. Simpson recalled lecturing around 1906 to mothers' meetings on infant feeding and infant diseases (*My Life and Family Reminiscences,* 1931, 52). For lectures in Portsmouth Gaol, see *BMJ* (20 August 1904): 397; for Holloway Prison, *BMJ* (22 October 1904): 118.

106. The principle of the milk depot was to provide milk suitable for infants whose mothers were unable to suckle them. (In France the bottles bore the motto "Faute de Mieux"—"for want of better.") The milk in poor districts was often very unsatisfactory: even if it had come from cow to shop without contamination or delay, it was often sold in very unhygienic conditions, and sometimes diluted with water. So to provide milk less likely to convey infection to susceptible infants was certainly a good idea. Unfortunately, they were fairly expensive to run, and some local authorities thought it either too great an expenditure or beyond their powers anyway; while for the purchasers it was not as cheap as the treacherous condensed milk, so demand was sometimes unexpectedly low. See McCleary, *Infantile Mortality and Infants Milk Depots,* 1905, and *Infant Welfare Movement;* also *BMJ* (9 January 1904): 97 (Belfast Public Health Committee refusing a donation to help establish one); *BMJ* (9 April 1904): 848 (the London Milk Supply); *BMJ* (16 April) and (13 August 1904), for depots projected in Lambeth and Shadwell, London; (27 August 1904) (criticisms by Newman as tending to lessen maternal responsibility); (17 September 1904): 693 (discussion at Sanitary Inspectors' Association); (24 September 1904): 768 (details including cost of Bradford depot); and arguments in favor in *The Present Conditions of Infant Life,* Infants' Health Society, 1905, 13–14, and J. J. Buchan, "Milk Depots and Kindred Institution," in Kelynack, *Infancy,* 1910.

107. McCleary, *Development of British Maternity and Child Welfare Services,* 1945, 10; Newsholme, *Fifty Years,* 335.

108. *Public Health* (Aug. 1899): 721.

109. Newman, *Infant Mortality,* 264.

110. Somerset Maugham, *Of Human Bondage,* 1915, 560. In Huddersfield, however, they were not supposed to enter unless invited or come inside to sit down without being asked. See McCleary, *Infant Welfare Movement,* 264.

111. Thomas Gautrey, *Lux Mihi Laus,* 1937, 91.

112. See Anna Davin, *Board School Girls,* forthcoming.

113. See Local Government Circular to the Board of Guardians on the Administration of Outdoor Relief, 1910, 34–35; and Pat Thane, "Women and The Poor Law in Victorian and Edwardian England," *History Workshop* 6 (1978): 29–51. See also her point that the 1908 Children's Act was opposed by working-class organizations because it "licensed intrusions into the working-class family which would not have been countenanced by or for the better-off."

114. This account is based mainly on Dora Bunting, "Schools for Mothers," in Kelynack, *Infancy,* and McCleary, *Infant Welfare Movement,* 123–130. For detail on the school for mothers in Birmingham, see Dyhouse, "Working-Class Mothers and Infant Mortality."

115. Sykes, *School for Mothers,* 8.

116. Sykes, preface to Miss Bibby, Miss Colles, Miss Petty, and Dr. Sykes, *The Pudding Lady: A New Departure in Social Work,* 1912 (reprint 1916 by National Food Reform League), 13; *Infant Welfare Movement,* 35. (Lady Meyer was quoted as using "mothercraft" in 1911 [*Progress* (1911): 52], which is the earliest mention of the word I have found, but as she was closely involved in the school for mothers that does not disprove McCleary's attribution.)

117. The importance of the Notification of Births Act (1907) was that it made it much easier for the local authorities (if they wanted) to trace newborn babies and send out visitors. Saleeby, after its passage, "occupied himself in various parts of the country in the efforts which were necessary to persuade local authorities to adopt" its provisions. See *Woman and Womanhood,* 132.

118. See Alys Russell, "The Ghent School for Mothers," *The Nineteenth Century and After* (December 1906); and *Infant Welfare Movement,* 126. She and Mrs. Gordon spoke on 1 May 1907 to a meeting of people interested in developing something similar in St. Pancras.

119. *School for Mothers,* 39.

120. For recent work on differences in diet within the family, see Laura Oren, "The Welfare of Women in Labouring Families: England, 1860–1950," in ed. Hartman and Banner, *Clio's Consciousness Raised,* ed. M. S. Hartman and L. Banner, 1974; and D. J. Oddy, "The Working-Class Diet, 1880–1914," in *The Making of the British Diet,* ed. D. J. Oddy and D. S. Miller, 1976, chap. 18.

121. *School for Mothers,* 39

122. Such accusations provoked the submission of the Infant Life Insurance Bill in 1890, and they are plentiful in evidence of doctors and coroners to the Select Committee of the House of Lords set up to report on the bill. See PP.1890, xl, minutes of evidence throughout. D. L. Thomas, medical officer of health for Limehouse, in a detailed analysis (1899) of infant mortality there, felt constrained to discuss the possible role of insurance, though he felt unable to prove or disprove it. The other factors he considered were poverty, illegitimacy, overlaying, unhealthy surroundings, and hereditary diseases (not maternal ignorance). "On Infantile Mortality," *Public Health* (September 1899): 810–817.

123. *School for Mothers,* 38–39.

124. Kanthack, *Preservation of Infant Life,* 2, 4.

125. As the infant death rate was declining quite sharply in these years, it was always tempting to attribute the fall to the strenuous efforts being made. Already in 1907 Sykes was claiming that the reduction of infant deaths that summer was the result of their system of visiting. *Progress* (1907): 56. In retrospect Newman, McCleary, and even Newsholme all explain the twentieth-century decline by the rise of the infant welfare movement. See especially Newman, *Building of a Nation's Health,* 244, *English Social Services,* 19.

126. McCleary, *Infant Welfare Movement,* 129. For comparable but less publicized work in neighboring St. Marylebone, see Pritchard, *Infant Education,* introduction.

127. Eric Pritchard, *Proceedings of the Infant Mortality Conference,* Liverpool, 1914, 51–59. The word "mothercraft" was being freely used at the conference. Besides the usual papers (and an evening lecture by Saleeby, "The Nurture of the Race") a competition in mothercraft was judged and prizes presented.

128. Newman, *The Building of a Nation's Health,* 1939, 243.

129. Ibid., 247.

130. Pritchard, *Proceedings,* 51.

131. McCleary, *Infant Welfare Movement,* 17–18.

132. LGB Circular, 30 July 1914, quoted in *Infant Welfare Movement,* 142.

133. Board of Education yearly regulations for Grants to Schools for Mothers, in PP. 1914, Cd.7534, lxiv; PP.1914–6, Cd.7985, 1; PP.1918, Cd.9154, xix.

134. See, for example, PP.1917–18 (86), xxv, Return of Grants from Board of Education 1916–1917 to voluntary schools for mothers in London, Birmingham, Manchester, Liverpool, Leeds, and Bradford.

135. The Maxim gun, introduced into the British army in 1889 (after it had been tried out on a punitive expedition in the Gambia) and by World War I being used in an improved version by both British and German troops, was vastly more lethal than previous weapons and along with high explosive shells and mines was responsible for the unprecedented casualties of 1914–1918.

136. T. N. Kelynack, ed. *Child Welfare Annual,* 1916, vii.

137. *Maternity and Child Welfare* (January 1917): 32.

138. *Maternity and Child Welfare* (April 1917) (''How the National Baby Week Can be Made a Success''); June 1917 (''National Baby Week''—three articles including ''A Justification of Baby Week'' by Mrs. A. E. Barnes).

139. *Maternity and Child Welfare* (February 1917): 60; Newman, *Public Education in Health,* 1924, 21.

140. Gloden Dallas, introduction to *Maternity: Letters from Working Women,* ed. Margaret Llewellyn Davies, 1978 ed.

141. Herbert Samuel, preface to *Maternity.*

142. *Maternity,* letter 41, 68.

143. Ibid., figures bearing on infant mortality, 194–195.

144. Ibid., letter 20, 46.

145. Ibid., letter 33, 60–61.

146. Ibid., letter 63, 91.

147. Ibid., letter 21, 48–49.

148. Ibid., letter 16, 40.

149. Ibid., letter 62, 89–90.

150. Ibid., 212.

151. Newman, *Public Education in Health,* 1924, 7.

152. Three reports on maternal mortality and morbidity by Dr. Janet Campbell were issued by the Ministry of Health in 1924, 1927, and 1932; and there was an interdepartmental committee on the same subject whose interim report in 1930 considered half of maternal deaths to be preventable and stressed the role of anemia and malnutrition in the mother.

153. Margaret Balfour and Joan C. Drury, *Motherhood in the Special Areas of Durham and Tyneside,* 1934.

154. See Catherine Hall, ''Married Women at Home in Birmingham in the 1920s and 1930s,'' and Diana Gittins, ''Women's Work and Family Size between the War,'' both in *Oral History* 5 (Autumn 1977) (Women's History Issue).

155. Enid Charles, *The Twilight of Parenthood,* 1934 (and her *Menace of Underpopulation,* 1936); McCleary, *British Depopulation.*

156. Hilary Land, "The Introduction of Family Allowances: An Act of Historic Justice?" *Change, Choice and Conflict in Social Policy,* ed. P. K. Hall, H. Land, R. A. Parker, and A. Webb, 1975, 174.

157. See Tim Mason, "Women in Nazi Germany," *History Workshop* 1 (Spring 1976) and 2 (Autumn 1976).

158. There is a useful article on women and the Front by Richard Marlen in the *Leveller,* March 1978.

159. M. Bruce (*The Coming of the Welfare State,* 314) points out that family allowances were nearly paid to the father rather than the mother: only a last-minute vote in the House of Commons secured them as primarily the mothers' right.

160. Beveridge, quoted by Hilary Land in "Women, Supporters or Supported?" in *Sexual Divisions in Society: Process and Change,* ed. D. L. Barker and S. Allen, 1976, 109.

161. This is discussed in Elizabeth Wilson, *Women and the Welfare State,* 1976; and in the work of Hilary Land: "Women, Supporters or Supported?" "Who Cares for the Family?" *Journal of Social Policy* (July 1978); "Income Maintenance Systems and the Division of Labour in the Family," *Social Security Research* (DHSS Report) HMSO, 1977, and "The Introduction of Family Allowances."

162. R. A. Bray, *The Town Child,* 1907, 116. Compare L. Haden Guest, London County Council doctor, on the necessity of feeding hungry schoolchildren—"We must insist on parental responsibility, but we must also insist on our responsibility as members of the big family of the State, for the feeding of all our children." *Rearing on Imperial Race,* 35. See also opposing view of Miss Elliot from Southwark Health Society, 47, and discussion pp. 71–73.

163. B. M. Richardson, "Woman as Sanitary Reformer," *Fraser's Magazine,* November 1880, 669–671. Richardson, a well-known and authoritative "sanitarian," was vice president of the Education Society and very much opposed to women's education (see *Journal of Education* 1 [February, 1880]: 34).

164. Saleeby, *Woman and Womanhood,* 18–19.

165. Burns, as chairman of the Local Government Board, had prescribed that the local committee that arranged the fostering of children should be at least one-third women (Boarding Out Order 1911). For a detailed account of the expansion, see Edith Maynard, *Women in the Public Health Service,* 1915.

166. *The Times,* 4 May 1909 (quoted in *Rearing an Imperial Race,* xxxviii).

167. Saleeby, *Woman and Womanhood,* 269–271, quotes approvingly a correspondent to *The Times* on 24 December 1909, Sophie Bevan, who had pointed out the imbalance created both in the colonies and at home by the emigration of young men but not young women. Her letter emphasized that one result was "the appalling number of half-castes, a blot on the civilization of the State . . . the very worst type of population." Saleeby was anxious about the low (white) birthrate in the colonies and the "surplus" of women at home and points out that the emigrant woman would be better placed to exercise her "rightful function of choosing the best man to be her husband and the father of the future."

168. Sir William Church, at a meeting of the National Health Society, reported *BMJ* (2 July 1904): 32.

169. Rachel McMillan, as a traveling teacher of hygiene for Kent County Council in the 1890s, realized "that fragmentary help was almost useless": Margaret McMillan, *Life of Rachel McMillan*, 94. The books of Margaret Loane, district nurse, give a vivid picture of the way in which working-class housewives struggled against almost impossible conditions. See, for example. *An Englishman's Castle*, 1909, 75, 104–141, 167, 224–225; *Neighbours and Friends*, 1910, 294; and also T. C. Horsfall, *The Improvement of Dwellings and Surroundings of the People*, 1904, 167 passim.

170. Cadbury, Matheson, and Shann, *Women's Work and Wages*, 1906, 235.

171. Ibid., 161.

172. *An Englishman's Castle*, 64.

173. A not infrequent metaphor: see, for example, "Child Feeding, Motherhood and National Well-being," *Progress* (April 1907) (where in spite of the stress on the mother the actual suggestions made cater only to her children); and Saleeby, *Woman and Womanhood*, 323.

174. Elizabeth Sloan-Chesser, *Perfect Health for Women and Children*, 1912, 54.

175. William Hill-Climo, "Army Organization: The Recruit," *Empire Review* (1903): 361.

176. McCleary, *Infant Welfare Movement*, appendix, 159, 158. The socialist Robert Blatchford idealized home and mother in much the same way.

177. PP.1910, Cd.5131, xxiii. Report on the Working of the Education (Provision of Meals) Act. 1906.

178. See discussion on tablecloths versus easily cleaned oilcloth, at National Food Reform Association Conference. *Rearing an Imperial Race*, 88–89, and also pp. 17, 29–30.

179. Pritchard, *Infant Education*, 133.

180. For origins of society, see address by Sir J. A. Cockburn. *Child Study* 1 (April 1908); for its composition, see reports from branches, *Child Study* 3 (July 1910): 80. Besides Pritchard, Alice Ravenhill, Mary Scharlieb (eugenist doctor with strong line on women, author of a number of manuals on problems of infancy, girlhood, motherhood, venereal diseases, etc.,), and James Crichton Browne (a doctor with a long-standing interest in child health and national efficiency, and a firm belief in the powers of motherhood), all addressed meetings of the society and contributed to the journal.

181. H. Davy, "The Cultivation of the Mind in Children," *Child Study* (July 1908): 51–52. (He also recommends the mother of Little Lord Fauntleroy as ideal.)

182. C. T. Ewart, "Parenthood," *Empire Review* (February–July 1910): 319.

3

Of Mimicry and Man

The Ambivalence of Colonial Discourse

Homi Bhabha

Mimicry reveals something in so far as it is distinct from what might be called an itself that is behind. The effect of mimicry is camouflage. . . . It is not a question of harmonizing with the background, but against a mottled background, of becoming mottled—exactly like the technique of camouflage practised in human warfare.

—Jacques Lacan,
"The Line and Light," *Of the Gaze*

It is out of season to question at this time of day, the original policy of conferring on every colony of the British Empire a mimic representation of the British Constitution. But if the creature so endowed has sometimes forgotten its real insignificance and under the fancied importance of speakers and maces, and all the paraphernalia and ceremonies of the imperial legislature, has dared to defy the mother country, she has to thank herself for the folly of conferring such privileges on a condition of society that has no earthly claim to so exalted a position. A fundamental principle appears to have been forgotten or overlooked in our system of colonial policy—that of colonial dependence. To give to a colony the forms of independence is a mockery; she would not be a colony for a single hour if she could maintain an independent station.

—Sir Edward Cust,
"Reflections on West African Affairs . . .
addressed to the Colonial Office,"
Hatchard, London, 1839

The discourse of post-Enlightenment English colonialism often speaks in a tongue that is forked, not false. If colonialism takes power in the name of history, it repeatedly exercises its authority through the figures of farce. For the epic intention of the civilizing mission, "human and not wholly human" in the famous words of Lord Rosebery, "writ by the finger of the Divine"[1] often produces a text rich in the traditions of trompe l'oeil, irony, mimicry, and repetition. In this comic turn from the high ideals of the colonial imagination to its low mimetic literary effects, mimicry emerges as one of the most elusive and effective strategies of colonial power and knowledge.

Within that conflictual economy of colonial discourse that Edward Said[2] describes as the tension between the synchronic panoptical vision of domination—the demand for identity, stasis—and the counterpressure of the diachrony of history—change, difference—mimicry represents an *ironic* compromise. If I may adapt Samuel Weber's formulation of the marginalizing vision of castration,[3] then colonial mimicry is the desire for a reformed, recognizable Other, as *a subject of a difference that is almost the same, but not quite.* Which is to say that the discourse of mimicry is constructed around an *ambivalence;* in order to be effective, mimicry must continually produce its slippage, its excess, its difference. The authority of that mode of colonial discourse that I have called mimicry is therefore stricken by an indeterminacy: mimicry emerges as the representation of a difference that is itself a process of disavowal. Mimicry is, thus, the sign of a double articulation; a complex strategy of reform, regulation, and discipline, which "appropriates" the Other as it visualizes power. Mimicry is also the sign of the inappropriate, however, a difference or recalcitrance that coheres the dominant strategic function of colonial power, intensifies surveillance, and poses an immanent threat to both "normalized" knowledges and disciplinary powers.

The effect of mimicry on the authority of colonial discourse is profound and disturbing. For in "normalizing" the colonial state or subject, the dream of post-Enlightenment civility alienates its own language of liberty and produces another knowledge of its norms. The ambivalence that thus informs this strategy is discernible, for example, in Locke's Second Treatise, which *splits* to reveal the limitations of liberty in his double use of the word "slave": first simply, descriptively as the locus of a legitimate form of ownership, then as the trope for an intolerable, illegitimate exercise of power. What is articulated in that distance between the two uses is the absolute, imagined difference between the "Colonial" State of Carolina and the Original State of Nature.

It is from this area between mimicry and mockery, where the reforming, civilizing mission is threatened by the displacing gaze of its disciplinary double, that my instances of colonial imitation come. What they all share is a discursive process by which the excess or slippage produced by the *ambivalence* of mimicry (almost the same, *but not quite*) does not merely "rupture" the discourse, but becomes transformed into an uncertainty which fixes the colonial subject as a "partial" presence. By "partial" I mean both "incomplete" and "virtual." It is as if the very emergence of the "colonial" is dependent for its representation upon some strategic limitation or prohibition *within* the authoritative discourse itself. The success of colonial appropriation depends on a proliferation of inappropriate objects that ensure its strategic failure, so that mimicry is at once resemblance and menace.

A classic text of such partiality is Charles Grant's "Observations on the State of Society among the Asiatic Subjects of Great Britain" (1792),[4] which was only superseded by James Mill's *History of India* as the most influential early nineteenth-century account of Indian manners and morals. Grant's dream of an evangelical system of mission education conducted uncompromisingly in English was partly a belief in political reform along Christian lines and partly an awareness that the expansion of company rule in India required a system of "interpellation"—a reform of manners, as Grant put it, that would provide the colonial with "a sense of personal identity as we know it." Caught between the desire for religious reform and the fear that the Indians might become turbulent for liberty, Grant implies that it is, in fact, the "partial" diffusion of Christianity and the "partial" influence of moral improvements will construct a particularly appropriate form of colonial subjectivity. What is suggested is a process of reform through which Christian doctrines might collude with divisive caste practices to prevent dangerous political alliances. Inadvertently, Grant produces a knowledge of Christianity as a form of social control that conflicts with the enunciatory assumptions that authorize his discourse. In suggesting, finally, that "partial reform" will produce an empty form of "the *imitation* of English manners which will induce them [the colonial subjects] to remain under our protection,"[5] Grant mocks his moral project and violates the Evidences of Christianity—a central missionary tenet—which forbade any tolerance of heathen faiths.

The absurd extravagance of Macaulay's *Infamous Minute* (1835)—deeply influenced by Charles Grant's *Observations*—makes a mockery of Oriental learning until faced with the challenge of conceiving of a "reformed" colonial subject. Then the great tradition of European humanism seems capable only of ironizing itself. At the intersection of European learning and colonial power, Macaulay can conceive of nothing other than "a class of interpreters between us and the millions whom we govern—a class of persons Indian in blood and colour, but English in tastes, in opinions, in morals and in intellect"[6]—in other words, a mimic man raised "through our English School," as a missionary educationist wrote in 1819, "to form a corps of translators and be employed in different departments of Labour."[7] The line of descent of the mimic man can be traced through the works of Kipling, Forester, Orwell, Naipaul, and to his emergence, most recently, in Benedict Anderson's excellent essay on nationalism, as the anomalous Bipin Chandra Pal.[8] He is the effect of a flawed colonial mimesis, in which to be Anglicized is *emphatically* not to be English.

The figure of mimicry is locatable within what Anderson describes as "the inner incompatibility of empire and nation."[9] It problematizes the signs of racial and cultural priority, so that the "national" is no longer naturalizable. What emerges between mimesis and mimicry is a *writing,* a mode of representation, that marginalizes the monumentality of history, quite simply mocks its power to be a model, that power which supposedly makes it imitable. Mimicry *repeats* rather than *re-presents,* and in that diminishing perspective emerges Decoud's displaced European's vision of Sulaco as

> the endlessness of civil strife where folly seemed even harder to bear than its ignominy . . . the lawlessness of a populace of all colours and races, barbarism, irremediable tyranny. . . . America is ungovernable.[10]

Or Ralph Singh's apostasy in Naipaul's *The Mimic Men:*

> We pretended to be real, to be learning, to be preparing ourselves for life, we mimic men of the New World, one unknown corner of it, with all its reminders of the corruption that came so quickly to the new.[11]

Both Decoud and Singh, and in their different ways Grant and Macaulay, are the parodists of history. Despite their intentions and invocations they inscribe the colonial text erratically, eccentrically across a body politic that refuses to be representative, in a narrative that refuses to be representational. The desire to emerge as "authentic" through mimicry—through a process of writing and repetition—is the final irony of partial representation.

What I have called mimicry is not the familiar exercise of *dependent* colonial relations through narcissistic identification so that, as Fanon has observed,[12] the black man stops being an actional person for only the white man can represent his self-esteem. Mimicry conceals no presence or identity behind its mask: it is not what Césaire describes as "colonization-thingification"[13] behind which there stands the essence of the *présence Africaine.* The *menace* of mimicry is its *double* vision, which in disclosing the ambivalence of colonial discourse also disrupts its authority. And it is a double vision that is a result of what I've described as the partial representation/recognition of the colonial object. Grant's colonial as partial imitator, Macaulay's translator, Naipaul's colonial politician as play actor, Decoud as the scene setter of the *opéra bouffe* of the New World, these are the appropriate objects of a colonialist chain of command, authorized versions of otherness. But they are also, as I have shown, the figures of a doubling, the part-objects of a metonymy of colonial desire that alienates the modality and normality of those dominant discourses in which they emerge as "inappropriate" colonial subjects. A desire that, through the repetition of *partial presence,* which is the basis of mimicry, articulates those disturbances of cultural, racial, and historical difference that menace the narcissistic demand of colonial authority. It is a desire that reverses "in part" the colonial appropriation by now producing a partial vision of the colonizer's presence. A gaze of otherness, that shares the acuity of the genealogical gaze that, as Michel Foucault describes it, liberates marginal elements and shatters the unity of man's being through which he extends his sovereignty.[14]

I want to turn to this process by which the look of surveillance returns as the displacing gaze of the disciplined, where the observer becomes the observed and "partial" representation rearticulates the whole notion of *identity* and alienates it from essence. But not before observing that even an exemplary history like Eric Stokes's *The English Utilitarians in India* acknowledges the anomalous gaze of otherness but finally disavows it in a contradictory utterance.

> Certainly India played *no* central part in fashioning the distinctive qualities of English civilisation. In many ways it acted as a disturbing force, a magnetic power placed at the periphery tending to distort the natural development of Britain's character.[15]

What is the nature of the hidden threat of the partial gaze? How does mimicry emerge as the subject of the scopic drive and the object of colonial surveillance? How is desire disciplined, authority displaced?

If we turn to a Freudian figure to address these issues of colonial textuality, that form of difference that is mimicry—*almost the same but not quite*—will become clear. Writing of the partial nature of fantasy, caught *inappropriately,* between the unconscious and the preconscious, making problematic, like mimicry, the very notion of "origins," Freud has this to say:

> Their mixed and split origin is what decides their fate. We may compare them with individuals of mixed race who taken all round resemble white men but who betray their coloured descent by some striking feature or other and on that account are excluded from society and enjoy none of the privileges.[16]

Almost the same but not white: the visibility of mimicry is always produced at the site of interdiction. It is a form of colonial discourse that is uttered *inter dicta:* a discourse at the crossroads of what is known and permissible and that which though known must be kept concealed; a discourse uttered between the lines and as such both against the rules and within them. The question of the representation of difference is therefore always also a problem of authority. The "desire" of mimicry, which is Freud's *striking feature* that reveals so little but makes such a big difference, is not merely that impossibility of the Other which repeatedly resists signification. The desire of colonial mimicry—an interdictory desire—may not have an object, but it has strategic objectives that I shall call the *metonymy of presence.*

Those inappropriate signifiers of colonial discourse—the difference between being English and being Anglicized; the identity between stereotypes that through repetition, also become different; the discriminatory identities constructed across traditional cultural norms and classifications, the Simian Black, the Lying Asiatic—all these are metonymies of presence. They are strategies of desire in discourse that make the anomalous representation of the colonized something other than a process of "the return of the repressed," what Fanon unsatisfactorily characterized as collective catharsis.[17] These instances of metonymy are the nonrepressive productions of contradictory and multiple belief. They cross the boundaries of the culture of enunciation through a strategic confusion of the metaphoric and metonymic axes of the cultural production of meaning. For each of these instances of "a difference that is almost the same but not quite" inadvertently creates a crisis for the cultural priority given to the *metaphoric* as the process of repression and substitution which negotiates the difference between paradigmatic systems and classifi-cations. In mimicry, the representation of identity and meaning is rearticulated along the axis of metonymy. As Lacan reminds us, mimicry is like camouflage, not a harmonization or repression of difference, but a form of resemblance that differs/defends presence by displaying it in part, metonymically. Its threat, I would add, comes from the prodigious and strategic production of conflictual, fantastic, discriminatory "identity effects" in the play of a power that is elusive because it hides no essence, no "itself." And that form of *resemblance* is the most terrifying thing to behold, as Edward Long testifies in his *History of Jamaica* (1774). At the end of a tortured, negrophobic passage, that shifts anxiously between piety, prevarication, and perversion, the text finally con-fronts its fear; nothing other than the repetition of its resemblance "in part": "[Negroes] are represented by all authors as the vilest of human kind, to which they have little more pretension of resemblance *than what arises from their exterior forms.*"[18]

From such a colonial encounter between the white presence and its black semblance, there emerges the question of the ambivalence of mimicry as a problematic of colonial subjection. For if Sade's scandalous theatricalization of language repeatedly reminds us that discourse can claim "no priority," then the work of Edward Said will not let us forget that the "ethnocentric and erratic will to power from which texts can spring"[19] is itself a theater of war. Mimicry, as the metonymy of presence, is, indeed, such an erratic, eccentric strategy of authority in colonial discourse. Mimicry does not merely destroy narcissistic authority through the repetitious slippage of difference and desire. It is the process of the *fixation* of the colonial as a form of cross-classificatory, dis-criminatory knowledge in the defiles of an interdictory discourse, and therefore necessarily raises the question of the *authorization* of colonial representations. A question of authority that goes beyond the subject's lack of priority (cas-tration) to a historical crisis in the conceptuality of colonial man as an *object* of regulatory power, as the subject of racial, cultural, national representation.

"This culture . . . fixed in its colonial status," Fanon suggests, "[is] both present and mummified, it testified against its members. It defines them in fact without appeal."[20] The ambivalence of mimicry—almost but not quite— suggests that the fetishized colonial culture is potentially and strategically an insurgent counterappeal. What I have called its "identity-effects" are always crucially *split*. Under cover of camouflage, mimicry, like the fetish, is a part-object that radically revalues the normative knowledges of the priority of race, writing, history. For the fetish mimes the forms of authority at the point at which it deauthorizes them. Similarly, mimicry rearticulates presence in terms of its "otherness," that which it disavows. There is a crucial difference between this *colonial* articulation of man and his doubles and that which Foucault describes as "thinking the unthought,"[21] which, for nineteenth-century Europe, is the ending of man's alienation by reconciling him with his essence. The colonial discourse that articulates an *interdictory* "otherness" is precisely the "other scene" of this nineteenth-century European desire for an authentic historical consciousness.

The "unthought" across which colonial man is articulated is that process of classificatory confusion that I have described as the metonymy of the substitutive chain of ethical and cultural discourse. This results in the *splitting* of colonial discourse so that two attitudes towards external reality persist; one takes reality into consideration while the other disavows it and replaces it by a product of desire that repeats, rearticulates "reality" as mimicry.

So Edward Long can say with authority, quoting variously, Hume, Eastwick, and Bishop Warburton in his support, "Ludicrous as the opinion may seem I do not think that an orangutang husband would be any dishonour to a Hottentot female."[22]

Such contradictory articulations of reality and desire—seen in racist stereotypes, statements, jokes, myths—are not caught in the doubtful circle of the return of the repressed. They are the effects of a disavowal that denies the differences of the Other but produces in its stead forms of authority and multiple belief that alienate the assumptions of "civil" discourse. If, for a while, the ruse of desire is calculable for the uses of discipline, soon the repetition of guilt, justification, pseudoscientific theories, superstition, spurious authorities, and classifications can be seen as the desperate effort to "normalize" *formally* the disturbance of a discourse of splitting that violates the rational, enlightened claims of its enunciatory modality. The ambivalence of colonial authority repeatedly turns from *mimicry*—a difference that is almost nothing but not quite—to *menace*—a difference that is almost total but not quite. And in that other scene of colonial power, where history turns to farce and presence to "a part," can be seen the twin figures of narcissism and paranoia that repeat furiously, uncontrollably.

In the ambivalent world of the "not quite/not white," on the margins of metropolitan desire, the *founding objects* of the Western world become the erratic, eccentric, accidental *objects trouvés* of the colonial discourse—the part-objects of presence. It is then that the body and the book lose their representational authority. Black skin splits under the racist gaze, displaced into signs of bestiality, genitalia, grotesquerie, which reveal the phobic myth of the undifferentiated whole white body. And the holiest of books—the Bible—bearing both the standard of the cross and the standard of empire finds itself strangely dismembered. In May 1817 a missionary wrote from Bengal,

> Still everyone would gladly receive a Bible. And why?—that he may lay it up as a curiosity for a few pice; or use it for waste paper. Such it is well known has been the common fate of these copies of the Bible. . . . Some have been bartered in the markets, others have been thrown in snuff shops and used as wrapping paper.[23]

Notes

This chapter was first presented as a contribution to a panel on "Colonialist and Post-Colonialist Discourse," organized by Gayatri Chakravorty Spivak for the Modern Language Association Convention in New York, December 1983. I would like to thank Professor Spivak for inviting me to participate on the panel and Dr. Stephan Feuchtwang for his advice in the preparation of the paper.

1. Cited in Eric Stokes, *The Political Ideas of English Imperialism* (Oxford: Oxford University Press, 1960), 17–18.

2. Edward Said, *Orientalism* (New York: Pantheon Books, 1978), 240.

3. Samuel Weber, "The Sideshow, Or: Remarks on a Canny Moment," *Modern Language Notes* 88, no. 6 (1973): 1112.

4. Charles Grant, "Observations on the State of Society among the Asiatic Subjects of Great Britain," *Sessional Papers* 1812–13, 10 (282), East India Company.

5. Ibid., chap. 4, p. 104.

6. T. B. Macaulay, "Minute on Education," in *Sources of Indian Tradition,* vol. 2, ed. William Theodore de Bary (New York: Columbia University Press, 1958), 49.

7. Mr. Thomason's communication to the Church Missionary Society, September 5, 1819, in *The Missionary Register,* 1821, 54–55.

8. Benedict Anderson, *Imagined Communities* (London: Verso, 1983), 88.

9. Ibid., 88–89.

10. Joseph Conrad, *Nostromo* (London: Penguin, 1979), 161.

11. V. S. Naipaul, *The Mimic Men* (London: Penguin, 1967), 146.

12. Frantz Fanon, *Black Skin, White Masks* (London, Paladin, 1970), 109.

13. Aimé Césaire, *Discourse on Colonialism* (New York: Monthly Review Press, 1972), 21.

14. Michel Foucault, "Nietzsche, Genealogy History," in *Language, Counter-Memory, Practice,* trans. Donald F. Bouchard and Sherry Simon (Ithaca: Cornell University Press, 1977), 153.

15. Eric Stokes, *The English Utilitarians and India* (Oxford: Oxford University Press, 1959), xi.

16. Sigmund Freud, "The Unconscious" (1915), *SE,* XIV: 190–191.

17. Fanon, *Black Skin, White Masks,* 103.

18. Edward Long, *A History of Jamaica* (1774), 2:353.

19. Edward Said, "The Text, the World, the Critic," in *Textual Strategies,* ed. J. V. Harari, (Ithaca: Cornell University Press, 1979), 184.

20. Frantz Fanon, "Racism and Culture," in *Toward the African Revolution* (London: Pelican, 1967), 44.

21. Michel Foucault, *The Order of Things* (New York: Pantheon, 1970), pt. 2, chap. 9.

22. Long, *A History of Jamaica,* 364.

23. *The Missionary Register,* May 1817, 186.

Part Two

Making Boundaries

4

Images of Empire, Contests of Conscience

Models of Colonial Domination in South Africa

John L. Comaroff

This argument, vaguely political in nature, took place as often as the two men met. It was a topsy-turvy affair, for the Englishman was bitterly anti-English and the Indian [Dr. Veraswami] fanatically loyal. . . .

"My dear doctor," said Flory, "how can you make out that we are in this country for any purpose except to steal? It is so simple . . . the British Empire is a device for giving trade monopolies to the English—or rather gangs of Jews and Scotchmen."

"My friend, it is pathetic to hear you talk so. . . . [W]hile your businessmen develop the resources of our country, your officials are civilizing us, elevating us to their level, from pure public spirit. . . . [Y]ou have brought us law and order. The unswerving British Justice and Pax Britannica."

"Pox Britannica, doctor, Pox Britannica."

—George Orwell, *Burmese Days*

In the mid-1820s, John Philip, superintendent of the London Missionary Society at the Cape, stepped up his controversial campaign for the right of "coloured peoples" to sell their labor in a free market (Ross 1986: 77 ff.). His

arguments, laid out in *Researches in South Africa,* called on no less an authority
than Adam Smith: the "vassalage" of the coloreds, he declared (1828, 1:367),
not only violated the "principles of political economy"; it also had a "de-
pressing" moral effect on the entire population, making the "aborigines" into
worthless miscreants and their masters into idle tyrants. Anticipating both
Durkheim and Hegel, Philip, a technician of the soul, evoked the body corporeal
to drive home his organic vision of colonialism: "The different members of
a state [are] beautifully represented by the members of the human body: . . .
if one member suffers, all the members suffer"; a corollary being that "the
peculiar vices of all ranks of the inhabitants are the vices of the system" (pp.
386, 388). Hence it was that, by freeing the coloreds, "the colonists and their
families . . . [would themselves] be converted into useful farmers." With a
rhetorical, historical flourish the good reverend added: "To what does England
owe the subversion of the feudal system, and its high rank among the nations
of the world, but to the emancipation and elevation of its peasantry?" And that
through self-possessed labor, private property, and the removal of all forms of
servitude.

Such arguments had long been aired in Britain, of course. Questions about
the morality and the control of free labor lay at the heart of the abolitionist
debate—itself part of the reconstruction, during the Age of Revolution, of
bourgeois ideology in the image of industrial capitalism. Consequently, Philip's position had wide support in Whitehall, Exeter Hall, and church halls all
over England. But in South Africa the situation was different. The colonists
were simply not used to being told that they would become a useful agrarian
bourgeoisie if only they allowed their laborers to cultivate in freedom. Nor did
the missionary stop at delivering sermons on the theory of political economy.
He also confronted the colonial government with its practical failings. Official
policy might have spoken the language of free labor, but existing conditions,
he alleged, encouraged administrators to perpetuate sundry forms of vassalage.
Take this example, from a passage entitled "Interest of the Colonial Functionaries in the Oppression of the Aborigines":

> The landed proprietors of South Africa depend on the price of labour, and the
> number of hands they can command; and it is obvious, while things remain in
> this state, . . . magistrates [and other functionaries] are under . . . temptation to
> oppress the people by enslaving them, and keeping down the price of labour.
> (1828, 1:346 f.)

And many of them did so on a regular basis, he added—naming names. Pax
Britannica, for Philip as for the fictional Flory, left much to be desired.

Not surprisingly, John Philip was sued by one of those censured in his
Researches; the Supreme Court at the Cape awarded William Mackay substantial damages—and seriously admonished the missionary for his impolitic

behavior (Ross 1986: 116 ff.; Macmillan 1927). In England, however, the latter was seen as something of a martyr to a particular model of colonialism. His debt was paid by subscription among churchmen, philanthropists, and liberal politicians, and his crusade became a touchstone in the struggle, within the colonizing culture, to refashion the imperial project. For one thing became clear amid all the legalities and loud acrimony: Philip had done more than call into question the deeds of a few of His Majesty's servants at a remote British outpost. Whether he intended it or not, he had opened up to scrutiny some of the less obvious contradictions of the colonial enterprise itself. Such was the effect of his oft-repeated claim that the tensions of empire flowed not from the idiosyncratic intentions of its agents, their "peculiar vices"; that they grew, rather, out of the "vices of the system" at large. The nature of South African colonialism had become, as it remains today, the subject of an argument of structures and practices.

Images of Colonialism

The image of colonialism as a coherent, monolithic process seems, at last, to be wearing thin. That is why we are concerned here with the tensions of empire, not merely its triumphs; with the contradictions of colonialism, not just its crushing progress. This is not to diminish the brute domination suffered by the colonized peoples of the modern world, or to deny the Orwellian logic on which imperial projects are founded. Nor is it to deconstruct colonialism as a global movement. It is, instead, to broaden our analytic compass; to take in its moments of incoherence and inchoateness, its internal contortions and complexities. Above all, it is to treat as problematic the *making* of both colonizers and colonized in order to understand better the forces that, over time, have drawn them into an extraordinarily intricate web of relations. This goes much further than to restate the commonplace that the colonizing process is characterized by occasional conflict, as well as common interest, among its perpetrators—be they administrators or industrialists, merchants or militia, the crown or the cloth. To be sure, its contradictions everywhere run far deeper than are suggested by the tensions visible on the surface planes of empire.

In short, colonialism, as an object of historical anthropology, has reached a moment of new reckoning. My contribution to this moment is, by design, narrowly focused. I shall explore the making, as agents of empire, of the nonconformist missionaries to the Griqua and Tswana, the peoples of the northern frontier of early nineteenth-century South Africa. The shaping of these historical figures—which began on the changing ideological and social scape of contemporary Britain—reveals much about the contradictions of colonialism, here and elsewhere. It goes without saying that the making of any historical actor is crucial to his or her actions in the making of history; that the latter cannot be fully understood except in relation to the former. In the case of the evangelists of the London Missionary Society (LMS) and Wesleyan Methodist Missionary Society (WMMS) in South Africa, however, there are two unusually compelling reasons for this.

First, these men, the vanguards of empire and its most active ideological agents, came from the interstices of a class structure undergoing reconstruction; many of them, as we shall see, were caught uneasily between a displaced peasantry, an expanding proletariat, and the lower reaches of the rising British bourgeoisie (Beidelman 1982: 50). On the colonial stage itself, they were quite clearly a "dominated fraction of the dominant class" (Bourdieu 1984: 421), the ruled among the rulers. This was exacerbated by the fact that most of them regarded themselves—and were regarded by their compatriots—as "friends and protectors of the natives" (see for example Wilson 1976). It was a position that often set them at odds with others in the colonial division of labor, particularly those from different fractions of the dominant class (cf. Trapido 1980: passim; Legassick 1980: 46; Newton-King 1980: 198 f.; Bundy 1979). Consequently, in viewing the colonial process through their eyes—focused as they were by the ambiguities of their own social situation—we gain an especially penetrating insight into its internal struggles and inconsistencies.

Second, the nonconformist missionaries, bearers of the Protestant ethic in the capitalist age, saw themselves not merely as heroic figures in the creation of a new Empire of the Spirit in Africa. They also took themselves to be the conscience of British colonialism, its moral commentators; to wit, it was this self-appointed stance that was later to legitimize their occasional forays into colonial politics. In their writings are rehearsed all the arguments of images and ideology, of dreams and schemes, voiced among the colonizers as they debated the manner in which natives should be ruled, their worlds reconstructed. It is noteworthy that, for all the enormous literature on African missions, this aspect of their historical role is perhaps the least documented. And yet it gives their perspective a singular vantage—indeed, a significant advantage—in revealing the tensions of empire, the contradictions of colonialism.

I begin, then, by tracing the missions back to the society that spawned them, Britain circa 1810–1840. In so doing, I concentrate first on the spirit of the age: on those of its social features and ideological discourses that were to affect the colonial process and the part of the churchmen in it. Thereafter, I shall examine the background of these churchmen, locating them on the changing social landscape of the time. In all this, I seek to provide a kind of imaginative sociology—that is, a sketch of the social and cultural forms that shaped their imagined world, their life context as they regarded it. On the basis of that sociology, I shall follow the evangelists onto the colonial stage itself, looking through their gaze at its conflicts of images and practices.

The Origins of the Colonial Mission in South Africa: Britain 1810–1840

By 1810, the industrial revolution had cut deep into the physical, social, and cultural terrain of Britain. The very term *"industrial* revolution'' tends to direct our gaze toward its productive ecology and its technological bases; the machine, after all, was the dominant metaphor of the age. And there is no doubting the importance of its material and technical aspects, or its complex impact on the fabric of everyday life. At the same time, it is difficult to disagree with the many scholars, of both Right and Left, for whom the essence of the industrial revolution lay in the transformation of relations of production and, concomitantly, relations among classes. This is not to say that capitalist forms were not foreshadowed in eighteenth-century commerce and agriculture, or that social distinctions did not exist before the rise of the factory system; simply that the revolution hinged on the reconstruction of the division of labor and, with it, the social order at large.

Regarded in this light, the industrial revolution has been portrayed as the triumph of a "conquering bourgeoisie" (Hobsbawm 1962: 19) over a proletariat vanquished in the process of its making (Thompson 1963). Certainly, its polarizing effect on Britain was palpable at the time, signs of class consciousness and conflict being everywhere visible, from the passing of the Combination Acts to the outbreak of Luddism (Hobsbawm 1964: 5 f.). Moreover, it sparked an often bitter controversy over the effects of industrialization, an argument between "optimists" and "pessimists" that found its way into artistic and literary expression as well as scholarly debate (Briggs 1959: 14; 1979: 33). Nonetheless, for all the vital imagery that cast the common people against lordly tyrants (Shelley 1882: 164), "vulgar rich" against "ill-used" worker (Anon. 1847), or benign captains of industry against the ungrateful, improving masses, it would be simplifying matters to describe the emerging social structure purely in terms of two classes locked in mortal embrace.

The point will turn out to be crucial for us. Interestingly, it was appreciated by a remarkable man of the period, William Dodd. Dodd had no schooling and was forced into twenty-five years of mill work, during which he lost an arm but learned to write movingly of his experiences. His letters, published anonymously in 1847, are extraordinary enough; but more astonishing still is his introduction to them. In it, he gives an account of social and economic divisions in England, assessing that there existed eight classes. Four (royalty; nobility; capitalists; and gentlemen of trade, the professions, and the clergy) were "privileged"; they made the law and profited from the toils of others (p. 11 f.). The latter (skilled laborers; common laborers; honorable paupers; and the dishonorable poor) composed the nonprivileged mass, from which ascent was "attended with difficulty." Others had spoken of class in broadly similar terms before; notably, Charles Hall (1805). Dodd, however, made two observations of particular salience here: that neither of the strata, the privileged or the poor, was solidary or united, each being caught up in its own affinities and antagonisms; and that the "humbler . . . clergy," as the most poorly paid members of the privileged ranks, occupied their lowest, least secure reaches.

These observations were clearly correct. Within the upper orders, relations between the increasingly powerful industrial bourgeoisie and the landed aristocracy were often difficult and always ambiguous. And, for their part, the "nonprivileged" were differentiated according to their positions in the social division of labor—differences that fragmented the workforce and were used to exercise control over it. The dominant ideology of the period also separated laboring men from the undeserving poor. Where the deserts of the former would one day be recognized by the great accountant in the sky, the destiny of the latter was eternal condemnation to a satanic hell that looked for all the world like a Mancunian foundry.

An important corollary of the internal fragmentation of the classes was that upward mobility presented itself as a possibility for those who "improved" themselves. There was little to stop a common laborer from becoming a craftsman; or the son of a skilled worker, a clerk in the lower levels of the privileged orders. Or so the poor were told incessantly from the pulpit and in the press. Without such gradations across the major lines of class, this would have been implausible. A pauper could not envision becoming a prince, and only the most star-crossed chimneysweep aspired to be a captain of industry. Those who did make their way up the social ladder, though, often found themselves not secure members of a more elevated class but the bearers of anomalous rank; neither of the rich nor of the poor, of the ruling nor of the ruled. Caught in the fissures of the class structure, they were suspended between the privileged, whose values they shared, and the impoverished, from whence they came—and to whom, if they failed, they would return. This is where Dodd's second observation becomes significant. Low churchmen, more than anyone else, personified the process: many of them, especially in northern parishes, were former artisans or peasants who had climbed, unsteadily, into the middle class. And, lacking wealth or distinction, they clung tenuously to their new social position.

Here, then, is the thread that weaves together the general and the particular. In the large-scale processes of the industrial revolution was forged the specific context from which arose the army of nonconformist missionaries to South Africa. The fact that they came from here—from the ideological core yet the social margins of bourgeois Britain—was not only to affect their place in colonial society and its politics. It was also to shape the moral terms in which they were to deal both with other Europeans and with the "savage" on the frontiers of empire. For their own biographies, built on an unremitting commitment to self-improvement, were the very embodiment of the spirit of capitalism, a living testimonial to its ethical and material workings. And inasmuch as they were to evangelize and civilize by personal example—itself part and parcel of bourgeois morality—the road along which they were to lead the heathen was to retrace their own pathways through British society. Or, rather, toward an image of that society as they wished to see it. And what they wished to see was a neat fusion of three idealized worlds: the rational, capitalist age in its most ideologically roseate form, wherein unfettered individuals were free to better themselves; an idyllic countryside in which, alongside agrarian estates, hardworking peasants, equipped with suitable tools and techniques, produced gainfully for the market; and a sovereign ''Empire of God,'' whose temporal affairs remained securely under divine authority. Later, when we return to the roots of the South African evangelists, we shall see why these particular imagined worlds should have been so important to them. First, however, let us examine each in turn. Not only do they give us yet greater insight into the spirit of the era; they also bring us a step closer to the colonial encounter.

Imagined Worlds: (1) The Individual and Civilized Society

The triumph of the bourgeoisie in the age of revolution was most visibly expressed in the dominant worldview of early capitalism—in particular, its stress on utilitarian individualism and the virtues of the disciplined, self-made person; on private property and status as measures of success, poverty as appropriate sanction for failure; on enlightened self-interest and the free market as an instrument of the common good; on reason and method, science and technology, as the key to the progress of mankind. These values did not go uncontested, of course. For all the philosophical support they enjoyed in the liberalism of Bentham and Mill, they were freely questioned in the artistic work of the likes of Shelley and Blake; for all their backing in the political economy of Smith and Ricardo, they were subject to outspoken socialist critique and to the vocal objection of a fraction of the working class. Indeed, the entire history of the British labor movement from the late eighteenth century onward has been a discourse on precisely this ideology. Still, the revolution confidently forecast by Engels (1968 chap. 9) did not arise from the squalor of Manchester. As Matthew Arnold (1903: viii) was to muse in 1865, even such popular organs as the *Saturday Review* had observed that Britain had ''finally anchored itself, in the fulness of perfected knowledge, on Benthamism.''

Perfected knowledge or not, the rise of capitalism, by its very nature, entailed the inculcation of a set of signs and images into the collective consciousness of Britain. Among these, perhaps the most far-reaching concerned the essence of the person.[1] Classic liberalism posited a world consisting of self-contained, right-bearing individuals who created society by the sum of their actions. "Universal History," declaimed Carlyle (1842: 1), is the history of what great men accomplish. In its popular form, this philosophical individualism saw people less as products of a social context than as autonomous beings—Daltonian "atoms," says Élie Halévy (1924: 505)—with the capacity to construct themselves if they set their minds and bodies to the task. Further, the *self* was viewed as a divided entity (Foucault 1975: 197). On the one hand, it was the core of subjectivity: "I," the center from which a person looked out and acted on the world. On the other, it was an object: "me, myself," something of which "I" could become (self-) conscious and subject to (self-) restraint or indulgence. As Reed (1975: 289) and others note, this divided self was to be a ubiquitous presence in Victorian literature, colonizing popular consciousness through such vehicles as the novel, the theater, the tract, and the diary.

The immediate corollary of such a conception of self was that the social values of bourgeois ideology could be internalized as qualities of individual *person*ality. Thus the virtues of discipline, generosity, and ownership, to name a few, were embodied in self-control, self-denial, and self-possession; conversely, hedonism and indolence were, literally, self-destructive. No wonder that one archetype of the success story in contemporary heroic novels was the "self-made man," who often turned out to be a manufacturer.[2] This image of the person was cogently expressed in the doctrine of self-improvement; the notion that, through methodical behavior and the avoidance of indulgence, one might better oneself—the reward being upward mobility for men, upward nubility for women. In this respect, the outer shell of the individual was a gauge of inner essence. Neat dress and a healthy body spoke of a worthy heart and an alert mind (Haley 1978). What is more, the subjective "I" was in a position to monitor the progress of the objective self.

Self-evidently, this ideology of personhood saturated the popular discourses of the time. Take, for instance, the link between self-improvement and literacy. For all the debate in some circles as to whether the poor should be educated, reading took on a doubly positive connotation. Not only did it expand the mind; it also engaged the self in a properly profound manner. For, in addressing the written text, readers internalized it, reflected on it in the deepest recesses of their being, and entered with it into a silent conversation. And, in the process, they came to know better both the outer world and their inner selves. The rise of literacy in the nineteenth century might have been encouraged by the commoditization of the printed word (Anderson 1983: 38 f.). But its social impact was closely tied to the ascendance of the reflective, inner-directed self.

The partibility of the self—later to reappear as a "scientific" principle in, among other things, Freudian psychology—also manifested itself in the "natural" oppositions of mind and body, spirit and essence, consciousness and being, which came to loom so large in post-enlightenment thought (Spicker 1970). Even more crucial for the development of capitalism, it underlay the notion that individuals could separate from the rest of their being, and sell, a part of themselves: their capacity for work (Marx 1967: pt. 2, chap. 6). We all know the implications that follow. Inasmuch as commodity production entailed the exchange of labor power between worker and capitalist, it demanded a standardized measure of quantity (for human effort) and a universal medium of remuneration (for pay). The latter is money; the former, time. And both can be spent or used, wasted or owned.

As time and money became vehicles for dividing the self, so they came to mediate the rhythms of everyday life, detaching work time from leisure time, workplace from home, wage labor from unpaid domestic toil, production from consumption; imbricated in all this being the sanctification of the nuclear family with its engendered division of labor, the distinction between public and private domains, and other familiar signs and practices of a rising capitalist order. That time and money were explicitly equated in the early nineteenth century is nicely demonstrated by Thompson (1967: 87), who also shows that the growing salience of the clock resonated with both secular and Protestant ideas of discipline and self-improvement. So did the notion that wealth was a just reward for effort. Wesley, after all, had spoken of its "precious talents" (Warner 1930: 155); for him it was a true measure of human worth, at once spiritual and material.

It is not necessary, after Weber and Tawney, to labor the connections—ideological, symbolic, even aesthetic[3]—between industrial capitalism and Protestantism, bourgeois culture and liberal individualism. Notwithstanding theological differences over such questions as predestination and salvation, Protestantism envisaged the human career as a cumulative moral voyage, unrelieved by the possibility of atonement or absolution. The person, as a self-determining being, laid up treasures in heaven in the same way as he or she did on earth—by ascetic effort, neighborly duty, and good works. This person could not be a slave—at least, not for the nonconformists who were to evangelize South Africa, some of whom were active abolitionists. For them, it was through free labor and commerce, self-willed moral and material improvement, that the heathen was going to pave the road to personal salvation.

At the same time, nonconformism was quick to affirm the premises of an unequal society—at home and abroad. In preaching self-realization through work and duty, it exhorted the poor to make peace with their lot. Thus, for example, while Wesley set out to give a sense of worth to the troubled masses, and to draw them into secure social and spiritual communities, he assumed that "the labor relationship was an ethical one" (Warner 1930: 146 f.). Employee and master had different functions by virtue of divine calling, the spiritual status of each depending on the manner in which he fulfilled his appointed role. As this implies, "a diversity of ranks" was taken to be perfectly natural and eternal (p. 125). At a stroke, the alienating experience of wage labor became the necessary cost of salvation, and inequality was made into a sacred instrument of moral sanction. Although he advocated fair pay and prices, Wesley was as vociferous as any industrialist in decrying agitation by workers: "meddling" on the part of "those who are given to change" might threaten the providential market and, even worse, encourage sloth on the part of the poor.

The nonconformist missions were to export these images of selfhood and society, transposing them from factory and foundry, mine and mill, pithead and pulpit onto African soil. But other members of the dominant class—settlers, merchants, and administrators among them—were also caught up in the spirit of the age. Not all of them read its signs and images in the same way, however—at least as they were to apply to the colonized. Quite the opposite: it was such things as the future of African personhood, labor, and literacy that the bearers of empire were to contest among themselves.

Imagined Worlds: (2) The City and the Countryside

For those who lamented a paradise lost to the cause of the industrial revolution, the idealized British past was situated in a pristine countryside cast timelessly in the early eighteenth century. This idyll was inhabited by three estates: (1) the feudal establishment, in which lord and servant were bound in a web of mutual obligation; (2) the yeomanry, independent peasants who "[produced] for the market, themselves employing wage-labour, and shared the outlook and interests of gentlemen and merchants rather than of landless labourers and subsistence husbandmen" (Hill 1969: 70); and (3) a mass of poor, honest smallholders engaged in both agriculture and domestic industry. In the public perception, the last two categories were often lumped together as one and romanticized as the "perfect Republic of Shepherds and Agriculturalists" (Wordsworth [1835] 1948: 54).

More than anything else perhaps, the transformation of the countryside was associated, in the British imagination, with the fall of the yeomanry—itself a process dramatized by the migration of many people to bleak northern cities. Its passing, typically ascribed to enclosure and the agrarian revolution that preceded industrialization, was taken by many to signal the unraveling of the social fabric at large.[4] In the eye of contemporary beholders, the yeomanry had embodied a "traditional" lifestyle in which domestic groups, with their customary division of labor, produced more than enough for their own needs and were free to enjoy the fruits of their toil; in which households were securely embedded in communities of kin and neighbors; in which the independence of the family was guaranteed by its private estate and its social position.[5]

This vision may have had a slim basis in history (Briggs 1959: 40). Yet its appeal is attested by the fact that the nineteenth-century reformers who sparked most public interest were those who undertook to stitch back together the torn social fabric. For example, Owen's popularity among workers seems to have lain in his attempt "to reconcile . . . industry with domestic employment," and his promise of "a return to the rural existence [with its] family and community life" (Thomis 1974: 148). In this respect, Hill (1969: 272) has suggested that the transformation of the landscape subsumed, in a nutshell, the antagonism between the new bourgeoisie and the working class. The bitterness of the poor, he argues, flowed as much from having been dispossessed of their land as from their resentment at being forced into factories. But that bitterness was directed at more than just larceny, however grand. It was fanned by the death throes of an epoch, the most tragic symptom of which was taken to be the scarring of the earth itself, the defacing of England-as-garden.

At the same time, the industrial revolution had a contradictory impact on contemporary images of the relationship between country and city. On the one hand, the chasm dividing them was seen to grow ever wider. Far from just a description of sociospatial realities, this contrast between mill town and moor, metropolis and meadow, became a key symbolic trope in British historical consciousness. Note that it was industrial workers, many of them with no experience of rural England, who agitated most loudly for a return to the land, a mythical world of contented labor, village cricket, and county entertainments (Thompson 1963: 231). In both poetry and popular conception, the country stood to the city as nature to worldliness, innocence to corruption, a harmonious past to the disjunctive present (Williams 1973).

On the other hand, as the mill and the mine made their noisy entry into the rural northern valleys, the industrial revolution blurred the ecological distinction between country and city. As Sir John Clapham put it,

> Rural labour and town labour, country house and town house, were divided by no clear line. In one sense there was no line at all. Very many of the industrial workpeople were countrymen, though their countryside might be fouling and blackening, their cottages creeping together and adhering into rows, courts, formless towns. (1926: 36)

That the contrast between country and city seemed simultaneously to be growing and disappearing is not paradoxical. As the ecological and social separation between them dissolved under the impact of industrial capitalism, the resulting dislocation was acutely felt throughout Britain, leaving fragmented and discontented working populations in its wake (Briggs 1959: 42). Some had to move to the city, others found that the city had moved to them. Either way, the sense of having crossed boundaries, both old and new, was unavoidable, often painful. And this, in turn, could not but highlight the contrast between the worlds separated by those boundaries.

As the perceived opposition between country and city grew in the popular imagination, then, it became a master symbol of the radical transformation of British society, picking out a counterpoint between mythic past and present reality. But the idealized countryside also stood for the possibility of paradise regained, a Utopian rhapsody for the future. That is why the dreams of the likes of Owen were paid so much attention. In practice, these dreams could not be realized in a greatly changed England. However, the open vistas of the non-European world seemed to offer limitless possibilities. The missionaries to South Africa—many of whom came from the rural communities most altered in the restructuring of Britain (see below)—were to resuscitate the rural idyll as a model for Africa.

Imagined Worlds: (3) The Empire of God

Notwithstanding the sheer vibrancy of the Protestant revival during the early nineteenth century, this was a secularizing age in which the suzerainty of religion was in decline (Toynbee 1969: 235). At the time of the Reformation, says Christopher Hill (1969: 34), ecclesiastical hegemony had been all-encompassing: not only were cloth and crown entailed in each other, but the parish church was the nub of political and social life for most Britons. What is more, the signs and practices of Christianity were taken-for-granted features of everyday existence, an unspoken condition of seeing and being. In these circumstances, temporal power appeared as a function of spiritual sovereignty—which made it hard to distinguish religion from politics, *lex Dei* from *lex naturae*. Indeed, James I, who openly identified kingly rule with divine command, equated sedition with blasphemy (Mill 1982, 6: 10 f.). No wonder that "the reformed Church of England . . . [was] inseparable from national consciousness" (Chadwick 1966: 3). With the profound economic turmoil of the mid-sixteenth century, however, all of Europe witnessed a spiritual crisis and a bitter struggle for control over religious life—one consequence of which was to be the steady growth of Christian dissent and, in particular, the birth of Congregationalism, an antiestablishment movement that would spread quickly among lower-class groups (Hill 1969: 111). The London Missionary Society, later to evangelize the Tswana, arose from this movement.

The breakdown of the unity and authority of Anglicanism in the 1640s, Hill (p. 190) goes on, was a critical moment: the Kingdom and God, and hence the Kingdom of God, could never again exist as one, or enjoy the same supreme hegemony. This is not to say that organized religion lost all influence in the political process, or that Protestant doctrine ceased to pervade public discourse. As nineteenth-century ecclesiastical history proves, the matter is much too complex to be captured in such general terms. The point, rather, is that spiritual sovereignty, sui generis, had lost its ineffability. Far from being an unquestioned order of signs and symbols through which nature and society were apprehended, Christianity had itself become an object of debate and struggle. The growing disunity of the church was an element in this. So, too, was the dissolution of doctrinal homogeneity among nonconformists after 1800 (Briggs and Sellers 1973: 6). But the most telling portent of authority undermined was the fact that the role of the church—and the relationship between the sacred and the secular—could be questioned at all. No longer did Christianity-as-culture have the capacity to dissolve the distinction between the law of God and the law of the land, the divine and the mundane; no longer was reality constructed by automatic reference to the moral language of Christendom. Its hegemony lost, English Protestantism, too, was to be transformed by the forces that drove the age of revolution. Like most other things, it was about to be refashioned in the ethical mold of capitalism (Anderson 1983: chap. 2).

There was, however, no reason why a Kingdom of God could not be re-created elsewhere, and nowhere seemed better than the fringes of the European world. Two things underscored this at the time. One was the abolition of the slave trade in 1807, an act taken by the mission societies as a moral mandate to right "the wrongs of Africa."[6] The other grew out of the collapse of the "Old British Empire" (Knorr 1941: 211), a reverse that made "colonial expansion so distasteful to the English that they even . . . abolished the Secretaryship of State for the Colonies" (Halévy 1924: 87).[7] To nonconformists, the chance to evangelize in an imperial vacuum was appealing: being strongly antiestablishment, and for the rigid separation of church and state, they did not welcome the presence of a colonial government (Briggs and Sellers 1973: 143); it curbed their freedom to minister to an unfettered spiritual sovereignty. As time passed and conditions changed, the Kingdom of God would pave a way for the Empire of Britain, a process in which some missionaries were to play a lively part. But at the dawn of the new century, the hiatus in colonial expansion enabled English Christians to dream of their own spiritual imperium.

This dream, nonetheless, was firmly grounded in the ethos of the age. The Kingdom of God—as the nonconformists said repeatedly in the abolition debate—was to be built on a moral economy of Christian commerce and manufacture, methodical self-construction and reason, private property and the practical arts of civilized life. Like all utopias, it offered a future that fused the values of the present with the myths of the past. Savage society would, by careful tending, be made into an independent peasantry, much like the late British yeomanry. In talking thus, the missions relied heavily on horticultural metaphors, evoking the re-creation of the spoiled English garden in Africa's "vast moral wastes" (Moffat 1842: 614). The countryside would be tilled anew, civilizing the heathen as he cultivated the soil.

But the African garden was to be part of the imperial marketplace. After all, commerce, like money, was an integral—even sanctified—aspect of civilization. For many, in fact, commercial agriculture was the panacea that would establish both the material and the moral infrastructure of the Kingdom of God—an imagined world that fused the Benthamite vision of liberation through free exchange, the Protestant notion of self-construction through rational improvement, and the bourgeois ideal of accumulation through hard work. From small seeds there grew large dreams; from modest biographies, heroic visions of deeds to be done.

Modest Biographies: The Social Roots of the Nonconformist Missionaries

I have noted that most nonconformist missionaries to South Africa were men who had risen from laboring, peasant, and artisan backgrounds to the lower end of the bourgeoisie, often via the church. Few had a university education—some had no schooling at all—and many would "have spent their lives as artisans had they not been invited to enter the ministry" (Etherington 1978: 28). Indeed, the LMS *Rules for the Examination of Missionaries* (1795) stressed that candidates did *not* have to be learned; Godly men who knew "mechanic arts" were also welcome. Beidelman (1982: 50) has reiterated that "the missionary movement in Britain cannot be separated from the . . . rise of the lower middle classes." Not only was it from here that most evangelists came; many of their biographies, marked by modest upward mobility and the acquisition of re-spectability, echoed the rise of the class itself. Nonconformism may have drawn its following from all strata (Briggs 1959: 69), but its missionaries were from a narrow band of the social spectrum. Hobsbawm's account of the "new sects" nicely summarizes the origins of these men.

> [The sects] spread most readily among those who stood between the rich and powerful on one side, the masses of the traditional society on the other: i.e., among those who were about to rise into the new middle class, those about to decline into a new proletariat, and the indiscriminate mass of small and inde-pendent men in between. (1962: 270)

But it is not only the reconstruction of class divisions that weaves missionary biography into the social history of the age. Also salient were the other major transformations of which I have spoken: the ascendance of a new moral economy; the social, ecological, and aesthetic despoliation of the countryside; and the secularization of the age.

The most heroic British figures in South African mission history, with the possible exception of John Philip, were Robert Moffat and his son-in-law, David Livingstone.[8] Their backgrounds, if not their later lives, were typical of the first generation of nonconformist evangelists. Moffat was the son of a ploughman who had risen to become a petty official in a Scottish salt tax office.[9] The elder Moffat's life was a model of disciplined, self-sacrificing improve-ment: he died leaving £2,351 and a freehold dwelling, great wealth in light of his origins. In 1795, when Robert was born, his parental home was at Ormiston, near Edinburgh. His grandparents' cottage still stands in the Ormiston public garden; the remains of his own home are now enclosed in a National Coal Board property. The one faces rural, horticultural Scotland; the other, industrial Britain. Moreover, Ormiston had been rebuilt by John Cockburn, a capitalist and reformer, who erected a distillery, introduced flax production, and revivified local agriculture. The young Robert, in short, saw the countryside and town begin to merge and the peasantry, of which his father had been part, become an agrarian and industrial workforce. The reconstruction of northern Britain reached to his doorstep.

Moffat came from a strict Calvinist family in which improvement was equated with industry, thrift, and good works. Apparently their sense of philanthropy included a "lively evangelical interest in foreign parts" (Northcott 1961: 17). For all the stress on improvement, however, Robert had almost no schooling, although reading, sewing, and knitting was a regular evening activity for both sexes. At fourteen, he became a gardener, and later moved to Cheshire, where he happened on a group of Independent Methodists whose views and style of worship attracted him. From this cottage prayer circle, through the good offices of a Congregationalist minister in Manchester, Moffat's path led to the LMS, ordination, and a long sojourn among the Tswana. Just as his youth was dominated by the currents of the age—hardening class lines, the transformation of the country and the peasantry, and the absorption of the poor into the bourgeois moral economy—so his later career was dedicated to the reenactment of his own life amid those currents. The African was to be led along similar paths, learning to read and reflect, to cultivate and sell his labor, and to see the value of industry—so that he, too, might better himself. Mission biography, as I said, was mission ideology personified.

The early life of David Livingstone closely resembled that of Robert Moffat. He also grew up in the fissures of the emerging class structure; his childhood, too, was spent at the intersection of the country and the city. Blantyre, his birthplace, was eight miles from Glasgow and boasted a major textile works; it was here that, at ten, he was employed when his family fell on hard times. His grandfather, Neil, like Moffat's father, had been a rural man—a small farmer—but lost his tenancy when the land was taken over by a commercial sheep farm. Forced to migrate to the industrial fringe of Glasgow, Neil slowly raised enough to leave mill work. However, his son, a tea salesman, could not hold on to hard-won respectability: he suffered repeated financial reverses, and the family had to move into Shuttle Row, a tenement owned by Blantyre Mill. This community, like Ormiston, was planned by the mill owner. It also abutted a park, the private garden of the works manager—thus highlighting the contrast between stark tenement and verdant countryside, laboring poor and new rich. From the Livingstone home, says Johnston (n.d.: 50–51), one could see "a peep of Glasgow . . . dimly discernible through [an] irridescent mist of smoke, sunshine, and rain." Between Blantyre and Glasgow, he goes on, lay clearly visible "strips of murdered country, fields of rye alternating with fields of baking bricks."

Like the Moffats, the Livingstones devoted themselves energetically to education and self-improvement; the atmosphere and daily routine in the two households seem to have been similar. Most accounts tell how David spent two hours each evening in the company school and then went home to read—all this after a twelve-hour workday. His family were also members of the es-tablished church until the 1830s, when his father, affected by nonconformist preaching, joined the independent Hamilton Church. From there, it is said, he took home a pamphlet on medical missions in China. David had long shown an interest in medicine and found the prospect appealing. The rest is well known: after saving the necessary funds, he went to study in Glasgow, and from there found his way, like Moffat, into the LMS.

The general pattern will be clear. Of the seventeen LMS and WMMS missionaries who began work among Southern Tswana before 1860, and for whom we have sufficient information, twelve came from Scotland or the north of England, two from Wales, and only three from southern England; thirteen of them being from the industrializing river valleys, the urban peripheries or proletarianized villages. Sixteen of the seventeen, moreover, fit Hobsbawm's description (p. 670)—that is, of persons caught between rich and poor, either indeterminate in their class affiliation or struggling to cross the invisible boundary into the bourgeoisie. Five of them came from peasant stock, five were from artisan backgrounds, three had been petty clerks or traders, and three had risen directly from the ranks of the laboring poor. Many, like Moffat and Livingstone, were from displaced rural families. For all of them, the church conferred respectability and a measure of security in their social position, even though it did not enrich them.

All this underscores the extent to which the nonconformists were creatures of their age and its contradictions. It also indicates why they should have been so caught up in its moral economy and ideological discourses; why, in par-ticular, they were so drawn to the idealized worlds of expansive bourgeois individualism, of a renascent countryside, of a resurrected Empire of God. Let us follow them to Africa and see how, thus socially and culturally endowed, they took up their role as the conscience of the colonizer.

Colonialisms in Conflict: The South African Frontier, circa 1820–1860

When the first generation of LMS and WMMS missionaries arrived in South Africa, they did not, despite their rhetoric of Africa-as-desert, encounter an empty landscape. The Cape of Good Hope, ruled earlier by Holland and now by Britain, was already a field of tension and conflict (see de Kiewiet 1941: chap. 2; Newton-King 1980: passim). From the perspective of the evangelists, as recorded in their accounts,[10] the terrain sported four sets of characters—aside from Africans—and three models of colonial rule. The former included (1) His

Majesty's administrators and officers, most of them gentlemen of high birth and/or rank; (2) British settlers, largely respectable middle-class burghers of Cape Town and farmers in the colony; (3) Boers (lit. "farmers") of Dutch, German, and French descent who were regarded as "rude"; and (4) themselves, agents of the various mission societies. Even more sharply distinguished were their models of colonial rule, though they would not have referred to, or labeled, them as such. The first, associated with the British administration (and, by extension, British settlers), may be dubbed *state colonialism;* the second, attributed to the Boers, was a form of *settler colonialism;* and the third, their own, was perceived as a *civilizing colonialism.* In the missionaries' view, if it may be so summarily stated, the three colonialisms were, respectively, bureaucratic, brutal, and benign (see, e.g., Philip 1828: 1).

I shall describe these models in a moment. But, before I do, a few qualifications are to be made. First, although each was associated with a specific set of characters, it did not follow that everyone on the colonial stage would act according to type; the Christians were quick to point out when, say, a government functionary or British settler behaved "like Boers." Second, while the three colonialisms were, in principle, quite discrete, evangelists often underplayed the differences between themselves and administrators, stressing their mutual involvement in the imperial project; for some churchmen, this was a deliberate part of the effort to persuade some officials to participate in their civilizing mission (e.g., Philip 1828; and later Mackenzie 1887). Third, the content of the different colonialisms was to be transformed, over time, by subcontinental and global forces. As this implies, the nonconformist vision was itself to alter, and increasingly to fragment, as the years went by. However, I am concerned here with the early 1800s, when the models were clearly delineated, and the evangelical voice unified.

Three Models of Colonialism

I repeat that the three "models" are drawn from the body of mission literature—letters, reports, published works—where they are *not* laid out in formal terms. Still, it will become clear that their content and coherence are beyond question. Each captures a pervasive, consistent set of stereotypic images; images that were held up as a template—literally, a model—against which to describe and evaluate the actions of whites toward blacks.

1. The *state* model, according to which the colonial government was seen to oversee the territory, had, as its first priority, *Pax Britannica:* the pacification of "tribes," under British law, in an ever-widening radius outward from the Cape. Ideally, this was to be achieved by trade and by making alliances with native chiefs.[11] To this end, the administration sponsored the exploration of the interior but did not

concern itself with the civilization of indigenes; their "improvement," in official rhetoric, would follow naturally from trade, pacification, and contact with whites. Nor did the state impose direct rule on inland peoples, although it kept an increasingly regulatory eye on the flow of black laborers and the terms of their employment. The obligation to "protect the aborigines"—from internecine war, unscrupulous whites, and Boer enslavement—was also part of the self-appointed mandate of the administration, especially after abolition. "It is a wise policy in Government," observed John Moffat (1842: 210), "to *render every facility* to the advancement of knowledge and civilization among the aborigines" (my italics). But to the evangelists, state policy was ambiguous on just this point (recall Philip; p. 662). It became even more so in the early 1850s when, by the Sand River Convention (1852) and Bloemfontein Conventions (1854), Britain ceded control over the hinterland and its black population to Boer settlers—and to their form of colonialism (see, e.g., Thompson 1969: 420–425; Davenport 1977: 62–63, 124).

State colonialism, as I said, was to change over time. It would involve, in due course, the imposition of taxes, the limitation of chiefly authority, and many other (typically legalistic, punitive) forms of regulation. Above all, from the late 1860s onwards, in the wake of the mineral revolution, it would be ever more concerned with the control of "native [wage] labor." But the essence of the missionary view of the state—that it was about bureaucratic regulation, not civilization, at least in their terms—would remain intact for a long time. Indeed, it was to be fed by the government: in 1878, for example, Sir Gordon Sprigg, prime minister of the Cape, was to go about the colony announcing his firm resolve to make blacks into laborers—and to punish any "native rebellion" by forcing the culprits to forfeit their land. The policy of his administration, he added in an obvious dig at the evangelists, "is to teach them to work, not to read and write and sing."[12]

2. *Settler colonialism,* the Boer model, was represented by the missionaries in starkly negative terms. To them, Boers were no more than half-savages: they led degenerate, unrefined lives, lacked a true European "spirit of improvement," and showed their "monstrous" character by treating blacks as prey to be hunted and enslaved.[13] As this suggests, settler colonialism was seen to be founded on brute coercion and domination by force—although it was justified by appeal to the biblical allegory of "the children of Ham," according to which eternal servitude was the divine calling of blacks.[14] For the evangelists, the Boer model was revealed most clearly in, and after, the Great Trek of the 1830s, when the settlers, loudly protesting

abolition, left the colony for the interior.[15] Their epic frontier movement, the mythological exodus of Afrikaner historical consciousness, did more than strike a blow for Boer independence from the state colonialism of Britain. It also established a new order of relations between these Europeans and the peoples of the interior. The encounter began with either war or alliance and ended, usually, with the subordination of local communities to Boer control. The latter was expressed in one or more of four ways: (1) the imposition of tax and/or demands for tribute; (2) the seizure of men, women, and children to toil as bonded servants and unpaid laborers on white farms; (3) the requirement that chiefs provide military assistance to the whites against "unfriendly natives"; and (4) the gradual appropriation of "tribal" lands. These measures, the churchmen pointed out in their various ways, added up to a deliberate, systematic process of domination. A few indigenous communities were destroyed as a result, their dispossessed members forced to become laborers and servants on the white farms that seemed to be multiplying across the South African hinterland. Others remained physically intact, but many lost their independence, their leaders emasculated by the irresistible demand for regular tax, tribute, and labor.[16]

3. The *civilizing colonialism* of the mission, as we would expect, was much more fully spelled out by the Christians than were the other models. Apart from all else, they believed their designs for the transformation of indigenous life to be more positively comprehensive, more finely detailed, than any other (see, e.g., Moffat 1842: 616 f.; Livingstone 1858: Lecture I). Nor were they alone in this view. It was to become an anthropological commonplace, a century later, that the mark of the early mission enterprise was its effort to reconstruct *totally* African society and culture (e.g., Bohannan 1964: 22 f.).

Distilled to its essence, the civilizing colonialism of the nonconformists sought to "cultivate" the African "desert" and its inhabitants by planting the seeds of bourgeois individualism and the nuclear family, of private property and commerce, of rational minds and healthily clad bodies, of the practical arts of refined living and devotion to God. All these things were of a piece; that, after all, was what was implied by *total* reconstruction. Hence, far from limiting themselves to religious conversion, the evangelists set out, at once, to (1) create a theater of the everyday, demonstrating by their own exemplary actions the benefits of methodical routine, of good personal habits, and of enlightened European ways; (2) banish "superstition" in favor of rational technique and Christian belief; (3) reduce the landscape from a chaotic mass of crude, dirty huts to an ordered array of square, neatly bounded residences (with rooms and doors, windows and furniture, fields and fences), enclosure being both a condition of private property and civilized individualism and an aesthetic expression of the sheer beauty of refinement;[17] (4) recast the division of labor by making men into hardworking farmers and bringing women "indoors" to the domestic domain, much along the lines of the English middle-class family; (5) encourage these families to produce for the market by teaching them advanced methods, the worth of time and money, and the ethos of private enterprise—the explicit model being the late British yeomanry (see above); all of which (6) demanded that Africans be taught to read and reason, to become self-reflective and self-disciplined. It followed, as axiomatic, that "heathen" society would be forever destroyed. But the evangelists were less sure of their attitude toward indigenous secular authority. In light of their commitment to the separation of church and state, they promised repeatedly not to interfere in "tribal" government and politics. However, in seeking "religious freedom" for their congregants, and by "fighting superstition," they tried hard to drive a wedge between (what *they* took to be) the temporal and ritual aspects of the chiefship—which brought them into open conflict with many chiefs. Of course, the ideal solution was to convert these rulers, a stroke that would replace the benighted rule of heathenism with a new Christian sovereignty. In sum, the nub of the civilizing colonialism of the mission—and it was, quite explicitly, a colonialism, in that it sought to subordinate Africa to the dominance of the European order—lay in replacing native economy and society with an imagined world of free, propertied, and prosperous peasant families. This latter-day yeomanry would inhabit a bounded and cultivated countryside, its beauty marred neither by the nakedness of savagery nor the despoliation of an ex-panding industrial city. It was a world in which God-inspired authority, per-vading the reasoning mind and the receptive soul of every person, would reign through ever more enlightened secular rulers.

It is in the details of this civilizing colonialism, to recall what I said at the outset, that the making of the evangelists may be seen to have shaped the way in which they sought to make history; patently, the substance of their imagined worlds, formed on the social and physical landscape of Britain, had been fused and transposed into a coherent model for Africa. Thus Moffat (1842: 616–617), leaning heavily on the rhetoric of Fowell Buxton, was fond of asserting that, if only the missions were careful to rebuild African life in all its aspects, "civilization [would] advance as the natural effect, and Christianity operate as the proximate cause of the happy change." He also took pains to point out (pp. 616–617) that his entire career was given over to leading the Tswana along the high road to refinement, at the apex of which lay European civil society. This objective justified all his efforts to remake the Tswana mode of production and consumption, to establish a large school and a busy printing press, to clothe the heathens and rehouse them in proper habitations, to stimulate trade and reform the social division of labor. The general point was echoed by Livingstone, who repeatedly proclaimed that he, too, was working toward the "el-evation of man" in Africa (1858: 46) through the "inestimable blessings" of "those two pioneers of civilization—Christianity and commerce" (p. 21); it was the latter, after all, that would gain the "negro family" entry into the "body corporate of nations" (1857: 84). Even when he took off for Central Africa, leaving his brethren to the more mundane tasks of the mission, he justified his exploration as a necessary step in attaining the goal of "civilization, commerce, and Christianity" (p. 18; also p. 7). And as it was for Moffat and Livingstone, so it was with their evangelical colleagues; elsewhere Jean Comaroff and John Comaroff (1991, 1: chap. 6; 2: chaps. 2–4) show that the model of civilizing reform—the scheme for reconstructing the very bases of "native life"—was shared by all the nonconformists.

As significant here is the fact that the three models, taken together, owed much to the missionaries' self-appointed role as the conscience of the colonizer. Each was a moral refraction of bourgeois ideology, a measure of the ethics of the imperial impulse. This is most obvious in the case of the settler model, which was represented as the very inverse of enlightened liberal humanism (see, e.g., Philip 1828, 2:318). Hence the claim that the Boers violated the principles of *free* labor and *self*-determination, the corollary being that they would happily banish Africans from the kind of personhood and society for which civilized Britain had come to stand. But bourgeois ideology and morality also permeated the churchmen's view of state colonialism—founded, as it was, on the separation of sacred from secular authority, on the recognized right of a ruling class to exercise temporal command over the people and places under its jurisdiction, and on the duty of His Majesty's functionaries to extend the imperial sphere of influence (e.g., Moffat 1842: chap. 13). Accordingly, the appointed role of government was not merely to administer the territory and population of the Colony. It was also—to recapitulate a popular opinion at home—the creation of a space, a "body of corporate nations" under *Pax Britannica* (Livingstone 1857: 84), within which British commerce, interests, and values might flourish. The spirit of the age, and its particular expression in the nonconformist imagination, emerges unmistakably in the terms which they chose to portray the colonial process.

So, too, does the social position of the missionaries—specifically, their class background and orientations—both at home and abroad. Thus, the state model took for granted the right of a cadre of "well-born" Britons to exercise authority over the colonial population, white and black, by virtue of their membership of a ruling *class;* a "*law-making* class," as William Dodd (1847: 11) called them, not knowing how well the term applied to the overseas ministers of *Pax Britannica.* A number of the churchmen did not especially admire the British aristocracy, and many disapproved of the actions and ethics of His Majesty's representatives at the Cape (e.g., Livingstone, in Schapera 1960: 81 f.; Philip 1828, 2: 253 passim). Yet they did not question the right of the ruling classes to govern (see, e.g., Macmillan 1963: 249 f.). At the other end of the spectrum, the settler model was thought to reflect the sheer "boorishness," the brute degeneracy of the Boers, who were compared explicitly with the "worst" of the "unimproved" masses back in Britain (e.g., Ludorf 1863: 203). For their part, the evangelists saw their own position as lying between ruler and settler: as I have said repeatedly, their social situation and their ideology alike were an embodiment of middle-class respectability, an expression of the assertive bourgeois Benthamism of which Arnold was to write. The upper-class gentlemen of His Majesty's administration might govern by right of their nobility and worldly authority, and the lowly Boers might dominate by brute force. But they, emissaries of the Empire of God, were there to implant a reign of civility, a state of colonization more pervasive and powerful than the colonial state, more enduring than the rancher republicanism of the Boers. So it was that the triumph of the bourgeoisie at home would be made into an imperial dominion of middle-class liberal virtue.

Measured on the uncompromising scale of political and military might, the churchmen did *not* occupy a niche between ruler and settler. As they well knew, they were the least potent whites in this colonial theater: subject to the authority of the Cape government, on the one hand, they lacked the social and material resources, the numbers, and the resolute strength of the Boers, on the other. As I noted above, it was just this—their being a "dominated fraction"—that makes the missionaries' reading of contemporary South Africa so revealing to us. Having to justify themselves to a frequently uncooperative administration, and to defend themselves against the (always suspicious, often belligerent) settlers, they were repeatedly sensitized to the different colonizing projects that were contesting the subcontinent. Moreover, their only weapons in this political arena were their rhetorical potency and their moral sanction. Add to this their assumed role as ethicists of empire and it is no wonder that few others on the scene were as articulate in discoursing on the competing colonialisms.

But two obvious questions follow from all this. Were the evangelists' models of colonialism similarly perceived by others—in particular, by those to whom they were attributed? And how accurately did they describe the various faces of colonization? The second question is, for present purposes, the less significant, since we are concerned here with arguments of ideology and representation; arguments that were themselves part of the colonial process and hence, by definition, only partial accounts of it. More salient is the issue of representation itself. Did those who spoke for the Boers—then or later—concur in the settler model? What of the functionaries of the state? And what difference did it make anyway?

The Boers, who reciprocated the evangelists' contempt in full (de Gruchy 1979: 12 f.), repudiated the negative moral charges made against them by the nonconformists, and they were loud in ridiculing accusations of personal brutishness and spiritual degeneracy. Indeed, a sympathetic German explorer and natural historian, Henry Lichtenstein (1928, 1:59), claimed not to recognize the "barbarians, [the] half-savages" described in British accounts of the settlers and bandied about by the churchmen. Also denied were the seizure of native land, the kidnapping of blacks for slaves, and unprovoked attacks on the various chiefdoms in pursuit of stock and prisoners. Where such attacks and seizures occurred, they were justified as due punishment for cattle theft and other infractions against European property and persons. Likewise, demands for tax, tributary labor, and military assistance were legitimized in a manner reminiscent of the constitutional spirit of *Pax Britannica:* the Boers, went the argument (see, e.g., Theal 1893: 517 f.), having established sovereign jurisdiction over the interior of South Africa by right of conquest during the Great Trek, had conferred free citizenship on peoples like the Southern Tswana. In return for protection, peace, and the right to live within the settler territories, these peoples had, like citizens everywhere, to undertake military service and to pay taxes in cash or labor. What is more, as Boer leaders liked to point out, Britain had signed the Sand River and Bloemfontein Conventions in 1852 and 1854, thereby recognizing their right to conduct "native policy" as they saw fit. As this suggests, the imputation of lawlessness or immorality was rejected out of hand—and has been ever since by a long tradition of Afrikaner historiography (see, e.g., Theal 1891, 1893; Cory 1919; Muller 1969). However, the *facts* of domination—its grounding in a theology of racial inequality; its practical application in various forms of regulation and extraction; its concentration on relations of land, labor, and taxation; its enforcement by coercive, even violent means—were not questioned. Just the opposite: they were assertively defended as legal and proper. In short, the missionaries' model of the *substance* of settler colonialism, if not their reflections on its moral and legal bases, were accepted by those to whom it was meant to apply. To be sure, the ideology of domination that it described was to be sustained in broadly similar form well into the postcolonial epoch in apartheid South Africa.

In the same vein, the stereotypic image of state colonialism shared by the nonconformists did not depart far from that essayed by the Cape authorities themselves, at least between about 1820 and the 1860s. It did not capture all the complexities, of course. For example, there was a great difference between the treatment of "coloureds" and blacks within the colony and the policy toward those who lived along or beyond the frontier. The latter, as the missionaries noted, were encouraged to retain the integrity of their polities, keeping intact the institutions of "tribal government." By contrast, the former, whose political communities had long been dismantled, had become a servant class dispersed within and around the white settlements and farms of the Cape; even after abolition, their "freedoms" were greatly restricted by both law and common practice. John Philip might have railed against this in his campaign for "civil rights" (1828, 2:308); and he well understood the sympathy with which the middle and lower echelons of "magistrates" regarded (and treated) the settlers prior to, and after, the Great Trek. But most evangelists did not fully grasp the degree to which the state had become an agency for regulating both the flow of labor and the terms on which coloureds and blacks served whites; and all this long before Sprigg's spirited defense of civilization-through-toil. Nonetheless, His Majesty's functionaries would not have disagreed with those churchmen who perceived state colonialism to be a form of limited, regulatory governance. Indeed, they, too, were often assertive in extolling the virtues of this form of imperial rule—as generations of South Africans have been told by their school history books.

Here, then, are the imaginative and ideological bases for the clash of colonialisms. At one level—the coda of domination—nineteenth-century South African history may be read as an unfolding confrontation between these three colonialisms. From the perspective of the victim, their coexistence made the encounter with Europe appear contradictory and, initially at least, difficult to fathom. It is, after all, something of an irony to the colonized that those who come to rule them spend so much time fighting among themselves over the terms of command. Indeed, African popular protest was to make a good deal of the irony, often turning it into a bitterly satirical commentary on the poetics— or, rather, the poetic injustice—of oppression. And some black South Africans were to find new forms of empowerment in the fissures among the whites. But all this was yet far into the future. In the early decades of the century, the differences among the colonialisms were to express themselves in a series of struggles over policy and the practices of power.

From Models to Struggles

It is obviously impossible to offer here a detailed account of these struggles. To do that would be to rewrite the colonial history of South Africa. For the present, let me give just one example, one piece of that history, and let the matter rest.

In June 1847, in a letter written before his antipathy to the Boers had reached its highest pique, David Livingstone (Schapera 1974: 5) lamented that the "Dutchmen" had "a great aversion to missionaries." Their enmity, he said, was caused by the "idea that we wish to furnish the natives with fire-arms." This letter, as it turns out, anticipated a long, angry round of hostilities among settlers, evangelists, and administrators; hostilities that were to break into open violence in the terrain beyond the Cape frontier, where the western edge of Boer-claimed territory met Bechuanaland. It is not surprising that the ostensible cause of the trouble was the alleged supply of weaponry to the Tswana. *Pax Britannica* notwithstanding, many chiefs had concluded that, in the interior, a little ordnance went much further than even the most far-reaching ordinance; hence they were trying desperately to lay their hands on some musketry. Furthermore, guns had taken on enormous significance for both the blacks and the Boers. To the former, they were an icon of the potency of *sekgoa* (European ways) at large, a power to be seized and harnessed; to the latter, they were an affirmation of the exclusive control over force, of the capacity to determine the lives and deaths of lesser beings—"baboons and Bechuanas" among them.[18] But the conflict ran to the very core of colonial contestation, bringing the three colonialisms into noisy collision. And it ended, after some years, in a striking denouement: the destruction—indeed, physical dismemberment—of Livingstone's house and his mission to the Kwena by settler commandos. For it was none other than Dr. Livingstone himself who was presumed by his enemies to be most guilty of gun running. He denied it, of course, arguing, in the *British Banner* (1849), that it was Boer traders who, tempted by huge profits, were selling firearms to the chiefs—despite the orders of their leaders (Livingstone, in Schapera 1974: 14). The traffic was so large, he added, that any settler authority who thought he could stop it "might as well have bolted his castle with a boiled carrot."

Carrots and castles aside, there is evidence that Livingstone did supply some guns to the Kwena (see Schapera 1974: 41). For all the Reverend Ludorf's insistence later that missions had been there "to furnish weapons not carnal, but spiritual,"[19] other churchmen were also drawn into the trade over the next decade or so. For example, William Ashton[20] told his LMS superiors that Moffat's son, a trader, had once brought ammunition to the Kuruman station. Some had been sold to Tswana who, at the time, were fighting a group of settlers. The rest "was stored away in his father's garden," buried, it seems, amid the carrots. "What will become of the Station," asked the nervous pastor, "if the Boers get to know [what] is in the missionary's garden?" To add to the irony, Ashton wrote again three weeks later,[21] complaining that all this had occurred while Moffat Sr. was in Cape Town trying to persuade the government to send ammunition to two "trustworthy" chiefs. Ordnance, he commented acidly, should not enter the country "by the means of either missionaries or their sons." Despite his plea, several evangelists continued willingly to help Tswana obtain weapons. But, as even the settlers knew, their efforts were far too limited to alter the balance of forces on the frontier (Schapera 1974). Effective access to the means of violence lay elsewhere.[22]

As this suggests—and this is the point—the strife over the supply of firearms to the Tswana was as much a symbolic as a material issue. But this does not mean that it was trivial. Apart from all else, the hostilities made it clear to all concerned that the deep interior had become a combat zone, alike political and ideological, in which the various protagonists were battling to lay down the terms on which black South Africa was to be ruled. Looking at this struggle from the standpoint of the Boers, and of settler colonialism, the involvement of the evangelists betokened two things, both extremely serious. The first was that, in procuring weapons for the Tswana—thereby handing them the power over human life and death—the churchmen were acknowledging their humanity and according them a place among *Homo sapiens*. It was as if the gift of a musket was a metonym for the gift of membership in mankind itself. The propriety of that gift might have been taken for granted by the civilizing mission, but it was deeply contested by the settlers: for them it was divine truth, not a mere pigment of the imagination, that humanity ended at the color bar. According to Livingstone (Schapera 1974: 19), their leaders had long made it plain to the LMS that "a Missionary should teach the natives that the boers were a superior race." It was in this context, in fact, that the simian simile had first arisen: the "Dutchmen" had told his brethren, says the good doctor, that they "might as well teach baboons as Bechuanas." To give them weaponry, then, was tantamount to taking a firearm from the hunter and handing it to his prey. The Tswana were right: guns were indeed an icon of European potency. In trying to stop the nonconformists from supplying even one to a black, the Boers sought to turn back the revolutionary tide of the civilizing mission at large.

There seems to have been little doubt among Boers that the evangelists stood for a competing colonialism—a colonialism that promised resistance and rebellion. Thus, for instance, one community went so far as to write into its constitution that members had to "take a solemn oath to have no connection with the London Missionary Society, . . . a political association, disseminating doctrines on social questions subversive of all order in society" (Theal 1902: 228). Settler leaders were well aware of the churchmen's intention to reconstruct the "native" world ab initio; the hated Philip (1828, 2:355), after all, had said over and over that "civilization supposes a revolution in the habits of the people." As Stow (1905: 268) was later to suggest, the Boers firmly believed that the LMS harbored the "Utopian idea of laying the foundation, under their own special priestly guidance, of a model kingdom of 'regenerated natives.'" Not Moffat or Philip or Livingstone, for all the clarity with which they envisaged an Eden of the Spirit, could have phrased better the charter for their civilizing colonialism.

If, for the settlers, one aspect of the conflict over guns was their struggle against civilizing colonialism, the second was their opposition to, and effort to free themselves from, state colonialism. For, as they saw matters, there was yet another side to the "interference" of the missionaries. It lay in the fact that these men continually threatened to appeal to the Cape authorities, petitioning them to restrain Boer efforts to assert their autonomy and to rule the interior. The settlers appear to have assumed that their shared Britishness would dispose Her Majesty's officials to listen to the churchmen; and, on occasion, the nonconformists *did* invoke a "British" sense of civility and justice to goad officialdom into action. Despite their claims of noninvolvement in colonial politics, the LMS and WMMS were quick to enter the public arena when they wished the state to exercise authority over the Boers (Comaroff and Comaroff 1991, 1:7). Recall that, while his garden was being filled with shot, Moffat had been in Cape Town to obtain armed support for the Tswana against the whites. Nor was this an isolated incident. During the trouble over the guns, the mission societies and their directors had made regular contact with the government, and had sometimes succeeded in persuading it to intervene, albeit on a limited scale, to protect black communities—thereby provoking yet further acrimony among Britons and Boers. Hence the accusation made in the annals of Afrikaner historiography some seventy years later: that the evangelists were responsible for "malicious calumny, native unrest, race hatred, and . . . warfare between British and Dutch" (Cory 1919: 295). Not only had they been responsible for a dangerous form of civilizing colonialism on their own account, but their intercession was also blamed for the perpetuation of state colonialism in the South African interior.

The immediate reaction of the Boers to the competing colonialisms, and to the actions of mission and government, was to assert their autonomy and their dominion over the black communities of the interior in ever more flagrant terms. In the late 1840s, well established in central South Africa, they spent a good deal of effort proving to the administration that *Pax Britannica*—and, more generally, the authority of the colonial state—was a dead letter, ever less enforceable as the distance from Cape Town grew larger. In making their point, and simultaneously nurturing the agrarian roots of settler economy and society, they set about laying the bases of the rancher republics of the Transvaal and Orange Free State. Among these was a "native policy" founded on the four elements of their model of domination: taxation, labor extraction, the demand for military service, and land appropriation.

Some liberal historians have argued that these actions were meant as a deliberate provocation to the colonial state; proof that, since it could no longer "protect the natives," the government could do little to arrest the settler march—the political Trek—to independence (see, e.g., Agar-Hamilton 1928). Perhaps. Official Boer rhetoric had it that the settlers bore "no hostile intention toward any native tribe—unless . . . they attacked" (Meintjes 1973: 74). But such attacks were held to occur all the time, allegedly, as we might guess, because the evangelists and other "unscrupulous" Europeans insisted on supplying guns to the blacks. Hence Ludorf[23] recounts how a Boer leader had personally reiterated to him that "we shall drive all [the missionaries] away for it is them who teach the natives to be rebellious [and] to resist the white man."

To be sure, as they tried to throw off the shackles of the state, the Boers made increasingly aggressive efforts to thwart the civilizing mission and to silence the political voice of the missionaries. The nonconformists were told that if they either interceded with the Cape government or encouraged the chiefs to resist the settlers any further, they would be attacked and their stations destroyed. So belligerent did the admonitions become that, in 1849–1850, rumors began to circulate in the LMS: two senior evangelists, it was said, had actually been taken prisoner. The report that bore the ''news'' to London[24] also announced gravely that ''the Dutch Boers . . . [had] peremptorily ordered Livingstone to remove from his station and never to return to it.'' For the next two years, the archival records of the LMS and WMMS are one long litany, much of it hearsay, of intimidation and abuse of churchmen. For their part, the societies appealed repeatedly to the colonial authorities for protection and support.

By late 1851, the British government had had enough of trying to contain the Boers. Afrikaner historiography has it that Britain eventually came to see positive advantage in drawing closer to them and their form of colonialism (Muller 1969: 149); to see, among other things, that the natives had indeed been spoiled by the civilizing mission and would no longer subject themselves easily to white authority. Whatever the reasons, and they are more complex than I can discuss here, when Britain signed the Sand River and Bloemfontein Conventions, they gave the settlers constitutional sanction for their rancher republicanism. In both the historical consciousness of black South Africa (Molema 1951: 85 f.) and in the eyes of the evangelists (e.g., Ludorf 1854; 1863: 203), this heralded the final triumph of settler colonialism over the other, more enlightened modes of colonial rule. The Reverend Roger Edwards captures well the ensuing despair:

> Oh! what have the Commissioners done by yielding all to the boers. Has England removed from her escutcheons one of her noblest titles—justice to the native tribes? Well may we weep over these evils, and the interruption if not the termination of mission work. (1853: 44)

If ever the churchmen felt the frustrations of being a dominated fraction of the dominant class, it was now. What is more, they were not thanked by the Tswana for their exertions. As one perspicacious parson had already noted in 1851, far from winning the gratitude of the blacks, ''we . . . are blamed by [them] as forerunners . . . of oppression and destruction from the hands of our fellow white men.''[25] There were few rewards in being the conscience of the colonizer. But the evangelists' feeling of impotence had yet to reach its nadir. That was to come with the final chapter of the story.

In the wake of Sand River and Bloemfontein, the settlers celebrated their independence by flexing their political muscle further, extending their domination, in its now familiar form, over an ever-wider circle of Tswana polities. Among those who did not take easily to Boer authority were the Kwena, the chiefdom in which David Livingstone had established his station. And so, in 1852, Transvaal commandos, citing native belligerence and missionary interference as justification, decided to attack their capital at Kolobeng. Before doing so, however, they demanded that the Tshidi-Rolong—among whom Reverend Ludorf lived and worked—join the expedition as footsoldiers of the republic of which they were now involuntary citizens. The Tshidi ruler refused, was attacked himself, and fled north into exile (Molema 1966).

The Boers were as good as their word. Kolobeng was sacked and the LMS outpost laid to waste, its contents—the books, medicines, and other signs and instruments of the civilizing mission—deliberately destroyed and strewn over the landscape (Schapera 1974: 171). One round in the argument over guns had come to a decisive end. Livingstone gave up his mission among the Kwena for the exploration of Central Africa. And Ludorf withdrew to Thaba 'Nchu, a distant Tswana settlement on the fringe of Basutoland where the WMMS had long had a station safe from the vicissitudes of the frontier. Like Edwards, he was sure that the Boer triumph tolled the end of the civilizing mission in Bechuanaland; his reports, significantly, were laced with images of a burned, despoiled countryside, much like accounts of rural England under the impact of industrialization. As a result, he joined in the task of making Thaba 'Nchu into a new Eden, replete with cultivated gardens and fenced properties, printing press and pulpit, and other accoutrements of yeoman life—indeed, into a "perfect republic of peasants" reminiscent of Wordsworth's romantic idyll. That project, too, was to become embroiled in a contest of colonialisms. When the discovery of diamonds in the 1860s led to yet another round of conflict throughout the interior, the irrepressible evangelist was to try to create a "United Nation" of Southern Tswana, free of both British and Boer suzerainty. He was even to write a constitution for this independent black nation-state, a constitution built on private property, peasant enterprise, and bourgeois individualism. But that is another story.

For the moment, at least, the unrelenting contest of colonialisms had reached an uneasy point of rest. Its brief denouement, interestingly, was written on the geopolitical topography of the subcontinent: the state colonialism of Great Britain was reined into the boundaries of the Cape Colony; the settler colonialism of the Boers occupied the central interior; and the civilizing colonialism of the mission was confined to stations either beyond the frontier or within insulated pockets dotted across the remote countryside. Each charted, for its protagonists, a total world; each represented the effort of one class fraction to assert its own form of hegemony over South Africa; and, as noted before, each was to be drawn back into the fray, albeit in somewhat altered form, when the pause was shattered by the mineral revolution.

Conclusion

This finally returns us, full circle, to John Philip and the fictional Flory, he of the Orwellian imagination. As Philip had foreseen long before, the battle for South Africa did not arise out of the idiosyncratic actions of individuals. It grew from a system of relations among members of the body politic at large. And it was, indeed, an argument of structures and images, perceptions and practices. If anything is revealed by this excursion—and it should now be clear why it was so valuably undertaken through missionary eyes—it is that the terms of domination were never straightforward, never overdetermined. They seldom are, of course. In most places, at most times, colonialism did (and does) not exist in the singular, but in a plurality of forms and forces—its particular character being shaped as much by political, social, and ideological contests among the colonizers as by the encounter with the colonized.

As I said earlier, there is a sense in which, for the latter, the niceties of competing colonialisms are beside the point. At core, subordination has an emotional and perceptual logic, a calculus of abasement, all its own. At another level, however, the struggles among fractions of a ruling class can make a difference. They certainly did in South Africa. Not only did those struggles create spaces and places in which some blacks were to discover new, if limited, modes of empowerment; others, of course, were to find novel sources of enrichment at an almost Faustian cost. But, more important over the long run, the tensions of empire—in the form of conflict among colonizers and colonialisms—were to reveal some of the contradictions of European expansionism. For they would, in due course, lay bare the hidden structures, the unspoken and undisclosed ideological scaffolding, on which its peculiar structure of domination rested. In South Africa, as in other parts of the globe, the revelation of such contradictions were to feed the rise of black protest and resistance.

If Philip was correct in seeing the inherent contradictions, the systemic "vices," in early nineteenth-century colonialism, Flory saw the cosmic pun in imperialism; that, far from *pax,* it was a *pox,* a condition that scars the body personal and social, and may eventually blind those afflicted by it. Remember who it was that failed to see the truth behind the fantasy, mistaking larceny for law, sickness for civilization: none other than Veraswami—very/swami—a highly intelligent Indian doctor. It is not difficult to misunderstand the nature of colonialism and imperialism: not for the dominant, not for the subordinate, not for the scholar-voyeur. Thus, for all the evident complexities in the colonization of Africa, there remains a tendency, in some anthropological quarters, to take an essentialist view of it; to treat it as, at bottom, a linear, inexorable process in political economy, cultural imperialism, political modernization, material expansionism, or whatever. This account confirms what a number of others have shown: that colonialism simply does not have a single, transhistorical "essence," neither political nor material, social nor cultural. Rather, its form and substance are decided in the context of its making. And its making, I repeat, is in serious part a product of struggles among dominant ideologies and their perpetrators. As it happens, the three colonialisms in South Africa each stressed one face of the imperial impulse: the state emphasized the politicolegal aspects of British rule; the settlers, the socioeconomic dimensions of race relations in a new agrarian society; and the mission, the signs and practices of bourgeois European culture. But the substance of the colonizing project, over the long term, was all of these things, in proportions determined on the battlegrounds of history—the bodies and societies, the territories and cultural terrains of South Africa, white and black.

Notes

The research for this chapter was funded by the National Science Foundation and National Endowment for the Humanities. I should like to thank both bodies. Some passages included in it are drawn, in amended and abridged form, from Jean Comaroff and John Comaroff, *Of Revelation and Revolution: Christianity, Colonialism, and Consciousness in South Africa* (1991).

1. The early nineteenth-century image of the person was not new; like much of the ontology of the age, it was foreshadowed in earlier epochs. But it was brought into sharp focus by the industrial revolution, and loomed large in the imagined world of the missionaries of the period.

2. A good example is Mrs. Bank's hero, Jabez Clegg, The Manchester Man.

3. Halévy (1924: 429 f.), for one, ascribes the "uniform ugliness" of British architecture to the combination of capitalism and Puritanism.

4. See Arbuthnot's study of contemporary agriculture (1773). Arbuthnot argues for large-scale farming, but adds (p. 139), "I most truly lament the loss of our yeomanry ... [who] kept up the independence of this nation; ... sorry I am to see their lands now in the hands of monopolizing Lords." See Thompson (1963: 219) for a less roseate view of the yeomanry.

5. One remarkable statement of the myth is in Wordsworth's (1948) sketch-of-the Lake District. An elegy for a disappearing world, it conjures up a yeomanry who live in a "pure Commonwealth," an "ideal society."

6. This was the title of a noted antislavery poem by Roscoe (1787: 31).

7. Of course, the ideology of imperialism had not died. Between the demise of the old and the rise of the new colonialism, there was much debate over the pros and cons of empire—fueled by Adam Smith's hostility toward a dominion of anything but free trade (Knorr 1941).

8. I focus on Moffat and Livingstone rather than on Philip because they actually worked among the Tswana, both devoting their energies directly to the civilizing mission—albeit, in Livingstone's case, only for the earlier part of his evangelical career. Philip, by contrast, spent most of his years in South Africa living in Cape Town as superintendent of the LMS. But the choice is largely a matter of convenience; it makes little difference to my characterization. As Ross's recent biography (1986) of Philip shows, his background in Scotland was not unsimilar to that of Moffat and Livingstone.

9. On Moffat, I draw from J. Moffat (1886), Smith (1925), and Northcott (1961); on Livingstone, from Johnston (n.d.), Jeal (1973), and others.

10. This perspective, summarily presented here, is drawn from, among other sources, Campbell (1813); Moffat (1842); Broadbent (1865); Livingstone (1857); Mackenzie (1871); and the LMS and WMMS archives.

11. Increasingly, this included paying annuities to allied chiefs. In one case, Moffat (1842: 209) adds with satisfaction, the payment was intended to promote education, an unusual departure from the state model.

12. See the *Diamond Fields Advertiser* (1 November 1878) for a report.

13. The words are from Barrow (1801—4:67, 273), whose views of the Boers were widely quoted, not least in missionary writings; see, for example, Philip (1828, 2:263, 273). For further evidence of the attitudes toward the settlers held by the British colonists in general, and the evangelists in particular, see Streak (1974) and Coetzee (1988: 28 ff.).

14. For evidence that the evangelists were aware of the theological justification for the settler model, see Philip (1828, 2:315–316).

15. For the missionaries, it was only Boer trekkers to whom the settler model really applied—not those, Livingstone explains (1857: 35), who chose to stay in the colony under English law.

16. Livingstone (1857: 35) gave much "eyewitness" evidence to support the claim that these practices were both brutal and common. He added that the Boers did not hide their acts, but assertively justified them.

17. In a passage often paraphrased by missionaries, Barrow (1801—4:57) had written: "As none of the [lands] are enclosed there is a general appearance of nakedness in the country . . . which . . . if divided by fences, would become sufficiently beautiful."

18. The phrase was attributed by Livingstone (Schapera 1974: 19, 19n) to "not a few" Boers and their leaders.

19. J. Ludorf, Thaba 'Nchu, 2.8.53 [WMMS South Africa Correspondence 315].

20. W. Ashton, Kuruman, 7.5.58 [LMS Incoming Letters (SA) 31-1-B].

21. W. Ashton, Kuruman, 7.25.58 [LMS Incoming Letters (SA) 31-1-B].

22. The Tswana had long tried to acquire arms. Their neighbors, the Griqua, had obtained weaponry from the colony early on and, as a result, controlled frontier trade. By midcentury, however, the Tswana had found no major source of supply (see, e.g., Shillington 1985).

23. J. Ludorf, Motito, 10.16.52 [WMMS South Africa Correspondence 315].

24. J. Freeman, Mabotsa, 12.25.49 [LMS Home Odds 2-4-D].

25. I. Hughes, Griquatown, 6.12.51 [LMS Incoming Letters (SA) 26-1-A].

References

Agar-Hamilton, John A. I. 1928. *The Native Policy of the Voortrekkers.* Cape Town: Maskew Miller.

Anderson, Benedict. 1983. *Imagined Communities.* London: Verso.

Anonymous [William Dodd]. 1847. *The Laboring Classes of England.* Boston: Putnam.

Arbuthnot, John ["a Farmer"]. 1773. *An Inquiry into the Connection between the Present Price of Provisions, and the Size of Farms.* London: T. Cadell.

Arnold, Matthew. 1903. *Essays in Criticism* [First Series]. London: Macmillan.

Banks, (Mrs.) G. Linnaeus. 1876. *The Manchester Man.* Altrincham: John Sherrat & Son.

Barrow, John. 1801–1804. *An Account of Travels in the Interior of Southern Africa . . .* London: Cadell and Davies.

Beidelman, Thomas O. 1982. *Colonial Evangelism.* Bloomington: Indiana University Press.

Bohannan, Paul. 1964. *Africa and Africans.* New York: Natural History Press.

Bourdieu, Pierre. 1984. *Distinction.* Cambridge, Mass.: Harvard University Press.

Briggs, Asa. 1959. *The Age of Improvement 1783–1867.* London: Longmans.

———. 1979 *Iron Bridge to Crystal Palace.* London: Thames and Hudson.

Briggs, John, and Sellers, Ian, eds. 1973. *Victorian Nonconformity.* London: Edward Arnold.

Broadbent, Samuel. 1865. *A Narrative of the First Introduction of Christianity amongst the Barolong Tribe of Bechuanas.* London: Wesleyan Mission House.

Bundy, Colin. 1979. *The Rise and Fall of the South African Peasantry.* London: Heinemann.

Campbell, John. 1813. *Travels in South Africa.* London: Black, Parry.

Carlyle, Thomas. 1842. *On Heroes, Hero-Worship, and the Heroic in History.* New York: Appleton.

Chadwick, Owen. 1966. *The Victorian Church* [Part I]. New York: Oxford University Press.

Clapham, John H. 1926. *An Economic History of Modern Britain: The Early Railway Age, 1820–1850.* Cambridge: Cambridge University Press.

Coetzee, John M. 1988. *White Writing: On the Culture of Letters in South Africa.* New Haven: Yale University Press.

Comaroff, Jean, and Comaroff, John L. 1991. *Of Revelation and Revolution.* Chicago: University of Chicago Press.

Cory, George E. 1919. *The Rise of South Africa.* Vol. 3. London: Longmans, Green.

Davenport, T. R. H. 1977. *South Africa: A Modern History.* Toronto: University of Toronto Press.

de Gruchy, John W. 1979. *The Church Struggle in South Africa.* Cape Town: David Philip.

de Kiewiet, C. W. 1941. *A History of South Africa, Social and Economic.* Oxford: Clarendon Press.

Edwards, Roger. 1853. ''Report from Mabotsa, 1852.'' In *Report of the Missions in South Africa . . . in connection with the London Missionary Society,* 31–44.

Engels, Friedrich. 1968. *The Condition of the Working Class in England.* Stanford: Stanford University Press.

Etherington, Norman. 1978. *Preachers, Peasants and Politics in Southeast Africa, 1835–1880.* London: Royal Historical Society.

Foucault, Michel. 1975. *The Birth of the Clinic.* New York: Vintage Books.

Halévy, Élie. 1924. *A History of the English People in 1815.* New York: Harcourt Brace.

Haley, Bruce. 1978. *The Healthy Body and Victorian Culture.* Cambridge, Mass.: Harvard University Press.

Hall, Charles. 1805. *The Effects of Civilization on the People in European States.* London: For the author and sold by T. Ostell and C. Chappel.

Hill, Christopher. 1969. *Reformation to Industrial Revolution, 1530–1780.* Harmondsworth: Penguin.

Hobsbawm, Eric J. 1962. *The Age of Revolution 1789–1848.* New York: New American Library.

———. 1964. *Labouring Men.* London: Weidenfeld and Nicholson.

Jeal, Tim. 1973. *Livingstone.* New York: G. P. Putnam's Sons.

Johnston, Harry H. n.d. *David Livingstone.* London: Charles H. Kelly.

Knorr, Klaus E. 1941. *British Colonial Theories, 1570–1850*. Toronto: University of Toronto Press.

Legassick, Martin. 1980. "The Frontier Tradition in South African Historiography." In *Economy and Society in Pre-Industrial South Africa,* ed. S. Marks and A. Atmore, 44–79. London: Longman.

Lichtenstein, Henry (Martin Karl Heinrich). 1928–1930. *Travels in Southern Africa . . .* Cape Town: Van Riebeeck Society.

Livingstone, David. 1857. *Missionary Travels and Researches in South Africa.* London: Murray.

———. 1858. *Dr. Livingstone's Cambridge Lectures,* Cambridge: Deighton, Bell and Co.; London: Bell and Daldy.

Ludorf, Joseph D. M. 1854. "Extract of a Letter from Rev. Joseph Ludorf, Thaba 'Nchu." *Wesleyan Missionary Notices—relating to Foreign Missions,* Third Series (December): 194.

———. 1863. "Extract of a Letter from Moshaning." *Wesleyan Missionary Notices— relating to Foreign Missions,* Third Series, (December): 203–207.

Mackenzie, John. 1871. *Ten Years North of the Orange River.* Edinburgh: Edmonston and Douglas.

———. 1887. *Austral Africa.* London: Sampson Low.

Macmillan, William Miller. 1927. *The Cape Colour Question.* London: Faber and Gwyer.

———. 1963. "Political Development, 1822–1834." In *The Cambridge History of the British Empire,* vol. 8. 2d ed., ed. A. P. Newton and E. A. Benians, 248–265. Cambridge: Cambridge University Press.

Marx, Karl. 1967. *Capital.* New York: International Publishers.

Meintjes, Johannes. 1973. *The Voortrekkers.* London: Cassell.

Mill, John Stuart. 1982. *Collected Works of John Stuart Mill.* Vol. 6. London: Routledge and Kegan Paul.

Moffat, John S. 1886. *The Lives of Robert and Mary Moffat.* New York: Armstrong and Son.

Moffat, Robert. 1842. *Missionary Labours and Scenes in Southern Africa.* London: Snow.

Molema, Silas Modiri. 1951. *Chief Moroka.* Cape Town: Methodist Publishing House.

———. 1966. *Montshiwa, Barolong Chief and Patriot.* Cape Town: Struik.

Muller, C. F. J. 1969. "The Period of the Great Trek, 1834–1854." In *Five Hundred Years: A History of South Africa,* ed. C. F. J. Muller, 146–182. Pretoria: Academica.

Newton-King, Susan. 1980. "The Labour Market of the Cape Colony, 1807–28." In *Economy and Society in Pre-Industrial South Africa,* ed. S. Marks and A. Atmore, 171–207. London: Longman.

Northcott, Cecil. 1961. *Robert Moffat: Pioneer in Africa 1817–1870.* London: Lutterworth.

Orwell, George. 1934. *Burmese Days.* New York and London: Harcourt Brace Jovanovich.

Philip, John. 1828. *Researches in South Africa.* London: James Duncan.

Reed, John R. 1975. *Victorian Conventions.* Athens: Ohio University Press.

Roscoe, William. 1787. *The Wrongs of Africa, a Poem.* London: R. Faulder.

Ross, Andrew. 1986. *John Philip (1775–1851): Missions, Race and Politics in South Africa.* Aberdeen: Aberdeen University Press.

Schapera, Isaac, ed. 1960. *Livingstone's Private Journals, 1851–1853.* Berkeley: University of California Press.

———. 1974. *David Livingstone: South African Papers, 1849–1853.* Cape Town: Van Riebeeck Society.

Shelley, Percy Bysshe. 1882. *The Poetical Works of Percy Bysshe Shelley.* London: Reeves and Turner.

Shillington, Kevin. 1985. *The Colonisation of the Southern Tswana, 1870–1900.* Johannesburg: Ravan Press.

Smith, Edwin W. 1925. *Robert Moffat, One of God's Gardeners.* Edinburgh: Turnbull and Spears.

Spicker, Stuart F., ed. 1970. *The Philosophy of the Body.* Chicago: Quadrangle Books.

Stow, George W. 1905. *The Native Races of South Africa.* London: Swan Sonnenschein.

Streak, Michael. 1974. *The Afrikaner as Viewed by the English, 1795–1854.* Cape Town: Struik.

Theal, George McCall. 1891. *History of South Africa [1795–1834].* London: Swan Sonnenschein.

———. 1893. *History of South Africa [1834–1854].* London: Swan Sonnenschein.

———. 1902. *The Progress of South Africa in the Century.* London and Edinburgh: Chambers.

Thomis, Malcolm I. 1974. *The Town Labourer and the Industrial Revolution.* London: Batsford.

Thompson, Edward P. 1963. *The Making of the English Working Class.* London: Gollancz.

———. 1967. "Time, Work-Discipline and Industrial Capitalism." *Past and Present* 38:56–97.

Thompson, Leonard M. 1969 "Co-operation and Conflict: The High Veld." In *The Oxford History of South Africa,* vol. 1, ed. M. Wilson and L. Thompson, 391–446. Oxford: Oxford University Press.

Toynbee, Arnold. 1969. *Toynbee's Industrial Revolution.* New York: Augustus M. Kelley.

Trapido, Stanley. 1980. "'The Friends of the Natives: Merchants, Peasants and the Political and Ideological Structure of Liberalism in the Cape, 1854–1910." In *Economy and Society in Pre-Industrial South Africa,* ed. S. Marks and A. Atmore, 247–274. London: Longman.

Warner, Wellman J. 1930. *The Wesleyan Movement in the Industrial Revolution.* London: Longmans, Green.

Williams, Raymond. 1973. *The Country and the City.* London: Oxford University Press.

Wilson, Monica. 1976. "Missionaries: Conquerors or Servants of God?" Address given at the opening of the South African Missionary Museum. Lovedale: South African Missionary Museum.

Wordsworth, William. [1835] 1948. *A Guide through the District of the Lakes in the North of England.* Malvern: Tantivy Press.

5

Sexual Affronts and Racial Frontiers

European Identities and the Cultural Politics of Exclusion in Colonial Southeast Asia

Ann Laura Stoler

This essay is concerned with the construction of colonial categories and national identities and with those people who ambiguously straddled, crossed, and threatened these imperial divides. It begins with a story about *métissage* (interracial unions) and the sorts of progeny to which it gave rise (referred to as *métis*, mixed-bloods) in French Indochina at the turn of the century. It is a story with multiple versions about people whose cultural sensibilities, physical being, and political sentiments called into question the distinctions of difference that maintained the neat boundaries of colonial rule. Its plot and resolution defy the treatment of European nationalist impulses and colonial racist policies as discrete projects, since here it was in the conflation of racial category, sexual morality, cultural competence, and national identity that the case was contested and politically charged. In a broader sense, it allows me to address one of the tensions of empire that this chapter only begins to sketch: the relationship among the discourses of inclusion, humanitarianism, and equality that informed liberal policy at the turn of the century in colonial Southeast Asia and the exclusionary, discriminatory practices that were reactive to, coexistent with, and perhaps inherent in liberalism itself.[1]

Nowhere is this relationship between inclusionary impulses and exclusionary practices more evident than in how métissage was legally handled, culturally inscribed, and politically treated in the contrasting colonial cultures of French Indochina and the Netherlands Indies. French Indochina was a colony of commerce occupied by the military in the 1860s and settled by *colons* in the 1870s with a métis population that numbered no more than several hundred by the turn of the century.[2] The Netherlands Indies, by contrast, had been settled since the early 1600s with those of mixed descent or born in the Indies—

numbering in the tens of thousands in 1900. They made up nearly three-fourths of those legally designated as European. Their *Indische* mestizo culture shaped the contours of colonial society for its first two hundred years.[3] Although conventional historiography defines sharp contrasts between French, British, and Dutch colonial racial policy and the particular national metropolitan agendas from which they derived, what is more striking is that similar discourses were mapped onto such vastly different social and political landscapes.[4]

In both the Indies and Indochina, with their distinct demographics and internal rhythms, métissage was a focal point of political, legal, and social debate. Conceived as a dangerous source of subversion, it was seen as a threat to white prestige, an embodiment of European degeneration and moral decay.[5] This is not to suggest that the so-called mixed-blood problem was of the same intensity in both places or resolved in precisely the same ways. However, the issues that resonated in these different colonies reveal a patterned set of transgressions that have not been sufficiently explored. I would suggest that both situations were so charged in part because such mixing called into question the very criteria by which Europeanness could be identified, citizenship should be accorded, and nationality assigned. Métissage represented, not the dangers of foreign enemies at national borders, but the more pressing affront for European nation-states, what the German philosopher Johann Gottlieb Fichte so aptly defined as the essence of the nation, its "interior frontiers."[6]

The concept of an interior frontier is compelling precisely because of its contradictory connotations. As Etienne Balibar has noted, a frontier locates a site both of enclosure and contact and of observed passage and exchange. When coupled with the word *interior,* frontier carries the sense of internal distinctions within a territory (or empire); at the level of the individual, frontier marks the moral predicates by which a subject retains his or her national identity despite location outside the national frontier and despite heterogeneity within the nation-state. As Fichte deployed it, an interior frontier entails two dilemmas: the purity of the community is prone to penetration on its interior and exterior borders, and the essence of the community is an intangible "moral attitude," "a multiplicity of invisible ties."[7]

Viewing late nineteenth-century representations of a national essence in these terms, we can trace how métissage emerges as a powerful trope for internal contamination and challenge conceived morally, politically, and sexually.[8] The changing density and intensity of métissage's discursive field outlines the fault lines of colonial authority: in linking domestic arrangements to the public order, family to the state, sex to subversion, and psychological essence to racial type, métissage might be read as a metonym for the biopolitics of the empire at large.

In both Indochina and the Netherlands Indies, the rejection of métis as a distinct legal category only intensified how the politics of cultural difference were played out in other domains.[9] In both colonies, the *métis-indo* problem produced a discourse in which facile theories of racial hierarchy were rejected, while confirming the practical predicates of European superiority at the same time. The early Vietnamese and Indonesian nationalist movements created new sources of colonial vulnerability, and some of the debates over the nature and definition of Dutch and French national identity must be seen in that light. The resurgence of European nationalist rhetoric may partly have been a response to nationalist resistance in the colonies, but it cannot be accounted for in these terms alone.[10] For French Indochina, discourses about the dangers of métissage were sustained in periods of quiescence and cannot be viewed as rhetorics of reaction *tout court*. This is not to suggest that there was no correspondence between them.[11] But anticolonial challenges in Indochina, contrary to the discourse that characterized the métis as a potential subversive vanguard, were never predominantly led or peopled by them. And in the Indies, where persons of mixed descent made up a potentially powerful constituency, the bids they made for economic, social, and political reform were more often made in contradistinction to the demands of the native population, not in alliance with them.

Although the content of the métis problem was partially in response to popular threats to colonial rule, the particular form that the securing of European privilege took was not shaped in the colonies alone. The focus on moral unity, cultural genealogy, and language joined the imagining of European colonial communities and metropolitan national entities in fundamental ways. Both visions embraced a moral rearmament, centering on the domestic domain and the family as sites in which state authority could be secured or irreparably undermined.[12]

At the turn of the century, in both metropole and colony, the liberal impulse for social welfare, representation, and protective legislation focused enormous energy on the preparatory environment for civic responsibility: on domestic arrangements, sexual morality, parenting, and more specifically on the moral milieu of home and school in which children lived.[13] Both education and upbringing emerged as national projects, but not as we might expect, with a firm sense of national identity imported to the periphery from the metropolitan core. As Eugene Weber has argued for late nineteenth-century France, "patriotic feelings on the national level, far from instinctive, had to be learned."[14] As late as 1901, six out of every ten French army recruits had not heard of the Franco-Prussian War.[15] Thus the Gallicization of France and its colonies through compulsory education, moral instruction, and language was not a one-way process with a consensual template for that identity forged in the metropole and later transported by new metropolitan recruits to colonial citizens. Between 1871 and 1914, French authorities were preoccupied with the threat of national diminishment and decline, with the study of national character a "veritable industry in France."[16]

French anxieties over national identity are commonly attributed to the loss of Alsace-Lorraine in 1870, but of perhaps equal import was the collective assimilation of more than one hundred thousand Algerian Jews under the Crémieux Decree of the same year.[17] Debates over who was really French and who was not intensified over the next twenty years as increasing numbers of working-class Italians, Spanish, and Maltese in Algeria were accorded French citizenship. A declining birthrate (accelerating in the 1880s) placed a premium on expanded membership in the French national community but prompted a fear of internal aliens and pseudocompatriots at the same time.[18] The Dreyfus affair coupled with concerns over the suspect loyalties of the new French of Algeria gave particular urgency to debates about the cultural contours of what it meant to be French.[19]

Heightened debates over the mixed-blood question in the Dutch context converged with domestic and colonial social reform, crystallizing in a civilizing offensive of a somewhat different order. It targeted the "dangerous classes" in both locales—Holland's paupered residuum (as distinguished from its respectable working class) and the Indies' growing population of impoverished (Indo) Europeans, the majority of whom were of mixed descent but legally classified as European. The domestic project joined liberals and conservatives, Protestants, and Catholics in a shared mission, with middle-class energies concentrated around the "uplifting" of the working-class family and its moral reform. This "civilizing offensive" focused in large part on child welfare and particularly on those "neglected" and "delinquent" children whose "upbringing" ill-prepared them for "their future place in the social system" and thus marked them as a danger to the state.[20]

Although national anxieties were not at the same pitch as in France, there is evidence that, at the turn of the century, Dutch national feeling—what Maarten Kuitenbrouwer has called an "extreme nationalism"—"underwent something of a revival," then later subsided again.[21] In tandem with the domestic offensive was also an imperial one that spanned concerns about both Dutch paupers in the Indies and "vagabond Hollanders" in South Africa. Efforts to counter "the perils of educational failure" and the increased mixing, marrying, and interaction of poor whites with colonized populations in the two locales gave rise to increased investments in the education of poor white children and assaults on the parenting styles those children were subject to at home.[22] The securing of Dutch influence in South Africa on the eve of the Boer War centered on strategies to instill a cultural belonging that was to mark the new boundaries of a "Greater Netherlands" embracing Flanders, South Africa, and the Indies.[23] In both metropolitan class and imperial projects, questions of national identity, child rearing, and education were on the public agenda and intimately tied.

Thus the question of who might be considered truly French or Dutch resonated from core to colony and from colony to core.[24] In the Indies and

Indochina, cultural milieu, represented by both upbringing and education, was seen to demarcate which métis children would turn into revolutionaries, patricides, loyal subjects, or full-fledged citizens of the nation-state. As T. H. Marshall has argued, "when the State guarantees that all children shall be educated, it has the requirements and the nature of citizenship definitely in mind."[25] Métis education raised issues about retaining colonial boundaries and regenerating the nation. At issue were the means by which European *beschaving* (civilization or culture) would be disseminated without undercutting the criteria by which European claims to privilege were made.

As such, the discourses about métissage expressed more pervasive, if inchoate, dilemmas of colonial rule and a fundamental contradiction of imperial domination: the tension between a form of domination simultaneously predicated on both incorporation and distancing.[26] This tension expressed itself in the so-called métis problem in quintessential form. Some métis were candidates for incorporation, but others were categorically denied. In either case, the decision to grant citizenship or subject status to a métis could not be made on the basis of race alone, because all métis shared some degree of European descent by definition. How, then, could the state mark some candidates so they would be excluded from the national community while retaining the possibility that other individuals would be granted the rights of inclusion because French and Dutch "blood prevailed in their veins"? I explore that question here by working off of a seemingly disparate set of texts and contexts: a criminal court proceeding in Haiphong in 1898; the Hanoi campaign against child abandonment in the early 1900s; the protracted debate on mixed marriage legislation in the Indies between 1887 and 1898; and finally, the confused and failed efforts of the Indo-European movement itself in the Indies to articulate its opposition to "pure-blood" Dutch by calling on race, place, and cultural genealogy to make its demands.

In each of these texts, class, gender, and cultural markers deny and designate exclusionary practices at the same time. We cannot determine which of these categories is privileged at any given moment by sorting out the fixed primacy of race over gender or gender over class. On the contrary, I trace an unstable and uneven set of discourses in which different institutional authorities claimed primacy for one over another in relationship to how other authorities attempted to designate how political boundaries were to be protected and assigned. For mid-Victorian England, Mary Poovey argues that discourses about gender identity were gradually displaced in the 1850s by the issue of national identity.[27] However, the contestations over métissage suggest nothing linear about these developments. Rather, class distinctions, gender prescriptions, cultural knowledge, and racial membership were simultaneously invoked and strategically filled with different meanings for varied projects.

Patriarchal principles were not always applied to shore up government priorities. Colonial authorities with competing agendas agreed on two premises: children had to be taught both their place and race, and the family was the crucial site in which future subjects and loyal citizens were to be made. These concerns framed the fact that the domestic life of individuals was increasingly subject to public scrutiny by a wide range of private and government organizations that charged themselves with the task of policing the moral borderlands of the European community and the psychological sensibilities of its marginal, as well as supposedly full-fledged, members.

At the heart of this tension between inclusionary rhetorics and exclusionary practices was a search for essences that joined formulations of national and racial identity—what Benedict Anderson has contrasted as the contrary dreams of "historical destinies" and "eternal contaminations."[28] Racism is commonly understood as a visual ideology in which somatic features are thought to provide the crucial criteria of membership. But racism is not really a visual ideology at all; physiological attributes only signal the nonvisual and more salient distinctions of exclusion on which racism rests. Racism is not to biology as nationalism is to culture. Cultural attributions in both provide the observable conduits, the indexes of psychological propensities and moral susceptibilities seen to shape which individuals are suitable for inclusion in the national community and whether those of ambiguous racial membership are to be classified as subjects or citizens within it. If we are to trace the epidemiologies of racist and nationalist thinking, then it is the cultural logics that underwrite the relationship between fixed, visual representations and invisible protean essences to which we must attend. This convergence between national and racial thinking achieves particular clarity when we turn to the legal and social debates in the colonies that linked observable cultural styles of parenting and domestic arrangement to the hidden psychological requirements for access to French and Dutch citizenship in this period.

Cultural Competence, National Identity, and Métissage

In 1898 in the French Indochinese city of Haiphong, the nineteen-year-old son of a French minor naval employee, Sieur Icard, was charged with assaulting without provocation a German naval mechanic, striking his temple with a whip and attempting to crush his eye. The boy was sentenced by the tribunal court to six months in prison.[29] Spurred by the father's efforts to make an appeal for an attenuated prison term, some higher officials subsequently questioned whether the penalty was unduly severe. Clemency was not accorded by the governor-general, and the boy, referred to by the court as "Nguyen van Thinh *dit* Lucien" (called Lucien) was sentenced to bear out his full term. The case might have been less easily dismissed if it were not for the fact that the son was métis, the child of a man who was a French citizen and a woman who was a colonial subject, his concubine and Vietnamese.

The granting of a pardon rested on two assessments: whether the boy's cultural identity and his display of French cultural competence supported his claim to French citizenship rights. Because the governor-general's letters listed the boy as Nguyen van Thinh dit Lucien, they thereby not only invoked the double naming of the son, privileging first Nguyen van Thinh over Lucien, but also suggested the dubious nature of his cultural affinities, giving the impression that his real name was Nguyen van Thinh, although he answered to the name Lucien. The father, Sieur Icard, attempted to affirm the Frenchness of his son by referring to him as Lucien and eliminated reference to Nguyen. But the angry president of Haiphong's tribunal court used only the boy's Vietnamese name, dropping Lucien altogether, and put the very kinship between the father and son in question by naming Icard as the "alleged" father.

Icard's plea for pardon, which invoked his own patriotic sentiments as well as those of his son, was carefully conceived. Icard protested that the court had wrongly treated the boy as a "*vulgaire annamite*" (a common Annamite) and not as the legally recognized son of a French citizen. Icard held that his son had been provoked and only then struck the German in retaliation. But more important, Lucien had been raised in a French patriotic milieu, in a household in which Germans were held in "contempt and disdain." He pointed out that their home was full of drawings of the 1870 (Franco-Prussian) war and that like any impressionable [French] boy of his age, Lucien and his imagination were excited by these images.

The tribunal's refusal to accept the appeal confronted and countered Icard's claims. At issue was whether Nguyen van Thinh dit Lucien could really be considered culturally and politically French and whether he was inculcated with the patriotic feelings and nationalist sentiments that might have prompted such a loyal response. The tribunal argued that Icard was away sailing too much of the time to impart such a love of *patrie* to his son and that Icard's "hate of Germans must have been of very recent origin since he had spent so much time sailing with foreigners."[30] The non-French inclinations of the boy were firmly established with the court's observation that Lucien was illiterate and knew but a few French words. Icard's argument was thus further undermined since Icard himself "spoke no annamite" and therefore shared no common language with his offspring.

Although these counterarguments may have been sufficient to convince the governor-general not to grant leniency, another unclarified but damning reason was invoked to deny the son's case and the father's appeal: namely, the "immoral relations which could have existed between the detainee and the one who declared himself his father."[31] Or as put by Villeminot, the city attorney in Haiphong charged with further investigating Icard's appeal, the boy deserved no leniency because "his morality was always detestable" and the police reports permitted one "to entertain the most serious suspicions concerning the nature of the relations which Nguyen van Thinh maintained with his alleged father."[32]

Whether these were coded allegations of homosexuality or referred to a possibly illegal recognition of the boy by Icard (pretending to be his father) is unclear. Icard's case came up at a time when acts of "fraudulent recognition" of native children were said to be swelling the French citizenry with a bastard population of native poor.[33] Perversion and immorality and patriotism and nationalist sentiments were clearly considered mutually exclusive categories. As in nineteenth-century Germany, adherence to middle-class European sexual morality was one implicit requisite for full-fledged citizenship in the European nation-state.[34]

But with all these allusions to suspect and duplicitous behavior perhaps what was more unsettling in this case was another unspeakable element in this story: namely, that Icard felt such a powerful sentiment between himself and his son and that he not only recognized his Eurasian son but went so far as to plead the case of a boy who had virtually none of the exterior qualities (skin tone, language, or cultural literacy), and therefore could have none of the interior attributes, of being French at all. What the court seemed to have condemned was a relationship in which Icard could have shown such dedication and love for a child who was illiterate, who was ignorant of the French language, and who spent most of his time in a cultural milieu that was much less French than Vietnamese. Under such circumstances, Icard's concern for Lucien was inappropriate and improper; his fatherly efforts to excuse his son's misdeeds were lauded by neither the lower courts nor the governor-general. On the contrary, paternal love and responsibility were not to be disseminated arbitrarily as Icard had obviously done by recognizing his progeny but allowing him to grow up Indo-Chinese. In denying the father's plea, the court passed sentence on both Icard and his son: both were guilty of transgressing the boundaries of race, culture, sex, and patrie. If Icard (whose misspellings and profession belied his lower-class origins) was not able to bring his son up in a proper French milieu, then he should have abandoned him altogether.

What was perhaps most duplicitous in the relationship was that the boy could be both Nguyen van Thinh in cultural sensibilities and Lucien to his father, or, from a slightly different perspective, that Lucien's physical and cultural non-French affinities did not stand in the way of the father's love. Like the relationship with the boy's mother, which was easily attributed to carnal lust, Icard's choice to stand up for his son was reduced to a motive of base desires, sexual or otherwise. Neither father nor son had demonstrated a proper commitment to and identification with those invisible moral bonds by which racist pedigrees and colonial divides were marked and maintained.

Cultural Neglect, Native Mothers, and the Racial Politics of Abandonment

The story invokes the multiple tensions of colonial cultures in Southeast Asia and would be of interest for that alone. But it is all the more startling because it so boldly contradicts the dominant formulation of the "métis question" at the turn of the century as a problem of "abandonment," of children culturally on the loose, sexually abused, economically impoverished, morally neglected, and politically dangerous. European feminists took up the protection of abandoned mixed-blood children as their cause, condemning the irresponsibility and double standards of European men, but so too did colonial officials who argued that these concubinary relations were producing a new underclass of European paupers, of rootless children who could not be counted among the proper European citizenry, whose sartorial trappings merely masked their cultural incompetence, who did not know what it meant to be Dutch or French. The consequences of mixed unions were thus collapsed into a singular moral trajectory, which, without state intervention, would lead to a future generation of Eurasian paupers and prostitutes, an affront to European prestige and a contribution to national decay.

If we look more closely at what was identified as abandonment, the cultural and historical peculiarities of this definition become more apparent. In his comprehensive history of child abandonment in western Europe, John Boswell commonly uses "abandonment" to refer to "the *voluntary* relinquishing of control over children by their natal parents or guardians" and to children who were exposed at the doors of churches or in other public spaces and less frequently for those intentionally exposed to death.[35] Boswell argues that ancient and contemporary commentators have conflated abandonment with infanticide far more than the evidence suggests. Nevertheless, perceptions and policies on abandonment were integrally tied to issues of child mortality. Jacques Donzelot argues that in nineteenth-century France abandonment often led to high rates of child mortality and that the intensified policing of families was morally justified for those reasons among others.[36] This does not suggest that abandonment always led to death or that this was always its intent. The point is that in the colonial context, in contrast, discussions of abandonment rarely raise a similar concern for infanticide or even obliquely address this eventuality.

The abandonment of métis children invoked, in the colonial context, not a biological but a social death—a severing from European society, a banishment of "innocents" from the European cultural milieu in which they could potentially thrive and where some reformers contended they rightfully belonged.[37] Those officials who wrote about métis children argued that exposure in the colonial context was to the native milieu, not the natural elements, and to the immoral influence of native women whose debased characters inclined them to succumb to such illicit unions in the first place. Moreover, abandonment, as we shall see, was not necessarily voluntary, nor did both parents, despite the implication in Boswell's definition, participate in it. The statutes of the Society for the Protection and Education of Young French Métis of Cochinchine and Cambodia defined the issue of abandonment in the following way.

> Left to themselves, having no other guide than their instincts and their passions, these unfortunates will always give free rein to their bad inclinations; the boys will increase the ranks of vagabonds, the girls those of prostitution.
>
> Left to their mothers and lost in the milieu of Annamites, they will not become less depraved. It must not be forgotten that in most cases, the indigenous woman who consents to live with a European is a veritable prostitute and that she will never reform. When, after several years of free union with Frenchmen, the latter disappear or abandon her, she fatally returns to the vice from which she came and she nearly always sets an example of debauchery, sloth, and immorality for her children. She takes care of them with the sole purpose of later profiting from their labor and especially from their vices.
>
> For her métis son, she seeks out a scholarship in a school with the certainty that when her child obtains a minor administrative post, she will profit from it. But, in many cases, the child, ill-advised and ill-directed, does not work and when he leaves school, abandons himself to idleness and then to vagabondage; he procures his means of existence by extortion and theft.
>
> Abandoned métisse girls are no better off; from the cradle, their mothers adorn them with bracelets and necklaces and maintain in them a love of luxury innate in the Annamites. Arriving at the age of puberty, deprived of any skills which would help them survive, and pushed into a life by their mothers that they have a natural tendency to imitate, they will take to prostitution in its diverse forms to procure the means necessary to keep themselves in luxury.[38]

Here, abandonment has specific race, cultural, and gender coordinates. Most frequently, it referred to the abandonment of métis children by European fathers and their abandonment of the children's native mothers with whom these men lived outside of marriage. The gaze of the colonial state was not directed at children abandoned by native men but only at the progeny of mixed unions. Most significant, the child, considered abandoned whether he or she remained in the care of the mother, was most frequently classified that way precisely because the child was left to a native mother and to the cultural surroundings in which she lived. But the term "abandonment" was also used freely in another context to condemn those socially déclassé European men who chose to reside with their mixed-blood children in the supposedly immoral and degraded native milieu. In designating cultural rather than physical neglect, abandonment connoted at least two things: that a proper French father would never allow his offspring prolonged contact or identification with such a milieu and that the native mother of lower-class origins would only choose to keep her own children for mercenary purposes.

If abandonment of métis offspring by European men was considered morally reprehensible, the depraved motives of colonized women who refused to give up their children to the superior environment of state institutions were considered worse. Thus the president of the Hanoi Society for the Protection of Métis Youths in 1904 noted that "numerous mothers refuse to confer their children to us . . . under the *pretext* of not wanting to be apart from them, despite the fact that they may periodically visit them at school."[39] But if maternal love obscured more mercenary quests to exploit their young for profits and pleasure, as was often claimed, why did so many women not only refuse to hand over their children but also reject any form of financial assistance for them? Cases of such refusal were not uncommon. In 1903 the Haiphong court admonished a métisse mother who was herself "raised with all the exterior signs of a European education" for withdrawing her daughter from a government school "for motives which could not be but base given the mother's character."[40] Resistance also came from the children themselves. In 1904, the seventeen-year-old métisse daughter of an Annamite woman cohabited with the French employer of her mother's Annamite lover, declaring that she *volontairement* accepted and preferred her own situation over what the Society for the Protection of Métis Youths could offer.[41] Numerous reports are cited of métisse girls forced into prostitution by *concubin,* that is, by native men who were the subsequent lovers of the girls' native mothers. These cases expressed another sexual and cultural transgression that metropolitan social reformers and colonial authorities both feared: namely, a "traffic in *filles françaises*" for the Chinese and Annamite market, not for Europeans.[42]

The portrait of abandonment and charitable rescue is seriously flawed, for it misses the fact that the channeling of abandoned métis children into special state institutions was part of a larger (but failed) imperial vision. These children were to be molded into very special colonial citizens; in one scenario, they were to be the bulwark of a future white settler population, acclimatized to the tropics but loyal to the state.[43] As proposed by the French feminist caucus at the National Colonial Exposition of 1931, métisse young women could

> marry with Frenchmen, would accept living in the bush where young women from the metropole would be hesitant to follow their husbands, . . . [and would form] the foundation of a bourgeoisie, attached at one and the same time to their native land and to the France of Europe.[44]

This perspective on mixed marriages was more optimistic than some, but it echoes the commonly held view that if métisse girls were rescued in time, they could be effectively educated to become *bonnes ménageres* (good housekeepers) of a settled Indochina, wives or domestics in the service of France. Similar proposals, as we shall see, were entertained in the Indies in the same period and there too met with little success. However, in both contexts, the vision of fortifying the colonial project with a mixed-blood yeomanry was informed by a fundamental concern: What could be done with this mixed population, whose ambiguous positioning and identifications could make them either dangerous adversaries or effective partisans of the colonial state?

Fraudulent Recognitions and Other Dangers of Métissage

The question of what to do with the métis population prompted a number of different responses, but each hinged on whether métis should be classified as a distinct legal category subject to special education or so thoroughly assimilated into French culture that they would pose no threat. In French Indochina, the model treatment of métis in the Netherlands Indies was invoked at every turn. In 1901, Joseph Chailley-Bert, director of the Union Colonial Française, was sent on a government mission to Java to report on the status of métis in the Indies and on the efficacy of Dutch policy toward them. Chailley-Bert came away from Batavia immensely impressed and convinced that segregation was not the answer. He was overwhelmed by the sheer numbers of persons of mixed descent who occupied high station in the Indies, with wealth and cultivation rivaling those of many "full-blooded" Europeans. He argued that the Dutch policy not to segregate those of mixed descent or distinguish between illegitimate and legitimate children was the only humane and politically safe course to pursue. He urged the government to adopt several Dutch practices: that abandoned métis youth be assigned European status until proof of filiation was made; that private organizations in each legal grouping (i.e., European and native) be charged with poor relief rather than the government; and that European standing not be confined to those with the proper "dosage of blood" alone. In the Indies he noted that such a ruling would be impossible because the entire society was in large part métis and such a distinction "would allow a distance between the aryan without mix and the asiatic hybrids."[45]

Monsieur A. July, writing from Hanoi in 1905, similarly applauded "the remarkably successful results" of the Indies government policy rejecting the legal designation of métis as a caste apart. He argued that France's abolition of slavery and call for universal suffrage had made a tabula rasa of racial prejudice; however, he was less sanguine that France's political system could permit a similar scale of naturalization as that practiced by the Dutch, since not all young métis could be recognized as *citoyen français* for reasons he thought better not to discuss. Firmin Jacques Montagne, a head conductor in the Department of Roads and Bridges also urged that French Indochina follow the Indies path, where the Dutch had not only "safeguarded their prestige, but also profited from a force that if badly directed, could turn against Dutch domination."[46] Based on the account of a friend who administered a plantation on Java, he urged that métis boys in Indochina, as in the Indies, should be educated in special institutions to prepare them to be soldiers and later for modest employment in commerce or on the estates.

These appeals to Dutch wisdom are so curious because they reflected neither the treatment of the poor Indo-European population in the Indies nor what administrative quandaries were actually facing Dutch officials there. In the very year of Chailley-Bert's visit to Batavia, the Indies government began a massive investigation of the recent proliferation of European pauperism and its causes. Between 1901 and 1903 several thousands of pages of government reports outlined the precarious economic conditions and political dangers of a population legally classified as European but riddled with impoverished widows, beggars, vagrants, and abandoned children who were mostly Indo-Europeans.[47] The pauperism commission identified an "alarming increase" of poor Europeans born in the Indies or of mixed parentage, who could not compete for civil service positions with the influx of "full-blooded" Dutch educated in Europe or with the growing number of better-educated Indonesians now qualified for the same jobs.[48]

The Dutch did investigate Indo-European adult life and labor, but the focus of the commissions' concern was on children and their upbringing in the parental home (opvoeding in de ouderlijkewoning).[49] Among the more than seventy thousand legally classified Europeans in the Indies in 1900, nearly 70 percent knew little Dutch or none at all. Perhaps the more disturbing finding was that many of them were living on the borderlands of respectable bourgeois European society in styles that indicated not a failed version of European culture but an outright rejection of it.[50]

The causes of the situation were found in the continued prevalence of concubinage, not only among subaltern European military barred from legal marriage but also among civil servants and European estate supervisors for whom marriage to European women was either formally prohibited or made an economically untenable option. Although government and private company policies significantly relaxed the restrictions imposed on the entry of women from Europe after the turn of the century, nonconjugal mixed unions, along with the gendered and racist assumptions on which they were based, were not about to disappear by government fiat. In Indochina, French officials had to issue repeated warnings against concubinage from 1893 to 1911 (just when the societies for protection of métis youth were most active), suggesting the formation of another generation that threatened not to know where they belonged.[51] The pauperism commission condemned the general moral environment of the Indies, targeting concubinage as the source of a transient "rough and dangerous pauper element" that lived off the native population when they could, disgracing European prestige and creating a financial burden for the state.[52]

But Indo-European pauperism in the Indies could not be accounted for by concubinage alone. The pauperism commission's inquiry revealed a highly stratified educational system in which European youths educated in the Indies were categorically barred from high-level administrative posts and in which middling Indo-Europeans were offered only a rudimentary training in Dutch, a basic requisite for any white-collar job.[53] European public (free) schools in the Indies, like those in Indochina, were largely schools for the poor (*armenscholen*) attended by and really only designed for a lower class of indigent and mixed-blood Europeans.[54]

A concrete set of reforms did form a response, to some extent, to concubinage and educational inequities, but European pauperism was located in a more unsettling problem: It was seen to have deeper and more tenacious roots in the surreptitious penetration of inlanders into the legal category of European.[55] Because the European legal standing exempted men both from labor service and from the harsher penal code applied to those of native status, officials argued that an underclass of European soldiers and civilians was allegedly engaged in a profitable racket of falsely recognizing native children who were not their own for an attractive fee. Thus, the state commission argued, European impoverishment was far more limited than the statistics indicated: The European civil registers were inflated by lowlife mercenaries and, as in Indochina, by *des sans-travail* (the unemployed), who might register as many as thirty to forty children who did not have proper rights to Dutch or French citizenship at all.[56]

The issue of fraudulent recognition, like concubinage, hinged on the fear that children were being raised in cultural fashions that blurred the distinctions between ruler and ruled and on the fear that uneducated native young men were acquiring access to Dutch and French nationality by channels, such as false filiation, that circumvented state control. Such practices were allegedly contingent on a nefarious class of European men who were willing to facilitate the efforts of native mothers who sought such arrangements. Whether there were as many fraudulent recognitions of métis children in Indochina or *kunstmatig gefabriceerde Europeanen* (artificially fabricated Europeans) in the Indies as authorities claimed is really not the point. The repeated reference to fictitious, fraudulent, and fabricated Europeans expressed an underlying preoccupation of colonial authorities, shared by many in the European community at large, that illicit incursions into the Dutch and French citizenry extended beyond those cases labeled fraudulent recognition by name. We should remember that Nguyen van Thinh dit Lucien's condemnation was never explicitly argued on the basis of his suspect parentage, but on the more general contention that his behavior had to be understood as that of an indigene in disguise, not as a citizen of France. Annamite women who had lived in concubinage were accused of clothing their métisse daughters in European attire, while ensuring that their souls and sentiments remained deeply native.[57]

Colonial officials wrestled with the belief that the Europeanness of métis children could never be assured, despite a rhetoric affirming that education and upbringing were transformative processes. Authorities spoke of abandoned métisse daughters as *les filles françaises* when arguing for their redemption, but when supporting segregated education, these same authorities recast these youths as physically marked and morally marred with ''the faults and mediocre qualities of their [native] mothers'' as ''the fruits of a regrettable weakness.''[58] Thus abandoned métis children represented not only the sexual excesses and indiscretions of European men but also the dangers of a subaltern class, degenerate (*verwilderen*) and lacking paternal discipline (*gemis aan vaderlijke tucht*), a world in which mothers took charge.[59] To what extent the concern over neglected métis children was not only about the negative influence of the native milieu but also about the threat of single-mother families as in Europe and America in the same period is difficult to discern.[60] The absence of patriarchal authority in households of widows and native women who had exited from concubinary domestic arrangements was clearly seen as a threat to the proper moral upbringing of children and sanctioned the intervention of the state. Métis children undermined the inherent principles on which national identity thrived—those *liens invisibles* (invisible bonds) that all men shared and that so clearly and comfortably marked off *pur-sang* French and Dutch from those of the generic colonized.

The option of making métis a legal category was actively debated in international colonial forums through the 1930s but was rejected on explicitly political grounds. French jurists persuasively argued that such a legal segregation would infest the colonies with a destructive virus, with a ''class of *déraciné*, déclassé,'' ''our most dangerous enemies,'' ''insurgents, irreconcilable enemies of our domination.''[61] The legal rejection of difference in no way diminished the concern about them. On the contrary, it produced an intensified discourse in which racial thinking remained the bedrock on which cultural markers of difference were honed and more carefully defined.

This was nowhere clearer than in the legal discussion about whether and by what criteria children of unknown parents should be assigned French or native nationality.[62] Under a 1928 *décret,* all persons born in Indochina (that is, on French soil) of unknown parents of which one was presumed to be French could obtain recognition of ''la qualité de français.''[63] Presumed Frenchness rested on two sorts of certainty: the evaluation of the child's ''physical features or race'' by a ''medico-legal expert'' and a ''moral certainty'' derived from the fact that the child ''has a French name, lived in a European milieu and was considered by all as being of French descent.''[64] Thus French citizenship was not open to all métis but restricted by a ''scientific'' and moral judgment that the child was decidedly nonindigene.[65] As we have seen in the case of Nguyen van Thinh dit Lucien, however, the name Lucien, the acknowledged paternity by Icard, and the patriotic ambience of the household were only sufficient for the child to be legally classified as French, not for him to be treated as French by a court of law. Inclusionary laws left ample room for an implementation based on exclusionary principles and practices.

The moral outrage and crusade against abandonment attended to another underlying dilemma for those who ruled. Métis youth not only had to be protected from the "demoralization of the special milieu" in which they were raised but, as important, educated in a way that would not produce unreasonable expectations or encourage them to harbor desires for privilege above their station simply because French or Dutch blood flowed in their veins. The aim of the Hanoi society for the protection of métis youth was "to inculcate them with our sense of honor and integrity, while only suggesting to them modest tastes and humble aspirations."[66] Similarly, in the Indies, Indo-European pauperism was commonly attributed to the "false sense of pride" of Indos who refused to do manual labor or take on menial jobs, who did not know that "real Dutchmen" in the Netherlands worked with their hands. The assault was double-edged. It blamed those impoverished for their condition but also suggested more subtly that if they were really Dutch in spirit and drive, such problems of pauperism would not have arisen.

The Cultural Frontiers of the National Community

Fears of white impoverishment in the colonies were held by many different constituencies: by social reformers concerned with child welfare, by European feminists opposed to the double standard of European men, and by colonial officials who fiercely debated whether increased education would diffuse the discontents of the European poor or, as with the peasants of France, turn them into empowered enemies of the state.[67] However, none of these fears was very far removed from the more general concern that European men living with native women would themselves lose their Dutch or French identity and would become degenerate and *décivilisé*. Internal to this logic was a notion of cultural, physical, and moral contamination, the fear that those Europeans who did not subscribe to Dutch middle-class conventions of respectability would not only compromise the cultural distinctions of empire, but waver in their allegiances to metropolitan rule.

Such fears were centered on mixed-bloods but not on them alone. In the Indies, at the height of the liberal Ethical Policy, a prominent doctor warned that those Europeans born and bred in the colonies, the *blijvers* (those who remained), lived in surroundings that stripped them of their *zuivere* (pure) European sensibilities, which "could easily lead them to metamorphose into Javanese."[68] A discourse on degeneracy with respect to the creole Dutch was not new in the Indies but in this moment of liberal reform took on a new force with specific moral coordinates. This discourse was directed at poor whites living on the cultural borderlands of the *echte* (true) European community, at some European men who married native women, at all European women who chose to marry native men, and at both European and Indo-European women who cohabited with, but chose not to marry, men of other nationalities.

These specific fears may have been intensified by the surge of political activity at the turn of the century, coalescing around an Indisch population of "mixed-blood" and "pure-blood" Dutch of Indies origin. Their distinct economic interests, cultural style, and legal positioning produced equivocal loyalties to the colonial state. The Indische voice, evident in a range of new publications and associations, identified itself in two ways: by its cultural rooting in the Indies rather than the Netherlands and by an ambiguous appeal to the notion of race. At a time when the native nationalist project was not yet under way, this Indische press articulated a new notion of a fatherland loyal to, but distinct from, the Dutch fatherland and firmly opposed to the Dutch-born elite who managed the state. Between 1898 and 1903 various Indisch groups rose, fell, and reassembled as they each sought viable programs to promote the "uplifting" of the Indo-European poor without linking their own fate to them. To do so, they resorted to principles of racial hierarchy that accorded those of a certain upbringing, sexual morality, and cultural sensibility a right to privilege and to rule.[69]

What underwrites this common discourse is a new collusion between race and culture: As race dropped out of certain legal discriminations, it reemerged, marked out by specific cultural criteria in other domains. The contemporary discourse on the new racism in Europe situates "cultural racism" as a relatively recent and nuanced phenomenon, replacing the physiological distinctions on which earlier racisms had so strongly relied.[70] The "novelty" of the new racism is often located in its strong cultural inflection, embedded in wider structures of domination, based in the family, and tied to nationalist sentiments in ways that make it more relevant to a wider constituency and therefore more pervasive and insidious to weed out.[71] But are these features of the "new racism" really new at all? I would argue, on the contrary, that they are firmly rooted in a much earlier discourse that linked race, culture, and national identity, a discourse elaborated at the turn of the century in Europe's "laboratories of modernity"—the colonies—not at home.[72]

It is striking how critical the concept of cultural surroundings (*milieu* in French, *omgeving* in Dutch) in this period was to the new legal stipulations on which racial distinctions and national identity were derived. Paul Rabinow makes a strong case that the concern about milieu permeating French colonial thinking on education, health, labor, and sex in the late nineteenth century can only be understood in terms of the scientific *episteme* on which it relied.[73] Medical guides to the acclimatization of Europeans in tropical regions frequently warned that Europeans would lose their physical health and cultural bearings if they stayed in the tropics too long. Debates over whether European children should be schooled in France or the Netherlands were prompted by efforts to create the social habitus in which sentiments and sensibilities would be shaped.[74] These debates drew not so much on Darwin as on a popular neo-Lamarckian understanding of environment in which racial and national essences could be secured or altered by the physical, psychological, climatic, and moral surroundings in which one lived. The issue of omgeving and the linkages between national, racial, and cultural identity were, however, most thoroughly thought out in the colonial legal discourse on the criteria for European status and inscribed, not in the laws themselves, which self-consciously disclaimed racial difference, but in the cultural logic and racist assumptions underpinning the legal arguments. What is apparent in these documents is a tension between a belief in the immutability and fixity of racial essence and a discomforting awareness that these racial categories are porous and protean at the same time. More unsettling still was the cultural perception that the essences embodied by the colonized and colonizer were asymmetric. Thus Javanese or Vietnamese might at any moment revert to their natural indigenous affiliations, while a Dutch essence was so fragile that it could unwittingly transform into something Javanese.

Jus Soli, Jus Sanguinis, **and Nationality**

"In the civilized world, no one may be without a relationship to the state."[75] J. A. Nederburgh, one of the principal architects of Indies colonial law in 1898, engaged the question of national identity and membership more directly than many of his contemporaries. He argued that in destroying racial purity, colonialism had made obsolete the criteria of *jus soli* (place of birth) and *jus sanguinis* (blood descent) for determining nationality. Colonial *vermenging* (mixing or blending), he contended, had produced a new category of "wavering classes," large groups of people whose place of birth and mixed genealogies called into question the earlier criteria by which rights to metropolitan citizenship and designations of colonial subject had once been assigned. Taking the nation to be those who shared "morals, culture, and perceptions, feelings that unite us without one being able to say what they are," Nederburgh concluded that one could not differentiate who had these sensibilities by knowing birthplace and kinship alone. He pointed to those of "pure European blood" who "for years remained almost entirely in native surroundings [*omgeving*] and became so entirely nativized [*verinlandschen*] that they no longer felt at ease among their own kind [*rasgenooten*] and found it difficult to defend themselves against Indische morals and points of view."[76] He concluded that surroundings had an "overwhelming influence," with "the power to almost entirely neutralize the effects of descent and blood."[77] Although Nederburgh's claim may seem to suggest a firm dismissal of racial supremacy, we should note that he was among the most staunchly conservative legalists of his time, a firm defender of the superiority of Western logic and law.[78] By Nederburgh's cultural account, Europeans, especially children "who because of their age are most susceptible and often the most exposed" to native influence in school and native servants at home, who remained too long in the Indies "could only remain *echte-Europeesch* (truly European) in thought and deed with much exertion."[79] While Nederburgh insisted that he was not "against Indische influence per se,'' he recommended that the state allocate funds to bring up European children in Holland.[80] Some eight years later, at the height of the Ethical Policy, another prominent member of the colonial elite made a similar but more radical recommendation to close all schools of higher education in Batavia and to replace them with state-subsidized education in Holland to improve the quality of the colored (*kleuringen*) in the civil servant ranks.[81] Both proposals derived from the same assumption: that it was "impossible for persons raised and educated in the Indies to be bearers [*dragers*] of Western culture and civilization."[82]

Attention to upbringing, surroundings, and milieu did not disengage personal potential from the physiological fixities of race. Distinctions made on the basis of *opvoeding* (upbringing) merely recoded race in the quotidian circumstances that enabled acquisition of certain cultural competencies and not others. The focus on milieu naturalized cultural difference, sexual essence, and moral fiber of Europeanness in new kinds of ways. I have discussed elsewhere how the shift in the colonies to white endogamy and away from concubinage at the turn of the century, an intensified surveillance of native servants, and a sharper delineation of the social space in which European children could be brought up and where and with whom they might play not only marked out the cultural borders of the European community but also indicated how much political security was seen to reside in the choices of residence, language, and cultural style that individuals made. Personal prescriptions for inclusion as citizens of the Dutch state were as stringent and intimate as those that defined the exclusion of its subjects.[83] The wide gap between prescription and practice suggests why the prescriptions were so insistently reiterated, updated, and reapplied. Among those classified as European, there was little agreement on these prescriptions, which were contested, if not openly defied.

In 1884 legal access to European equivalent status in the Indies required a "complete suitability [*geschiktheid*] for European society," defined as a belief in Christianity, fluency in spoken and written Dutch, and training in European morals and ideas.[84] In the absence of an upbringing in Europe, district authorities were charged with evaluating whether the concerned party was "brought up in European surroundings as a European."[85] But European equivalence was not granted simply on the display of a competence and comfort in European norms. It required that the candidate "no longer feel at home" (*niet meer thuis voelt*) in native society and have already "distanced" himself from his native being (*Inlander-zijn*). In short the candidate could neither identify nor retain inappropriate senses of belonging or longings for the milieu from which she or he came.[86] The mental states of potential citizens were at issue, not their material assets alone. Who were to be the arbitrators? Suitability to which European society and to which Europeans? The questions are disingenuous because the coding is clear: cultural competence, family form, and a middle-class morality became the salient new criteria for marking subjects, nationals, citizens, and different kinds of citizens in the nation-state. As European legal status and its equivalent became accessible to an ever-broader population, the cultural criteria of privilege was more carefully defined. European women who subscribed to the social prescription of white endogamy were made the custodians of a new morality—not, as we shall see, those "fictive" European women who rejected those norms.

Colonial practice contradicted the moral designations for European national and racial identity in blatant ways: Which European morality was to be iconized? That embraced by those European men who cohabited with native women, became nativized, and supported their offspring? Or the morality of European men who retained their cultural trappings as they lived with native women who bore métis children, then departed for Europe unencumbered when their contracts were done? Or was it the morality of colonial officials who barred the filing of paternity suits against European men by native women or the morality of those who argued for it on the grounds that it would hinder fraudulent acknowledgments and easy recognitions by lower-class European men? What can we make of the ruling on European equivalence for non-native residents that stipulated that candidates must be from regions or states that subscribed to a monogamous family law?[87] How did this speak to the thousands of Indisch Dutch men for whom concubinage was the most frequently chosen option? And finally, if national identity was, as often stated, "an indescribable set of invisible bonds," what did it mean when a European woman on marriage to a native man was legally reclassified to follow his nationality? As we shall see, these invisible bonds, in which women only had a conjugal share by proxy to their husbands, were those enjoyed by some but not all men. The paradox is that native women married to European men were charged with the upbringing of children, with the formative making of Dutch citizens, and with culturally encoding the markers of race. Colonial cultures created problematic contexts in which patriarchal principles and criteria for citizenship seemed to be at fundamental odds. At a time when European feminists were turning to motherhood as a claim to citizenship, this notion of "mothers of citizens" meant something different in colonial politics, where definitions of proper motherhood served to clarify the blurred boundaries of nation and race.[88]

The Mixed-Marriage Law of 1898

The mixed-marriage law of 1898 and the legal arguments that surrounded it are of special interest on several counts. Nowhere in the Dutch colonial record is the relationship among gender prescription, class membership, and racial category so contentiously debated and so clearly defined; nowhere is the danger of certain kinds of mixing so directly linked to national image while references to race are denied.[89] This is a liberal discourse ostensibly about the protection of native (men's) rights and later viewed as the paragon of ethical intent to equalize and synchronize colonial and metropolitan law. But, as Willem Wertheim noted nearly forty years ago, it did far more to buttress racial distinctions than to break them down.[90]

Legal attention to mixed marriages was not new in the Indies but had never been formalized as it was to be now.[91] Mixed marriages had been regulated by government decree and church decretals soon after the East Indies Company established a settlement in Batavia in the early seventeenth century. The decree of 1617 forbidding marriages between Christian and non-Christian remained intact for over two hundred years. With the new Civil Code of 1848, the religious criteria were replaced with the ruling that marriage partners of European and native standing would both be subject to European law.

The legislation on mixed marriages prior to 1898 was designed to address one kind of union but not others. The 1848 ruling allowed European men already living in concubinage with non-Christian native women to legalize those unions and the children born from them. Although the civil law of 1848 was derived from the Napoleonic civil code, a dominant principle of it had been curiously ignored: that on marriage a woman's legal status was made that of her husband. As Dutch jurists were to argue a half-century later, because mixed marriages had then been overwhelmingly between European men and native women, the latter's legal incorporation could be easily assumed. This, however, was no longer the case in the 1880s when Indies colonial officials noted two troubling phenomena: first, more women classified as European were choosing to marry non-European men; and second, concubinage continued to remain the domestic arrangement of choice over legal marriage.[92] Legal specialists argued that concubinage was a primary cause of Indo-European impoverishment and had to be discouraged. However, the mixed-marriage rulings, as they stood, were so complicated and costly that people continued to choose cohabitation over legal marriage. Perhaps more disturbing still, some European, Indo-European, and native women opted to retain their own legal standing (thereby protecting their own material assets and those they could bestow on their children), thus rejecting marriage altogether.[93]

Colonial lawyers were thus faced with a conundrum: How could they implement a ruling that would facilitate certain kinds of mixed marriages (over concubinage) and condemn others? Two basic premises were accepted on all sides: that the family was the bulwark of state authority and that the unity of the family could only be assured by its unity in law.[94] Thus legitimate children could not be subject to one law and their father to another, nor could women hold native status while their husbands retained that of a European.[95] Given this agreement there were two possible solutions: either the "superior European standing" of either spouse would determine the legal status (and nationality) of the other; or, alternately, the patriarchal principle—that is, a woman follows the legal status of her husband (regardless of his origin)—would be applied.

Principles of cultural and male supremacy seem to be opposed. Let us look at why they were not.

Those who argued that a European woman should retain her European standing in a mixed marriage did so on the grounds, among others, that European prestige would be seriously compromised. The liberal lawyer J. H. Abendanon cogently argued that European women would be placed in a "highly unfavorable and insecure position"; by being subject to *adat,* she risked becoming no more than a concubine if her native husband took a second wife, as polygamy under Islamic law was not justification for divorce. Others pointed out that she would be subject to the penal code applied to those of native status. Should she commit a crime, she would be treated to "humiliating physical and psychological punishment," for which her "physical constitution" was unsuited. Her relegation to native status would thus cause an "outrageous scandal" in the European community at large.[96]

The argument above rested on one central but contested assumption: that all women classified as European deserved the protection and privilege of European law. However, those who made the countercase that the patriarchal principle be applied regardless of origin, argued that the quality of women with European standing was not the same. Although the state commission noted that mixed marriages between European women and native men were relatively few, it underlined their marked and "steady increase among certain classes of the inhabitants."[97] Such mixed marriages, all but unthinkable in 1848 but now on the rise among Indo-European and even full-blooded European women with native men, were attributed to the increasing impoverishment and declining welfare of these women, on the one hand, and to the "intellectual and social development" among certain classes of native men, on the other.[98] The latter issue, however, was rarely addressed because the gender hierarchy of the argument was contingent on assuming that women who made such conjugal choices were neither well-bred nor deserving of European standing.

One lawyer, Taco Henny, argued that the category European was a legal fiction not indicative of those who actually participated in the cultural and moral life of the European community and that the majority of women who made such choices were "outwardly and inwardly indistinguishable from natives." Because these women tended to be of lower-class origin or mixed racial descent, he held that they were already native in culture and inclination and needed no protection from that cultural milieu in which they rightly belonged. Similarly, their subjection to the native penal code was no reason for scandal because it was appropriate to their actual station. They were already so far removed from Dutch society proper that it would cause no alarm.

If Taco Henny's argument was not convincing enough, Pastor van Santen made the case in even bolder terms: "The European woman who wants to enter into such a marriage has already sunk so deep socially and morally that it does not result in ruin, either in her own eyes or those of society. It merely serves to consolidate her situation."[99] Such arguments rested on an interior distinction between echte Dutch women and those in whom "very little European blood actually flowed in their veins" within the category of those classified as European. Pastor van Santen's claim that this latter group had already fallen from cultural and racial grace had its "proof" in yet another observation: "that if she was still European in thought and feeling, she would never take a step that was so clearly humiliating and debasing in the eyes of actual [werkelijk] European women."[100] This reasoning (which won in the end) marshaled the patriarchal tenets of the civil code to exclude women of a certain class and cultural milieu from Dutch citizenship rights without directly invoking race in the legal argument.

But this gendered principle did more work still and could be justified on wider grounds. Such legislation defined a "true" European woman in accepted cultural terms: first, by her spousal choice, and, second, by her maternal sentiments. She was to demonstrate that she put her children's interests first by guarding their European standing, which would be lost to her future progeny if she married a non-European under the new law. As such, it strongly dissuaded "true" European women from choosing to marry native men. This was its implicit and, according to some advocates, its explicit intent. In addition, it spoke on the behalf of well-to-do native men, arguing that they would otherwise lose their access to agricultural land and other privileges passed from fathers to sons under adat law.[101] Finally, the new legislation claimed to discourage concubinage, as native men could thus retain their customary rights and would not be tempted to live with Indo-European and "full-blooded" European women outside of marriage. But perhaps most important, this appeal to patriarchy prevented the infiltration of increasing numbers of native men into the Dutch citizenry, particularly those of the middling classes, who were considered to have little to lose and much to gain by acquiring a Dutch nationality. Those who supported "uplifting" native men to European status through marriage would in effect encourage marriages of convenience at the expense of both European women who were drawn to such unions and those who prided themselves on the cultural distinctions that defined them as European.[102] Here again, as in the fraudulent recognitions of métis children, at issue was the undesirability of an increase in "the number of persons who would only be European in name."[103]

In the end, the mixed-marriage ruling and the debates surrounding it were more an index than a cause of profound changes in thinking about sexual practice, national identity, and colonial morality. Mixed marriages increased between native women and European men between 1900 and 1920. This was evident in the declining number of acknowledgments of children born out of wedlock and in an increased number of single European men who now married their huishoudster (housekeeper or sexual companion or both).[104] Condemnation of concubinage came simultaneously from several sources. The Pauperism Commission had provided new evidence that concubinage was producing an underclass of Indos that had to be curbed. By treating prostitution and the huishoudster system in the colonies as similar phenomena, the Nederlandschen Vrouwenbond (Dutch Women's Association) conflated the distinct options such arrangements afforded women and rallied against both.[105] The Sarekat Islam, one of the strongest native nationalist organizations, also campaigned against concubinage on religious grounds, which may have discouraged some native women from such unions.[106] Still, in 1920 half the métis children of a European father and native mother were born outside of marriage. After 1925 the number of mixed marriages fell off again as the number of Dutch-born women coming to the Indies increased fourfold.

Hailed as exemplary liberal legislation, the mixed-marriage ruling was applied selectively on the basis of class, gender, and race. By reinvoking the Napoleonic civil code, European men were assured that their "invisible bonds" of nationality remained intact regardless of their legal partner. European women, on the other hand, were summarily (but temporarily) disenfranchised from their national community on the basis of conjugal choice alone.[107] Those mixed marriages that derived from earlier cohabitations between European men and native women were not the unions most in question, and jurists of different persuasions stated as much throughout the debate. These marriages were considered unproblematic on the assumption that a native woman would be grateful for, and proud of, her elevated European status and content with legal dependence on a European man. Were native women easily granted European legal standing and Dutch citizenship because there was no danger that they could or would fully exercise their rights? The point is never discussed because racial and gender privileges were in line.

But what about the next generation of métis? Although the new ruling effectively blocked the naturalization of native adult men through marriage, it granted a new generation of métis children a European standing by affixing their nationality to their father's. Would this generation be so assuredly cut from their mother's roots as well? The persistent vigilance with which concern for omgeving, upbringing, class, and education were discussed in the 1920s and 1930s suggests that there were resounding doubts. The Netherlands Indies Eugenics Society designed studies to test whether children of Europeans born in the Indies might display different "racial markers" than their parents.[108] Eugenicist logic consolidated discussions about national identity and cultural difference in a discourse of "fitness" that specified the interior frontiers of the nation, reaffirming yet again that upbringing and parenting were critical in deciding who would be marked as a fictive compatriot or true citizen.

Although the race criterion was finally removed from the Indies constitution in 1918 under native nationalist pressure, debates over the psychological, physical, and moral makeup of Indo-Europeans intensified in the 1920s and

1930s more than they had before. A 1936 doctoral dissertation at the University of Amsterdam could still "explain the lack of energy" of Indo-Europeans by the influence of a sapping and warm, dank climate; by the bad influence of the "energyless Javanese race" on Indo-Europeans; and by the fact that "half-bloods" were not descended from the "average European" and the "average Javanese."[109] In the 1920s, the European-born Dutch population was visibly closing its ranks, creating new cultural boundaries while shoring up its old ones. Racial hate (*rassenhaat*) and representation were watchwords of the times. A renewed disdain for Indos permeated a discourse that heightened in the depression as the nationalist movement grew stronger and as unemployed "full-blooded" Europeans found "roaming around" in native villages blurred with the ranks of the Indo poor. How the colonial state distinguished these two groups from one another and from "natives" on issues of unemployment insurance and poor relief underscored how crucial these interior frontiers were to the strategies of the emerging welfare state.[110]

Indo-Europeans and the Quest for a Fatherland

The slippage between race and culture as well the intensified discussions of racial membership and national identity were not invoked by the *echte-Europeesche* population alone. We have seen that the moral geography of the colonies had a metonymic quality: Despite the huge numbers of Europeans of mixed parentage and substantial economic means, the term "Indo" was usually reserved for that segment who were *verindische* (Indianized) and poor. Less clear are the cultural, political, and racial criteria by which those of mixed descent identified themselves. The contradictory and changing criteria used by the various segments of the Indo-European movement at the turn of the century highlight how contentious and politically contingent these deliberations were.

It is not accidental that the term "Indo-European" is difficult to define. In the Indies it applied to those of *mengbloeden* (mixed blood) of European and native origin, to Europeans born in the Indies of Dutch nationality and not of native origin, and to those pur-sang Europeans born elsewhere who referred to the Indies as a "second fatherland."[111] The semantics of mixing thus related to blood, place, and belonging to different degrees and at different times. *Soeria Soemirat,* one of the earliest publications of the Indo-European constituency in the late 1890s, included among its members all Indies-born Europeans and took as its central goal the uplifting of the (Indo-)European poor. The Indisch Bond, formed in 1898, was led by an Indies-born European constituency that spoke for the Indo poor but whose numbers were rarely represented in their ranks. At the heart of both organizations was the push for an *Indisch vaderland,* contesting both the popular terms of Indonesian nationalism and the exclusionary practices of the Dutch-born (*totok*) society.[112]

The Indo-European movement never developed as a nationalist movement. As "socially thin" as Benedict Anderson suggests its creole counterpart was in the Americas, it could neither enlist a popular constituency nor dissociate from its strong identification with the European-born Dutch elite. The Indisch movement often made its bids for political and economic power by invoking Eurasian racial superiority to inlanders while concurrently denying a racial criteria for judging their status vis-à-vis European-born Dutch. The subsequent effort in 1912 to form an Indische Partij (with the motto "Indies for the Indiers") was stridently antigovernment, with a platform that addressed native as well as poor Indo welfare. Despite an inclusionary rhetoric, its native and poor Indo constituency was categorically marginalized and could find no common political ground.[113] By 1919, when native nationalist mobilization was gaining strength, the need for a specifically Indo-Bond took on new urgency and meaning. As its founder argued, "it would be a *class-verbond* (class-based association) to support the interests of the larger Indo-group."[114] This organization, eventually called the Indo-Europeesch Verbond (IEV), with more than ten thousand members in 1924, continued to plead the cause of the Indo poor while remaining unequivocally loyal to the Dutch colonial state. This truncated version of a much more complicated story, nevertheless, illustrates the unsettling point that the poor Indo constituency never achieved a political voice. However large their numbers, they were silently rejected from the early Indonesian nationalist movement and could only make their demands based on claims to a cultural and racial alliance with those Dutch who ruled.[115]

Questions of cultural, racial, and national identity were particularly charged around proposals for Indo-European agricultural settlements. This utopian project for white settler colonies peopled with those of mixed descent joined persons of widely disparate political persuasions in curious ways. In 1874 and 1902 state commissions on European pauperism had begun to explore the agricultural possibilities for the Indo poor. Their proposals focused on beggar colonies, self-sufficient rural confinements in which (Indo-)European paupers would be housed, fed, and kept out of sight. Other, more ambitious schemes advocated intensive horticultural and small-scale estates that would compete with neither native peasant production nor the agribusiness industry. These rural solutions to the mixed-blood problem, entertained in both the Indies and Indochina, were based on a common set of premises: that native blood ties would make them more easily acclimatized to tropical agriculture, while their European heritage would provide them with the reason and drive for success. Thus brawn and brains, tropical know-how and European science, and government assistance and private initiative were to come together to produce an economically self-sustaining, morally principled, and loyal *volk*. The Indische Bond first, and the IEV later, made land rights and agricultural settlements for needy Indos one of its principal platforms. Conservative and fascist-linked organizations concerned with European unemployment in Holland and

European prestige in the colonies also proposed a New Guinea settled by white people that would serve their imperial plan. As a province of a Groter Nederland, New Guinea might absorb an economically weak underclass in the metropole, alleviate Dutch unemployment, and foster a settler colonialism in the Indies for continued rule.[116]

The vision of turning potential patricides into pastoral patriots never worked, but its discussion raised critical national issues for different constituencies. The state viewed the poor Indo population as déraciné, rootless, and therefore dangerous. The Indisch movement clearly could not claim a fatherland without territorial rights and roots within it (since many Indo-Europeans had European standing, they could not own land). The movement's appeal to an Indisch nationalism lacked a proper mass-based constituency, a volk, and a homeland to make its claims. For the conservative Vaderlandse Club, rural settler colonies in the 1930s were part of a wider effort to ward off a Japanese invasion while reducing overpopulation in the Netherlands. The Fatherlands' Club and the IEV joined in a short-lived alliance to support the settler schemes, to oppose the *ontblanking* (unwhitening) of the Indies, and to attack the ethical policy that had fostered the increased entry of educated Javanese into subaltern civil service jobs. However, as the IEV became increasingly anti-Totok, their conflicting images of the future fatherland became difficult to deny.[117]

For the Indo-European movement, their *vaderland* was an Indisch fatherland independent of Holland. For the Indies fascists, who defined their task as the self-purification of the nation (*zelfzuivering der natie*), their notion of the vaderland juxtaposed images of "a tropical Netherlands," uniting the Netherlands and Indies into a single state.[118] Neither of these imaginings concurred with that of the native nationalists who were to oppose them both.

Rootlessness and Cultural Racism

With rootedness at the center stage of nationalist discourse, the notion of rootlessness captured a range of dangers about métissage.[119] Abandoned métis youths were generically viewed as vagrants in Indochina, as child delinquents in the Indies, as de facto stateless subversives without a patrie.[120] In times of economic crisis "free-roaming European bastards" were rounded up for charity and goodwill in efforts to avert a racial disgrace. Liberal colonial projects spent decades creating a barrage of institutions to incorporate, inculcate, and insulate abandoned métis youths. But the image of rootlessness was not only applied to those who were abandoned.

In 1938 government officials in Hanoi conducted a colonywide inquiry to monitor the physical and political movements of métis. The Resident of Tonkin recommended a comprehensive state-sponsored social rehabilitation program to give métis youths the means to function as real *citoyens* on the argument that with "French blood prevailing in their veins," they already "manifested an instinctive attachment to France."[121] But many French in Indochina must have been more equivocal about their instinctive patriotic attachments. The fear that métis might revert to their natural inclinations persisted, as did a continuing discourse on their susceptibility to the native milieu, where they might relapse into the immoral and subversive states of their mothers.

Fears of métissage were not confined to colonial locales. We need only read the 1942 treatise, *Les Métis,* of René Martial who combined his appointment on the faculty of medicine in Paris with eugenic research on the *anthrobiologie des races.* For him, métis were categorically persons of physical and mental deformity. He saw métis descent as a frequent cause both of birth defects in individuals and of the contaminated body politic of France. As he put it,

> Instability, the dominant characteristic of métis, . . . is contagious, it stands in opposition to the spirit of order and method, it generates indeterminable and futile discussion and paralyzes action. It is this state of mind that makes democracies fail that live with this chimera of racial equality, one of the most dangerous errors of our times, defended with piety by pseudo-French who have found in it a convenient means to insinuate themselves everywhere.[122]

That Martial's spirit continues to thrive in contemporary France in the rhetoric of LePen is not coincidental. The discourses on métissage in the early twentieth century and in LePen's rhetoric on immigrant foreigners today are about both external boundaries and interior frontiers. Both discourses are permeated with images of purity, contamination, infiltration, and national decay. For both Martial and LePen, cultural identities refer to human natures and psychological propensities inimical to the identity of the French nation and a drain on the welfare state.[123]

On Cultural Hybridity and Domestic Subversions

These historically disparate discourses are striking in how similarly they encode métissage as a political danger predicated on the psychological liminality, mental instability, and economic vulnerability of culturally hybrid minorities.[124] But could we not re-present these discourses by turning them on their heads, by unpacking what the weakness of métissage was supposed to entail? Recast, these discourses may be more about the fear of empowerment, not about marginality at all; about groups that straddled and disrupted cleanly marked social divides and whose diverse membership exposed the arbitrary logic by which the categories of control were made.[125] These discourses are not unlike those about Indische women that, in disparaging their impoverished and hybrid Dutch and non-European tastes, eclipsed the more compelling reality that they could "sometimes pass between ethnic communities, cross lines drawn by color and caste and enter slots for which they had no birthright, depending on their alliance with men.''[126] The final clause is critical because through these varied sexual contracts citizenship rights were accorded and métis identities were contested and remade.[127] The management of sexuality, parenting, and morality was at the heart of the late imperial project. Cohabitation, prostitution, and legally recognized mixed marriages slotted women, men, and their progeny differently on the social and moral landscape of colonial society. These sexual contracts were buttressed by pedagogic, medical, and legal evaluations that shaped the boundaries of European membership and the interior frontiers of the colonial state.

Métissage was first a name and then made a thing. It was so heavily politicized because it threatened both to destabilize national identity and the Manichaean categories of ruler and ruled. The cultural density of class, gender, and national issues that it invoked converged in a grid of transgressions that tapped into metropolitan and colonial politics at the same time. The sexual affront that it represented challenged middle-class family order and racial frontiers, norms of child rearing and conjugal patriarchy, and made it increasingly difficult to distinguish between true nationals and their sullied pseudocompatriots. The issue of fraudulent recognition could be viewed in a similar light. Poor white men and native women who arranged legal recognition of their own children or those of others defied the authority of the state by using the legal system to grant Dutch and French citizenship to a younger generation.[128]

The turn of the century represents one major break point in the nature of colonial morality and in national projects. In both the Indies and Indochina, a new humanitarian liberal concern for mass education and representation was coupled with newly recast social prescriptions for maintaining separatist and exclusionary cultural conventions regarding how, where, and with whom European colonials should live. Virtually all of these differentiating practices were worked through a psychologizing and naturalizing impulse that embedded gender inequalities, sexual privilege, class priorities, and racial superiority in a tangled political field. Colonial liberalism in its nationalist cast opened the possibilities of representation for some while it set out moral prescriptions and affixed psychological attributes that partially closed those possibilities down.

But the exclusionary strategies of the colonial state were not meted out to a passive population, nor is it clear that many of those who inhabited the borderlands of European colonial communities sought inclusion within them. At the core of the métis problem were cultural contestations of gender and class that made these ''laboratories of modernity'' unwieldy sites of engineering.[129] The experiments were reworked by their subjects, not least of all by women who refused to give ''up'' their children to charitable institutions for European training and by others who chose cohabitation (not concubinage) over marriage. Women and men who lived culturally hybrid lifestyles intercepted nationalist and racist visions. Without romanticizing their impoverishment, we might consider the possibility that their choices expressed a domestic subversion, a rejection of the terms of the civilizing mission. For those who did not adhere to European bourgeois prescripts, cultural hybridity may have affirmed their own new measures of civility.

Notes

Earlier versions of this chapter were presented at the American Anthropological Association meetings, "Papers in Honor of Eric Wolf," in New Orleans, December 1990, and at the TNI Conference, "The Decolonization of Imagination: The New Europe and Its Others," Amsterdam, May 1991. I thank Talal Asad, Val Daniel, Geoff Eley, Lawrence Hirschfeld, Barbara Laslett, Jeffrey Weeks, Luise White, and fellows of the Histories of Sexuality Seminar at the Institute of the Humanities, the University of Michigan, for their comments.

1. Uday Mehta outlines some features of this relationship in "Liberal Strategies of Exclusion," *Politics and Society* 18, no. 4 (1990): 427–454. He cogently argues for the more radical claim that the theoretical underpinnings of liberalism are exclusionary and cannot be explained as "an episodic compromise with the practical constraints of implementation" (p. 429).

2. Cochinchina's European population only increased from 594 in 1864 to 3,000 by 1900 (Charles Meyer, *Le Français en Indochine, 1860–1910* [Paris: Hachette, 1985], 70). By 1914 only 149 planters qualified as electors in the Chamber of Agriculture of Tonkin and Annam; on Java alone there were several thousand (John Laffey, "Racism in Tonkin before 1914," *French Colonial Studies,* no. 1 [1977]: 65–81). In 1900 approximately 91,000 persons were classified as European in the Indies. As late as 1931 there were just under 10,500 French civilians in Indochina, when the Indies census counted 244,000 Europeans for the same year (see A. van Marle, "De groep der Europeanen in Nederlands-Indie, iets over ontstaan en groei," *Indonesie* 5, no. 5 (1952): 490; and Gilles de Gante, *La population française au Tonkin entre 1931 et 1938* [Mémoire de Maitrise, Université de Provence, 1981], 23.

3. See Jean Taylor's subtle gendered analysis of the mestizo features of colonial culture in the Netherlands Indies (*The Social World of Batavia* [Madison: University of Wisconsin Press, 1983]). The term *Indisch* is difficult to translate. According to Taylor, it is a cultural marker of a person who "partook of Mestizo culture in marriage, practice, habit and loyalty" (p. xx). It is most often used in contrast to the lifestyle and values of the Dutch *totok* population comprised of Hollanders born and bred in Europe who refused such cultural accommodations and retained a distinct distance from *in-lander* (native) customs and social practice. Thus, for example, the European *blivjers* (those who stayed in the Indies) were commonly referred to as *Indisch* as opposed to *vertrekkers* (those Europeans who treated their residence in the Indies as a temporary assignment away from their native metropolitan homes).

4. See Martin Lewis, "One Hundred Million Frenchmen: The 'Assimilation' Theory in French Colonial Policy," *Comparative Studies in Society and History* 3, no. 4 (1961): 129–151. While the social positioning of Eurasians in India is often contrasted to that in the Indies, there are striking similarities in their changing and contradictory

legal and social status in the late nineteenth century. See Mark Naidis, "British Attitudes toward the Anglo-Indians," *South Atlantic Quarterly* 62, no. 3 (Summer 1963): 407–422; and Noel Gist and Roy Wright, *Marginality and Identity: Anglo-Indians as a Racially Mixed Minority in India* (Leiden: E.J. Brill, 1973), esp. pp. 7–20.

5. For an extended discussion of the politics of degeneracy and the eugenics of empire, see my "Carnal Knowledge and Imperial Power: The Politics of Race and Sexual Morality in Colonial Asia," in *Gender at the Crossroads: Feminist Anthropology in the Post-Modern Era,* ed. Micaela di Leonardo, 51–101 (Berkeley: University of California Press, 1991).

6. In the following section I draw on Etienne Balibar's discussion of this concept in "Fichte et la Frontière Intérieure: A propos des *Discours a la nation allemande,*" *Les Cahiers de Fontenay* 58/59 (June 1990).

7. Fichte quoted in Balibar, "Fichte et la Frontière Intérieure," 4.

8. See my "Carnal Knowledge and Imperial Power" on métissage and contamination. Also see Pierre-André Taguieff's *La Force du Préjugé* (Paris: La Découverte, 1987), in which he discusses "la hantisse du métissage" and argues that the métis problem is not a question of mixed-blood but a question of the indeterminate "social identity" that métissage implies (p. 345).

9. This is not to suggest that the French and Dutch rejection of métis as a legal category followed the same trajectory or occurred in the same way. As I later show, the legal status of métis children with unknown parents was still a subject of French juridical debate in the 1930s in a discourse in which race and upbringing were offered as two alternative criteria for judging whether a métis child should be granted the rights of a *citoyen.* See Jacques Mazet, *La condition juridique des métis dans les possession françaises* (Paris: Domat-Montchresiten, 1932).

10. Paul Rich, *Race and Empire in British Politics* (Cambridge: Cambridge University Press, 1986), argues that the antiblack riots in Liverpool and Cardiff in 1919 represented "the extension of rising colonial nationalism into the heart of the British metropolis itself at a time when nationalist ferment was being expressed in many parts of the empire" (p. 122).

11. The profusion of French juridical tracts in the 1930s debating whether métis should be made a separate legal category (distinct from European and indigene) and what were the political effects of doing so were forged in the tense environment in which Vietnamese nationalists were making their opposition most strongly felt. See David Marr's two important studies of the Vietnamese nationalist movements, *Vietnamese Anticolonialism, 1885–1925* (Berkeley: University of California Press, 1971) and *Vietnamese Tradition on Trial, 1920–1945* (Berkeley: University of California Press, 1981). It is noteworthy that Marr makes no reference to the métis problem (generally or as it related to citizenship, immigration, and education) in either text.

12. This is not to suggest, however, that the battles for legal reform regarding, for example, paternity suits, illegitimate children, and family law waged by jurists, feminists, and religious organizations in the Netherlands and the Indies at the turn of the century were animated by the same political projects or fears; on the contrary, in the colonies, the social menace of illegitimate children, as we shall see, was not only about future criminals and prostitutes but also about mixed-blood criminals and prostitutes, about European paternity, and native mothers—and thus about the moral landscape of

race and the protection of European men by the Dutch colonial state. For contrasting discourses on paternity suits in the Indies and Holland, compare Selma Sevenhuijsen's comprehensive study of this political debate (*De Orde van het Vaderschap: Politieke debatten over ongehuwd moederschap, afstamming en huwelijk in Nederland 1870–1900* [Amsterdam: Stichting Beheer IISG, 1987]) to R. Kleyn's "Onderzoek naar het vaderschap" (*Het Recht in Nederlandsch-Indie* 67 [1896]: 130–150).

13. On the relationship between racial supremacy and new conceptions of British motherhood at the turn of the century, see Anna Davin's "Imperialism and Motherhood," *History Workshop*, no. 5 (1978): 9–57, and Lucy Bland's "'Guardians of the Race' or 'Vampires upon the Nation's Health'? Female Sexuality and Its Regulations in Early Twentieth-Century Britain," in *The Changing Experience of Women*, ed. Elizabeth Whitelegg et al., 373–388 (Oxford: Oxford University Press, 1982). On the European maternalist discourse of the emerging welfare states, see Seth Koven and Sonya Michel's "Womanly Duties: Maternalist Politics and the Origins of the Welfare States in France, Germany, Great Britain, and the United States, 1880–1920," *American Historical Review* 95 (October 1990): 1076–1108.

14. See Eugene Weber's *Peasants into Frenchmen* (Stanford: Stanford University Press, 1976), 114. Although Weber's argument that much of France's rural population neither considered itself French nor embraced a national identity has been refuted by some scholars, for my purposes his ancillary argument holds: Debates over the nature of French citizenship and identity were heavily contested at the time.

15. Weber, *Peasants into Frenchmen*, 110.

16. Raoul Girardet, *Le nationalisme français* (Paris: Seuil, 1983), 30–31; and Robert Nye, *Crime, Madness and Politics in Modern France: The Medical Concept of National Decline* (Princeton: Princeton University Press, 1984), 140.

17. See Pierre Nora, *Les Français d'Algerie* (Paris: R. Julliard, 1961).

18. French fertility rates began to decline in the late eighteenth century, much earlier than in other European countries, but then they decreased most sharply after 1881 (see Claire Goldberg Moses, *French Feminism in the 19th Century* [Binghamton: SUNY Press, 1984], 20–24).

19. Thus, of the 200,000 "Français d'Algerie," more than half were of non-French origin. Coupled with the 20,000 Parisian political undesirables deported there by the Second Republic in 1851 (commonly referred to as "les sans-travail," "les révoltés," "les déracinés"), the equivocal national loyalties of Algeria's French colonial population were reopened to question. See Pierre Nora's *Les Français d'Algerie* (Paris: René Julliard, 1961). Also see Stephen Wilson's comprehensive study of French anti-Semitism at the turn of the century, in which he suggests that violent cultural racism in the colonies against Jews provided a "model" for anti-Semitism at home (in *Ideology and Experience: Antisemitism in France at the Time of the Dreyfus Affair* [Teaneck: Fairleigh Dickinson University Press, 1982], esp. pp. 230–242).

20. See Ali de Regt's "De vorming van een opvoedings-traditie: Arbiederskinderen rond 1900," in *Geschiedenis van opvoeding en onderwijs,* ed. B. Kruithof, J. Nordman, Piet de Rooy (Nijmegen: SUN, 1982). On the relationship between the development of the modern Dutch state and the new focus on family morality and motherhood at the turn of the century, see Siep Stuurman's *Verzuiling, Kapitalisme en Patriarchaat: Aspecten van de ontwiddeling van de moderne staat in Nederland*

(Nijmegen: SUN, 1987). For France, see Jacques Donzelot's *The Policing of Families* (New York: Pantheon, 1979), which traces state interventions in family life and child rearing practices to a half-century earlier.

21. See I. Schoffer's "Dutch 'Expansion' and Indonesian Reactions: Some Dilemmas of Modern Colonial Rule (1900–1942)," in *Expansion and Reaction,* ed. H. Wesseling, 80 (Leiden: Leiden University Press, 1978): and Maarten Kuitenbrouwer's *The Netherlands and the Rise of Modern Imperialism: Colonies and Foreign Policy, 1870–1902* (New York: Berg, 1991), 220.

22. See Colin Bundy's "Vagabond Hollanders and Runaway Englishmen: White Poverty in the Cape before Poor Whiteism," in *Putting a Plough to the Ground: Accumulation and Dispossession in Rural South Africa, 1850–1930,* ed. William Beinart, Peter Delius, and Stanley Trapido, 101–128. (Johannesburg: Raven Press, 1987). On the colonial state's concern about Dutch paupers in the Indies, see *Rapport der Pauperisme-Commissie* (Batavia: Landsdrukkerij, 1902). I discuss these issues at more length in "Children on the Imperial Divide: Sentiments and Citizenship in Colonial Southeast Asia" (Paper prepared for the conference "Power: Working Through the Disciplines" held by Comparative Study of Social Transformations at the University of Michigan, January 1992).

23. See Kuitenbrouwer, *The Netherlands,* 223.

24. For the Netherlands, compulsory education was only instituted in 1900, about the same time it was introduced to the Indies (see Jan Romein, *The Watershed of Two Eras: Europe in 1900* [Middletown, Conn.: Wesleyan University Press, 1978], 278).

25. See T. H. Marshall, *Class, Citizenship and Social Development* (Westport, Conn.: Greenwood, 1963, reprint 1973), 81.

26. See Gerard Sider, "When Parrots Learn to Talk, and Why They Can't: Domination, Deception, and Self-Deception in Indian-White Relations," *Comparative Studies in Society and History,* 27, no. 1 (1987): 3–23.

27. See Mary Poovey's *Uneven Developments: The Ideological Work of Gender in Mid-Victorian England* (Chicago: University of Chicago Press, 1988).

28. Benedict Anderson, *Imagined Communities* (London: Verso, 1983), 136.

29. Archives d'Outre Mer, Protectorat de l'Annam et du Tonkin, no. 1506, 17 December 1898.

30. See Archives d'Outre Mer, December 1898, no. 39127, Report from Monsieur E. Issaud, Procureur-Général to the Résident Superieure in Tonkin at Hanoi.

31. "Relations immorales qui ont pu exister entre le détenue et celui qui s'est déclaré son père" (Archives d'Outre Mer [hereafter AOM], Fonds Amiraux, no. 1792, 12 December 1898).

32. AOM, Aix-en Provence, no. 1792, 12 December 1898. Report of M. Villemont, Procureur in Haiphong, to the Procureur-Général, Head of the Judicial Service in Hanoi.

33. According to the procureur-général, Raoul Abor, these fraudulent acknowledgments were threatening to submerge the French element by a deluge of naturalized natives (see Raoul Abor, *Des Reconnaisances Frauduleuses d'Enfants Naturels en Indochine* [Hanoi: Imprimerie Tonkinoise, 1917], 25).

34. George Mosse, *Nationalism and Sexuality* (Madison: University of Wisconsin Press, 1985).

35. John Boswell's *The Kindness of Strangers: The Abandonment of Children in Western Europe from Late Antiquity to the Renaissance* (New York: Pantheon, 1988). According to Boswell, this relinquishment might occur by "leaving them somewhere, selling them, or legally consigning authority to some other person or institution" (p. 24). As we shall see, abandonment in colonial practice did not fit this definition at all.

36. See Donzelot's *The Policing of Families*, 29.

37. I do not use this term in the sense employed by Orlando Patterson with regard to slavery but to suggest the definitive exile from European society that abandonment implied.

38. AOM, Amiraux 7701, 1899, Statute of the "Société de protection et d'éducation des Jeunes Métis Français de la Cochinchine et du Cambodge."

39. AOM, No. 164, 11 May 1904 (my emphasis).

40. AOM, 13 November 1903.

41. Letter from the Administrative Resident in Bac-giang to the Résident Superieure in Hanoi.

42. AOM, Letter (no. 151) to the Governor-General in Hanoi from Monsieur Paris, the President of the Société de Protection et d'Education des Jeunes Métis Français abandonnés, 29 February 1904. This concern over the entrapment of European young women in the colonies coincides with the concurrent campaigns against the white slave trade in Europe (see Frank Mort, *Dangerous Sexualities: Medico-Moral Politics in England Since 1830* [London: Routledge and Kegan Paul, 1987], 126–127).

43. For such recommendations, see A. Brou, "Le métis franco annamite," *Revue Indochinois* (July 1907): 897–908; Douchet, *Métis et congaies d'Indochine* (Hanoi, 1928); Jacques Mazet, *La conditions juridique des métis* (Paris: Domat-Montchrestien, 1932); Philippe Gossard, *Études sur le métissage principalement en A.O.F.* (Paris: Les Presses Modernes, 1934).

44. Etats-Generaux du Feminisme, *Exposition Coloniale Internationale de Paris 1931, rapport général présenté par le Gouverneur Général Olivier*, 139 (Paris: Imprimerie Nationale, 1931).

45. AOM, Amiraux 7701, *Report on Métis in the Dutch East Indies* (1901).

46. "Courte notice sur les métis d'Extrême Orient et en particulier sur ceux de l'Indochine," Firmin Jacques Montagne, AOM, Amiraux 1669 (1903), 1896–1909.

47. The fact that the issue of poor whites loomed large on a diverse number of colonial landscapes at this time may derive, in part, from the fact that white poverty itself was coming to be perceived in metropole and colony in new ways. In Calcutta nearly one-fourth of the Anglo-Indian community in the late nineteenth century was on poor relief (Gist and Wright, *Marginality and Identity*, 16. Colin Bundy argues for South Africa that white poverty was redefined "as a social problem to be tackled by state action rather than as a phenomenon of individual failure to be assuaged by charity" (p. 104). In the Indies, this reassignment of poor relief from civic to state responsibility was hotly contested and never really made.

48. *Rapport der Pauperisme-Commissie* (Batavia: Landsdrukkerij, 1902); *Uitkomsten der Pauperisme-Enquete: Algemeen Verslag* (Batavia: Landsdrukkerij, 1902); *Het Pauperisme onder de Europeanen in Nederlandsch-Indie*, pts. 3, 5 (Batavia: Landsdrukkerij, 1901); *Uitkomsten der Pauperisme-Enquete: Gewestelijke Verslagen* (Batavia: Landsdrukkerij, 1901); *De Staatsarmenzorg voor Europeanen in Nederlandsch-Indie* (Batavia: Landsdrukkerij, 1901).

49. See Petrus Blumberger's *De Indo-Europeesche Beweging in Nederlandsch-Indie* (Haarlem: Tjeenk Willink, 1939), 26.

50. See J. M. Coetzee, *White Writing: On the Culture of Letters in South Africa* (New Haven: Yale University Press, 1988), in which he argues that the British railed against Boer idleness precisely because authorities refused the possibility that an alternative, native milieu may have been preferred by some European men and have held a real attraction.

51. AOM, Archives Centrales de l'Indochine, nos. 9147, 9273, 7770, 4680.

52. *Encyclopedie van Nederlandsch-Indie* (1919), 367.

53. In 1900, an educational survey carried out in Dutch elementary schools in the Indies among 1,500 students found that only 29 percent of those with European legal standing knew some Dutch and more than 40 percent did not know any (Paul van der Veur, "Cultural Aspects of the Eurasian Community in Indonesian Colonial Society," *Indonesia*, no. 6 (1968): 45.

54. See Dr. I. J. Brugmans, *Geschiedenis van het onderwijs in Nederlandsch-Indie* (Batavia: Wolters, 1938).

55. See J. F. Kohlbrugge, "Prostitutie in Nederlandsch-Indie," *Indisch Genootschap*, 19 February 1901, 26–28.

56. See n.a., "Ons Pauperisme," *Mededeelingen der Vereeniging "Soeria Soemirat,"* no. 2 (1892), 8. One proof of the falsity of the claim was that these fathers often conferred upon these children "repulsive and obscene" names frequently enough that a government ruling stipulated that no family name could be given that "could humiliate the child" (G. H. Koster, "Aangenomen Kinderen en Staatsblad Europeanen," *De Amsterdammer,* 15 July 1922).

57. Letter from the Administrative Resident in Bac-giang to the Resident Superieure, Hanoi, AOM, no. 164, 11 May 1904.

58. See Jacques Mazet, *La Condition Juridique de Métis* (Paris: Domat-Montchrestien, 1932), and Douchet, *Métis et congaies d'Indochine.*

59. Kohlbrugge, "Prostitutie in Nederlandsch-Indie," 23.

60. See Linda Gordon's discussion of this issue for early twentieth-century America in *Heroes of Their Own Lives: The Politics and History of Family Violence* (New York: Vintage, 1988).

61. See Mazet, *La Condition Juridique de Métis,* 37, 42.

62. Questions about the legal status of métis and the political consequences of that decision were not confined to the French alone. The International Colonial Institute in Brussels created by Joseph Chailley-Bert in 1893 engaged this question in at least three of its international meetings in 1911, 1920, and 1924. See *Comptes Rendus de l'Institut Colonial International* (Bruxelles: Bibliothèque Coloniale Internationale, 1911, 1920, 1924).

63. Mazet, *La Condition Jurdique de Métis,* 114.

64. Ibid., 80.

65. Ibid., 90.

66. Statute of the "Societé de protection des enfants métis," 18 May 1904. Article 37.

67. Similar debates occurred at the International Colonial Congress of 1889, in which scholars and administrators compared and contrasted pedagogic strategies for

natives in the colonies to those for the peasants of France. See Martin Lewis, ''One Hundred Million Frenchmen: The 'Assimilation' Theory in French Colonial Policy,'' *Comparative Studies in Society and History* 3, no. 4 (1962): 140.

68. J. Kohlbrugge, ''Het Indische kind en zijne karaktervorming,'' in *Blikken in het zielenleven van den Javaan en zijner overheerschers* (Leiden: Brill, 1907).

69. Michel Foucault's discussion of the historical shift from a ''symbolics of blood'' to an ''analytics of sexuality'' in the mid- and late nineteenth century would be interesting to explore in this colonial context, where the mixed-blood problem invoked both of these principles in resolving issues of paternity and citizenship rights (*An Introduction,* vol. 1 of *The History of Sexuality* [New York: Pantheon Books, 1978], esp. pp. 147–150). Although a discussion of race and sexuality is notably absent from all but the very end of *The History of Sexuality,* Foucault once remarked that it was ''the fundamental part of the book'' *Power/Knowledge: Selected Interviews and Other Writings, 1972–1977* (New York: Pantheon, 1980), 222.

70. See, for example, the contributions of those in British cultural studies, such as by Stuart Hall and Paul Gilroy; also compare the discussion of nationalism and racism in France by Etienne Balibar, who does not mark cultural racism as a recent phenomenon but does argue for a new intensification of the force of cultural difference in marking the interior frontiers of the modern nation-state. See Etienne Balibar and Immanuel Wallerstein, *Race, Nation, Class: Ambiguous Identities* (New York: Verso, 1991).

71. Thus Paul Gilroy (*There Ain't No Black in the Union Jack,* London: Hutchinson, 1987), 43, for example, argues that the ''novelty of the new racism lies in the capacity to link discourses of patriotism, nationalism, xenophobia, Englishness, Britishness, militarism, and gender differences into a complex system which gives 'race' its contemporary meaning. These themes combine to provide a definition of 'race' in terms of culture and identity. . . . 'Race' differences are displayed in culture which reproduced in educational institutions and, above all, in family life. Families are therefore not only the nation in microcosm, its key components, but act as the means to turn social processes into natural, instinctive ones.''

72. It is not coincidental that this is precisely the period in which George Stocking identifies a shift in the meaning of culture in the social sciences from its singular humanistic sense of refinement to the plural anthropological notion of cultures as shared values of specific human groups. Although Stocking argues that Franz Boas made the analytic leap from culture to cultures as an antiracist response, it is clear that these two connotations joined to shape the exclusionary tenets of nationalist and racist projects (*Race, Culture, and Evolution: Essays in the History of Anthropology* [New York: Free Press, 1968], esp. pp. 200–204).

73. See Paul Rabinow's *French Modern: Norms and Forms of the Social Environment* (Cambridge: MIT Press, 1989), esp. pp. 126–127, where he traces the effects of neo-Lamarckian thinking on colonial pacification policies. I am more concerned here with how this attention to milieu fixed the boundaries of the European community and identified threats to it. On the contaminating influences of milieu, see my ''Carnal Knowledge and Imperial Power,'' 51–101.

74. The similarity to Pierre Bourdieu's notion of ''habitus'' as a stylization of life, an unconsciously embodied set of rules of behavior that engenders durable schemes of thought and perception, is striking. These colonial discussions of milieu denote not only

a social ecology of acquired competencies but a psychological environment in which certain dispositions are promoted and affective sensibilities are shaped (Pierre Bourdieu, *Outline of a Theory of Practice* [Cambridge: Cambridge University Press, 1977], 82).

75. "In de beschaafd wereld, niemand zonder staatsverband mag zijn" (K. H. Beyen, *Het Nederlanderschap in verband met het international recht* [Utrecht, 1890]), quoted in J. A. Nederburgh, *Wet en Adat* [Batavia: Kolff and Co., 1898], 83). The word *staatsverband* literally means "relationship to the state." Nederburgh distinguishes it from nationality and defines it as "the tie that exists between the state and each of its members, the membership of the state" (p. 91). Dutch scholars of colonial history say the term is rarely used but connotes citizenship.

76. Ibid., 87–88.

77. Ibid., 87.

78. See Willem Wertheim's incisive review of R. D. Kollewijn, *Intergentiel Recht* ('s-Gravenhage: Van Hoeve, 1955), in *Indonesie* 19 (1956): 169–173. Wertheim mentions Nederburgh in his criticism of Kollewijn, whose liberal rhetoric and opposition to such conservatives as Nederburgh belied the fact that he praised the virtues of the Indies mixed-marriage legislation of 1898, despite the racist principles that underwrote it.

79. Nederburgh, *Wet en Adat,* 88.

80. Ibid., 90.

81. Resident of Solo, Heer Kooreman, *Indische Genootschap,* 9 October 1906, referenced in J. Kohlbrugge, *Blikken in Het Zieleleven van den Javaan en Zijner Overheerschers* (Leiden: E. J. Brill, 1907), 150–151.

82. Ibid.

83. See my "Rethinking Colonial Categories: European Communities and the Boundaries of Rule," *Comparative Studies in Society and History,* 31, no. 1 (1989): 134–161; and "Carnal Knowledge and Imperial Power."

84. W. E. van Mastenbroek, *De Historische Ontwikkeling van de Staatsrechtelijke Indeeling der Bevolking van Nederlandsch-Indie* (Wageningen: Veenam, 1934), 70.

85. See W. F. Prins, "De Bevolkingsgroepen in het Nederlandsch-Indische Recht," *Koloniale Studien* 17 (1933): 652–688, esp. p. 677.

86. Ibid., 677; Van Marle, "De groep der Europeanen in Nederlands," *Indonesie* 5, no. 2 (1951): 110.

87. See Mastenbroek, *De Historische Ontwikkeling van de Staatsrechtelijke Indeeling der Bevolking van Nederlandsch-Indie,* 87.

88. See Karen Offen's "Depopulation, Nationalism and Feminism in Fin-de-Siècle France," *American Historical Review* 89, no. 3 (1984): 648–676.

89. The following discussion is based on several documents that I will abbreviate in referencing in the section below as follows: *Verslag van het Verhandelde in de Bijeenkomsten der Nederlandsch-Indische Juristen-Vereeniging* on 25, 27, and 29 June 1887 in Batavia [hereafter *JV*]; "Voldoet de wetgeving betreffende huwelijken tusschen personen behoorende tot de beide staatkundige categorien der Nederlandsch Indische bevolking (die der Europeanen en met hen, en die der Inlanders en met hen gelijkgestelden) aan de maatschappelijke behoefte? Zoo neen, welke wijzigingen zijn noodig?" (1887) [hereafter *VW*]; J. A. Nederburgh, *Gemengde Huwelijken, Staatsblad 1898, No. 158: Officiele Bescheiden met Eenige Aanteekeningen* [hereafter *GH*].

90. Wertheim, review of *Intergentiel Recht.*

91. The term "mixed marriages" (*gemengde huwelijken*) had two distinct but overlapping meanings in the Indies at the turn of the century. Common usage defined it as referring to contracts between a man and a woman of different racial origin; the state defined it as "a marriage between persons who were subject to different laws in the Netherlands Indies" with no reference to race. The distinction is significant for at least two reasons: (1) because the designations of legal standing as inlander versus European cut across the racial spectrum, with generations of mixed-bloods falling on different sides of this divide, and (2) because adat (customary) and Dutch law followed different rulings with respect to the marriage contract, divorce, inheritance, and child custody.

92. Although the hierarchies of gender and race of Indies colonial society account for the fact that in 1895 more than half of the European men in the Indies still lived with native women outside of marriage, this may only tell one part of the story. The juridical debates on legal reform of mixed marriages suggest that there were women who chose cohabitation over legal marriage. At the very least, this suggests that concubinage may not have been an appropriate term for some of these arrangements, nor does it necessarily reflect what options women may have perceived in these arrangements.

93. W. F. Prins, "De bevolkingsgroepen in het Nederlandsch-Indische recht," *Koloniale Studien* 17: 665. That some women chose cohabitation over legal mixed marriages is rarely addressed in the colonial or secondary literature on the assumption that all forms of cohabitation could be subsumed by the term "concubinage," signaling the moral degradation of a "kept woman" that the later term implies. References in these legal debates to the fact that some women chose not to marry suggests that this issue needs further investigation.

94. Nederburgh, *GH,* 17.

95. As the chairman of the commission poignantly illustrated, a woman with native legal standing could be arrested for wearing European attire at the very moment she emerged from the building in which she had just married a European. Nor could a European man and his wife of native standing take the short boat trip from Soerabaya to Madura without prior permission of the authorities since sea passage for natives was forbidden by law (*JV,* 29–30).

96. Nederburgh, *GH,* 20.

97. Ibid., 13.

98. Ibid., 13.

99. *JV,* 39.

100. Idem.

101. Ibid., 51.

102. Ibid., 40. The arguments presented over the mixed-marriage ruling are much more numerous and elaborate than this short account suggests. There were indeed those such as Abendanon (the lawyer friend of Kartini), whose proposals raised yet a whole different set of options than those offered in these accounts. He argued that both man and woman should be given European status, except in those cases in which a native man preferred to retain his rights under adat law. Abendanon also single-handedly countered the claim that any European woman who chose to marry a native man was already debased, arguing that there were many Dutch girls in the Netherlands for whom

this was not the case. But these arguments were incidental to the main thrust of the debate and had little sway in the final analysis.

103. Nederburgh, *GM,* 64.

104. See A. van Marle's "De Groep der Europeanen in Nederlands-Indie, iets over ontstaan en groei," *Indonesie* 5, no. 3 (1952): 322, 328. Van Marle suggests that the much larger number of illiterate women of European standing in central Java and the Moluccas compared to the rest of the Indies indicates that the number of mixed marriages in these regions was particularly high (p. 330). But this was not the case everywhere. In East Java, European men acknowledged more of their métis children but continued to cohabit with the native mothers of their children outside of marriage (p. 495).

105. Mevrouw Douaire Klerck, *Eenige Beschouwingen over Oost-Indische Toestanden* (Amsterdam: Versluys, 1898), 3–19.

106. S. S. J. Ratu-Langie, *Sarekat Islam* (Baarn: Hollandia Drukkerij, 1913), 21.

107. A woman who had contracted a mixed marriage could, on divorce or the death of her husband, declare her desire to reinstate her original nationality as long as she did so within a certain time. However, a native woman who married a European man and subsequently married and divorced a man of non-European status could not recoup her European status.

108. Ernest Rodenwalt, "Eugenetische Problemen in Nederlandsch-Indie," *Ons Nageslacht* (1928): 1–8.

109. Johan Winsemius, "Nieuw-Guinee als kolonisatie-gebied voor Europeanen en van Indo-Europeanen" (Ph.D. dissertation, Faculty of Medicine, University of Amsterdam, 1936), 227.

110. Jacques van Doorn emphasizes the dualistic policy on poverty in the 1930s in "Armoede en Dualistisch Beleid" (unpublished); I would refer to it as a three-tiered policy, not a dualistic one.

111. J. Th. Petrus Blumberger, *De Indo-Europeesche Beweging in Nederlandsch-Indie* (Haarlem: Tjeenk Willink, 1939), 5.

112. See Paul van der Veur's "The Eurasians of Indonesia: A Problem and Challenge in Colonial History," *Journal of Southeast Asian History* 9, no. 2 (September 1966): 191–207, and his "Cultural Aspects of the Eurasian Community in Indonesian Colonial Society," *Indonesia* 6 (October 1968): 38–53.

113. On the various currents of Eurasian political activity, see van der Veur's "The Eurasians of Indonesia." On the importance of Indo individuals in the early Malay press and nationalist movement, see Takashi Shiraishi's *An Age in Motion: Popular Radicalism in Java, 1912–1926* (Ithaca: Cornell University Press, 1990), esp. pp. 37, 58–59. Neither account addresses the class differences within Eurasian groups and where their distinct allegiances lay.

114. Blumberger, *De Indo-Europeesche Beweging,* 50.

115. According to the historian Rudolph Mrazek, the early silent rejection of the Indo-European community from the Indonesian nationalist project turned explicit under Soekarno in the mid-1920s, when Indo-Europeans were categorically barred from membership in nationalist political organizations. Mrazek suggests that this silence among Dutch-educated nationalist leaders on the Indo question should be understood as a response from their own cultural formation and identification as cultural hybrids themselves (personal communication).

116. See P. J. Drooglever's discussion of this failed effort in *De Vaderlandse Club* (Franeker: T. Wever, 1980), 193–208.

117. Drooglever, *De Vaderlandse Club,* 285.

118. *Verbond Nederland en Indie,* no. 3 (September 1926): 3. In the late 1920s, this publication appended the subtitle "A Fascist Monthly" to the name above.

119. This issue of rootlessness is most subtly analyzed in contemporary contexts. Liisa Malkki explores the meanings attached to displacement and uprootedness in the national order of things ("National Geographic: The Rooting of Peoples and the Territorialization of National Identity among Scholars and Refugees," *Cultural Anthropology* (1992). Pierre-André Taguieff examines LePen's nationalist rhetoric on the dangers of the rootlessness of immigrant workers in France. See Taguieff's "The Doctrine of the National Front in France (1972–1989)," *New Political Science,* no. 16/17, 29–70.

120. See A. Braconier, "Het Pauperisme onder de in Ned. Oost-Indie levende Europeanen," *Nederlandsch-Indie,* no. 1 (1917): 291–300, at p. 293.

121. Enquête sur Métissage, AOM, Amiraux 53.50.6.

122. René Martial, *Les Métis* (Paris: Flammarion, 1942), 58.

123. See Taguieff, "The Doctrine of the National Front."

124. On the recent British discourse on Britishness and the cultural threat of Islam to that identity, see Talal Asad's rich analysis in "Multiculturalism and British Identity in the Wake of the Rushdie Affair," *Politics and Society* 18, no. 4 (December 1990): 455–480.

125. Hazel Carby ("Lynching, Empire and Sexuality," *Critical Inquiry* 12, no. 1 [1985]: 262–277) argues that Afro-American women intellectuals at the turn of the century focused on the métis figure because it both enabled an exploration and expressed the relations between the races, because it demythologized concepts of pure blood and pure race while debunking any proposition of degeneracy through amalgamation. Such black women writers as Pauline Hopkins embraced the mulatto to counter the official script that miscegenation was not the inmost desire of the nonwhite peoples but the result of white rape (p. 274). In both the Indies and the United States at the same time, the figure of the Indo-mulatto looms large in both dominant and subaltern literary production, serving to convey strategic social dilemmas and political messages. It is not surprising, then, that the portrayal of the Indo in fiction was widely discussed in the Indies and metropolitan press by many more than those who were interested in literary style alone.

126. Taylor, *The Social World of Batavia,* 155.

127. Carole Pateman argues that the sexual contract is fundamental to the functioning of European civil society, in that the principle of patriarchal right defines the social contract between men and the individual and citizen as male (*The Sexual Contract* [Stanford: Stanford University Press, 1988]).

128. I thank Luise White for pressing me to think out this point.

129. Gwendolyn Wright, "Tradition in the Service of Modernity: Architecture and Urbanism in French Colonial Policy, 1900–1930," *Journal of Modern History* 59 (June 1987): 291–316, at p. 297.

6

"The Conversion of Englishmen and the Conversion of the World Inseparable"

Missionary Imperialism and the Language of Class in Early Industrial Britain

Susan Thorne

When the Rev. George Greatbatch arrived in North Meols, a small village in western Lancashire, his "heart sank" before the widespread "ignorance and general behavior" of the native population.[1] The area to which Greatbatch had been sent by the Lancashire Itinerant Society shortly after its founding in 1801 (Greatbatch was the society's first appointment) would be described by one of his successors as "probably one of the most unenlightened and uncivilized parts of the kingdom."[2] Greatbatch himself decided to submit to an arduous fifteen-mile commute from Newburgh rather than bring his wife and children to live among such a people: "I recollect the awkward gaze wherewith the people looked upon me, and the painful feelings of my heart when I retired to a little hovel from among them. . . . The thought of living among them would have overwhelmed me." Greatbatch explained his visceral recoil from the people to whom he had been sent to minister by saying, "I had little thought there was a station for me at home which so much resembled the ideas I had formed of an uncivilised heathen land."[3]

Such invocations of "uncivilised heathen lands" and their inhabitants were a ubiquitous feature of social discourse in early industrial Britain. While often observed in passing by social and cultural historians of this period, such discursive gesticulations in the Empire's direction have not as yet been engaged in a systematic way.[4] This essay focuses on the evangelical and missionary association of the heathen classes at "home" with the heathen "races" that populated Britain's rapidly expanding colonial empire at the turn of the nineteenth century. It will ask when—and why—evangelical ministers like the Reverend Greatbatch began to view the laboring poor as somehow comparable to the Empire's "heathen races." What did heathens abroad and heathens at home have in common in the minds of contemporary evangelicals? What meanings did imaginative associations with the Empire attach to the religious public's perceptions of the laboring poor? And what were the political and social consequences of this linguistic gesture to the colonies in the evangelical language of class?

There is considerable empirical justification for attending to evangelicals. The evangelical contribution to British political culture from this "age of revolution" through the "age of empire," simply put, cannot be overstated.[5] As late as the 1860s and 1870s, "the churches were still the great arbiters of public attitudes towards social issues"; indeed, for most of the nineteenth century, British public opinion was "educated from the pulpit."[6] Not only did almost half the adult population attend church on a regular basis; the overwhelming majority of the unchurched remainder were exposed to religious influences when they were children in Britain's massively popular Sunday schools.[7] And within organized religion in nineteenth-century Britain, evangelicalism's influence was without effective rival. Evangelicalism "set the tone of British society" for much of the nineteenth century; indeed, much of what we think about when we think of "Victorian values" was of evangelical inspiration.[8] Thus whatever we might learn about the impact of colonialism on evangelical social discourse will have important implications for British society as a whole.

Colonialism's prominence in the evangelical imagination was the result of the extensive "home" organizational labors of foreign missionary societies, the effectiveness of which was registered in contemporary depictions of "the missionary spirit" as "the characteristic feature of religion."[9] In their efforts to raise funds and volunteers for their foreign operations, missionary societies produced and disseminated a voluminous body of propaganda representing the colonial encounter to which the Victorian religious public proved enormously receptive. The attractions of foreign missionary intelligence were considerable in an age before alternative means of enlightenment, entertainment, and even assembly were widely available. This was particularly true of public missionary meetings at which audiences were treated to a foreign missionary's eyewitness account of travels and battles among the heathen or the testimony of a convert from the colonies resplendent in exotic "native" dress. Missions were an extremely important source of information about the outside world as well as entertainment in rural areas like North Meols, where it must be remembered that most of the British population lived until 1850 and a significant minority thereafter. Add to this the wide distribution of religious publications (in which missionary themes figured very prominently) and the privileged location of missionary imperial propagandists becomes, I think, apparent.[10]

Missions were not only an effective conduit of information about the Empire; they were also a primary source of the information available to the British public about the poor and laboring classes at home. The missionaries deployed by organizations like the Lancashire Itinerant Society were arguably the most visible bourgeois presence in the working-class community for most of the first half of the nineteenth century, when police, social welfare, and public educational provisions were minimal. These organizations were also very effective in broadcasting their "findings" about the poor to the middle-class audiences who financed their operations. Like their foreign missionary counterparts, home missionary institutions involved a large cross-section of the evangelical community in their activities—through fund-raising campaigns, sermons, printed propaganda, and the numerous opportunities available for voluntary service in the home mission "field" itself. In combination, these discursive practices and organizational structures comprised the principal occasions, I would argue, on which the respectable classes in Britain came into contact with the poor.[11]

Although historians have generally approached home and foreign missions as separate undertakings, functionally and ideologically independent, contemporary evangelicals experienced them as two fronts of the same war, separated by geographic happenstance and little more.[12] Foreign missions, for example, were often applauded for their "reflux" benefits at home. The prestige of the mission field was widely portrayed as a means through which even the hardest of heathen hearts at home might be softened. In a letter to his son, the Rev. William Alexander (who had succeeded Greatbatch in North Meols) described a local husband's outraged response to the conversion of his wife at a cottage meeting; the husband "threatened violence if she persisted in her course." Yet even someone as hostile to religion as this man claimed to be was compelled by "curiosity" to attend a missionary prayer meeting in the chapel, where he was so impressed "by the missionary facts which were narrated, that he determined to attend the service on the Sabbath." It will come as no surprise to discover that this gentleman was shortly thereafter to convert or that he "became a holy and useful member of the church."[13]

The geographically dispersed and culturally diverse fronts of the evangelical war on heathenism were connected on many levels. Although the national and regional organizations were institutionally distinct, home and foreign missions were promoted by the same individuals on the local level, a circumstance duly noted by contemporaries. To the rhetorical question "Whose names appear in support of foreign missions?" home missionary activists across the nation gave the standard reply: "Unquestionably those of men most forward to promote the spiritual welfare of their countrymen."[14] Greatbatch himself, along with many of his contemporaries, had originally intended to become a foreign missionary, and he claimed that the foreign cause remained forever "near my heart." Indeed, home and foreign missions were sufficiently interchangeable that many chapels took up a single missionary collection each month and simply divided the proceeds between home and foreign fields.[15]

The institutional and social connections between home and foreign missions encouraged their evangelical audiences to think about subaltern groups in Britain and its colonies in relation to one another, thereby rendering evangelical religious practice a principal site at which conceptions of race emanating from the colonies entered metropolitan social discourse. This is not to say that the evangelical language of class simply mirrored the language of race (or vice versa), that evangelical conceptions of race and class simply "recapitulated or reproduced or even 'expressed'" the other, or that they were "defined by the same determinations" or had "exactly the same conditions of existence."[16] The relationship between race and class is better understood in terms of Stuart Hall's concept of "articulated" discourses; while their connections were influential, their histories remained distinct. Put in a slightly different way, the historical developments that gave rise to home missionary conceptions of the poor invariably reverberated in the foreign mission field and were refracted in foreign missionary discourse—and vice versa; but such influences did not take the same form or develop in the same directions in the very different sociopolitical contexts of Britain and its colonies. It is on the metropolitan consequences of their uneven and complex intersection that this essay focuses.

Charity Begins at Home

The history of British missions typically begins with the Evangelical Revival; but it was not until the 1780s and 1790s that a specifically missionary philanthropy—that is to say, a mode of philanthropy primarily oriented to spiritual conversion—found widespread support. By contrast with Catholic Europe, the missionary involvements of Protestant Britain were minimal for most of the eighteenth century. There were only two missionary organizations at work in the British Empire during this period, the Society for the Propagation of the Gospel (founded in 1701) and the Society for Promoting Christian Knowledge (founded in 1699). Neither of these societies was evangelical in inspiration, nor were they primarily oriented to the Empire's indigenous inhabitants in the manner of their evangelical successors. Their efforts were primarily pastoral rather than missionary: they were primarily designed to keep European settlers in the church rather than to convert the surrounding "heathen" populations.

Missionary outreach was also minimal on the British missionary home front, again until the decades bracketing the nineteenth century's turn. The philanthropic enthusiasm for which eighteenth-century Britain is renowned was primarily humanitarian rather than missionary in its orientation: eighteenth-century philanthropy was largely concerned to redress the corporeal consequences of poverty. Lying-in hospitals for pregnant women, foundling societies for abandoned children, lock-hospitals and Magdalene societies for the treatment of venereal disease and the reclamation of prostitutes, all endeavored to protect the health of especially the young and female poor—either by addressing the problem of infant mortality or by restoring to social usefulness the bodies as much as the souls of those lost to vice.[17]

These "humanitarian" philanthropies served the vital imperial function of augmenting the physical health and reproductive well-being of those sectors of the British population from which potential settlers were recruited, during a period when the establishment of European settlements was viewed as the paramount purpose of British expansion.[18] This imperial imperative for relieving poverty at "home" would lose much of its force in the aftermath of the American Revolution. Britain's expansionist aspirations were directed thereafter in easterly directions, for the most part, including first and foremost the heavily populated regions of South Asia. These regions were not demographically "available" for European settlement on anything like the North American scale, and the physical well-being of poor people in Britain was deprived of much of its former imperial value. These imperial developments coincided with developments in the metropolitan economy that further reduced the demand for and value of the labor of Britain's poor. The great economic transformations of this period—the commercialization of agriculture and the tumultuous onset of industrialization—resulted in near-catastrophic levels of un- and underemployment that contributed considerably to the political tensions which transformed this age of revolution.

The resulting pressure on the poor rates prompted the propertied classes to react with varying degrees of alarm. The more paternalistically inclined responded to the emergency by expanding "outdoor" provisions of relief, drawing on their parish's provisions for the poor to supplement plummeting agricultural wages and to offset temporary unemployment (the so-called Speenhamland solution). The dismal science of political economy was the other and increasingly common response—and the one to which our evangelicals were decidedly more prone. Malthusian anxieties about overpopulation encouraged the view that however well meaning, interventions in the operation of a free market would bring calamitous results. The politically correct response in times of distress, however difficult it might be to maintain, was to do as little for the poor as possible.[19]

These imperial and domestic developments combined to transform the religious community's outreach to the poor during the closing decades of the eighteenth century.[20] Secular assistance (in the form of alms, health care, housing, food, coal, blankets, etc.) would increasingly be viewed as a very cruel form of kindness that simply fostered the "irresponsible" behavior on which Britain's alleged overpopulation was blamed.[21] "It fosters habits of idleness and vice, of luxury and waste, of thoughtlessness and improvidence, of servility and discontent" and was itself responsible for "most of the evils which have lately pressed so severely upon the poorer classes of society."[22] The respectable classes were encouraged to assuage their consciences in the face of mounting popular distress by redirecting their philanthropic energies in the more spiritual direction of missions. Missionary philanthropy was embraced as "charity of the most enlightened nature; charity which no just view of political economy, no general speculations on the condition of mankind, can for a moment render questionable."[23] Reforming manners and saving souls would increasingly take precedence over saving lives as moral regeneration displaced material aid. The founding of the Proclamation Society in 1787, the Religious Tract Society in 1799, the Society for the Suppression of Vice in 1801, the British and Foreign Bible Society in 1804, as well as numerous itinerant societies and Sunday schools on the local level, were all manifestations of evangelical philanthropy's increasingly spiritual bent at the nineteenth century's turn.

Gentlemanly Capitalism and Its Discontents

My narrative thus far pits the propertied classes of evangelicalism against the poor. But the propertied elite in Britain was itself divided in ways that were registered and contested in the emergence of a missionary style of philanthropy. For religion was a critical marker of the considerable distance between the industrial middle classes and Britain's "gentlemanly capitalist" Establishment. It is worth reminding ourselves of how wide the divide remained between Britain's middling ranks and even this relatively "open" landed elite during those revolutionary decades bracketing the nineteenth century's turn. Even the most successful of Britain's industrial magnates (and it was industrial and to a lesser extent commercial rather than finance capital that predominated in evangelical and especially in Nonconformist circles) were outsiders from the point of view of Great Britain's established political elite. Although not without social status and economic clout from the point of view of the laboring poor, the middling ranks in British society were a "dominated fraction within the dominant class." Most could not vote, and their collective presence in Parliament was negligible (and would remain so until the second half of the nineteenth century). The social stigma that continued to be attached to "manufactured" wealth limited middle-class influence in the informal corridors of power (at Court and in society) as well.[24]

The Anglican Establishment was suspicious of the missionary project and its middle-class promoters from the outset. Beleaguered internally with endemic absenteeism and pluralism, the Established Church was simply not able to compete with the energetic and highly organized bevy of home missionaries championing the cause of Methodism and Dissent. Denominational rivalry—made serious enough in its own right by the political and economic advantages at stake for the Establishment—was intensified by the perceived challenge that evangelicalism presented to the established social hierarchy. Offensive enough was the often-proclaimed assertion by evangelicals that the upper classes of

England were "but little superior, in respect of morals, to the lower."[25] Home missionary advances were invoked in support of middle-class claims to be the nation's true spiritual leaders, "the chief support of its liberty and religion," as one home missionary spokesman proclaimed, "the great depositories of its moral truth, commercial honor, and Christian fabric."[26]

Even more disturbing to Anglican sensibilities, however, were the social relations of missionary philanthropy. In place of the gentry's traditional emphasis on distance and discipline, awe and fear, evangelicals sought to substitute what they considered to be a more effective internalization of authority. "The time is gone by," a Dissenting home missionary advocate pointedly proclaimed, "when it will be assumed, that ignorance is the mother of devotion, and that to keep men in subordination, it is necessary to debar them from education. . . . Religion is the surest foundation of the political edifice, and its principles constitute the moral elements, which must, eventually, cement and consolidate the several parts of the structure."[27]

Traditional elites, however, were not at all sure that the preservation of the established order was compatible with popularizing religion. Evangelical missionary organizations interposed middle-class functionaries between the nation's gentlemanly capitalist rulers and the laboring poor in what was then an unprecedented dispersal of authority. And however disciplinary their intent, to the extent that they were predicated on assumptions about the spiritual equality of believers, missionary practices were potentially subversive.[28] As Victor Kiernan has put it, " to invite peasants to read Scripture themselves, unguided, [the reference here is to the British and Foreign Bible Society] was to overthrow, in the end, all respect for law and order."[29]

While secure in its hegemony, Britain's landed Establishment tolerated, albeit uneasily, evangelicals' early missionary forays. This uneasy accommodation, however, was brought to an end by the outbreak of revolution in France. Evangelicals, particularly the Nonconformists among them, were widely suspected of Jacobin sympathies. Evangelicals were subjected to vituperative abuse in Establishment propaganda, physically assaulted by Church and King mobs, harassed by hecklers, and arrested by local authorities on the flimsiest of excuses. The suspension of habeas corpus and the imposition of severe penalties on those found guilty of encouraging "contempt for monarchy or constitution" put all evangelicals, but particularly Nonconformists, in an extremely vulnerable position.[30]

The wartime state went to extraordinary lengths to curtail the missionary expansion of evangelical influence. While the French Revolution is generally credited with convincing England's governing classes of the necessity of grounding their authority in religion, its short-term effect was to delegitimize the institutional means, such as itinerant preaching, popular literacy, and public assemblies, whereby religion might acquire genuinely popular assent. Landowners joined forces with the Anglican clergy to discourage home missionary operations in the districts over which they had influence. And their influence was still considerable. Those dependent on gentry largesse for housing, access to land to farm, custom, jobs, or justice were not likely to jeopardize these all-important services by home missionary involvements that were widely perceived as not just religious but political in nature.[31]

It was only now, in the 1790s, that evangelicals began to manifest the foreign missionary ambitions that would dominate British religious practice for most of the century to come.[32] This momentous decade witnessed the establishment of foreign missionary societies in connection with all of Britain's major evangelical denominations. The Baptist Missionary Society was founded in 1792, the London Missionary Society in 1795, and the Church Missionary Society in 1799. The Methodist Missionary Society was not established until 1818, although a longer-lived Methodist committee on missions had been sending missionaries abroad since at least 1785. By the end of the nineteenth century, British Protestants were sponsoring more than twenty missionary organizations expressly designed to spread the gospel to the indigenous "heathen" inhabitants of foreign lands.[33]

The evangelical missionary impulse of the nineteenth century differed from its predecessors in a number of important ways. First and most obviously, earlier missionary organizations had targeted European settlers for the most part, displaying only a cursory interest in indigenous populations and even then only in those living in the immediate vicinity of European settlements.[34] Second, these early missionary organizations were supported by a small circle of very wealthy and largely aristocratic sponsors and, as a result, did not involve a significant number of British Christians in their operations. The "modern" missionary movement, by contrast, was far more ambitious in the scale of its operations—taking all the world and the peoples therein within its scope. Moreover, its dependence on the financial support of large numbers of small contributors brought a far wider spectrum of the British philanthropic public in touch with the mission field and by extension with the Empire in which most of Britain's foreign missionaries operated.[35]

Britain's governing classes seem to have been more tolerant of the evangelical public's foreign missionary involvements. Foreign missions were not immune to the charges of political subversion so frequently directed against their home counterparts—and missionaries in the foreign field operated under stringent official restrictions.[36] But however onerous in their own right, the obstacles placed in the way of evangelical missions in the Empire were far less severe and efficacious than the restraints placed on evangelical missions at "home." At virtually the same time that the British East India Company was being forced to allow missionaries into its territories, evangelicals barely succeeded in averting legislation engineered by Home Secretary Lord Sidmouth which would have effectively precluded the itinerant ministries that comprised the evangelical missionary project at home.[37]

Establishment suspicions of home missions persisted into the volatile post-war period, and in an effort to avoid any semblance of controversy, respectable evangelicals increasingly avoided public association with or significant private support for home missionary activities. But, perhaps to ease their consciences, evangelical Britons began at this time to invest enormous quantities of money, time, and enthusiasm in the missionary cause abroad. By 1847, the Church Missionary Society, the British and Foreign Bible Society, and the Society for the Propagation of the Gospel all had incomes in excess of £100,000 per annum; the London Missionary Society's income was over £75,000 and the Baptist Missionary Society's income exceeded £25,000. By way of contrast, the income of the London City Mission, Britain's most generously supported home missionary agency, barely exceeded £14,000. As a result, then, of the primarily political struggles between Britain's gentlemanly capitalist Establishment and the Dissenting middle class, evangelical support for home missions would remain "negligible" while foreign missions "flourished" well into the second half of the nineteenth century.[38]

"As Heathen as Darkest Africa"

The pronounced disparity in evangelical support for home and foreign missions had important discursive consequences, shaping the terms on which home missionaries represented their operations as well as their beneficiaries to their evangelical audience. Home missionary advocates complain again and again about widespread disparities in press coverage, in attendance at public meetings, and, most important, in contributions to the home as opposed to the foreign cause—differences that were explicitly attributed to the respectable public's association of home missionary outreach with political radicalism.[39] Frustrated home missionaries and their supporters sternly reminded their fellow evangelicals that "if the obligation of Christian benevolence extends to men of every tongue and people of every nation, its claim must possess peculiar force at home."[40] Some occasionally went so far as to call it downright "preposterous to weep over the perdition of distant millions, and set at nought the claims of countless multitudes who are dropping into hell all around, at your doors, and before your eyes."[41]

But the important thing to note is that even when they were least sympathetic, home missionary advocates were forced to contest foreign missions' popularity to raise money and otherwise mobilize support for their own cause. Most home missionary advocates avoided the sort of resentful hyperbole cited above, finding it more productive in the long run to try to turn the popularity of their chief competition to home advantage. Home missions could be promoted, for example, as a way to enlarge the domestic social base from which foreign missions drew their financial support and field personnel. More and better Christians in England would translate into more contributions for foreign missionary coffers, argued the Rev. John Angell James in his aptly titled sermon "The Conversion of Englishmen and the Conversion of the World Inseparable": "Every minister who is raised up to preach the gospel at home, is another advocate for missions abroad. . . . [E]very new congregation that is formed is a new home and foreign mission at the same time. . . . See what a connexion [exists] between home operations and the spread of the gospel abroad?"[42] "I am convinced," urged another Congregational minister in 1850, "that if during the last five and twenty years we had been spending more in wise and well-directed effort in England, the London Missionary Society's income would be double what it is. I speak in the interests of India and China and Africa, when I appeal to you on behalf of our great English interests in this matter."[43] The resurgence of emigrationism at midcentury suggested yet another way by which home missionary exertions in Britain would benefit the foreign missionary and imperial cause.

> That large numbers, in the course of a few years, will emigrate, there can be little question; and if they are to go forth as a blessing, not as a blight, to aid distant missionary effort, not to neutralize and destroy it; to propagate not the worst evils which characterize the parent country, but the blessings which with all its faults, give it so high a place in the scale of nations;—they must be Christianized before they leave their native shores.[44]

Many home missionary proponents went still further, urging the importance of home missions by claiming that their practice and targets were essentially indistinguishable from those of the foreign field whose importance they did not pretend to challenge. Home missionaries complained incessantly that England suffered from a "heathenism as dense as any in Polynesia or Central Africa," comparing reports of local conditions in rural areas (such as that submitted by Greatbatch) to "the survey of some unknown district of Africa by a missionary" or describing the inhabitants of rural and village communities as "as heathen and barbarian as the natives of darkest Africa."[45] No more effective analogy was apparently to hand to underscore the vices of the unchurched in Britain than establishing that they needed "missionary interposition as energetic and devoted as in any heathen land."[46] At an 1830 service honoring a newly appointed city missionary of the Christian Instruction Society, the Rev. Joseph Fletcher bemoaned the "awful degradation" of those in London "as ignorant of 'the true God' as if they had lived under the meridian of heathen superstition, and paganism were still the religion of the villages!"[47] The scottish Congregationalist Ralph Wardlaw similarly pleaded on behalf of missions for those "many thousands of our own countrymen, who pass under the common name of Christian, and yet are living in the ignorance of heathens, and dying in this ignorance."[48]

That such comparisons were even possible suggests, I think, that "race" and "class" were not yet the antithetical or even discrete axes of identity that they have since become. By contrast to the contemporary scholarly propensity to view race and class as inimical modes of domination and subordination, the early Victorians seem to have assumed their underlying similarity, to have been struck, as Thomas Holt has recently put it, more by their similarities than their differences, convinced by the very symmetry between representations of poor and colonized peoples that both forms of subordination were just, both prejudices true.[49] Or to put it somewhat differently, sin was certainly a great equalizer in these discussions, but its circumventing of those social boundaries we distinguish today as "race" and "class" was done in such a way as to reinforce rather than subvert imperial as well as domestic social hierarchies. This was a profoundly and consistently negative equality, from which neither "heathen" grouping derived moral or political benefit. As the Rev. James Stephen grimly concluded in 1811, "In surveying the moral condition of mankind, of every age and country, whatever varieties may be found amongst them in colour, language, customs, and manners; the same gloomy features of inherent depravity, the same sad proofs of estrangement from God are visible in all."[50]

Evangelical Political Economy and Popular Racial Identities

The argument thus far is that class struggles between competing factions of the propertied elite contributed to the articulation of racial discourses generated in the Empire with languages of class taking shape at "home."[51] To reiterate, it was largely in response to reprisals from the "gentlemanly capitalist" Establishment that middle-class evangelicals began to redirect their growing missionary ambitions in foreign and imperial directions. This, in turn, encouraged home missionary supporters to promote their own cause by relating its operations and comparing its beneficiaries to the more respectable foreign field. Again, this is not to say that either discursive structure (home missionary representations of the working classes and foreign missionary representations of the colonized) replicated the other in any simple or unmediated way. The many influences that made their way between Britain and its Empire via missionary institutions rarely made the trip intact. As Ann Stoler has put it, "seemingly shared vocabularies . . . [that] may sometimes remain the same, at other times diverge and transpose into distinct and oppositional political meanings."[52]

For example, among the imperial influences whose traces can be discerned on the evangelical language of class, the perception of "heathenism" was preeminent. And this perception, it is important for us to note, was acquiring increasingly negative connotations as a result of developments in the colonies. Heathenism is, of course, an intrinsically derogatory label, but its moral implications grew considerably worse after the abolition of slavery. Evangelicals were actively involved in the abolitionist movement, opposing slavery as a violation of their Christian political economy. "Free" labor and "legitimate" trade were viewed by evangelicals as the economic mechanisms through which Christianity distributed its political and social benefits, as well as, and perhaps more important, its punishments.[53]

Antipathy to slavery remained prominent among evangelical concerns even after the slave trade was abolished in 1807 and slavery itself in 1834. By this time, however, the geographic focus and political signification of antislavery sentiment had shifted considerably, from a moralizing condemnation of European demand for slaves to work its plantations in the New World to Africa's willingness to supply. The rationale for foreign missions shifted accordingly, from atonement for European guilt to a mechanism through which Africans might be lured into alternative forms of trade. The expansion of Christianity was increasingly promoted as an adjunct to the expansion of "legitimate" commerce, a means of "civilizing" the world's "barbaric races," now considered peculiarly susceptible to savage cruelties like slavery.[54] Thus were Africa and Africans transformed in the course of Britain's age of reform from the victims to the villains of antislavery invective.

Heathenism, in the meanwhile, became the ideological repository for the British religious public's newfound repugnance for slavery. And its application to the working class then being made at home played an important role, I would argue, in helping to contain the radical potential of evangelical missions that had raised the alarm of the Establishment. Whatever sympathy for the poor generated in home missionary contacts was avoided or dispelled by a language of heathenism imported from the colonies. In this way did foreign missions help to foreclose the possibility of the sort of cross-class political alliances that established elites had earlier feared and that they sought to squelch with their clampdown on home missionary encounters.

Interestingly enough, the power of such comparisons was reinforced by the numerous occasions on which evangelicals were moved to contrast the beneficiaries of home and foreign missions.[55] Home missionary propagandists frequently tried to press the urgency of their claims by comparing negatively their beneficiaries to those encountered in foreign fields. To underscore Britain's need for missions, in other words, they characterized the heathen classes at home as even more degraded than their overseas counterparts. As one report put it, "The outcast thousands of the people, whom we have culpably suffered to grow up in the heart of our country, [are] more profligate and more perverted than Hindoos."[56]

> If they could be selected and separated into a city by themselves, they would present a population as blind, corrupt, and brutish, as could be furnished from any city of the heathen world—they are seared in conscience, almost divested of moral sense, and sunk into all but hopeless degradation. They are in all respects "earthly, sensual, devilish," without God and without hope in the world.[57]

In 1847, the *Annual Report* of the London City Mission similarly urged its claims on the public purse by portraying its targets as more sinful than heathens elsewhere.

> Of all places in the world, London has the first claims upon us. Here within a walk of this place [St. John's] we know that hundreds of thousands are living without the public worship of God; and we have reason to fear that they are living without religion altogether; we know that many are sunk in vice and sorrow; more guilt than the Heathen, because they have greater means of knowledge, and they have the prospect of a more awful end. Untaught and unreclaimed, they disgrace the kingdom. . . . NEVER WAS THERE, I THINK, SO LARGE A MASS OF UTTERLY UNREGARDED HEATHENISM IN IT AS AT THIS MOMENT.[58]

This rhetorical strategy was not without risk, however. Foreign missionary activists occasionally turned the tables on their home missionary competitors by arguing that even if British heathens were more degraded than their foreign counterparts, their degradation was the reward of their own perverse moral choice and thus neither susceptible to nor deserving of missionary redress. Such was the logic of William Carey, founder of the Baptist Missionary Society, who pointed to the fact that "our own countrymen have the means of grace, and may attend on the word preached if they chuse it" to argue for the priority of the foreign cause.[59]

Implicit in the moral economy of this latter formulation was a widespread belief that the poor at home had been "coddled" enough. It was at this point in missionary discussions that representations of the British poor and of colonized subjects diverged. What is interesting here, however, is the disciplinary function this racial distinction performed in the social discourse of home missions. Even, or perhaps especially, those characteristics that the poor had in common with the missionary middle classes—their race or national heritage—constituted benefits whose apparent waste served merely to indict more fully their possessor. And it was this racial kinship, oddly enough, that helped to rationalize the aggressive social distancing that characterized the period in which the British working class got "made," social distancing that culminated in the widely resented Poor Law reforms of 1834.

Self-help was the only cure for poverty that our missionary political economists acknowledged, and charities that stimulated self-help were regarded as the most effective means of alleviating the suffering of exceptional "deserving" individuals, as well as a revealing index of a beneficiary's potential worth (the logic being that those who would help themselves were deserving).[60] At the same time, the act of philanthropy was itself considered one of the more important stimulants of the most crucial components of self-help, namely, thrift and responsibility.[61] The problem, of course, lay in finding sufferers in sufficiently dire straits to evoke the philanthropic pity of the poor. Foreign missions were among the more popular solutions to this problem. Foreign missions purportedly "elevated" the poor at home by exposing them to the uplifting example of middle-class missionary activism as well as by stimulating their fiscal prudence—all the while redeeming heathens abroad by financing the global spread of gospel truth.[62]

Foreign missionary societies targeted popular constituencies in Britain from their beginnings. The 1807 *Annual Report* of the London Missionary Society praised the formation of "Auxiliary Societies (in which the poor of the flock, by the periodical contribution of small sums, may materially enlarge the funds, and be induced by regular information in their stated meetings to offer up their intercessions for the prosperity of this Institution)."[63] The "auxiliary" movement itself was expressly designed to facilitate the collection of "contributions to the poor."[64] Foreign missionary representatives canvassed working-class Sunday schools and mission chapels—inviting them to send representatives to local auxiliary committees established to organize the annual missionary meeting in their locale. These celebrations of the foreign mission cause lasted from one to two full weeks, during which time special services, including a public meeting, a prayer service, a ladies meeting, a juvenile meeting, and a missionary bazaar, would be held at all or most of those chapels and Sunday schools belonging to the auxiliary. The imaginative resonance of these meetings owed a great deal to the presence of foreign missionaries who toured provincial auxiliaries while on their periodic furloughs from the mission field. Occasions on which a John Williams, Robert Moffat, David Livingstone, James Chalmers, Griffith Johns, or perhaps a local son or daughter made good in the mission field addressed a congregation would be recalled years later as "red letter days" in the life of a town, auxiliary, or chapel.[65]

The missionary presence on the local level extended far beyond these annual meetings. Subscriptions were collected on a regular basis (collectors came round once a week to collect the pennies of the poor), with missionary "intelligence" provided by free literature, conversation, and the illustrations on the "missionary box."[66] The London Missionary Society hired special agents, often retired missionaries, to prod auxiliaries into greater effort on its behalf and to conduct missionary meetings during the "off-season," particularly for home mission chapels and Sunday schools whose ministerial resources were stretched thin.[67] The foreign missionary cause was also the frequent subject of the weekly sermon in chapels across the social spectrum of Nonconformity, and family services often took missionary themes as their subject as well. Robert Moffat, a Scottish gardener's apprentice before entering the foreign field, traced his own missionary calling to his mother's instruction: "On the long winter evenings the lads were gathered by the fireside, and . . . she would read aloud, in such missionary publications as were then to be had, the story of the dauntless pioneers of the gospel."[68] The effectiveness of missionary organization throughout the British countryside was such that contemporaries could claim that "many a small tradesman or rustic knows more of African or Polynesian life than London journalists."[69] And according to F. K. Prochaska, of all the bourgeois philanthropies that plied their wares in the working-class community, foreign missions "were probably the most adept at getting the cooperation of the poor."[70]

The fact that so many "precious pennies" were coaxed from working-class pockets by foreign missionary fund raisers was a source of outrage for many contemporary radicals. Unfortunately, their resentment of missionary intrusions in the working-class community found expression, not in solidarity with colonized comrades in the Empire, but in easily "racialized" protests against the audacity of middle-class evangelicals who dared to compare freeborn Englishmen of however humble a station to the heathen savages of the Empire. William Cobbett was perhaps the best known and certainly the most popular of the radical intelligentsia who juxtaposed working-class interests to the duplicitous and hypocritical machinations of Exeter Hall.[71] Breaking up antislavery meetings became "a statement of class consciousness by working-class radicals," who, according to the historian Patricia Hollis, believed that "the exploitation of factory children financed the very philanthropy of their masters, their subscriptions to Bible Societies, to anti-slavery societies and to chapel building." In addition to Cobbett, Hollis singles out Richard Oastler, the Tory paternalist who led the campaign for factory reform, and Bronterre O'Brien, the Chartist journalist, as vociferous in their antipathy toward those missionary philanthropists who "preferred their objects of benevolence at a distance and possessing 'a black hide, thick lips and a wooley head.' "[72] In 1840 a group of Norwich Chartists broke up a meeting of the African Civilization Society (in which evangelical missionary representatives figured prominently), shouting, "Emancipate the white slaves before you think of the black" and "Look to the slavery and misery of the New Poor Law."[73]

Conclusion

This essay has tried to demonstrate something that few historians of colonialism would probably question, that British and imperial histories intersected in profound and important ways. British historians, unfortunately, continue to try to downplay the Empire's significance for understanding Britain's historical development. Linda Colley has gone so far as to argue that "for most of the time . . . empire simply did not loom all that large in the minds of most men and women back in Europe."[74]

This has been especially true of British historians who work on class. Social historians have looked for the catalysts and consequences of the world's first industrial revolution in the peculiarities of English politics, culture, and geography instead.[75] That imperialism might have mattered, either to the course of British industrialization or to the makings and remakings of popular identities in its wake, has been effectively ignored and even actively resisted.[76] This insular inattention to imperial influences has survived intact British social history's recent "linguistic turn." While far-reaching doubts have been expressed about many other of its underlying precepts—the very existence of social classes and the viability of class analysis, the revolutionary character of industrialization, and even social causality itself—the British historical subject continues to be conceived within the geographic confines of the nation.[77]

There are many and important exceptions to the insular tendencies of which I complain; but the imperial history of class explored here seems to have fallen between their historiographical cracks. While eighteenth-century historians have been more willing than their nineteenth-century counterparts to take the Empire into account, they are, and rightly enough, more interested in imperialism's contribution to the emergence of national rather than class identities.[78] As far as nineteenth-century studies are concerned, imperialism's effective saturation of popular as well as canonical cultural practices has attracted the attention of cultural historians. But the general assumption has been that imperial preoccupations displaced rather than informed class consciousness.[79] "Race" figures similarly in twentieth-century histories that attribute the upsurge of popular conservatism during the 1970s and 1980s to the corrosive effects of racial prejudice on working-class consciousness.[80] The most interesting and ambitious efforts to rethink British history from its imperial "bottom up," however, have been made by feminist historians, who have transformed our understanding of gender relations, the family, and even feminism itself in Britain by taking into account British women's identification with the colonizing project.[81] Here too, however, imperialism and race are typically invoked as alternatives to the class concerns that have until recently distinguished (and in a positive way, I think) British feminist historiography from its North American counterpart.[82]

We owe most of what we know about the *connections* between class and race to scholars whose primary research interests are in "Third World" studies. To better understand the disparate and divisive visions of empire that battled for hegemony on the colonial ground, literary critics, historians, and historically minded anthropologists have been increasingly drawn on to European historiographical terrain.[83] Class formation in Europe has figured prominently in these discussions. European communities in the colonies were riddled by class tensions, which racial prejudices were deliberately fostered to counteract. Race was also and even more importantly invoked to justify and mediate Europeans' hegemony over colonized social groupings. Here too historians have found that European conceptions of class played the important role of providing a model on which the racial logics deployed in the colonies were patterned.[84]

Scholarly discussions of the intersections of class and race in colonial discourse have emphasized the many and important ways in which metropolitan ideas about class were transformed in the colonies into a discourse about "race." Or, to put it another way, the primary concern has been to illuminate the ways in which the language of race spoken in the Empire—as well as at home—was "classed." The history of evangelical missions recounted here, however, suggests that the ideas about class that British colonizers brought with them to the Empire might already have been "raced," constructed on the basis of a social nomenclature whose primary referent was the colonial encounter.

The extraordinary scale of British imperial expansion at the end of the nineteenth century has obscured the magnitude of Britain's colonial involvements at the eighteenth century's turn, which is when historians generally agree that "class" first entered the English social lexicon.[85] By 1820, the British Empire had already absorbed almost a quarter of the world's population, most of whom were incorporated between the Seven Years War, which began in 1756, and the Napoleonic Wars, which ended in 1815.[86] The rapid accumulation of such geographically immense and culturally diverse territories was brought "home" to Britain by any number of institutional and cultural channels—travelers, colonial officials, correspondence with emigrants, service in the military, and so on—but among these I would argue missions were preeminent. The missionary movement obviously failed to suppress the domestic social resentments against which its representations of empire were directed—indeed, it provided fuel for their fire in many instances. At the same time, the class struggles generated therein were effectively contained within the racialist parameters on which the Empire's continuance was predicated. This was one of the more paradoxical results of the missionary movement's rendering the conversion of Englishmen and the conversion of the world inseparable.

Notes

I am grateful to Anna Clark, Fred Cooper, Geoff Eley, Cynthia Herrup, Nancy Hewitt, Susan Juster, Catherine Peyroux, Nathan Quandt, Ann Stoler, Tim Schrand, Richard Soloway, Jennifer Thorn, and Karen Wigen for their helpful comments on various incarnations of this chapter.

1. Quoted in B. Nightingale, *The Story of the Lancashire Congregational Union, 1806–1906: Centenary Memorial Volume* (London: John Heywood, 1906), 37.

2. *Memoirs of Rev. William Alexander,* by his son, John Alexander (Norwich: Fletcher and Alexander, 1856), 182. William Alexander succeeded Greatbatch in 1824, and found the inhabitants "'most of them, wretchedly poor. . . . Except the farmers, all are weavers. Almost all of them have been idle during that time; many are idle now; and if winter overtake them in this state, I know not what will become of many families. I am sorry to say that hardships seem to exasperate rather than to humble'" (p. 226).

3. Nightingale, *Story of the Lancashire Congregational Union,* 37. Nightingale himself describes the choice of western Lancashire as mission field in very similar terms: "As the founders of the London Missionary Society selected the South Sea Islands as their first sphere of labour, than which none was more distant, dark, unpromising and

perilous, so acted the promoters of the Lancashire Itinerant Society. No part of the county could have been more remote from the center of operations, and certainly none was more hopelessly heathen and lost than Western Lancashire'' (p. 19).

4. Although preliminary steps in this direction are taken by Deborah Epstein Nord, ''The Social Explorer as Anthropologist: Victorian Travellers among the Urban Poor,'' in *Visions of the Modern City: Essays in History, Art, and Literature,* ed. William Sharpe and Leonard Wallock, 118–130 (New York: Proceedings of the Heyman Center for the Humanities at Columbia University, 1983): and Douglas Lorimer, *Colour, Class and the Victorians: English Attitudes to the Negro in the Mid-Nineteenth Century* (Leicester: Leicester University Press, 1978). Lorimer, however, focuses on a later period and assumes that class preexisted and gave birth to race—a chronology of influence that I attempt to complicate.

5. The reference here is, of course, to E. J. Hobsbawm's three-volume history of nineteenth-century Britain: *The Age of Revolution, 1789–1848* (London: Weidenfeld and Nicolson, 1962); *The Age of Capital, 1848–1875* (New York: Charles Scribner's Sons, 1975); *The Age of Empire, 1875–1914* (New York: Random House, 1987).

6. Olive Anderson, ''Women Preachers in Mid-Victorian Britain: Some Reflexions on Feminism, Popular Religion and Social Change,'' *Historical Journal* 12, no. 3 (1969): 467; and J. F. C. Harrison, *The Early Victorians, 1832–1851* (New York: Praeger, 1971), 133.

7. For a compelling evaluation of the persisting influence of organized religion in Britain throughout the nineteenth century, see Hugh McLeod, ''New Perspectives on Victorian Class Religion: The Oral Evidence,'' *Oral History Journal* 14, no. 1 (1986): 31–49; and Thomas Walter Laqueur, *Religion and Respectability: Sunday Schools and Working-Class Culture, 1780–1850* (New Haven: Yale University Press, 1976).

8. D. W. Bebbington, *Evangelicalism in Modern Britain: A History from the 1730s to the 1980s* (London: Unwin Hyman, 1989), ix, 105.

9. I am quoting here from the Rev. Arthur Tidman's address to the annual meeting of the London Missionary Society in 1845; see Richard Lovett, *The History of the London Missionary Society, 1795–1895,* vol. 2 (London: Oxford University Press, 1899), 675. Evangelicals were frequently ridiculed for the missionary obsessions; to Dickens's Mrs. Pardiggle and her accomplice Mrs. Jellyby, one might add Thackeray's Pitt Crawley and the Countess of Southdown, or Eliot's Mr. Bulstrode.

10. See Leslie Howsam, *Cheap Bibles: Nineteenth-Century Publishing and the British and Foreign Bible Society* (Cambridge: Cambridge University Press, 1991); F. K. Prochaska, ''Little Vessels: Children in the Nineteenth-Century English Missionary Movement,'' *Journal of Imperial and Commonwealth History* 6, no. 2 (January 1978): 103–118; and Brian Stanley, ''Home Support for Overseas Missions in Early Victorian England, c. 1838–1873'' (Ph.D. dissertation, Cambridge University, 1979).

11. See John Seed, ''Unitarianism, Political Economy and the Antinomies of Liberal Culture in Manchester, 1830–1850,'' *Social History* 7, no. 1 (January 1982): 1–25; Alan J. Kidd, ''Charity Organization and the Unemployed in Manchester c. 1870–1914,'' *Social History* 9, no. 1 (January 1984): 45–66; Gertrude Himmelfarb, *The Idea of Poverty: England in the Early Industrial Age* (London: Faber and Faber, 1984).

12. I have been greatly influenced by Ann Stoler's powerful demonstration of the connectedness of ''bourgeois 'civilizing missions''' in Europe and its colonies; see, most recently, *Race and the Education of Desire: Foucault's ''History of Sexuality''*

and the Colonial Order of Things (Durham, N.C.: Duke University Press, 1995), which I am grateful to Dr. Stoler for sharing with me in its early stages.

13. Alexander, *Memoirs,* 194.

14. See Robert Burls, *A Brief Review of the Plan and Operations of the Essex Congregational Union for Promoting the Knowledge of the Gospel in the County of Essex and Its Vicinity* (Maldon: P. H. Youngman, 1848), 12.

15. See Susan Elizabeth Thorne, "Protestant Ethics and the Spirit of Imperialism: British Congregationalists and Foreign Missions, 1795–1926" (Ph.D. dissertation, University of Michigan, 1990), esp. chaps. 1, 2.

16. Stuart Hall, "Race, Articulation and Societies Structured in Dominance," in *Sociological Theories: Race and Colonialism* (Paris: UNESCO, 1980), 305–345.

17. See David Owen, *English Philanthropy, 1660–1960* (Cambridge, Mass.: Harvard University Press, 1964), pt. 1: "Philanthropy in the Age of Benevolence (1660s–1780s)"; and especially Donna Andrew, *Philanthropy and Police: London Charity in the Eighteenth Century* (Princeton: Princeton University Press, 1990), chaps. 5, 6.

18. For most of the eighteenth century, Britain's colonial ambitions were directed toward establishing colonies of British settlers to provide markets, goods, and services for the metropolitan economy. This emphasis on establishing European settlements distinguished Britain's colonial ambitions from those of its primary rivals on the Continent. The Dutch, the French, and the Spanish had long been engaged in more extractive colonial practices dependent on the exploitation of indigenous labor.

19. See K. D. M. Snell, *Annals of the Labouring Poor: Social Change and Agrarian England, 1660–1900* (Cambridge: Cambridge University Press, 1985). This period would also see the beginnings of a new variant of settler colonialism, with Australia and New Zealand being developed to absorb Britain's "surplus" (unemployed and/or criminal as well as radical) population. These latter colonies figured into British colonial calculations in a different way than their North American predecessors, valued less for their contribution to the metropolitan economy than as political safety valves.

20. See also Deborah Valenze, "Charity, Custom and Humanity: Changing Attitudes towards the Poor in Eighteenth-Century England," in *Revival and Religion since 1700: Essays for John Walsh,* ed. Jane Garnett and Colin Matthew, 59–78 (London: Hambledon Press, 1993).

21. According to Snell, poverty and unemployment were the cause rather than the consequence of the increased birthrate in this period. The decline in arrangements whereby agricultural laborers "lived in" with their employers coupled with the drastic drop in the availability of agricultural opportunities for women forced women and allowed men to marry earlier, which was accompanied by married couples producing more children.

22. Both quotes from "Christian Missions: An Enlightened Species of Charity," by the Rev. S. C. Wilks (London, 1819), 8, 12–13.

23. Ibid.

24. See P. J. Cain and A. G. Hopkins, *British Imperialism,* vol. 1: *Innovation and Expansion, 1688–1914* (London: Longman, 1993); Perry Anderson, "The Figures of Descent," in Anderson, *English Questions* (London: Verso, 1992), 121–192.

25. John Campbell, *Jethro: A System of Lay Agency in Connexion with the Congregational Churches, for the Diffusion of the Gospel among our Home Population* (London: CUEW, 1839), 16–17, 55.

26. Ibid.

27. John Reynolds, "The Necessity and Propriety of Home Missions," a sermon preached at Crown Court Chapel, on Tuesday morning, May 18, 1824, before the committee and friends of the Home Missionary Society (London: R. Baynes, 1824).

28. Deryck W. Lovegrove, *Established Church, Sectarian People: Itinerancy and the Transformation of English Dissent, 1780–1830* (Cambridge: Cambridge University Press, 1988), 109–110, 123–125; D. W. Bebbington, *Evangelicalism in Modern Britain: A History from the 1730s to the 1980s* (London: Unwin Hyman, 1989), 99–100.

29. Victor Kiernan, "Evangelicalism and the French Revolution," *Past and Present* 1 (February 1952): 53. Kiernan suggests that this was primarily the position of diehard High Churchmen, to whom he contrasts the forward-looking vision of evangelicals like Wilberforce. According to E. P. Thompson, however, the French Revolution at least temporarily had the effect of frightening evangelical Anglicans away from their former interdenominational home missionary alliances and, indeed, away from missionary ministrations to the poor altogether. Their philanthropy became increasingly conservative and authoritarian, more in line with High Church sensibilities (see *The Making of the English Working Class* [New York: Vintage Books, (1963) 1968], 56–57).

30. E. R. Norman, *Church and Society in England, 1779–1970* (Oxford: Clarendon Press, 1976), 31; Lovegrove, *Established Church, Sectarian People,* chaps. 6, 7; and Thompson, *The Making of the English Working Class,* esp. chap. 5.

31. Lovegrove, *Established Church, Sectarian People,* chap. 7.

32. A coincidence that has not escaped scholarly attention. See Élie Halévy, *The Birth of Methodism in England,* trans. and ed. Bernard Semmel (Chicago: University of Chicago Press, 1971); Kiernan, "Evangelicalism and the French Revolution"; Bernard Semmel, *The Methodist Revolution* (New York: Basic Books, 1971); and Stuart Piggin, "Halévy Revisited: The Origins of the Wesleyan Methodist Missionary Society: An Examination of Semmel's Thesis," *Journal of Imperial and Commonwealth History* 11, no. 1 (October 1980): 17–37.

33. See A. N. Porter, ed., *Atlas of British Overseas Expansion* (London: Routledge, 1991), 124–127.

34. Rev. William Fleming Stevenson, *The Dawn of Modern Missions* (Edinburgh, 1887).

35. Kenneth Scott Latourette, *A History of the Expansion of Christianity,* vol. 3: *Three Centuries of Advance, 1500–1800* (New York: Harper and Brothers, 1939–1944), 49.

36. Emilia Viotti da Costa, *Crowns of Glory, Tears of Blood: The Demerara Slave Rebellion of 1823* (New York: Oxford University Press, 1994).

37. Lovegrove, *Established Church, Sectarian People,* 135–137; Penelope Carson, "An Imperial Dilemma: The Propagation of Christianity in Early Colonial India," *Journal of Imperial and Commonwealth History* 18, no. 2 (May 1990): 169–190.

38. K. S. Inglis, *Churches and the Working Classes in Victorian England* (London: Routledge and Kegan Paul, 1963), 11; and Norris Pope, *Dickens and Charity* (New York: Columbia University Press, 1978), 105.

39. George Hoskings Wicks, "Bristol's Heathen Neighbors: The Story of the Bristol Itinerant Society, 1811–1911" (1911), 21.

40. The Rev. Ralph Wardlaw continued, arguing that "the claim begins with the family, and enlarges its range progressively, to kindred, and friends, and country, and

mankind.'' See his ''The Early Success of the Gospel and Evidence to Its Truth, and an Encouragement to Zeal for Its Universal Diffusion'' (1823), 41–42.

41. Campbell, *Jethro*, 24.

42. Rev. John Angell James, ''The Conversion of Englishmen and the Conversion of the World Inseparable'' (1835), 3.

43. Joshua Wilson, ''A Plea for Home Evangelisation'' (1859).

44. Baptist Home Missionary Society, *Annual Report for 1857*, 25–26.

45. These are characteristic examples of a rhetoric common to home missionary reports from the early nineteenth century; these particular quotes are recorded in the following local histories: ''The History of Headingly Hill Congregational Church,'' 20; Wicks, ''Bristol's Heathen Neighbors,'' 33; and Rev. C. E. Darwent, *The Story of Fish Street Church Hull* (London: Wm. Anderson and Co., 1899), 128.

46. Home Missionary Society of the Congregational Union of England and Wales, 39th Annual Report (1858), 9.

47. ''An Address Delivered by Rev. Joseph Fletcher MA of Stepney to the Rev. John Pyer on his Public Designation to the Office of City Missionary in the Service of the Christian Instruction Society, on Wednesday Evening, April 21, 1830, at Claremont Chapel, Pentonville,'' 3–4.

48. Wardlaw, ''The Early Success of the Gospel,'' 41.

49. See Holt, *The Problem of Freedom*, 308–309.

50. ''Christianity, the True Light to Illuminate the World,'' 56.

51. See Hall, ''Race, Articulation and Societies Structured in Dominance,'' 325.

52. Stoler, *Race and the Education of Desire*, 13.

53. See David Brion Davis, *The Problem of Slavery in the Age of Revolution, 1770–1823* (Ithaca: Cornell University Press, 1975); and Boyd Hilton, *The Age of Atonement: The Influence of Evangelicalism on Social and Economic Thought, 1785–1865* (Oxford: Clarendon Press, 1985).

54. Ralph Austen and Woodruff D. Smith, ''Images of Africa and British Slave Trade Abolition: The Transition to an Imperialist Ideology, 1787–1807,'' *African Historical Studies* 2, no. 1 (1969): 69–83.

55. Again, to quote from Stuart Hall, the articulation of race and class invariably forms a ''complex structure: a structure in which things are related as much through their differences as through their similarities'' (''Race, Articulation and Societies Structured in Dominance,'' 325).

56. Newcastle Town Mission, *Annual Report* (1829), 4.

57. Campbell, *Jethro*, 8.

58. *An Appeal for the London City Mission*, 5. It was initially the rural north, the birthplace of industrialization, that was described in such quasi-imperial terms, as ''a breeding-ground for 'barbarians,' '' ''so wild a country nurses up a race of people as wild as the fen'' (Thompson, *The Making of the English Working Class*, 219), although the darkness at the heart of urban ''civilization'' would eventually displace its agrarian progenitor. By the middle of the nineteenth century, the deployment of racial and imperial imagery intensified in the form of ever more elaborate efforts to distinguish ''respectable'' working people from the ''residuum.'' Henry Mayhew was simply continuing what had already become a well-established rhetorical strategy when he described the ''moral and intellectual'' difference between skilled and unskilled workers

in 1851 as "so great that it seems as if we were in a new land and among another race."
Cited in Norman McCord, *British History, 1815–1906* (Oxford: Oxford University
Press, 1991), 225. See also Himmelfarb, *The Idea of Poverty;* and for the later period,
see Joseph McLaughlin, "Writing the Urban Jungle: Metropolis and Colonies in Conan
Doyle, General Booth, Jack London, Conrad, and T. S. Eliot" (Ph.D. dissertation, Duke
University, 1992).

59. Quoted in Catherine Hall, "Missionary Stories: Gender and Ethnicity in England in the 1830s and 1840s," in Hall, *White, Male, and Middle Class: Explorations
in Feminism and History* (New York: Routledge, 1988), 216, 218.

60. The effort to distinguish between the deserving and the undeserving poor was
apparently one of the central motivations for the reform of the Poor Law. The New Poor
Law did not, however, achieve these desired results. According to Gertrude Himmelfarb,
"The stigma of pauperism, which was meant to differentiate the pauper from the poor,
had the perverse effect of stigmatizing the entire body of the poor, thus reinforcing the
very ambiguity the reformers had so strenuously tried to remove." See *The Idea of
Poverty,* 525.

61. The moral and fiscal capacity for philanthropy was an important mechanism of
class differentiation—separating the respectable from the residuum as well as the
wealthy from the poor; see Peter Mandler, "Christian Political Economy and the
Making of the New Poor Law," *Historical Journal* 33, no. 1 (1990): 87.

62. Recall the violently antievangelical if not anti-Christian husband of North
Meols, whose heart was softened to Christianity by foreign missionary intelligence.

63. Cited in Lovett, *The History of the London Missionary Society,* 1:81–83. According to the Rev. W. Walton, "The poor and artisan classes came in at first [ca. 1790s]
as missionaries. . . . Only after twelve years, when the auxiliary system was started, did
the Society come to depend on smaller gifts than those provided by middle class
people." See "Other Men Laboured . . . A grateful tribute to the men and women of
Nottinghamshire for their faithful service to the London Missionary Society" (1945),
12–15; and Stanley, "Home Support for Overseas Missions in Early Victorian England," esp. chap. 6.

64. Circular of 1812 quoted in Irene Fletcher, "The Fundamental Principle of the
London Missionary Society," pt. 3, *Transactions of the Congregational Historical
Society* 19, no. 5 (September 1963): 227.

65. See, e.g., Patton, "The Triple Jubilee of the London Missionary Society,
1795–1845," 19; Rev. James Sibree, *Recollections of Hull During Half a Century* (Hull:
A. Brown and Sons, 1884), 67–70.

66. Collectors were instructed to distribute one of these missionary collection boxes
in every Congregational home in their district and to visit the home to collect from the
box at least once each quarter. Collectors were to open the box on every visit "in the
presence of those belonging to the house and at the same time relating some fact or
incident in connection with Mission work." See Leeds Auxiliary Committee of the
London Missionary Society, Committee Minutes, 20 June 1904 (Dr. Williams's Library).

67. Lovett, *History of the London Missionary Society,* 2: 723–724.

68. J. S. Moffat, *The Lives of Robert and Mary Moffat* (London: T. Fisher Unwin,
1885), 4.

69. *London Quarterly Review* 7 (1856): 239; quoted in Cecil Peter Williams, "The Recruitment and Training of Overseas Missionaries in England Between 1850 and 1900" (M.L. dissertation, University of Bristol, 1976), chap. 1, n. 25.

70. F. K. Prochaska, "Philanthropy," in *The Cambridge Social History of Britain, 1750–1950*, vol. 3: *Social Agencies and Institutions*, ed. F. M. L. Thompson (Cambridge: Cambridge University Press, 1990), 367.

71. Exeter Hall was the London site of the annual public meetings of nationally based philanthropies, prominent among which were foreign missionary societies.

72. Patricia Hollis, "Anti-Slavery and British Working-Class Radicalism in the Years of Reform," in *Anti-Slavery, Religion and Reform*, ed. Christine Bolt and Seymour Drescher (Folkestone, Kent: William Dawson and Sons, 1980), 298–299, 311.

73. Quoted in Pope, *Dickens and Charity*, 100.

74. See "The Imperial Embrace," *Yale Review* 81, no. 4 (October 1993): 97–98, a review of Edward W. Said's *Culture and Imperialism* (New York: Vintage, 1993). C. J. D. Duder similarly qualifies his appreciation of John M. Mackenzie's *Imperialism and Popular Culture* with the disclaimer that "despite the often fascinating work contained in this book, I still conclude that the British Empire was a factor of more importance in the life of Nigeria than of Neasden" (*Victorian Studies* 30, no. 4 [Summer 1987]: 529). See also Miles Taylor, "John Bull and the Iconography of Public Opinion in England, c. 1712–1929," *Past and Present* 134 (February 1992): 94, and "Patriotism, History and the Left in Twentieth-Century Britain," *Historical Journal* 33, no. 4 (1990): 987; and Peter Marshall, "No Fatal Impact? The Elusive History of Imperial Britain," *Times Literary Supplement*, 12 March 1993, 8–10. The insular proclivities of British historians are powerfully contested in John M. Mackenzie's introduction to *Imperialism and Popular Culture* (Manchester: University of Manchester Press, 1986), 1–16; Shula Marks, "History, the Nation and Empire: Sniping from the Periphery," *History Workshop Journal* 29 (1990): 111–119; and, most recently, Antoinette Burton, "Rules of Thumb: British History and 'Imperial Culture' in Nineteenth- and Twentieth-Century Britain," *Women's History Review* 3, no. 4 (1994): 483–500.

75. E. J. Hobsbawm and Victor Kiernan have been exceptional in this as in so many other regards. See especially Hobsbawm's *Industry and Empire* (New York: Penguin, 1969); and Kiernan's *Imperialism and Its Contradictions*, ed. and introd. Harvey J. Kaye (New York: Routledge, 1995).

76. Lack of interest is, by definition, difficult to document, but for more or less explicit denials of imperialism's influence on popular and working-class culture, see Henry Pelling, "British Labour and British Imperialism," in *Popular Politics and Society in Late Victorian Britain* (New York: St. Martin's Press, 1968), 82–100; and Richard Price, *An Imperial War and the British Working Class* (London: Routledge, 1972). Geoff Eley has recently complained about the continued insularism of the social historical project in "Playing It Safe, Or How Is History Represented? The New Cambridge Social History of Britain," *History Workshop* 35 (Spring 1993): 206–220.

77. The most important of these revisionist interventions remains Stedman Jones's *Languages of Class: Studies in English Working-Class History, 1832–1982* (Cambridge: Cambridge University Press, 1983), esp. "Rethinking Chartism," 90–178. The geographic parameters of the British historical subject are being broadened in other promising directions. See, for example, Hugh Kearney, *The British Isles: A History of*

Four Nations (Cambridge: Cambridge University Press, 1989), which challenges the hegemony of English developments in the historiography of modern Britain. Historians working on nineteenth-century Britain are increasingly attentive to their subjects' interest in and identification with developments on the Continent; see, for example, Eugene Biagini, *Liberty, Retrenchment, and Reform: Popular Liberalism in the Age of Gladstone, 1860–1880* (Cambridge: Cambridge University Press, 1992); Margo Finn, *After Chartism: Class and Nation in English Radical Politics, 1848–1874* (Cambridge: Cambridge University Press, 1993); and Maura O'Connor, *A Political Romance: Italy and the Making of the English Middle Class, 1800–1864* (forthcoming).

78. See, for example, Linda Colley's "Britishness and Otherness: An Argument," *Journal of British Studies* 31, no. 4 (October 1992): 309–329; and J. G. A. Pocock's "The Limits and Divisions of British History: In Search of the Unknown Subject," *American Historical Review* 87, no. 2 (April 1982): 311–336, although note that Pocock explicitly excludes from his broadened British history the nonwhite colonial "dependencies."

79. The general thrust of the argument in *Imperialism and Popular Culture* is that the martial dramas and material superprofits of the "new imperial" era transformed popular political identities in ways that precluded—or at least sharply limited—social divisions along class lines; although see also Price, *An Imperial War and the British Working Class.*

80. See, for example, the Centre for Contemporary Cultural Studies, *The Empire Strikes Back: Race and Racism in '70s Britain* (London: Hutchinson, 1982); and Paul Gilroy, *"There Ain't No Black in the Union Jack": The Cultural Politics of Race and Nation* (Chicago: University of Chicago Press, 1987).

81. This imperial rethinking of the feminist project was initiated in response to the critical interventions of black and Third World feminists; see, for example, Valerie Amos and Pratibha Parmer, "Challenging Imperial Feminism," *Feminist Review* (Autumn 1984): 3–20; and Chandra Mohanty, "Under Western Eyes: Feminist Scholarship and Colonial Discourses," *Feminist Review* 30 (Autumn 1988): 61–88. See also Hall, *White, Male, and Middle Class;* Margaret Strobel, *European Women and the Second British Empire* (Bloomington: Indiana University Press, 1991); Vron Ware, *Beyond the Pale: White Women, Racism and History* (London: Verso, 1992); Clare Midgley, *Women Against Slavery: The British Campaigns, 1780–1870* (New York: Routledge, 1992); Nupur Chaudhuri and Margaret Strobel, eds., *Western Women and Imperialism: Complicity and Resistance* (Bloomington: Indiana University Press, 1992); and, most recently, Antoinette Burton, *British Feminists and India* (Chapel Hill: University of North Carolina Press, 1995).

82. Contrast Anna Davin's "Imperialism and Motherhood," *History Workshop* 5 (Spring 1978): 9–66, to the retreat from class analysis announced in Michelle Barratt's introduction to the revised edition of *Women's Oppression Today* (London: Verso, 1988); and, to a lesser extent, in Catherine Hall's biographical introduction to *White, Male, and Middle Class.*

83. As a Europeanist trying to engage these discussions, I am very conscious here that any simple reversal of the historiographic "gaze" from colonialism's impact on the Third World to its metropolitan or European reverberations could well be construed in such a way as to reinforce Eurocentric assumptions about where "history" happens

or which histories are important, assumptions that are themselves the ideological refraction of Western imperial hegemony. At the same time, I think it is important to contest that other Eurocentric assumption, the assumption that influence, like rivers, flows down the hills of power, moving historically ever outward from all-determining European centers to appropriating if not supine peripheries. This assumption is manifest in that scholarly asymmetry about which Dipesh Chakrabarty has complained, whereby Third World scholars have to incorporate in their narratives European historical and historiographical developments to be taken seriously in a Western academy that indulges European scholars' disinterested ignorance about the history of and historiography on Europe's colonies. See "Postcoloniality and the Artifice of History: Who Speaks for 'Indian' Pasts?" *Representations* 37 (Winter 1992): 1–26.

84. Ann Laura Stoler, "Rethinking Colonial Categories: European Communities and the Boundaries of Rule," *Comparative Studies in Society and History* 31 (1989): 134–161; Lorimer, *Colour, Class and the Victorians.*

85. Asa Briggs, "The Language of 'Class' in Early Nineteenth-Century England," reprinted in R.S. Neale, ed., *History and Class: Essential Readings in Theory and Interpretation* (New York: Basil Blackwell, 1983), 2–39. *The Oxford English Dictionary* lists as the first reference to "class" as a sociological category, Josiah Hanway's pamphlet of 1772, "Observations on the Causes of the Dissoluteness which reigns among the lower classes of people."

86. For a thoughtful account of the importance of this period in British imperial history, see C. A. Bayly, *Imperial Meridian: The British Empire and the World, 1780–1830* (New York: Longman, 1989).

7

Race, Gender, and Citizenship in the German Colonial Empire

Lora Wildenthal

One of a recent series of antiracism posters in Berlin has asked, "When you think, Who is German, is the thought at the back of your mind really, Who is Aryan?" It is an unkind but accurate analysis of widely held, powerful assumptions that pervade discussions of xenophobic and racist violence, political asylum, citizenship, and naturalization. Antiracists as well as proponents and passive supporters of racist violence often take it for granted that victims and potential victims, particularly people of color, are foreign. However, the image of a homogeneous white German people confronting a legally and culturally distinct foreign people was as inaccurate a hundred years ago as it is today. The law is one site where the lives of "Germans" and "others" have been intertwined.

In this essay, I analyze several cases of disputed citizenship drawn from the German colonies before the First World War. Cases of marriage between white German men and colonized women of color show how citizenship law—organized by gender hierarchy—worked in a political context of colonial empire that was organized by gender hierarchy and race. They show how German citizenship law was intended to preserve "Germanness" and yet divided those self-designated heroes of German cultural work, colonialists. During the last ten years before the First World War, political and economic processes in Germany's "settlement colonies" (Southwest Africa and, to a lesser extent, East Africa and Samoa) led to debate on political representation and development policy for colonists. The issue of mixed marriage (marriage between German men and female colonial subjects) arose within that debate. The themes of culture, sexuality, and control in the issue of "race mixing"

(*Rassenmischung*) made mixed marriage easy to use in polemics; once raised, however, it was a difficult issue to control or resolve.

Ultimately, the debate counterposed German men's rights to German "racial purity." Advocates of the latter position included men who wished to insert racial categories into law and colonialist women whose response to the issue was shaped by their own specific position in existing citizenship law and in the cultural understandings of marriage that stood behind it. I consider gender first in terms of German men's rights, then in terms of German women's legal and cultural subordination in marriage.

As a point of departure, I take a widely received example of recent scholarly interest in the legal issues and cultural meanings of citizenship: the historical sociologist Rogers Brubaker's book *Citizenship and Nationhood in France and Germany* (1992). Brubaker asks why France and Germany now have such divergent modes of assigning citizenship and argues that "the French understanding of nationhood has been state-centered and assimilationist, [while] the German understanding has been *Volk*-centered and differentialist" (Brubaker 1992: 1). His discussion focuses largely on the years 1880–1914 and the 1980s in both states. He concludes that Germany's 1913 citizenship law—still in effect today—has been shaped by an "ethnocultural" or "ethnonational" understanding of statehood, based on a "community of descent" both within and beyond the boundaries of Germany (Brubaker 1992: 1, 122, 114). Brubaker does not argue specifically that the German conception of citizenship has been racial; instead, he uses terms such as "Volk," "ethnocultural," or "ethnonational" to describe ideas in historical debates on citizenship.

Brubaker's work focuses our attention on the big differences between the cases of France and Germany. The divergent legal principles for attributing citizenship of *jus soli* and *jus sanguinus* play a central role in his account (Brubaker 1992: 81). French law draws on both principles. According to jus soli, those born on a state's soil, or territory, receive citizenship in that state. German law makes use only of the principle of jus sanguinus, or descent. According to jus sanguinus as it was applied in the German Empire (1871–1918), those born to married parents received the father's citizenship. If there was no recognized father, the child received the citizenship of the mother.

In what follows, I develop aspects of the history of German citizenship that Brubaker has neglected, using additional historical sources from the German colonies and paying attention to the workings of gender and family. The cases of disputed citizenship I discuss are marginal to the history of German citizenship in some respects. They took place, not in Germany, but in colonial German Southwest Africa, East Africa, and Samoa; and they arose within unusual families, in which German men had married African and Samoan women. However, it was precisely such unusual cases that tested the limits of citizenship law and forced Germans to clarify their terms. After introducing some modifications to Brubaker's approach, I present some historical material that illustrates the importance of gender and conclude with some new comparative possibilities.

The first step is to pick up a dropped term of Brubaker's comparison: although he gives extended attention to the French colonial empire and its impact on citizenship issues in France, he does not mention the German colonial empire. Between 1884 and the First World War, Germany controlled roughly what is now Namibia, Tanzania, Togo, and Cameroon, as well as parts of Samoa, New Guinea, and further Pacific Islands and Kiao-Chow, an area on China's Shantung Peninsula that included the city of Tsingtau.

The second step is to consider the workings of gender and family in citizenship cases. Citizenship was one of many areas in which German men and women belonged to distinct categories of rights bearers. German men had the right of passing on their citizenship to the women they married and to their children.[1] On marriage, the man's citizenship erased and replaced that of the woman—and this is the key point for cases of colonial mixed marriage. Women did not have such rights regarding children and spouse when they participated in the institution of marriage. A hierarchical relationship between men and women was built into citizenship law. Therefore, one cannot speak of a "person" in a gender-neutral sense when analyzing German citizenship law.

Citizenship law dealt with persons as members of a normatively defined family, with its gender and generational categories; any case of disputed citizenship was necessarily a family story.[2] This fact becomes more obvious if we investigate how the law worked *within* the family. Brubaker's analysis assumes families whose members shared a homogeneous national origin, not individual persons, as the objects of citizenship law. The cases I consider below concern families made up of members with differing initial citizenship statuses. In these cases, the 1913 citizenship law rendered the "community of descent" of which Brubaker speaks radically permeable in a gender-specific way: the wife's initial citizenship and her ancestry were beside the point.

The cases below concern German men married to African and Samoan women. A much smaller number of cases involved German women married to African men, but these had completely different legal implications. Technically, such women assumed their husbands' citizenship, even if that meant colonial subject status. I have found no case in which matters escalated to the point where that status was in fact definitively pronounced. In all cases, however, the women were roundly denounced for having forsaken German civilization. Individual women were expelled from the German colonies and forced to live in Germany or abroad (Wildenthal 1994: 311–314). Certainly, the legal situation was intimidating for such women, as they could easily be denied rights as a German altogether if they pressed their cases. Racial and sexual fears about white German women's relations with African men formed a backdrop to the colonial mixed marriage debate, even when cases involving German men were technically at issue.

Third, the place of race in German citizenship law needs to be indicated more clearly. While ideas of race were certainly present in the formulation of law and the law contributed to the racialization of contemporary thinking about Germanness, nowhere did German imperial (*Reich*) law offer racial definitions. (The Nazis were the first to insert race formally into law.) Neither the 1913 law nor its predecessor, the citizenship law of 1870, allowed for the explicit insertion of a category of race in its interpretation. It is important to appreciate this state of affairs, since it lay at the center of the mixed marriage debate and the more general citizenship debate that Brubaker discusses. The relevant categories of citizenship were: Reich citizen (*Reichsangehörige/r*), foreigner (*Ausländer/in*), and colonial subject (*Eingeborene/r*, lit. "native").[3] The colloquial designation "mixed-blood" (*Mischling*) was irrelevant to citizenship law; citizenships could not be "mixed" (Fleischmann 1910: 561).[4]

"Native" legally indicated that group of persons under the jurisdiction of colonial law (rather than German Reich law), not race per se. The term itself was never qualitatively defined; that task was explicitly put off to a future decree. As the Colonial Office stated, "The concept 'native' is not legally specified" (Colonial Office 5424: 24). Nevertheless, colonial governors formulated working definitions of "native" in their administrative decrees that did offer racial definitions (Hedrich 1941: 11–12 n 26). Indeed, two governors and a former governor just promoted to colonial secretary issued administrative decrees that banned mixed marriage on racial grounds in Southwest Africa, East Africa, and Samoa. The conflict between Reich law, which refused racial definitions, and local governors' administrative actions fueled the mixed marriage debate.

Jus sanguinus was not a racial principle in any simple way. That citizenship based on paternal descent was not the same as citizenship based on race was exactly what troubled those who took race seriously enough to consider the "racial" attributes of mothers. The issue of inserting race into law extended beyond the colonial empire, though the colonial mixed marriage bans suggest that it reached its most extreme point there. A concurrent debate developed in Germany over the Polish minority in the Prussian east, which reflected concern about defining who was a real, or "racial," German within the European borders of Germany (Brubaker 1992: 127–137). A political alliance of male radical nationalists in Germany interested in colonial expansion either overseas or in Eastern Europe, settlers in the colonies, and most organized colonialist women called for a specific definition of race in law.

As Brubaker discusses, the 1913 citizenship law emerged in response to years of agitation by German nationalists who feared that jus sanguinus was failing to protect the integrity of Germandom—variously termed a "race," "culture," or "nation"—around the world. The 1913 law did contain some changes over against the 1870 law that appeased some of the colonialists' and nationalists' demands, primarily that Germans residing abroad for ten years without registering with a consul would no longer lose their citizenship. It also introduced an ''imperial citizenship'' (*Reichsangehörigkeit*) unmediated by citizenship in one of Germany's federal states (Maßfeller 1953: 13–14). The 1913 law represented an interesting juncture of public debate but did not constitute a genuine turning point in the history of German citizenship (Maßfeller 1953: 14). Most important, it did not allow for the insertion of a legal category of race any more than its predecessor had. It did not change a thing as far as colonial mixed marriages were concerned. Therefore, radical nationalists and many colonialists took up their call for legal bans on mixed marriages again immediately after the 1913 law was passed.

German Male Settlers and Fathers' Rights

Mixed marriage was banned in three colonies: Southwest Africa (1905), East Africa (1906), and Samoa (1912) (Schulte-Althoff 1985). These were unique at that time among the European colonial empires. Colonial officials cited U.S. antimiscegenation laws as precedents. The bans, which were not laws that had received the approval of the Reichstag but rather administrative decrees issued by colonial governors and the colonial secretary, did insert race as a legal category into citizenship. The bans infringed on German men's legal right to pass on citizenship to their wives and children. For this and other reasons, many jurists considered the bans illegal.

The two governor's deputies in Southwest Africa who drafted the first ban openly intended to introduce race into citizenship law. They presented grounds for the 1905 ban as follows:

> The native woman, the mixed-blood children produced by both [her and her German husband] and their offspring [become] German citizens and are thereby subject to the laws valid for the Germans here. The male mixed-bloods will be liable for military service, capable of holding public offices, and will partake of the right to vote to be established sometime in the future, as well as other rights tied to citizenship. These consequences are of a high degree of seriousness. . . . Not only is the preservation of the purity of the German race and of German civilization here very substantially impaired because of them, but also the white man's position of power is altogether endangered. (Cited in Hintrager 1955: 76)

The Southwest African ban, like the East African ban the following year, must be seen in the context of contemporary rebellions that seriously challenged German rule. When the governor's deputies penned the above in October 1905, the colony had already seen almost two years of stubborn armed resistance that ultimately cost the combatant African peoples between 60 and 80 percent of their populations. Although German victory was a foregone conclusion, the great expense of conducting the 1904–1907 war and the fact that the German public could no longer overlook African resistance to the supposed benefits of German rule created a political crisis in Germany. In

1905–1906, East Africa also endured an immensely destructive war, the "Maji Maji Rebellion" (Drechsler 1980; Iliffe 1969). Threats to the "white man's position of power" in those colonies were very real when—or moments before—the bans were decreed. In fact, the 1905 and 1906 bans were part of an overall reformulation of German colonial rule in the immediate wake of the wars. Germans at the time referred to the postwar period as the era of "colonial reform" (1906–1910) and explained the wars as the result of settlers' brutal excesses and the lack of law and order in the colonies. The colonial warfare between 1904 and 1907 not only led to new measures for controlling the often-decimated African colonial subject populations but also to a reconsideration of what white German colonial society should look like. This, in turn, involved criticizing certain practices of early frontier settlers, including their sexual and family lives.

Historians have stressed the mixed marriage bans' importance for reiterating the division between colonizers and colonized basic to colonial rule, and as symptoms of larger efforts to align class with status as ruler or ruled (Bley 1971; Schulte-Althoff 1985). These interpretations of class and race division are undoubtedly accurate, but the mixed marriage bans were not controversial on those grounds. Even the colonial opposition in the Reichstag accepted those hierarchies. The bans became sources of lasting controversy in the colonies and in Germany because of their impact on German men. How could the legal and cultural prerogatives of German men be reconciled with the necessary attributes of male colonizers—now that those attributes had come to encompass the public display of sexual and racial purity?

Limiting the patriarchal rights of German men proved to be the most controversial aspect of the debate over mixed marriage. Nevertheless, advocates of strict "race separation" (*Rassentrennung*) in Southwest Africa forged ahead with additional measures. In 1907 the colony's highest court interpreted the ban as retroactively valid, so that marriages concluded before the 1905 ban were declared null. This highly controversial decision affected thirty marriages and was eventually moderated in 1912 to invalidate only those marriages concluded after the 1905 ban (Bley 1971: 212). In January 1909, a new self-administration charter provided for the voting rights of which the governor's deputies had spoken. One clause (par. 17f) stripped German men of their municipal voting rights if they were married to or living with a "native woman" (Bley 1971: 212).

The case of Carl Becker illustrates the outcomes for a German male settler. Becker's wife, whom he had married in 1897, was a Rehobother. The Rehobothers were one of several peoples living in Namibia at the time of German annexation. They were descended from an early nineteenth-century colony of intermarried Boers and Africans originally resident in what is now South Africa. Rehobothers' European ways (they spoke Cape Dutch, followed the Dutch Reformed faith, and lay emphasis on their European ancestry) as well as their land and cattle holdings made them good candidates for intermarriage in German male settlers' eyes. Most Southwest African mixed marriage cases that came before the Colonial Office concerned German-Rehobother couples.

Becker's letter of protest to Southwest Africa Governor Bruno von Schuckmann is a catalog of the male rights that were upheld by German citizenship and family law but violated by the mixed marriage bans.

1 September 1909

Your Excellency,

. . . By Paragraph 17f of the self-administration charter, I, as the husband of a Rehobother woman, am disenfranchised. Paragraph 17f stems from the idea that Southwest Africa is a white man's country. As a white man I make no comment, for the white man is in power at the moment and the final source of law is power. A study of Prussian history, however, shows that in her many annexations Prussia proceeded in each individual case with the greatest regard and respect for historical tradition. . . . I believe that this well-tried principle should be applied here too. My marriage came about with the collaboration of the moral and legal agencies of the state, before the publication of Paragraph 17f. I am utterly convinced that no retrospective legislation may deprive me of my rights.

The consequences of Paragraph 17f are absolutely shattering for me: I pay annually 5,000 marks to educate my five children, two of whom are in Germany. With the same number of children and a European wife I should receive an annual grant of 1,500 marks to meet the cost of their boarding fees at school. I receive nothing.

If I go anywhere with my wife, who is almost white (a picture of my family is enclosed) and in moral and intellectual respects is the equal of any white woman in the colony, I have to face unpleasantness.

All this happens to me despite the fact that I keep 30,000 acres of farmland in perfect order, that I personally carry all the costs associated with it and willingly shoulder the burden of taxes and expenses entailed in running a household of eight whites and forty natives. This is the thanks I get for contributing, as an old soldier, to the conquest and pacification of this country for Germany. Why does it happen to me? Because I haven't done as so many others (I could give their names) who have lived with native women and brought children into the world, only to abandon them and to live now partly in respect and honor, some of them in rags, but all enjoying their franchise. . . . Will my children, all of whom are receiving a German education, be my heirs? Will my boys become soldiers and later have the vote? There are questions which I must see positively answered, or I shall lose all joy in life and all my delight in work.

Nevertheless, there is no power in this world which will make me leave my wife, who has been a true companion for the past twelve years.

If my civic rights remain denied me, if my marriage is not recognized in law, it will finish my joy and pride in the country which I have served with all my strength these many years. [. . .] In anticipation of a favorable answer, I remain,

Yours faithfully,
Becker, Farmer (Cited in Bley 1971: 217–218; translation slightly altered here)

In his letter Becker drew eloquently on Prussian history, legal precedent, his own contributions to Southwest Africa's development, and his moral duties as family patriarch. Becker claimed not only that his wife was "almost" indistinguishable from a supposed real German but also that his whole way of life as a citizen, father, and property owner exemplified the German colonizing ideal. Altogether, the letter presented Becker's exclusion from respectable settler society as an actual disruption of colonial progress. His arguments were difficult to counter. Becker was in fact able to convince the colonial administration that his marriage was consonant with colonial reform and public morality, and he regained his civic and family rights. In 1912, Southwest African male settlers in Becker's situation were regranted their rights as long as they were able to pass a property qualification and show through language and other "cultural" aspects of their household that their "way of life" (*Lebensführung*) was respectable.

The Becker case showed that the Colonial Office would protect the rights of German men—*if,* like Becker, they were married, prosperous, and otherwise "respectable." Two other cases showed the limitations of that protection and the continuing frustration of German male settlers. One concerned Wilhelm Grevel, a planter in Samoa who wished to marry the Samoan woman with whom he had been living. The Colonial Office decided to crack down on mixed marriage in Samoa just as Grevel attempted to marry—but the outcome of the case shows how difficult the prevention of mixed marriage was even when the Colonial Office threw its authority behind bans. Another example from Southwest Africa, which concerned the Panzlaff family, demonstrates the Colonial Office's reluctance to move beyond formal recognition of German citizenship, to ensure that German citizens of color were treated as equal to "whites" in German colonial society.

Dr. Wilhelm Grevel of Samoa was a prosperous, articulate farmer and landowner who had been living with a Samoan woman, Savali, since 1907 and who had fathered some children with her. Although this was a case of simple cohabitation according to German law, actually Samoan custom and many European colonists recognized "Samoan-style" (*fa'a Samoa*) marriage not certified by the marriage registry. In 1910, Grevel applied for a marriage certificate. The local judge, Adolf Schlettwein, an opponent of "race mixing," rejected the application (Colonial Office 5432: 63–71, 77, 79).

Where Becker had depended on moral suasion to obtain an exception to an existing government measure, Grevel fought his case on legal grounds. At the time, there was no existing bar to mixed marriage, but Grevel sensed, accurately, that his planned marriage was the test case for a Samoan mixed marriage ban. He had the self-confidence and money to hire a lawyer and argue aggressively, even going so far as to sue Schlettwein (Colonial Office 5432: 64–65, 68–69, 77). Grevel cited legal treatises that stressed the absence of race-based restrictions on marriage in German law. Grevel's lawyer declared that there was no legal basis for forcing a German man to consign himself to Samoan-style marriage and thereby risk his children's legitimacy as heirs. Grevel had the right, "as a German citizen, to demand marriage according to German law" (Colonial Office 5432: 77). Grevel's lawyer even threatened that Grevel would take Savali to Germany, marry her there, and bill the government for all expenses (Colonial Office 5432: 77).

Along with his legal onslaught, Grevel defended himself with arguments that resembled Becker's. He insisted on his own cultured and reputable status, and on his wish to fulfill his obligations to his children and Savali. It was customary in Samoa, Grevel explained, for a German husband to live in Samoan-style marriage to ascertain whether the Samoan woman would adjust to Europeanized life; he had always intended to marry Savali (Colonial Office 5432: 65). As for the children, Grevel assured Governor Wilhelm Solf,

> My personage, my social position, and my financial circumstances offer a sure guarantee that my children will be raised as Europeans and Germans (in the case of my death, my family in Germany will take responsibility for that). (Colonial Office 5432: 65)

However, Solf (who became colonial secretary in December 1911) chose not to interfere with Judge Schlettwein's actions. In January 1912, Solf pronounced a ban on mixed marriage in Samoa that explicitly upheld Schlettwein's position. Moreover, he forbade Savali to leave German Samoa. Two months later, Grevel petitioned the Reichstag and succeeded in having the petition accepted for consideration in committee (*Stenographische Berichte* 11 March 1913: 8015). In August 1913, Savali gave birth to a son, and Grevel renewed his efforts to marry her (Colonial Office 5432: 192). Finally, Grevel and Savali were allowed to leave Samoa, and they married before an English judge in 1914 (Colonial Office 5432: 176–177, 192, 215). Marriages concluded abroad had to be and were recognized by German law, and so the bans could be successfully evaded (Colonial Office 5418: 275). After January 1912, new mixed marriages could not be concluded in Southwest Africa, East Africa, and Samoa. Nevertheless, in highly mobile colonial societies, couples simply evaded the bans by crossing the border from Southwest Africa to the Cape Colony, or by traveling from Samoa to Australia and marrying there.

The Southwest African settler Panzlaff's appeal was still under consideration at the Colonial Office in 1914 when the First World War broke out (Colonial Office 5418: 267–274). Panzlaff had been in Southwest Africa even longer than Becker, having settled in 1891 and married in 1894. He protested against the conditions in the colony that prevented his children from being white: they were exposed, for example, to daily insults and were excluded from first- and second-class train compartments, he wrote. Most of all, Panzlaff was concerned that his children's unclear citizenship status would not allow him to pass on to them the "fruits of his work of long years" (Colonial Office 5418: 271). His three children had attended school in Germany since the age of nine; at the time of the appeal the oldest son was eighteen.

As his complaints indicated, Panzlaff sought not only legal certification of his children's German citizenship status, which the Colonial Office supported, but also "social equalization" (*gesellschaftliche Gleichstellung*). At this point, the Colonial Office declared the necessity of discriminating against Panzlaff's children.

> They do not obtain a *social* equalization thereby [i.e., from legal citizenship] and they should not obtain it in the interest of the prestige and preservation of the white race. These public interests are stronger than the wishes of the small number of colored Germans in the colony. If the children do not want to be seen as second-class citizens or shunned by educated Germans, then they should refrain from emigrating [*sic*] in a new land in which race oppositions must be upheld, and should submerge themselves among the great mass of blood-crossings of all possible kinds in Germany. (Colonial Office 5418: 271)

Even as the Colonial Office acknowledged the Panzlaff children's claim to German citizenship—using the still rare phrase "colored Germans" (*farbige Deutsche*)—it denied their right to live freely and without discrimination where they were born, Southwest Africa. The Colonial Office freely defended the Panzlaff children's status as German citizens but angered Panzlaff *père* by refusing to defend the social attributes of that citizenship.

The rights of German men, then, were both the foundation of legal approaches to the "problem" of mixed marriage and the central source of persistent controversy. Men's rights and interests could not easily be disengaged from those of their families, as colonial officials discovered. As late as 1914, a German medical doctor in Samoa wrote to the liberal newspaper *Berliner Tageblatt* to warn against assaults on male colonial settlers of long and respectable standing.

> One could not do anything worse precisely to the old pioneers of Germandom than *to attack their family honor and drag their sons and daughters through the mud.* In some cases, their embitterment has gone so far that it *threatens to halt the progress of Germandom,* and that some German fathers have even sent their children to America and New Zealand to be educated, not only for convenience's sake but also in order not to expose them to insults in Germany. It can hardly be doubted that children thus educated soon return as fully American or English. (Colonial Office 5432: 202; emphasis in original)

The author cited above rejected the notion that race mixing necessarily damaged "Germandom" (*Deutschtum*). Rather, the assault on "old pioneer" men by way of an overly energetic pursuit of racial purity was damaging it. His argument suggests that commentators saw Germandom differently, depending on whether they interpreted it in racial or patriarchal terms.

Jurists in the Berlin Colonial Office decided in favor of upholding existing "respectable" mixed marriages and thereby upheld the rights of German husbands and fathers. Hardly anyone wished to argue publicly that mixed marriage presented no problem at all, but there was sufficient public controversy over restricting the rights of German men that, for example, Grevel obtained a friendly hearing in the Reichstag. In opposition to Solf's ban, the Reichstag passed a resolution that the legality of mixed marriages and the fate of mixed-descent children be clarified (*Anlagen* 1912: 325). The sympathy for German male settlers' plight was met by a vigorous faction in favor of "race separation," however. The bans turned out to be too volatile politically to be reversed. The legal status of the bans and of individuals in mixed families remained in limbo. In the years just before the First World War, the sons of early German male settlers were themselves reaching manhood.

Sons of German Pioneers and Men's Rights

In a legal and political context that focused on the rights of German men, the figure of the male "mixed-blood" who might hold those rights was highly politicized. Cases concerning male mixed-bloods were legally similar to mixed marriage cases, since determining citizenship was only possible by examining their family story. However, their cases were different in that while the "whiteness" of their fathers was recognized by all concerned, these young men were Germans of color. Their cases reveal how wide the gulf was between the recognition of formal citizenship such as the Colonial Office was willing to grant and the exercise of civic rights in the everyday life of German colonial society.

One well-publicized case concerned Ludwig Baumann of Southwest Africa. Baumann was a certified engineer who had been trained in Germany. While working in Southwest Africa, he was convicted of embezzlement, and in 1913 he appealed his conviction to the colony's highest court. At that point, he was suddenly "revealed" to be a "mixed-blood" by a member of the trial audience. Baumann stated that his maternal great-grandfather had married a Rehobother or part-Rehobother woman. Baumann's father, maternal grandfather Kleinschmidt, and maternal great-grandfather Schmehl had all been missionaries of the Rhenish Missionary Society, which had been active in Southwest Africa since the 1840s (Colonial Office 5424: 29, 51, 64). At the time of the trial, Baumann was thirty-two years old, which suggests that his parents were married no later than the year of his birth, 1881.

It is difficult to believe that the history of one of the oldest German families of Southwest Africa, as Baumann's family evidently was, could be "revealed" in this way. German male settlers' precolonial and early colonial marriages with

Rehobother women were a well-known part of the history of German South-west Africa. Nevertheless, the court proceeded to act on this "revelation" in an extreme and apparently self-consciously ahistorical way. The presiding judge declared,

> Each person whose family tree can be traced back to a native through the paternal or maternal line, and therefore every mixed-blood as well, must be considered and treated as a native. The degree of the blood relationship with the native is beside the point. (Colonial Office 5424: 51)

The judge rejected the relevance of the missionaries' valid marriages as legal evidence of Baumann's status as German citizen, citing instead Baumann's ancestry as proof that he was a "native." He then refused to try the case, stating that Baumann came under the jurisdiction of the Native Court (Colonial Office 5424: 51).

Such a "one-drop rule" was unheard of in German colonial law and administration, though familiar to experts in U.S. law. The Colonial Office was furious but legally unable to overturn the court's judgment. Now the conflicting legal interpretations concerning race and citizenship were out in the open. The Southwest African court stated, "Whether a person is a native or a member of the white race is a question of fact" (Colonial Office 5424: 51). The Colonial Office responded, "The question of who is a native or member of the white race is not merely a fact, but rather primarily a legal question" (Colonial Office 5424: 52).

In speech and appearance, even Baumann's opponents agreed that he seemed "white" (Colonial Office 5424: 29, 48). Nevertheless, fellow settlers reinterpreted Baumann's social attributes in the light of the revelations. Remarks about Baumann in the press show how settlers used racial, economic, and moral criteria as mutually reinforcing factors to create a false consistency. Rather than simply carry on his missionary family's tradition of education, Baumann had "raised himself up to the cultural level of whites" by becoming an engineer (Colonial Office 5424: 29). A Southwest African newspaper noted that he had held good positions but could not keep them and that he had amassed debts (Colonial Office 5424: 48, 29). The governor of Southwest Africa, Theodor Seitz, commented that he had considered hiring Baumann but had heard that Baumann was not dependable (Colonial Office 5424: 49). Seitz praised the Baumann decision as contributing to "an ever purer separation of whites and colored" and as helping to prevent "mixed-bloods" from being "considered socially equal to whites" (Colonial Office 5424: 48). The local newspaper pronounced the judgment "tragic," in the sense of a hero whose fatal flaw had finally emerged: an educated man, a man who, the newspaper admitted, probably belonged to the Association of German Engineers, was to be "thrust down to the Kaffirs and Hottentots!" (Colonial Office 5424: 29).

The lesson to be drawn was that every mixed marriage was "disastrous"; "if our colony is to remain German, we must adhere unconditionally to the principle of race purity" (Colonial Office 5424: 28). As for Baumann, he left Southwest Africa for Cape Town. He later requested, and received, a suspension of his sentence on the grounds that he had found a job in the Cape Colony and did not intend to return to Southwest Africa (Colonial Office 5424: 49). In Cape Town, as German "race purists" complained, racial boundaries were less strictly imposed.

The Baumann case, which took place almost eight years after the original 1905 mixed marriage ban, showed how stubborn the opponents in the mixed marriage debate remained. The court's decision dramatically extended the notion of retroactively determining "race" regardless of existing citizenship. In so doing, it contradicted a decision made just one year earlier to uphold marriages such as his parents' in order to avoid hardships for men like Becker— something a local colonial newspaper conceded (Colonial Office 5424: 29). Nevertheless, Baumann's combined attributes of individual wrongdoing, proven African ancestry, and failure to prosper as a model colonist eradicated the possibility of being accepted as "white" again in the eyes of colonial society.

A final example of a "mixed-blood" German man's petition also gained notice in Germany in 1913. Willy Krabbenhöft of Southwest Africa was at that time employed at a trading company in Cameroon, apparently having left Southwest Africa in anger over his treatment there as a "native." He wrote a furious letter to the Progressive People's Party (*Fortschrittliche Volkspartei*) in Germany to petition for the reinstatement of his German citizenship (Colonial Office 5418: 331–335). Like Ludwig Baumann, Krabbenhöft was descended from a settler family that established itself in the precolonial period. His German father, a trader, and British-Rehobother mother, Lucie Forbes, were married in 1881 before a Rhenish missionary. Lucie Forbes's mother belonged to the prominent Rehobother Cloete family (Colonial Office 5424: 70). Like Baumann, Krabbenhöft had the misfortune to lodge an appeal at the Southwest African highest court. The terms in which Krabbenhöft described his offense are revealing of his view of his own social position in the colony. Out on his land one day, he saw what he thought was a jackal and shot it. In fact, it was a dog that belonged to an African, who demanded compensation from Krabbenhöft "rudely" and "in a presumptuous manner" and finally summoned the police (Colonial Office 5418: 334). While Krabbenhöft freely admitted that he had done wrong, he resented the social humiliation of having to apologize to the African. It was decided that Krabbenhöft pay twenty marks compensation, which he found excessive and chose to appeal in January 1910. At that point, he was told that he did not fall under the German court's jurisdiction because he was a "mixed-blood" (Colonial Office 5424: 20, 24).

Much as Becker did, Krabbenhöft relied on the juxtaposition of his own hardworking, good-faith conduct and the unfair, even arbitrary actions of the government. In addition, he clearly partook of the German colonial ideology of racial superiority. Like Baumann, Krabbenhöft did not deny that he had some African heritage, but he was furious at what he saw as the favoring of a ''truly'' black African's interests over his own.

> It is unheard of that the court protects the interests of a pitch-black Kaffir and barred from defending himself a mixed-blood—if I absolutely am to be seen as one—of the fourth degree, who until then had counted as a German citizen and had risked goods and life itself (*Gut und Blut*) for the state. Such treatment is degrading and nothing less than a gross injustice. (Colonial Office 5418: 334)

Krabbenhöft clearly thought that the ''one-drop rule'' was not the right way to distinguish colonizers from the colonized—and he obviously saw himself as one of the former. His response to the court's application of the one-drop rule was a remark that constructed Jews as another race and then mocked German pretensions to purity: ''The German (*Deutscher*) injures himself in his pride as a Jew-German (*Judo-Germane*)'' (Colonial Office 5418: 334). He clearly thought that a new rule ought to be defined.

Krabbenhöft thus did not reject the views of white supremacists and the Southwest African government. He wished to prove, however, that the existing measures had created ''the opposite of any logical concept of law'' (Colonial Office 5418: 331). ''I want to say first of all that *today* I am *treated as a mixed-blood* by the Southwest African government, before I was not'' (Colonial Office 5418: 331). The very uncertainty created by the mixed marriage debate was an infringement of his and others' rights. The marriages of Germans such as his father had been repeatedly questioned, Krabbenhöft continued; children such as himself had been threatened with the status of illegitimate birth and the loss of inheritance rights, as well as with social treatment as mixed-bloods. For ten years, he pointed out, public discussion had sifted through the matter, and yet still those affected had to live in uncertainty. The 1909 self-administration charter (which had led to Becker's protest) was yet another instance of official arbitrariness: Krabbenhöft's own name was put on the voting list, while German men of undisputed whiteness married to wives of mixed descent were excluded—''An odd situation'' (Colonial Office 5418: 333). Then, in 1910, some of the disenfranchised men regained their suffrage while others did not—''also odd'' (Colonial Office 5418: 333). Like Becker, Krabbenhöft emphasized the white physical appearance of the families in question, as well as their ''white'' economic and social qualities.

> I am speaking of marriages in which the wife is already a mixed-blood of the *third* degree and whose child from a German husband is of the *fourth* degree. If the child is certainly in principle still a mixed-blood, there must still be a point at which it is to be counted among the whites. (Colonial Office 5418: 332)

As had Becker, Krabbenhöft stressed the demoralizing and even subversive effect of the state's new discrimination against such families.

> The families have been very strongly degraded. This measure of the government [i.e., retrospective invalidation of mixed marriages] weighed heavy on the minds of those affected and aroused a general uneasiness, because it was felt to be an injustice. Besides, trust in the German government is gone. Such is the general mood. (Colonial Office 5418: 332)

Krabbenhöft went on to describe his personal disillusionment, stressing above all his military service. Krabbenhöft was drafted into the colonial army in early 1903 and served for the next three years, which saw the heaviest fighting of the 1904–1907 war.

> As is evident, I have in many cases taken my hide to market for the state. For that, my citizenship was later revoked; I may not demand the protection of any German courts and am thereby robbed of all rights since I cannot even assert them by way of justice and law. That I have taken offense at the judgement to that effect is comprehensible to every fair-thinking person; frankly, I doubt the existence of justice, of law. I was good enough to fulfil my duties, but am no longer good enough to enjoy rights. (Colonial Office 5418: 333)

Krabbenhöft cited his military service as an especially strong claim to German citizenship; of course, noncitizens could not be drafted. If his German citizenship was not recognized, he threatened to sue for compensation for his army duty.

Colonial Secretary Solf confronted the governor of Southwest Africa, Theodor Seitz, and demanded that he confirm Krabbenhöft's German citizenship (Colonial Office 5424: 69–71). In September 1914, just after the First World War had broken out, a marriage took place without any fuss between Johannes Wilhelm (Willy) Krabbenhöft—described in a newspaper announcement of the wedding as a German citizen—and Margarete Götz, a twenty-year-old Bavarian woman who had come to Southwest Africa (*Keetmanshooper Zeitung*, 24 September 1914, 1). It is possible that Krabbenhöft soon afterward became the father of his own children. The end of German colonial rule, however, meant that the mixed marriage debate was relegated to legal scholarship.

The notion of a legal race certification parallel to citizenship law never died out before the First World War, but neither did it prevail. The creation of a new supreme court for all the colonies was planned, where it was to be decided once and for all whether mixed marriage was legal. The war in 1914 interrupted those plans. It is hard to know how (or if) that court would have decided the matter. The above examples demonstrate that the limitations on German men's rights proved a formidable obstacle to those who wished to secure bans on mixed marriage and race mixing.

German Women's Culture versus German Men's Rights

The centrality of men's rights is a necessary context for understanding the reaction of colonialist women to the debates. Colonialist women objected to jus sanguinus and refused to resolve the problem back into "necessary" rights of German men. Instead, they drew attention to the German woman's supposed importance for reproducing "truly" German children and culture. There was a strong precedent for this approach in Germany's various women's movements, whose members had long formulated claims for female citizenship on the basis of woman's supposedly essential bond with German culture. The phrase "cultural tasks of woman" (*Kulturaufgaben der Frau*) frequently appeared in such contexts, indicating those activities that German women were uniquely capable of undertaking for the good of the German nation and that men could not do for themselves (Wildenthal 1994: 3–4). In the colonial movement, too, men had not appreciated "that colonial work could not do without the hand and heart of women" (Frobenius 1918: 12). The "racially inferior" woman, colonialist women insisted, made a German marriage impossible. German women's entry into the colonial movement created a new, woman-centered ideology of racialized colonial reproduction. Nowhere did this ideology emerge more clearly than in the mixed marriage debate.

It should not be surprising that colonialist women approached the mixed marriage debate in ways distinct from men, given that German women and men were treated so differently under the citizenship laws of 1870 and 1913 and by the Civil Code generally. (Indeed, a well-publicized campaign had been going on in Germany since the 1880s to revise the Civil Code in favor of increased rights for married women.) Moreover, the colonies transformed the relations between German women and men in ways that were unsettling to colonialist women. The very disparity between numbers of German men and German women in the colonies gave German women their strongest argument for inclusion in the colonial project. But it also established the precedent of German male colonists managing wholly without German women. As I have noted, sexual and familial relationships with female colonial subjects held certain advantages for German male settlers. German men did not absolutely need German women for either menial or "cultural" tasks. German women faced the predicament of, in effect, having to ask German male colonists to accept them as sexual substitutes for colonized women. Altogether, "civilized" gender relations appeared fragile in the colonies.

Some German women clearly had a sense of collective sexual betrayal by German men. Paula Mueller, the leader of the German-Evangelical Women's Association (Deutsch-Evangelischer Frauenbund), asked of German men,

Have you, those of you who have had relations with colored women, asked yourself the question, how the German woman is stricken at her most vulnerable, how she is injured in her dignity, when a man enters into marriage with a white woman after living illegitimately with a colored woman? (Cited in Hasenkamp 1913: 65)

But more than simple sexual betrayal was at stake. Mixed marriages in the colonies seemed capable of affecting gender relations in Germany.

The reasons why German men chose colonized women as wives were far from reassuring for German women. For German men in the colonies, colonized women were cheap and were not able to place many demands on their husbands or sexual partners. Furthermore, the German men could beat them with impunity. Just prior to the 1905 mixed marriage ban in Southwest Africa, the highest court there decided a divorce case between a German man and his Rehobother wife. The man severely beat his wife, and she asked for a separation. The court, however, declared that the marriage had been invalid from the beginning, because "the law forbids natives to conclude such a marriage, in consideration of their cultural level and moral views, as well as the state-law and private-law effects" (Colonial Office 5424: 15; see also Hintrager 1955: 75). The woman was denied any kind of compensation through the annulment of her marriage. As the wife of a German man, she had had some rights; as a female colonial subject, she had far fewer. The fact that indigenous women were legally and physically vulnerable to the demands of German male colonizers appealed to many of those men as a simpler, more "naturally" hierarchical form of relations between the sexes. German men in the colonies could ignore "civilized" standards of the treatment of women.

All this flew in the face of German women's cultural ideal of marriage and its importance as the organic unit on which society was founded. In the words of Marianne Weber (1907: 571), author of a massive comparative study on marriage and critique of the Civil Code's marriage law, the cultured marriage (*Kulturehe*) was the "union of two intellectually and morally fully developed personalities." Such a union of moral equals created "the highest and least doubtful ethical values that life can offer us" (Weber 1907: 571). The mixed marriage, colonialist women insisted, was a perversion of all those things, because the husband and colonized wife could never be equals.

Many Europeans linked gender relations in their own societies to colonial projects through the widespread notion that civilizations could be ranked in terms of advancement by how women were treated in them. In the last decade before the First World War, debate over the treatment of women in Europe itself was intense. It seems that colonial mixed marriages highlighted to German colonialist women their own vulnerability in marriage and in other legal and social relationships with German men. In the eyes of colonialist women, mixed marriage was in no way a possibility of extending "civilized" principles or women's rights (such as they were) to colonized women. Instead, colonialist women saw mixed marriages as a dangerous example that threatened to throw

German marriages back into a state of "primitive" male brutality. Indeed, German men themselves used this supposed syndrome of "going native" as an excuse for their own documented brutality and rape of African women, as in the case of East African explorer Carl Peters's murders (Reuss 1981; Wildenthal 1994: 71–74). German colonialist women were repelled at this—but hardly ever, it seems, on behalf of the African and Samoan women involved. One colonialist woman author, Clara Brockmann, commented on the 1905 court case mentioned above to the effect that the justice of the wife's case was beside the point. She stressed the "good" that came of the case, namely, the 1905 mixed marriage ban.

> Because of an individual case—an old Herero [sic] woman demanded a separation from her white husband on grounds of severe maltreatment—this decision [the 1905 ban] was reached, a very controversial position. . . . But this incisive measure has also done some good; in the future the native woman will be more and more dislodged from unlawful situations. (Brockmann 1910: 4)

Brockmann blamed the wife and never suggested that the husband, or other German husbands in mixed marriage, were in "unlawful situations" instead.

The conflict between the German men's rights and racial principles was many-sided. The narrative I have sketched with cases of disputed citizenship suggests the overall primacy of the former, rather than the continuously successful assertion of ideas of descent as Brubaker has argued. On the basis of that conclusion, several larger narratives of the history of German citizenship may be considered for cross-national comparison.

Placing the Nazis' insertion of race into law at the center of the last hundred years of German citizenship debates would be a promising approach. Brubaker has relatively little to say about Nazi law (Brubaker 1992: 165–168), as he wishes to stress continuities across the Nazi period rather than the new aspects of Nazi law. Most important in Brubaker's reading, the 1913 citizenship law remained in place during the Third Reich and up to the present day. There are some alternative continuities, however. I have already questioned the extent to which the 1913 law represented a real change from its predecessor, the 1870 Prussian law stemming from before the unification of Germany in 1871. Taking a different approach, we can ask if Nazi law, which was a real turning point, has also had lasting effects on German jurists' understandings of race, family, and law after 1945.

A focus on the changing status of women in marriage with regard to citizenship has perhaps the greatest potential for leading us to such alternative continuities. How did the Weimar Republic and the Nazi period affect women's citizenship law? The principle by which a husband's and father's citizenship determined that of his wife and children was only removed in 1949, through article 3 of the West German Basic Law. Thereafter, children might inherit German citizenship through mothers or fathers; likewise, a wife's citizenship became independent of her husband's (Beitzke 1960: 42; Hoffmann and Stephan 1950: 64). That was a major turning point in the history of German citizenship law.

A remark by Franz Maßfeller, a German jurist who specialized in family and racial law in the Nazi period and continued to publish on legal topics in the Federal Republic of Germany, is suggestive of how the themes of race and gender in the history might have converged during and after the Third Reich. In 1953, Maßfeller wrote that two outstanding issues in citizenship needed to be resolved in the new Federal Republic. One was the relationship between federal citizenship and centralized Reichsangehörigkeit—a question formally created by the 1913 law and given additional weight by the Nazi legal preference for centralized citizenship. The other was "the realization of the principle of equal rights of the sexes in the area of citizenship law" (Maßfeller 1953: 16). It is doubtful that Maßfeller experienced a sudden conversion to feminism after 1945. However, his interest in the matter makes sense if we think of how the issue of women has worked historically in German citizenship debates. Developing article 3 of the Basic Law would render German citizenship law more racialized, because the attributes of the mother as well as the father would be taken into account. The father's Germanness would no longer subsume the mother's citizenship or ancestry. Not surprisingly, Nazi law inaugurated legal investigations of mothers' as well as fathers' "racial" backgrounds, though Nazi racial laws added to rather than replaced the 1913 law. Maßfeller's remark tells us nothing about the intentions and realization of article 3 of the Basic Law, or about his own probably minor role in developing citizenship law after 1949. However, it does reveal an unexpected constituency for changing women's status in citizenship and family law.

With attention to turning points in German citizenship law and to ideas of gender and race in debates, German racial measures in the colonies and after the First World War need to be compared with U.S. antimiscegenation laws and with mixed-marriage bans and related measures in the post-1918 European empires. Finally, a comparison of German and French (or other European) appropriations of each state's colonial past with attention to the issue of citizenship suggests itself. In the German case, the relative repression of that past has permitted the widespread belief there that "Germandom" has survived "untouched" by Africans, Asians, and Pacific Islanders, among others. That, in turn, is a key part of the image of the Aryan German.

Notes

1. These were the forms of automatic attribution of citizenship. I am leaving aside discussion of forms that existed for naturalization.

2. One such family story of citizenship (inter alia) may be found in Opitz, Oguntoye, and Schultz 1991:56–76.

3. The relevant laws on citizenship and its attribution through marriage and birth in effect between 1884, when German colonial rule began, and 1914 included *Gesetz vom 4, Mai 1870* ("concerning marriage and the registration of family status of federal citizens abroad"), *Gesetz vom 1, Juni 1870* ("on the acquisition and loss of federal and state citizenship"), *Gesetz vom 6, Februar 1875* ("on the registration of family status and marriage"), and the *Gesetz vom 22.7.1913* ("Law for Reich and State Citizenship") (Riebow et al. 1893: 53–66; Maßfeller 1953: 13–14).

4. In practice, the legal status of the vast majority of mixed-descent persons as "natives" was undisputed because they were born outside of marriage and their fathers did not choose to legitimate them. They therefore received their mothers' status as colonial subjects.

References

Unpublished Sources

Federal Archive, Potsdam Division, Potsdam, Germany
Records of the Colonial Office
RKA5418 Mischehen und Mischlinge in rechtlicher Beziehung. Allgemeines. 1912–1924.
RKA5421 Mischehen und Mischlinge in rechtlicher Beziehung. Deutsch-Ostafrika. 1906–1913.
RKA5424 Mischehen und Mischlinge in rechtlicher Beziehung. Deutsch-Südwestafrika. 1913–1919.
RKA5426 Mischehen und Mischlinge in rechtlicher Beziehung. Kamerun. 1902–1913.
RKA5432 Die Mischehen und die Rechtsverhältnisse der Mischlinge in Samoa. 1900–1920.

Published Sources

Beitzke, Günther. 1960. *Familienrecht*. 9th ed. Munich: C. H. Beck.
Bley, Helmut. 1971. *South-West Africa under German Rule, 1894–1914*. Trans. Hugh Ridley. Evanston: Northwestern University Press. Original German edition 1968.
Brockmann, Clara. 1910. *Die deutsche Frau in Südwestafrika: Ein Beitrag zur Frauenfrage in unseren Kolonien*. Berlin: E. S. Mittler.
Brubaker, Rogers. 1992. *Citizenship and Nationhood in France and Germany*. Cambridge, Mass.: Harvard University Press, 1992.
Drechsler, Horst. 1980. *Let Us Die Fighting: The Struggle of the Herero and Nama against German Imperialism (1884–1915)*. London: Zed Press.
Fleischmann, Max. 1910. "Die Mischehen in den deutschen Schutzgebieten vom Rechtsstandpunkte." In *Verhandlungen des Deutschen Kolonialkongresses 1910*, 548–567. Berlin: Dietrich Reimer.
Frobenius, Else. 1918. *10 Jahre Frauenbund der Deutschen Kolonialgesellschaft*. Berlin: "Kolonie und Heimat."

Hasenkamp, Hans. 1913. "Unsere Stellung zum Verbot der Rassenmischehe." *Evangelisches Gemeindeblatt für Deutsch-Südwestafrika* 3 (July):61–65.

Hedrich, Kurt. 1941. *Der Rassegedanke im deutschen Kolonialrecht: Die rechtliche Regelung der ehelichen und außerehelichen Beziehungen zwischen Weißen und Farbigen.* Schramberg: Gatzer & Hahn.

Hintrager, Oskar. 1955. *Südwestafrika in der deutschen Zeit.* Munich: R. Oldenbourg.

Hoffmann, Edgar, and Walter Stephan. 1950. *Ehegesetz nebst Durchführungsverordnungen: Kommentar.* Munich: C. H. Beck.

Iliffe, John. 1969. *Tanganyika under German Rule, 1905–1912.* Cambridge: Cambridge University Press.

Maßfeller, Franz. 1953. *Deutsches Staatsangehörigkeitsrecht von 1870 bis zur Gegenwart.* Frankfurt am Main: Verlag für Standesamtswesen.

Opitz, May, Katharina Oguntoye, and Dagmar Schultz, eds. 1991. *Showing Our Colors: Afro-German Women Speak Out.* Trans. Anne V. Adams, introd. Audre Lorde. Amherst: University of Massachusetts Press.

Reuss, Martin. 1981. "The Disgrace and Fall of Carl Peters: Morality, Politics and *Staatsräson* in the Time of Wilhelm II." *Central European History* 14, no. 2 (June):110–141.

Riebow, Otto, et al., eds. 1893–1910. *Die deutsche Kolonialgesetzgebung: Sammlung der auf die deutschen Schutzgebiete bezüglichen Gesetze, Verordnungen, Erlasse und internationalen Vereinbarungen mit Anmerkungen und Sachregister.* 13 vols. Berlin: E. S. Mittler.

Schulte-Althoff, Franz-Josef. 1985. "Rassenmischung im kolonialen System: Zur deutschen Kolonialpolitik im letzten Jahrzehnt vor dem Ersten Weltkrieg." *Historisches Jahrbuch* 105:52–94.

Anlagen. 1912. Vol. 2: *Stenographische Berichte über die Verhandlungen des Deutschen Reichstages.*

Stenographische Berichte über die Verhandlungen des Deutschen Reichstages. 1912–1913. Berlin: Reichsdruckerei.

Straehler. 1920. "Schutzgebietsangehörigkeit." In *Deutsches Kolonial-Lexikon,* ed. Heinrich Schnee, 312–313. Leipzig: Quelle & Meyer.

Weber, Marianne. 1907. *Ehefrau und Mutter in der Rechtsentwicklung. Eine Einführung.* Tübingen: J. C. B. Mohr (Paul Siebeck).

Wildenthal, Lora. 1994. "Colonizers and Citizens: Bourgeois Women and the Woman Question in the German Colonial Movement, 1886–1914." Ph.D. dissertation, University of Michigan.

Part Three

Colonial Projects

8

"Le bébé en brousse"

European Women, African Birth Spacing, and Colonial Intervention in Breast Feeding in the Belgian Congo

Nancy Rose Hunt

Today we do not make any decisions about spacing the births of our children. . . . Our ancestors had stronger children because they were not born too close together. Today parents no longer worry about their children getting sick. They think that they can always buy medicine and then the child will get well. This is why couples no longer separate their beds after the birth of a child, as they used to in the time of our ancestors.[1]

A group of Western family planning experts elicited this remark from one Zairian while investigating "traditional" methods of birth control in Kasai and Shaba in 1976 and 1977. The survey team was interested in the "cultural precedent" of Zairian mothers abstaining from sexual intercourse while nursing. This way of "regulating fertility and spacing children" seemed to indicate that "long before the influx of Western ideas, the understanding of the importance of child spacing to maternal and infant health was widespread in these cultures." The researchers were alarmed by Zaire's population growth rate, and feared the country's 27 million people would double in size within the next twenty-five years. They recommended that family planning projects "capitalize" on "this ancestral precedent" by using it as a "banner" in encouraging the use of biomedical contraceptives. Their assumption was that African birth spacing customs had disappeared because of "the breakdown of their traditions in the face of modernization."[2] Some fifty years earlier, other groups of Western experts—colonial doctors, missionaries, mine owners, and officials— also viewed these African reproductive practices as a kind of birth control. They were not interested in making it a "banner" of any of their projects, however.

Birth spacing in Africa, and in the Third World in general, is of growing interest to demographers, health professionals, development policy planners, and anthropologists. There is an extensive interdisciplinary literature on the relationships among postpartum abstinence, birth intervals, and breast feeding; their effects on fertility and maternal and infant health; the socioeconomic factors responsible for their decline; and the cultural resiliency of birth spacing customs due to beliefs about sperm, breast milk, sexuality, and infant survival.[3] This literature implicitly poses the historical question of how changes in breast feeding and postpartum abstinence contributed to the decline in birth spacing intervals and to population growth and the deterioration of maternal and infant health in twentieth-century Africa.[4] This paper will broach qualitative dimensions of this question by examining colonial efforts to alter infant feeding and to distribute milk to mothers and infants in the Belgian Congo. It will show how these colonial initiatives were linked to a discourse which viewed African birth spacing customs as insidious and saw a solution in European women. The frankness of this discourse highlights the inadequacy of assuming that changes in birth spacing and infant feeding customs can be ascribed to an amorphous, ineluctable erosion of "traditional" African life in the face of "Westernization."[5]

The Belgian Congo as a colonial regime intervened more substantially and on a wider scale in maternal and infant health than any other colonial power in sub-Saharan Africa. White colonial women were the first to organize maternal and infant health programs, called *gouttes de lait* (drops of milk), in the Congo. Mme van den Perre, president of a comparable network in Belgium, the Gouttes de Lait de Saint-Gilles, was concerned by reports of high infant mortality in the colony.[6] She founded the Ligue pour la Protection de l'Enfance Noire in Brussels under the high patronage of the Belgian queen in 1912.[7] The Ligue's first goutte de lait was opened in Kisantu in the same year. The Ligue's purpose was to reduce infant mortality in the colony by teaching African women the "art" of child rearing, cleanliness, and hygiene, and to struggle against harmful "errors and prejudices": the supplementary feeding of infants from birth and the "superstition" forbidding postpartum sexual relations.[8]

The Commission pour la Protection des Indigènes voted unanimously during its 1912–1913 session to support Mme van den Perre's organization of "generous women."[9] The Ligue's work was met, however, with skepticism and disdain by some doctors, missionaries, and colonial officials until the early 1920s.[10] The medical corps was particularly hostile, and the name goutte de lait, also used for infant welfare centers in Belgium, was disliked. Some feared that white women were "preaching to their African sisters the abandonment of maternal milk for artificial milk."[11] Mme van den Perre defended her organization in 1920: "Never, contrary to what has been said to hurt us, have we urged any black woman nor white woman to feed her infant with a baby bottle when she could feed it at the breast."[12]

The Ligue was little appreciated until the emergence of colonial concern about the impact of population loss, infertility, and low birthrates on growing industrial labor requirements in the early 1920s. Doctors and missionaries began applauding the Ligue's work, and the Départment des Colonies agreed to subsidize it.[13] There was growing awareness that a drastic decline in the population and a considerable growth in infertility had occurred since the colonial conquest.[14] High infant mortality rates and the labor shortage of the early 1920s enhanced the sense of crisis. Depopulation and a low birthrate became dominant themes in a burgeoning, colonial demographic literature. The scare culminated in 1924 with a report on the "social question" to the Congrès Colonial National. It found that the Congolese population was threatened by excessive mortality and minimal natality among those leaving their villages for wage work, an alarming rate of sleeping sickness, and extremely common infant mortality. Moreover, it complained of prostitution and immorality in urban and industrial centers, polygamy, and wrongheaded African infant rearing practices.[15] A sufficient population was an absolute necessity for the colony's "harmonious development."[16] One of the chief recommendations of this and subsequent Congrès Colonial National reports of the 1920s and early 1930s was to develop puericulture,[17] or infant welfare, programs. The 1924 report argued that the Ligue's work was a model that should be "extended and generalized" because "for the repopulation of the Congo . . . [it] could be a precious aid."[18] Some were claiming that the consultation efforts of weekly health check-ups, weighing infants, and teaching mothers their "educating duties," under the direction of European women, had done more than anything to reduce infant mortality.[19]

The new interest in the Ligue's work gave Mme van den Perre a new tack by which to promote her organization. In 1926, she twice addressed colonial audiences with a patriotic plea:

Without black labor, our colony would never be able to send to Europe the wealth buried in its soil.[20]

Help us by all means in our ability to protect, to care for the child while educating indigenous mothers, it is a duty. We need black labor. . . . To protect the child in the Congo is a duty, not only of altruism, but of patriotism.[21]

The call for puericulture, gouttes de lait, and infant consultations was not a new outcry: it was a transposed one. Before depopulation and infant mortality were colonial problems, they were national problems. Comparable concerns about fertility decline, infant welfare, and providing sterile breast milk substitutes had swept France, England, and Belgium earlier in the century as each country took its turn fretting about depopulation and infant mortality. As Anna Davin has shown, the infant welfare movement in England was inspired by worries about fertility decline and "imperialism and motherhood." In the wake of the Boer War and summer epidemics of infant diarrhea, eugenicist fears about "race degeneration" were linked to a "matter of Imperial importance," the menace of depopulation at home and in the Dominion. There was a "surge of concern about the bearing and rearing of children—the next generation of soldiers and workers, the Imperial race." Motherhood was redefined in this period, as child rearing became "a national duty not just a moral one." The problem of infant mortality was blamed on the ignorance and negligence of mothers, especially those of the working class, and mothercraft (instruction on how to be a proper mother), infant milk depots, and well-baby clinics were the declared panacea.[22] In Belgium, the fall in the birthrate prompted concerns for the "plague of Onanism," that is, the widespread use of coitus interruptus as a form of fertility regulation. The Belgian church took the lead in the Catholic drive against birth control in Western Europe in 1909.[23] France, however, was the forerunner: the sense of panic over fertility decline emerged there about a half-century sooner, and its gouttes de lait and infant consultations were the models of subsequent infant welfare efforts in England and Belgium.

Gouttes de lait or infant consultations opened up in Belgium, particularly in industrial areas among working-class populations, in the early twentieth century. The Ligue Nationale pour la Protection de l'Enfance du Premier Age was founded in 1903.[24] Infant mortality in Belgium was associated with the decline or, in some cases, absence of breast feeding, especially among mothers working in the industrial or agricultural sectors.[25] Although most gouttes de lait seem to have favored breast feeding, their provision of sterile breast milk substitutes also permitted mothers *not* to nurse under medical supervision.

In Belgium—and elsewhere—the infant welfare movement had distinct class dimensions. It was frequently a private, philanthropic activity. A paternalistic tone, concerned to reduce maternal and working-class ignorance, was common.[26] This tone resurfaced in the colonial context with distinct racial dimensions. We turn now to the colonial scene, the novelties it contained for Europeans, and the ways puericulture and gouttes de lait were recast within colonial settings.

Colonial Logic and African Birth Spacing

That African women would abstain from sexual intercourse for up to two or three years after giving birth had always puzzled the colonial imagination. Europeans pictured that Africans' wish to avoid this "ordeal" led to infanticide and abortion.[27] At the 1912–1913 meeting of the Commission pour la Protection des Indigènes, colonial officials and missionaries were concerned that abortion was a widespread practice. They argued that African women feared pregnancy.

> When realizing that in indigenous society the woman nurses her child for two years or more, and that during all this time . . . she no longer counts for her husband, one understands better those among them who do not maintain the sentiment of maternal duty, preferring not to have children than to undergo this ordeal.[28]

Focusing on abortion provided one resolution to the contradiction which postpartum abstinence represented to Europeans, accustomed to assuming that sexuality in the tropics, especially among Africans, was uncontrollable.[29]

In the 1920s and early 1930s colonial discourse about depopulation, infertility, and a shrinking birthrate usually divided the causes into those that could be attributed to European occupation (introduction and spread of disease, or psychological trauma, for example) and those considered indigenous in origin, predating conquest. African marital, sexual, and infant feeding practices were key among these indigenous causes.[30] The health-related reasons that local Africans extended to explain these practices—that having sexual relations during this period would lead to the newborn dying, the mother's milk drying up, the child being puny,[31] and "numerous calamities for her, for the child and for the father"—were deemed superstitious.[32] Polygamy was blamed, although there was uncertainty about whether it should be considered the consequence or the cause of the problem.[33] Polygamy could not in and of itself be identified as a cause of lower fertility. If postpartum abstinence was strictly adhered to it was possible that a polygamous marriage would be more prolific than a monogamous marriage. Nevertheless, postpartum abstinence was thought to encourage polygamy: "It results . . . that the African appreciates polygamy a lot which permits him to continue his habits without interruptions. This belief is certainly harmful in the domain of repopulation and in the moral order because it detracts from monogamy."[34] Some thought that African women would ask their husbands to take extra wives because of the custom.[35]

Changing the family structure by encouraging monogamy and educating couples in their duties as spouses was the envisaged corrective. Missionaries were well known to combat the custom by advising "couples to resume conjugal commerce a certain while after birth."[36] There were mixed reports about how effective these efforts were. It was known that around missions like Kisantu and Baudouinville, families with numerous children were prospering in the early 1920s: "mothers with three to seven children are not rare."[37] This was attributed not to monogamy alone but also to "a higher conception of marriage and the social duties which are incumbent on spouses."[38] This "higher conception" was not easily inculcated, however, usually requiring Christian education for both spouses, and was most likely among "girls raised among the nuns."

> In the sufficiently Christianized milieu, marriage, even monogamous, undergoes too many injurious influences of the setting: the pagan parents retake the woman from the husband, the powerful chiefs intervene for the profit of their friends. . . .
> In many Christian households, the woman, even if baptized, conserves very tenacious pagan prejudices; after each birth she will refuse during three years all relations with the husband; she fears imaginary perils, and especially the jeers of all the old pagan women of the tribe. Only the girls, who have *during several years,* been raised among the nuns, or at least in an already well Christianized village, dare to put themselves above these prejudices and mockeries and give many children to their husband.[39]

Another factor that appeared to be promoting prolonged lactation and sexual abstinence was lack of food, particularly milk. Colonial commentators viewed the weaning of infants as irrational.

> It is conceived in reality not as the gradual substitution of a more varied and better equilibrated nourishment to the diet of maternal milk, but as the gradual addition of customary foods to a lactation which is continued very late and constitutes the basis of the infant's diet for two years, indeed three years.[40]

Stories of some mothers giving their infants thick, not easily digestible foods at the age of one month by holding the child horizontally and pushing it into the child's throat, despite cries and breathing difficulties, were among those considered alarming.[41] As expressed in *La Question sociale* report, "they nurse them too long. . . . [T]his practice was perhaps indispensable because the blacks have not, like us, powdered milk (*farines lactées*) and other numerous milk substitutes."[42]

Europeans sought the underlying function of what seemed to be superstitious beliefs about the need for abstinence. They identified it as compensation for a lack of adequate food alternatives to breast milk and the generally poor nutritional level of mothers. Besides, they reasoned, changing sexual abstinence habits alone would not necessarily achieve the desired increase in fertility because of lactation's potential for suppressing ovulation.

> The abandonment of this practice of abstention during the nursing period would probably not by consequence augment the number of children as much as one would believe. In effect, normally, the woman should not be fertile during the period of full nursing. A new pregnancy should occur only at the decline of this period and while the milk of the mother is no longer indispensable to the child.[43]

The colonial remedy was to make other food available to children, by distributing milk and milk products so mothers' milk *would* be dispensable.

> The lack of milk [substitutes] causes infantile mortality; it slows even the fertility of families, because it delays weaning, before which spouses do not resume conjugal relations. It is necessary to have animal milk to supplement the deficiency of maternal milk.[44]

The raising of dairy livestock was encouraged.[45] The distribution of free milk would be accompanied by "nurseries of propaganda" or puericulture clinics.

> To inculcate the notion of utilizing milk, one can act by example. In face of the present difficulty of procuring this food, the government could put . . . cartons of milk at the disposition of hospitals and charities for children. Orphans should be raised through the intervention of private, subsidized agencies, missions,

infant charities, etc. which would organize a hygienic alimentation. There is room
to establish true nurseries of propaganda aided by the State.[46]

African marital, sexual, and infant feeding practices were regarded as related
phenomena. Each was associated in the colonial mind with the "irrational"
practice of women abstaining during what were perceived to be exceedingly
long periods of breast feeding. Altering these indigenous causes of low fertility
could put an end to what was seen as a form of birth control. The notion that
shortening birth intervals would increase fertility, with no unfortunate health
consequences, was explicitly expressed:

> The present situation is certainly irrational. Sometimes women breast feed during
> three years. In the course of the approximate thirty years during which women
> are susceptible of becoming mothers, to place periods of three to four years during
> which they can have only a single child, while nature would certainly permit them
> to support more frequent pregnancies without harm.[47]

Colonial perceptions of customary birth spacing practices prompted calls for
a "crusade to combat the prejudices that separate the spouses."[48] European
women were expected to play a prominent role in this crusade.

Colonial Anxieties about White Women in the Tropics

Colonial assumptions about sexuality and fertility in the tropics were implicit in the desire to alter African reproductive practices. They were also
behind doubts about whether white women belonged in the colony. The historical ambivalence that surrounded the activities of Mme van den Perre's
league may also have reflected shifting opinions about whether the presence
of European women in the colony was desirable. As one colonial woman
explained, it was not until after World War I that Belgian women "matured
by the war . . . [and] less fearful, left more voluntarily for the colony."[49] The
change in attitude about European women involved a growing conviction that
their presence was essential to protect white male morality. A second factor was
a newly perceived need for and acceptance of European women as practitioners
within puericulture programs, a charitable activity that would also keep them
entertained. Opinions about white women's capacity to give birth safely,
provide child care, and find breast milk substitutes in the colony had also been
revised.

For years it was thought that white women would be rendered sterile by the
tropical climate. Whether due to a climatic suppression of menstruation[50] or
an anticonceptual effect of quinine, fertility in the tropics was considered rare.

> The primordial marital duty is to apply oneself to creating a sound and large
> family, to continue a vigorous race, to not expose oneself to the temptation of

a voluntary and degrading sterility, and this duty well understood must keep the wife in her natal country.[51]

Fears for the health of *l'éternelle blessée* multiplied when one tried to imagine a white woman giving birth in the colony. Without her mother or other relatives, and a doctor often at a considerable distance, no one would be there to help her except a "black chambermaid, very often incompetent, negligent and unclean. . . . And what a long convalescence awaits her under this debilitating climate." The health of the infant was also a worry: "the difficulty of procuring it a good nursemaid (*nourrice*) and even good goat's milk." No one seemed sure that a child raised in the colony would not be "degenerate."[52]

Yet the assumed association between degeneration and the tropics was altered by the 1920s demanding rather than forbidding the presence of white women. The panic in the 1920s over fertility levels, depopulation, and labor requirements was articulated around issues of morality. Concubinage was widespread in the Congo, and in the early 1920s still openly practiced under the euphemism of "ménagère" (housekeeper).[53] European male promiscuity was considered a factor in the spread of venereal disease, and infertility was frequently perceived as most severe in those industrial areas such as the Copperbelt, where the concentration of single men—both European and African—was most dense. In the early 1920s, there were outcries to increase the number of European households on the Copperbelt, keep whites out of certain bars, prohibit pornographic posters suggesting the idea of interracial sexual relations, and recruit whites more carefully.[54] The underlying logic was that it was "antinatural to force a single man to live in a hot climate which is inclined more than here [in Belgium] towards sexuality (*porte plus qu'ici à la sexualité*)."[55] "Excess" rather than health became the more pressing problem.

> Formerly, women did not set out for Africa. . . . Why? The climate is improper for the woman, it was said. Today [in 1944], there are almost as many white women as men. The climate, has it changed? But no, it hasn't. But the first women who arrived in Africa created a familial atmosphere and a pattern of living that showed that it was not climate but rather excess that killed.[56]

The need to preserve Belgian honor and the thirst for colonial prestige made concubinage increasingly unacceptable.[57] The moral influence of the European woman was needed to preserve the honor of the white man. Her presence in the home would comfort her husband, and he would no longer need to go to clubs. She would "free him especially of this evil which consumes a good number of colonials and which has the name: the 'Ménagère.'"[58]

The solution was to stabilize the European family. This was especially evident on the Copperbelt, where European workers were increasingly accompanied by their wives during the 1920s and 1930s.[59] We need to know more about how this rhetoric about European women was translated into practice and the class dimensions involved in whose presence was desired, who actually came, the total numbers over time, and what women did.[60] The moral benefits that the emigration of wives of those of the "superior classes" would bring to the colony had been recognized as early as 1910. Greater reserve was felt necessary for wives of subordinate agents and functionaries, especially considering that "it might happen that one or another of these women would not exactly be an ameliorating element."[61] Whether white women should go to the colony remained an issue of debate during the 1920s,[62] but by the mid-1940s was assumed and embodied in principles disseminated at colonial training courses. Whatever the risks, the tenet by 1944 was that it was necessary to depart as a family.

> Discipline in sexuality: Here is posed a large problem which is tied to that of the colonial family. The first principle is the following: colonization costs in money, in human lives; we do not colonize with men, but with men and women. The colonizing country must not take into consideration possible losses in masculine and feminine personnel. . . . The conditions of modern life are such that these sacrifices are more and more reduced, and families start to be able to live under the tropics. . . . By consequence, the first law must be: it is necessary to leave as a family, whatever the risks.[63]

European women were to have a double and connecting role, intended to instill a sense of propriety in white males and save the honor of the colonial power while also serving as a model for and teacher of African women.[64] Belgian women began to be encouraged to make sacrifices for Congolese women in the mid-1920s.

> Men and women of good will, devoting their existence to the good of tomorrow, we have never had enough of them in the Congo: women particularly could play an eminently useful role there. Many charities to be found are charities to be realized by women and for women.[65]

The heroic image of the arduous, monotonous lives of white women in the colony evoked numerous burdens as well as endless devotion.

> Accompanying their husbands in the course of long, fatiguing and monotonous journeys, in good as in bad weather, under an implacable sun or under torrential rains, deprived of comfort, living under the tent or in road-posts, often burdened themselves with giving attention to their children, they devote themselves benevolently and modestly to a highly humanitarian purpose of which they can be proud.[66]

Charitable activity directed at Congolese mothers and children was considered an appropriate, honorable activity for white women. It would also prevent boredom and idleness.

> One would hope then that all white women who stay in the Colony have the devotion to bring their aid to this beautiful charity. Unfortunately, this is not always the case, and the idleness makes many white women find the time in the Congo very long. They are disinterested in this question and thus lose the occasion to save a large number of black children from dying.[67]

Crucial to the residence of European women in the colony was their being able to feed their own children there. In 1924, in response to the growth in the number of white children in the mining area of Katanga, the local medical journal printed an article for doctors about proper infant feeding. Breast and bottle feeding schedules and advice on milk substitutes in the absence of cow's milk were included. The same advice, derived from "authorized specialists," was being distributed to white mothers at the hospital's infant consultation program and supplied at the day nursery.[68]

A series of articles in the bulletin of the Union des Femmes Coloniales published in the late 1930s, entitled "Le bébé en brousse" (Babies in the Bush), assured white women that they would be able to find milk and coolers in even the most remote areas, advised how to prepare and clean baby bottles, find a scale from a state post or trader, and suggested feeding schedules and types of artificial milk. "Even in commerce in the bush" one could find Nestlé and Renaux powdered milks, Delacré food and Phosphatine Fallières.[69] The development of a cattle raising industry in Katanga was linked to this need for a source of fresh milk for infants. White women were told to avoid feeding infants at night because this was a frequent cause of digestive problems. If the infant had insomnia or was crying, it was important to "search for other causes. . . . [R]egularity is the most important point for the health of young children."[70] The infant was to be fed at three-hour intervals and was allowed to sleep at the breast. Mixed feeding was preferred to total artificial feeding in the event that breast milk was lacking.[71] Under no pretext were " 'boys' to be allowed to prepare baby bottles or baby's meals."[72]

The availability of milk and infant health programs was not only important for African women: they *enabled* the colonial presence of European women. Colonial doctors were aware that while African mothers were the principal focus of such programs, European women would also benefit.[73] Segregated services somewhat analogous to those operating for African women were available for some European women, and some facilities provided for both populations. Regardless, programs for white women were never direct copies of those for Congolese mothers, as they were permeated with a racism intent on protecting European children from African hands. In Stanleyville, the

Crèche Prince Léopold, founded by Mme Urbain, served the needs of European mothers for fresh milk while operating a nursery for African children. A stock of dairy goats was assembled to nourish the larger African children, and African women were encouraged to become wet nurses for other women's children. Europeans joined the program in order to buy *lait en bôite*.[74]

Among European children living in the colony, infant mortality fell from 17.8 percent in 1929 to 2.81 percent in 1946. This was attributed to the careful selection of parents before departure from Belgium, prenatal care, good hygiene and nourishment, the absence of heavy labor for women, and medical assistance at birth.[75] Even working-class children received special protection. There is evidence that European wives of working-class men did not come to the colony in as great numbers as wives of other Europeans. When they did come, they, like African women, might become the objects of charitable programs run by the local *comité* of the Union des Femmes Coloniales, similar to what they might have experienced in an industrial center in Belgium. In 1923, a day nursery for white children under four years of age opened in Elisabethville, the administrative capital of Katanga and the largest city on the Congolese Copperbelt. Within a year over a dozen babies were regularly watched and fed in this institution. It was established by the provincial medical service to meet the needs of white mothers "who the high price of life forces to do salaried work" in order to remove their "anxiety of entrusting their children to the care of a boy."[76]

Colonial Puericulture for Africans on the Copperbelt

Colonial attitudes about African birth spacing customs and the activity of European women concerned sexual and family formation practices of Africans and Europeans—when, where, how often, and with whom people should reproduce. Anxieties about the immorality of single men, depopulation, and infant mortality emerged in the early 1920s on the Copperbelt. Attention turned to stabilizing not only European but also African families. These phenomena were roughly parallel not only chronologically but ideologically as well. The discourse calling for the moral, stabilizing influence of European wives marked similar pleas for the increased presence of African wives. African children, like European children, received special care and facilities.

The need for African labor was acutely felt at the same time that about 50 percent of young infants in the camps of the colony's largest copper mining company, Union Minière du Haut-Katanga, were dying. The two major solutions proposed at this time were African labor stabilization and the development of maternal and infant health programs. By 1924, Union Minière was operating a goutte de lait service to encourage births and reduce infant mortality. Weekly visits, gifts in kind, special birth gifts, and complete rations for mothers during the first six months of pregnancy and the first year of nursing were part of the program.[77] In 1925, Union Minière decided to create a service to protect the health of African mothers and their infants. This program was part of a larger stabilization effort to increase wages, provide long-term contracts, and recruit workers who would be taught skills and encouraged to live in company compounds with their wives and children.[78] According to the company's medical service, the camps' reputation for immorality and the "sterility of industrial households"—attributed to a population composed mostly of single men and occasional prostitutes—"constituted the principal arguments of this [stabilization] policy." The medical staff encouraged launching the Oeuvre de Protection de l'Enfance Noire (OPEN) program. Its explicit aims were to reduce infant mortality, which was attributed to maternal ignorance, and to increase the birthrate.[79]

"Surveillance of weaning" was part of this social program, which included maternity wards and infant and prenatal medical clinics. It operated with daily schedules that varied according to the age of the child and were "strictly respected."[80] Weaning was considered a "delicate period," and the medical service disapproved of periods of prolonged breast feeding followed by what appeared to be an abrupt abandoning of the child to fend for itself.

Rations had previously been given in kind to the worker for his wife and infants, but under this system "no control was possible as to the amount given to children."[81] Union Minière decided to make the feeding of children a direct company affair. The medical service organized mess halls to assure that infant feeding became scientifically controlled quantitatively and qualitatively. In 1931, children aged two to five went to mess halls twice a day to eat their meals, and those over five went three times a day.[82] Within two years, the age at which children began to be fed in mess halls had been lowered to one year. White "dames" and nuns watched over the meals and taught the children "to eat properly, to serve themselves with spoons and forks, to wash their hands before and after meals."[83] Attendance was carefully noted, and if a child was absent one of the staff would go to the parents' house to investigate. The company physician was convinced that the "functioning of these refectories . . . notably improved" the health of the children,[84] while house visits contributed to family education.[85]

Mothers were supposed to attend the infant consultation program once a week, where their infants were examined, weighed, and given quinine. Nurses taught the mothers how to clothe, feed, and care for their children. Daily attendance in order to bathe infants in large bath halls was encouraged. Women received gifts of sugar, soap, and children's clothes, enticing them to attend regularly. Mothers also received a gift if they gave birth at the hospital, the OPEN center, or even at home, as long as a company doctor or midwife was present. Women who were not nursing received milk to feed their infants, and those who were received a double ration.[86]

Rations for wives were a way to manipulate women's use of time and secure discipline. Vegetables were excluded from women's rations but not from men's to ensure that women cultivated the garden plots provided.[87] Although women's rations were deemed important for their health, they were not, like men's, required by law. This was considered a "wise policy" by Union Minière.

> But the absence of a legal obligation leaves him [the employer] the possibility of occasionally suppressing the ration of the wife of the worker who does not submit to the discipline of the camp and notably to useful occupations and jobs, either for themselves and their family or for the whole collectivity, that it is indispensable to impose on them: maintain the yard and hut, bring the children to medical consultations and to school, do some farming work, etc. . . . The possibility of this sanction suffices in itself to obtain good discipline among the women.[88]

The extra ration distributed to pregnant or nursing women, although considered nutritionally important, would have doubled as an inducement to adhere to OPEN activities and schedules.

Although the specific instructions given are unknown, Union Minière's infant feeding program clearly involved direct intervention in breast feeding practices and in fertility. It is well established that the volume of breast milk a woman produces depends on the frequency and intensity of nursing, and frequency and intensity of nursing are also chief factors in lactational anovulation.[89] The feeding of children in mess halls at one to two years of age was a kind of supplementary feeding which would have tended to decrease the volume of mothers' breast milk and the frequency of nursing and consequently to precipitate the resumption of ovulation.

OPEN is an example of excessive colonial intervention in breast feeding and weaning practices in an effort to maximize fertility and minimize infant mortality.[90] It was possible given the extensive social control within the confines of a mining compound. Stabilization as a labor strategy emerged on the Katangan Copperbelt partly due to the shortage of workers in the early 1920s and to the company's desire to save costs by replacing white labor with black. It also surfaced during a larger colonial demographic crisis, evident not only within the camps, where the sex ratio was imbalanced and venereal disease on the rise, but also in the rural areas where miners were recruited. The company's advancing of bridewealth payments for recruits and offers of better housing, rations for spouses and children, primary schooling, and medical care were used to tempt married workers to sign longer contracts. These inducements were simultaneously part of a company strategy to increase fertility and survival rates within the camps.[91]

George Chauncey argues convincingly that stabilization of labor on the other side of the border, on the Northern Rhodesian Copperbelt, was a labor strategy intending to "localise . . . women's reproductive labour not in the rural areas . . . but under company domain and on company property." Reproductive labor in Chauncey's sense, the "daily reproduction of labour power, that is, the daily maintenance of the worker,"[92] was part of Union Minière's strategy as well, yet at least during the heyday of the OPEN program, it was women's role in biological reproduction which was considered of supreme importance.[93] As Bruce Fetter has expressed it, the Union Minière "management decided to 'breed' its own labor force."[94] By 1931, Union Minière was convinced that its efforts to "be attentive to guide these indigenous families grouped around it" had shown that "the reputation of immorality and sterility of industrial households is false, that the families are as stable and even more prolific than in the customary areas."[95]

Union Minière's stabilization policy and maternal and infant health program succeeded in creating a milieu of monogamous families in the camps, in reducing the adult and infant rates of mortality, and in increasing the birthrate (50 per 1,000 in 1950).[96] The company was pleased to report that the sex ratio went from 26 women to 100 men in 1925 to 71 women to 100 men in 1945. Whereas there were 41 children for 100 women in the camps in 1925 (children representing 8 percent of the total population), there were 136 children for 100 women in 1945 (or 36 percent of the population).[97] By 1946, children under five years of age were no longer fed in mess halls, but continued to be fed paps at the infant consultations to facilitate weaning.[98] Weaning generally occurred in the twelfth month.[99] A 1950 study revealed that the children of one Union Minière camp had weight curves comparable to those found among French children, while weights were lower in the *centre extra-coutumier* of Jadotville and even lower in the rural areas.[100] This was explained by the fact that all one- to three-year-old infants of the company compounds were given 200 cubic centimeter of powdered milk and 20 grams of maize semolina each day the OPEN center was open. The mothers consumed this supplement during the first months of life[101] . . . instead of the infant.

Outside Union Minière: Numbers, Lures, Milk, and Time

Union Minière's OPEN program was an extreme, due to its capacity to be explicitly authoritarian and coercive. No one ever suggested a colonywide program for feeding young infants in mess halls, but most of the basic institutional elements of the OPEN program—maternity wards, prenatal and infant consultation programs, moral advice and incentives—were duplicated throughout the colony as missionaries, colonial doctors, and lone white women established programs. Although the OPEN program may have been excessively rigid and its direct impact limited to a small fraction of the colony's population, certain elements and tensions reemerged in other industrial and rural contexts in subsequent years.[102]

By 1940, it was evident that the Belgian Congo possessed a network of prenatal and infant consultations, maternities, midwife schools, and orphanages exceeding in number and importance what had been realized in any other sub-Saharan African colony.[103] Numerous sets of colonial actors participated. Maternal and infant health efforts ranged from those attached to government hospitals to those operated by missions and private companies to the "modest action made by the wife of a European agent at a detached post, alone in the bush."[104] An influential philanthropic, para-governmental organization, the Fonds Reine Elisabeth pour l'Assistance Médicale aux Indigènes (FOREAMI), was founded in 1930 by royal decree to meet the dire health needs of the people in Bas-Congo.[105] Due to the presence of numerous Catholic and Protestant missions FOREAMI managed to establish fifty-eight consultation sites, and 22,300 children were enrolled annually by 1935. In 1936, when it expanded into Kwango, a light missionary presence permitted only twenty consultation sites to be established. By making a call for help to the wives of colonial agents and FOREAMI personnel, another twenty-two consultation programs were founded.[106]

In 1938, the government was subsidizing 262 infant consultation programs, and most private companies were operating additional programs, including Huilever, Vicicongo, Otraco, Compagnie minière des Grands Lacs, Mines d'or de Kilo-Moto, Union Minière, and Forminière.[107] By the 1950s, an array of private and public organizations were involved in maternal and infant health. These included missions, the governmental medical service, FOREAMI, FOMULAC (Fondation Médicale de l'Université de Louvain au Congo), Croix-Rouge du Congo, Oeuvre de la Maternité et de l'Enfance Indigènes (OMEI), Fonds du Bien Etre Indigène, Aide aux Maternités et Dispensaires du Congo, and most industrial, commercial, and agricultural companies. In 1955, the Oeuvre Reine Astrid pour la Mère et Enfants Indigènes (OREAMI) was created as a third section of FOREAMI to inventory and oversee the various programs.[108] A 1956 survey reported that there were 884 infant consultation programs in the colony. About two hundred thousand young children were estimated to attend these weekly, and one-third of the colony's infant population (aged 0–2 years) was thought to have been reached by the programs. Colonial statistics on births in maternity wards were also high: it was claimed that nearly 19,000 or one-third of births took place in maternities in 1956. Over half of the women giving birth during the year were estimated to have attended prenatal consultations during their pregnancies.[109]

Incentives to participate in the programs took various forms. Rewards for giving birth in a maternity ward were common, and ranged from gifts paid to Force Publique soldiers whose wives had just given birth (to live infants) to gifts in kind to mothers who gave birth in clinics and hospitals.[110] Lures for regular attendance at infant clinics were routine. One Union des Femmes Colonials member explained, "I must say they are assiduous about the visits,

I think it is especially due to the little clothes that I give to them for having come regularly."[111] Others distributed soap and small clothes to attract mothers while preaching bodily cleanliness and protection from the cold.[112] Cooperation with other charitable organizations facilitated these efforts.[113] In Costermansville, the local *comité* of the Union des Femmes Colonials ran a consultation program where they distributed rice, salt, and soap as well as clothes, sheets, and covers each week.[114] Those programs operated by private companies, like Union Minière, had more leverage over women's lives. In the Forminière diamond mining camps, a list of absent women was drawn up after each consultation session. The chef de camp would investigate.[115]

Milk products were increasingly used within infant welfare programs, while, as we have seen above, the popular name "goutte de lait" indicates that it was an aspect from the early days of the Ligue's activities. Different programs reported proudly on their accomplishments in nurturing orphans and infants of mothers with insufficient milk. Wet-nursing experiments were not very successful. The Berceau du Kasai saved the life of one orphan through a diet of breast milk substitutes for seven months. It also purchased a dairy goat that it would lend to a mother unable to nurse if she was the wife of a nurse or domestic servant. If she instead was rated incapable of managing herself, the Berceau would prepare baby bottles and the infants would be brought each day to drink in front of the staff.[116] Five to eight orphans were going to the infant consultation in Usumbura daily in 1938 for a baby bottle and the necessary milk for the day.[117] Work with orphans was an opportunity to intervene more directly in infants' lives, demonstrate the importance of alternative sources of milk, and establish trust among the population.

> An orphanage . . . must have baby bottles, sterilizers, beds, swaddling clothes, etc. available. . . . "No matter what is better than nothing" mustn't be expounded. If the natives think that in institutions run by European personnel, mortality is greater than in the customary milieu, it will be difficult to get them to accept the infant rearing advice that is given to them.[118]

In 1947, the Commission pour la Protection des Indigènes encouraged the government to produce propaganda encouraging soya cultivation and the use of soya milk for feeding children, especially when breast milk was lacking.[119] Milk distribution programs began in earnest in the 1950s, largely out of concern for kwashiokor and a growing international "obsession" that there were widespread protein deficiency problems.[120] In the late 1940s, soya milk was being distributed at the Kilo-Moto gold mines, and *lait écremé*—"a food of high interest because it is cheap and has high protein value"—was already being given to two- to five-year-olds in Jadotville.[121] Experiments with the nutritional benefits of supplementing mothers and children's diets with lait écremé were conducted by FOREAMI, beginning in 1952, with the assistance of the Fonds International de Secours à l'Enfance. Two and a half to three tons of powdered milk were dissolved and distributed to the homes of 2,500 to 3,000 persons in Kwango each month.[122] After fifteen months, it was concluded that each category of "beneficiary"—o to two-year-old infants, two- to five-year-old children, pregnant and nursing women—had profited remarkably. Nursing women, in particular, had more abundant and rich breast milk.[123]

The quality and volume of Congolese women's breast milk became a concern of scientific research in Kwango and Kivu in the 1950s. Several studies were conducted to measure and evaluate its chemical composition, protein and amino acid content, and the quantity secreted monthly and in relation to those receiving milk supplements.[124]

Within infant welfare programs, there was a general emphasis on earlier weaning and on breast feeding according to a strict time schedule rather than on infant demand. In 1952, the *Congo Mission News* ran a story about brides' courses being given by the Church Missionary Society in Matana. Every girl of the mission's district in Urundi was required to attend these courses before being married. With the help of baby dolls, the future mothers received motherhood training. Separate beds for babies were encouraged, and the "need of regular hours for feeding the baby, instead of every time it cries" was stressed. This was explained

> by comparing the stomach to a cooking-pot on the fire; the girls quickly tell me that it is senseless to put in more beans when the first lot are half cooked: "You would spoil them *all:* first empty the pot and then cook some more." When this is applied to the baby we consider other causes for crying than hunger and they realize that baby has no language except a cry to express everything, and so mother must learn to understand the language.[125]

The need to discipline infants and a fear of spoiling them was at the heart of the preference for scheduled feeding. One Belgian researcher thought that the key to the Congolese attitude was that "a baby must never cry; all its whims must be satisfied."[126] This was thought to lead to "certain dangers of a psychological order."

> During early infancy, the relationship of the infant with its mother is made at the same time of dependence: he counts upon all from her and uniquely her, and of domination: she is always there to satisfy his needs. Not undergoing any frustration, he lives in a climate of absolute security. . . . The lack of development of the sense of initiative, the absence of all learning of frustration will render more difficult the surmounting of the critical period which weaning represents.[127]

Health was used as a rationale for scheduled feeding in literature directed at both European and African women. This was the case in a booklet published in the early 1950s by FOREAMI and the Fonds du Bien Etre Indigène.

Containing advice for Congolese mothers on child care, breast feeding, and hygiene, it was printed in the colony's four vehicular languages. In 1953, 41,000 copies were printed and disseminated in Kikongo. The Swahili version, *Mashauri kwa Mama wa Kongo,* is a rare source on what was prescribed as appropriate maternal behavior for Congolese women within maternal and infant health care programs. Women were told not to carry heavy loads during pregnancy, not to "grasp for African medicine" if they had health problems, not to call other women of the village together for help during childbearing, and to give birth in a hospital or clinic. Mothers were also told to nurse their children six times a day, on a regular three-hour feeding schedule, beginning at seven in the morning until nine at night. The page of "don'ts" was revealing.

> Don't breast feed your child because he cries: he will silence himself. . . . At night don't nurse him even a little: the infant will suckle in the evening and will suckle again in the morning. Don't ever give him "malafu" (beer) or coconut water: milk will suffice. Before the seventh month, flour gruel is bad. You will not nurse at all [at night] if he sleeps in [his own] bed. If you get cow's or goat's milk, you will go to the dispensary, the doctor will give you good advice, you will know what to do.[128]

Mothers were advised to introduce supplementary foods during the seventh month, and by the tenth month to feed the child milk with a bottle and other foods.

This booklet also illustrates how the white woman and her habits were held up as the correct model to be emulated, especially for house cleaning and interior decoration.[129] The European woman was not only a moral model and an actual practitioner through whose voluntarism many of the maternal and infant health programs were to be sustained. Her breast feeding patterns and practices also became a measure and guide for what was expected of Congolese women. It was assumed by one colonial author, for example, that exclusive natural breast feeding would, as in Europe, become insufficient around the fourth or fifth month. This became a rationale for encouraging earlier weaning, and changes in birth spacing practices would be a harmonious consequence.

> It is necessary to advise them that weaning is less dangerous for the baby and to lead those nursing to separate themselves more quickly from the infant being nursed. The weight curves show that exclusive natural breast feeding, as in Europe besides, becomes insufficient around the fourth or fifth month. The mother and the infant will both profit from a more intelligent diet, and subsequently good marital relations will often be promoted: [due to] certain customs prohibiting sexual relations before the end of breast feeding.[130]

By the 1950s, colonial authors began to express the idea that African birth intervals had declined. "These sexual taboos have a tendency to become shorter and the weaning to become more precocious: It would be irrelevant to regret and rejoice this: these sociological facts only demand to be stated."[131] One author, calling them "victims" of monogamy, remarked on African women's increasing work loads as they gave birth to more children, while lacking the aid they might have received from co-wives in a polygynous situation.

> Presently, we often see in the bush, a woman carrying on the back a small child and leading by the hand another, who walks with pain. This last, precociously weaned, is in a certain measure, a victim of monogamous marriage.[132]

In Elisabethville's urban quarters (not the mining compounds) in the late 1950s, 62.7 percent of the women's children were spaced at two-year intervals and 21.4 percent at three-year intervals. The same study indicated that 73.9 percent of the mothers were weaning their children after 12 to 18 months, and 20.3 percent after 19 to 24 months. Fifty-two percent said they stopped nursing when they became pregnant, indicating that postpartum abstinence was not maintained during the entire lactation period. Thirty-six percent stopped breast feeding (or weaned their children) in order to resume sexual relations.[133] A 1959 study of rural diets, covering the entire colony except Katanga, argued that there were virtually no cases where mothers ran the risk of getting pregnant while still nursing.[134]

There is evidence that most Congolese women did not turn to scheduled feeding.[135] When research was conducted in Kwango in the early 1950s, it was assumed that women were feeding their children on demand, so they were separated from their children for three-hour intervals during the experiments.[136] In the late 1950s very few women of Elisabethville had adopted the Western model of fixed feeding times. Of the 4.5 percent of one study's sample who did, two-thirds were wives of clerks, monitors, or nurses, that is, of the *évolué* class of educated, elite Africans. Of the thirteen women in the sample who had adopted fixed schedules, eleven were less than twenty-five years old and ten had attended a *foyer social,* a center for Europeanized domestic and maternal training.[137] Most women, however, nursed whenever and as often as the child desired. At night, 83 percent of the infants slept in bed with their parents, and there was no evidence of spousal separation. The mothers were giving the children a porridge of manioc or corn beginning in the fourth or fifth month, and some were using bottles to make the transition to weaning.[138]

Widespread "superstitious beliefs" associated with imbibing milk may have led to coercive methods in infant clinics in some regions.

> In the remote areas . . . mothers offer milk to children only under coercion, so great is the suspicion that surrounds all non-traditional food presented under the form of industrial conservation. The aged in particular only talk of milk with the greatest disgust.[139]

Artificial and dairy milk did become more widely available though still out of reach to most of the population due to "the scantiness of the native's revenues."[140] For European women, imported milk was associated with health: Swiss milk "A l'Ours," a sterilized whole, canned milk was advertised regularly in the *Bulletin de l'Union des Femmes Coloniales* with a picture of a white nurse as "the sign of confidence of the medical corps in the tropics."[141] Among Africans, processed milk was generally consumed either for medicinal purposes or as a symbol of Europeanization. A study conducted in the 1950s indicated that of the 95 percent of the rural population relying on subsistence agriculture, only 12 percent of the children ever consumed milk and then for medicinal purposes only. Of the 5 percent with cash incomes (government workers or traders, for example), 42 percent of the children consumed milk, but irregularly, 28 percent of the women did as a luxury item, and men rarely consumed it.[142] The impact of milk distribution in hospitals, especially due to the "intensive propaganda carried on by FOREAMI," was thought to have changed attitudes towards its consumption: "It remains nevertheless considered as a medicine, destined especially for weak children."[143] Near missions and in colonial posts and urban areas, "by the contagion of example," milk was "interven[ing] more and more."[144] It tended to be bought in powdered form or as concentrated, sugared milk and served to children as a dessert.[145] "Certain powdered milks are ingested as is as a delicacy for their sugared taste. The natives of a higher social class consume milk either as a delicacy or to show openly the degree of Europeanization that they have attained."[146] The use of milk-based flours and oatmeal was becoming less rare among "evolved" populations in cities and near missions.[147] Thus although the "prejudice" against milk was found to be "crumbl[ing] bit by bit," this was only true for European imported forms or "industrial milk," whose "prohibitive cost . . . constitute[d] the principal obstacle to its spread."[148] Except in those areas, such as the Ituri region, where cattle raising was a customary pursuit, the milking of cows and goats was still rare, and fresh milk was not consumed.[149]

By the end of the colonial period, "far from the threats of extinction of the population as was feared at a certain moment,"[150] the population crisis had diminished, and in fact reversed itself. Attitudes about the "irrationality" of indigenous breast feeding practices subsided. Although African breast feeding had known nostalgic admiration, it began to be analyzed with greater scientific equanimity. In 1960 Holemans pointed to the rationality of indigenous practices in Kwango, while arguing that European and Kwango women's breast milk production followed very different patterns.[151] Since the quality of milk Kwango women secreted was often insufficient near the beginning of lactation, he contended that it was not surprising that mixed feeding was begun quite early, as it was a response to insufficient maternal milk.[152] He asserted that it was useless to try to "Westernize" indigenous practices, even though he also thought that "logically" the former were preferable. Accepting that mother's milk was an important nutritional source and that weaning occurred after three years, he identified two periods when infants were particularly susceptible to malnutrition.

> The logical solution to the problem would be that of administering cow's milk in adequate dilution and in sterile bottles. It is impossible to put this solution in practice: the bottle must be given every day and one cannot multiply to infinity infant consultations. Besides the intellectual level, habitation, work and household utensils of indigenous women do not permit proper preparation of this food in the customary milieu. The technique of supplementary feeding actually in use . . . might seem highly undesirable to us, but we can affirm that as long as the present circumstances persist, the natives will not abandon it, because they are perfectly aware that children are hungry. We cannot then discourage the customary method as long as it is impossible for us to replace it with adequate Western methods.[153]

Conclusion

This paper has examined one colonial regime's efforts to increase the birthrate, promote infant and maternal clinics, and socialize African women as biological reproducers and mothers. The colonial call for a "crusade to combat the prejudices that separate the spouses" led to the development of the most massive network of maternal and infant health programs in sub-Saharan Africa. Diet and health, the quality and volume of Congolese women's breast milk, the frequency and timing of nursing, and the appropriate time for and method of weaning became issues of Belgian concern in the Congo, during and following the demographic panic of the 1920s. Widespread distribution of milk invited dependence on imported foodstuffs and contributed to alterations in infant feeding patterns.

European women played a charitable role as paragons and practitioners, while they were beneficiaries of maternal and infant health endeavors aimed at Africans.[154] Colonial perceptions of European women's infant rearing tendencies—at home and in the colony—animated the goals and operations of these health programs. Neither Madame van den Perre's Ligue, the Congrès Colonial National, Union Minière, or FOREAMI were *against* breast feeding. Thinking about the history of colonial infant welfare in terms of a bottle versus breast dichotomy is as likely to distort the cultural practices of African mothers as it is the wishes of Belgian doctors and other interested colonial actors. Colonialists understood something about the immunological advantages of breast feeding from experience in Europe, where it was known that breast-fed babies were less likely to succumb to infant mortality. European women who bottle fed their infants were lamented, and African breast feeding could inspire a sense of nostalgia and envy. In 1920, it was remarked that "the *négresses* have, in the matter of child rearing, an important superiority over most white

women, . . . they nurse their children."[155] In 1950, in the colony more than
in Europe, breast feeding (of European infants) was being replaced by bottle
feeding even within the first few months after birth, "and that too often with
the complacency of the medical personnel." This was regretted because of the
increasing dangers for the infant's health, particularly dyspepsia and enteritis,
"so difficult to avoid in a tropical or hot climate."[156] Premature weaning and
early supplemental feeding were considered dangerous whether practiced by
working-class Belgians or the colonized women of the Congo. Nevertheless,
earlier and medicalized weaning of Congolese infants was generally favored
in colonial programs.

Colonialism entered into some of the most intimate aspects of African
women's lives: the birthing process, breast feeding, weaning, dietary choices,
and sexual activity. In an extreme form, in the early 1930s at least, a colonial
mining company entered into the heart of the processes of social reproduction,
colonizing African women's and children's time, space, and bodies. Time
became regularized. Women had daily schedules and weaning schedules.
Children were fed and bathed within new colonial public spaces. Even private
space was controlled and monitored to ensure hygiene and particular sleeping
arrangements.

These colonial initiatives were linked to a discourse which explicitly objected to prolonged lactation and postpartum abstinence practices, and argued
the pro-fertility benefits of reducing birth intervals. The consequences of these
maternal and infant health programs remain enigmatic. They were certainly not
uniform throughout the colony, and it is likely that colonial intentions also
varied across time and by place. There was a wide range of programs, undertaken by a multiplicity of colonial actors in settings with assorted limits on
social control and disparate reproductive, infant feeding, and dietary customs.
Population growth and declining sterility rates in Zaire have been linked by
others to colonial medicine, especially the widespread use of penicillin in
antiyaws campaigns after World War II.[157] Subsequent quantitative research
might establish a decline in birth intervals and its impact on fertility and
maternal and infant health. Even so, the decline in birth spacing customs and
intervals in twentieth-century Africa appears less an innocent and inescapable
outcome of "modernization" in light of candid colonial aspirations to shorten
them in the Belgian Congo.

How Africans interpreted, countered, structured, and slighted colonial intentions and deeds remains an open and important question. Infant welfare
clinics were not mere sites of colonial imposition, but of negotiation. European
and African women would have been important both as negotiators and in terms
of the objects, practices, and meanings which were negotiated. What to Europeans was a scientifically approved breast milk substitute could be to Africans a medicine or a European delicacy. What was prescribed was not
necessarily followed. There is evidence of Congolese women shaping programs

and negotiating the care they received, whether through insisting on being given a "matabish" (gift or bribe)[158] or demanding to be examined and cared for by female staff.[159] In the confines of a mining compound or a scientific experiment, women could be forcibly separated from their children for certain periods of time to secure changes in breast feeding practices. Significant changes in diet and labor requirements, too, whether due to colonial handouts and corvées or not, might have had an impact on the frequency of nursing and the timing of weaning. But ultimately most Congolese women rejected nursing their infants according to a tight and regular time schedule and continued to nurse them at night.[160] The small minority who did conform to this European image of proper motherhood were among a small elite who could also afford "industrial milk" imported from Europe. As one woman expressed it, "We can't let the child cry like the whites."[161]

Notes

I benefited from the advice and critical comments of several people during various stages of the conceptualization, research, and writing of this chapter. Gracious thanks go to Steven Feierman, Paul Landau, Ann Stoler, Jan Vansina, Jean-Luc Vellut, and James Wood.

1. Ronald S. Waife, *Traditional Methods of Birth Control in Zaire,* Pathfinder Papers No. 4 (Chestnut Hill, MA, 1978), 4.

2. Ibid., 12, 15, and 17.

3. See, for example, Hilary J. Page and Ron Lesthaeghe, eds., *Child-Spacing in Tropical Africa: Traditions and Change* (London and New York, 1981); Valerie Hull and Mayling Simpson, eds., *Breastfeeding, Child Health and Child Spacing: Cross-cultural Perspectives* (London, 1985); John Bongaarts, Frank Odile, and Ron Lesthaeghe, "The Proximate Determinants of Fertility in Sub-Saharan Africa," *Population and Development* 10, no. 3 (1984): 511–537; Beverly Winikoff, "The Effects of Birth Spacing on Child and Maternal Health," *Studies in Family Planning* 14 (1983): 231–245; Barbara B. Harrell, "Lactation and Menstruation in Cultural Perspective," *American Anthropologist* 83 (1981): 796–823; Jacqueline M. Mondot-Bernard, *Relationships between Fertility, Child Mortality and Nutrition in Africa* (Paris, 1975); Caroline Bledsoe, "Side-stepping the Postpartum Sex Taboo: Mende Cultural Perceptions of Tinned Milk in Sierra Leone," 101–124, in *The Cultural Roots of African Fertility Regimes,* Proceedings of the Ife Conference, Department of Demography and Social Statistics, Obafemi Awolowo University and Population Studies Center, University of Pennsylvania.

4. Little attention has been paid to explaining the decline in postpartum abstinence and breast feeding in an historically specific way. I am grateful to Rima D. Apple for directing my attention to an exception; see Lenore Manderson, "Bottle Feeding and Ideology in Colonial Malaya: The Production of Change," *International Journal of Health Services* 12, no. 4 (1982): 597–616. On the historical importance of the decline of postpartum abstinence in twentieth-century Africa, see Steven Feierman, "Struggles

for Control: The Social Roots of Health and Healing in Modern Africa," *African Studies Review* 28 (1985): 92–93. For exemplary work on related issues in England, Brazil, and the United States, see Angus McLaren, *Reproductive Rituals: The Perception of Fertility in England from the Sixteenth to the Nineteenth Century* (New York, 1984); Nancy Scheper-Hughes, "Infant Mortality and Infant Care: Cultural and Economic Constraints on Nurturing in Northeast Brazil," *Social Science and Medicine* 19 (1984): 535–546; and Rima D. Apple, *Mothers and Medicine: A Social History of Infant Feeding, 1890–1950* (Madison, 1987).

5. For a critique of "modernization" as a conceptual framework, see Magdalene S. David, "Determinants of Milk Choice in Infant Feeding among Urban Liberian Mothers," *Liberian Studies Journal* 12 (1987): 117–134.

6. In 1913, the Ligue conducted a survey that revealed infant mortality rates of 50, 75, and 90 percent in some areas. *Congrès Colonial National,* 1926, 157–158.

7. Mme van der Kerken, "Les oeuvres sociales et humanitaires au Congo Belge," in *Congrès Colonial National,* V^e session, no. 15, 1941, 8.

8. *Congrès Colonial National,* 1920, 102–104; Leo Lejeune, "L'enfance noire," *Bulletin de l'Union des Femmes Coloniales* 15, no. 88 (February 1938): 10–11.

9. It also urged that maternities should be created in all stations where a doctor was present and "practical teaching" instituted. Léon Guebels, *Relation complète des travaux de la Commission Permanente pour la Protection des Indigènes* (Brussels, n.d.), 130.

10. *La question sociale, Rapport au Comité du Congrès Colonial National* (Brussels, 1924), 159, 221.

11. Van der Kerken, "Les oeuvres sociales," 6. What exactly this hostility was about is not clear. It may have reflected divisions within Belgium over gouttes de lait, or an assertion by doctors of their exclusive professional prerogatives to counter the autonomous, unsupervised activity of Ligue women, or both. If the colonial medical profession did not have such control before 1924, it seems to have had afterward. The question of divisions among different sets of metropolitan and colonial actors vis-à-vis the infant welfare movements in Belgium and its colony needs more research.

12. *Congrès Colonial National,* 1920, 104. This comment is in keeping with a goutte de lait as theorized and practiced by Dr. Pierre Budin, the French doctor who founded one of the first infant consultations in France in 1892. The French idea was to encourage breast feeding whenever possible and to provide sterile milk as a substitute only when and to the extent necessary. The notion that "*the* food of infants is human milk" had been known to get lost as programs multiplied, however. In many, particularly in Paris, artificial feeding was "the rule," and some were dealing only with weaned infants; Pierre Budin, *The Nursling: The Feeding and Hygiene of Premature and Full-Term Infants* (London, 1902), 34, 156. This was the trend in England, too, where "infant milk depots" focused on providing clean milk, and there was little if any medical supervision; Deborah Dwork, *War Is Good for Babies and Other Young Children* (London and New York, 1987), 104. Mme van den Perre's statement not only asserts the importance of breast feeding for African women but is also an indication of a corresponding fear that white women in the colony were inclined to turn to unnecessary bottle feeding more readily than those remaining in the metropole. Why this may have been so needs further research.

13. Van der Kerken, "Les Oeuvres sociales," 7.

14. Although attempts to quantify the extent of depopulation which occurred in the Congo during the Leopoldian period (1885–1908) have and will falter, colonial claims that the population had been at least halved during this rapacious "red rubber" period were probably not exaggerated. The exact numbers involved in depopulation during the Congo Independent State period cannot be computed given the "wild guesses" and "farcical" calculations involved in Henry Morton Stanley's estimates of population figures at the beginning of this period. On the problems with Stanley's calculations and the way they have gone uncorrected by subsequent authors, see William Roger Louis and Jean Stengers, *E. D. Morel's History of the Congo Reform Movement* (London, 1968), 252–256.

15. *La question sociale,* 40–42, 81–87. For an excellent annotated bibliography of this literature, see Anne Retel-Laurentin, *Infécondité en Afrique noire: Maladies et conséquences sociales* (Paris, 1974), 141–188. For more recent interpretations of the factors involved in depopulation and infertility in colonial Zaire, see Anatole Romaniuk, *La fécondité des populations congolaises* (Paris, 1967), 129–170; Retel-Laurentin, *Infécondité en Afrique noire;* David Voas, "Subfertility and Disruption in the Congo Basin," in *African Historical Demography,* Vol. 2 (Edinburgh, 1981), 777–799; Bogumil Jewsiewicki, "Toward a Historical Sociology of Population in Zaire," in *African Population and Capitalism,* ed. Dennis Cordell and Joel W. Gregory, 271–279 (Boulder, 1987); John C. Caldwell and Pat Caldwell, "The Demographic Evidence for the Incidence and Cause of Abnormally Low Fertility in Tropical Africa," *World Health Statistics Quarterly* 36 (1983): 2–34; and Sabakinu Kivilu, "Les sources de l'histoire démographique du Zaire," *Etudes d'Histoire africaine* 6 (1974): 120.

16. Pro-natalist policies emerged out of this crisis in the Belgian Congo. They included family allocations; expansion of medical services; laws to repress abortion, prostitution, and polygamy; maternity gifts; and tax exemptions for monogamously married men with more than four children; Ghu-Gha Bianga, "La Politique démographique au Congo Belge," *Population* 33, no. 1 (January-February 1978): 189–194.

17. The word "puericulture" was coined by a French doctor of the name Carot in 1865 when he wrote a manual on the proper methods and means to assure the growth and health of infants; Paul Robert, *Dictionnaire alphabétique et analogique de la Langue Française,* vol. 5 (Paris, 1962), 679. The idea of "rearing of children, as an art, or branch of sociology" came into the English language in the first years of this century as doctors, and then the popular press, took note of the infant welfare movement in France; James A. H. Marray, ed., *Oxford English Dictionary* (London, 1961), 1568.

18. *La question sociale,* 159–160.

19. Ibid., 96, 159. These assessments of the Ligue's success should be treated with caution; such social work efforts were often introduced on a very limited scale.

20. Mme van den Perre, "A la Ligue pour la Protection de l'Enfance Noire," *Notre Colonie* 7, no. 103 (February 1926):44.

21. *Congrès Colonial Belge,* 1926, 159–160.

22. Anna Davin, "Imperialism and Motherhood," *History Workshop* 5 (1978): 9–65, esp. pp. 12–14. See also Dwork, *War Is Good.*

23. Ron J. Lesthaeghe, *The Decline of Belgian Fertility, 1800–1970* (Princeton, 1977), 135–139.

24. Lucien Garot, *Médecine sociale de l'Enfance* (Liège, 1946); and Camille Jacquart, *La mortalité infantile dans les Flandres* (Bruxelles, 1907).

25. Garot, *Médecine sociale;* Lesthaeghe, *Decline,* 174; and Jacquart, *La mortalité infantile.*

26. This attitude can be seen in Garot, *Médecine sociale;* and Jacquart, *La mortalité infantile.*

27. Guebels, *Relation complète,* 113.

28. Ibid., 128–129.

29. On European and African beliefs about African abortion, see Retel-Laurentin, *Infécondité en Afrique Noire,* 105–112.

30. Most of the colonial discourse (chiefly dating from the 1920s and early 1930s) on which this paper is based assumes near-universality in lactation and postpartum abstinence practices. It is not my intention here to specify variations and exceptions according to locality, social organization, seasonality, colonial work demands, migration patterns, or historical periods, although these certainly existed. It is my intention to examine this discourse and to sketch out in a preliminary, also generalized way, how it was translated into colonial practice. Extensive archival and field work would shed further light on the actual veracity of colonial generalizations and the impact of *and response to* colonial programs, interventions, and prescriptions within particular rural and urban contexts. For an ethnographic overview concerning postpartum abstinence practices in Africa, including in Zaire, see R. Schoenmaeckers et al., "The Child-spacing Tradition and the Postpartum Taboo in Tropical Africa: Anthropological Evidence," in Page and Lesthaeghe, *Child-Spacing in Tropical Africa,* 25–71.

31. *Congrès Colonial National,* 1930, I: 162–163.

32. *La question sociale,* 92.

33. Ibid., 94.

34. Ibid., 92.

35. *Congrès Colonial National,* 1930, I: 163.

36. *La question sociale,* 92.

37. Ibid., 144.

38. Ibid., 94–95.

39. Ibid., 175–176.

40. W. Bervoets and M. Lassance, *Modes et coutûmes alimentaires des Congolaise en milieu rural; Résultats d'une enquête portant sur le Congo belge et le Ruanda-Urundi à l'exclusion du Katanga, 1955–1957,* Mémoire, Académie royale des sciences d'outre-mer, Classe des sciences naturelles et médicale, n.s., t. IX, f. 4, 1959, 62.

41. Ibid., 67. Bervoets and Lassance assumed that these were "traditional" methods. Careful research might reveal changes in patterns of supplementary feeding practices due to demands on women's time, and to larger changes in the subsistence diet and in meeting basic nutritional needs due to forced labor and increased burdens on women. Evidence from Bangladesh about the seasonality of suckling patterns indicates that nursing and supplementary diets vary according to the availability of other foods and other labor demands on women's time. See S. Huffman et al., "Breast-Feeding Patterns in Rural Bangladesh." *American Journal of Clinical Nutrition* 33 (1980): 144–154. For a study on seasonal fluctuation in breast milk production as related to seasonal differences in dietary intake within the subsistence economy among the Shi

and Havu in Zaire, see Ph. Hennart and H. L. Vis. "Breast-Feeding and Post Partum Amenorrhoea in Central Africa, I. Milk Production in Rural Areas," *Journal of Tropical Pediatrics* 26 (October 1980): 177–183.

42. *La question sociale,* 95.

43. Ibid., 93. Lactation's suppressive effect on ovulation is exaggerated here.

44. Ibid., 242.

45. The first enterprise was founded in 1924 in Katanga, and by 1930, 135 million Belgian francs were invested in this activity that potentially would serve both European and African women; *Congrès Colonial National,* 1930, II: 47. The Congrès Colonial National recommended in 1930 that contests with financial and honorary prizes be encouraged; *Congrès Colonial National,* 1930, I:164–166.

46. *Congrès Colonial National,* 1930, I: 167.

47. *La question sociale,* 93. Doctors Trolli (of FOREAMI) and van Nitsen (of Union Minière) expressed the same logic to the Congrès Colonial National in 1941, calculating the length of the average Congolese woman's reproductive years and the number of births which could be attained if the "interconceptual space" could be reduced. See *Congrès Colonial National,* V^e session, 1941, no. 7, p. 15.

48. *Congrès Colonial National,* 1930, I: 167. It is interesting to note the parallel between this "crusade" in the colony and the crusade in Belgium against the "plague of Onanism" mentioned above. Coitus interruptus was the most important form of birth control, largely responsible for Belgium's sudden and silent fertility decline in the late nineteenth century. (The birthrate fell below 30 live births per 1,000 population in 1880.) A small group of Belgian neo-Malthusians had little impact because Socialists, Liberals, and Catholics were united in their stance against fertility regulation. An important 1909 pastoral letter to Belgian parish priests instructed them to question women in the confessional and advise them not to cooperate in the "plague." Lesthaeghe, *Decline,* 135–139. We can only guess what may have been occurring in confessionals in the Belgian Congo.

49. Van der Kerken, "Les oeuvres sociales," 9.

50. Jean-Luc Vellut, "Matériaux pour une image du blanc dans la société coloniale du Congo Belge," in *Stéréotypes nationaux et préjugés raciaux aux XIXe et XXe siècles,* ed. Jean Pirotte, Université de Louvain, Recueil de Travaux d'Histoire de Philologie, 6e série, fasc. 24 (Leuven, 1982), 100.

51. "La femme blanche au Congo," Instituts Solvay, Institut de Sociologie, Travaux du Groupe d'Etudes coloniales, no. 4, extract from *Bulletin de la Société Belge d'Etudes Coloniales,* no. 5, May 1910 (Brussels, 1910?), 9–10.

52. "La femme blanche," 8–9. Infant deaths among those 0 to 1 year old were recorded as 136.8 per 1,000 in 1930, dropping to 94.22 in 1935 and 31.4 in 1945. Belgium, Ministère des Colonies, *Rapports aux Chambres législatives sur l'administration du Congo Belge,* 1930, 12; 1935, 27; 1945–1946, 61. Mortality rates are rarely available in the annual reports. In 1925, 4.5 percent of white women died, 9 percent of white men died, and 24.7 percent of white children died; ibid., 1925, 10.

53. Vellut, "Matériaux," 97, 102.

54. This was partly in response to the murder of a European by an African, an incident which was interpreted as being committed in retribution for an adulterous episode between the European and the African's woman. Guebels, *Relation complete,* 318–321, 333, 423–424.

55. The passage continues, "In Africa, the sexuality of the native, his immoderate need of women, and the variety of them forms an atmosphere which impregnates bit by bit the white man. . . . Briefly, we can say that to send a single man into the bush and for a long time is against the nature of man as well as against the laws of sociability. Here it is necessary to talk of the danger of the black mistress. . . . [T]he nervous system of the white is not made to withstand the length of indigenous love which is not counted by hours and instants, but by days. Here, as elsewhere, sensations which are too strong brutalize the mind. This is why the little mischievous Negro, lively and industrious, becomes at puberty, a brute." Jean-Marie Habig, "Enseignement médical pour coloniaux, 2éme Partie, Psychophysiologie de l'européen et du noir," unpublished manuscript, Brussels: Ligue Coloniale Belge, Cours Coloniaux de Bruxelles, 1944, 10–11.

56. Ibid., 10.

57. Vellut, "Matériaux," 97, 103.

58. Etienne Glorieux, "La femme blanche au Congo," *Les Carnets de l'AUCAM,* 4 série, no. 8 (May 1929): 357.

59. In Elisabethville, the European population grew from scarcely 100 people in November 1910 to 1,031 in December 1911, including about 140 women. Twenty-five of these women were considered prostitutes; see Bruce Fetter, *The Creation of Elisabethville, 1910–1940* (Stanford, 1976), 29–31. Union Minière preferred to hire only single white men, and in the teens (1914) married men were permitted only if their wages reached a certain level and then only after a first term alone; see Charles Perrings, *Black Mineworkers in Central Africa* (London, 1979), 52. By the 1920s, the white population of Elisabethville became less one of single men of working age, as men began to be accompanied by their wives and children. White workers insisted that they be allowed to leave company compounds and live in bungalows in the European quarter of the town. In 1924, the disproportion between men and women remained more pronounced among white copper company employees (390 men per 100 women) than among the rest of the European population (170 men per 100 women); see Fetter, *Creation,* 95. Nevertheless, a general trend toward stabilizing white workers is evident. The proportion of the white workforce hired in Europe between 1929 and 1932 increased from 85 to 95 percent, while the proportion of them accompanied by their families during the same period increased from 33.3 percent to 68.7 percent; see Perrings, *Black Mineworkers,* 104 n. 20. For an important analysis of the relationship between the coming of European women to colonial settings and the stabilization of colonial rule, see Ann Laura Stoler, "Rethinking Colonial Categories: European Communities and the Boundaries of Rule," *Comparative Studies in Society and History* 31 (1989): 134–161.

60. The numbers of white women in the colony are rarely available in the annual reports. The number of white births is an indication of the increase in white women. Seventy births were registered in 1916, 104 in 1922, 507 in 1928, 612 in 1930, and 767 in 1940; Belgium, Ministere des Colonies, *Rapports aux Chambres législatives sur l'administration du Congo Belge,* 1916, 10; 1922, 22; 1928, 15; 1930, 12; 1945–1946, 62. There were 5,923 white women for 14,741 men in 1930 (40 percent); 4,357 for 9,094 in 1935 (47 percent); 11,989 for 17,746 in 1940 (61 percent); and 8,158 for 15,054 in 1945 (54 percent); ibid., 1945–1946, 62. On European women in the Belgian Congo, see the interesting collection of essays and documents in a special issue of *Enquêtes et*

Documents d'Histoire Africaine 7 (1987). On the *comité*'s work for poorer whites, see "La vie de nos comités," *Bulletin de l'Union des Femmes Coloniales* 15, no. 91 (May 1938): 4.

61. "La femme blanche," 11. Women of the best Belgian families avoided going until the 1940s; Vellut, "Matériaux," 97.

62. Glorieux, "La femme blanche," 356.

63. Habig, "Enseignment colonial," 10.

64. Glorieux, "La femme blanche," 357–358.

65. *La question sociale,* 103.

66. Laure Trolli, "Les femmes coloniales et l'enfance noire," *Bulletin de l'Union des Femmes Coloniales* 17, no. 112 (February 1940): 34.

67. *La question sociale,* 161.

68. "Puericulture," *Bulletin Médical du Katanga* 1, no. 2 (March 1924): 65. This journal was published by the medical services of the colonial government, Chemin du Fer du Katanga, and the principal copper mining company in Katanga, Union Minière du Haut-Katanga.

69. Dr. Boldyreff, "Le bébé en brousse," *Bulletin de l'Union des Femmes Coloniales* 14, no. 86 (December 1937): 20.

70. Ibid., 14, no. 85 (November 1937): 17; 14, no. 86 (December 1937): 20; 15, no. 87 (January 1939); 15, no. 89 (March 1938): 15.

71. Ibid., 15, no. 92 (June 1938): 14.

72. *La femme au Congo, Conseils aux partantes,* Publié par l'Union des Femmes Coloniales du Congo Belge et du Ruanda-Urundi sous l'égide du Ministère des Colonies (Brussels, 1956?), 74.

73. V. Cocq and Fr. Mercken, "L'assistance obstétricale au Congo Belge (y compris le Ruanda-Urundi)," *Gynécologie et Obstétrique* 31 (1935): 507–508.

74. Van der Kerken, "Les oeuvres sociales," 8.

75. R. Calonne, "Protection de l'enfance blanche et noire au Congo Belge," *Congrès Scientifique, Comptes Rendus, Elisabethville, 13–19 août 1950* (Brussels, 1950?), 137–138. Exactly what Calonne meant by the careful selection of parents is unclear.

76. "Puericulture," *Bulletin Médical du Katanga* 1, no. 2 (March 1924): 65. On the Union des Femmes Coloniale's work for poor whites, see "La vie de nos comites," *Bulletin de l'Union des Femmes Coloniales* 15, no. 91 (May 1938): 4.

77. *La question sociale,* 188.

78. L. Mottoulle, "Historique, organisation et résultats obtenus d'une oeuvre de protection de l'enfance noire dans la population indigène industrielle de l'Union Minière du Haut-Katanga," *Institut Royal Colonial Belge, Bulletin des Séances* 2, no. 2 (1931): 531. Perrings states that this program was founded in 1927, the same year that the mandatory contracts, the "main feature" of stabilization were introduced; see Perrings, *Black Mineworkers,* 79–83. Mottoulle's date of 1925 was the first year that recruits were authorized to bring their wives; later they were encouraged to do so.

79. Mottoulle, "Historique," 531–533.

80. R. van Nitsen [Médecin en Chef de l'UMHK], *L'Hygiène des travailleurs noirs dans les camps industriels du Haut-Katanga,* Mémoire, Institut Royal Colonial Belge, Section des Sciences naturelles et médicales, t. 1, fasc. 5, 1933, 137.

81. Ibid., 134–135.

82. Mottoulle, "Historique," 544.

83. Van Nitsen, *L'Hygiène des travailleurs*, 134–135. How the timing of this age reduction fits into the curtailment of production and the repatriation of numerous unskilled workers in 1931, the increase in production in 1933, and related changes in ratios of types of workers (skilled/unskilled, white/black) is unclear. Fetter argues that medical services were drastically cut in the early 1930s, whereas Perrings shows that increases in OPEN, hospital, and other "stabilization" costs increased between 1930 and 1932 at the same time that the proportion of women to men in the compounds increased from 40.7 to 64.4 percent. Fetter, *Creation*, 146, and Perrings, *Black Mineworkers*, 101–104. The role of nuns in the program is an indication of the close collaboration between the Catholic church and Union Minière. The extent to which the OPEN program as described by Van Nitsen and Mottoulle was actually a Benedictine "model camp" run for the company is unclear. See Jean-Luc Vellut, "Mining in the Belgian Congo," in *History of Central Africa*, Vol. 2, ed. David Birmingham and Phyllis M. Martin, 135 (London and New York, 1983).

84. Van Nitsen, *L'Hygiène des travailleurs*, 60.

85. Ibid., 134–135.

86. Ibid., 132–133. The double ration would have represented an incentive to breast feed, so clearly nursing was encouraged in the first months after birth. This encouragement of breast feeding in the early months after birth was in keeping with the ideas of puericulture experts and the operations of infant consultation programs in Belgium at the time; there was an appreciation of the immunological properties of breast feeding, even if the physiological factors involved were not yet entirely understood. It is also possible that, in keeping with Budin's teachings, breast milk substitutes might have been given during these months only to those women deemed *unable* to produce an adequate quantity of milk.

87. *Ibid.*, 57–58.

88. L. Mottoulle, *Politique sociale de l'Union Minière du Haut-Katanga et ses résultats au cours de vingt années d'application*, Mémoire, Institut Royal Colonial Belge, Section des Sciences Morales et Politiques, t. 14, f.3, 1946, 25.

89. A. S. McNeilly, "Effects of Lactation on Fertility," *British Medical Bulletin* 35, no. 2 (1979): 151–154. See also Harrell, "Lactation and Menstruation in Cultural Perspective."

90. From today's vantage point, it might seem that there would be increasing infant morbidity and mortality rates because weaned, mess hall-fed infants would no longer be protected by the immunological properties of breast milk. The Union Minière doctors' intentions were as much to reduce infant mortality as they were to increase fertility, and as will be shown below, they achieved both. It is likely that hygienic conditions and milk substitute preparations were excellent; Miriam H. Labock, "Contraception During Lactation: Considerations in Advising the Individual and in Formulating Programme Guidelines," *Journal of Biosocial Science*, Supplement, 9 (1985): 46.

91. In addition to cash allowances of 10 francs for wives and a comparable figure for each child, a bonus of 25 francs was paid every time a child was born in the compounds. The amount was doubled if the mother was under OPEN care. Perrings, *Black Mineworkers*, 81–83.

92. George Chauncey, Jr., "The Locus of Reproduction: Women's Labour in the Zambian Copperbelt, 1927–1953," *Journal of Southern African Studies* 7 (1981): 135–164.

93. It appears that social welfare and maternal and infant medical services were generally introduced later on the Zambian Copperbelt, and more as a way to keep idle women busy than to change their infant care practices and reduce birth intervals. See Jane Parpart, "Class and Gender on the Copperbelt: Women in Northern Rhodesian Copper Mining Communities, 1926–1964," in *Women and Class in Africa*, ed. Claire Robertson and Iris Berger (New York, 1986); and Perrings, *Black Mineworkers*, 199. Fetter argues that the Union Minière camps were more paternalistic and authoritarian than those of the Zambian Copperbelt, in *Creation*, 150.

94. Bruce Fetter, "Relocating Central Africa's Biological Reproduction, 1923–1963," *International Journal of African Historical Studies* 19, no. 3 (1986): 466. The fact that it was not only stabilization but reproduction that the company desired is evident in the birth gifts given to women, the training of sons as apprentices of their fathers, and the general emphasis on birth statistics in the company literature. On the training of boys as apprentices, see Van Nitsen, *L'Hygiène des travailleurs*, 119.

95. Mottoulle, "Historique," 532.

96. Calonne, "Protection de l'enfance," 142.

97. Mottoulle, "Politique sociale," 62.

98. Ibid., 31.

99. Calonne, "Protection de l'enfance," 145.

100. J. Lenelle and M. Parent, "Le problème du nourrisson noir au Katanga," *Congrès Scientifique, Comptes Rendus, Elisabethville 13–19 août 1950* (Brussels, 1950?), 127–132.

101. Ibid.

102. Jean-Luc Vellut has sketched a history of changes in the "moral economy of the [Belgian] colonizers." It represents an important beginning for thinking about the periodic shifts in medical and philanthropic intervention in the Belgian Congo. Jean-Luc Vellut, "Détresse matérielle et découvertes de la misère dans les colonies Belges d'Afrique Centrale, ca. 1900–1960," in *La Belgigue et l'étranger aux XIXe et XXe siècles,* ed. Michel Dumoulin and Eddy Stolls, 147–186 (Louvain-La Neuve, 1987). Future research might do better in terms of integrating the chronological swaths and the trends I shall suggest here in a more complete, illuminating way.

103. Trolli, "Les femmes coloniales," 33–34.

104. Neujean, "Protection maternelle et infantile," 928.

105. René-Jules Cornet, *Bwana Muganga (Hommes en blanc en Afrique noire),* Mémoire, Académie Royale des Sciences d'Outre-mer, Classe des Sciences morales et politiques, n.s., t. 41, fasc. 1, 1971, 274–278.

106. Trolli, "Les femmes coloniales," 34. The number of local children enrolled in Kwango consultations were estimated to rise from 30 to 85 percent between 1938 and 1959. Between 1932 and 1959, infant mortality for Kwango children under one dropped from 15.6 to 6.6 percent. The growth rate of the Kwango population, which was estimated as nil in 1942, reached 25 percent in 1958; G. Neujean, "La protection maternelle et infantile," in *Livre Blanc,* vol. 2 (Brussels, 1962), 931.

107. Trolli, "Les femmes coloniales," 33. On company programs, see General Moulaert, "Les oeuvres sociales aux Mines de Kilo," *Bulletin de l'Union des Femmes*

Coloniales 15, no. 98 (December 1938): 12–13; and E. Dupont, "Le développement des Oeuvres médico-sociales dans le Haut-Uele," *Bulletin du Comité Cottonier Congolais* 8, no. 23 (December 1948): 51–52.

108. G. Neujean, *L'Oeuvre Reine Astrid pour la mère et l'enfant indigene,* Mémoire, Académie Royal des Sciences Coloniales, Classe des sciences naturelles et médicales, n.s., t. 6, fasc. 1, 1957, 9–11.

109. Of those infant consultations inventoried, 146 were personally supervised by a doctor, 233 were operated by a nurse directed monthly by a doctor, 105 by nurses occasionally supervised by a doctor, and 400 "annex" consultations. FOREAMI, *Rapport annuel,* 1956, 67.

110. Bianga, "La politique démographique," 192.

111. Leo Lejeune, "L'enfance noire," *Bulletin de l'Union des Femmes Coloniales* 15, no. 88 (February 1938): 10–11.

112. "Les oeuvres sociales féminines au Congo, Le berceau du Kasai," *Bulletin de l'Union des Femmes Coloniales* 15, no. 96 (October 1938): 7.

113. The Oeuvre du Vêtement Congolais, founded in 1903, had 65 workshops in Belgium in 1938 when it sent 12,000 pieces of clothing to the colony; Mme van der Kerken, "Les Oeuvres sociales," 5–6. The Union des Femmes Coloniales received knitted cotton clothes made by the Dames de la Métropole and young girls in Belgian schools. FOREAMI supplied cotton to anyone who wanted to participate; 1,088 items were received in 1935 and 6,000 in 1938; Trolli, "Les femmes coloniales," 34.

114. "La vie de nos comités," *Bulletin de l'Union des Femmes Coloniales* 15, no. 19 (May 1938): 4.

115. "Les oeuvres sociales," 7.

116. Ibid., 8.

117. "Rapport des different comités locaux aux Congo," *Bulletin de l'Union des Femmes Coloniales* 15, no. 93 (July 1938): 19.

118. K. Holemans, *Contribution à la protection maternelle et infantile en milieu rural du Kwango,* Mémoire, Académie royale des sciences d'outre-mer, Classe des sciences naturelles et médicales, n.s., t. X., fasc. 1, 1960, 252.

119. Guebels, *Rélation complète,* 651–652.

120. Jean King and Ann Ashworth, "Historical Review of the Changing Pattern of Infant Feeding in Developing Countries: The Case of Malaysia, the Caribbean, Nigeria and Zaire," *Social Science and Medicine* 25 (1987): 1315.

121. Lenelle and Parent, "Le problème du nourrisson," 136.

122. K. Holemans, *Les carences alimentaires au Kwango,* Mémoire, Institut Royal Colonial Belge, Section des Sciences naturelles et médicales, t. 25, fasc. 3, 1954, 8. This program of milk distribution began in 1952 and was still under way in 1954.

123. Ibid., 3, 35.

124. Holemans, *Les carences alimentaires;* Holemans, *Contribution à la protection Maternelle;* K. Holemans and H. Martin, "Etude de l'allaitement maternel et des habitués du sevrage chez les indigènes du Kwango." *Annales de la Société Belge de Médicine Tropicale* 34 (1954): 915–923; J. Close, A. Van de Walle, and E. Robyans, "La composition du lait de femme au Congo belge, L, L'azote total." *Annales de la Société Belge de Médecine Tropicale* 37 (1957): 191–201; and J. Close and A. Van de Walle, "La composition du lait de femme au Congo belge, IL., Les acidés aminés

totaux du Colostrum," *Annales de la Société Belge de Médicine Tropicale* 37 (1957): 203–224.

125. "Brides' Courses at Matana," *Congo Mission News* (April 1954), 20–22. This British missionary society had posts in both the Belgian Congo and in the adjacent Belgian territory, Ruanda-Urundi.

126. Robert Maistriaux, *La femme et le destin de l'Afrique* (Elisabethville, 1964), 237.

127. Ibid., 240–241. Abrupt weaning was further thought to have a harmful impact on physical, affective, and intellectual development so that the child would "often take refuge in a desolate passivity, punctuated by aggressive somersaults"; ibid., 244. Although Maistriaux's psychological notion of "aggressive somersaults" may have been inspired by the turbulence of decolonization in the Congo, the idea that unscheduled breast feeding was a "deadly habit" was expressed by a French doctor in a manual on infant feeding and infant consultation programs in 1902; A.-B. Marfan, *Traité de l'Allaitement et de l'Alimentation des enfants du premier age* (Paris, 1902), 286, 561–562.

128. Maurist Dony, *Mashauri kwa Mama wa Kongo* (Brussels, 1953?), 32. The fact that the Swahili version somewhat garbled the instruction—saying "kwa muda wa saa tatu" (for periods of three hours) rather than "kila muda wa saa tatu" (every three hours)—would not have facilitated acceptance of the instructions; ibid., 31. There is no evidence that the emphasis on separate beds for mothers and children, the avoidance of nighttime nursing, and scheduled feeding also entailed conscious awareness that this reduction in suckling episodes might reduce the period of lactational anovulation. There has been research done indicating that this is the case. See McNeilly, "Effects of Lactation"; and Harrell, "Lactation and Menstruation." Short mentions the particular importance that abandoning nighttime feeding may have for the resumption of ovulation; R. V. Short, "Breast Feeding," *Scientific American* 250, no. 4 (April 1984): 38.

129. Dony, *Mashauri,* esp. p. 24.

130. G. Janssens, *La mortalité infantile aux Mines de Kilo, Etude basé e sur 1873 autopsies,* Mémoire, Institut Royal Colonial Belge, Section des Sciences naturelles et médicales, t. 20, f. 4, 1952, 117–118. There is a discrepancy between Janssens's argument that supplementary feeding should begin after four to five months and the instructions given in the FOREAMI booklet of the same era noted above (at seven months). The issue of when weaning and supplementary feeding should commence was clearly one of disagreement. In 1902, Doctor Marfan recommended that European infants [in Europe] be given no other food but milk for 8 to 9 months; Marfan, *Traité de l'Allaitement,* 565. While it was recommended that Congolese children be weaned at around 12 months in 1922 ("at this moment your milk is no longer worth anything"), by 1931, weaning was recommended after 8 to 9 months. Docteur Spire, *Conseils d'Hygiène aux Indigènes* (Brussels, 1922), 43; M. le Dr. David and M. le Dr. Dubois, *Vade-Mécum à l'usage des Infirmiers et des Assistants médicaux indigènes* (Brussels, 1931), 203. A Belgian puericulture guide written by the chief medical adviser of the Belgian infant welfare movement in the mid-1940s advised beginning weaning [in Belgium] in the seventh month, ending in the ninth or tenth month; Garot, *Médicine sociale,* 234. These instructions concur closely with those of the FOREAMI booklet.

Janssens, then, appears to have been an advocate of yet even earlier weaning—both in the colony and in the metropole.

131. Docteur Vincent, "L'enfance noire," *La femme et le Congo* 28, no. 161 (April 1958): 2–6.

132. Lenelle and Parent, "Le Problème du nourrisson," 133–134.

133. Maistriaux, *La femme,* 93–94.

134. Bervoets and Lassance, *Modes et coutûmes,* 64.

135. Many nurse according to the "self-demand principle" today, as has been pointed out for Shi and Havu women in the Kivu region. Hernart and Vis, "Breast-feeding," 177.

136. Holemans, *Les carences alimentaires,* 28–29.

137. Maistriaux, *La femme,* 98, 235.

138. Ibid., 236, 243.

139. Bervoets and Lassance, *Modes et coutûmes,* 48. As one of the IJAHS readers of this piece kindly pointed out, lactose intolerance (genetic deficiency of the lactase enzyme in adulthood) may have been one factor in this food avoidance. On this topic, see Frederick J. Simoons, "The Determinants of Dairying and Milk Use in the Old World: Ecological, Physiological and Cultural," *Ecology of Food and Nutrition* 2 (1973): 83–90; and G. Eichinger Ferro-Luzzi, "Commentary: Lactase Malabsorption Reconsidered," *Ecology of Food and Nutrition* 9 (1980): 247–356.

140. Bervoets and Lassance, *Modes et coutûmes,* 47.

141. See *Bulletin de l'Union des Femmes Coloniales* 15, no. 88 (February 1938): 11. Raising livestock was impossible in extensive areas of the Congo, so the use of imported substitutes is not surprising.

142. Bervoets and Lassance, *Modes et coutûmes,* 48.

143. Ibid., 47.

144. Ibid.

145. This was also because of colonial policy: imported products had fixed prices and were in constant supply in the cities, whereas oddly enough local foods could be difficult to find in the market. In the cities of Equateur and Kasai provinces condensed milk was respectively the tenth and fourth most commonly purchased imported product. In Orientale province, condensed milk was the third most commonly purchased imported product in the urban areas and powdered milk the sixteenth; condensed was the third in the rural areas. Ibid., 96–98.

146. Ibid., 50.

147. Ibid., 64.

148. Ibid., 49.

149. Ibid., 48–50.

150. Neujean, "Protection maternelle et infantile," 931.

151. "The volume of the milk secretion does not diminish before two and one-half years. If during the first semester of lactation, the milk volume of the indigenous woman is inferior (on the order of 50 percent) to the normal volume conceded for the white woman, one cannot but be struck by the great quantities of milk produced after two years of lactation. In fact, these quantities are superior to those produced around three to four months, a period in which, in the white woman, the production of milk achieves its maximum." Holemans, *Contribution à la protection maternelle,* 47. The contrast likely

reflected differences in the frequency and intensity of nursing, maternal diet, and supplementary infant feeding patterns.

152. Ibid., 51.

153. One susceptible period identified by Holemans was between 4 and 12 months if breast milk was insufficient, because supplementary foods appropriate for an infant of this age were not available; and the other was after weaning, that is, at the age of 3 years. Holemans, *Contribution à la protection maternelle*, 243–244.

154. There is no question that European women were extolled as paragons and practitioners in colonial discourse. The extent to which they played a critical role in the functioning and shaping of programs should not be exaggerated, however, more research is needed on their numbers, backgrounds, activities, and changing relations with other colonial actors.

155. *La question sociale*, 95. On problems with bottle vs. breast dichotomies, see Dana Raphael, "Weaning Is Always: The Anthropology of Breastfeeding Behavior," *Ecology of Food and Nutrition* 15 (1984): 203–213.

156. *La question sociale*, 138.

157. Caldwell and Caldwell, "The Demographic Evidence," 12.

158. "Les oeuvres," 7.

159. Holemans, *Contribution à la protection maternelle*, 255.

160. More research is needed on the extent to which African women in particular cultural areas historically changed and have since resumed aspects of customary infant feeding practices. In a recent important article, King and Ashworth assume that because most Zairian mothers use "traditional paps" today and because artificial milk and especially infant formula are widely unavailable that "most mothers still adhere to their traditional feeding practices." King and Ashworth, "Historical Review," 1310. It would be a mistake to assume that "tradition" has been either continuous or unchanged, especially in light of colonial agendas and programs.

161. Maistriaux, *La femme*, 235.

9

Tradition in the Service of Modernity

Architecture and Urbanism in French Colonial Policy, 1900–1930

Gwendolyn Wright

When the Parisian art critic Léandre Vaillat visited Morocco in the 1920s, he was enraptured with what he saw. Casablanca and especially Rabat seemed to represent the convergence of two diametrically opposed paths for twentieth-century cities: a modern vision of wide, orderly streets coexisted, apparently peacefully, with the picturesque charm of the indigenous North Africa madina, a setting adapted to a more traditional way of life. Morocco, Vaillat wrote, is "a laboratory of Western life and a conservatory of Oriental life."[1]

Like other astute European visitors, Vaillat recognized that this cultural imagery constituted an essential element of the French colonial presence. For historians today the strategies become even more clear: urban design—sometimes used in radically different ways within the same city—assumed a major role in efforts to make colonialism more popular among Europeans and more tolerable to the colonized peoples. Administrators of three French colonies of the early twentieth century—Indochina, Madagascar, and, most notably, Morocco—consciously used urban culture as a cornerstone of their political endeavors. Their notion of culture, by no means monolithic, emphasized variety and simultaneity—what the literary critic Mikhail Bakhtin, describing an earlier period in French cultural life, called "heteroglossia."[2] The colonial understanding of the term derived from a new appreciation of different aesthetics, both vernacular and refined, traditional and contemporary, indigenous and European; it also signaled a recognition of culture in a more anthropological sense, as values, as ways of living that varied from one group to another, even within a city. Administrators brought in professional advisers to interpret these various cultural meanings and then applied the research to their political goals.

For colonial officials, each aspect of culture had definite references to power. If social conventions acted out in public and private spaces formed a complex ritual of order, then upholding certain conventions seemed a way to prevent resistance to colonial authority—seen as a breakdown of social order. In Morocco, for example, when the French took power in 1912, Sultan Moulay-Hafid was forced to abdicate in favor of his more conciliatory brother, Moulay-Youssef; this required, the French resident-general then explained, "reviving around the [new] sultan the ancient traditions and old ceremonies of the court," as well as building and maintaining opulent palaces for the ruler.[3] Such officials hoped to preserve an established sense of hierarchy and propriety, buttressing it with what they perceived to be traditional rituals, spatial patterns, and architectural ornament, believing that this would reinforce their own super-imposed order.

Simultaneously, however, officials also experimented with settings and policies conducive to a technologically advanced, economically diversified urban world. This was most evident in the streamlined office buildings and apartment buildings of the European sections of colonial cities, but it also appeared in the public health dispensaries, the public works, and the industrial expansion that involved the entire colonial population. The modernist imagery of buildings paralleled efforts to stimulate more investment and train more productive workers, in keeping with the budgetary requirements of 1900 that all French colonies become economically self-sufficient. The goal, in sum, was to protect certain aspects of cultural traditions while sponsoring other aspects of modernization (fig. 9.1).

Because of its rich complexity and the extreme milieu of power in which it was carried out, this colonial urbanism helps orient us to the possible uses and inequities of various urban policies. As Vaillat made clear, the proposals and achievements of Morocco in the 1910s and 1920s, like those of Indochina and Madagascar, represent a particular version of modern urbanism, an approach more responsive to local history and culture than that of the European architectural avant-garde. Yet the two versions should not be seen as antagonistic. The cities of these three colonies, especially their European districts, exemplified many of the principles espoused by avant-garde modernists: more standardized construction, more rationalized organization of public services and industry, efficient circulation routes, and greater attention to the hygienic aspects of design, such as the need for ample fresh air and sunlight. For us, this alternative model, by the absolutist and authoritarian ways in which it was implemented, actually brings into focus some of the underlying problems of the modernist vision as a whole. Unequal access to the benefits of modern urbanism, while more visible in colonial cities, affected other metropolises as well; so, too, with the loss of autonomy and even livelihood for many handicraft workers, an uneconomical com-mitment to inappropriate materials and techniques, the tendency toward

Figure 9.1.   An idealized mural of a skyscraper rising from the jungle wilderness at the Colonial Exposition of 1931 in Paris symbolized the synthesis of modernity and tradition. (Reprinted with the permission of the Musée des Arts Africains et Océaniens, Paris.)

class and ethnic segregation implicit in zoning policies, and overreliance on expertise.

Moreover, one can discern some of the inherent problems in what we now call postmodernism, in many ways a legacy of the historically minded urbanism of the colonies, by studying this somewhat exaggerated case.[4] As specialists chose certain historic monuments to isolate and venerate, promoting particular stylistic idioms as prototypical forms, architectural design could no longer be considered the complex product of a diverse culture. The variety of forms and uses within any society, the ongoing adaptations of styles, now seemed inchoate to educated professionals. The gulf between ''architecture'' and ordinary building grew wider, while the historic fabric of cities was commercialized into a tourist commodity, an expression of quaint charm. Most important, the effort to replace certain groups' actual involvement in political life with a purely visual expression of their cultural autonomy demonstrates one of the ways in which historicist design, in many different settings, can be used for political power.

Common elements between metropolitan and colonial urban policies make it easier to understand, and therefore to evaluate, some of the implications of both resolutely modernist and more traditionalist approaches to urban design, wherever they are used. Such parallels and comparisons should not be dismissed as far-fetched. Indeed, in the early decades of the twentieth century, the accomplishments of colonial policies seemed to offer a direct and highly regarded contrast with the situation in France itself. Years later, after he had returned to France from Morocco, the urbanist Henri Prost looked back on the frustration that had characterized this period at home: ''One had to have lived in Paris around 1900 to understand the motives [for the urban reforms that followed in the colonies]. One had to have witnessed the disintegration of the grand STATE ADMINISTRATION that, from Sully to Colbert to Haussmann, had assured the harmony of our cities, in order to understand the anguish that afflicted young people before 1900.''[5] Such young people included future colonial urbanists like Prost, Ernest Hébrard of Indochina, and Georges Cassaigne of Madagascar, and also French leaders of the European avant-garde like Le Corbusier (who undertook his first plan for Algiers in 1930) and Tony Garnier (a close associate of Prost and Hébrard in their youth). Each of these architects had sought to reorient his work from the individual building to the larger urban conglomeration, albeit each with a personal cast. Yet most modernists and traditionalists alike were thwarted in their efforts to find meaningful work in France. In terms of urban theory, legislation, and actual policies, the country seemed at an impasse, despite the fact that many nonarchitects were equally concerned that their cities now lagged behind those of England, the United States, and, most disturbingly, Germany. Issues as varied as the low national birthrate, the dramatic rise in suicides and other expressions of mental illness, morbidity rates (especially for tuberculosis) that surpassed those of other European countries, poor industrial productivity, class antagonisms and regional conflicts, an inadequate housing stock, and a perceived decline in national prestige since the humiliation of the Franco-Prussian War—all these had urbanistic implications. But even though moral degeneracy and physical debilitation seemed especially grave in metropolitan areas, proposals to correct the situation could seldom generate enough support to be implemented.[6]

The cities of the French colonies did provide an exception to the apathy, a setting for transforming the concerns of intellectuals and architects into policies, for putting theories into practice. After all, colonial officials needed policies that could effectively quell the possibility of social unrest and encourage economic development; they required homes and workplaces for French settlers and for the indigenous populations drawn to the new colonial metropolises; and most of all, the political system provided policy makers with a degree of authority for carrying out their plans that simply did not exist in Paris, Marseille, or Lille. Writing in Morocco in 1914, Hubert Lyautey, head of the new protectorate, expressed his belief that the regulations he had recently promulgated would bring stability and prosperity and relieve the "urban malaise," much as similar legislation was doing "in New York, Brussels, Frankfurt, and Lausanne"—each in distinct contrast to Paris.[7]

Given this impetus, theory and practice in the colonies always, to a great extent, referred back to France—both its capital city and its provincial centers. The contrast between the *métropole* and the *outre-mer* suggests some of the reasons these experiments generated so much interest in France. For many fin-de-siècle Frenchmen, experimentation in the colonies seemed a way of inducing new spirit and vigor for all aspects of their national life. As Joseph Chailley-Bert wrote in 1903, introducing the French public to the impassioned speeches of Theodore Roosevelt, "New blood is infused by youth into the elderly, by the young colonies into the old *métropole.*"[8] On both the Right and the Left, the outre-mer seemed a place for working out the social, political, and aesthetic dilemmas of France, to apply the positive results to the mother country. An article on Hébrard's plan for the Indo-Chinese mountain station of Dalat praised his insistence on strict zoning, commenting that a policy "at first criticized in the name of liberty was, several years later, accepted as a safeguard against the kinds of industrial intrusions we suffer from so much in the *métropole.*" "In Morocco people believe in urbanism," wrote Vaillat in 1931, "while in France they do not. I cannot help comparing the results of this faith and skepticism."[9]

Indochina, Madagascar, and, above all, Morocco were much talked and written about throughout the French-speaking world and beyond during these years. They were seen as "laboratories"; again and again they were called *champs d'expérience,* or experimental terrains.[10] But in fact the colonial cities did not provide a significant model or even a much-needed incitement for replanning cities at home. Only with the Vichy government and post–World War II reconstruction would France enact and carry out major urban reforms, and this in a modernist vein that was openly hostile to history and regionalism.[11] Nonetheless, the concept of colonial cities as laboratories is important. First, the very idea drew together an extraordinary amount of professional talent. Second, the work of these individuals—administrators, architects, physical and social scientists—provides insights into the beliefs and strategies that fueled twentieth-century colonialism. Finally, the writings and accomplishments of these professionals provide us with a vantage for analyzing two contemporaneous variations of modernism in architecture and urban design—a more avant-garde or universalist version and a more traditionalist or cultural-relativist approach—and thereby an understanding of how each can be allied with power, in the past or in our own day. Considering the important recent efforts of historians to integrate cultural phenomena into social and political history, these experiments offer a striking example of how culture and politics could each be formative, one helping to shape the other.[12]

The very word "laboratory" resounded in many different circumstances in the early twentieth century, of course, but the colonial context gave it a very definite meaning. Here one could appraise firsthand the actual conditions of quite diverse settings and, simultaneously, distill general principles, whether about the nature of cities or the influence of religion; moreover, it was possible to consider and even act on the political ramifications of various ideas. In particular, two professions just emerging in France at the turn of the century but as yet unable to find official support for their expertise—urbanism and the social sciences—discovered in the colonies the opportunities denied them at home. Many French social scientists, including the anthropologist Lucien Lévy-Bruhl and the geographer Augustin Bernard, found the chance there to explore their theories about social structure or residential environments, among other topics.[13] They discussed ideas in prestigious research centers like the Institut des Hautes Études Marocaines, the École Française d'Extrême-Orient, or the Académie Malgache and often evolved their speculations into directives for the colonial governments. And it was in the colonies that would-be urban planners like Prost and Hébrard were given their first opportunities to plan and build on a genuinely metropolitan scale, for their predilections, too, fit in with the political strategies of a new generation of colonial administrators.

Indeed, at the turn of the century, the social and aesthetic issues championed by these social scientists and urbanists quickly became key aspects of a new French colonial policy called "association." To most observers, the underlying premises of the earlier nineteenth-century approach, called "assimilation," were twofold: French cultural predominance in language, laws, and even architectural style—the famous *mission civilisatrice*—and French military prowess demonstrated through destruction of indigenous cities and towns and embodied in a continuing, visible military presence. In contrast, most advocates of association called for the preservation of distinctive local cultures, including tribal councils and historic monuments, and they believed that this respect, when combined with social services like schools and hospitals, could counter resistance far more effectively than military strength.[14] Precisely at the moment that the nineteenth-century policy of assimilation was coming under attack—partly for moral reasons, but as much on the pragmatic grounds that it had proved to be politically and economically inefficient—colonial opportunities for the new generation of French urbanists and social scientists opened up. The policy of association that they implemented thus tended to have a strong basis in cultural sensibility and urban planning, ranging from issues of historic preservation and building style to the distribution of public services.

Let us now follow the basic principles of this phase of colonial urbanism into actual practice. Morocco, Indochina, and Madagascar each represent archetypical and distinct examples of an urbanistic association policy. In each case political problems were defined in cultural terms that gave urban planning and architectural design a central importance in consolidating political power. These problems—residential and commercial development, administrative centralization and industrial expansion, and the creation of a healthy, trained labor force—were familiar in France as well as in the colonies, articulating clearly the colonies' potential role as laboratories for metropolitan cities. In each instance, as part of their experimental mode, administrators and their consultants sought specifically to mitigate the disruption caused by modernist urban reforms by actively engaging traditional architectural forms and attuning themselves to the ways in which various cultural groups typically responded to the city.

The first example is also the best known. As resident-general of the new protectorate of Morocco between 1912 and 1925, Hubert Lyautey refined his concept of the "dual city," which we would call a form of geographic "association."[15] This entailed, first, the strict preservation of ancient artifacts, mosques, street fronts, and other kinds of ordinary cultural forms in the Arab cities. The Service des Antiquités, Beaux-Arts, et Monuments Historiques, established during the early months of the protectorate, gave its director, a former Beaux-Arts student by the name of Maurice Tranchant de Lunel, unprecedented powers to regulate new construction and protect existing buildings in the old Moroccan madinas. The policies of this office even show a certain awareness of the dangers of speculation in historic districts. The staff was advised that "the beauty and historic interest of Moroccan architecture resides not only in the important monuments but also—even especially—in the ensemble of constructions."[16] Administrative measures to protect a single monument could not prevent its being surrounded by new buildings as land values increased, thereby losing its historic character even if the structure itself remained untouched. Accordingly, Tranchant de Lunel promulgated a detailed set of aesthetic requirements for all new buildings and renovations in the major Moroccan madinas.

Prost's Service d'Architecture et des Plans des Villes, established in 1914 (making it the first such governmental agency in the French world), was then charged with overseeing all forms of building in the *villes nouvelles* alongside the existing Moroccan cities (fig. 9.2).[17] The two settlements were always separated by a zone of *non aedificandi* where construction was forbidden, although the method and scale varied from one city to another. Fez, Marrakesh, and Meknes exemplify Prost's vision, with greenbelts ranging from two to three kilometers surrounding the walls of the old city, reinforced by geological

Figure 9.2. Prost's 1918 zoning plan for Casablanca shows the *ville nouvelle*—including the habous district in the *nouvelle madina*—fanning out from the small core of the original madina. (Reprinted with the permission of the Académie d'Architecture, Paris.)

barriers like the ravines of Meknes or the steep hills of Fez. In Rabat and Casablanca, European construction before Prost's arrival precluded this strategy, and he resigned himself to thoroughfares, two hundred fifty meters wide, augmented by large public parks. These barriers marked the distinctions between two parts of a city, setting off two scales of construction, two periods of history, and often two races. The term "sanitary corridor" suggests the health precautions also inherent in this familiar colonial policy. In an off-guard moment, Prost later acknowledged that the zone existed as well "for military reasons," allowing the rapid mobilization of French troops—yet we should not reduce all his intentions to any single motive.[18]

Sizable extensions beyond the existing Arab cities—from two to (in the case of Casablanca) twenty times larger than the madinas—served the minority population of French *colons.* This land, while sometimes purchased from previous Moroccan owners, was more often opened to development through changes in title or outright expropriation "in the public interest," using justifications from French and Quranic law.[19] The French villes nouvelles proudly displayed the tenets of modern urban design. Yet in these colonial settings, the urban imagery involved a self-conscious cultural synthesis that stressed its particular locale: from the West came the clean lines and strict design guidelines for buildings, the spacious thoroughfares and zoning regulations; from Morocco, local ornamental motifs in porcelain mosaics and cedar, together with architectural adaptations to the climate such as the *menzeh* (a pavilion with courtyard), *mashribiya* (interlaced screen), and walls of white *naqsh nadida* (stucco).

French administrators disputed charges that they were segregating the different races. They even claimed that their urban policies liberated Moroccan Jews by offering them greater economic and residential mobility since Arabs and Jews alike were allowed to live in the European districts—if they agreed to abide by its urbanistic principles and thereby adopt modern Western culture.[20] Lyautey claimed that his dual-city approach to urban design could clearly distinguish between the two districts and give each its particular form of expression. "Touch the indigenous cities as little as possible," he explained. "Instead, improve their surroundings where, on the vast terrain that is still free, the European city rises, following a plan that realizes the most modern conceptions of large boulevards, water and electrical supplies, squares and gardens, buses and tramways, and also foresees future extensions."[21] The system, while radical, drew on certain urban precedents in the area, for segregation of foreigners had ancient roots in North Africa, reaching back to Greek and Egyptian towns, to medieval Muslim *funduq* (hotel-warehouses) for Christians, and *mēllahs* for the Jews.[22] The French innovation extended such geographic divisions to an elaborate interplay of spatial and architectural distinctions, all the while paying homage to the indigenous culture they had isolated.

However, Lyautey's assertion that improvements and extensions could be limited to the European districts and still benefit the Moroccans did not anticipate the rapid growth of the Arab populations in the expanding cities. By the time of World War I, overcrowding and the growth of bidonvilles had become inescapable problems, especially in Casablanca and Rabat, where the French villes nouvelles effectively walled in the older madinas; for reasons of health, political unrest, and cultural image, the French now had to consider new urban settlements for the Moroccans.

Claiming land from Islamic religious foundations called habous (*hubus*)—land known even now as habous districts (Derb el-Hubus, in Arabic)—colonial urbanists in Prost's service undertook the design of streets, houses, and public buildings that would harmonize, though not be continuous, with those in the old madinas. These sites featured services that had been lacking or grossly inadequate in the older Arab cities, even under French occupation, including better drainage and public water supplies, wider commercial streets for cars (side streets were kept narrow and cars prohibited there), and some municipal upkeep. In site plan and detail the referents were not modern but, rather, the traditional principles of Moroccan architecture and the established mores of Moroccan urban life. In the smaller habous district of Rabat, overseen by Pierre Michaud, one finds an appreciation of the basic tenets of local urban design: the plain facades of private houses, relieved by distinctive doorways that never faced the entry across the street, contrast strikingly with the elaborate complexity of the market areas. The principal architect of Casablanca's habous district, Albert Laprade, had filled sketchbooks with watercolors and measured drawings of "the poor dwellings of Rabat and Salé" in preparation for the project. "Every house was designed with love," he wrote of the new designs. "We taxed our ingenuity to create the maximum impression of serendipity, so dear to the Muslim."[23]

Laprade's oversimplified generalization about Islamic aesthetics suggests a darker side to the apparent cultural sensitivity, quite similar to the academic prejudices and policies Edward Said has labeled "Orientalism."[24] The habous districts are Western stage settings for Moroccan life, evoking the supposed harmonies of a traditional way of life that, in the Westerner's eyes, did not change over time. These architects fell prey to the desire for stopping time and history that is always implicit in a preservation campaign, yet the rationale goes deeper than their own tendency to romanticize. Colonialism did not provide for innovation or progress in the Moroccan districts; this prospect the French had reserved for themselves. Aesthetic predilections therefore had a definite political aspect, freezing Moroccan economic and political development at an archaic level of the picturesque, in sharp contrast to the visible advances and opportunities available to Europeans. Lyautey once again explained the matter straightforwardly when he told a gathering in Paris, "Since the recent, intense development of large-scale tourism, the presentation of a country's beauty has taken on an economic importance of the first order. To attract a large tourist population is to gain everything for both the public and the private budgets."[25]

This dual urban agenda therefore sought to control the cultural vitality of colonial cities, even as it assiduously studied the local culture. The villes nouvelles exhibited both European and Moroccan themes in their urban design, suggesting there was no inherent conflict. Similarly, the French promoted modernity for the Arabs through the exploitation of indigenous people and natural resources by French commercial interests, while at the same time they sustained the past, both for political reasons and for exploitation by French tourists who wanted to see charm and authenticity.

One finds an intriguing parallel, both aesthetic and political, in the French efforts to control the governmental apparatus of their far-distant colony, Indochina. Here, too, urbanism, balancing contemporary concerns with historicist sympathies, played a key role in defining political strategy. The very decision, in 1921, to bring in a professional urbanist as a governmental adviser derived from the renown of Lyautey's and Prost's work in Morocco, and it was with Prost's recommendation that Ernest Hébrard was chosen for the post.[26] Like Prost, his friend and colleague in the small but determined Société Française des Urbanistes, Hébrard wanted to strike a balance between industrial growth and cultural respect, between modernism and tradition. In this case, the political goal involved increased administrative prestige and efficiency, tempered with a suggestion of greater Vietnamese involvement in the government, in an effort to turn the colony into an asset for France. Hébrard's first duties therefore all concerned administrative design: a new scheme for the governmental quarter of Hanoi, capital of the Indo-Chinese Federation; an urban plan for the future summer capital of Dalat, in the Lang-Bian mountain range; and then, as part of these two larger projects, the design of several exemplary administrative buildings, ranging from the finance ministry to state schools and the museum of the École Française d'Extrême-Orient (fig. 9.3).

Both the decision to rely on large-scale, coordinated complexes of buildings and the specification that individual structures respond more visibly to their local context signaled a major shift from nineteenth-century colonial practice in Vietnam. Since the French took control of Saigon in 1862, their public buildings had been sited almost randomly, the individual grandiose forms derived solely from the principles of Beaux-Arts formalism—ornamental references to classical and baroque monuments, the plan generating the basic proportions of the elevation, the whole a visible expression of the supposed universality of Western concepts of order and beauty. This was, in other words, an architectural expression of the assimilationist policy toward colonial cultures, criticizing any intrusion of indigenous architectural forms as "métis."[27] By the post–World War I years, however, it no longer seemed prudent to insist on a single, unified image for French culture. Even at home, postwar rebuilding,

Figure 9.3.   Hébrard's museum of the Ecole Française d'Extrême-Orient in Hanoi, completed in 1931, grafted Southeast Asian decorative motifs and climactic accommodations onto a colonial institution. ("Musée Louis Finot," *Bulletin de l'Ecole Française d'Extrême-Orient*, 1933.)

whether for housing or public buildings, relied heavily on vernacular motifs from the region—and in 1920 the minister of colonies suggested that overseas administrators should study these efforts.[28] Consequently, Hébrard spent much time photographing and sketching indigenous architecture, from the high art of Angkor Wat or Buddhist pagodas to simple rural habitations, to find local antecedents for his official structures.[29]

Both instances actually signaled a rather superficial acknowledgment of cultural differences. Activists in the French provinces demanded economic and political decentralization, but they received only a formal deference to their particular needs in the newly fashionable regionalist architecture.[30] Even more insistent were the Vietnamese nationalists (Cochinchinese, Tonkinese, and especially Annamites were the most outspoken of the five nationalities brought together in the Indo-Chinese Federation) who, especially after their contribution to the French war effort, wanted greater respect and in many cases full autonomy for their own culture.[31] They, too, received only architectural concessions to their demands for local control. The substitution of what we could call "visual decentralization" for meaningful reform again suggests how political strategy could rely directly on aesthetics.

Political reality went beyond architectural details, to be sure. But the desire to decentralize authority often proves a difficult and ambiguous undertaking—certainly in a highly authoritarian situation like the colony of Indochina, and even in a highly centralized country like France. Thus when reformist governor-generals like Albert Sarraut and Maurice Long insisted on more positions for educated Indochinese, the result was simply a duplication (at lesser pay and prestige) of existing positions for French functionaries. Consequently, the government needed even more revenue to build more governmental offices, ministries, and customhouses for the larger staffs now at work in provincial towns and capital cities.[32] Neither "lateral cadres," as the new positions were called, nor indigenous styles for official buildings signaled a real shift in power relations.

The associationist suggestion of greater Vietnamese participation in colonial affairs also extended to industry. Governor-General Maurice Long, who created the Service d'Urbanisme for the colony in 1923, followed Sarraut in office, and he, like his predecessor, wanted to build up local industry—notably rubber plantations in the south and coal mining in the north. This, too, ultimately required a stronger governmental presence throughout the colony: new financial societies were founded; new public works projects, as well as private factories with governmental subsidies, were initiated; land for these "public purposes" had to be appropriated from the peasantry.[33] In addition, more offices for tax collection became necessary since most of the money for the public-sponsored work came from a state "loan," of which the Indochinese people themselves contributed 95 percent through increased taxes.[34] The 1920s were the decade of great economic expansion in Vietnam, and this *mise en valeur,* in the words of Albert Sarraut (now minister of colonies), relied in part on artificial expressions of mutual engagement and benefits.[35]

Such was the administrative system Hébrard was charged with designing. Yet his buildings, like those of lesser architects in the colony, superimposed a pastiche of exotic details on a Beaux-Arts plan. In any case, the main priority involved arrangements that would both aggrandize the colonial government and make it more efficient, even as it expanded. Long hoped Hébrard would bring the buildings and open space together in a manner that was "worthy of a great country."[36] This meant the familiar diagonal boulevards and isolated monuments of baroque urban design, looking back to France's "grand siècle."

Hébrard responded to his own century, too, with his careful planning for urban factories and automobile traffic. He outlined a zoning plan that restricted uses for different districts in every city. Although he insisted on the need for separation, it was to be primarily a juxtaposition of different classes and functions, overseen by the master urban planner, rather than the phobic racial segregation espoused by the local colons. Contact between the races was an inevitable part of colonial life, Hébrard contended, and it needed to be organized, sanitized, and rationalized.[37] Thus, by late 1922, the city of Saigon established a zone reserved for construction of "European-type houses"—permanent, detached, of minimum size and maximum occupancy.[38] Yet what amounted to racial segregation on medical or pseudofunctional grounds could easily lead to racial segregation on other grounds as well, as Philip D. Curtin has pointed out.[39] Hébrard's false trust in rational organization parallels his naive belief that zoning, joined with statistical studies of population growth and industrial expansion, could counter rampant speculation, another negative aspect of modern urban development.[40]

One should certainly not confuse these efforts at aesthetic reform, with their interplay of modernist and contextual themes, or the semblance of decentralization that accompanied them with a critique of colonialism and its inequalities. Hébrard and the officials with whom he worked wanted to modernize the forms of control, in part through demonstrations of their enlightened attitudes toward the cultures they dominated, in part through modern administrative efficiency and industrial expansion. Hébrard's Dalat fit the prescription for a modern colonial metropolis: it represented, wrote one of his associates, "a plan responding not only to the needs of a military camp, but also of a complete administrative capital that brings together all the functions of a government."[41] This more sophisticated concept of an urban center for political power went beyond earlier notions of military surveillance; it relied instead on modern industry and financial development, on education, art, and supposed cultural tolerance—all these unified and celebrated in new administrative surroundings.

New colonial settings were perhaps even more necessary in Madagascar, for this country had resisted occupation for almost a century, until 1895 (despite the presence of merchants and missionaries along the coast), in part by refusing to build roads or public services that would allow European access to the island's mountainous capital, Tananarive. General Joseph-Simon Galliéni, the first governor-general, initiated a massive public works campaign between 1896 and 1905, but, like his protégé Lyautey (who served under Galliéni in Indochina and Madagascar), Galliéni insisted on a modernizing effort that would not unnecessarily disrupt traditional patterns of life.[42] One exception was the abolishment of the institution of slavery. On September 27, 1896, after declaring Madagascar to be a possession of France, the chamber of deputies voted the immediate emancipation of all slaves in the new colony. This resulted in a large number of former slaves migrating to the capital, where they were recruited—forcibly, between 1896 and 1898, if they were vagabonds—for the construction of roads, hospitals, schools, and other services.

By the time of World War I, a combination of such immigration from the countryside and the challenge of an intensified nationalist movement seemed to warrant more extensive urban reforms for the capital city. But it was an epidemic of plague in 1918, augmenting the high mortality rates from malaria, that precipitated the first official plan for Tananarive, under the supervision of Governor-General Abraham Schrameck and Georges Cassaigne, a Beaux-Arts trained architect who had served as an urban adviser in the colony since 1900. Aware of Lyautey's and Prost's accomplishments in Morocco, Schrameck and Cassaigne emphasized a balance of traditionalist forms and modernist reforms.[43] Houses, markets, and other public buildings maintained the familiar, steeply pitched roof of local wood and thatch dwellings, albeit with more hygienic materials like tiles and brick, which were also native to the region.

For Cassaigne and the several officials he was to serve, public health represented the essence of modern urban planning, and, here as elsewhere, health seemed to depend on the separation of populations. A ring road of broad boulevards (completed in 1926, following Cassaigne's new plan of that year) provided both a modern traffic artery and a cordon sanitaire, in this case isolating the city from its medical zone: the Institut Pasteur and six quarantine hospitals for plague victims. Separation also referred to the "garden cities" on the outskirts of the capital, some for Malagasy workers near industrial sites, others for French functionaries near the administrative Place Colbert. Ideally the garden cities, three of which were built, would be linked to their respective workplaces and to the city center by a rapid transit system, but this was never put into effect because of budget constraints. Improvements, in Cassaigne's eyes at least, involved uncoercive changes that would not forcibly disrupt the temper of Malagasy life, so many aspects of his 1926 plan for the city, like that of 1918, were never realized.[44] The regional development, for instance, anticipated a spontaneous process of "decongestion" as colons and colonial subjects moved out of the central city—but crowding remained a problem. Moreover, building roads and extensions outside the city did not, as hoped, fully eliminate the mosquito-infested marshes and rice fields surrounding Tananarive, acknowledged to be a major source of malaria and still considered a critical menace to public health even today.

While public health remained a central concern, the tenor of Malagasy urban design began to change when Marcel Olivier became governor-general in 1924, championing a colonial policy more geared toward planned industrial productivity and social control. He hoped to solve the "crisis of manpower" by providing indigenous workers with "the maximum of moral health in the maximum of material comfort."[45] Like his friend Lyautey, Olivier saw urbanism as a key aspect of his political strategy. Accordingly, within two years, he created an official Conseil Supérieur d'Urbanisme to generate plans for every city on the island—the first of which was Cassaigne's 1926 plan for Tananarive.

The major impetus for the changes Olivier wished to see came in 1927 when a cyclone destroyed most of the coastal city of Tamatave—the first French capital and still an important port—requiring a new plan that would be implemented immediately.[46] The chief of this rebuilding effort, Jean de Cantelou, endorsed standardized construction and insisted on reinforced concrete as the most advanced, and hence the only acceptable, building material for official buildings. By the end of the year, de Cantelou was overseeing new construction throughout the colony. His Office d'Habitations Economiques designed flat-roofed *modèle-types* for Malagasy workers and functionaries, as well as larger prototypes for French bureaucrats; similarly, uniform models for administrative buildings, markets, and commercial structures emanated from the new Service d'Architecture et Urbanisme that he also headed (fig. 9.4).[47]

De Cantelou's unilaterally modernist approach to urban design fit with the more directive governmental policy under Olivier and his successor, Léon Cayla. As the urbanist told a conference in Paris, "We have quit the technical terrain to enter into the realm of social politics, of which urbanism is evidentally one of the principal means of action."[48] However, the new policy illuminates certain problems that can emerge when modernist approaches to urbanism become a basis of "social politics." For example, the decision to rely on reinforced concrete proved to be exceedingly expensive since there were no limestone deposits on the island and cement had to be imported. Nonetheless, the new technology continued to dominate official construction, even after national independence in 1960. Moreover, the commitment to modern construction techniques had to use a system of forced labor to meet the government's new standards. In 1925 Olivier announced that all public works would henceforth be carried out by the Service de la Main d'Oeuvre des Travaux d'Intêret Général. Known as SMOTIG, the service consisted of Malagasy military recruits, all of whom were required by law to serve three years. In this way, as Olivier explained in a *charte de travail* that same year, governmental public works would not take potential laborers away from the colonial plantations and factories; in fact, "like a veritable school," SMOTIG camps would train future employees through environmental and work discipline in their new surroundings.[49]

The twenty-three "pioneer camps" for some eight thousand to ten thousand SMOTIG workers per year also show another effort to incorporate tradition into modern industrialization, for Olivier pointed out that corvées had been an aspect of earlier Merina tribal rule, of Galliéni's first French government, and even of the eighteenth-century French ancien régime.[50] In addition, the houses for SMOTIG workers, while well ventilated and neatly arranged in rows, were built of inexpensive local materials like bamboo, rather than concrete. Each settlement, with three hundred to four hundred men, half of them with their families (although some camps had up to a thousand recruits), was likened to "a native village . . . except for the benefits of order and hygiene."[51]

For the most part, Olivier tried to defend his system by pointing to SMOTIG's positive impact on modernization through building up the colony's industrial base and reorganizing its cities, arguing that the "conception of the camps could serve as a model for urban centers."[52] Therefore, following the directive of de Cantelou's Service d'Architecture et Urbanisme, SMOTIG workers undertook major improvements in Tamatave, Tananarive, and other

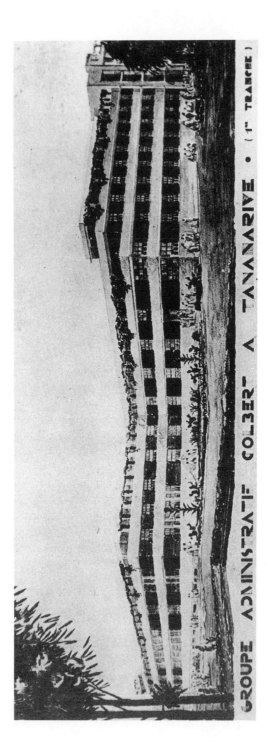

Figure 9.4. Jean de Cantelou's proposed new buildings at the administrative Place Colbert in Tananarive, designed as part of the 1930 public works campaign in that colony, were based on modern principles of aesthetics and efficiency. (*L'urbanisme aux colonies et dans les pays tropicaux* [La Charité-sur-Loire, 1932], vol. 1.)

Malagasy cities. Once again, urban settlements served as both means and ends for political and economic policy. Unconvinced, the International Labor Organization attacked SMOTIG in the French parliament, and, in 1930, the government agreed to begin disbanding the system—a process not completed until the Popular Front took power in 1936.

In Madagascar, then, as in Europe, political leaders considered construction technology and housing production integral parts of their program for urban improvements and economic growth. Yet the call for rationalization did not generate a close analysis of truly economical local materials or a labor system that valued people as construction workers as well as future occupants. Here, too, as in the other prominent French colonies of the period, traditional forms were utilized in an effort to downplay resistance while mitigating the more disruptive aspects of modernization. Traditionalism and modernism thus formed a unified urban policy. Emphasizing this two-part agenda, a 1936 article contended, echoing Vaillat, that Madagascar's "inhabitants do not fully realize that this little Continent is simultaneously one of the most extraordinary laboratories and museums that the universe has offered civilized man."[53] The usefulness of this cultural strategy, in other words, pertained primarily to French interests, to "civilized man" at home and abroad.

The synthesis of these two approaches to urbanism—one protecting tradition, the other promoting development—formed an important element of political strategy during this phase of French imperialism. The apparent successes of Morocco, Vietnam, and Madagascar generated considerable interest in Europe and, for a few decades, seemed to be accomplishing the goal of modernizing, while simultaneously stabilizing, the cities of three important colonies. Yet the tables would turn before long as nationalist movements arose in these colonial settings, beginning in the very cities whose development the French had hoped would defuse resistance. Young people, trained in French institutions, in contact with the villes nouvelles and their own cultures' urban heritage, used *both* traditions as the basis for their demands. Their arguments for political independence, first put forth in the cities of these French colonies, relied in large part on cultural ideals: a synthesis of the Western concepts of *liberté* and *egalité* with the integrity and autonomy of their own traditions.

This episode in French colonial history deserves a final comment on its historical and urbanistic significance. Historically, these different cultural tactics point to changes in French colonial policies in the early twentieth century, as administrators sought subtler ways to assert their power and more captivating techniques for winning support at home. In many instances, in fact, the colonial policies even reveal efforts to develop policies that could work in France itself, promoting modern improvements without disrupting national traditions or destroying the charm of French towns. Urbanistically, the examples illuminate an important phase of modernism, a debate involving both architectural design and urban planning policies between advocates of universalistic principles and those who believed in the need to respect existing cultures, even as they Westernized and brought them "up to date" in economic and political terms. The overwhelming political power of the colonial context allowed each side to experiment with a vision of the city and their professional role in the city; it also allows us to comprehend the ways in which both approaches to urban design can be allied with power, relying on the support of political administrators and using artistic skills to further political goals.

The social, political, and cultural pattern of the colonial laboratory has remained attractive for planners and architects. From Le Corbusier's modernist work in Chandigarh to Robert Venturi's and Denise Scott-Brown's current postmodern experiment in "traditional Iraqui architectural forms" in Baghdad, these former colonial cities remain a favored place to distill and experiment with one's ideas.[54] The close association of centralized power and culture still seems, at least in part, to define the appeal. If culture and politics are inevitably interwoven in such endeavors, past and present, the historical experience of French imperialism then suggests the kinds of questions we must ask when we analyze the intentions, and certainly the effects, of Western-sponsored urban reforms, whether in colonial or postcolonial settings.

Notes

Much of the early research for this project was carried out in collaboration with Paul Rabinow of the University of California, Berkeley, under a research grant from the National Endowment for the Humanities. I wish to thank him for those initial discussions on the relation between France and its colonies. I also wish to thank the Stanford Humanities Center for providing support and encouragement during a fellowship there in 1982–1983. Thomas Bender, Burton Benedict, Kenneth T. Jackson, and Philip Khoury offered helpful comments on an earlier draft of the present chapter, which represents my work published in *The Politics of Design in French Colonial Urbanism* (Chicago, 1991).

1. Léandre Vaillat, *Le périple marocain* (Paris, 1934), 55.

2. Mikhail Bakhtin, "Discourse in the Novel," in *The Dialogic Imagination,* ed. Michael Holquist, trans. Caryl Emerson and Michael Holquist (Austin, 1981), 259–422 (essay written in 1934–1935); also see Bakhtin's *Rabelais and His World* (Cambridge, Mass., 1968).

3. Hubert Lyautey, *Rapport général sur la situation de protectorat du Maroc au 31 juillet 1914* (Rabat, 1916), xiv. In another colonial context, see Bernard Cohn, "Representing Authority in Victorian India," in *The Invention of Tradition,* ed. Eric Hobsbawm and Terrence Ranger, 165–209 (Cambridge, 1983).

4. On architectural postmodernism and historicism, see Alan Coloquhoun, "Three Kinds of Historicism," *Oppositions* 26 (1984): 29–39, and *Essays in Architectural Criticism: Modern Architecture and Historical Change* (Cambridge, Mass., 1981).

5. Henri Prost, unidentified speech, n.d., Prost papers, Académie d'Architecture, Paris.

6. For later appraisals of such urban problems and apathetic responses, see Anthony Sutcliffe, *The Autumn of Central Paris: The Defeat of Town Planning, 1850–1970* (London, 1970), 167–251, and *Towards the Planned City: Germany, Britain, the United States, and France, 1780–1914* (Oxford, 1981), 126–162; and Norma Evenson, *Paris: A Century of Change, 1878–1978* (New Haven, Conn., 1979). The most notable exception to this urbanistic impasse was the innovative architecture of Tony Garnier in Lyons, his hometown; see Cinquantième Congrès de l'Association Française pour l'Avancement des Sciences, *Lyon, 1906–1926* (Lyons, 1926); and Tony Garnier, *Les grands travaux de la ville de Lyon* (Paris, n.d.).

7. Speech, July 14, 1914, Casablanca, in Hubert Lyautey, *Paroles d'action: Madagascar—Sud Oranais—Oran—Maroc (1900–1925)* (Paris, 1927), 116–117.

8. Joseph Chailley-Bert, *La vie intime: Les discours du Président Roosevelt* (Bordeaux, 1903), 32, cited in Raymond F. Betts, "The French Colonial Frontier," *From the Ancien Régime to the Popular Front*, ed. Charles K. Warner (New York, 1969), 131. Also see Bernard Semmel, *Imperialism and Social Reform: English Social-Imperial Thought, 1895–1914* (Garden City, N.Y., 1968); Henri Brunschwig, *Mythes et réalités de l'imperialisme coloniale française, 1871–1914* (Paris, 1960): Raoul Girardet, *L'Idée coloniale en France, 1871–1914* (Paris, 1978); and Phillip Mason, *Patterns of Dominance* (New York, 1970).

9. "Ernest Hébrard en Indochine," *Urbanisme* 2 (1933): 170; Léandre Vaillat, *Le visage français du Maroc* (Paris, 1931), 40.

10. Representative books that emphasize this theme include the works of Vaillat; Joseph Chailley-Bert, *La France et la plus grande France* (Paris, 1902); J. B. Piolet, *La France hors de France* (Paris, 1910); and Alfred de Tarde, *Le Maroc, école d'énergie* (Paris, 1915). In 1945 the engineer E. Joyant singled out these three colonies as prime examples of colonial successes—and metropolitan models—in his exposé to the Commission d'Urbanisme Colonial for the Secretariat d'Etat à la Marine et aux Colonies, p. 2, carton 407, Affaires Politiques, Archives d'Outre-Mer, Paris.

11. Jean-Louis Cohen, "L'Union sacrée: Technocrates et architectes modernes à l'assaut de la banlieue parisienne," *Les cahiers de la recherche architecturale*, no. 9 (1982): 6–25; and Anatol Kopp, *L'architecture de la reconstruction en France, 1945–1954* (Paris, 1982).

12. The most notable and best-known example of this endeavor is Carl E. Schorske's provocative *Fin-de-Siècle Vienna: Politics and Culture* (New York, 1980).

13. Edmund Burke III, "The Sociology of Islam: The French Tradition," in *Islamic Studies: A Tradition and Its Problems*, ed. Malcolm H. Kerr, 73–88 (Malibu, Calif., 1980); Marwan Buheiry, "Colonial Scholarship and Muslim Revivalism in 1900," *Arab Studies Quarterly* 4 (1982): 1–16; Terry Nichols Clark, *Prophets and Patrons: The French University and the Emergence of the Social Sciences* (Cambridge, Mass., 1973), 122–247; Lucien Lévy-Bruhl, *La mentalité primitive* (Paris, 1922); Augustin Bernard, *Le Maroc* (Paris, 1913); Augustin Bernard, Henri Labouret, Georges Julien, Charles Robequain, and Maurice Leenhardt, *L'Habitation indigène dans les possessions françaises* (Paris, 1931); and "Fondation de l'Académie des Sciences Coloniales," *Comptes-Rendus de Séances et Communications de l'Académie des Sciences Coloniales* (Paris) 1 (1922): 19–23.

14. Raymond F. Betts, *Assimilation and Association in French Colonial Theory, 1890–1914* (New York, 1961); Martin Deming Lewis, "One Hundred Million

Frenchmen: The 'Assimilation' Theory in French Colonial Policy," *Comparative Studies in Society and History* 4 (1962): 129–151; and M. M. Knight, "French Colonial Policy—the Decline of 'Association,'" *Journal of Modern History* 5 (1933): 208–224.

15. An excellent short overview of Lyautey's urbanistic policies is Brian Brace Taylor, "Planned Discontinuity: Modern Colonial Cities in Morocco," *Lotus International* 36 (1979): 52–66. For criticisms of Lyautey's tactics, see, in particular, Janet Abu-Lughod, *Rabat: Urban Apartheid in Morocco* (Princeton, N.J., 1980); François Béguin, *Arabisances: Décor architectural et tracé urbain en Afrique du Nord, 1830–1950* (Paris, 1983); and Melvin Knight, *Morocco as a French Economic Venture* (New York, 1937). Analyses of similar spatial policies in English colonies, also based on a version of the dual city, include Robert Grant Irving, *Indian Summer: Lutyens, Baker and Imperial Delhi* (New Haven, Conn., 1981); Anthony D. King, *Colonial Urban Development: Culture, Social Power and Environment* (London, 1976); and Thomas R. Metcalf, "Architecture and the Representation of Empire: India, 1860–1910," *Representations* 5 (1984): 37–65. However, the French were far more thorough and articulate in their efforts to manipulate the symbolism of indigenous and European settlements in pursuit of political goals.

16. Henri Descamps, "L'Urbanisme: L'oeuvre de M. Prost," *La construction moderne* 46 (December 14, 1930): 173. Also see Direction Générale de l'Instruction Publique, des Beaux-Arts et des Antiquités, *Historique (1912–1930)* (Rabat, 1931); E. Pauty, "Rapport sur la défense des villes et la restauration des monuments historiques," *Hésperis* 2 (1922): 449–472; and Hubert Lyautey, "Note, Rabat, le 18 juin 1913," carton 19, dossier 88, Fonds Lyautey, Archives Nationales, Paris.

17. For overviews of Prost's work, see J. Marrast, "Maroc," in *L'Oeuvre d'Henri Prost* (Paris, 1980), 49–119; René Jactel, "Veilles villes et cités modernes au Maroc," *Revue générale des sciences pures et appliqués* 24 (1914): 379–383; Résidence Générale de la République Française au Maroc, *La renaissance du Maroc: Dix années de protectorat, 1912–1922* (Poitiers, 1923); E. Joyant, "L'Urbanisme au Maroc," *La technique sanitaire et municipale* 17 (1922): 88–103; Henri Descamps, *L'Architecture moderne au Maroc,* 2 vols. (Paris, n.d.), based on his 1930 series for the journal *La construction moderne.*

18. Henri Prost, cited in Pierre Pelletier, "Valeurs financières et urbanisme au Maroc (I)," *Bulletin économique et social du Maroc* 19 (1955): 39.

19. "Consultation juridique sur l'expropriation pour cause d'utilité publique: Si Larbi Naciri," carton 19, dossier 88, Fonds Lyautey, Archives Nationales, Paris; Abu-Lughod, *Rabat,* 164, 170, 174–195.

20. Georges Hardy, *Les colonies françaises: Le Maroc* (Paris, 1930), 32–34; Jacques Berque, *French North Africa: The Maghrib between Two World Wars,* trans. Jean Stewart (New York, 1962), 159; Henri Prost, "Notes—Général—Maroc," n.d., Prost Papers, Académie d'Architecture, Paris; but also see Lyautey's "Note, fin novembre 1913 sur Marrakech," carton 55, Fonds Lyautey, Archives Nationales, Paris.

21. Hubert Lyautey, speech to the Université des Annales, Paris, December 10, 1926, in Lyautey, *Paroles d'action,* 452–453.

22. Philip Khoury, "Syrian Urban Politics in Transition: The Quarters of Damascus during the French Mandate," *International Journal of Middle Eastern Studies* 16

(1984): 507: T. H. Greenshields, "'Quarters' and Ethnicity," in *The Changing Middle Eastern City*, ed. G. H. Blake and R. I. Lawless, 124 (London, 1980); Kenneth L. Brown, *People of Salé: Tradition and Change in a Moroccan City, 1830–1930* (Cambridge, Mass., 1976), 34–39.

23. Albert Laprade, "Une ville crée specialement pour les indigènes à Casablanca," in *L'Urbanisme aux colonies et dans les pays tropicaux*, 2 vols., ed. Jean Royer, 1:97 (La Charité-sur-Loire, 1932).

24. Edward W. Said, *Orientalism* (New York, 1978). Also see Abdallah Larouri, *The Crisis of the Arab Intellectual*, trans. Diarmid Cammell (French ed., 1974; English ed., Berkeley, 1976).

25. Hubert Lyautey, speech at the Université des Annales, in Lyautey, *Paroles d'action*, 451.

26. Telegram from the minister of colonies to the governor-general of Indochina, June 24, 1921, and "Rapport sur le fonctionnement du Service, Années 1922–1923," p. 6, Direction des Travaux Publics de l'Indochine, Archives d'Outre-Mer, Aix-en-Provence; letter to Ernest Hébrard, February 18, 1921, Prost Papers, Académie d'Architecture, Paris. For an overview of Hébrard's early career in Rome, Greece, and Indochina, see Gwendolyn Wright and Paul Rabinow, "Savoir et pouvoir dans l'urbanisme moderne colonial d'Ernest Hébrard," *Les cahiers de la recherche architecturale*, no. 9 (1982): 26–43.

27. Tran Van Tat, "Mémoire sur l'évolution et l'aménagement de la ville de Saigon-Cholon," mémoire, Institut d'Urbanisme, Paris, 1928, p. 22: Jean Bouchet, "La naissance et les premières années de Saigon, ville française," *Bulletin de la Société des Études Indochinoises* 2 (1927): 63–132; M. A. Brébion, "Monographie des rues et monuments de Saigon." *Revue indochinoise* 16 (1911): 357–468; and Lê Thi Ngoc Ánh, "Étude de quelques monuments réprésentatifs de l'art française à Saigon dans les années 1877–1908," resumé of a mémoire, Faculté des Lettres de Saigon, 1973, Archives d'Outre-Mer, Paris.

28. Letters from the governor-general of Indochina to the minister of the interior, March 5, 1920, and February 28, 1923. Direction des Travaux Publics de l'Indochine, Archives d'Outre-Mer, Aix-en-Provence. On French postwar regionalist design, see Achille Duchêne, *Pour la reconstruction des cités industrielles* (Paris, 1919); Léon Rosenthal, *Villes et villages françaises après la guerre* (Paris, 1918); and D.-Alfred Agache, Marcel Aubertin, and Edouard Redont, eds., *Comment reconstruire nos cités détruites* (Paris, 1915).

29. Ernest Hébrard, "L'Architecture locale et les questions d'esthètique en Indochine," and "La conservation des monuments anciens et des vielles villes indigènes de l'Indochine," both in Royer, *L'Urbanisme aux colonies*, 2:32–34, 2:25–32; Tran Van Tat, "Mémoire," 70.

30. On economic and political regionalism, see Jean Charles-Brun, *Le régionalisme* (Paris, 1911); Henri Hauser, *Les régions économiques* (Paris, 1918); and Jules Milhau, "Le mouvement régionaliste," *Histiore économiques de la France entre les deux guerres*, 4 vols. ed. Alfred Sauvy, 3:128–151 (Paris, 1965–1975).

31. David G. Marr, *Vietnamese Anticolonialism, 1885–1925* (Berkeley, 1971), and *Vietnamese Tradition on Trial, 1920–1945* (Berkeley, 1981); Huynh Kim Khanh, *Vietnamese Communism, 1925–1945* (Ithaca, N.Y., 1982); and William J. Duiker, *The*

Rise of Nationalism in Vietnam, 1900–1941 (Ithaca, N.Y., 1976). The Indo-Chinese Federation, created in 1891, consisted of Cochinchina (South Vietnam), which remained an Algeria-style colony, and four protectorates: Tonkin (North Vietnam), Annam (Central Vietnam), Laos, and Cambodia, in the order of their conquest and the degree of French domination.

32. J. de Galembert, *Les administrations et les services publics* (Hanoi, 1931); Charles Bénard, *Au service de l'Indochine: L'Oeuvre de Maurice Long (1919–1923),* preface by Maréchal Lyautey (Paris, 1931); and "Situation de l'ensemble, Mission 1920, Tonkin," carton 169, Direction des Travaux Publics de l'Indochine, Archives d'Outre-Mer, Paris.

33. Martin J. Murray, *The Development of Capitalism in Colonial Indochina (1870–1940)* (Berkeley, 1980), 119–129; Charles Robequain, *L'Évolution économique de l'Indochine française* (Paris, 1938); and A. A. Pouyanne, "Les travaux publics de l'Indochine et le développement économique du pays," *Bulletin économique de l'Indochine,* n.s., 28 (1925): 513–542.

34. Thomas E. Ennis, *French Policy and Developments in Indochina* (French ed., 1936; English ed., New York, 1973), 92.

35. Albert Sarraut, *La mise en valeur des colonies françaises* (Paris, 1923).

36. Ernest Hébrard, "L'urbanisme en Indochine," in Royer, *L'Urbanisme aux colonies,* 1:282.

37. Ibid., 285; Ernest Hébrard, Emmanuel Durand, and M. Cohen-Stuart, "A propos de la séparation des villes au Maroc et aux Indes Néerlandaises," in Royer, *L'Urbanisme aux colonies,* 1:277. In "L'Urbanisme en Indochine," *L'Architecture* 36 (1923): 1–16, Hébrard was more straightforward about "the necessity for the specialization of quarters, especially where it concerns indigenous quarters, which should not, for multiple reasons, be mixed with European quarters" (p. 1).

38. Tran Nguyen Chan et la Ville de Saigon, "Recueil des textes concernant l'hygiène et la santé publique," Saigon, 1929, p. 338, carton 169, Direction des Travaux Publics de l'Indochine, Archives d'Outre-Mer, Paris.

39. Philip D. Curtin, "Medical Knowledge and Urban Planning in Tropical Africa," *American Historical Review* 90 (1985): 594–613.

40. Hébrard, "L'Urbanisme en Indochine," 1:284.

41. Louis-Georges Pineau, "Le plan d'aménagement et d'extension de Dalat," *La vie urbaine,* no. 49 (1939): 34.

42. Hubert Deschamps, *Histoire de Madagascar* (Paris, 1960), 237–254; Michel Massiot, *L'Administration publique à Madagascar* (Paris, 1971), 92–165: Joseph-Simon Galliéni, *Neuf ans à Madagascar (1896–1905)* (Paris, 1908).

43. Léon Rosenthal, "Le plan d'aménagement et d'extension de Tananarive," *La vie urbaine* 1 (1919): 298–310; Georges Cassaigne, "Le plan de Tananarive," *Le Musée Social* 31 (1924): 273–275, "Il faut décongestioner Tananarive," *Le Tribune de Madagascar* (November 21, 25, 28, and December 2, 1924), and "Les plans d'aménagement des villes de Madagascar," in Royer, *L'Urbanisme aux colonies* 1:128–131; H. Razafindralambo, "Extension de la ville de Tananarive dans la zone ouest et ses problèmes" (thèse du 3ème cycle, Institut d'Urbanisme, Paris, 1971), 24–30; Gérard Donque, "Les problèmes fondamentaux de l'urbanisme tananarivien," *Madagascar: Revue de géographie* 13 (1968): 43–51. Among the forums Lyautey, Prost, and Cassaigne shared in France during the 1920s were the Musée Social, the Académie des Sciences Colo-

niales, the Société Française des Urbanistes, and the 1923 Congrès de Strasbourg on postwar urbanism.

44. On the 1926 plan, see Cassaigne, "Les plans d'aménagement," 129, 131, and "La ville moderne, la circulation," *Bulletin économique de Madagascar et dépendances* 24 (1927): 74–78; A. Bruggeman, "Tananarive, son passé, son évolution, son avenir," *La vie urbaine* 14 (1933): 69–112; E. Weithas, "L'Urbanisme en Afrique Tropicale: Rapport général," in Royer, *L'Urbanisme aux colonies,* 1:112; M. C., "Tananarive et ses environs," *Bulletin économique de Madagascar et dépendances* 23 (1926): 31–39; "Plans d'aménagement et d'extension des villes à Madagascar," Rapport du Ministère des Colonies, December 24, 1926, carton 330, Direction des Travaux Publics de Madagascar, Archives d'Outre-Mer, Paris; Marcel Olivier, *Six ans de politique sociale à Madagascar* (Paris, 1931), 190–200.

45. Olivier, *Six ans,* 69, 271.

46. "Les travaux publics. 1927–1928," and "Activité du Service des Travaux publics en 1928–1929," carton 330, Direction des Travaux Publics de Madagascar, Archives d'Outre-Mer, Paris: M. A. Leblond, "Tamatave," *La revue de Madagascar* 4 (1933): 93–125: "L'ère des grands travaux," *Le monde colonial illustré,* no. 71 (1929): 176–177: Pierre Razaly-Andriamihaingo, "Urbanisme de Tamatave," *Bulletin de Madagascar,* no. 103 (1954): 1051–1062.

47. "Activité du Service des Travaux Publics en 1928–1929"; J. de Cantelou, "L'Architecture et l'urbanisme à Madagascar," in Royer, *L'Urbanisme aux colonies,* 1:132–140; Charles Lebel, "La standardisation à Madagascar" (thèse de doctorat, Faculté de Droit, Université de Paris, 1937), 2–21; "Grands travaux de Madagascar," *Le courier colonial* (May 8, 1927); "Une grande métropole coloniale: Tananarive," *L'Illustration* 94 (December 1936): 527–529.

48. De Cantelou, "L'Architecture," 132.

49. Olivier, *Six ans,* 69–132; "SMOTIG: Rapport de l'Inspection Général des Travaux Publics sur l'emprunt autorisé par la loi du 22 février 1931," report from the ministry of colonies, Tananarive, August 3, 1934, carton 334, Direction des Travaux Publics de Madagascar, Archives d'Outre-Mer, Paris. Also see "Rapport de M. Lebeque, Mission d'Inspection, 1933–1934," April 1, 1934, carton 334, Direction des Travaux Publics de Madagascar, Archives d'Outre-Mer, Paris: "Note sur le Régime de la main d'oeuvre à Madagascar," carton 331, Affaires Politiques de Madagascar, Archives d'Outre-Mer, Paris; François Valdi, "Le SMOTIG malgache," *Afrique française* 38 (1929): 510–516; Virginia Thompson and Richard Adloff, *The Malagasy Republic: Madagascar Today* (Stanford, Calif., 1965), 444–446.

50. Olivier, *Six ans,* 73–76, 100–101; R. Cherrier, "La legislation concernant le travail indigène à Madagascar" (thèse de doctorat, Faculté de Droit, Université de Paris, 1932), 7.

51. Olivier, *Six ans,* 116.

52. Ministère des colonies, cabinet de ministère, "De l'emploi du 2ème contingent," February 10, 1927, p. 6, carton 2942, Affaires Politiques, Archives d'Outre-Mer, Paris.

53. Maurius-Ary Leblond, "Madagascar et les sciences," *Revue de Madagascar,* no. 15 (1936): 18.

54. Norma Evenson, *Chandigarh* (Berkeley, 1966); "Venturi, Rauch & Scott Brown," *Progressive Architecture* 65 (1984): 88–89.

10

Educating Conformity in French Colonial Algeria

Fanny Colonna
Translated by Barbara Harshav

[Editors' note: The following selection is excerpted from Fanny Colonna's book *Instituteurs Algériens:* 1883–1939 (Paris: Presses de la Fondation Nationale des Sciences Politiques, 1975). Her principal focus is on the role of French schools in colonial Algeria and on selection and formation of a well-managed indigenous elite. She provides a unique perspective on the relationship between schooling in metropole and in colony and on the cultural and political logics of the moralizing colonial state. Above all, she attends to how specific criteria of "excellence" worked both to maintain France as a cultural standard and to sustain distance between colonizer and colonized. The two sections reproduced below are part 1, chapter 3, and part 3, chapter 2, of the original book. Some of the tables and a few passages have been excised from the text and are marked by ellipses.]

Part I: "It Is in the Colonies that the Secret of Capitalism Is Revealed"

In 1912, Rector Jeanmaire answered a journalist who had accused him of being the tool of an educational policy that clearly favored the natives: "I won't believe that what is good for our children is bad for native children." These words became famous and are often cited as a definitive and irrefutable expression of the neutrality of the school system in Algeria.[1] According to the republican version, proof that the educational system stood independent of the colonial power lay in its indisputably assimilationist instruction of the Algerians and in its desire to maintain in the colony the same objectives as in France. But should that version be accepted? Or perhaps we can conclude instead that if reformers and representatives of the school system were so sure of their techniques and their success, it was because the school system had already proved itself in a context and in relation to a situation that was not without analogy to the Algerian context. Or, in other words, that it was in a way preadapted to the integrative role it was to play in Algeria.

At that period, the conservative effects of the school were probably not known even to those who set them in motion. Those effects, both for those who benefited and for those who suffered from them, could only be seen after a study over enough time to demonstrate them objectively. Nevertheless, a sort of "intuition" seemed to allow the republicans to take full advantage in Algeria of the transposition of a system of instruction so laboriously devised and dearly imposed against the opposition of the right; a system, that is, that was consistent with their political plan and their deeply held ideology.

In fact, it was the reformers themselves, followed closely by the representatives of the school system, who drew constant parallels between the two contexts. People were compared: E. Combes wrote "The [Kabyles'] . . . character, physiological constitution, love of the soil, sobriety, and resistance to fatigue . . . are comparable to our highlanders of Auvergne."[2] Or: "The Kabyle and the native of Jura are both sturdy, made for changes of season as well as the differences of altitude."[3]

Aptitudes were compared. Concluding a long parallel between the performances of French students and native students, a parallel that favored the latter,[4] Combes stated, "This similarity is emphasized with dazzling clarity in Kabylia; it emerges almost spontaneously from the reports, all the more strikingly given the small brains of the native highlanders, who are forced to assimilate our nimble forms of language and nuanced habits of style, yet who catch up more quickly and easily in small schools as well as in large ones, with our highlanders of Cevannes or Auvergne in the immediate solutions of mental calculation and in the practical study of arithmetic."[5]

But this parallel is not the simple statement of a de facto similarity; it takes its meaning from, or more precisely its function is grasped only in light of, the profound similarity of situations, which is evident to men like Combes and Emile Burdeau. This similarity is so obvious even outside the colonial group that it becomes commonplace to assert it. "The indifference of the natives of Algeria to the education of their children is exactly like that of our rural population," writes Combes. "Its source is their own ignorance or their poverty."[6] This assertion is echoed by Burdeau, more subtly but just as staunchly: "As for the natives' aversion to education, it is surely much more violent and blinder than the reluctance encountered by our recent school laws in some parts of the [metropolitan] territory. But is it of a completely different nature?"[7]

The spread of the school in France in the nineteenth century encountered obstacles comparable in many ways to those it encountered in Algeria. The inspectors sent through France by Guizot in 1833 to assess the school situation heard testimony quite similar to that recorded by the senatorial committee of the XVIII during its travels in Algeria.[8] Like Algerian peasants, French peasants did not feel involved in the school that was imposed on them. As late as 1850, school attendance in the French countryside was insignificant.[9] In his monograph on the school of Mazières-en-Gâtine, Roger Thabault points out that, in 1851, out of forty-five students enrolled in school in January, only three attended school all year long. And those three were not sons of peasants: one was the son of the farrier, another of the innkeeper, and the third of a well-to-do farmer.[10]

Moreover, the indifference toward the school in France should not be interpreted as a sign of passivity and inertia. There are several indications that, at least in some regions, it was a truly cultural reaction, absolutely analogous to the one observed in Algeria in the same period.

In the late nineteenth century, the language and cultures of Flanders, the Basque region, and Brittany, those provinces where the problem was most acute, were still viable: those "citadels" constituted real missionary regions for the school.[11] Those peasants in whom "there was no trace of the French language," who "have barely been grazed by the civilization of the French language,"[12] had to be assimilated, first by disseminating the French language with French teachers: "Frenchmen are needed to make the Bretons French, they won't do it by themselves."[13]

Representatives of the school system described Breton children with the same categories used for young Algerian natives. M. Pointrineau, school inspector in Vannes, wrote,

> The little Breton peasant is left alone as soon as he can walk; no one is concerned with him anymore; he is the object of no care, either moral or physical; at most, he is taught to say a few words of prayer morning and night; and even that is rare. . . . When he is eight or nine years old, if the school isn't too far away, they think of sending him there: he has to learn his catechism and he can make his first communion. There he is in school, which he will attend quite irregularly, and where he will spend three years at most. If, physically, he is eight years old, in terms of intellectual development, he is barely three. Under these conditions, is it necessary to count the few Breton words that have been enough for him to lead a rather rudimentary life up to then?[14]

And this is how teachers [in Algeria] at the turn of the century described their students:

> The native child who enters the preparatory course is literally a little savage who knows nothing of our language, our customs, our ways. His range of ideas is narrow, and it takes miracles of ingenuity to interest him in what is totally alien to him, to raise him slowly from the few things he knows to the relatively large

number of things to which we want to introduce him; in a word, to rouse him, to excite and hold his attention. We pay attention only to what is interesting, and we are most often interested only in what maintains a certain relationship with familiar objects, acquired and well-assimilated ideas. The young native has seen little, observed little, and has few ideas. And, too often, he passively receives the education given him, and stores it in his memory as a foreign body. He neither understands nor assimilates.[15]

Clearly, the animal nature of the Breton child is no less than that of the Algerian child.

Confronted both domestically and externally with cultural differences, the reformers judged that the policy of the tabula rasa was to be practiced in both cases and that civilizing practices had to be imposed since the children are semisavages, reduced to a vegetative existence and living, as it were, in a state of nature. Hence it is the similarity of both the project and the situation that makes the school in France and the school in Algeria comparable in the reformers' minds; but to a certain extent, it is also inherent in the facts themselves. This was the source of the optimism of the promoters of educational reforms in Algeria, since they were aware that in France—from the time of the Ferry Laws (1881–1882), no matter what difficulties still existed—the school had been set on a victorious and irreversible path.

In France, we have gradually succeeded in relieving those feelings, assuaging poor parents with the aid of 4 million [francs] in school supplies, clothing, and food distributed by the school funds to the children. We have gone beyond the objections of religion, acceding to them to some degree by guaranteeing the neutrality of the school and giving students legitimate facilities for performing their religious duties. Analogous means would have a similar effect in Algeria.[16]

In fact, Burdeau outlined an entire Algerian program here: the *thaleb* who will teach the children a few verses of the Koran with the educator's indulgence is equivalent to the catechism on Thursday in France, something "to soothe the conscience of the parents."[17] Finally, the necessity of imposing a uniform and homogenizing education in both France and Algeria was based on symmetrical arguments: "I understand," wrote Guizot in 1860,

how the English came to this conclusion [of preserving their empiricist and differentiated educational system], and I agree with them. In France, we don't even have to ask the question that leads to that. Here, all the distinguished and diverse establishments of public education have disappeared—the teachers and the buildings, the corporations and the endowments. . . . In public education as in our whole social organization, a general system established and maintained by the State is a necessity for us; it is the condition that has made our history and our national spirit; we want unity, only the State can give it. We have destroyed everything, we much create.[18]

This assessment of the French situation applied just as well, and for the same reasons, to Algeria, where the argument was based, equally and above all, on the decay of the traditional system of instruction practiced in 1880. In both cases, the educational institution was presented as the only possible response in a cultural vacuum. In reality, however, many other attitudes toward this vacuum were possible: the attempt of the Arab-French school is one; the plan of the Duke d'Aumale to restore traditional education by changing it from inside was another. Tocqueville had also noted that, in France, the Revolution had not provided an opportunity for local cultures and energies, but had completed the work of centralization and destruction begun by the ancien régime and had even gone beyond it in leveling and uniformity.[19] We have seen above an example of the school system of Brittany, which, as Tocqueville stressed, at the time of the Revolution was one of two provinces where a certain local freedom still existed; the other was Languedoc. "Elsewhere the institution [of provincial States] had become mere shadows of their former selves, ineffectual and inert."[20]

Rather than prove the neutrality of the school in Algeria, the transposition of French methods and French schooling, one might say, proves the colonial nature of the school in France. Moreover, since similar recent research has shown that this is how the republicans' plan must be considered, this is only an additional proof; and from this perspective, that plan was perfectly consistent with Guizot's school.

It is no longer necessary to prove that Ferry's plan, like Guizot's, was aimed primarily at social stability. In his work on the educational ideology of the Third Republic, L. Legrand writes, "Ferry is mainly a man of order, and his pedagogical work is in keeping with a deliberately conservative perspective. If he worked for the proletariat, it was primarily out of concern for collective discipline, to improve the functioning of the social organism, in short, and in accordance with the positivist inspiration, to put an end to the revolution. . . . For Ferry in 1880, as for Combes in 1848, the issue was to establish amidst order the progress that was achieved."[21]

Finally, the spread of the school, like the spread of child care and modern medicine in late nineteenth- and early twentieth-century France, was dependent on an enterprise of colonization in the strict sense of the term, aimed at "realizing the acculturation of the lower classes to the values and goals of the middle classes."[22]

A missionary school in the strictest sense of the term, the system for the education of Algerians that transposed onto Algeria the methods and design of mass education in France was only a transition toward the position of the French masses. Coming later, indigenous education took its lessons and especially its hope [from French mass education], but it also bluntly reveals its ideology and function. The reasons for this clarity and admission make one wonder. The situation of the colonial school is somewhat analogous to the one analyzed by

Marx regarding "the modern theory of colonization."[23] Discussing English colonization in the nineteenth century, Marx explained how, in the new world, the political economy of the old world discovered—and revealed—the secret of capitalism, that is, the expropriation of the worker, since private property based on personal labor and property based on the labor of another person are contradictory; and the latter can be born only from the tomb of the former. This secret is discovered in the colonial situation because the conditions for the development of capitalism in the colonies are less favorable, or, in any case, are profoundly different.

In the English colonies, free access of workers to landed property resulted in the dispersion of the means of production, thus making it impossible to form "long-term enterprises." Analogously, in Algeria, the ill-advised dissemination of knowledge without morality, of science without conscience, would make the formation of a coherent and hierarchical society—with economic and social functions distributed harmoniously and above all consented to—much more difficult to realize than in Europe, because of the many contradictions between the opposing parties.

The recognition and sometimes even the claim for the colonial role of the school in the discourse of the reformers can also be understood as a tactic to overcome the violent opposition within the dominant society. But the situation was essentially similar in France, where the school also had to be defended against the right. The radical difference of the Algerian situation is that unlike class relations, which were never explicitly recognized in that period, at least not in official discourse, the colonial relationship was completely explicit and legitimate, or at least legitimated. In the late nineteenth century, no one, including Algerians, questioned the right to colonize Algeria. In fact, as Ferry explained, because colonization is a right, it implies duties for the stronger nations; one of those duties is to bring education. Ferry reminded his readers that the colonial enterprise involved an economic aspect, a civilizing aspect, and a political aspect.

> Gentlemen, we must speak louder and truer! We must say openly that, in fact, the superior races have rights with regard to the inferior races. . . . I repeat, the superior races have a right, because they have a duty, the duty to civilize the inferior races. (Applause from the same benches on the left. New interruptions on the extreme left and on the right.) Can you deny that there is more justice, more moral and material order, more equality, more social virtues in North Africa since France conquered it?[24]

Whether duties derived from rights or rights derived from duties—the variations in colonial discourse on this subject are legion—what is important is, on the one hand, this circular and inextricable causality; and on the other, the fact that the school is always ranked as one of the duties. And the legitimacy of a duty is harder to challenge than the legitimacy of a right. That was the great feat of the school system, justifying the possibility of the double reading of all discourse about it, however triumphant it may be. By defining itself from the start as a duty, it anticipated all future reappraisals, and it answered a question that was never asked, that was never even allowed to be formulated: Can the colonizer's school be neutral in the colonial relationship?

Finally, because of the power relationship that developed, because it was no longer enough to proclaim that the school was a duty, and because the school also fulfilled the first part of its mission, transforming the pressure for education into a demand for education, the links between the school system and the colonial system became less explicit. Thus, over the decades, the conquering function of the school, stated so brilliantly in 1887 by Paul Bert, disappeared completely and was retranslated by Violette in terms of "a native claim."[25]

Demonstrating that the colonial school before 1939 was almost bereft of any influence on social mobility is not to deny that it was a factor of change in many ways; but it does emphasize the fact that the effects of the school were systematically and usually successfully curbed, oriented, and manipulated. Clearly, education would not have been demanded by the dominated society if it had not proved to be relatively effective and perceived as a marketable commodity. Nevertheless—and this must be emphasized—it was a rare commodity. In fact, one of the functions of school selection was to make education scarce, thus increasing its value and the demand for it.

Clearly, there are several functions that can be fulfilled only by the school. It is the perfect vehicle for material innovation in housing, agriculture, hygiene, and health, both because of the knowledge it bestows and because of the attitudes and expectations it develops.[26] The fact remains, as admitted by the institution itself, that technical goals were only the means and pretext for a truly missionary initiative aimed at effecting a profound change in the morals and lifestyle, that is, in the ethos, of the conquered society. Is the classical missionary technique different in other contexts? Obviously, it was through the introduction of new ways of living that Christianity was effectively realized in non-European societies.[27] Symbolized by the teaching of morality, but conveyed in fact by all disciplines, especially "impartial disciplines" like history, this cultural teaching was the essential function of the school.

"The school is opened to the native to teach him and especially to improve his moral standard," according to the programs of 1890.[28] "If it is useful to learn reading, writing, and arithmetic, it is indispensable to think honestly and to act well. . . . In school, instruction is only a means, education alone is the end."[29]

The spread of complete, civilizing, and moralizing instruction, as opposed to the limited manual instruction demanded by the colonists, targeted primarily the proper acculturation of manpower for the colonists or for emigration, since the school bestowed both knowledge and ways to use it well. It was also propitious for the selection of the thin layer of indigenous elite required by the colonial administration, whose primary emphasis was on the moral programming of needs and aspirations. Last, but not least, with all its functions, education responded to a more fundamental, but always implicit, demand to create in Algeria, as in France, a situation in which domination was never questioned, recognizing that such a task was more difficult to perform in Algeria.

The clearest proof of this proposition is a statement dating from 1935, when the success of the school was guaranteed, written by a journalist favorable to the Algerians:

> Because of the instruction they are given, the Moslem natives of Algeria do not despair of the country that has become their homeland. . . . In many foreign colonies, the native mistreated by the representative of the conquering country directed his resentment first against his oppressor, and then into the anger of an immediate generalization against the conquering country itself. The Moslem native of Algeria may feel some irritation against a French representative; but there his spite stops, and far from bearing a grudge against France, personified by its bad representative, he says to himself: "Oh, if France only knew about it, nothing like that would happen."[30]

Because of its apparent neutrality, because of the distance it kept from the army, and because the white settlers hated it for defending and winning the right to teach the values of the Revolution of 1789, the school was the most effective colonial institution in legitimizing and disseminating the crucial opposition in the colonial discourse of Algeria between *ideal France* and *real France*. In a way, this opposition, internalized and experienced by groups of the dominated society, made the existence of a colonial elite logically possible and politically operative.

Part II: The Principle of the Proper Distance

Between the Ferry reform and World War II, the teacher training school produced about a thousand future teachers. Rather quickly, in a few decades, a certain pessimism developed within the institution; the enterprise seemed more challenging than had been predicted. Yet a small number of individuals turned out to be truly fit to meet the expectations of the school. By approving these few and censuring those students who were considered not up to par, the value system of the colonial schools emerged; this was a difficult compromise between values that were strictly educational and ruled out neither brilliance nor facility and values that were more "solid," "safer," so to speak, that they wanted to convey to those who in fact were intended to be the missionaries of the colonial order.

Educational Excellence and
Social Distance

The main concern of the educational authority was the moral value of the native student-teachers. The development of the teacher training school can be understood almost entirely as the desire to improve its "productivity" in this respect, that is, to be capable of effecting a more radical transformation of the individuals enrolled in it. This no doubt also explains the existence of the "graduation evaluation" by the principal, the supreme court of the school, which was recorded ostentatiously in a register. The final sanction of a three-year course, the evaluation was a final judgment in more than one sense: it determined the assignment of the new teacher (to a city or a tribe, in a disadvantaged or favored position, "independent" or "supervised"); but it also largely determined his professional future.[31] Strictly educational performances or pedagogical aptitudes had less weight in this evaluation than the so-called personal qualities, especially the moral inclination, the "total person." In short, this evaluation produced a second-degree selection and a hierarchization, by creating another category in a population that was already highly selective in relation to the total native school population at that time. In this second selection process, the school distinguished those it "recognized," and stigmatized those who did not take advantage of its instruction.[32]

Keeping strictly to the vocabulary of the various principals, between 1883 and 1939, the teacher training school of Bouzaréah produced 11.1 percent excellent teachers, 31.0 percent good teachers, 31.5 percent average teachers, and 26 percent fair or bad teachers. Such a high proportion of bad teachers is surprising. In fact, at that period teacher training school education was one of the most demanding branches of French education, hence of the French school in Algeria. Indeed, the failure rate of the teacher training school of Bouzaréah was rather low during the period in question (10%), an indication of a considerable return, in view of the distance separating the environment from which the students from the teacher training school originally came. What must be understood is that one-fourth of the students were considered to have met only the minimal demands of the school system, two-thirds of the student body would make adequate or very adequate teachers, and a little more than one-tenth were considered to be a complete pedagogical success.

First, the category "excellent"—that is, that 11.1 percent of the total population of the teacher training school defined by the educational institution as those who will make *excellent* or *very good* teachers—is distinguished from the other categories by a combination of social advantages, on the one hand, and by better scholarly performance, on the other. For the most part these students came from well-to-do families who enjoyed a high social status, more precisely a prestigious status . . . ; their fathers were more often literate in French than those of the other categories. They were more often of urban or suburban

Table 10.1   Variations of Some Social Characteristics of Algerian Teacher Training School Students According to the Judgment on Graduation from the Teacher Training School (in %)

Ranking by Judgment on Graduation	1	2	3	4	5	6	7	8
Excellent (11.1)	22.2	31.6	54.4	31.6	43.8	12.2	24.7	44.2
Good and average (62.5)	15.7	9.4	49.8	20.2	33.4	14.9	24.8	35.8
Satisfactory (26.4)	14.4	26.4	41.9	25.8	30.9	15.8	24.0	41.1
Total	16.9	24.3	46.3	29.8	36.9	14.9	27.5	42.0

Categories corresponding to the columns:
1. From a predominantly European city
2. Prestigious family
3. From an urban or semiurban milieu
4. Well-to-do family
5. Father literate in French
6. Father or relative teacher
7. Father employed in the public sector
8. Father peasant

origin and from population centers where Europeans outnumbered Algerians. One's position in the educational hierarchy rose steadily with the spread of acculturation: the countrysides provided average teachers, population centers where the number of Europeans was equal to or less than that of the Algerians produced average or good teachers, and those where Europeans were the majority supplied excellent teachers (see table 10.1).

Thus students designated as excellent were not only closer geographically and physically, as it were, to the dominant society; not only did they possess a considerable cultural advantage in the fact that their fathers could at least sign their name in French; but they were also the ones who offered an education profile closest to that of a good European student: unlike their classmates who finished primary school at thirteen or earlier, they usually entered the teacher training school at sixteen or younger and most often had a stellar educational record, the assessment of the original headmaster evaluating not only performance during the final year of school but also growth and consistency. In fact, nothing is more opposed to educational norms than the final, brilliant, last-minute "spurt," and students who were accepted for teacher training school had been selected long before, as a function not only of their aptitude but also of their consistency and their seriousness. Finally, excellent students were also characterized by the consistency of their efforts, since most of them have never had to repeat a class. In addition, they were most often ranked in the first third of their graduating class and were most often deemed worthy of being placed "upcountry," in charge of a tribal school. This was the educational definition of excellence, composed of consistent effort, scholarly performance, and moral attitudes judged necessary for the singular exercise of a cultural vocation. . . .

Coming from a well-to-do family was clearly a circumstance favoring excellence in rural students, but it seems to have had a negative influence in an urban milieu. Without claiming too much for correlations observed in a limited population, if we refer to the concrete knowledge of the group of former teacher training school students and to the history of the teacher training institution in Algeria, we can propose that the social profile of the excellent teacher of urban origin was symmetrically inverse to that of his rural counterpart. In the urban situation, the school recruited its students from families of lowly craftsmen or very low-level merchants (hairdressers, grocers, shoemakers) who were barely educated in Arabic. In the rural setting, we are dealing with the sons of rich peasants, who themselves had contact with the French school. Some model profiles (models both because they are those of teachers who achieved excellence and because they are illustrations of defined types) show that social conditions that are inverse, or reversed in city and country, succeeded in producing almost identical conduct, one that best predisposed to the maximum internalization of educational values.

Conversely, marginal or atypical individuals who ''could have done better'' (in their own terms, because they could have gone to the academic high school; and in terms of the school, because they lacked the tact and discretion that constitute the excellent individual) were either those from urban areas more favored by birth (sons of teachers or well-to-do merchants) or those from rural settings who were not part of the peasantry. Thus acceptable individuals in the rural area more often had fathers in the public sector than did excellent ones (9.5% as opposed to 7.0%). In the urban area, in contrast, good and average individuals more often had fathers who were officials or were assimilated than did acceptable students (42.6%, as opposed to 32.6% and 37.7%). This is because rural public jobs carried authority (magistrate, teacher, local policeman), which did not encourage the docility of the peasant; whereas urban positions here were often considered very lowly (nightwatchman, *chaouch,* porter).

These ostensibly paradoxical correlations are explained by the possibility that urban and semiurban students were systematically favored in the educational competition and were better located in relation to the dominant culture than were rural students. Because they were geographically, socially, and culturally distant from Western culture, rural students could reduce that distance and achieve excellence only if they possessed characteristics to a greater degree than their counterparts among other rural students; and these are characteristics found more frequently among all rural students than among all urban students even if we add education in French—for rural students were most often from well-to-do or prestigious families than were urban students.[33] Conversely, because they were closer to the legitimate culture, more often in contact with Westerners, handled French better, and in most cases were subjected to a more systematic pedagogy, urban and semiurban students could achieve excellence only if they suffered from one or several handicaps (in the strict sense of a lead that equalizes chances). Nevertheless, they obviously could not accumulate too many handicaps either, at the risk of being excluded from the student population. The function of these handicaps was to prevent them from overminimizing the distance separating them from Western culture, to remain at a respectful distance, and not to move too far from their original culture.

The principle that the social characteristics allowing one to achieve excellence differed according to the distance or the position of the individuals vis-à-vis the dominant [French] culture, enables us to understand the significance of features that have been unintelligible thus far. This is especially the case with the fact that fewer excellent students had characteristics that objectively could be considered to provide them with more proximity to Western culture than did students in other categories. For example, none of the fathers of excellent students were naturalized Frenchmen (while for average students, this is true in 2.4% of the cases). Excellent students were less often the sons or relatives of teachers than those in the other strata, including those in the category "satisfactory."[34] Similarly, their fathers were employed in the public sector no more often than those of the good or average students. Conversely, more often than all other categories, excellent students were of peasant origin (sons of *fellahin* or of landowners—but we can assume that the distance to scholarly culture and Western culture is equally great in both cases).

It is as if residing in a city and/or in a population center with many Europeans entailed one or several handicaps and the characteristics that were themselves the mark or the cause of a greater proximity to the dominant culture, and that these should have been enough to prevent the attainment of excellence, since those characteristics could also lead to too much familiarity, in the sense that it was frowned on that inferiors should allow themselves to be too familiar.

Thus the limits of urban privilege are clear. An urban background no doubt allowed students to enter teacher training school more easily: if we limit ourselves to an overall numerical ratio between urban and rural, there are almost as many rural as urban students in the population studied (45% and 55%), while the urban-rural population ratio varied from 1:20 to 1:10 in the period under consideration in Algeria. Moreover, [urban background] allowed higher scholarly performances than did any other geographic origin in this population, but it also forbade—save as a compensatory handicap—access to the highest elite, probably because this class did not favor a suitable internalization of educational values.[35]. . . .

The fact that the non-Kabyle rural populations in general were inadequately and badly educated evidently led to an overall underrepresentation of rural students [in the applicant pool] and hence an apparent overselection [of them]. But a consideration of the "concrete schooling" in each milieu is enough to show that the rural students no doubt were more frequently selected than their companions who became shepherds or migrants, but slightly less so than the urban students whose classes were overcrowded and who were even less motivated to prolong their education since those who completed primary school could find low-paying jobs in the city. . . .

Hence, if the relative overselection of the rural students . . . cannot be invoked to explain the fact that they attained excellence almost as often as urban students, even though in almost all cases (except the graduation examination) they turned in the worst performances, it is clear that criteria other than scholarly or even moral ones entered into defining excellence. The rural students had the special advantage of entering the school at a young and malleable age. Accounts of entrance examinations consistently mention the importance the school attached to a certain precocity of the adolescent who was both gifted and open-minded. The profile of the ideal candidate in these accounts in fact indicates the urban candidate,[36] possessing above all a good knowledge of French, both oral and written,[37] that is, able to prove "a good understanding of the texts," good pronunciation,[38] and the sense for methodical[39] but also "intelligent" composition, which displays "open-mindedness," and "flexibility."[40] They also had to demonstrate "their ideas" and "a bit of method in discussion,"[41] as well as "in reasoning,"[42] and "original and good ideas." Nevertheless, "educable" candidates, youths "with their minds on the future," who were "capable of acquiring knowledge," "those who promise the most in terms of the future," still had more chances than the "pillars of the school."[43]

In 1905, the principal of the teacher training school wrote,

> We are seeking intelligent young people, with open minds and a lively curiosity, rather than well-prepared candidates who have been stuffed with facts. The teacher training school is not a point of arrival, it is a point of departure. It is less about having a lot of varied knowledge, than about being able to acquire it. For us, the good candidate is not one who knows a lot but one who has the future in mind. This consideration should induce all teachers who have intelligent students' to prepare them for the teacher training school without thinking that they are obliged to get them through the intermediate stage of supplementary courses. . . . Of course, students from supplementary courses have an ease of preparation not possessed by their rivals coming directly from tribal schools, and under excellent conditions, they have completed a program that makes them able to cope with the examination; but a student with straightforward judgment and a flexible mind always attracts the attention of the examiners no matter what his origin or the school he has attended. Hence, out of twenty students admitted in the first year (1906), six come directly from tribal schools.[44]

This text is instructive for its detailed description of the mechanism of selection for entrance to the teacher training school: rural residents selected according to this principle were not likely to be ranked in the first third of the entrance examinations,[45] but they would be able to take advantage of the opportunity given them.[46] Their age, their distance from the dominant culture, expressed even in the most concrete details of clothing or the most mundane physical conduct,[47] the extraordinary adventure that happened to many of them, their well-to-do or often prestigious origin, insofar as it made social mobility conceivable—all combined to make the rural students very competitive, much more than a hypothetical affinity of values between the school and peasant values, or the Kabyles' greater aptitude for Westernization, and to enable them to take better advantage than their urban classmates of the exceptional conditions of acculturation offered them in the teacher training school. It enabled them to benefit fully and voluntarily from the "effect of shaping" exercised perhaps more intensely than any other in that educational branch. Moreover, a certain rustic bearing—meaning an absence both of malice and of physical and moral resistance—was not considered negative by the school when it could be translated into straightforwardness and firmness, and not into narrow-mindedness and fanaticism. Thus one teacher attributed his success in the teacher training school primarily to this feature.

> My excessive honesty and my way of answering earned me a reputation as a good mind. However, I was quite aware that they were very indulgent toward me. Without ever wanting to be different from the others in any way, I was, however, not like them; having lived thus far in a condition of independence, I remained natural, without affectation or malice. Having suffered and struggled early on, I had willpower, and I had acquired enough experience to avoid unpleasant surprises.[48]

Thus social origin, or more precisely, the relation to the dominant culture and the school that social origin produces, played an important role in the selection of elites, including those who were the object of a prolonged selection. This "elective election" evident in the political elites chosen mainly because of their position in the local social hierarchy, their prestige, and their clientele also played an unconscious role—conveyed through the bias of the educational apparatus—for the elites of a lower stature.

The Hidden Rule

An examination of the structure of the school discourse concerning the choice of students and the meaning of excellence is useful for completing this analysis.[49] Knowing who is excellent certainly tells a great deal about this distinction and its functions. But the analysis of the semantic field of excellence is no doubt necessary to avoid the risk of overinterpreting the statistics. Conversely, the reading attempted here avoids being completely risky only because it is based on those [statistical] consistencies. Last, but not least, when the school spoke of excellence, that is, of what is or should be most strictly educational, it was most clearly speaking of something else.

The logic that underwrote graduation evaluations is not visible at first glance. More precisely, the evaluations are surprising as long as their unity, one of their key elements, is not understood—that is, the primacy of the group over the individual, of morality over knowledge or pedagogical know-how, of the person over technical advantage. So, although they generally took account of character, intellectual aptitudes, work submitted, progress achieved, and pedagogical conduct, the standard of comparison between these different levels was in fact very unequal. Indeed, nothing could compensate for a lack of conformity to the moral demands of the school, while conversely, goodwill, docility, and consistency in effort were always recognized and rewarded. A considerable number of pairs of judgments, from the most caricatured to the most subtle, can be juxtaposed:

Very intelligent but fanatic.
(1887, student from Médéa)

Fanatic, sly, intelligent, works—will probably make only a mediocre assistant.
(1887, student from Beni Yenni)

Barely educated, hardly intelligent, good Frenchman—will make a good teacher.
(1887, student from Biskra)

Sickly, quite serious, not very intelligent, hardworking—will make a good instructor.
(1887, student from Tizi-Ouzou)

Lively mind and quite curious; has worked diligently and is one of the good native students. There may be some reservations about his character, which is not very open; about his mind, which is too disposed to systematic criticism—despite everything, seems apt to do good service in teaching.
(1931, student from Sidi-Aïch, ranked 4th out of 15 students)

Rather timid and awkward, but a good fellow, accommodating, gets along with his classmates and tried to do well. Not one of the quickest minds, but thanks to a tenacious effort, progress has been constant—will do his best as a teacher.
(1931, student from Mekla, ranked 3rd)

Between 1887 and 1931, years chosen arbitrarily, so-called technical (hence ethically neutral) categories were substituted for the moral categories initially used. This evolution was slow and apparently quite difficult, as indicated by the following evaluation from an intermediate period.

Nervous character, violent, irritable. Yields easily to impulses of a still uncouth and barbaric nature. Gifted with respect to intelligence and judgment. Worked in fits and starts. Has a rather solid education. A boy who is hardly susceptible to improvement and who will have to be watched very closely.
(1906, student from Beni Oughlis)

The abrupt and sometimes cynical nature of the evaluations of the late nineteenth century gradually gave way to a discourse more suited to the situation of the school and the nature of the power relation between the two world wars. However, despite the length of the period under consideration (a half century all told), there is no doubt of the homogeneity of the categories contained here, hence of the implicit ideology. The uncensored formulation at the end of the nineteenth century clearly expressed the truth of the institution: in the colonial situation, primary school teachers were shaped mainly in terms of a moral and civilizing initiative; the pedagogical objective came second. It was the same in France, slightly earlier.[50] If the school in Algeria in the late nineteenth and early twentieth century resorted to the ideological selection and dressage used in France fifty years earlier, it was because the situation of the teacher training school confronting students from Kabyle, the major component of the student body of Bouzaréah in 1890, was not fundamentally different from the teacher training schools of Auvergne or Alsace in 1860. In both cases, the attempt was to shape cultural mediators who came from a "barbarian" culture and were assigned to spread the legitimate culture. In shaping such mediators, it was risky to privilege qualities of mind. Hence excellent teachers were those who joined qualities of heart and mind, guaranteeing an honest use of intellectual "gifts," whereas good teachers were those whose moral attitudes made them fit at least to "set an example."

Stopping here would be to impoverish the analysis considerably. For the rule of the absolute priority of morality, if true, does not take into account the totality and complexity of the system of educational values. Perhaps it is only by the distribution of individuals into hierarchical strata that we can grasp the effect of a complex process in which the contradictions—both those between educational values and colonial values, on the one hand, and those at the heart of the educational ideology itself, on the other—would confront one another. In fact, the school and the colonial power did not necessarily have the same expectations vis-à-vis the educated individuals who were destined to become agents of dissemination of the dominant culture, even if, in other respects, the school was intimately linked to that power. The latter required teachers who were competent, but especially those who were politically safe. The school, however, expected much more from the teacher training school students. Insofar as it reproduced itself by shaping them, insofar as in other respects it believed more in the action of the total person than in that of techniques and knowledge, it was reluctant to ratify individuals who were not deeply acculturated to and steeped in Western values. However, the school's system of expectations was itself ambiguous, and strictly scholarly excellence was most often the product of a compromise between what might be called the demand for brilliance and the demand for seriousness.[51] Therefore, despite their definitive formulation, these evaluations are the product of an elaborate ideological alchemy. Only a deeper analysis can reveal what values were

invested in each operation of ranking and how contradictory demands were
reconciled.

First, all ways of being a satisfactory (that is, bad) teacher can be reduced
to two: one was *bad* because one was *heavy, closed, obtuse, violent,* and *has
remained Arabic* (or *Kabyle*); or, on the contrary, because one was *flighty,
pretentious, fickle,* and *lacking moral sense.* Similarly, one was (only) *good*
either because one was *diligent but not very intelligent* or because one was
gifted but might do better (fig 10.1).

The structure of these oppositions shows that we are dealing with two series
of oppositions with relation to a median term and not with two terms defining
an axis, like the gradation of *satisfactory, average, good, excellent* would seem
to suggest. Thus excellent was opposed on one side to *obtuse, closed,* and
diligent; and on the other to *immaturity, flightiness,* and *pretension.* It would
be defined, then, not only as a fortunate combination of qualities of mind and
heart but also as the proper mix of ascetic virtues and intellectual gifts. Thus:

> Character firm and manly—a large base of sincerity—bright intelligence—honest
> and healthy judgment—education already extensive and solid. . . . In brief, a
> teacher who can be counted on.
> (1904, from Beni Yenni)

Or, even better:

> Excellent individual—energetic and honest character—solid intelligence—a lot
> of fervor in work. Has given complete satisfaction with his behavior and his
> work—should very rapidly become a very good teacher.
> (1911, from Beni Yenni)

The text on excellence can also be deciphered differently by establishing that
excellence occupies a central position that marks off two halves: that of a lack
of acculturation and that of an excess of acculturation. Clearly, that for which
those on the side of *heaviness* and *diligence* were criticized was symmetrically
inverse to that for which those on the side of *amateurism* and *lack of conscience*
were criticized. Another structure opposing two types of relationships in conflict with the legitimate culture can be superimposed on this structure. It is no
accident that, when the hundred evaluations sampled for in-depth analysis[52] are
subjected to a simple selection on the basis of the categories used, 70 percent
of the individuals ranked as being overly acculturated were of urban origin
while 60 percent of those ranked in the other half were of rural origin. And
everything in their language and manners opposed the teacher training school
student of urban origin to the teacher training school student of rural origin.

In 1911, in an article entitled ''Advice to Monitors and Native Assistants,''
the director of the teacher training school wrote: ''According to the common
proverb, habit makes everything familiar to us. That is quite true of language.

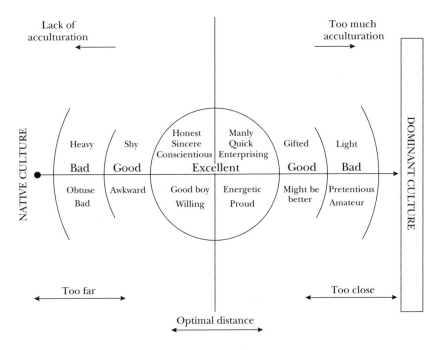

Figure 10.1.   Types of relations toward the school and the dominant culture.

Look at the instructor in the city, constantly in contact with French people, he truly speaks like a Parisian; his rustic colleague, on the other hand, searches for his words and stammers: he always seems to be on tenterhooks."[53]

Similarly, it was always students of rural origin who were accused of being "heavy of bearing and intelligence,"[54] "rough in manners, language, and feelings."[55] The opposition of the two halves of the system of educational values led to the term-for-term opposition of the two kinds of good and bad, if not to the existence of two distinct paths: that of obsolete rusticity and that of restrained urbanity, as the following two evaluations demonstrate.

A firm character, goodwill with good sense. A bit awkward and shy, but very dedicated and conscientious. Sustained and methodical work. Quite extensive and solid education. Will very likely make a good teacher.
   (1904, from Aït Lahsen)

Character already shaped. Knows what he wants and as a result imposes on those around him. Strong willed. Very sustained work. In all, a personality. Ordinary intelligence. Will very likely make an excellent assistant schoolmaster.
   (1897, from Saïda)

In fact, the school constantly vacillated between ratifying the aptitudes and especially the know-how—which usually amounted to knowing how to speak—of urban students whose acculturation had been loosely acquired by contact with Europeans and recognizing the diligent efforts of rural students whose only relationship with the legitimate culture was in school. Therefore, what defined excellent students was not only a compound of good qualities and defects but also a kind of relationship to the legitimate culture; and from that perspective, the ranking into one or the other half was ultimately as important for what it said about the individual and what it allowed to be predicted of his professional future as the ranking into whatever stratum. It is particularly revealing of the organization of the system of educational values; the school simultaneously showed a predilection for those who were closest to—or least far from—it and the dominant society. The school system maintained a hidden preference for them. But it had to yield not only to the external demand that regarded docility and loyalty as paramount necessities but also to its own requirements for asceticism and rigor, which were particularly strong in the formation process of the teacher training school.[56] Without denying an essential element of this training since the time of Guizot, the school could not renounce the exemplary function of its representatives.[57]

However, the system of educational values must not be presented as symmetrical, or more precisely, symmetrically organized with relation to excellence. In fact, not enough acculturation, like too much acculturation, was defined not in relation to excellence but in relation to the legitimate culture that then constituted a second center, indeed the actual center of the semantic field. What characterized all individuals located in the *defect* hemisphere was that they were too far from the legitimate culture. Conversely, those in the *excess* hemisphere were too close to it. Consequently, excellence was defined primarily in terms of distance, that is, as the sum of the images and behaviors adopted when one was neither too far nor too close to Western culture.

The vocabulary of the institution is very significant in this respect: "Excellent character, very resourceful, prudent. Customs and habits: has taken on too much of ours, even the bad ones" (1890, student from Tlemcen). Spatial notations even appear: "Very nice boy. Open, frank, cheerful character; polite and friendly manners: one of those who has gotten close to us during his stay in the teacher training school" (1911, student from Kerkera, a community of Collo).[58]

Clearly, however, the teacher training school students were never told explicitly that they must not get too close to the legitimate culture and that there was a rule dictating that evolution is not linear and unlimited: on the path of acculturation, there was a boundary that must not be crossed, a limit that was the precise indication of excellent. But if violations of this rule were severely sanctioned, the rule itself was never clearly stated. Furthermore, all measure of distance in relation to the legitimate culture involved an implicit measure

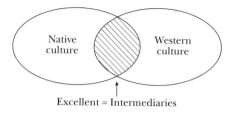

Figure 10.2.   Circles of traditional and Western cultures.

of the distance in relation to the traditional culture of origin. Someone who was too far from the West was too close to his culture of origin; he had ''remained an Arab'' (or a Kabyle). But someone who was too close to the West was too far from his culture of origin; he was de-Islamicized, uprooted in the colonialist lexicon: ''He takes himself for a Frenchman.'' So one ceased to be excellent whenever one crossed the circle of traditional culture. One was excellent as long as one has not penetrated the circle of Western culture (fig. 10.2).

Figure 10.2 not only accounts for the strict logic of the pedagogy designed for natives; it also allows us to explain both the existence and the failure of what might be called the assimilationist movement in Algeria. The ''in-between'' position of the excellent students coincides perfectly with the position of intermediary claimed by the middle-class elites of the subjugated society.

''The native intellectuals,'' wrote S. Faci, founder of *La Voix des humbles,* ''are the best intermediaries between France and the Moslem masses; their knowledge of the various milieus, their culture, their respectability, their independence, their impartiality, their attachment to France, are so many guarantees for the public powers.''[59]

This congruence is expected, since those elites were most often shaped in the French school. It was simply the product of internalizing the school's expectations. But we can also understand why the assimilationist ideology (expressed, for example, in a corporative publication like *La Voix des humbles*)[60]—consisting essentially of maximizing the distance separating the elites from the masses and minimizing the distance separating those same elites from the legitimate culture, more precisely, from the Europeans—was inherently bound to fail. For it explicitly went against a concealed but imperative rule of the colonial game. In their interpretation of the expectations of the school and in their eagerness to adopt them, these good students committed an error of judgment, or to put it more precisely, they did not recognize the implicit rule.

If the policy of assimilation demanded by the rising middle class failed—even though it had supporters in France—it was, of course, because it was incompatible with the totality of colonial interests. But it is significant to find proof that, right in the heart of the institution that was both the vehicle of that ideology and the declared means of that policy, the dice were loaded from the start.

Notes

1. Charles-Robert Ageron, *Les Algériens musulmans et la France* (Paris: Presses universitaires de France, 1968), 940; and H. Desvages, "L'enseignement des musulmans en Algérie sous le rectorat Jeanmarie," *Le Mouvement Social* 70 (1970): 137.

2. E. Combes, "Rapport fait au nom de la commission chargée d'examiner les modifications à introduire dans la législation et dans l'organisation de divers services de l'Algérie (instruction primaire des indigènes)," reproduced in *Bulletin Universitaire de l'Académie d'Alger,* 1892, p. 223.

3. "A. Cote, Schoolmaster," *Bulletin de l'enseignement des indigènes,* 1901, p. 28.

4. Combes clearly preferred external barbarians to domestic ones, as shown by several indications in his report: "No one I know claims to measure Arab brains and Breton brains by the same standard, and to close to the former the horizons of ideas and knowledge that are beyond the reach of the latter." "Rapport," 323.

5. Ibid., 177.

6. Ibid., 134.

7. Emile Burdeau, *L'Algérie en 1891, Rapports et discours à la Chambre des députés* (Paris: Hachette, 1892), 205.

8. For Guizot's inspectors, see Antoine Prost, *L'enseignement en France, 1800–1967* (Paris: Armand Colin, 1968), 97–99. For the committee of the XVIII, see the extracts of several statements in Combes's report cited above.

9. [. . .] Prost, 110.

10. R. Thabault, *1848–1914, l'ascension d'un peuple, son village, ses hommes, ses routes, son école* (Paris: Librairie Delgrave, 1914), 80.

11. "There are still areas in France where the inhabitants neither understand nor speak French, the language in which their obligations as men and as citizens are stipulated. These groups include the Flemish part of the districts of Dunkirk and Hazebrouk, the Basques in the Pyrenees, and the Bretons of Lower Brittany (the entire Department of Finistère and about half of Côtes-du-Nord and Morbihan, except of course for the inhabitants of the cities and the sailors on the coasts)." J. Carré, Inspector-General of Primary Education, quoted in *Bulletin de l'enseignement des indigènes,* 1888, 235.

12. Ibid., 238.

13. Ibid.

14. Ibid., 239.

15. P. Bernard, "Difficultés de l'enseignement au cours préparatoire," *Bulletin de l'enseignement des indigènes,* 1905. These teachers found confirmation of their own experience elsewhere. For example, in this text on "the education of the natives in the central provinces of British India": "After all, we should not be too surprised at the slow pace of the spread of education in those very backward countries and the minimal profit gained from attending school. No child in the world is worse prepared to learn than that young native. A European learns everything at school, in his family, on the

street. But let us remember the condition of a native child: his father and mother don't know anything; at home, there are no books, no furniture, nothing but three or four essential implements: a copper or clay jug, and a pot for cooking.'' Joseph Chailley, *Bulletin de l'enseignement des indigènes,* 1905.

16. Burdeau, *L'Algérie en* 1891, 205.

17. But, as we know, in Algeria, this concession did not last very long.

18. *Mémoires,* 3:24. Quoted in Thabault, 1848–1914, 53.

19. *The Old Régime and the French Revolution,* trans. Stuart Gilbert (Garden City, N.Y.: Doubleday, 1955).

20. Ibid., 212.

21. Louis Legrand, *L'influence du positivisme dans l'oeuvre sociale de Jules Ferry* (Paris: Marcel Rivière, 1961), 193.

22. Luc Boltanski, *Prime éducation et morale de classe* (Paris, Mouton, 1968), 29: ''Today we can hardly imagine the hopes placed in the school: what the school was to realize was a total transformation of minds, a peaceful and internal revolution. It allows everyone to rise to a decent, moral, orderly, and cultivated life. It was also, if not to level conditions, at least to create uniform ways of living and thinking, as well as uniform sensibilities.''

23. *Capital,* trans. by Samuel Moore and Edward Aveling (New York: International Publishers, 1967), vol. 1, chap. 33, pp. 765–774.

24. Speech in the Chambre, 28 February 1885.

25. [Ed. note: quotations omitted. Reference is to Paul Bert, speech, 14 April 1897, in *Bulletin de l'enseignement des indigènes,* p. 29; Jonnart, Speech at Tlemcen, *Dépêche Algérienne,* 8 May 1895; Viollette, *Algérie vivra-t-elle,* 1931, p. 258.] Similarly, the ''class function'' of secondary education in France is much more manifest and explicit at the beginning of the century than later on. See Viviane Isambert-Jamati, ''Essai d'analyse sociologique d'une réforme scolaire française au debut du siècle,'' paper presented to the 7th World Congress of Sociology, Varna (Bulgaria), 14–19 September 1970.

26. ''In a semibarbaric country,'' wrote Combes in his report to the Senate, ''the school building itself is a lesson for the eyes. It indicates the superiority of the people who built it over the people whose youth it shelters. For simple men, used to judging by appearances, a shack-school would not have a moral effect. It would look too much like other residences to give the idea of a considerable superiority. If we want our civilization to become more refined simply by the sight of the school, let us build schools worthy of it and worthy of us.'' Combes, ''Rapport,'' 669–670.

27. Claude Lévi-Strauss, *Tristes Tropiques* (Paris, Plon 1962 [1st ed. 1955]), 185. For example, the Salesian missionaries understood that if they convinced the Bororos to give up building their village in the traditional concentric plan, they would gain control of them. Such examples can be multiplied.

28. ''Morale-Conseils pédagogiques,'' *Bulletin de l'enseignement des indigènes,* 1890, 254.

29. While the text designed for French schools barely ten years earlier is more subtle, it strictly translates the same priority of moral action: ''Moral instruction is designed to complete and connect, elevate and ennoble all school instruction. While other studies each develop a special category of aptitudes and useful knowledge, moral instruction develops the man himself, that is, a heart, an intelligence, a conscience.'' Decree of 27

July 1882, determining the pedagogical organization and curriculum of public primary schools. III-1: "Object of moral instruction." . . .

30. J. Melia, *Le triste sort des indigènes musulmans de l'Algérie* (Algiers, 1935), 2. Melia's comments are corroborated by F. Abbas: "The European surrounded by his Arab mandarins (cadis, pasha, and marabouts) was feudal. France was the King—'Oh, if the King only knew,' this pathetic and trusting cry of the serfs of the ancien régime seems to hold for us. The essential thing is that liberal France hears him." *La nuit coloniale* (Paris: Juillard, 1962), 116–125.

31. As indicated in the school archives, an unfavorable assessment on completing the teacher training could definitively compromise a career in education and shut all doors to a career in the public domain.

32. The following analysis is based on the statistical processing of all the evaluations of the 993 teacher training school students studied previously (part 2), and on the relationship of the categories of those evaluations with the economic, social, and geographic characteristics of those students.

33. These characteristics were, in fact, compensatory advantages and could be turned into educational advantages.

34. It is clear why teachers' sons did not have good grades, since they were practically the only ones who said in interviews that they should (or could) have gone to the academic high school and criticized the teacher training school: "Teacher training school was oppression. I felt there was progress in relation to the other natives, but it didn't come out" (teacher of Kabyle origin, son of a teacher, appointment 1923–1926). "I returned to teacher training school because of the way things worked out. . . . For my part, I would haved liked to go to the academic high school, then to study law. I felt drawn toward eloquence" (teacher of Arab origin, son of a teacher of Oran, appointment 1924–1927).

35. It was always and only the urban students who could display dilettantism (a rare quality in this population) and who could boast: "I was the first native to get in. In the first quarter, I was in the first 10 (we were ranked with the Europeans). Afterward I was average. I had talents, but I didn't work; I practically didn't study. I often wrote an essay an hour before turning it in, even though we had two weeks. I should have done much better than my less talented classmates" (teacher of urban origin, from a very modest family, West Algeria, appointment 1924–1927).

36. Since the urban students were those ranked first.

37. "We attach particular importance to French: a written French composition and a reading explained orally constitute the two decisive tests." "Concours d'admission au cours normal," *Bulletin de l'enseignement des indigènes,* 1900, 161.

38. "It is necessary to insist on pronunciation, articulation, delivery, emphasis. A clear reading in which the tone is modulated to express different feelings is itself an intelligent commentary on the text." "Concours d'admission au cours normal (suite): Épreuves orales et pratiques," *Bulletin de l'enseignement des indigènes,* 1905, 6.

39. Which must not exclude "the small sincere, experienced, personal note: candidates are censured for reciting with a pen instead of letting their heart or their experience speak." Ibid., 175.

40. "Compte rendu du concours d'entrée," *Bulletin de l'enseignement des indigènes,* 1905.

41. Ibid., 1904, 7.
42. Ibid., 1903.
43. Ibid., 1905.
44. Ibid., 1906, 110.
45. In the entrance examination, there is the following order: urban 36.0%; semi-urban 34.8%; rural 31.2%.

46. And in fact, in the graduation examination, rural students rank ahead of semi-urban students, 34.4% in the first third, as opposed to 32.6% for semiurban, and 36.4% for cities.

47. Describing his costume on the day he came to the city to qualify for the certificate of studies in 1920, one teacher said, "I was a country boy, he [a colleague and friend who was present at the interview] was a city boy. I reported for the certificate of studies in a turban with small cords on top, you know, the ones worn only by riders or adults. It's because I was a spoiled child. But in the schoolyard, everybody looked at me: I was the only one" (teacher of rural, Arab origin, appointment 1924–1927).

48. S. Faci, *Mémoires d'un instituteur algérien d'origine indigène*, supplement to *La Voix des humbles*, April 1931.

49. This [section] is based on the content analysis of a sample of one hundred evaluations from eight complete graduations, at a regular interval (every seven years). Graduation and not evaluation has been chosen as the unit of analysis based on the hypothesis that individuals' perception of their virtues and defects, in the pedagogical relationship more than in any other situation, is spontaneously structural: one is a good or bad student in relation to a group of defined students.

50. This is certainly the explanation of certain features and some vicissitudes of teacher training education in the nineteenth century, especially that "in-depth inquiry" which was to take into account not only the candidate's knowledge but especially his conduct and his moral attitudes. Instituted by the Guizot law in 1830, this inquiry completely replaced the recruitment competition in the reform of 1861. See Maurice Gontard, *La question des écoles normales primaires de la Révolution de 1789 à 1869* (Toulouse, Centre régional de documentation pédagogique, 1962). Notably, the author specifies: "Recruitment by competition which could open the school to elements not offering religious guarantees (this is right after the Falloux law) and moral requisites is abandoned as insufficient and risky. It is replaced by an in-depth inquiry guided by the concerns of the rector and the primary inspectors."

51. See Pierre Bourdieu and Monique de Saint-Martin, "L'excellence scolaire et les valeurs du système d'enseignement français," *Annales (Economies, Sociétés, Civilisations)* 25, no. 1 (January–February 1970): 147–175.

52. The sample included an equal number of rural and urban students.

53. *Bulletin de l'enseignement des indigènes,* 1897, 98.

54. 1897, from Aït Kherma, a mixed community of a national fort.

55. 1904, from Aït Lahsen, Beni Yenni.

56. In fact, the social origin, generally low/middle, and the shaping of the teachers of teacher training schools predisposed them to reject what might be called intellectual "Parisianism" in favor of solidity, the provincial, and "scholarly" seriousness.

57. Hence contradictions like the following text of 1911. Given the period, "Arab" can be translated as "urban" and "Kabyle" as "rural," without any serious risk of

error: "And we are threatened in June by a new Berber invasion. I certainly don't ask anything better than to have students of that origin. They are diligent, hardworking, labor very zealously and consistently. They are not gentlemen as our Arabs so easily become. But in terms of a diploma, they inspire much more confidence in me. In any case, even if the needs of the department weren't so unambiguous, I must admit that I fear the sharp ferment of the Kabyle mind in an establishment. The schoolmasters of Kabylia complain quite rightly of their assistants—and I have sometimes had occasion to note the symptoms that make me fear the intensification of the evil in the next generation of schoolmasters from Bouzaréah. So we need Arabs." (Letter of the director of the teacher training school to the director of the Academy of Alger, 23 February 1911, Archive de l'Ecole normale de Bouzaréah, série K.)

58. And conversely: "Secretive, lying, brash character. Has hardly been changed by contact with the French" (1911, student from Beni Oughlis).

59. *L'Algérie sous l'égide de la France* (Alger: Published by the author, 1936), 277.

60. *La voix des humbles* (The voice of the humble), publication of teachers of indigenous origin, was a collective journal that appeared in Algeria from 1920 to 1939. It was edited by graduates of the teacher training program of Bouzaréah. One could consider that it expressed more or less exactly the aspirations and the social project of the ensemble of middle elites trained in French schools and which the lexicon of the era called "évolués."

Part IV

Contesting the Categories of Rule

11

The Difference—Deferral of a Colonial Modernity

Public Debates on Domesticity in British Bengal

Dipesh Chakrabarty

In nationalist representations, the colonial experience of becoming modern is haunted by the fear of looking unoriginal. This is understandable, for some of the founding myths of European imperialisms of the last two hundred years were provided by narratives that, as Meaghan Morris has recently reminded us, always portrayed the modern as something that had already happened somewhere else.[1] Nationalist writings therefore subsume the question of difference within a search for essences, origins, authenticities, which, however, have to be amenable to global-European constructions of modernity so that the quintessentially nationalist claim of being "different but modern" can be validated.[2] While nationalist thought thus mobilizes for its own ends the cultural field of difference, its resolutions, whether of the "woman question" or that of the "nation" itself, are inherently unstable and require, for their continued survival, much more than just the force of persuasive rhetoric. Differences are too heterodox for the nationalist project of modernity to contain them.

The issue of domesticity helps me to chart the movement of some of these questions in colonial Bengal. That English education often brought in its trail a sense of crisis in Bengali families—a certain degree of waywardness in young men that led to their neglecting their duties toward their families and the elders—was a most commonly voiced complaint against the Young Bengal of the early nineteenth century. The British in India pushed the question further by promoting the idea that husbands and wives should be friends/companions in marriage. "Friendship," of course, had a very particular range of meaning in these nineteenth-century discussions on domestic life. It reflected the well-known Victorian patriarchal ideals of "companionate marriage" that the

373

British introduced into India in the nineteenth century and that many Bengali male and female reformers embraced with great zeal.[3]

It is the debates around this question—in particular, those around the ideals of the Bengali housewife—that act as my starting point. What interests me, however, is a particular problem. Hidden in these debates were statements about how the personal/domestic was to be distinguished from the communal/public, the distinction itself reflecting some of the compulsions that modern colonial rule brought with itself. This essay is an effort to understand the many contradictory and heterodox moves through which the Bengali modern has negotiated this distinction in (re)constituting itself within a world system fashioned by imperialism. My aim is to attend carefully to nineteenth-century Bengali contestations over received bourgeois models for relating the personal to the public world of civil and political life.

The British instituted some kind of a civil society in colonial Bengal. The modern civil society carries with itself the distinction of the "public" and the "private." This distinction, in turn, raises the question of the state. As Philippe Ariès says, the modern public/private split fundamentally relates to the positioning of the individual with regard to the (modern) state, that is, the casting of the individual into the role of the citizen.[4] Since the colonial relationship was one that denied the colonized the status of the citizen, Bengali engagements with "modernizing" the domestic cannot be discussed in separation from nationalism, the ideology that promised citizenship and the nation-state, and thus the ideal civil-political society that the domestic order would have the duty of servicing. What I discuss, however, are the ways the project of creating citizen-subjects for Bengal/India was/is continually disrupted by other imaginations of family, personhood, and the domestic.

The debates about domesticity that I examine here took place within what I would call "*public* narratives of the nature of social life in the family." I emphasize the word "public" because the documents on which I base this essay are both products as well as constituents of a modern print culture or the public sphere—in the European, or even Habermasian, sense—that arose in Bengal (and elsewhere in India) as a result of our encounter with a post-Enlightenment European imperial nation. The texts discussed here are prescriptive, many of them written by Bengali authors, male and female, attempting to adapt that very Victorian subject, "domestic science," to nineteenth-century nationalistic programs for educating women. What these documents capture are fragments of Bengali self-fashioning in the context of the formation of a modern public life, for these writings were definitely subject to a growing body of conventions about desirable forms and topics of speech in public.[5] This entailed, as it has elsewhere, the development of rules for representing, within this so-called public, aspects of life seen as constituting its opposite—the private, the personal, the domestic. Bengali modernity has thus produced its own share of artifacts that narrate "the private" in "public," for example, novels, autobiographies, diaries, letters, etc.

This history, then, tells us very little about what went on in the everyday lives of actual, empirical, *bhadralok* families. Something of those lives can indeed be traced in my documents—and there is evidence to suggest the existence of relatively autonomous domains for women that the coming of a print culture may have significantly eroded.[6] But what I focus on is primarily a conflict of attitudes that marked what was said *in print,* within the emergent conventions of bookish writings, about the ideals of the housewife and about desirable forms of marriage and domestic life.

I should also explain as part of these preliminaries that it is a small group of people whose history is discussed in this essay. I write about the so-called Hindu bhadralok, the respectable people of the middle classes. It is partly my lived, intimate knowledge of this group that informs the questions I discuss here.

I

In many ways, the expression "domestic life" as it is used here was a European category of thought. The assumption that cultures were not properly understood until the "domestic" had been opened up to scholarly (or governmental) scrutiny, itself belonged to an intellectual tradition that objectified the idea of "culture" and that seems to have marked much European writing and thinking on India in the eighteenth and early nineteenth century. James Mill in his *History of British India* (1817) quotes Bentinck, then the governor of Fort St. George, Madras, as expressing the opinion that the Europeans knew "little or nothing of the customs and manners of the Hindus, . . . their manner of thinking; their domestic habits and ceremonies, in which circumstances a knowledge of the people consists."[7] Mill's quotation of Henry Strachey from the *Fifth Report* also points to a similar train of thought: "We cannot study the genius of the people in their own sphere of action. We know little of their domestic life, their knowledge, conversation, amusements, their trades and casts [*sic*], or of any of those national or individual characteristics, which are essential to a complete knowledge of them."[8]

Mill, as is widely known, was to erect upon this concern with the domestic and "women's question" an entire edifice, his voluminous *History,* that condemned India as an inferior civilization. The concern with "domesticity" was very much a part of this civilizational critique of India. The idea of "civilization," a product, as Lucien Febvre has shown, of European thought in the 1760s, saw the world as both united and hierarchical. The hierarchy was defined by a scale of civilization that constructed the world as one—why else would a single scale be universally valid?—while dividing it up into more and less civilized countries.[9]

The universalist indictment of this civilizing discourse aroused in Bengali (male) social reformers of the nineteenth century a strong desire to participate in what was now seen as a world community of countries, peoples, or nations (these words being used in this period somewhat interchangeably). "Each country has its own language," said *Bodhoday,* one of the earliest "modern" children's primers (written by Vidyasagar).

> The language we speak is called Bengali. The people of Kashi and the surrounding regions speak a language called Hindi. The people of Persia speak Persian. In Arabia, the language is Arabic . . . The language of the people of England is English.[10]

This awakening to a wider world, however, was qualified by the hierarchical view that was part and parcel of the concept of "civilization" itself. Literature produced in Bengali for consumption in schools also showed that long before the new colonial intelligentsia became "Indian" in any geopolitical sense, they had become ensnared in this competitive and hierarchical imagination of the world. In a book on morality, in the writing of which Vidyasagar collaborated with his friend Rajkrishna Bandyopadhyay, this is how the civilizing language expressed itself in an essay on "labour."

> Countries where people are averse to labour and live on the flesh [of animals] obtained by hunting or on fruit and roots [*phalmool*], are uncivilized [*asabhya*]. The aboriginals of America and Australia as well as the Negroes are still in this state. They live in great hardship without adequate food and clothing, and they do not save anything for hard times. It is not surprising that so many of them die from hunger. . . . The Germans, the Swiss, the French, the Dutch and the English are the most industrious peoples [*jati*] of the world. That is why they enjoy the best circumstances among all nations.[11]

The promise of "improvement," of being allowed into the tiny coterie of the "leading" nations of the world—a possibility of which this quotation speaks and to which it sees "hard work" as the key—was, of course, what theoretically made the community of civilized nations look "open." It was also what drew, and has since drawn—as Ranajit Guha has shown—generations of nationalists of this idea of "improvement."[12]

As this civilizing-cum-nationalist body of thought proliferated in the second half of the nineteenth century to incorporate influences coming out of Victorian England, the personal and the domestic came to be tied ever more closely to the idea of the nation. Bengali books on education of the young now argued, following the likes of Samuel Smiles, that "the individual was a physical embodiment of the nation" and the latter improved "only if the individual had undergone all-round improvement."[13] The Victorian fetishes of "discipline," "routine," and "order" became some of the most privileged elements in

Bengali writings on domestic and personal arrangements, constituting in themselves objects of desire and beauty.

The internal "discipline" of "the European home" was now seen as a key
to European prosperity and political power. Bengali books on "domestic
science" extolled the "attractive" qualities of "the house of any civilized
European," which was now compared to "the abode of gods." It was a place
where *srinkhala* (discipline) reigned, things were clean, attractive, and placed
in order. The Bengali/Indian home—itself a colonial construct, as we shall
see—suffered badly in comparison. It was said to be like hell—dirty, smelly,
disorderly, unclean, and unhealthy.[14] In her book on domesticity published in
the 1880s Nagendrabala Saraswati combined (the ancient Hindu lawgiver)
Manu with Samuel Smiles to say,

> There cannot be any improvement in the state of the nation without improvement
> first in the domestic and political spheres. Obedience is the fundamental aspect
> of life in both politics and the family; in the latter the father or the husband is
> the master. The degree to which a society will obey rules depends on [practices]
> at more fundamental levels.[15]

Order was thus linked to notions of cleanliness, hygiene, health, and a certain
regimentation of time expressed in the "virtue" of punctuality. The question
of health, in turn, reflected the relations of power under colonial rule, the idiom
of gender (the imperial theme of the emasculation of the colonized) in which
it was often manifested, and the extent to which the male body itself had become
a signifier for these relationships.[16] Several of the books on health and medicine
written in the 1860s and 1870s were concerned with the supposed laziness of
the Bengali male body. Radhanath Basak's *Sarirtattvasar,* the author said, was
written to help the Bengali body grow strong.[17] Radhikaprasanna Mukhopadhyay's seemingly popular book, *Sasthyaraksha* (to which he gave the English
title *Preservation of Health*) put the question in a straightforward manner.

> For as long as there will be wars and other similar acts of a base nature, the
> meat-eating races will dominate the vegetarian ones. . . . Respectable middle-class
> people of our country are sometimes seen to be humiliated by lower-class
> Europeans in public places. . . . Indeed, there is need for valour and strength in
> the country.[18]

The happiest human races, argued the author of another book on physical
education, were those who had been able to develop "a balanced growth of
mental and physical faculties." Sound moral judgment (*dharmabuddhi*), he
said, did not prevail until the brain was strongly developed. This was apparently
what "the scholars of Europe and America [had] recently discovered," and
they had accordingly devised rules for regulating life in the family—regulating
the practices to do with love, food, procreation, and child rearing. The critical

task in all this was to reform women, for these arrangements could not be put in place until women were educated in the new rules of the body. "Food soaked in ghee or oil, sweets and unripe fruit are all like poison to the child," complained our author, yet "uneducated [Bengali] housewives" continued to bring the nation's children up on just such a diet.[19] Nationalism was thus also at work in redefining childhood. Anukulchandra Datta, one of the early writers on "domestic science," wrote, "Well-trained children are the pride of the country. With bad training and corrupt morals, they only bring disgrace to the family and [become] the scum of the nation."[20] A regimen of routine regulating children's eating habits, games, work, and manners was what the housewife was now being called on to administer.[21]

Time was of the essence of this regimen. Its proper management was seen as the key to dovetailing "domestic" time with the time of the civil-political and the public sphere. In Datta's book on "home training," a mother tells her daughter,

> How the English appreciate the value of time! They work at the right time, eat at the right time, attend office at the right time, and play at the right time. Everything they do is governed by rules. . . . It is because of this quality that the English get the time to accomplish so much. Nowhere among the educated, civilized nations/races [*jatis*] are instances to be found of people disregarding the value of time and misusing it as we do.

"Obedience," the mother explains (with echoes, once again, of Samuel Smiles), is a "principal virtue" of civilization; without it there could be no peace or discipline in the family.[22] Without a sense of time, said another author, even the nursing of the sick was difficult. In administering doses of medicine, he said, "one should not deviate from the intervals prescribed by the doctor. . . . This is why it is absolutely essential that there is a clock in every house and that . . . the women are taught to read it."[23]

The civilizing discourse that propelled both imperialist and nationalist thought thus produced the figure of the "uneducated housewife/mother" as one of the central problems that the project of making Bengalis into citizen-subjects had to negotiate. The lack of books in Bengali on the subject of domestic science was now deplored by authors who came forward, with a sense of patriotic duty, to fill in this perceived void. "In our country," said Datta, whom we have already quoted, "we don't have a subject called 'home-training.' Yet the prospects of our improvement . . . depend one hundred per cent on this." "The country needs nothing so much to promote its regeneration as good mothers," declared an epigram on the title page of the book.[24]

It was thus that the idea of the "new woman" came to be written into the techniques of the self that nationalism evolved, which looked on the domestic as an inseparable part of the national. The public sphere could not be erected without reconstructing the private.

II

My attempt to understand how the question of difference was played out in this (re)construction of the domestic realm in bhadralok life will take as its point of departure a generally accepted observation often made about this history: that in nineteenth- and early twentieth-century Bengali tracts supporting women's education and even the idea of "friendship" between husbands and wives, the ideal of the "modern," educated housewife was almost always tied to another ideal, the older patriarchal imagination of the mythical divine figure of the goddess Lakshmi.[25]

Lakshmi, regarded as Vishnu's wife by ca. A.D. 400, has for long been upheld in puranic Hinduism as the model Hindu wife, united in complete harmony with her husband in a spirit that combined submission with loyalty, devotion, and fidelity. The goddess Sri-Lakshmi, as David Kinsley points out, "is today one of the most popular and widely venerated deities of the Hindu pantheon. Her auspicious nature and her reputation for granting fertility, luck, wealth and well-being seem to attract devotees in every Indian village."[26] Paul Greenough and Lina Fruzzetti have dealt at length with the role that Lakshmi plays in contemporary Hindu-Bengali culture and her continuing association with notions of abundance, wealth, beauty, and prosperity.[27]

Lakshmi, however, has a reverse side, Alakshmi (Not-Lakshmi), her dark and malevolent Other. The innately heterogeneous puranic literature ascribes the origins of this malicious mythical woman to diverse sources. Her genealogy is complex and is embedded, as Upendranath Dhal shows, in the claims and contestations around Brahmanical ideologies. "The Linga-Purana . . . says that Visnu created the universe in two-fold ways. One part consisted of Sri-Padma, four Vedas, the rites prescribed by the Vedas and Brahmanas. And the other part consisted of Alakshmi, Adharma and the rites deprecated by the Vedas."[28]

However she originated, Alakshmi came to embody a gendered conception of inauspiciousness and the opposite of all that the Hindu lawgivers upheld as the *dharma* (proper moral conduct) of the householder. When she entered a household, she brought jealousy and malice in her trail, brothers fell out with one another, families and their (patri)lineages (*kula*) faced ruin and destruction, the highest misfortune that Hindu patriarchal minds could ever imagine. As Dhal puts it on the basis of *Padmapurana,*

> The choice of Alakshmi rests with a residence where there is constant family feud, where the guests are not honoured, where thieves and scoundrels are in plenty, where people . . . [engage in] illicit love [—] in other words, whatever has been proscribed by lawmakers like Manu, Yajnavalka have been portrayed as the most cherished thing for Alakshmi.[29]

Lakshmi and Alakshmi were mutually exclusive categories. A house where the spirit of Alakshmi prevailed was said to be unbearable for Lakshmi, who always left such a household and bestowed her favors on others who, and in particular whose women, did not flout the rules and rituals that made them auspicious. The Lakshmi-Alakshmi cycle has often been used in pre-British and folk literature to explain family (mis)fortunes and social mobility.[30]

What kind of women would be termed Alakshmis in our nineteenth-century tracts on new domesticity? Two kinds, of which the first were women without any formal education, for it was they who were bringing the nation into disrepute. As one author said, "Women are the Lakshmis of the community [*samaj*]. If they undertake to improve themselves in the sphere of *dharma* and knowledge, and thus exercise a good influence on the youth, . . . [there will be] an automatic improvement in social life."[31] Much of this literature agreed that it was women's innate propensity to jealousy that, when left uncontrolled by the auspicious rituals of domestic work (*grihakarya*), invariably sapped the vitality of the Bengali institution of the (extended) family.[32] One important argument often advanced in favor of educating women was that education of the right kind would help to get rid of the poison of jealousy that ignorance produced and would thus help to restore in women their true Lakshmi-like nature.

Clearly, then, the invocation of Lakshmi was not an instance of a "tradition" fighting "modernity." The "modern" Lakshmi, to be produced through education, was an indispensable part of a nationalist, and self-consciously articulated, search for domestic "happiness." "Education is what brings happiness to the human race. It is the lack of it . . . that is causing unhappiness in women. Their faults are growing. Malice and feelings of hostility toward one another are to be found particularly in uneducated women."[33] Converting women into grihalakshmis (Lakshmi of the household) through the novel means of formal education was the self-appointed task of a civilizing nationalism. One cannot miss the urgency of what a well-known female author of this period, Kailashbashini Devi, wrote in this regard.

> O [the Spirit of] Delusion! When will you leave this land of Bengal? Mother [Bengal], when will your daughters be liberated from the darkness of illusion and find happiness in the light of knowledge? . . . O Lord of Destiny! How many more years will it be before the minds of the women of Bengal are purged of this terrible disposition [to quarrel]?[34]

That it was the lack of knowledge and education that made the women of this country "uncivilized," "lazy," "quarrelsome," and therefore bad for domestic happiness, was now regarded by many authors as a self-evident proposition.[35]

But a lack of education was not the only factor that made some women behave in an Alakshmi-like spirit. Education itself could also be dangerous. It could produce its own variety of Alakshmis, women who were allegedly arrogant, lazy, immodest, defiant of authority, and neglectful of domestic duties. As one author of a textbook on domestic science put it, "in today's women, education produces an [inordinate] fondness for luxury and comfort. They do not have much sympathy for others in the family, nor much modesty, and unlike [women] in the past, do not look on their husbands as divine beings. . . . The proper aim of women's education is to correct these faults."[36]

Several negative terms were used to describe such women or their behavior: *bibi* (the feminine form for *babu*, a dandy), *memsahib* (European women), *boubabu* (a housewife who behaves like a *babu*), *beshya* (slut), etc. Kundamala Devi, a woman writing in the women's magazine *Bamabodhini patrika* in October 1870, said, "Oh dear ones! If you have acquired real knowledge, then give no place in your heart to memsahib-like behavior. This is not becoming in a Bengali housewife."[37] These imaginary "ultra-modern" women were portrayed in fiction and nonfiction as selfish and self-indulgent people who had overturned the domestic order by their disrespectful attitude toward the *grihini* of the household, the mother-in-law: "The present situation [is that] . . . the boubabus are spending all their time massaging themselves with soap, . . . in doing up their hair in a variety of styles, painting their lips red, etc., . . . leaving [all] domestic work to the [poor] old mother-in-law."[38] The alleged neglect of *grihakarma* (domestic work or duties) by "(over)educated" women was the subject of complaint and banter in Manomohan Bosu's book on Hindu rituals. Speaking of "the effort to destroy" the Hindu home now apparently at work in the *antahpur* (the inner apartments or women's quarters), he said,

> On all sides we hear the cry: Be civilised, learn manners, don't touch cow dung [traditional purifier/cleanser] or dirty cooking pots, don't handle the broomstick, and don't even go near the hearth! After all, you are the ladies of the household, does it suit you to do the work of the maidservant? If you spend the whole day in the kitchen, when will you apply yourselves to the cultivation of the mind? Or when, for that matter, will you find the time to do needlework, . . . a must [for civilised women]? How else would you acquire the civilization of the *bibis* [European women]? Henceforth, devote yourselves [only] to reading books, knitting wool, dressing up, attending the [Brahmo] Samaj. Speak chaste Bengali, and spend the whole day discussing [the fashionable] subjects of health, cleanliness, discipline, . . . agitate for moderation in lifestyle and spending, and thus turn yourselves into a [race] of precocious little aunts![39]

Bosu's reference to the maidservant is a reminder that what was at issue was not the question or even the quantum of actual physical exertion by middle-class women. The physically harder part of domestic labor, one could reasonably assume, would have been performed by hired servants (or retainers) in many bhadralok families—subaltern groups whose histories we have not even begun to imagine. The invocation of "household duties," or grihakarma/grihakarya, worked rather as a cryptic cultural code for the qualities of personhood that made a woman both "modern" and desirable. Education was essential to the production of this desirability, for "an uneducated woman," as a book on *naridharma* (women's dharma) put it, "cannot be skilled in grihakarya [domestic work]. At the same time, a woman who neglects grihakarya for the sake of learning, will find her learning to be useless. The most successful wife is she who combines education with skills in household tasks."[40] Grihakarya, or household work, was a culturally shared way of referring to the qualities of grace/modesty and obedience which were described in this literature as the two signs of Lakshmi-like auspiciousness in a woman. The attainment of both required modern education. A book on female education (*streesiksha*) waxed eloquent on "true modesty," which it distinguished from the "uncivilized" expression of modesty in uneducated women. The latter, it was said, giggled loudly, their physical movements were rushed and lacked grace, and they ran away at the sight of unfamiliar men (i.e., did not know how to conduct themselves in the company of male strangers), while women with true modesty were easily told by their "downcast eyes, blushing cheeks . . . and [their tendency to] speak softly and little."[41] Yet another book called *Advice to Women* spelled out clearly the differences in behavior that distinguished the ideal housewife (*kulastree:* wife belonging to the *kula* or lineage) from a whore (*kulata/beshya*):

> *Kulastree:* of calm and composed movements; speaks little; eyes downcast; avoids men; covers up her body; without lust; dresses simply.
>
> *Kulata/beshya:* fickle/restless; garrulous; looks everywhere; seeks male company; parts of body exposed; lusty; dresses up.[42]

Students of the social history of the bhadralok will know that it was not only the male writers of the period who wrote in this vein. Very similar points of view, in different forms, were often expressed by women (which is not to deny the dissimilarities that could distinguish women's writings from men's). I will also take for granted the by now familiar point that the literature discussed originated as part of the historical process through which a modern patriarchal discourse was fashioned by the Hindu Bengali bhadralok under the twin pressure of colonial rule and emerging nationalist sentiments.[43] The very interchangeable use made in these writings of words such as beshya (whore) and memsahib (European woman) suggest a nationalist insistence on cultural stereotypes in a gesture of creating and maintaining boundaries that were patently false. Nor is there much intellectual mileage to be had from regarding the use of the Lakshmi figure as an instance of the so-called modernity of tradition, for that only leaves all modernities looking the same.

For the purpose of this analysis, I will also take for granted another obvious point: that Alakshmi, beshya, boubabu, memsahib, etc. were terms that stood for individual assertiveness on the part of women and its undesirability. They were the figures of imagination that helped demonize the "free" and "private" (female) individual whom the European writers on conjugality idealized. "Friendship" between husbands and wives, grown in the privacy and freedom of bourgeois patriarchy, appears here to have run into opposition from the patriarchal structures that already existed. "Freedom" in the West, several authors argued, meant *jathechhachar,* to do as one pleased, to be self-indulgent and selfish. In India, it was said, "freedom" meant freedom from the self, the free person being one who could serve and obey voluntarily.

> To be able to subordinate oneself to others and to dharma . . . [and] to free the soul from the slavery of the senses, is the first task of human freedom. . . . That is why in Indian families, boys and girls are subordinate to the parents, wife to the husband and the parents-in-law, the disciple to the guru, the student to the teacher, . . . the king to dharma, . . . the people to the king . . . [and one's] dignity and prestige to the community [*samaj*].[44]

To read this conflict over the ideals of the Bengali housewife (the *sugrihini*)—grihalakshmi versus the memsahib—as a debate about the "freedom" of the autonomous bourgeois self, on the one hand, and the idea of subordinating the individual to the will of the clan or the extended family, on the other, is not so much to misread it as to stay completely within the very terms of these colonial texts themselves.[45] After all, as is known, for nationalist and imperial historians alike, the "woman question" has often acted as a measure of "freedom" and quality of civilization.[46]

Freedom, undoubtedly, was a key idea that shaped the Bengali modern. The emergent and new (bourgeois) individuality in Bengal in the nineteenth and twentieth centuries was deeply embroiled in the question of defining personal freedom in the context of the norms of the extended family. Debates over "free will" versus "determination" or "necessity" (sometimes read as "fate" or "destiny"), for example, provided some of the central motifs in quite a few of Bankimchandra's novels, an early edition of *Kapalkundala,* in fact, carrying a whole essay on the subject of "freedom versus destiny."[47] Bipinchandra Pal's autobiography, itself an artifact of our modernity, framed its own narrative by posing free will as one of its central organizing themes. Pal's preface to the book said,

> The biggest lesson I have learned in this life is this: while I may not always [consciously] admit it, I can never deny that I am not the master of my own life. . . . Debates over questions of *free will and determination* [the italicized words are in English in the text] or [the] *moral responsibility* [of the individual] will never detract from the truth and value of this lesson. I do not know whether or not I really possess individual freedom . . . nor do I deny that there may be such freedom. . . . But above all stands the truth that I am not the lord of this life.[48]

It is not my purpose here to sit in judgment over the nineteenth-century question of whether or not Bengali lives were "free." I do not want to essentialize or fetishize the idea. Investigations into "unfreedoms" are obviously a matter of investigating concrete contexts that cannot be contained by the merely textual. Here, however, as I have already said, I am concerned with the textual alone. I want to read these texts—in particular, the debate over the ideals of the grihalakshmi—as illustrations of the different possible, often noncommensurable, worlds we created for ourselves as we embraced our (colonial-nationalist) modernity. What I read in the terms in which the Bengali debates over new forms of domesticity were conducted are two radically different, though not unconnected, constructions of the social life of the family as narrated in public. They are both constitutive of our "modernity," yet each of them posits a relationship between domesticity and civil-political life that is contradicted by the other. They can come together only by bringing each other into crisis. I do not claim that my reading of these texts exhausts the possibilities created in our modernity. But it may enable us to question the narratological closures that give this "modernity," or its "history," a semblance of homogeneous unity.

III

At the heart of the grihalakshmi/memsahib debate, then, were at least two contradictory articulations of the public/private distinction, both called into being by the exigencies of our colonial modernity. I have explained the way this relationship was conceived within the view that took as its task the "civilizing" of Bengal/India. I will now demonstrate the structure of the second articulation by moving to an earlier period in the history of British colonialism in Bengal and begin by considering two documents from the year 1823. I choose these documents simply because they help me to lay bare the structure of a practice which, over time, got routinized and hence all too codified.

Both of these documents involved the prominent resident, journalist, and social commentator of early colonial Calcutta, Bhabanicharan Bandyopadhyay. One of these documents is a well-known tract that Bhabanicharan authored in 1823: *Kalikata Kamalalaya* (Calcutta: The Abode of Kamala [Lakshmi]). The other one, a relatively obscure pamphlet published in the same year from Calcutta and now held in the British Library, is entitled *Gauradeshiya samaj sangsthapanartha pratham sabhar bibaran* (literally: Minutes of the first meeting held in connection with the establishment/foundation of Gauradeshiya samaj [society/association]). Bhabanicharan was one of the founders of this association. The other organizers were such contemporary Bengali stalwarts as Dwarkanath Tagore, Radhakanta Deb, Ramkamal Sen, Tarachand Chakrabarti, Ramdulal De, and Kashinath Mullick.

Gauradeshiya Samaj, one should remember, was itself part of a fledging civil society already visible in the schools, offices, workshops, press, and voluntary associations in Calcutta of the 1820s. As the editor of the magazine *Samachar*

Chandrika, Bhabanicharan was a luminary of the "public sphere" that was emerging in Calcutta in this period. The published minutes of the Samaj themselves constitute interesting historical evidence of this: they show the organizers of this voluntary association adopting some of the rituals of "public life" that the Europeans would have brought to the country. At this "meeting" of the Samaj of which the published "minutes" now form the source of our information, a "chairman" (this word is transliterated in the document as *charman*) was nominated and elected, and resolutions proposed, seconded, moved, discussed, and voted on, rituals that would have been unimaginable in pre-British India. More importantly, what makes this text a witness to the emergence of a "public life" for the Bengali middle classes in Calcutta is the main subject that was discussed at the meeting. It was nothing other than "the state of the country" and the possibilities of "improvement."

The country—variously named Hindusthan, Bharatvarsha, a Hindu kingdom, Gauradesh, etc.—is described in this document as being in a state of misery brought about by a combination of factors including the following: (a) lack of unity among "us" [Hindus] and (b) declining status of scriptures and Brahmins, all compounded by ignorance on the part of the rulers (the British) of the dharma (moral order, proper action) of the land.[49] The appeal that this document makes to a dharmic code in discussing a political and social order will not surprise students of Bengali history. Books written early in the first decade of the nineteenth century by Bengali intellectuals patronized by the British interpreted the coming of the Raj by invoking this code. Mrityunjay Vidyalankar, "for many years the Chief Pundit in the college of Fort William," saw the restoration of dharma, that is, the practice of *rajdharma* (the dharma of the king) as the divine purpose behind British rule.[50] In Rajivlochan Mukhopadhyay's biography of the eighteenth-century zamindar Krishnachandra Ray of Nadia, the British were described in terms directly borrowed from the Mahabharata.

> They hail from *vilat* [Persian, *vilayat* = foreign land] and they are English by *jati.* They live in Calcutta in their *kothis* [official buildings]. . . . Their qualities are these: they are truthful, possess complete self control [*jitendriya:* one who has conquered (the temptations of) the sense organs], do not envy others, and they are great warriors who feel compassion towards their subjects. . . . As intelligent as Vrihaspati, as wealthy as Kuvera, as strong as Arjuna, they rule in the manner of a Yudhisthira, nurturing good and suppressing evil. . . . It is only if they become the possessors and controllers of this country that we all will be saved. Otherwise the *yavana* [the Muslims] will destroy everything.[51]

There is no doubt a significant trace of this language in the way the minutes of Gauradeshiya Samaj use dharma as a shorthand for both land/country for order/rule, that is, for a moral community. However, while in Rajivlochan's or Mrityunjay's prose dharma does not speak to any idea of "nation" or "civilization," the minutes of the Samaj are interestingly different. In the language of the minutes, dharma is made to work in tandem with the hierarchical and competitive European discourse of "civilization." One aim of the Samaj's resolve to "protect Hindu dharma" was to prevent "the humiliation of . . . the country, scriptures and dharma" by especially the European missionaries. The theme of the decline of the country, though expressed in terms of dharma, differed from Mrityunjay's or Rajivlochan's treatment of the subject in that it now included explicit comparison with European countries and their histories. Even the desire for the unity of the Hindus reveals itself here as an emulative desire on the part of the colonized: "It is not possible for an individual to achieve by solitary effort things that would be of use and benefit to this country. . . . European people . . . accomplish even the most difficult tasks with ease because they organise themselves into societies." "In the very distant past," the minutes continue,

> the people of India [Bharat] were superior to the inhabitants of other islands. . . . They have become dependent and have been humiliated [and are now] immersed in abject misery. The unspeakable degree of our degradation can be comprehended if we compare our current state with the way intelligence and knowledge have influenced [other people]. But a combination of vanity and [our] current customs . . . prevents us from either acknowledging our sad circumstances or from making any effort to overcome them.[52]

The premise of this whole discussion was the idea of "improvement" that we have already recognized as central to the idea of "civilization." The first requirement, Ramkamal Sen argued at this meeting, was unity, and this was to be achieved by forming voluntary associations or "societies" as he put it: "That we seldom unite on any issue can be put down to the fact that the Hindus have no society [the English word is used here] . . . to make [the holding of] meetings and discussions possible." It was resolved at this meeting that the new "Gauradeshiya Sabha of the bhadralok" would strive to eradicate the evil customs of the country by publishing Bengali translations of informative books from other countries, by promoting discussions among the scholars and pundits, by starting a school, and by acquiring European machinery to help the cause of knowledge, for, as it was observed in the minutes, "a country lacking in printing presses and printed material . . . [to help disseminate] advice on conduct and rituals, will find the spread of harmful behaviour impossible to check, far less stop."[53]

These minutes thus anticipate many of the features of that which came to characterize nationalist thought as the century wore on: the desire for a "national" (still unclear in its outlines) unity, the desire for improvement in the state of the country, and the desire, finally, for a vigorous "public sphere"—voluntary associations, presses, and printed material promoting discussion on matters of public interest, and formal meetings with all the rituals of "public" life—elections, votes, resolutions, the recording of minutes and other related practices—built into them. There is not yet an explicit desire for the modern nation-state here, but words like "humiliation" and "dependence" do refer back to a protonational spirit that runs through this document and that distinguishes it from the texts of Rajivlochan Mukhopadhyay or Mrityunjay Vidyalankar who wrote in the early 1800s.

It is instructive, in this context, to consider Bhabanicharan Bandyopadhyay's tract *Kalikata Kamalalaya* (hereafter *KK*) published in the same year as the minutes of the Samaj, 1823, as a guide to "good conduct" in the urban life of Calcutta. Bhabanicharan, readers will recall, was one of the architects of Gauradeshiya samaj and was an important editor in the emergent world of Bengali journalism. He had also worked in various capacities for a number of European business firms in the city. In other words, his participation in what we would now categorize as Bengali "public life" was by no means negligible. Yet, as his book *KK* shows, public/private, home/world, and domestic/official were not the distinctions that he would have applied to his own life. *KK* is an interesting instance of the dharmic code being used to produce and organize an articulation of the relationship between domestic and civil-political life which was quite antithetical to that produced under the sign of "civilization."

KK is written in the form of a dialogue between an "urban dweller," a Brahmin who lives and works in Calcutta, and a "stranger," a newcomer from the country, who handles the city with a certain degree of anxiety and trepidation and who is therefore eager to find out about its ways. It is a book written very much in the colonial context and shares some of the sentiments expressed by Rajivlochan Mukhopadhyay and Mrityunjay Vidyalankar, on the one hand, and Gauradeshiya samaj on the other. As in the writings of the former, there is a tendency in *KK* to please the British, a trait quite in keeping with the history of Bengali Brahmins who, unlike, say, their Maharashtrian counterparts, had for generations occupied the position of a subordinate elite serving powerful rulers including the Muslims. A certain spirit of sycophancy therefore came "naturally" to these people. Being able to win praise from one's employers was something to be proudly displayed—a biography of Bhabanicharan published in 1849 after his death devoted a whole section to listing the occasions on which he had secured such praise (*kartadiger prashangsha*).[54] In the same spirit of obsequiousness, *KK* described the English as a "dharmic and fair-minded people" who were only performing their royal duty by providing education (i.e., schools) "to protect dharma."[55]

Unlike the texts of the Fort William College pundits, however, *KK* displays an inherent anxiety over the changes brought about by social mobility in Calcutta, in particular, the role that "new" money could play in undermining the "proper" model of social order and the place of the Brahmins within it.[56] The word *kamalalaya* describing Calcutta as the abode of the goddess of wealth, Kamala (or Lakshmi), betrays this concern. This dissolution of kinship bonds in the city is mourned by the urban dweller in *KK*, for it allowed people to engage in "shameful acts." Even religious ceremonies, he says, were not being observed in the proper spirit, ostentatious displays of money and wealth often being more important than any sacred intent. The celebration of Durga Puja (worshiping of Goddess Durga) in Calcutta, said Bhabanicharan, had already acquired a bad name among many who called it, mockingly, "chandelier puja," "festival of *baijis* [dancing girls]," "occasion for the worship of one's wife's jewelry and sarees," etc.[57] One sees why Bhabanicharan participated in the efforts of Gauradeshiya Samaj: constructing proper rules of proper conduct for the residents of colonial Calcutta is a concern shared by *KK* and the minutes of the Samaj.

"I hear that in Calcutta a large number of people have given up the right codes of conduct," the stranger says in *KK*. Is it true, he asks, that they eat too early (a reference, I think, to the emerging ritual of the breakfast), leave home too early in the morning, "spend the entire day working," return home late, and retire immediately after the evening meal? To continue with this list of complaints against the people of Calcutta:

> [They] do not any longer observe the [life-cycle] ceremonies. . . . [They] have given up the daily rite of *sandhya bandana* [evening prayers] and other similar actions. . . . They give no thought to what they wear or eat and [in these matters] just please themselves. . . . They have stopped reading the scriptures and learn only Persian and English. They cannot read or write Bengali and do not consider Bengali scriptures worthy of their attention. . . . On the death of their parents, they participate in the funeral ceremonies only by proxy, as they find these ceremonies repulsive. . . . Uncut hair is the only sign of mourning they [are prepared to] wear, some even going to the length of shaving their beards on the plea that they have to attend office. . . . They have abandoned the dhoti and have taken to wearing tunic, pants, and black leather boots that come in all different shapes—high heels, plain head, blunt nose—complete with shoelaces. . . . They would employ [without checking] any stranger that came along and claimed to be a Brahmin cool. . . . Their speech is a mixture of their own language and those of foreign races. . . . Perhaps they have not read any *shastras* [scriptures] in Sanskrit, why else would they want to use *yavanic* [Muslim/foreign] speech when one's own language would do just as well?[58]

These charges brought against the Calcutta bhadralok are self-explanatory, but let me highlight the important ones: salaried (or paid) work demanding long and fixed hours ("the whole day"); impurity of language, food, and clothes; neglect of daily, sacred observances.

The "urban dweller" in *KK* begins by conceding the validity of these charges. "What you have heard is true," he says, and adds, "—but a Hindu who behaves like that is a Hindu only in appearance [*Hindubeshdhari:* one dressed as a Hindu]." In spite of the new structuring of the day that the colonial civil-political society required, the true Hindu strove to maintain a critical symbolic boundary between the three spheres of action (karma) that defined life: *daivakarma* (action to do with the realm of gods), *pitrikarma* (actions pertaining to the realm of one's ancestors), and *vishaykarma* (action to do with the realm of worldly interests, that is, undertaken in pursuit of wealth, livelihood, fame, power, etc.). The most commendable of the *vishayi bhadralok* (i.e., bhadralok with worldly interests) were always able to separate the self-in-the-world from a transcendental, higher self.

> People with important occupations such as *diwani* or *mutasuddiship* wake up early and meet with and talk to different kinds of people [visitors] [only] after completing their morning ablutions. . . . Later on they rub their bodies with oil. . . . Before eating, they engage in [different] puja [worship] ceremonies [including] *homa* sacrifice, *valivashya,* etc. Having rested for a while after the meal, they put on beautiful garments and proceed to their places of work in palanquins or other handsome carriages. They do not stay at work any longer than necessary. . . . On returning home, they change into a fresh set of clothes, wash themselves, and touch Ganga water to purify themselves. They say their evening prayers, eat, and then entertain visitors. . . . Middle-class people who are not wealthy . . . follow the same pattern, with the difference that they work harder, have less to give away in charity, and can afford to entertain only a smaller number of [importunate] visitors. The more indigent bhadralok also live by the same ideas. But they have to work even harder and have even less to eat or give away.[59]

Of particular interest to us is how Bhabanicharan handled the question of the polluting effects of using foreign languages. True, his urban dweller says, in effect, many foreign words had equivalents in Sanskrit and the bhadralok were indeed at fault when they did not use them. But "what should we do," he asked, "when dealing with words that do not translate into Bengali or Sanskrit?" Bhabanicharan actually produces a list of such unavoidable words of which the following are in English. The list speaks for itself: "nonsuit, summons, common law, company, court, attachment, double, decree, dismiss, due, premium, collector, captain, judge, subpoena, warrant, agent, treasury, bills, surgeon [sergeant?], discount."[60]

It is clear that these words belonged to the sordid domain of vishaykarma, the realm of worldly interests, which is where (British) rule was, and Bhabanicharan's ideal was to prevent these words from polluting the purer domains of daivakarma and pitrikarma. Using clothes, Ganga water, etc. to mark the boundaries between the domains seems to have been a common practice among the upper castes in Calcutta in the early part of the nineteenth century. A later description of Calcutta in the days of Rammohun Roy said,

> The worldly [vishayi] Brahmins of Calcutta conducted their vishaykarma under the English but took special care to protect the dominance and prestige of the

Brahmins in the eyes of their own people. They washed themselves every evening
on returning home from work and thus cleansed themselves of the bad effects
[*dosha*] born of [the daylong] contact with the *mlechha* [untouchable; i.e., the
English]. They would then complete their *sandhya* [evening prayer] and other
[rituals of] puja [worship], and eat in the eighth part of the day [about midnight]....
Those who found this routine too difficult made a habit of completing their
evening prayer, homa, and other pujas in the morning before they left for office.
Further, they would offer Brahmins money and other objects [*naivedya:* objects
offered to sacred powers] and that itself cancelled out all their *dosha*.[61]

Let us pause a little over this classificatory framework, this "art of living"
that Bhabanicharan and his contemporaries had developed for themselves in
the face of the demands that the coming of a modern civil society made of them.
Where would the state and the civil society belong in terms of this framework?
How indeed would Bhabanicharan classify his own involvement in the public
sphere, his own act of writing and publishing *KK,* for example, or his own
involvement in the Gauradeshiya samaj? What kind of karma was it to advocate
and work for the "enlightenment" and "improvement" of one's own country
or people? Was it vishaykarma, or was it simply unclassifiable in Bhabanicharan's terms?

In the first place, one has to note that the self-in-the-world of Bhabanicharan's construction cannot be a nationalist self, for it has at the outset abnegated
the capacity to rule in the material world. In the face of British rule, the author
of *KK* can only plead his lack of power and the force of circumstances. The
king must uphold dharma, it is the duty of the Brahmin to assist the king in
this task, and so the latter must learn the ways of the foreigner king—thus went
his argument regarding English education for Indians. "I see no dosha [bad
effect] coming from [Brahmins or Hindus] learning the knowledge of the rulers
of the land, as otherwise the business of the state [rajkarma] would be impossible to pursue."[62] Very similar was his defense of the use of English words
by Bengalis: "Rulers of every race [jati] put into circulation words or expressions belonging to their own tongue. What else could one do but adopt
them, especially in matters to do with the administration of royal justice
[*rajbichar*]?"[63]

Or mark his pragmatism as well as the somewhat pathetic declaration of
helplessness in handling English words that did not translate into Bengali but
were nevertheless "unavoidable" in the pursuit of material well-being:
"Dosha accrues to a person if he uses those [English, Arabic, or Persian] words
in the conduct of daivakarma and pitrikarma. But what harm is done in using
them in conducting vishaykarma or indeed in the context of jokes and lighthearted conversations?"[64]

KK thus does not share the (later) nationalist urge to translate into Indian
languages English words that had to do with modern statecraft or modern
technology. An unmistakable expression of the nationalist and civic desire to

appropriate the instruments of "modern" rule is absent from this text. *KK* instead marginalizes the state (and by implication, the nation) by separating it from the purer aspects of personhood, by looking on it as a contingency and an external constraint, one of the many one has to negotiate in the domain of vishaykarma. As a later publication on the moral conduct of the Hindu male householder put it, "one might engage in improper karma if that was essential to the maintenance of one's family."[65] The pursuit of wealth and well-being— that is, life in civil-political society—could not be a sacred task as it took one into relationships that necessarily admitted of exceptions to the more serious rules of living, as did jokes and lighthearted exchanges. That is why Bhaban-icharan mentioned vishaykarma and jokes together, in the same breath, as it were, for they both belonged to an area of life where the burden of existence was made bearable only by a spirit of lightheartedness. The serious business of "nationalism"—or indeed the all-consuming conception of the nation itself that one day, by dint of its sacredness, would demand the sacrifice of life at its altar—could not be born of such a spirit.

Bhabanicharan's trichotomous division of "action" into *vaishayik, paitrik,* and *daiva* is thus incapable of classifying, say, his own involvement in a protonationalist voluntary association like Gauradeshiya Samaj. If it were to be placed in the category of vishaykarma, for instance, where the Brahmin, theoretically, was happy to forsake all claims to rule and play second fiddle to the king, there would be no recognition of the (nationalist) desire to rule that the Samaj itself articulated, or of the dynamics of power relations that led to the emergence of such a desire.

This separation of the purer part of the self from the more polluting pro-ceedings of public life and of the civil society had implications for Bhaban-icharan's understanding of domesticity. He does not even mention women or children; their existence is contained within the definition of the life of the male, upper-caste, patriarchal householder. Nor does griha, or home, play any part in his thought as a spatial entity. There is no conception here of the "home" being the man's castle, his personal refuge in love from the competitive world of the public sphere. The *grihini,* the housewife, is not a separate subject of discussion here, presumably because it was assumed that she was only a derived aspect of the male *grihi.* After all, says Manu of the female life cycle, "Know that for a woman, marriage is her *upanayana* [the ritual that makes a man twice-born], cohabiting with and serving the husband is [the equivalent of] staying with and serving the guru, and *grihakarma* [household work] her service to *agni* [the fire god]."[66] The house, too, as a spatial entity, would not have been relevant as such to the way Bhabanicharan outlined the dharma of the grihi. This dharma was made up of all the three karmas. And certain actions to do with pitri and daiva karma were indeed to be undertaken outside of the domestic space—pilgrimage, or *tirthayatra,* would be a prominent example— while certain actions pertaining to vishaykarma (dealing with importunate visitors, say) could be conducted from home.[67] The internal cultural organization of the domestic space, such as the question of segregation of the sexes, would have been subject to this overall framework.

There is, in addition, nothing in Bhabanicharan's text that suggested any attraction to the idea that the time of the household should keep pace with the time of the civil-political society. The themes of discipline, routine, punctuality, all those particular constructions of human sociality that the themes of "progress" and "civilization" made both desirable and necessary and that so characterize what later nationalists wrote on domestic life, do not resonate through *KK*. If anything, there was an emphasis to the contrary. In the world that *KK* depicts, the ideal householder never spent more time at work than was minimally needed and concentrated on the higher levels of pitri and daiva karma. The self, in its highest form, was visualized as a part of the *kula,* the self-conception of the patriarchal, patrilineal, and patrilocal extended family, a self-conception that was more tied to a mythoreligious idea of time than to the temporality of secular history. The civil society here was a matter of compulsion, of unfreedom, a forced interruption of more important/purer acts.

IV

Let me highlight the nature of the opposition between the two articulations of the domestic and the civil-political that Bengali modernity entailed, an opposition that I read into the neologism grihalakshmi, the two horizons as it were to which this compound word (griha = house + Lakshmi) points us. One is the horizon of the nineteenth-century European imagination of progress that was predicated on a split structure of consciousness, a consciousness that always perceived the present as "unhappy" and therefore defined its worldly engagement as a struggle for "happiness" (treated as synonymous with "freedom"), which was to be achieved within a historicized future. Elsewhere I have discussed "history" itself as a sign of this consciousness and described how the nineteenth-century Bengali imagination of the griha (home/house) came to embody this split whereby Bengali homes, standing for our present, were always found lacking in the discipline and beauty that marked the typical English "home," which embodied the desired historical future.[68]

Discipline in public and personal life called for a dislodgment of the self from the mythoreligious time of the kula and its insertion into the historical narrative of "freedom/happiness." The Bengali modern, to the extent that she or he was the subject of this fable, was the embodiment of this unhappy consciousness struggling to transform itself. "We become very sad," wrote Krishnabhabini Das in the 1880s in her account of her travels in England, "when we realize how unhappy the couples of our country are. . . . Very few persons in our country know how the ideal husband-wife relationship should be. This is the reason why . . . Indian [couples] prove to be extremely unhappy."[69] One did not have to go to England to find out about domestic happiness or its alleged absence in Bengali/Indian homes. An essay that young Madhusudan Dutt wrote in 1842 on women's education while he was still at school was eloquent on the subject: "The happiness of a man who has an enlightened partner is quite complete. . . . The people of this country do not know the pleasure of domestic life, and indeed they cannot know, until civilization shows them the way to attain it."[70] This was precisely the voice of the colonial modern looking to orient domesticity to the requirements of the civil-political. Historical time was saturated here with the message of "improvement."

Yet Bengali public narratives of the social life of the family were replete at the same time with the opposite theme, that of "degeneration," a view of the nineteenth century as "the dark ages," or *kaliyuga,* a feature to which Sumit Sarkar has recently drawn our attention.[71] This was a theme that articulated the personal/domestic with the national in such a way that the civil-political society itself came to be seen as the site, if not the source, of unhappiness. To a degree, this was the flip side of the narrative of improvement. It followed the civilizing discourse in picturing the present as unhappy and therefore in need of reform anyway. We also see the same use of "woman" as a signifier of the quality of the times, with the difference, however, that the value of the sign was changed from positive to negative.

Rajnarayan Bose's essay *Se kal ar e kal* (1873) (Then and Now), an eclectic, heterogeneous nationalist text irreducible to any one simple argument, offers one well-known example of this genre. It shares something of Bhabanicharan's positions in *KK* in the way it situates the question of labor by connecting domestic life and civil society. *Se kal ar e kal* is an impressionistic comparison of "then"—defined as the period "from the beginning of English rule to the time of the founding of the Hindu College [1817]"—with "now" (which covered the years since).[72] The latter, for Rajnarayan, is a period of decline, and this is a cultural fact he reads off the (gendered) Bengali, body which he locates, depending on the particular gender of the body in question, in very different histories of labor. Both male and female bodies signify degeneration for Rajnarayan but the reasons are interestingly different. The female body is weak because of the neglect, by "the women of the present times," of the routine of grihakarya, the rituals of auspiciousness that were meant to bind women to the order of the kula.

> The women of those times were more hardworking than women at present. These days, women in well-to-do families are completely dependent on the [labor of the] servants and averse to grihakarya. The women of older times were not like that. . . . The educated women of our country now are reluctant to do physical labor or grihakarya. . . . The women of the past were [also] capable of more compassion and affection than women today.[73]

However, if the women of "now" did not work hard enough at home and this contributed to their declining physical strength, their male counterparts, according to Rajnarayan, worked only too hard under the new office routine instituted by the British. Besides, their working hours were all too inappropriate.

> Another factor reducing the vitality of the men of our times is the excessive and untimely labour they have to undertake. There is no longer any doubt that the introduction of English civilization into this country has seen an excessive rise in [the demand for] labour. We can never work as hard as the English. . . . The English [style of] exertion is not right for this land. The rule that the present rulers have introduced of working continuously from ten to four, is not at all suited to this country. The body tires quickly if one exerts oneself when the sun is strong. Especially, the practice of children having to rush to school immediately after their [morning] meal and [being obliged] to spend the day in company of hundreds of others, their perspiring bodies subjected to the confined air of one building, is definitely something that causes their health to break down.[74]

Once again, this is not a univocal text. Rajnarayan is no doubt in part responding to the imperialist charge of "effeteness" that the British brought against Bengali men and their sense of masculinity.[75] In the passage that follows the one quoted, he bemoans the absence of physical sports and exercise facilities for children. But the complaint against the rushed "morning meal" (breakfast?) repeats a theme that we have already come across in *KK* and refers to a conception of an alternative rhythm/structure of everyday life autonomous of the civil society. It is within this autonomy that this text (as does *KK*) locates the question(s) of labor/action (karma) and domesticity. Civil-political life itself is the object of criticism in this mode of thinking.

Rajnarayan's contemporary Bhudev Mukhopadhyay's essays on the rituals of the Hindu domesticity, *Achar prabandha,* repeats this demand of autonomy by illustrating some of the contradictions that nationalist thought had to carry with it in attempting to assimilate to its own ends the ideology of the kula. On the one hand, Bhudev's enthusiasm for these rituals is derived from the nationalist desire for discipline in private and public life—he explains, using the English words "drill" and "discipline," how the practice of these rituals enhanced "one's vitality and capacity for work."[76] On the other hand, his critique of British rule on the strength of a theory of karma, strongly reminiscent of that of *KK,* doubles up as a powerful critique of civil-political society itself, of capitalism, work, and bourgeois regimes of discipline and historical time, all of which he marginalizes in portions of his text as simply external constraints imposed on a more permanent and deeper rhythm of life revealed in the Hindu cycles of *nityachar* (everyday rituals) and *naimittikachar* (rites of passage). This is how, for instance, Bhudev handles the problem of the "new" work routine that takes up the whole day.

It is the first half of the third part of the day, i.e. from 9 to 10:30 [A.M.], that is the time [assigned in the scriptures] for work related to the earning of one's livelihood. How different our circumstances are now from those of the ancients! One and a half hours' work was [once] sufficient to enable one to earn money. Nowadays even twenty-four hours do not seem enough. . . . These days the working [*chakuria*] people are *forced* to have their [midday] meal between 9 and 10:30 so that they can be at work on time. Many of them, therefore, *have* to complete their afternoon and evening prayers in the morning.[77]

Written about sixty years after *KK,* these words acknowledge the powerful and inexorable presence of the new order of work and civil society and their capacity to disrupt violently the dharmic arrangement of time for the male householder. The public sphere, however, in this understanding is not embraced within the higher meaning of life. One has to bend to its compulsion but not let it enter one's soul. There is, of course, no better example of this in bhadralok history than the phenomenon of the nineteenth-century Bengali saint Ramakrishna whose (posthumously published) *Kathamrita* (Gospel), as Sumit Sarkar and Partha Chatterjee have shown, consistently exhorted the male Bengali householder (*grihi*) to separate himself from the nationalist impulse and denigrated the public sphere and the regimen of salaried employment (*chakri*) as a conflicted, corrupting world where one was necessarily compromised.[78]

What was heard in the compound word *grihalakshmi* in the nineteenth century, then, were at least these two contrary ways of bringing together the domestic and the national in public narratives of the social life of the family. One way was to subordinate domesticity and personhood to the project of the citizen-subject and the goals of the civil-political sphere, which, in turn, were seen as the site of work for the acquisition of improvement and happiness. The other was to imagine a connection between the domestic and a mythoreligious social—often equated in conscious nationalist writing with "community" or the "nation"—whereby the civil society itself became a problem, a constraint whose coercive nature was to be tolerated but never enjoyed.

V

What all this amounts to saying, it seems to me, is that the Bengali modern, implicated as it is in the structures and relationships of power that produce the social justice narratives of the public sphere, is constituted by tensions that relate to each other asymptomatically. There cannot, therefore, be any one unitary history of its becoming. This "history" that is ceaselessly gathered up as one by the exigencies of the historian's profession and by the needs of the state and governmentality is always already not-one. Questions of this history/modernity have to be situated within a recognition of its "not-oneness."

This produces a fundamental problem for the construction of historical narratives, for if this subject is, at one and the same time, both historicist and not, how can the historicist imagination of the historian speak for it (except by subordinating the whole to what is in effect only a part of it)? This is where I cannot agree with Sumit Sarkar's reduction, for instance, of the bhadralok critique of chakri (waged/salaried work) and civil society to a problem of historical time without in any way problematizing that very conception of time itself. "The precise nature and implications of this [bhadralok] aversion to chakri . . . needs some analysis," comments Sarkar in his valuable essay on Ramakrishna, and then adds the following:

> What made chakri intolerable was—its connotation of impersonal cash nexus and authority, embodied above all in the new rigorous discipline of work regulated by clock-time. Disciplinary time was a particularly abrupt and imposed innovation in colonial India. Europe had gone through a much slower, and phased, transition spanning some five hundred years. . . . Colonial rule telescoped the entire process for India within one or two generations. . . . Chakri thus became a "chronotype" [sic] of alienated time and space.[79]

Let us put aside the completely rhetorical figures of quicker and slower, or smoother and bumpier, passages in histories. Let us also not consider the obvious question that suggests itself if one takes the historicist argument here seriously: are the bhadralok today necessarily more enamored of office discipline than their nineteenth-century ancestors, now that more historical time has elapsed and a larger number of generations subjected to its regime?

It is unfortunate that Sarkar buries the question/histories of personhood in a phrasing that he does not himself contemplate: "What made chakri intolerable was . . . its connotation of *impersonal* [emphasis added] cash nexus and authority." The sociologese of this sentence, its use of "impersonal," "cash nexus," and "authority," bespeaks a familiar narrative of transition to capitalist-modernity that renders all "precapitalist" relations the same— "personal," "face-to-face," embedded in kinship, and so forth. The modern or capitalist, then, is precisely its other—and therefore the same again the world over—and the transition is best understood by essentializing, hence sociologizing, the difference between the two!

Yet this "difference" is what has been at issue in my reading of Bengali public narratives of the social life of the family. The Bengali modern is not an "incomplete" modern or even a "bad" colonial one compared to some "good" metropolitan model. The grihalakshmi is not a Rousseauian solution of the question of "womanhood" in phallocratic bourgeois modernity—the model of Sophy, educated and companionable but modest and obedient at the same time.[80] True, colonial rule introduced this model into bhadralok lives and the expression grihalakshmi partakes of it. But the concept of grihalakshmi, being tied to the mythoreligious time of the kula, also escapes and exceeds bourgeois time in all the three different senses that Lyotard has read into the word "exceed" in a different context: to pass beyond, to fall outside of, to excise.[81] The expression "grihalakshmi" shares in ideas of personhood that do not owe their existence to the bourgeois projects that European imperialism brought to India. Nor are these ideas mere historical residues, remnants of a past, left there only because the colonial-Bengali transition to modernity did not afford us the allegedly leisurely pace of the transformation in Europe. To say this is not to deny the cruelties of the patriarchal orders that this neologism of Bengali modernity, grihalakshmi, entails; it is, however, to claim that no adequate critique of this modernity can be mounted or practiced from within secular-historicist narratives alone, which, by their very nature, are incapable of representing what is not secular-historicist, except in an anthropologizing mode.

Let me elaborate a little further on this by discussing an obscure but by no means untypical text from the nineteenth century: a booklet called *Patibrata dharma* (with the English title *A Treatise on Female Chastity*) written around 1870 by a Bengali woman called Dayamayi Dasi. The stamp of the bourgeois project of European modernity, of educating women to be both companions to their husbands as well as being devoted to them, is unmistakably present here. The very title of the book speaks of its concern with such feelings of devotion and its given English title places it firmly within the tradition of Bengali Victoriana. Encouraged by her husband to learn to read and write, Dayamayi Dasi wrote this tract on *kulakaminir kartabya* (duties of the woman of the kula) which her husband published after her death. (Perhaps it would not be unkind to suggest that, in nineteenth-century Bengal, men who fancied themselves as "modern" in relation to their own times took pride in possessing wives who could read, write, or, even better, publish.) In that sense, kula here was a term that tied the domestic to the national. As Dayamayi Dasi said, quoting from the *Brahmavaivartapurana,* to express her sense of nationalism, "The land blessed with women of such nature [i.e., devoted to their husbands] is comparable to heaven, and the people of that country should treat their women as goddesses."[82] Besides, the very act of writing such books was part of becoming the new woman that the ideal of citizen-subject demanded. Not only that. Women whose writings circulated in the public sphere were often those who had indeed experienced some measure of "companionship" with their husbands, a "friendship" that permitted this diffusion of knowledge between the sexes. Literacy itself was part of their experience of a newfound individuality, and, in the context of the families structured by the patriarchal principle of kula, this was never achieved without struggle and pain.[83]

Yet the ideology of the patriarchy of the kula drips out of every word of what Dayamayi wrote in praise of this friendship and intimacy.

A woman has no better friend than her husband. It is because he helps cover [woman's shame] that he is called *bharta*. He is *pati* because he nurtures. He is *swami* because it is to him that the body belongs, he is the lord of the body. He fulfills [woman's] desires, that is why he is [called] *kanta.* He is a *bandhu* as he shares happiness, *parampriya* as he gives affection, and *raman* because he gives pleasure. It is he who, through his own semen, returns as the son, and that is why the son is valued. But for a *kulastree,* the husband is dearer than even a hundred sons.[84]

How would we understand this speech if we were not to classify it as some specimen of a "low" or "false" consciousness waiting to be "raised" by the political subject? What kind of a modern was Dayamayi Dasi? To be sure, the project of bourgeois individuality was a strong factor in her modernity, the idea of the autonomous individual existing for her own ends was something that animated this modern. But kula, grihalakshmi, etc., for all their undeniable phallocentrism, were also ways of talking about formations of pleasure, emotions, and ideas of a good life that associated themselves with models of nonautonomous, nonbourgeois, and nonsecular personhood. Women writing in *Bamabodhini patrika* argued that knowledge would "become graceful" in women only if they could at the same time retain "all the good qualities to be found in Hindu women" such as "modesty, humility, softness, patience [and] self-sacrifice."[85] This is a recurrent theme in modern Indian public life—worked out here in public narratives of the social life of the family—that the highest form of personhood was one constituted by the idea of self-sacrifice, the idea of living for others, not in the secular spirit of civic virtue that Rousseau would have applauded but in a spirit of subordination to the nonsecular and parochial principle of dharma. The idea, as I have argued elsewhere, was not at all innocent of power, domination, and even cruelty and violence, but, whatever else it may have been, it was never merely a ruse for staging the secular-historicist project of the citizen-subject.[86]

The kula, then, was an integral part of the categories with which the patriarchal Bengali modern consolidated its ideology of new domesticity in the context of a growing public sphere that colonialism had instituted. I want to make two points relating to Dayamayi Dasi's and others' affectionate description of the patriarchy of the kula.

My first point is that an irreducible category of "beauty," a nonsecular and nonuniversalistic sense of aesthetics, circulates in these writings, pointing us to a certain subject of pleasure/emotion that speaks through these documents. These texts on modern Bengali domesticity harp on the association between "womanhood" and "pleasantness." Alakshmi was not only inauspicious, she was unpleasant as well, or, correspondingly, what was unpleasant in a woman was also inauspicious. "*Mukhara* [sharp-tongued] is another name for women of unpleasant speech. Even the presence of a single mukhara woman can drive peace away from a household for ever," said a book called *Bangamahila* (The Women of Bengal).[87] A booklet on methods of examining prospective brides warned that women with names that evoked feelings of terror should not be married.[88] Some texts quoted Manu to emphasize the connection between the pleasant and the auspicious in the feminine: "A girl should be given a name that is pleasant to pronounce [and] that has no oblique meanings. . . . The [name] should fill the heart with feelings of affection [and] joy. It should signify *mangal* [auspiciousness], end in a long vowel and bring to [the bearer of the name] blessings from the utterer of it."[89]

That is why, our author explained, all the Sanskrit terms for "wife" were meant to sound pleasant, all significantly ending with a long vowel—*jaya, bharya, grihalakshmi, ankalakshmi, grihini, sahadharmini, ardhangarupini.*

> Even a five-year-old child will be able to tell from these names that the Hindu woman is not a slave even if she is skilled in domestic work. She is not a maidservant. Serving her husband does not make her a kept woman. . . . The Hindu woman is an object of great affection, care, and pride.[90]

My second point follows from this. The connection between these pleasures and the ideology of the auspicious grihalakshmi, which is intimately tied to the concern for well-being of the kula, always exceeds a straightforward bourgeois project of domesticating women in order to allow them into the modern and male public sphere. For the conception of mangal associated with the idea of "auspiciousness," on which the survival of the line of the kula depends, can be only very inadequately translated as "material prosperity" or simply "well-being." It is not a concept embedded in the secular time of the historicist imagination. An idea celebrated in the so-called medieval Bengali texts, the *Mangalkavyas* (Mangal Poems), where the human realm is never separated from the realms of gods and spirits, the word "mangal" is a matter of everyday performance, clichéd no doubt but rooted deep in (chronologically pre-British) narratives/practices of kinship and family where Christian or historicist distinctions between the divine and the human do not apply. Space will not allow me to develop the point, but anybody with some intimate knowledge of Hindu-Bengali pleasures will know how intertwined the narratives of Bengali domesticity and familial emotions are, for example, with the popular tales and songs that have celebrated, at least for three centuries now, the most important Hindu-Bengali mother-goddesses, Durga and Kali.

Needless to say, this imagination was at work in the nationalist aesthetics that marked the texts on domesticity that I have discussed here. Grihalakshmi signified a conception of the nationalist sublime which made the country ("not an object of the senses," as Kant would remind us)[91] "comparable to heaven" (to return to the language of Dayamayi Dasi). And it was nationalism that used the term "Alakshmi" interchangeably with "memsahib," European woman, a negative word charged with the impossible task of policing a false boundary between cultures.

But even this does not wrap up the Bengali modern. Dayamayi Dasi's own text provides us with a critical example of how even in these public narratives of domesticity and personhood, caught between the asymptomatic perspectives of the citizen-subject and of the grihalakshmi, there remained possibilities of other maneuvers creating speaking positions that looked far beyond the patriarchy of the Bengali modern. Her book, which is a paean to the patriarchy of the kula, breaks completely out of its own framework at one point in the preface where she records the exhilarating sense of liberation that literacy brought to her: "I had never entertained the thought that I would learn to recognize the alphabet or to read books. . . . But, in the end, I developed such a thirst for prose and poetry that I began to neglect my duties toward *samsar* (the world, the household, the family) and my husband."[92]

This statement, which survives the patriarchy of the Bengali modern that speaks through the rest of Dayamayi's book, reminds us of the other struggles that modernity helped unleash.[93] But it is also a statement that, in its uncompromising resistance to duty (whether modern or ancient, civic or familial), is not assimilable to the emancipatory visions that Eurocentric imaginations of civil-political life have bequeathed to us.

This conclusion cannot offer a closure, far less an explanation, for a modernity that, as I have said, is itself not one. The modern, no doubt, is a myth in that it naturalizes history. The "true" bourgeois does not exist except in representations of power and domination. Colonizing relationships, however, are not created through the complex attention to "truth" that is often in evidence in academic debates. European imperialists would not have been able either to legitimize their colonial domination by using the idea of "progress" or to sell this idea to the colonized, if their own representations of "progress" were explicitly riddled with self-doubt. The certitudes that constitute the colonial theater have not vanished with the demise of formal imperialism. The compulsion (and the temptation, as Heidegger once said) to think and translate the world through the categories of the European imperial-modern is real and deeply rooted in institutional practices, both within and outside the university.[94] One cannot simply opt out of this problem, or not suffer, by a sheer act of will, the "epistemic violence" that has been a necessary part of nation- and empire-making drives of the last two and a half centuries.[95] History therefore cannot be a "talking cure" from "modernity"; the analyst is not the addressee of this story of colonial Bengal. I think of it, as Barthes once said with reference to Shaharazad of the *Arabian Nights,* more as a merchandise, a narrative traded "for one more day of life."[96] To attempt to write difference into the history of our modernity in a mode that resists the assimilation of this history to the political imaginary of the European-derived institutions—the very idea of the civil-political, for instance—that dominate our lives, is to learn from Shaharazad's technique of survival. It is to say, to every perpetrator of epistemic violence and in the voice of the woman-subject Shaharazad, "Don't fuck me yet, for I still have (an)other story to tell."

Notes

An earlier version of this chapter was read at a workshop in Brighton, U.K., sponsored by the Social Science Research Council, New York. I am grateful to the participants for their criticisms. In addition, I thank Fiona Nicoll, Christopher Healy, Anthony Low, Eugene Irschick, Martin Jay, Robin Jeffrey, Thomas Metcalf, Hilary Standing, Vivek Dhareswar, and Patrick Wolfe for their helpful comments. I am deeply indebted to all my colleagues in *Subaltern Studies,* but especially to David Arnold, Partha Chatterjee, Ranajit Guha, Gyan Pandey, and David Hardiman, for comments on this paper. I also recall with sadness the many helpful discussions I had on this subject with my dear departed friend Hitesranjan Sanyal. I shall always miss his criticisms.

1. This is an idea forcefully and illuminatingly argued in Meaghan Morris, "Metamorphoses at Sydney Tower," *New Formations* (Summer 1990): 10.

2. One of the best discussions of this argument is Partha Chatterjee's book *Nationalist Thought and the Colonial World: A Derivative Discourse?* (London, 1986).

3. The story is told in Meredith Borthwick, *The Changing Role of Women in Bengal, 1849–1905* (Princeton, 1984), and Ghulam Murshid, *Reluctant Debutante: Response of Bengali Women to Modernization* (Rajshahi, 1983).

4. Philippe Ariès, Introduction, in *A History of Private Life: Passions of the Renaissance,* ed. Roger Chartier, 9 (Cambridge, Mass., 1989).

5. For examples of the way (male) reviewers controlled and regulated literary output of women, see Yogendranath Gupta, *Bange mahila kabi* (Calcutta, 1953), 33–34, 58–59, 65–71, 125–128, 139, 220–221.

6. See Sukumar Sen, *Women's Dialect in Bengali (1928)* (Calcutta, 1979). Sen shows the prevalence in women's speech (of the 1920s) of older words that had gone out of use in male speech and writing.

7. James Mill, *The History of British India,* 5th ed., ed. H. H. Wilson, 1:xxiv (London, 1858).

8. Ibid., xxx.

9. Lucien Febvre, "Civilisation: Evolution of a Word and a Group of Ideas," in *A New Kind of History: From the Writings of Febvre,* ed. Peter Burke, 219–257 (London, 1973).

10. Ishvarchandra Vidyasagar, *Bodhoday,* 10th reprint (Calcutta, 1858), 8.

11. Rajkrishna Bandyopadhyay, *Nitibodh* (Calcutta, 1858), 12–13. The preface to the first edition mentions that many of the essays in this book were written by Vidyasagar himself.

12. On the critical role that the idea of "improvement" played in British India in stitching together imperialist and nationalist ideologies, see Ranajit Guha, "Dominance without Hegemony and Its Historiography," in *Subaltern Studies* VI, ed. R. Guha, 210–309 (Delhi, 1989).

13. Somrath Mukhopadhyay, *Sikshapaddhati* (Dhaka, 1870), 4, 33. This was one of the many books that self-consciously borrowed from Samuel Smiles.

14. Nagendrabala Saraswati, *Garhasthyadharma ba naridharmer parishista* [in Bengali] (Jamalpur, Burdwan, 1904), 1, 29.

15. Anon., *Streesiksha* [in Bengali], vol. 1 (Calcutta, 1877), 28–29.

16. Ashis Nandy, *The Intimate Enemy: Loss and Recovery of Self under Colonialism* (Delhi, 1987), has a stimulating discussion of this problem.

17. Radhanath Basak, *Sarirtattvasar* [in Bengali] (Calcutta, 1864), 100.

18. *Sasthyaraksha* [in Bengali] (Calcutta, 1870), 2.

19. Rangalal Bandyopadhyay, *Sarirsadhani vidyar gunokirtan* [in Bengali] (Calcutta, 1869?), 5, 38, 43, 46–47. The book bears the English title *On the Importance of Physical Education.*

20. Atulchandra Datta, *Grihasiksha* [in Bengali] (Calcutta, 1906), 13.

21. Ibid., 3–4, 34–39, 78, 80.

22. Ibid., 55, 62, 65.

23. Chandranath Bosu, *Garhasthyapath* [in Bengali] (Calcutta, 1887), 15–16.

24. Datta, *Grihasiksha,* preface and title page; Tarasankar Sharma, *Streeganer vidyasiksha* [in Bengali] (Calcutta, 1851), 25–26.

25. Both Borthwick and Murshid document this.

26. David Kinsley, *Hindu Goddesses: Visions of the Divine Feminine in the Hindu Religious Tradition* (Berkeley, 1988), 19–32. See also Manomohan Bosu, *Hindu achar byabahar* [in Bengali] (Calcutta, 1873), 60.

27. Paul R. Greenough, *Prosperity and Misery in Modern Bengal: The Famine of 1943–1944* (New York, 1982), 12–41; and Lina Fruzzetti, *The Gift of a Virgin: Women, Marriage, and Ritual in a Bengali Society* (Delhi, 1990).

28. Upendranath Dhal, *Goddess Lakshmi: Origin and Development* (Delhi, 1978), 136.

29. Ibid., 141 n. 20.

30. See Baikunthanath Majhi, *Baromaser Srisri lakshmidevir bratakatha o panchali* [in Bengali], revised by Madhusudan Bhattacharya (Calcutta, n.d.); Pasupati Chattopadhyay, *Baromese srisri lakshmidevir panchali o bratakatha* (Calcutta, n.d.).

31. Bhikshuk [Chandra Sen], *Ki holo!* (Calcutta, 1876), 77.

32. Anon., *Kayekkhani patra* [in Bengali] (Calcutta, 1882), 25–26; Gupta, *Grihastha-jiban* [in Bengali], 21; Gopinath Dasgupta, *Hitabodh* [in Bengali] (Calcutta, 1869), 44–45; Gopenath Dasgupta, *Neetigarbha* [in Bengali] (Calcutta, 1869), 60; Ramsundar Ray, *Streedharmabidhyak* [in Bengali] (Calcutta, 1859), 29.

33. Yogendranath Ray, *Bangamahila* [in Bengali] (Chinsurah, 1881), 87–88.

34. Kailashbashini Devi, *Hindu mahilaganer heenabastha* [in Bengali] (Calcutta, 1863), 6–7, 63.

35. See, in addition to the references already cited, Kailashchandra Tarkaratna, *Reetimool* [in Bengali] (Hooghly, 1862), 78–79, 83–96 (the book bears the English title *Roots of Conduct,* which places it in the tradition of Bengali Victoriana); Kaleeprasanna Ghosh, *Nareejati bishayak prastab* [in Bengali] (Calcutta, 1865?), 66.

36. Gupta, *Grihastha-jiban,* 14.

37. Quoted in Borthwick, *Changing Role,* 105.

38. Bhikshuk, *Ki holo!* 96–97.

39. Bosu, *Hindu achar,* 57.

40. Anon., *Naridharma* [in Bengali] (Calcutta, 1877), 27, puts this gloss on a *sloka* from the Mahabharata, which says, ''[Only] she is [the true] wife who is skilled in domestic work, who bears children and who lives for and is devoted to her husband.''

41. Anon., *Streesiksha,* 84–87.

42. Ishanchandra Bosu, *Streediger prati upadesh* [in Bengali] (Calcutta, 1874), 8–11. See also Shibchandra Jana, *Patibratyadharmasiksha* [in Bengali] (Calcutta, 1870), 35.

43. Partha Chatterjee, "The Nationalist Resolution of the Women's Question," in *Recasting Women: Essays in Indian History,* ed. Kamkum Sangari and Sudesh Vaid, 233–253 (New Brunswick, 1990); Tanika Sarkar, "Nationalist Iconography: Images of Women in Nineteenth-Century Bengali Literature," *Economic and Political Weekly* (hereafter *EPW*) (21 November 1987): 2011–2015; Malabika Kaelekar, "Kadambini and the *Bhadralok:* Early Debates over Women's Education in Bengal," *EPW* 21, no. 17 (26 April 1986): WS-WS31; Jasodhara Bagchi, "Representing Nationalism: Ideology of Motherhood in Colonial Bengal," *EPW* (20–27 October 1990): WS65-WS71.

44. Deenanath Bandyopadhyay, *Nanabishayak prabandha* [in Bengali] (Calcutta, 1887), 30–31.

45. Srabashi Ghosh's extensively researched article "Birds in a Cage," *EPW* 21, no. 43 (October 1986): 88–96, demonstrates the continuing relevance of nineteenth-century questions.

46. Thus Altekar's nationalist study of Hindu women begins with a statement that could have come from Mill: "One of the best ways to understand the spirit of a civilization and to appreciate its excellences and realize its limitations is to study the history of the position and status of women in it." A. S. Altekar, *The Position of Women in Hindu Civilisation: From Prehistoric Times to the Present Day* (Banaras, 1956), 1. For a statement typically seeing the extended family as an institution inimical to the growth of individuality, see Margaret M. Urquhart, *Women of Bengal: A Study of the Hindu Pardanashins of Calcutta* (Calcutta, 1926), 33, 43–44.

47. See Amitrasudan Bhattacharya, *Bankimchandrajibani* [in Bengali] (Calcutta, 1991), 90–91; and Sabyasachi Bhattacharya, "Bankimchandra and the Subjection of Women: Kapalkundala's Destiny." I am grateful to Professor Bhattacharya for allowing me access to this manuscript.

48. Bipinchandra Pal, *Sattar batshar* (Calcutta, 1955/56), 7–8.

49. *Gauradeshiya samaj sangsthapanartha pratham sabhar bibaran* [in Bengali] (Calcutta, 1823), 9–10, 12–14, 16–17, 21–22.

50. Mrityunjay Sharmanah [Vidyalankar], *Rajabali* [in Bengali] (Serampore, 1808), 294–295, and the posthumously published *Prabodh chandrika* [in Bengali] (Serampore, 1846), 6.

51. Rajivlochan Mukhopadhyay, *Srimaharaj krishnachandra rayashya charitram* [in Bengali] (London, 1811), 43–47.

52. *Bibaran,* 6–9.

53. Ibid., 4, 19–20, 27–28.

54. See the editor's introduction to Bhabanicharan Bandyopadhyay, *Kalikata Kamalalaya* (1823), ed. Brajendranath Bandyopadhyay, 8–10 (Calcutta, 1952).

55. Ibid., 43.

56. S. N. Mukherjee, "Class, Caste and Politics in Calcutta, 1815–38," in Leach and S. N. Mukherjee (eds.), *Elites in South Asia,* ed. Edmund Leach and S. N. Mukherjee, 33–78 (Cambridge, 1970).

57. Ibid., 5–6.

58. Ibid., 8, 10–13.

59. Ibid., 8–9.

60. Ibid., 22. There is one word—*sarip* [?]—that I have left out of this list as I could not understand it. Partha Chatterjee has suggested to me that the word could be a transliteration of the word "sheriff."

61. *Tattvabodhini patrika* (n.d.), quoted in Sibnath Sastri, *Ramtanu lahiri o tatkalin bangasamaj* [in Bengali] (Calcutta, 1957), 58.

62. *KK,* 12.

63. Ibid., 22.

64. Ibid.

65. Kashinath Bosu comp., *Darshandeepika* [in Bengali] (Calcutta, 1848), 14–18.

66. Cited in Shyamapada Nyayabhusan, *Bidhababibahanishedhak* [in Bengali] (Calcutta, 1877), 13.

67. An 1849 biography of Bhabanicharan gave detailed descriptions of his pilgrimage trips. *KK,* editor's introduction, 11–14. *Tirthayatra,* or pilgrimage, was later incorporated as a subject in Bengali books on domestic science. "The life of someone who has never set foot on a place of pilgrimage is devoid of much significance. Every grihi must budget for *tirthayatra*": Ambikacharan Gupta, *Grihasta-jiban* [in Bengali] (Calcutta, 1887), 309.

68. See my "Postcoloniality and the Artifice of History: Who Speaks for 'Indian' Pasts?" *Representations* 37 (1992): 1–26.

69. Krishnabhabini Das, quoted in Murshid, 148.

70. *Mudhusudan racanabali* [in Bengali], ed. Kshetra Gupta (Calcutta, 1965), 518–519.

71. Sumit Sarkar, "The Kalki-Avatar of Bikrampur: A Village Scandal in Early Twentieth Century Bengal," in Guha, *Subaltern Studies* VI, 1–53.

72. Rajnarayan Bose, *Se kal ar e kal* [1874], ed. Brajendranath Bandyopadhyay and Sajanikanta Das (Calcutta, 1976/7), 2.

73. Ibid., 86–87.

74. Ibid., 39–40.

75. See John Rosselli, "The Self-Image of Effeteness: Physical Education and Nationalism in Nineteenth-Century Bengal," *Past and Present* 86 (February 1980): 121–148.

76. Bhudev Mukhopadhyay, *Achar prabandha* [in Bengali] (Chinsurah, 1908), 6, 12–13, 35.

77. Ibid., 52, 60–61 (emphasis added).

78. Sumit Sarkar, "'Kaliyuga,' 'Chakri,' and 'Bhakti': Ramakrishna and His Times," *Economic and Political Weekly* 27, no. 29 (18 July 1992); and Partha Chatterjee, "A Religion of Urban Domesticity: Sri Ramakrishna and the Calcutta Middle Class," in *Subaltern Studies* VII, ed. Partha Chatterjee and Gyanendra Pandey, 40–68 (Delhi, 1992).

79. Sarkar, "Kaliyuga," 1549–1550.

80. See Jean-Jacques Rousseau, *Emile,* trans. Barbara Foxley (New York, 1977), Bk. V, and the discussion in Sarah Kofman, "Rousseau's Phallocratic Ends," in *Revaluing French Feminism: Critical Essays on Difference, Agency and Culture,* ed. Nancy Fraser and Sandra Lee Bartky, 46–59 (Bloomington, 1992).

81. Jean-François Lyotard, *Heidegger and "the Jews,"* trans. Andreas Michel and Mark Roberts (Minneapolis, 1990), 17.

82. Dayamayi Dasi, *Patibrata dharma* [in Bengali], 1–2.

83. Bharati Ray, "Bengali Women and Politics of Joint Family," *EPW* 28, no. 32 (28 December 1991): 3021–3051.

84. Dasi, *Patibrata dharma,* 1–2.

85. Saraswati Sen quoted in Borthwick, *Changing Role,* 55–56. See also Indira Devi, *Narir Ukti* [in Bengali] (Calcutta, 1920), dedication.

86. See my *Rethinking Working-Class History: Bengal 1890–1940* (Princeton, 1989).

87. Yogendranath Ray, *Bangamahila* [in Bengali] (Chinsurah, 1881), 87–88.

88. Radhikanath Thakur, comp. and trans., *Patripariksha* [in Bengali] (Murshidabad, 1880), 17.

89. Bosu, *Hindu achar,* 15–16.

90. Ibid., 58–60.

91. Immanuel Kant, *The Critique of Judgment,* trans. J. C. Meredith (Oxford, 1973), 97.

92. Dasi, *Patibrata dharma,* preface.

93. See the discussion in my "Postcoloniality and the Artifice of History."

94. See Martin Heidegger, *On the Way to Language,* trans. Peter D. Hertz (New York, 1982), 15. The problem receives attention in my "Postcoloniality and the Artifice of History" and "Labour History and the Politics of Theory: An Indian Angle on the Middle East," in *Workers and Working Classes in the Middle East: Struggles, Histories, Historiographies,* ed. Zachary Lockman, 321–334 (Albany: State University of New York Press, 1994).

95. I have borrowed the idea of "epistemic violence" from the work of Gayatri Spivak.

96. Roland Barthes, *The Grain of the Voice: Interviews 1962–1980,* trans. Linda Coverdale (New York, 1985), 89.

12

The Dialectics of Decolonization

Nationalism and Labor Movements in Postwar French Africa

Frederick Cooper

Patterns of decolonization are particularly difficult to unravel because we know the end point: the emergence of the independent state from colonial rule. It is tempting to read the history of the period from 1945 to 1960 as the inevitable triumph of nationalism and to see in each social movement taking placing within a colony—be it by peasants, by women, by workers, or by religious groups—another piece to be integrated into the coming together of the nation. What is lost in such a reading are the ways in which different groups within colonies mobilized for concrete ends and used as well as opposed the institutions of the colonial state and the niches opened up in the clash of new and old structures. Whether such efforts fed into the attempts of nationalist parties to build anticolonial coalitions needs to be investigated, not assumed. As this chapter will show, at the very moment that the distinct but related struggles of labor movements and parties became increasingly powerful in the mid-1950s, a direct clash emerged between the principle of class struggle and African unity.

The clash is important not just for its place in the history of twentieth-century Africa but for the implications it had for what kinds of Africas would be imaginable in the postcolonial era and what kinds of Africas would be excluded from political debates. Beyond that, the clash is an instance of a profound conflict of aspirations that the end of colonial rule did more to reveal than to resolve: for some, the end of empire meant that impoverished and oppressed people could share in the universal good, could aspire to a generally defined minimum standard of living, could insist on certain rights, as workers, as citizens, as women, as individuals. But for others, liberation had a different meaning—as an expression of aspirations that were specific to Africa, that postulated a notion of community against the pretentions of universal progress. In such an argument, universality was a mask for Eurocentrism, a confusion of Europe's peculiar history with standards that Europe expected the rest of the world to meet, an assumption that European categories like "class" or "rights" displaced African ideas of affinity. Yet as African labor movements were among the first to learn, the very insistence on the primacy of "African" community can constitute a denial of solidarities and differences that people experience in their daily lives.

I will focus on one sort of social movement, labor, and on a particular example, the transition of the French West African labor movement from a class-centered, internationalist organization from roughly 1945 to 1955 to a nationalist organization that insisted that workers subordinate their own concerns, interests, and collective awareness to the emerging national struggle. As much as this is a story of the ambivalent relationship of two sorts of movements in a colony, it is also a story of a complex engagement of an African labor movement and a colonial state: how workers' collective actions forced officials to rethink their conceptions of labor as much as their policies, how workers seized the new colonial discourse and turned attempts to articulate control to claims to entitlements, and how the colonial state finally began to move away from the implications of the universalistic language in which it had asserted its authority. Ironically, France found relief from such demands by reaching an understanding with the nationalist parties, whose vision of African autonomy promised an end to insistence on wages and benefits equal to those of European workers. My goal is thus an interactive, dynamic analysis of the relationship between the political strategies and discourses of a colonial regime and social and political movements within African colonies.

The National Question and the Labor Question

The metanarrative of anticolonial triumph takes two forms.[1] One, the narrative of social mobilization, shows that inchoate, often local, resistance to colonial rule which had been evident since the conquest, was channeled into a unified anticolonial movement in the years after World War II by Western-educated intellectuals. Mobilizing African teachers, clerks, workers, and peasants—working through organizations ranging from ethnic associations to groups of market women to alumni of secondary schools—and bringing people into modern political parties, the postwar leaders forged a movement that attacked head-on the racist construction of the colonial state and claimed its territory, its symbols, and its institutions to bring material progress and a sense of national identity to the people of each African colony.[2]

The second metanarrative is the revolutionary one, denying legitimacy to the modernizing national elite as much as to the colonial regime. Frantz Fanon argued that wage workers, aspiring only to the privileges of white workers in the colony, could not consistently challenge colonial dominance. Rather, it would be peasants and the lumpenproletariat who would spearhead the struggle, for only they were willing to face up to the absolute denial of identity that colonialism necessarily entailed and to use violence to end it. Fanon was not in fact a nationalist, and had little sympathy for the rhetoric of racial unity or the invocation of symbols of the African past that "bourgeois nationalists" found easy to embrace as they set themselves up as brokers between African "tradition" and postcolonial "modernity." His imagined future was actually a reversal of an imperialist past: " 'The last shall be first and the first last.' Decolonisation is the putting into practice of this sentence."[3]

These metahistories of decolonization imply particular readings of colonialism itself. The first version accepts the image of progress associated with Western education, the expansion of markets, and global linkages. It insists that the fundamental contradiction of colonialism lay in its inability fully to embrace modernity: maintaining the coherence of a colonial state and its ability to exploit colonial labor and resources required racial exclusions that denied a role in bringing about that progress to those among the colonized who were best adapted to the task. The blocked path could only be cleared by national liberation, hence a focus on social struggles in colonies insofar as they led to and were subsumed in the national struggle. The second version sees colonialism as destructive at every level, the only possible change a total reversal of a political and social order.

The irony of Fanon's position is that his quest to define the True Anticolonialist allows colonialism, by the logic of inversion, to define the only politics to which he can accord legitimacy. That different groups among a colonized population might bring their own histories and their own interests to a complex engagement with colonial power is lost in a powerful rhetoric that not only demands a singular focus but also delegitimizes any other kind of contestation.

There is a great deal at stake, politically and morally, in these arguments. In the triumphant emancipation of a people from colonialism—by a modernizing elite or through revolutionary mobilization—any voice for a particular interest represents divisiveness or a colonialist reaction. It is the claim to have arrived, to represent a True Anticolonialism or a True Nation, that forms a crucial ideological basis for postcolonial authoritarianism. The African single-party state is only one manifestation of such a trend; the widespread suppression or marginalization of trade unions is, in this context, the most ironic result.

Wage workers—like other social categories—were simultaneously confronting the general condition of selling labor power in a capitalist economy, the institutions (from job hierarchies to trade unions) through which the experience of capital and labor in Europe was transferred to colonies, the power relations specific to the colonial state, and the particular historical and cultural patterns through which each act of creating a labor force took place.[4] My focus here is on how workers resisted, appropriated, and redefined the economic and social institutions and discursive frameworks through which colonial regimes tried to organize work, and the relationship of these processes to the denouement of colonial power itself. I am making an argument different from Ranajit Guha's stress on the "autonomy" of the "subaltern" or James Scott's vision of "hidden transcripts" among the colonized allowing a collective ethos to emerge that suddenly bursts into public confrontation.[5]

The problem with such arguments is not that distinct modes of communication and practices of opposition did not exist within colonies, but that historical accounts that privilege this form of opposition in a colonial context miss the long-term dynamics of the interplay of "hidden" and "public" transcripts, underestimate the way in which this dynamics could destabilize colonial regimes and their officials' conceptions of their own power, and misleadingly imply that certain forms of oppositional politics within a colony have an inherent legitimacy that others do not. My goal in this chapter is not simply to show that social movements that used and engaged the institutions and ideologies of institutions imported by colonizers could be as important challengers of colonial power as those that steadfastly resisted their blandishments, but to trace the implications of such engagement over time. Colonial regimes changed the way that they deployed power and articulated legitimacy in response to such pressures, and this redeployment defined new terms in which power was articulated and contested.

Colonial Power and African Labor

Colonizers brought with them not so much "colonialism"—a coherent set of practices and discourses intended to dominate conquered people while maintaining their distinctiveness—as a series of hegemonic projects.[6] Realizing these projects, however, brought colonizers into relations with indigenous elites and subalterns, and at each step along the way, these elements reshaped each other. Much of the history of colonization in Africa can be seen as a series of failed hegemonic projects, each of which was subverted as much by its "collaborators" as by those who "resisted" it.

Late nineteenth-century imperialism justified itself by playing up tyranny and slaving on the African continent, insisting that only the benevolent exercise of European power could bring the continent into a world of peaceful commerce and social and cultural progress. Early colonial regimes at times took seriously the reformist implications of such arguments, but immediately ran into the consequences of the limited spatial and cultural domains over which they could exercise effective power and the necessity for alliances with the very people whose tyranny they had pledged to uproot. In effect, colonial regimes had to link themselves to the attempts of a wide range of African elites to establish their own hegemonies and protect or enhance their own resources. Despite the efforts of colonial regimes to awe the populace with symbols of their own superiority and to channel African aspirations in specified directions, their cultural work was fragmented by the multiple local idioms in which power was articulated and the limited coercive and economic means they brought to bear. By the 1920s, Great Britain and France were downplaying their "civilizing missions" and trying to portray their compromises and weaknesses as sound policy, termed "indirect rule" or "association."[7]

The strongest attempts to use African labor in new ways, such as labor recruitment in Upper Volta or Kenya, actually deepened regimes' reliance on indigenous intermediaries to do their dirty work. Colonial regimes had to foster chiefs' ambitions and at times restrict their own, for fear that excessive demands for labor or overzealous subimperialism on the part of chiefs might undermine the stability of rural authority.[8]

Colonial officials went a long way to convince themselves that Africa was a continent of "tribes," that its people were deeply and immutably immersed in the social relations of the village and the politics of deference to chiefly authority.[9] They were therefore anxious about the emergence of social categories that fell outside their boundaries. Such people were often called "detribalized," and they included mission converts and educated Africans—the very minds imperial powers seemed to be colonizing—and wage laborers, the necessary condition of a capitalist future. The political language of colonial states was thus only capable of labeling such people by what they were not—it could not think through what they were.

Indeed, the discussion of labor issues within colonial bureaucracies in the 1920s and early 1930s was meager and impoverished. Officials in French or British Africa were above all interested in numbers—and saw Africa as suffering an endemic labor shortage—yet their formal adherence to free labor ideology meant they could not discuss the ways in which power was exercised over young men within the jurisdiction of chieftancies. Nor could they say much about the social conditions at places of work—or residential conditions for workers in towns—for the myth of the "tribal" African dictated that such people should be shuttled back to rural villages as rapidly as possible or that "chiefs" should be brought to town to reproduce a "traditional" structure of authority. Early critics of labor policy—missionaries, travelers, and the occasional dissident voice within colonial administration—operated within such a framework, documenting the horrors of forced labor in French Equatorial Africa or the Ivory Coast (where it was legal until 1946), arguing for the end of all coercive recruitment practices, and showing that migratory labor undermined the integrity of rural societies while assuring the maladaptation of Africans to wage labor and urban life. Wage labor in Africa was not discussed as if it posed a particular set of social problems; the kinds of discussions regarding European workers taking place in the International Labour Office and national legislatures in the 1920s and 1930s seemed remote from Africa.[10]

By the 1920s, French and British policy makers had turned the reformable "other" of the days of conquest into a frozen being whose otherness colonial governments now claimed to protect. The problem was that the systems of authority articulated and legitimated through local authorities could not handle the extent of social change that the uneven development of colonial economies entailed. Cities, commercial pathways, mines, and other sites not easily contained in the idea of "traditional Africa" were to prove especially troublesome precisely because colonial officials did not want to think of Africans as belonging there. Colonial regimes would swing back to the universalistic, change-oriented project, only to find that this hegemonic ideal was even more contradictory and even more open to subversion than the fragmented idioms of rule of the 1920s and 1930s.

Colonial Authority Challenged

Colonial states had created a system vulnerable to challenges in precisely those areas they did not want to think about. However unimpressive and uneven efforts to build imperial economies in Africa were, colonial regimes had created islands of wage labor production as well as nodes on commercial networks, through which cash crops produced by peasant farms and the narrow range of European commodities sold by European firms passed.

Colonial regimes were able to diffuse the strains of the depression of the 1930s into the countryside, but the revival of export production reconcentrated African labor and led to the first wave of strikes in the British copper mines of Central Africa and in some railroad and port centers. In much of British Africa, World War II—when Britain had little to supply to African workers and much to demand of them—led to endemic labor crisis, forcing officials to raise wages and more important to think seriously for the first time about the category of labor. French Africa, relatively isolated after the fall of France, had rather different wartime experiences, but labor protest caught up soon after the war ended, in a period when exports were increasing, labor forces were growing, and urban inflation was rampant.[11]

The postwar strike wave took place in a changed political and economic context. France and Great Britain, their economies in shambles and their ability to sell their own products for foreign exchange cruelly limited, saw their tropical colonies as the only way they could save the franc, the pound, and national autonomy from the new hegemon on the international horizon, the United States. India was going, Indochina was threatened, and officials said in so many words that Africa was their great hope, its underdeveloped state itself a sign of how much its productive capacity could be improved. Ideologically, the great war against conquering tyrannies—and the language of "self-determination" that emerged in the propaganda wars against Hitler—put colonial powers on the defensive, and the Soviet Union was eager to attack colonialism while the United States was less than eager to defend it.

In this context, the two leading colonial powers had to articulate a compelling justification for what they were doing in the colonies. The idea of "development" simultaneously promised that Africa would make an enhanced contribution to production—saving the empires—and that Africa would receive the benefits of the technical knowledge and newfound ability to plan, as well as whatever capital these powers could afford to invest. The developmental initiative was both an assertion of a coherent and unified rationale for the continuation of colonial rule and a process in which Africans could join in their own interests but under government direction. Here was a hegemonic project, although it would prove to be so weighted down with contradictions and unrealizable goals that it would barely last a decade.

The continued strikes in Africa were both a disruption of the economic project and an embarrassment to the ideological one. They represented a telling instance of the "powerless" making the "powerful" reconfigure both ideology and the apparatus of government. Both governments had thought that "development" would be a framework they could control. French officials, in particular, thought that an infusion of capital, planning, and technical assistance would be compatible with allowing African societies to evolve in their own milieu, without the dangers of proletarianization. That was not to be.

Both governments found that the subcontracted power structure and the subcontracted and multiple hegemonies they had elaborately constructed in rural Africa meant nothing in the workplace. The perceived loss of control had a double effect on the exercise of power in colonial regimes in this critical conjuncture. First, African strike action diminished within the bureaucracy the once-dominant provincial administrators who knew their natives and had long tried to keep Africans inside their "tribal" categories in favor of a rising generation of technocrats whose interventions were rooted in the universalities of European social engineering. Labor officers and inspecteurs du travail became key actors. Second, the need to reassert control in mines, railways, ports, and cities disciplined officials to take their new hegemonic project seriously and to make a closer effort to articulate that project with the intimacies of actual social life. Trying to think of ways to get Africans back to work, officials turned to the precedents they thought they knew: the efforts to tame class conflict in Europe itself.

In British Africa, the series of key, dramatic strikes in the few key mines and communications networks in Central, West, and East Africa on which the colonial economy depended, which lasted from 1935 until the late 1940s, led to a slowly growing recognition that the labor question was a reality that had to be faced. In French Africa, the ideological journey from the peculiarity of the African to the universality of the worker was a surprisingly fast one. On the eve of the Dakar general strike of 1946, the governor-general still thought it was possible to have development without proletarianization.[12] But a series of strikes in the port that began in December with minimal labor organization turned into larger union-led strikes in early January. By mid-January, a general strike lasting eleven days emerged out of a movement that was part carefully planned strike, part mass urban collective action. The unions came together in a citywide organization that brought in civil servants, clerks in commercial establishments, bakery workers, skilled workers, dockers, and manual laborers in a variety of trades. Market women refused to sell anything to white customers. A daily mass meeting became the focus of organization and sense of collective empowerment. The unions demanded ''equal pay for equal work and output,'' a minimum wage triple official calculations, equal rates of indemnities for family obligations and local cost of living for civil servants, and union participation in classifying jobs. Colonial officials were constrained from using their most obvious old weapon—the colonial army—because of their belief that Africans were a naturally rural people and that wage workers would desert the city if handled too roughly, because of concerns that violence in a highly visible city would be an international embarrassment, and because of their new hope that if treated as a modern man the African worker might eventually act like one. The governor-general, symbol of colonial power, telegraphed Paris in despair that he saw no way to get Africans back to work.[13]

In the heat of the strike, officials called in a form of knowledge that was familiar to them in the metropole but which had not appeared relevant to the colonies. Inspector Masselot, an expert in labor affairs, was flown in from Paris, and he set about negotiating with commercial workers, with metalworkers, and with government workers in different unions. He brought with him model collective bargaining agreements based on a form standardized in France: the contracts—with significant wage increases at the bottom and wider increments at the top—eventually induced workers, group by group, to peel away from the general strike. The general strike lasted eleven days, the strike movement as a whole two and a half months. At its end, most workers were considerably better off, the unions that had organized the strikes had become self-confident, and the more privileged government workers who had struck alongside their brethren had acquired such benefits as family allowances. Not only were the monetary victories substantial, but by conceding that low-level civil servants receive family allowances—even if not at rates equal to those of French officials or the small number of African ''évolués'' at the senior ranks—the government was in effect admitting that the needs of an African worker were of the same kind as those of a European worker. The myth that Africans were not really workers fell before the strikers' insistence on equal pay for equal work and the labor specialist's belief that French models of industrial relations could solve problems anywhere. Masselot saw this not so much as a victory for labor as the advent of a new approach to managing African society: ''There is a technique in organizing work, as with anything, and it cannot be improvised.''[14]

The process of channeling a wide conflict into specific, negotiable issues was soon institutionalized within the Inspection du Travail in French West Africa. These techniques—and the entire fabric of French claims to be "assimilating" or "developing" Africans—were promptly turned by African labor leaders into claims to entitlements. Even during the first strike wave, one labor leader rendered his opposite number in the administration speechless at a bargaining session by commenting, "Your goal is to raise us to your level; without the means we will never get there."[15] Over the years, African trade unionists used the rhetoric of imperial policy and the institutions of French industrial relations to claim the emoluments won by metropolitan workers.

Collective action continued to make clear that African voices would not just set off a rethinking of the labor question in colonial bureaucracies but would struggle to make themselves heard over the details of each dispute. The Dakar strike was followed by the massive railway strike in all of French West Africa from October 1947 to March 1948. This strike of some twenty thousand workers revealed that the combination of union organizing and the networks among railway workers could bring about collective action over a vast space, and the union showed its determination to exercise its voice about the details of a program of "stabilizing" and restructuring work organization.[16] Meanwhile, such issues as minimum wages were at the center of citywide general strikes in Conakry, Guinea, and Cotonou, Dahomey. The strike wave in British Africa also continued—the Gold Coast mines and railways in 1947, Dar es Salaam, and, again, Mombasa in 1947, the riots in the Gold Coast in 1948. These strikes were deeply rooted in the conjuncture of the postwar years. French West African wage labor forces were small—perhaps 2 or 3 percent of the total population and concentrated in transport, commerce, and government (plus scattered mines, the agricultural processing industry in Senegal, and plantation agriculture in Guinea and the Ivory Coast). But the narrowness of colonial economies gave them considerable power: a few nodal points (Dakar, Conakry, Abidjan, Cotonou, and the railway lines extending inland from those points) were essential to the all-important import-export trade and to government services. Yet at this time, the wage spectrum was narrow and provided little incentive to stay in a particular job. The strikes of the late 1940s followed linkages within a workforce that was poorly attached to specific jobs, that was involved in networks linking city and country, but that nonetheless vitally needed wages to survive.

The strikes crossed the boundaries of employment categories to embrace people moving into and out of particular occupations and into and out of urban areas, taking place in cities where rapid increases in employment were not countered by parallel growth in housing and services, following on the rampant inflation that upset the possibilities both migrant and fully proletarianized workers had for assuring their families' survival, reflecting the breakdown of tacit understandings between workers and employers about questions of discipline and remuneration, and proving difficult for officials to control as expanding urban economies and fledgling union organization added to workers' ability to withdraw their labor. These strikes did not turn out to begin a linear expansion of worker collective action toward an ever-widening compass: they were part of a conjuncture, and states' subsequent moves as well as changing circumstances channeled labor protest in a number of different directions.[17]

In the French case, the approach that Inspector Masselot had taken in the 1946 general strike acquired a strong institutional base within the Inspection du Travail. "Since May 1946," stated the next annual report on labor in French West Africa, "the constant preoccupation of the Inspection du Travail has been to avoid the repetition of events of the same nature and to bring about . . . the conclusion of a package of collective bargaining agreements discussed in an atmosphere of mutual comprehension."[18]

Officials came to think trade unions were a good idea, since an orderly process of negotiation could be carried out with them.[19] The idea of masses of cheap labor power circulating among jobs and between workplace and village lost its appeal, for it was this seemingly amorphous nature of an urban labor force that was blamed for the fact that strikes rapidly became general strikes. Officials set about attaching workers to particular occupational categories and fracturing the almost uniform low level of wages through substantial raises to workers in the most vulnerable sectors. They began to talk of "stabilization," of making a career, not just a few months of employment, attractive to African workers.

And officials soon began to think that the labor force had to be reproduced in a different way. The old model of the worker—and officials thought almost exclusively about male workers—as a single man who need only be paid an individual subsistence, leaving the costs of maintaining households, raising children, and caring for anyone not actually at work to a village economy increasingly peopled by women, seemed to be reproducing the wrong kind of workforce. Now, they wanted workers to be socialized and acculturated to urban life and industrial discipline from childhood.[20]

As the drive to turn the African worker from unruly primitive into industrial man accelerated in the late 1940s, colonial officials read the significance of "tradition" in increasingly negative terms. Such an African was no longer a quaint figure whose well-being and cultural integrity the wise colonial ruler was to maintain, but an obstacle to progress. This was why the brutality of colonial regimes in the 1940s and 1950s—beyond the occasional detention of "agitators"—was usually aimed at people whose dissidence could be conceptualized as atavistic, as the dangerous violence of primitive people. Such was the case in the terror unleashed against rural rebels in Madagascar in 1947 and Kenya in 1952, even as British and French regimes handled "modern" forms of protest with considerably more diffidence.[21] Indeed, as the governor of

Senegal made clear in his postmortem on the 1946 strike, the fear that a spreading strike could extend to "the most remote corners of the bush" was very much in officials' minds, and a reason for handling strikes with care and trying to mark them off as *labor* disputes solvable through orderly procedures rather than as challenges to colonial power that could not be so clearly bounded.[22] The quest for the modern African was not limited to the field of labor: cautious attempts to bring select Africans into European-modeled political institutions and to make African agriculture more scientific were being made. But the labor question struck in the most visible and vulnerable parts of empire, and forced officials to come to grips with the concrete realities of Africans acting in ways that transcended the old boundaries of control.

The discourse described above represented an effort to reassert control. Organized around a single vision of progress in a European image, focused on specific institutions and practices, it represented a hegemonic project couched in universalistic language. But even before the notions of stabilization and reproduction had been fully spelled out, African labor leaders were trying to seize the discourse. They turned a language of social engineering into a language of entitlement, seizing on the desperate hope of officials that Africans would behave in predictable ways to claim that wages and benefits should also be determined on a European model.

From Working Class to Nation: Trade Unionism in French Africa

What made the demands of labor particularly powerful was that they were set forth within disciplined, effective strike movements and that they were posed in the very rhetorical structures on which French officials placed their claims to legitimate rule over its subjects. In the general strike of 1946 and several subsequent strikes, unions won substantial gains and acquired the confidence to demand more. Even as officials tried to divide workers by occupation and rank, the victories of some encouraged others to try, while the fledgling organizations of workers focused demands on the state itself for a "code du travail" that would set minimum standards of wages and working conditions for all wage workers.

This was also a demand that officials thought paralleled their own desire for a clear map—based on French labor codes—of what industrial relations were supposed to be. Such a code had to apply to workers of all races, unless France wished to undermine its own claim, made in response to critics of its empire, that Overseas France was an integral part of France itself, and the presumption of a nonracial code raised the stakes of the debate over how the universal worker would be defined. Business groups saw the danger, but could not jettison either the rhetoric of imperial unity—depending as they did on the protection of the colonial state—or the rhetoric of regulation, for they too wanted industrial relations channeled into predictable directions. So they could only plead that the special conditions of the colonies be taken into consideration in drafting the code.

Meanwhile, worker organizations began to affiliate with the rival labor federations into which unions in France itself were grouped, and by far the most popular was the Confédération Générale du Travail (CGT), closely linked to the French Communist party (PCF). The CGT's efforts in the colonies have been the subject of some scholarly debate, and the organization's claim to have assisted colonial proletariats has been challenged by scholars who insist that the CGT was in its own way imperialist. Irwin Wall has pointed out the condescending attitude of CGT and PCF leaders toward colonial aspirations for self-determination and their insistence that only French communists could lead colonized peoples on the path to socialism. In short, he argues, they missed the paramount importance of nationalism to the people of the colonies.[23]

But this argument itself assumes that a historical judgment can be passed on the basis of a discussion that took place in France. At the same time, the argument naturalizes nationalism—treating it as an inevitable drive toward a future of political independence, as a train that one either boards or misses. Whatever the limits of the vision of CGT leaders in France, African trade unionists could use the institutions of the CGT and the legitimacy it had in French politics in their own ways.[24] By associating themselves with the CGT, African trade unionists not only let colonial officials think that their approach to work issues was fundamentally modern and progressive—modeled on France—but reminded them that claims to universalism could take more than one form.

In practice, the CGT-affiliated unions in French West Africa waged a number of campaigns in different colonial cities, with uneven but significant success, for higher wages and other benefits, while they developed a French West Africa-wide organization to mobilize politically for the code du travail. The CGT unions insisted throughout the late 1940s and 1950s that their fundamental goal was "equal pay for equal work," and indeed equal benefits for equal work.[25]

Given the universalistic, nonracial definition of the wage laborer, the costs of whatever guarantees workers won could be high. The elevated stakes of the debate over the code du travail caused it to drag on for six years, until November 1952. Its final passage came after a one-day, highly effective general strike throughout French West Africa, organized by all the trade union federations and spearheaded by the CGT. The code guaranteed all wage workers a forty-hour week, paid vacations, and other benefits; it guaranteed the right to organize unions and, with certain restrictions, the right to strike; it created consultative bodies in the state apparatus with union representation. The code pronounced in principle for wage workers to receive family allowances to help them raise children.

It did all this for a strictly bounded workforce—wage laborers only. Officials' assumption that wage workers were male was so ingrained it was only occasionally commented on, and trade unions' version of "equal pay for equal work" was focused on a comparison of male breadwinners across the races. The code was quite explicit in focusing only on workers who received a wage. So-called customary labor—which included most labor done by women as well as most of the forms of labor on African farms that shaded into tenancy—was left to an African world that officials did not have to probe. This realm, in fact, was where several leading African politicians, like Léopold Senghor and Félix Houphouët-Boigny, were building political machines, and they were content to keep the inspecteurs du travail from asking too many questions there.

The African deputies to the French National Assembly in Paris had played an active role in the debate, and their threats to drop their support for the code if certain provisions that they cherished were left out had swayed some metropolitan politicians who feared polarization and a new strike wave.[26]

This was the high point of cooperation between the leaders of African political parties and the trade unions. Earlier, the leading political activists had retained a certain distance from the labor movement: Lamine Guéye, then the leading Socialist politician in Dakar, had sat out the 1946 strike and accordingly earned the contempt of the strikers. Senghor and Houphouët-Boigny had at times seemed more concerned with the damage the railway strike of 1947–1948 was doing to commerce than with helping the railwaymen achieve victory, and Houphouët-Boigny was credited by the French labor inspectors with persuading the railwaymen in his territory, the Ivory Coast, to give up the strike two months before the rest of the workers settled.[27] The leading politician from the Soudan, Fily Dabo Sissoko, conspired with French officials to split Soudanese railwaymen off from their Senegalese brethren on the crucial Dakar-Niger line, a move that failed ignominiously when the railwaymen whom Sissoko thought of as his clients ignored his call to break the strike.[28] Houphouët-Boigny remained distrustful of the labor movement, although Senghor, *after* the railway strike, moved to bring its leaders into his party's orbit, pushing Ibrahima Sarr, the hero of 1947–1948, into an elected office. But in the strike wave of 1946–1948, it was clear that electoral mobilization and labor mobilization were two processes, with considerable tension between them.[29] After the victory of 1952, the tension would soon become manifest again.

The most interesting figure in this regard is Sékou Touré of Guinea. He had been a humble clerk in the French bureaucracy and made his start in a civil servants' union. He became leader of the Guinean national federation of CGT unions and led a bitter general strike, largely over the government's setting of the minimum wage, in 1950. This gave him a reputation throughout CGT circles, and he was one of the prime movers behind the strike of November 1952 for the code. He more than anyone stood in the early 1950s for CGT trade unionism: aggressive tactics, detailed demands for one after another of the perquisites enjoyed by French workers, and the rhetoric of proletarian internationalism. He was a true "cégétiste" (CGTist).[30] There were curious sides to his political persona even then: outside of union matters, he cooperated with the more conservative Houphouët-Boigny, and within the CGT he was a rival of the Soudanese leader Abdoulaye Diallo, who had the inside track in internationalist circles, having become a vice president of the leftist World Federation of Trade Unions (WFTU).[31] But at the time of victory in the struggle for the code, Sékou Touré seemed fully committed to making the French working class the reference point for the aspirations of African workers. When the code was voted, he directed his union leaders, "*Résponsable,* your bedside reading is the Code du Travail, which you can never study enough."[32]

When business interests tried to stall implementation of key provisions of the code and the government temporized, another French West Africa-wide strike movement materialized, while in Guinea Sékou Touré led a strike lasting sixty-seven days and resulting in acceptance of the labor movement's interpretation that a key article of the code entitled workers to a 20 percent increase in the minimum wage. This strike, officials admitted, was a "remarkable personal success" for Sékou Touré.[33] He took a less personal interest—but the CGT and other union forces were in any case well prepared—in the next great campaign culminating in 1956, for family allowances for wage workers. By then, strike threats were sufficiently intimidating to get the government to make the necessary concessions before the scheduled strike took place. The union movement in French West Africa had at that time signed up an impressive 35 percent of the region's five hundred thousand wage workers.[34]

But already the politics of African trade unionism were shifting, with Sékou Touré leading the new direction as he had led the old. In 1953, the year of his triumph in the Guinea strike, Sékou Touré ran for the territorial council, the principle legislative body at the level of the individual colony. He was not the only trade unionist to realize that labor offered a launching platform for politics, but that it was no more than that. In fact, the precision with which the code du travail defined the working-class—and the partial success of union efforts at raising wages and government efforts at stabilizing the labor force—meant that the population with a direct interest in labor's success was narrower than it might have been in the days of the amorphous laboring mass. Houphouët-Boigny was explicit in downplaying workers as a political base; the relatively well off farmers who constituted his own base may not have been more numerous, but their networks of tenancy, clientage, and affiliation penetrated much more deeply into the Ivory Coast's rural population.[35] Sékou Touré seems to have begun by following Houphouët-Boigny's tutelage in his political career, and in those years he kept his union activity compartmentalized so as not to antagonize his patron.[36]

Herein lies the best way for understanding the shift in the French labor movement from a predominantly internationalist (cégétiste) orientation to a nationalist one. Most writing on the subject of the antimetropolitan turn among African trade unionists does not consider any explanation necessary: the nationalism of the African masses is self-evident. But there is not much evidence that this turn originated among the rank and file. There is, on the contrary, evidence that the shift came from above, from labor leaders anxious to enter the political arena, and that as they did so, the autonomist labor movement they had spawned itself became subject to rank-and-file pressures for old-style demands, for higher wages and for equality with metropolitan workers. For someone like Sékou Touré, electoral support required mobilizing people of diverse interests through multiple networks of organization and affiliation and finding a language of broad appeal. The language of the labor movement had, since the war, urged African workers to cast their gaze toward French workers and demand entitlements accordingly. It was, of course, filled with attacks on colonialists, but above all on colonialists who had not lived up to the assimilationist and universalistic rhetoric of French imperialism. The peasant or pastoralist in rural Guinea had no French person whose entitlements were a relevant basis of comparison. Yet peasants and pastoralists had much in the structure of colonial society to feel constricted by. The common denominator that a budding politician in the early 1950s could mobilize was not equality but reactions to the colonial state itself, however diverse the common base of grievances might be. Even at the height of his trade union militancy, Sékou Touré reportedly remarked that his support in his first electoral campaigns "is not solely due to the progressive ideas which I defended; it is the consequence of the affection which a part of the Guinean masses hold for me, because I am the descendant of an illustrious family."[37] The search was on for building multiple bases of support and finding an idiom of affinity that went beyond class-based appeals.

It was thus while workers were still engaged in struggles for equal wages and family allowances that some labor leaders in French West Africa began to try to disaffiliate their organizations from their metropolitan connections and turn them into truly African organizations—with changed slogans and mobilizing ideologies—that could be used in broad political struggles.[38] The reactions of French officials to all of this is quite interesting, for it reveals not only the tensions among Africans over the contradiction of the nationalist and social agenda but also the way in which French thinking about their own exercise of power was being transformed in dialogue and confrontation with African organizations. At first glance, one might guess that French officials would reject out of hand the autonomist position, for it negated every premise of postwar imperial ideology. In the immediate postwar years, officials had seemed to see something positive in the CGT for affirming that French standards provided a model for African aspirations. But by 1954 or 1955, officials were not so sure—for the CGT had been far too successful using this rhetoric—

and greeted the autonomist surge in the labor movement with something akin to relief. As the chief inspecteur du travail commented,

> [The CGT leaders] have succeeded in trapping the public powers and rival union confederations in a kind of cycle that one can break out of only with great difficulty. If in effect one satisfies demands, these serve as a point of departure for new, more elevated demands, which threaten at this pace to break open the structure of the country and lead to a crisis, with unemployment, misery, discontented masses.[39]

Even earlier, French officials had thought that Sékou Touré might lead a nationalist exodus from the CGT, and they had welcomed the possibility. They were premature, but kept hoping.[40] And in 1955, open confrontation burst out between Sékou Touré, who insisted that the French CGT and the WFTU were out of touch with "African realities" and needed to give expression to a distinct "personality of African trade unionism," and Abdoulaye Diallo, who heaped contempt on "so-called African trade unionism."[41]

Meanwhile, African politicians were calling for a specifically African trade unionism that would work alongside African political parties. The feuding gave rise to a new federation, the Confédération Générale du Travail–Autonome (CGTA), independent of the French CGT, in which Sékou Touré played a leading role but which forged alliances with political parties in the respective territories of French West Africa. The loyalists—thinking the autonomists were playing into the hands of the government—promptly dubbed the new organization "CGT–Administrative." French officials in fact were pleased over the split, although worried lest the new organization be too successful and reestablish unity on a different basis. The noncommunist federations also went through a similar process, with most forming specifically African federations independent of the metropolitan *centrales*. In 1957, most of these organizations—the CGT in effect conceding it had lost its vanguard role—decided to combine forces in a single trade union federation that would express aspirations to African unity. It became known as the Union Générale des Travailleurs d'Afrique Noire (UGTAN).[42]

Sékou Touré became the most articulate spokesman of the new African trade unionism. He argued that the fundamental issue was African unity in the struggle against imperialism. The old rhetoric of equality, like that of class struggle, was gone. Indeed, Sékou Touré insisted, "although the classes of metropolitan and European populations battle and oppose each other, nothing separates the diverse African social classes." Because of the common identity of Africans, there was no need for a plurality of trade unions. The claim to unity and uniformity came in the same breath.[43] UGTAN debated the issue of class struggle, and refused a proposal that the organization act not only against "white colonialism, but also against Africans who exploit their racial brothers, like the planters of the Ivory Coast." Instead, delegates—with considerable unease and disagreement—insisted that the liquidation of colonialism should "take pride of place over the class struggle."[44] Class struggle was being labeled un-African; the national struggle was to supersede all others. In secret, French officials welcomed the new direction in African trade unionism: "the movement could a priori be considered—and it has not failed to be this in effect—as favorable to our future in Africa."[45]

In 1956 the context in which the African struggles for power and for social justice intersected underwent a dramatic change. The French government, frustrated in its efforts to shape economic and social change in its own way, fearing a second Algeria, and seeking to distance itself from all the demands for parity that followed from its assimilationist and universalist imperial ideology, pulled back. Developmentalist thinking, in the end, did not offer an answer to the question that had bedeviled Africa's conquerors for over sixty years: how to harness the resources and labor power of the continent.[46] The French government redefined political institutions under the *loi cadre* (framework law) devolving effective government (except for foreign affairs, defense, etc.) to the individual territories, operating under elected legislatures, a "vice-président du conseil" chosen by the party controlling the legislature, and African ministers. Most decisions and budgets were devolved from the federations (French West Africa and French Equatorial Africa) to the territories (Senegal, Ivory Coast, Dahomey, Niger, etc.).

France made it clear that the civil service in each territory, with certain transitional provisions, would be the responsibility of each government; if government workers were to get any more perquisites, the territorial legislatures would have to raise the money to pay for them. The effect of this was to put the French reference point at one remove from African civil servants and workers. The civil service unions realized quickly that "territorialization" threatened the rhetorical and institutional basis for all their demands.[47] But the tide was against them: African politicians were eagerly seeking the legislative and executive offices, and trade union leaders were prominent among them.

French officials thought they had got themselves out of the trap that their own rhetoric and CGT organization had got them into. As one political observer noted, as soon as trade union leaders won office they would be in the same position as their French predecessors in facing workers' demands for new entitlements, and—having to pay the bills—they would offer "meager satisfaction." Workers would be held in check by "their respectful fear of local African authorities, who will not lack the means to make their point of view prevail."[48] It would now be African trade unionists who would fall into a trap baited by their own nationalism and sprung by the takeover of state institutions by ambitious men of power.

French officials guessed right: as African politicians, including those of trade union background, moved into state offices, they would seek to tame the labor movement. Trade union leaders did well in the 1957 elections. In eight of the nine territories of French West Africa, trade union leaders were named minister of labor or minister of the civil service, and seven of these eight were UGTAN members. Sékou Touré became vice-président du conseil in Guinea. Even Diallo gave up his communist connections and his communist rhetoric to join the government in the Soudan.[49] The level of strike activity went down, and UGTAN itself intervened to cool off some strike movements. This soon led to considerable tension from the rank and file, whose interests in the old demands of equality with French workers, higher minimum wages, better benefits, and guarantees against the loss through territorialization of already-won privileges were now threatened by the very success of anticolonial politics.[50] A particularly long and bitter strike—entailing riots, imprisonments, and death—took place in Dahomey, in which a militant rank and file stood opposed to a government labor minister who was himself a CGT and UGTAN veteran, with the union caught in between. As the dispute dragged on to only partial resolution, a pro-labor speaker at a rally commented, "It was easier to obtain satisfaction from a European inspecteur du travail than it is now from an African minister." The minister, for his part, was trying to turn his comrades' discourse about African-French equality and universal standards of labor policy into a discourse on the scarcity of local resources.[51]

Sékou Touré, as he moved toward power, told trade unionists that the game had changed, and they now would have to fall in line to express the unity of the African personality and the unity of the anti-imperialist struggle. A strike against "the organisms of colonialism" was one thing.

> But when it is directed against an African government, it affects African authority, reinforcing by this means, in the relations of force established between the dependent power and the dominant power the authority of the latter. . . . Trade unionism for trade unionism's sake is historically unthinkable in current conditions, trade unionism of class just as much. . . . The trade union movement is obligated to reconvert itself to remain in the same line of emancipation.[52]

His minister of labor, Camara Bengaly, also lectured trade unionists on their new duties.

> The workers, without renouncing any of their rights but convinced of the necessity to use them in good earnest, will go through a reconversion to become the precious collaborators of the elected authorities of the people and more particularly of the young Conseil de Gouvernement in its mission to realize the happiness of all Guineans through work done in love. . . . [T]he orientation of our trade union movement must necessarily correspond to the general policies desired by our populations. Any conception of trade unionism contrary to this

orientation must be discarded, and courageously fought in order to be eliminated definitively.[53]

Coming on the eve of Guinean independence, the words were chilling. The assertions that Africans were an undivided people, that Africans now ruled themselves, and that Africans were engaged in an ongoing struggle with outside forces would be used to ensure that Africans spoke with a single voice. One of Sékou Touré's collaborators and rivals in years of trade union action, David Soumah, already understood the implications.

A unity which stifles the voice of free trade unionism sets back the emancipation of the laboring masses instead of facilitating it. A unity which ends up in reality in subordinating trade union action to the goodwill of governments and employers, which submits trade unionism, the very expression of liberty, to a too narrow obedience toward political parties and political men, neutralizes the action of the masses for social progress.[54]

Sékou Touré practiced what he preached—far more than French officials, who had thought him a useful tool against universalistic trade unionism, expected. He led Guinea out of the French empire in 1958, rejecting de Gaulle's program for close Franco-African relations during the devolution of power. He duly set about consolidating his personal authority and those of his henchmen, repressing—among other groups—any vestige of autonomous trade unionism. Unions were forcefully amalgamated into a single confederation, which was in turn subordinated to Sékou Touré's political party as Guinea became a single-party state. As one commentator put it, ''Trade unionism was forbidden to trade unions,'' and the unions became ''an organization of the party for the control of the masses.'' When Sékou Touré humiliated the teachers' union and jailed some of its leaders during their pathetic attempt in 1961 to secure a pay raise, it was clear that unions as an organism to advance members' interests had no place in this kind of political independence.[55]

Guinea—presided over by a former trade unionist—represented an extreme in the extent of government destruction of union rights and organizations. In places like Nigeria, Ghana, Zambia, or Senegal unions struggled more successfully to remain a part of political and social life. Trade unions, in those countries, have proven difficult to repress and able—as in the colonial era—to mobilize new discourses in their defense; in Zambia and Nigeria trade unions have in the 1990s proved to be the nucleus of opposition to authoritarian governments. But co-optation of the top layer of union leadership and considerable repression in many countries have reduced the room for maneuver they seized during the postwar decade.[56] Veterans of the labor movement in Senegal refer in interviews to trade unionists taking off the ''le boubou syndical'' in favor of ''le boubou politique,'' trading in the robes of union power for the robes of political office, asserting that the unions contributed to political struggle but only became the "auxiliaries" of political parties even as many trade union leaders were co-opted into the government.[57] Senegal's prime minister in 1958 dismissed trade unionists' concerns as "secondary." Later, the leader of the railway strike of 1947–1948, Ibrahim Sarr, who was never jailed by the French, was imprisoned by the government of Senghor for his role in trying to forge a populist political movement in 1962, and the most influential Senegalese in UGTAN, Alioune Cissé, who had been able to lead a nationalist labor organization without running afoul of the police, served time in jail in 1968 for his role in a general strike.[58]

Repression and co-optation must be understood in relation to the politics of patronage: labor leaders were never pure embodiments of proletarian solidarity but people inserted in diverse webs of affiliation. They could fit into wider structures of political mobilization or else use their own connections to tie working-class communities into rival structures—hence the central importance to new regimes of fracturing the class-based potential of the labor movement while incorporating its leaders and its component parts into structures of patronage. Even before coming to power, political-cum-labor leaders within UGTAN were trying to bring about an ideological shift within the labor movement that would put the claim to state power at the apex of political relationships, focusing on workers' relationship with a nationalist leadership rather than their solidarity among themselves. The French move in 1956 to put significant resources in the hands of elected African politicians fundamentally changed the context of party-union relations. However much nationalist sentiments among the labor rank and file evolved from 1946 to 1956, the sharp break in 1956–1958 reflected the shift of state resources from a colonial power to African political leaders, eager to turn their complex political networks into an effective political machine. The new rhetorical strategies would be underscored by the new resources, yet the aspiring leaders' sense of the fragility of their position made them anxious to eliminate rival modes of organizing collectively and rival ideologies of mobilization.[59]

There was, of course, a case to be made that African trade unionists had done well enough in the final years of colonialism that they should have exercised restraint in the early years of independence, but the government of Guinea, for one, was not calling for a debate over priorities. Sékou Touré's version of unity and anti-imperialism—and other regimes similarly posited "development" as a national goal that no one could legitimately oppose—refused debate as it proclaimed that the dialectic of nation and class had been resolved in favor of the former.[60] The irony of this pattern of decolonization was that the vision of a unified Africa that animated political rhetoric in the mid-1950s, and which Sékou Touré and others used to shift attention from "equal pay for equal work," was itself lost. As African leaders consolidated power in their respective territories—focusing patronage, repression, and political symbolism within the borders they inherited—the possibilities of cooperation within francophone West Africa faded, and UGTAN soon ceased to function.

Conclusion

Looking back on the moment in 1957 when Africans were first entering ministerial office in French West Africa, there is something strange and revealing about the way the "colonizers" and the "colonized" were portraying their own actions. French administrators were congratulating themselves on having found a way to end the cycle of demands that trade union organization and French imperialist rhetoric had unleashed: they would give up power to Africans. African leaders were perfecting rationales for repressing, more vigorously than the colonial regime, social movements of the sort from which they had sprung. The colonizers could no longer see themselves as very colonial; the self-conscious leaders of the colonized were taking over the colonial state's claim to define the meanings of progress and legitimacy. Both sides seemed to hope—vainly it turned out—that the nationalists' authoritarianism would be more effective than the colonial variety in creating a developmentalist state.

In the end, the French colonial effort was trapped by the logical and political consequences of the universalism it claimed to stand for—knowledge did not prove to be power. Officials had since World War II shed their ambivalence about France as a social model for Africa and moved away from their alliances with indigenous elites. The notion of development through European knowledge reasserted a metropolitan right to reshape the most intimate social processes—remaking family as well as workplace. But in labor, as in other domains, the assertion of a scientific vision of social restructuring was turned by African labor movements into claims to entitlements, while the actual program of social reform failed, officials soon realized, to turn the workplace, the farm, or the family into a reflection of French images. Development efforts were leading to new forms of struggle without showing signs of making Africa into the productive junior partner of the postwar colonial imagination.

African labor movements, as their leaders became caught up in the quest for state power, also fell into an ideological trap. It became more difficult for them to assert that the metropolitan standard for wages and benefits should apply to all workers, or indeed to frame their political position around the notion that workers existed both within the nation and across the globe and that the condition of "the worker" posed problems that required specific attention, both within and among nations. The tension between workers' claims as workers and Africans' assertions of political rights as Africans was, during the 1940s and early 1950s, a creative and empowering one. But when "nation-building" became a state project and national identity was held to subsume all other forms of affiliation, that tension was pushed from the arena of politics.

The notion of sovereignty itself has its traps, and global acceptance of self-determination as the ultimate value in international politics has often occluded discussion of the content of that sovereignty. In the 1960s and 1970s, the denial of meaningful citizenship to black South Africans was a worldwide concern, but the destruction of labor movements in Guinea was not.[61] Yet the silences and exclusions of concepts like sovereignty and citizenship do not necessarily remain that way; political movements seeking to push a shared set of principles in new directions can use them, and have, as points of departure. The successes of the labor movement in Africa in the 1940s and 1950s is an important instance of a discourse of control that could not be contained.

As Dipesh Chakrabarty and Partha Chatterjee have argued, assertions that universalistic rationality provides the key to improving human life have come to Africa or Asia attached to the historical baggage of colonization. But exposing the parochialism of universality leaves a fundamental issue on the table.[62] A rejectionist stance—condemning everything with a European connection as imperialist—would still allow European categories to define the discourse even if the values attached to each category were reversed. Carried to its logical conclusion, an antiuniversalist argument allows no possibility for dialogue about moral issues across cultural borders, even though what those borders are is as much in question as the kinds of social and political practices that can be considered emancipatory. Aimé Césaire has expressed the dilemma brilliantly: ''There are two ways to lose oneself: by a walled segregation in the particular or by a dilution in the 'universal.' ''[63]

The forms of postcolonial states and the attitudes they projected in their moment of triumph toward social questions seem at first to represent the latter: francophone African states let the French Code du Travail be the blueprint for their labor legislation, just as they maintained colonial bureaucracies and expanded the modernist architecture of colonial cities into a symbol of national sovereignty. The colonial code's contribution to defining a sharp boundary between the working class and all those excluded from the legislation's purview continued in the form of invidious distinctions between a regulated ''formal sector'' and an ''urban informal sector'' of self-employed or irregularly employed people unprotected by legislation and subject to harassment for unlicensed activities. Such distinctions became part of the discourse not only of national bureaucracies but also of the international organizations that African states eagerly joined, such as the International Labour Office or the United Nations.[64] The failings of decolonization, it might seem, lie in the way colonial regimes, even as their sense of command failed, determined the institutional and discursive parameters for future social policy.

Such an argument would miss two crucial points. First, the bounded and regulated labor force did not emerge full blown from the late colonial imagination, but came about as colonial states and African labor movements struggled with and influenced each other. The discourses of stabilization, unionization, and industrial relations were brought to Africa only when Africans forced the labor question onto the imperial agenda. The labor movement thought it could achieve material gains for its members by operating within the system the colonial governments were moving toward and insisting that all workers, regardless of race, be treated as equals within it. Both sides, as they negotiated and struggled with each other, immersed themselves ever more deeply within a discursive structure that treated wage labor as a universal construct, and both tried to use that structure for different ends.

Second, the hegemonic project of postwar imperialism, passed on to post-colonial states, never did confine Africa into its developmentalist categories. Instead, it narrowed into a gatekeeper's ideology. In taking over capital-city institutions, African governments soon learned how thin was the wave of "nationalism" that had carried them into office, and how much they had merely taken over a sovereignty often better defined by its linkage to organizations overseas than within the territory of the state. Some scholars have even argued that such states exist largely by virtue of their international recognition—their seats in the United Nations and above all their being the locus for administering aid programs and as targets for International Monetary Fund and World Bank interventions.[65] Developmentalist ideologies are crucial to the gatekeeper state: those are the terms in which aid is appealed for. The gate, of course, faces inward as well, and administering the juncture of local structures and the international economy represents a potent source of jobs and patronage. But now that the universalistic claims of development theories have failed to remake economy and society, these processes serve to maintain a tottering, constricted apparatus rather than to form the basis for the further penetration of a hegemonic ideology much beyond the site of the gatekeeper's tollbooth. Within the national boundaries, African leaders have had to make and remake their political bases by whatever means they could, building on the particu-laristic ties that the universalities of modernity were supposed to diminish.[66] The crisis of African states is not attributable to too much modernity or too little; uncovering its origins and its meanings requires a much deeper probing of pathways taken and pathways missed, of possibilities and constraints in global systems that are themselves changing and contested.

For a time, the labor movement was able to achieve significant material rewards and a sense of empowerment by turning the colonial state's assertion of its modernizing role into claims to the standards and resources of a European state. For a time, the debate between labor leaders who wanted to continue to claim entitlements in similar terms and those who wished to envelop the movement in struggles for political independence brought out issues and tensions in social and political movements that were important to confront. But when one sort of movement—which claimed a singular and exclusive role for the nation-state—insisted that all other movements be subsumed under it, the possibility of creative tension and fruitful debate was lost. African politics would benefit from confronting those tensions and that debate again.

Notes

I am grateful to Ann Stoler for her comments on the penultimate draft of this chapter. The first version was presented to the conference "Power: Thinking across the Disciplines" at the University of Michigan in January 1992, and various intermediate drafts were tried out in seminars and lectures at several universities in the United States, France, Great Britain, the Netherlands, and South Africa. I received many helpful comments at all these stages. The following abbreviations are used in the notes: AS, Archives du Sénégal (files K, labor, 17G, politics, and 21G, security), and ANSOM, Archives Nationales (France), Section Outre-Mer (files IGT, labor, and AP, political affairs).

1. A third metanarrative has surfaced among certain imperial historians in Great Britain: that the impetus for decolonization originated within the British bureaucracy before nationalist parties arose to challenge it, as a result of calculations of British interests and power and consistent with an older conception of colonial rule, based on the "white" Commonwealth, as a stepping-stone to self-government. This is a classic bit of Whig history and has been rightly attacked as such by John Darwin, "British Decolonization since 1945: A Pattern or a Puzzle?" *Journal of Imperial and Commonwealth Studies* 12 (1984): 187–209. A more sophisticated variant for the French case comes from Jacques Marseille, who argues that colonies were discarded because they did not pay except as the privileged preserves of weak metropolitan firms, and the timing can be explained by the increasingly European focus of the French economy in the 1950s, which further marginalized vested interests and sentimental attachments to empire. Marseille's focus is so resolutely metropolitan that he does not ask what inside of colonies accounts for the fact that they did not pay. *Empire colonial et capitalisme français: Histoire d'un divorce* (Paris: Albin Michel, 1984).

2. This theme characterized much writing by political scientists influenced by modernization theory in the 1950s and 1960s, but also the writings of certain scholars on the Left. The triumphalist version emerges most strongly in autobiographies and other publications by leading participants, including Kwame Nkrumah, Nnamdi Azikiwe, Jomo Kenyatta, and Sékou Touré. The argument in this and the following paragraphs is developed fully in my "Conflict and Connection: Rethinking African Colonial History," *American Historical Review* 99 (1994): 1516–1545, and in the introduction to my *Decolonization and African Society: The Labor Question in French and British Africa* (Cambridge: Cambridge University Press, 1996).

3. Frantz Fanon, *The Wretched of the Earth,* trans. Constance Farrington (New York: Grove, 1966; orig. 1961), 30; Frantz Fanon, *Black Skin, White Masks,* trans. Charles Lam Markmann (New York: Grove, 1967; orig. 1952), 226–229.

4. For a stimulating discussion of the tension between labor as an abstract category and as a concretely located one, see Dipesh Chakrabarty, "Marx after Marxism: History, Subalternity and Difference," *Meanjin* 52 (1993): 421–434.

5. Ranajit Guha and Gayatri Spivak, eds., *Selected Subaltern Studies* (New York: Oxford University Press, 1988), and James Scott, *Domination and the Arts of Resistance: Hidden Transcripts* (New Haven: Yale University Press, 1990).

6. Ranajit Guha considers colonial "dominance" to be quite distinct from "hegemony" as Gramsci applied the concept to European societies. Yet he deprives himself of the possibility of analyzing *attempts* at articulating hegemony—at building a culture of acquiescence if not consent—within colonial societies and the relationship of those attempts to colonial violence. See Ranajit Guha, "Domination without Hegemony and Its Historiography," in *Subaltern Studies VI: Writings on South Asian History and Society,* ed. Ranajit Guha, 210–309 (Delhi: Oxford University Press, 1989).

7. Anne Philips, *The Enigma of Colonialism: British Policy in West Africa* (Bloomington: Indiana University Press, 1989), shows the ambition of the first British administrators in British West Africa to remake the meanings of land and labor, followed only after World War I by more conservative policies, while a parallel process in the French case is analyzed in Alice Conklin, *A Mission to Civilize: The Republican Idea of Empire in France and West Africa, 1895–1930* (Stanford: Stanford University Press, forthcoming). See also my "Africa and the World Economy," in *Confronting Historical Paradigms: Peasants, Labor, and the Capitalist World System in Africa and Latin America,* ed. Frederick Cooper et al., 84–201 (Madison: University of Wisconsin Press, 1993).

8. John Lonsdale and Bruce Berman, "Coping with the Contradictions: The Development of the Colonial State in Kenya," *Journal of African History* 20 (1979): 487–506; Frederick Cooper, "'Conditions Analogous to Slavery': Imperialism and Free Labor Ideology in Africa," in *Beyond Slavery: Explorations in Citizenship, Labor, and Race,* ed. Frederick Cooper, Thomas C. Holt, and Rebecca J. Scott (forthcoming).

9. At the same time, it is important to emphasize that the chiefly authority being supported was only in a partial sense "traditional": ambiguous bonds of linguistic or cultural commonality were often institutionalized into political units that had never before existed; changing political and cultural relations of the nineteenth century were often frozen into bounded territories, gazetted power structures, and newly defined "ethnicities." Terence Ranger, "The Invention of Tradition in Colonial Africa," in *The Invention of Tradition*, ed. Eric Hobsbawm and Terence Ranger, 211–262 (Cambridge: Cambridge University Press, 1983); Leroy Vail, ed., *The Creation of Tribalism in Southern Africa* (Berkeley: University of California Press, 1989).

10. These points are developed and documented in my *Decolonization and African Society.*

11. During the brief rule of the French Popular Front in 1936–1938, some attempts were made to treat what wage labor there was as a normal part of social life, while trying to encourage peasant production and keep wage labor to a minimum. In this period, unions were formed and successful strikes conducted, but the fall of the Popular Front brought this to an end, and Vichy governors revived the essentialist argument that Africans were incapable of acting like true wage workers and would be productive only in direct response to authoritative command.

12. See the position papers prepared for the Brazzaville Conference of 1994 in AP 2201/4 and 2201/7, ANSOM.

13. Governor General to Minister, telegram, 10 January 1946, IGT 13/3, ANSOM. The story is told with full documentation in my "The Senegalese General Strike of 1946

and the Labor Question in Post-war French Africa," *Canadian Journal of African Studies* 24 (1990): 165–215.

14. Masselot to Minister of Colonies, 23 February 1946, AP 960/syndicalisme, ANSOM.

15. Transcript of a meeting between union leaders and officials of the Government-General, St. Louis, 15 January 1946, K 405 (132) AS.

16. Frederick Cooper, "'Our Strike': Equality, Anticolonial Politics, and the 1947–48 Railway Strike in French West Africa," *Journal of African History* 37 (1996): 81–118.

17. These arguments are amplified in particular contexts in Cooper, *Decolonization and African Society.* For conjunctural interpretations of South Africa strikes in the same era, see T. Dunbar Moodie, "The Moral Economy of the Black Miners' Strike of 1946," *Journal of Southern African Studies* 13 (1986): 1–35, and Gary Minkley, "Class and Culture in the Workplace: East London, Industrialisation, and the Conflict Over Work, 1945–1957," ibid. 18 (1992): 739–760.

18. Inspection du Travail, AOF, Annual Report, 1946, p. 74.

19. See the annual reports of the Inspection du Travail for 1946–1948. For an extended study of one instance of rethinking the labor question in British Africa, see Frederick Cooper, *On the African Waterfront: Urban Disorder and the Transformation of Work in Colonial Mombasa* (New Haven: Yale University Press, 1987).

20. Cooper, *Decolonization and African Society,* chaps. 6, 7.

21. It is in this sense—and in relation to postwar imperial ideology—that there is some truth in Fanon's remark, "The Colonial World is a Manichean world" (*Wretched of the Earth,* 33). For quite different reasons, Fanon and colonial officials wanted to deny the complex interplay of different forms of culture and power, and to see Africa in dichotomous terms, divided in the one case between colonizer and colonized, in the other between modern and backward.

22. Governor, Senegal, to Governor General, 9 February 1946, incl. Governor General to Minister, 23 March 1946, AP 960/syndicalisme, ANSOM.

23. Irwin Wall, *French Communism in the Era of Stalin: The Question for Unity and Integration, 1945–1962* (Westport, Conn.: Greenwood, 1983), chap. 9; Philippe Dewitte, "La CGT et les syndicats d'Afrique occidentale française (1945–1957)," *Le Mouvement Social* 117 (1981): 3–32.

24. When a French CGT leader came to Dakar in the midst of the general strike of 1946 and (this being the period when the CGT was cooperating with the government) counseled moderation, he was politely ignored. But the very leaders who ignored him were eager to affiliate their unions with the CGT and to be in a position to organize across different territories and use whatever political clout the CGT could muster in France. Cooper, "Senegalese General Strike."

25. This included family allowances—a valued piece of social legislation won by French workers in 1932—which fit into a picture of enlightened social engineering as a means of encouraging the reproduction of the working force, both in the biological sense and in the sense of fostering stability and continuity in the workforce. Before the war, the idea that family allowances could be applied to Africans was ridiculed: Africans bred too much anyway, and it was better that they not get attached to a place of work. But by the late 1940s, officials were rethinking this position, and the CGT was pushing them to apply the French system of family allowances to workers of all races in Africa.

The awarding of modest family allowances to low-level African civil servants in the 1946 strike was the first key victory; the second was won in the French legislature (on a bill introduced by a Senegalese deputy) in 1950, when it equalized all benefits for functionaries regardless of origins; the third came in general provisions of the 1952 code; and final victory came after strike threats and negotiation in 1956, when a specific program of family allowances was made compulsory in the private sector. Cooper, *Decolonization and African Society,* chap. 7.

26. The debate may be followed in the *Débats* of the Assemblée Nationale and the Conseil de la République through much of 1951–1952, reaching a climax in November 1952.

27. Inspecteur Général du Travail to M. le Deputé Dumas, 6 January 1948, IGT 13/2, ANSOM. Senghor quietly told union leaders on the eve of the strike that they had his support, made a private appeal to officials in Paris to work out a favorable settlement, but did nothing in public to support the railwaymen's case. Police officials noted the resentment among strikers of his aloofness, and strike veterans interviewed in 1994 remember both his private support and his public silence. Over two months into the strike, African deputies to French West Africa's main legislative body discussed intervening in the strike but could not agree on what to do or say. Sûreté, Renseignements, 17 December 1947, K 457 (179), AS; French West Africa, *Bulletin du Grand Conseil,* 23 December 1947, 80–81, and 31 January 1948, 320–321; and interviews conducted by the author along with a team of graduate students from the Université Cheikh Anta Diop, Dakar, with Oumar NDiaye, Amadou Bouta Guèye, and Mansour Niang, August 1994.

28. Note signed by Pillot to M. le Directeur Fédéral de la Régie des Chemins de Fer de l'A.O.F., incl. Directeur to President du Conseil de l'Administration, 19 January 1948, Secretary General of Government General to Sissoko, 29 January 1948, copy in Inspecteur du Travail, Bamako, to Inspecteur Général du Travail, 7 February 1948, plus the Inspecteur's letter, all in K 457 (179), AS.

29. Cooper, "'Our Strike.'"

30. Or a "notorious communist," as security officials sometimes put it. French West Africa, Service des Affaires Politiques, "Pointe de l'activité syndicale en A.O.F. au 31 Décembre 1950," AP 3408/5, ANSOM.

31. As early as 1951, French security agents picked up the extent of this rivalry and reported private remarks from Sékou Touré critical of French communist designs on the African masses and an insistence that the PCF "would not penetrate the African soul." Not coincidentally, Houphouët-Boigny, whose party had a cooperative relationship with the PCF in France (although this was never more than an alliance of convenience for this most bourgeois of African politicians), had broken with the PCF in 1950. FWA, Direction de la Sûreté, Renseignements, 5 October 1951, 17G 272, AS.

32. Quoted in R. W. Johnson, "Sékou Touré and the Guinean Revolution," *African Affairs* 69 (1970): 351.

33. Sûreté, Renseignements, 1956, on Sékou Touré, 17G 606, AS.

34. High Commissioner to Ministry, telegram, 22 November 1955, K 418 (144), AS; George Martens, "Industrial Relations and Trade Unionism in French-speaking West Africa," in *Industrial Relations in Africa,* ed. Ukandi Damachi, H. Dieter Seibel, and Lester Trachtman, 35 (New York: St. Martin's Press, 1979).

35. FWA, Revues trimestrielles, Ivory Coast, second and third trimesters 1953, AP 2230/4, ANSOM.

36. French security was keeping a good eye on all this, and became convinced that despite Sékou Touré's actions in the labor field, he would come around to an anti-communist, anticégétiste position. High Commissioner to Minister, 20 March 1954, IGT 11/2, ANSOM.

37. Sûreté, Renseignements, 5 October 1951, 17G 272, AS.

38. The outlines of this story are told in Dewitte, "La CGT et les syndicats," and Martens, "Industrial Relations."

39. Note from the Inspecteur Général du Travail to the Minister, 26 July 1954, IGT 2, ANSOM.

40. Affaires Courantes, Dakar, to Governor, Soudan, telegram, 16 November 1951, 17G 272, AS.

41. France, Overseas Ministry, 2e Bureau, report dated 21 October 1955, on comments of Sékou Touré on the meeting of the Comité de Coordination des Unions Syndicales CGT de l'AOF et du Togo, 1–14 March 1955, Saint-Louis, AP 2264/8, ANSOM; George Martens, "Le syndicalisme en Afrique occidentale d'expression française: De 1945 à 1960," *Le Mois en Afrique* 180–181 (1980–1981): 58.

42. Sûreté, Senegal, Renseignements, 5, 31 July 1956, 21G 215 (178), AS; IGT, "Evolution de la situation syndicale en A.O.F.," 28 July 1956, 17G 610, AS; Martens, "Le syndicalisme," 58–59.

43. The spy who reported Sékou Touré's speech to a Senegalese audience also noted that the audience showed signs of "impatience" as he spoke and that the Senegalese CGTA leader advised Sékou Touré to cut his remarks short—it is by no means clear that this was the message rank-and-file workers wanted to hear. Senegal, Sûreté, Renseignements, 21 February 1956, 21G 215, AS.

44. Governor, Dahomey, to High Commissioner, 22 January 1957, K 421 (165), AS, reporting on the UGTAN conference in Bamako.

45. They did have their worries about too much African unity but worried more that CGT veterans would take over UGTAN. "However, any solution would appear preferable to a reimposed seizure by international communism of African trade unionism." Minister to High Commissioner, draft of letter (not sent), dated 8 February 1957, AP 2264/8, ANSOM. The high commissioner even considered financial aid to UGTAN to make sure it didn't turn to the French CGT for help, although he decided not to do this and only to maintain a close and positive liaison. High Commissioner to Minister, 8 February 1957, IGT 11/2, ANSOM.

46. On the loss of confidence in the development initiative, see Marseille, *Empire colonial et capitalisme français,* and Cooper, *Decolonization and African Society,* chap. 10.

47. Officials quite explicitly saw territorial budgets paid for by local taxpayers as the best mechanism to "resist claims" regarding the "status and remuneration of civil servants in each territory," and accepted that the loi cadre was a repudiation of the costs of the previous policy of assimilation. Government General, French West Africa, "Mémoire sur la réforme des structures de l'A.O.F.," 11 July 1955, AP 491, ANSOM; Pierre-Henri Teitgen, statement of Assemblée Nationale, *Débats* 20 March 1956, 1072–1073. The union's realization of the danger territorialization posed is clear in

Resolution of Comité de Coordination des Unions Territoriales CGT de l'Afrique Occidentale Française-Togo, 17 February 1956, K 425 (165), AS.

48. FWA, IGT, "Note sur l'évolution du syndicalisme in A.O.F.," 19 April 1957, IGT 11/2, ANSOM.

49. Martens, "Le syndicalisme," 88–89.

50. FWA, Service de Securité, Bulletin d'Information, May 1957, 17G 630, AS.

51. Dahomey, Renseignements, October 1957–April 1958, 17G 588, AS; Governor, Dahomey, to Minister, 30 January 1958, AP 2189/12, ANSOM. Another instance of the discourse of scarcity coming from the new government in Senegal is Mamadou Dia, "Un régime d'austérité accepté par tous," Afrique Nouvelle 499 (26 February 1957).

52. "Exposé de M. le Vice-Président Sékou Touré à l'occasion de la conférence du 2 février 1958 avec les résponsables syndicaux et délégués du personnel RDA," "Le RDA et l'action syndicale dans la nouvelle situationpolitiques des T.O.M.," PDG (9)/dossier 7, Centre de Recherche et de Documentation Africaine, Paris.

53. Speech of Camara Bengaly in name of Conseil de Gouvernement to Congrès Constitutatif de l'UGTAN, Conakry, 23–25 May 1958, sous-dossier UGTAN, K 421 (165), AS.

54. Report of David Soumah, Secretary General, to Congrès de la CATC, Abidjan, 10–12 November 1958, 17G 610, AS. Soumah was Guinean leader of the church-affiliated trade unions. These were, as Soumah seemed to anticipate, suppressed shortly after independence.

55. Claude Rivière, "Lutte ouvrière et phenomène syndical en Guinée," Cultures et Développement 7 (1975): 53, 73–75. Guinean intellectuals' eventual verdict on their leader is suggested in the title of a book by a former collaborator who was later exiled, Ibrahima Baba Kaké, Sékou Touré: Le héros et le tyran (Paris: Jeune Afrique, 1987).

56. For guides to studies of trade unionism in Africa, see William Friedland, "African Trade Union Studies: Analysis of Two Decades," Cahiers d'Etudes Africaines 14 (1974): 575–589, and George R. Martens, African Trade Unionism: A Bibliography with a Guide to Trade Union Organizations and Publications (Boston: Hall, 1977).

57. Interviews, Moussa Konaté and Mory Tall, Dakar and Thiès, August 1994.

58. Sûreté, Senegal, April 1958, 17G 633, AS; Interview, Alioune Cissé, Dakar, August, 1994.

59. On resources, patronage, and politics, see Jean-François Bayart, L'Etat en Afrique: La politique du ventre (Paris: Fayard, 1989).

60. On the way African governing elites used the idea of a struggle for development to deny the legitimacy of opposition, see Aristide Zolberg, Creating Political Order: The Party-States of West Africa (Chicago: Rand-McNally, 1966).

61. James Ferguson, "Paradoxes of Sovereignty and Independence: 'Real' and 'Pseudo-' Nation-States and the Depoliticization of Poverty," in Siting Culture, ed. Kirstin Hastrup and Karen Fog Olwig (Oslo: Scandinavian University Press, forthcoming); Kathryn Sikkink, "Human Rights, Principled Issue-Networks, and Sovereignty in Latin America," International Organization 47 (1993): 411–441.

62. These scholars' call for a "provincialization" of European history points to the need for the making of universalistic claims to be considered part of the story rather than for such principles to be a standard for others to meet. One hopes such an effort

will get beyond present formulations that simply debunk "liberalism," "bourgeois equality," or "citizenship" as Western constructions, as if these concepts were themselves static and were not subject to continual appropriation, deflection, and redefinition in the process of politics, within colonies as much as within Europe itself. See Partha Chatterjee, *The Nation and Its Fragments: Colonial and Postcolonial Histories* (Princeton: Princeton University Press, 1993), 197–198, 237–239; and Dipesh Chakrabarty, "Postcoloniality and the Artifice of History: Who Speaks for 'Indian' Pasts?" *Representations* 37 (1992): 20–21

63. Aimé Césaire, *Lettre à Maurice Thorez* (Paris: Présence Africaine, 1956), 15.

64. On postcolonial codes du travail, see Côte d'Ivoire, Loi 64-290 du 1er août 1964; Sénégal, Code du Travail, Loi 61-34 du 15 juin 1961; Rivière, "Lutte ouvrière . . . en Guinée," 78–81. Important as the power to label is within national and international organizations, it has its limits. The negative connotations of "informal sector"—like "detribalized" Africans or "floating population" in earlier eras—does not mean that the bureaucracies that deploy such a term can control what goes on within its boundaries or contain its spread. In some countries the "second economy" is larger and more dynamic than the first.

65. Robert H. Jackson, *Quasi-States: Sovereignty, International Relations and the Third World* (Cambridge: Cambridge University Press, 1990).

66. On the state and social relations in postindependent Africa, see Bayart, *L'état en Afrique;* and for a provocative statement about the distinct idioms of power in contemporary Africa, see Achille Mbembe, "The Banality of Power and the Aesthetics of Vulgarity in the Postcolony," *Public Culture* 4, no. 2 (1992): 1–30.

Cars Out of Place

Vampires, Technology, and Labor in East and Central Africa

Luise White

This essay is about things that never happened. The African vampires discussed here are not the undead but men and occasionally women specifically employed—as firemen in East Africa and game rangers in Central Africa—to capture Africans and extract their blood.[1] Such vampires were said to exist throughout much of East and Central Africa; they were a specifically colonial phenomenon and were first noted in the late 1910s and early 1920s. In the colonial versions of these stories, most vampires were black men supervised on the job by white men, but in postcolonial versions who works for whom has become unclear. Although it seems plausible that these stories originated in botched medical procedures done in too great haste during World War I,[2] establishing their source does not account for their meaning thirty years later, or their power, or the passion with which they were retold and withheld. Stories in which colonial employees drained Africans of their blood may reveal more than the vivid imagination of their narrators; they disclose the concerns and anxieties of people at a specific time and place.

Vampires and Colonial Historiography

The problem of how to interpret the imaginary has haunted the historiography of colonialism like no other issue. "Believe me," wrote Frantz Fanon, "the zombies are more terrifying than the settlers; and in consequence the problem is no longer that of keeping oneself right with the colonial world . . . but of considering three times before urinating, spitting, or going out into the night." He envisioned a day when,

after centuries of unreality, after having wallowed in the most outlandish phantoms, at long last the native, gun in hand, stands face to face with the only forces
that contend for his life—the forces of colonialism. And the youth of the colonized
country, growing up in an atmosphere of shot and fire . . . does not hesitate to
pour scorn on the zombies of his ancestors, the horses with two heads, the djinns
who rush into your body while you yawn.[3]

But the opposite appeared to have happened. Survivors of a famine in
Malawi recalled that the goats they sold to buy food turned into snakes when
their new owners took them home;[4] Africans in colonial Northern Rhodesia
who opposed federation with white-dominated Southern Rhodesia believed
that sugar had been poisoned by the English "House of Laws" to sap their
will;[5] guerrillas in Zimbabwe's war of liberation not only believed in spirit
mediums, they claimed to have been supplied with goods by their ancestors'
spirits.[6]

How do we account for this? Michael Taussig offers two extremes, that
academic representations of superstition are "blind belief in blind belief" and
that such explanations reflect another level of reality, "in which faith and
skepticism easily coexist."[7] I want to suggest that both analyses are unsatisfactory; they treat imaginary events as make-believe, locating them firmly in
the gaze of the observer, not that of the people whom they terrify and fascinate.
We must ask instead what things that never happened meant to the people for
whom they were real—people who, in many cases, claimed these things
happened to them. Rewriting colonial histories means asking how the colonial
experience created what Ann Stoler has called "hierarchies of credibility."[8]
Dismantling those hierarchies so that phantoms and fantasies can be reinserted
into colonial historiography requires linking the revisionist histories themselves with the methodologies on which they are built.

Although postcolonial discourses have provided an undifferentiated account
of colonialism,[9] recent research has shown colonialism to be far more fragmented than earlier studies revealed. The colonialism that was, in Frederick
Cooper's words, "acceptable in polite company," policed itself, while the
colonized struggled to control their own lives.[10] The meaning of ethnicity now
seems to have been refashioned under colonial rule,[11] and white power has been
deconstructed from a monolith to a fractured group whose cohesion came from
the class-based critique of continually redefining who was white and the
privileges being white entailed.[12] Making the colonized a disciplined, exploit-
able labor force, or Westernized in any way, was not easy: ex-slaves, for
example, struggled to maintain their customary rights to land and crops rather
than work as free labor, while casual labor—the work men could do a few days
a week or a month to eke out a living—might have been exploited, but it was
beyond employers' control.[13] Every shantytown, beggar, and runaway wife
was an affront to the ability of colonialists to control the cities they designed.[14]
Where labor performed to imperial expectations, it nevertheless produced a

cycle of official violence and reform: colonial terrorism had its own aesthetic that made its victims dangerous and primitive, innocent and in need of protection.[15] All this suggests that the dichotomized categories of rulers and ruled are obsolete and that colonial situations might best be studied for their ambiguities as much as for their injustices.[16]

We know that colonialists understood this—their documents were obsessed with poor whites and the dangers of Africans in European clothing[17]—but how did Africans express the contradictions of their oppression? In African history, the search for African voices with which to write has been an academic obsession for almost thirty years. While the formal study of oral tradition was to provide a concrete methodology with which historians might study a pre-colonial past filled with mythical heroes and landscapes,[18] colonial historians were not supposed to have such images to interpret. Oral histories were by definition about things that were within a living memory; facts could be checked by interviewing a number of informants. The emphasis was on how to verify, not how to interpret.[19] Even a long overdue feminist critique of oral history addressed the politics of the collection of oral materials, not their interpretation.[20] As ethnography and anthropological objects have been de-centered in the last decade,[21] academic attentions have subtly shifted to the individual; methodological debates in oral history have concentrated, like those in literature, on establishing the authority and authenticity of the voice of the colonized.[22] Life histories have come to be considered more authentic than simple interviews; letting African voices speak for themselves has not only become a methodology, it has become a minor publishing enterprise.[23] But concerns about validity, authenticity, and letting Africans speak for themselves are concerns about how scholars may best represent African experiences, concerns that emerged from the very academic processes by which colonial history has been what Gyan Prakash calls "Third Worlded"—made into an object of study in the First World and given new and powerful meanings by subordinated groups there.[24] But in many cases, establishing the authenticity of the voice—or cacophony of voices—has left it disembodied and decontextualized. Colonial subjects have been enframed as they have been represented. Techniques of authenticating, as Timothy Mitchell has shown, position the observer: "The world is set up before the observing subjects as though it were a picture of something."[25]

The study of colonial vampires may reverse this trend. These vampires are described in a wide variety of oral accounts, and, as descriptions of things that never happened, should begin to subvert some of our ideas about what constitutes authenticity. The study of colonial vampires is authentic not because of any particular legitimacy of the voices I quote, but because it involves writing about the colonial world with the images and idioms produced by the subjects themselves. Like postcolonial rainmaking or the hybrid beasts of modern bridewealth payments, vampires are an epistemological category with which

Africans described their world.[26] I argue that these vampires are not simply generalized metaphors of extraction and oppression but that these images are, like other orally transmitted information, told at specific times to specific people for specific reasons.[27] They describe not only the extraction of blood but also how it occurs, who performs it, and under what conditions and inducements. I argue that it is possible to read—or more precisely, to hear—specific vampire accusations as a debate among working men about the nature of work: not its material conditions or remuneration, but how the experience of skilled or semiskilled labor and involvement with machines could change the men who were so engaged. This is not the only interpretation of vampire accusations that is possible, of course, but it is the one that conforms most closely to the details and the emplotment of working men's accounts. The men quoted here were colonial policemen, firemen, health inspectors, tailors, and railway workers who passed from unskilled apprenticeship to engine drivers. All described these vampires in similar terms, noting the secrecy of the work, the intensity with which it was supervised, and the impossibility of knowing who exactly did it, so that the vampires known to laboring men had definite characteristics. Interpreting vampires from working men's accounts does not tell us more about these vampires than other sources might, but it allows us to examine differentiation in the labor process and within the labor force in the words and categories of laboring men.

Most of the data presented here comes primarily from interviews with former laborers and artisans—men who were not specialized storytellers at all—conducted in rural western Kenya in 1986 and in and around Kampala, Uganda, in 1990. Although many women told these stories with passion and graphic detail as well,[28] this article is based on oral data that was presented to me as men's stories. Many of the returned migrants I interviewed in rural western Kenya claimed that once home they never told their wives these stories because "my wives were adults and could get the stories from other sources,"[29] or "none of my wives could realize the seriousness of these stories, but"— turning to my male research assistant—"a man like you can realize the value and seriousness of any story."[30] Men who claimed to have done the work of capture themselves said they could not tell anyone, not even my wife about it, even after they had told my assistant,[31] but a man who narrowly escaped the clutches of Nairobi firemen from a "town toilet" in 1923 told everyone about it: "Why not? I am lucky to have escaped and therefore must talk freely about it."[32] What kind of stories were these, that were so contested and so gendered, and that were withheld or broadcast according to individual experience, not the story?

These stories were about blood, but they were also about occupations. If blood is taken to be universal, then its power to terrify comes from that; if blood is taken to be a gendered bodily fluid, then the loss of blood is far more alarming to adult men than to adult women.[33] But in either case, blood is the most ambiguous of bodily fluids; according to context it can signify life or death. Other bodily fluids, semen or breast milk, do not. It is possible that stories about blood, and specific forms of its removal, articulate and point out ambiguities. When the systematic removal of blood is associated with a specific occupational group, it suggests that the ambiguities have to do with certain kinds of labor.[34] Read as stories about blood, vampiric firemen represent certain reservations about specific skills, and the alliances made through on-the-job training, hierarchy, and an extended working day.

While published accounts of these stories were not uncommon, most of the data presented are personal narratives. In many ways, these stories fit the format of urban legends—most people believed that it was a well-established fact that firemen captured people for their blood—but the use of folkloric categories does not adequately describe the extent to which these stories were debated and contested by their narrators. Many of my informants insisted that these stories were false because they never met anyone who knew a victim. A few others explained that these stories arose when Africans were unwilling to participate in colonial medical experiments. According to one man, ''When the Europeans were here we had a lot of diseases. . . . They were doing research . . . and it was not easy to convince somebody that they were going to do research on them so what they did was to kidnap those people.''[35] Another said he was ''convinced that these people came from hospitals because nowadays people are required to donate blood for their sick relatives.''[36] As late as 1972, a Tanzanian newspaper ran a half-page article explaining that firemen did not kill people.[37] One month later, ''Nearly Victim'' wrote to the editor refuting the article: ''Where did hospitals get their supply of blood in those grim days, before Independence? People used to disappear mysteriously in those days . . . or didn't you know that the blood was used to treat the white man only?''[38] But some people were aware of the ambiguity of these stories: ''It seems these stories were true, first of all considering that they existed as stories and those who lost their relatives . . . can prove it. However, those people whose relatives were not taken can say these stories were false.''[39]

Vehicles and Vampires

Stories about bloodsucking firemen, known in East Africa by variants of the Kiswahili term *wazimamoto,* the men who extinguish the fire (or heat, or light, as in brightness but not as in lamp), and in Central Africa as *banyama,* the men of the meat, or animals, as in game rangers or possibly hunters, cover a wide geographic range, from the East African coast to eastern Zaire to at least as far south as the Limpopo.[40] Many of these narratives contain generic fire brigade vehicles; more often than not, captured people were put into a vehicle and taken away, sometimes to be kept in a pit in the local fire station, ''the property of the government.''[41] Although there is an obvious association to be made of the red of fire engines and the red of blood—in the unimaginative words of one man, firemen's "equipment is always red and so is blood, therefore any African in the olden days could easily conclude that they were involved in bloodsucking"[42]—it should be noted that this was an association most of my informants generally did not make. In the late 1950s and 1960s Europeans had their own set of rumors about the dangers of driving red cars,[43] but my informants were more concerned with describing "cars which bore a cross"[44] or "a grey Land Rover with a shiny metal back,"[45] than they were with pointing out the dangers of the color red. Indeed, the vehicles they described had no lights and often no windows.

Vehicles in wazimamoto stories were not only dangerous, they were found in the most unlikely places and relationships. A sixty-year-old man in Kampala claimed that in the days when "the only departments with cars were the police and fire brigade," the yellow fever department captured people; "but since they had no motor vehicles of their own, they had to use the fire brigade department's motor cars," which was how this rumor began.[46] In rural Tanganyika during World War II a blood drive to supply plasma to troops overseas failed because a fire engine was always stationed by the small airstrip and Africans assumed the blood was to be drunk by Europeans. Years later, it was said that the blood of unconscious Africans was collected in buckets and then rushed to Dar es Salaam in fire engines.[47] In Dar es Salaam in 1947, according to a former superintendent of police, a blood transfusion service was established but had no transport of its own, and so fire engines carried blood donors to the hospital, giving rise to the rumor "that the vehicles, usually with a European volunteer in charge, were collecting African males for their blood and that it was a plot by Europeans to render them impotent."[48] Officials' folklore about the fear of fire engines had it that during Christmas 1959, police in Mbale, Uganda, patrolled the African townships in the local fire engine, to keep even the criminals inside their homes.[49]

Trucks and cars were out of bounds as well. Early in 1939 when the governor of Northern Rhodesia visited the liberal settler Gore-Browne in his unlikely estate in Northern Province, his car was followed by a vanette. This caused great suspicion; it was said that Gore-Browne and the new governor "were concocting plans for kidnapping on a large scale."[50] In Lamu, Kenya, in the mid-1940s, medical department trucks patrolled the streets "and, should it come upon a straggler, draws from his veins all his blood with a rubber pump, leaving his body in the gutter."[51] A dozen years later in western Kenya, "motor vehicles painted red" drained the blood from lone pedestrians captured along the Kisumu to Busia highway; the blood was then taken to blood banks in hospitals.[52] In eastern Zambia in 1948, children were lured to trucks on the road at nighttime, made helpless and invisible with the banyama's wands, and taken to towns across the border in Malawi where they were fattened on special foods while the European employers of banyama drank their blood; they returned home "very emaciated."[53] The domestic relations of Europeans, when enclosed in vehicles, were extremely suspicious. In rural Tanganyika in the late 1950s, a white geologist was attacked; he aroused local suspicions because there were curtains on the windows of his truck.[54] In 1959 in what was then Salisbury, Rhodesia, a "courting couple" in a parked car in an isolated spot were attacked because of "an almost firm belief" that Africans were being captured and drugged and loaded onto a Sabena aircraft on which their bodies were "cut up and canned during the flight" to the Belgian Congo.[55] Automobiles could be made to perform dreadful tasks. In western Kenya in 1968, travelers feared accepting rides because the wazimamoto had cars with specially designed backseats that could automatically drain the blood of whoever sat there.[56]

Representing Bureaucracy

What are these stories about? They are about vehicles in unexpected places, used for unintended purposes; these are stories about borrowed transport. But was this borrowing symbolic or literal? Did it represent permeable administrative boundaries or simple lapses in colonial funding and vehicle allocations? Were the signs and symbols of bureaucratic authority being contested in a popular discourse, or were official cars being appropriated by underfunded bureaucrats? While I doubt that the Ugandan yellow fever department took blood samples using fire brigade vehicles—Kampala did not have a fire engine until after 1932—everywhere but Nairobi fire-fighting equipment was routinely used, by all accounts badly, by police. Dar es Salaam did not have a fire brigade until 1939; Mombasa until 1940; and Kampala until 1953. Until then untrained police forces were usually unable to contain fires in those cities: "The manipulation of the fire appliances in the event of emergency is left to the unskilled, untrained, and undrilled efforts of a few African constables."[57] In many towns, "we only heard about *wazimamoto* but never saw any."[58] But where there was a formal and well-organized fire brigade, it did not do much better. Nairobi's fire brigade had its own quarters, a fire master, and two fire engines, but in 1926 there was a commission of inquiry to investigate why it was so incompetent, and nine years later it received only forty-two fire calls.[59] After World War II, fire stations became powerful images in some places. In 1947, a riot at the Mombasa Fire Station badly damaged a fire engine.[60] In Dar es Salaam in 1959, "one could observe an occasional African crossing the street to get as far away from the fire station as possible and running when in front of the station."[61] Elsewhere, fire stations did not carry the same meanings.[62] Indeed, the men and women in Kampala who named different departments in Entebbe that received the blood—the welfare department, the yellow fever department, the veterinary department—may not have been confused, they may have been stating the problem of these stories: How do you locate extraction in bureaucracy when bureaucracy seems so fluid?

Indeed, suppose our own academic questions were anticipated, or even essential, to how these stories were narrated? What if the confusion of services and terrors was in fact the emplotment? What if "What were fire engines doing in the places they did not belong?" meant "What sort of society puts fire engines on runways, and blood-draining vehicles on the streets at night?" The account of the blood-draining truck from Lamu, for example, puts the blame firmly on its intent, not its construction. Africans did not misrepresent ambulances—vans with tubes and pumps inside them—but they misrepresented their motives: the trucks did not cure sick people but attacked those unlucky enough to be walking alone at night. These stories may be a colonial, African version of a complaint one now hears daily in Africa: that officials have failed to keep the streets safe. These narratives make access, mobility, and safety into issues for debate and reflection. They make the concrete and the mechanical into problematics.

But it is unlikely that this is all they mean. The presentation of cars in stories, even stories about vampires, reveals popular ideas about the interaction between culture and technology, between bodies and machines.[63] Automobiles generate their own folklore in industrial societies,[64] where they literally become the vehicles for older symbols and associations and where their material value is at least equal to their symbolic value.[65] That vehicles could be controlled, modified, and transformed may have reflected the imagined powers of their manufacturers or the real needs of their owners.[66] Cars can take people away; motoring and roads are, by definition, ways of erasing boundaries and reclassifying space:[67] roads are someone's order and someone else's disorder. The vanette behind the governor's car, the fire engines on the runway, and the courting couple's darkened car implied the contradiction of orderly relations: they were parked in confusing spaces that blurred boundaries.[68] But the blurred boundaries may not have been those between the yellow fever department and the fire brigade; they may be those between certain kinds of employment and machines: someone's blurred boundaries was someone else's identity. Uniforms, drills, daily polishings of equipment[69]—men "dressed in fire brigade uniforms in the daylight . . . doing this job for Europeans who were at that time their supreme commanders"[70]—all these things made some jobs appear categorically different from the casual labor a man could take up and abandon with ease.

Concealing Men

These stories do not tell us anything about the living African men inside the vehicles.[71] Cars without windows cannot reveal the men inside; so either they were not an important part of these stories, or they were known to be hidden, or they were at least undetectable. One man said he could not be sure of the race of *bazimyomwoto* in Kampala because they always did their work at night.[72] Another claimed that they were chosen for their jobs with great secrecy and caution. "It was not an open job for anybody, you had to be a friend of somebody in the government, and it was top secret, so it was not easy to recruit anybody to begin there, although it was well paid."[73]

If vehicles without windows or lights concealed their occupants, they also hid the work of fighting fires and the labor process of capturing people: "I only heard that wazimamoto sucked blood from people, but I never heard how they got those people."[74] "The act was confidential."[75] The relationship of vehicles—and their specific sounds—to work obscured the work. In Nairobi in the 1940s, "their actual job was not known to us. All we were told was that they were supposed to put out burning fires. Whenever there was a burning fire we would hear bell noises, and we were told that the wazimamoto were on their way to put it out."[76] In general, the wazimamoto "ambushed people and threw them in a waiting vehicle,"[77] and "the victims used to call out for help when they were being taken in the vehicle,"[78] but even men and women who narrowly escaped capture did not know much more. In western Kenya late one night in 1959, a woman "found a group of men hiding behind a vehicle that had no lights of any sort." She ran and hid, but they looked for her until "the first cock crowed and one of them said, 'Oh oh oh the time is over.'"[79] In rural Buganda that same year—across eastern Africa, 1959 was a year of widespread blood accusations[80]—a man was awakened by villagers "saying that the place had been invaded by *bazimyomwoto.*" He hid behind a large tree and "narrowly evaded capture." In the full moon's light he could see their car and their clothes—"black trousers and white coats"—but could not describe what they did: "Afterwards I heard that several people had lost their blood."[81]

Even men who claimed to have done this work, either as firemen or policemen, described a labor process that had more to do with hierarchies and automobiles than with co-workers. One such man said that capturing Africans was essential to discipline, rank, and on-the-job seniority, but he described the organization of work as a relationship to a white man and a waiting vehicle.

When one joined the police force [in Kampala] in those olden days he would undergo the initial training of bloodsucking. . . . When he qualified there, he was then absorbed into the police force as a constable. This particular training was designed to give the would-be policeman overwhelming guts and courage to execute his duties effectively. . . . During the day we were police recruits. Immediately after sunset we started the job of manhunting. . . . We would leave the station in a group of four and one white man who was in charge. Once in town we would leave the vehicle and walk around in pairs. When we saw a person, we would lie down and ambush him. We would then take the captured person back to the waiting vehicle. . . . We used to hide vehicles by parking them behind buildings or parking a reasonable distance from our manhunt. . . . The precautions we took were to switch off the engine and the lights.[82]

Here, knowledge of the vehicle is described in much greater detail than is knowledge of the white man. Moreover, the extension of the working day is taken for granted in this account. What does it mean when people describe technology, equipment, and modified vehicles in ways that obscure descriptions of work and the time the work takes? The absence of light and useful windows, the "shiny metal back" made these vehicles closed, protected, and opaque. Their insides were not known. Men who could describe the insides of pits could not describe the insides of trucks.[83] Dangerous vehicles and the modifications specific to them made the men who performed the work of capture safe, secluded, and anonymous; even they could not describe what they did. But veiling labor with different mechanisms—curtains, no lights, shiny metal backs—kept it secret and indicated that something the public should not see was going on inside. Veiling labor focused attention on it, and on the need to maintain secrecy, and made it the object of scrutiny and speculation.[84] Making certain jobs hidden located them in the realm of the imagination; while certain kinds of workers might complain about a lack of public awareness of their jobs, that lack of awareness gave the public enormous control: their description of what went on in the hidden vehicle went unchallenged by the men in the cars.[85] Where Africans could describe the inside of vehicles, it was a site of fiendish production—the Sabena aircraft on which Africans recently turned into pigs were canned. To counter the fears of what was inside a curtained van a Tanganyikan district officer (and mystery writer) gave villagers a tour of the inside of a white geologist's van; he thought that if they saw what the curtains actually hid—a bed, a table and chairs, and a photograph of a fiancée—he could guarantee the young man's safety.[86]

Technology and Narrative

The veiling of labor was frequently done with metal and electrical equipment. In Kampala it was commonplace to explain that the term "bazimyomwoto" referred to the use of automotive equipment, not to fire fighting. "These people did their job at night, so when they approached somebody they would switch off the lights, and in Kiswahili to switch off is *kuzima* and the light is *moto.*"[87] This translation of Kiswahili into Luganda is wrong; *kuzima taa* means "to put out the light"; *kuzima moto* means "to put out the fire." But it is a mistranslation that reflects the importance of automobile equipment in Ugandan vampire stories.

And what is that importance? It seems to be a knowledge of the mechanics of engine sounds and electrical systems. Such technical knowledge is not only specialized and privileged, it conceals a labor process. But such a labor process, that "hidden abode of production," discernible only when one leaves the noise of the factory,[88] may have been kept secret by laborers themselves. Work routines learned on the job may have produced an unexpected camaraderie. A man who was a railway fireman in Nairobi from 1936 to 1958 described a fantastic subterranean system of technical sophistication.

> Pipes were installed all over the town. People never used to know the exact place where the pipes were, but us, we used to know. Whites were very clever. They used to cover the pipes and taps with some form of iron sheets. When a fire was burning anywhere we would go locate the tap and fix our hoses up. . . . Running water was there throughout the year, therefore we never experienced any shortage of water at any time of the year.[89]

This account praises informal knowledge, which could only be learned on the job or from co-workers' conversations and anecdotes, especially in places where recruits were hired off the street and did not graduate from training programs.[90] Nairobi in the mid-1930s had two fire engines and 508 hydrants, and virtually no funds for hydrant or water distribution system repair.[91] In this account the informal expertise of fire fighting—passed from white man to black man—was knowing where the pipes were hidden, not putting out fires. But in Kampala,

> they kept victims in big pits. Those pits were made in such a way that no one would notice them. Whites are very bad people. They are so cunning and clever. . . . The job of police recruits was to get victims and nothing else. Occasionally we went down the pits and if we were lucky saw bloodsucking in progress but nothing more. . . . Those pits were really hidden, and even those working within the police station could not notice them.[92]

My point is not that the knowledge of technology was more important than the work itself, but that the knowledge that was otherwise secret bonded a few select Africans to specialized procedures. In 1958 in eastern Zambia, prison warders overheard rumors that the local station of the Society of Missionaries for Africa, everywhere called the White Fathers, were about to kidnap Africans and had already marked their victims with "the Sign of the Cross which was not visible to the intended victim or to his fellows but only to the Europeans and their African henchmen."[93] The invisible signs, the secrets of the pipes and the pits, reveal another dimension to workers' own and popular perceptions of the advantages—technological and social—of skilled labor.

Occupational folklorists have described how technical expertise is parodied by those so skilled—the pilots who board a plane with a white cane and dark glasses—as a challenge to managerial authority.[94] Bolivian tin miners performed ceremonies that denied the importance of skill, "to make the tools help us in our work."[95] African historians who have been able to compare oral and written accounts of the same skilled labor have shown how specialized, skilled labor portrays itself and is portrayed in words of privilege and supe-riority. Mine managers' views of Basotho shaft sinkers in South Africa, for example, encouraged their sense of superiority but also praised their camara-derie; Basotho shaft sinkers spoke of their favored status in the mine com-pounds and of the high wages their specialization offered.[96] Workers' narra-tives may reveal the tensions and conflicts within the workplace that managerial accounts omit. Workers' oral narratives about technology, how-ever imprecise and inaccurate they are, might be a way to foreground the ambiguities and conflicts about the work itself. The man who boasted of the knowledge of hidden pipes he shared with "clever whites" was proud of his on-the-job training. He insisted that in his twenty-two years as a railway fireman he never saw anyone captured, although he admitted that "on seeing us people used to run in all directions."[97] But other men saw certain kinds of skills as inviting danger. A Ugandan man of about the same age said that bazimyomwoto "operated in villages during the night. A bell would be tied up to an electricity pole and when it was rung, immediately a vehicle would drive by to pick victims. Once a man was captured near my home. He was one of the Uganda Electricity Board workers."[98] African concerns about mechani-zation, about the technological nature of skilled jobs, may have been ex-pressed in vampire stories. These concerns do not seem to have been about the societal impact of mechanization, but were about a gendered boundary be-tween men and machines that could refashion potency and performance.[99] People in Dar es Salaam, for example, feared that the men who went to give blood in fire engines would become impotent, or that firemen had injections that could make men "lazy and unable to do anything."[100] Blood accusations were most public in the mines of colonial Katanga after mechanized shovels were timed and tested against a team of pick and shovel men.[101]

Vampire stories were most private when occupations were neither chal-lenged nor explained. The return home leveled the distinctiveness of the most extraordinary careers: "All policemen in those olden days were the agents of wazimamoto." But "when someone was a policeman he remains so even after leaving his job. Policemen are always careful what they leave out. Retired policemen cannot tell you what they were doing during their working time."[102] The same man who described how best to park a car when capturing unwary Africans said he could not tell anyone about it. "How could I do that after swearing to keep secrets? The works of policemen were very hard and involved so many awful things some of which cannot be revealed to anyone. Because of the nature of my work I could not tell anyone even my wife. . . . Even my brothers I could not tell."[103] Storytelling both presents personal identity and allows it to be negotiated and redefined by the audience; withholding stories may permit personal and professional identity to be rigidly maintained.[104] These stories were not explanations; they were accusations: they did not explain misfortune, but imputed work, identity, and loyalty.[105]

Tools of Empire

When studying narratives about vampiric firemen in Africa, it is important that we identify what was weird and unnatural in these stories to their tellers and not become overly concerned with what seems weird and unnatural to ourselves. It is easy for Western scholars to get bogged down in the issue of blood-drinking Europeans, but that is in fact the most natural part of the story, demonstrated over and over by community and common sense: "Of course the stories were true. . . . People used to warn each other not to walk at night."[106] But what was unnatural and weird to the people who told these stories may well have been those things that were rare and unnatural in their daily lives—cars and electricity.

But these stories are not simple condemnations of technological change and motor transport; medical technology and cars and electrical equipment were, in narrative and in daily life, mediated through a very African medium—working men. Specialized equipment was used by small specialized occupational groups, and for these men, technology had an intense meaning: they talked about it in interviews more than they talked about work. For the most part, technical knowledge was apportioned so sparingly and so slowly that it seemed to defy natural laws, so that railway firemen could claim that they had water even in the dry season. In reality, the allocation of specialized tools and tasks to a few skilled laborers kept most people in ignorance of how automobiles or electricity poles actually worked; on a symbolic level, this kept technology from becoming naturalized in any way.

The very peculiarity of cars, lights, and mirrors made the men who could use them a little peculiar as well. The new tools not only bonded men to machines in odd ways—whatever went on inside the curtained truck—but also bound men to mechanization. Marxist theorists of the labor aristocracy have described how the work rhythms required by the technological demands of new industries identified skilled workers with management in nineteenth-century England;[107] although the same processes did not take place in nonindustrialized Africa, it is likely that their specialized tools and techniques placed skilled labor under their employers' control in ways that unskilled labor had never been managed. These men might know where "the clever whites" hid their pipes, or pits, or signs, or have had the on-the-job training "to execute his duties effectively," but they were, in the process, never insulated from their employers' supervision and command.

Tools and technology have recently been studied as one of the ways Europeans dominated the colonized world; they were supposed to overpower Africans or to mystify them.[108] But the contradictory meanings of tools in these stories is too complex, and too layered, to be explained in any single way. The tools in these stories have been assimilated; to some extent, they were already familiar objects, whatever their origin.[109] What made them fearsome was how and why they were used—both in narrative and as narrative. On the Northern Rhodesian Copperbelt there was *mupila,* "white balls of drugs," thrown into the path of a lone traveler to whom the banyama then spoke. "If he answered all his power left him, his clothes fell off, and he no longer had a memory or a will."[110] In southeastern Zaire in the 1940s, rubber tubes and flashlights had the same effect.[111] In Dar es Salaam thirty years later: "They use many things to catch people. Sometimes they use a mirror. . . . Your mind changes and you just follow any place they go."[112] Tools themselves, properly used, could disempower ordinary Africans. Those who were skilled enough to use them lost something too, not direction, but their identity: they became invisible.

In these narratives, technology reveals unnatural acts—not bloodsucking, which is weird only to us, or even odd behavior in the backseats of parked cars, but the regimented labor process required by technology: on-the-job training, rank, time discipline, and intense supervision, even after hours. The cars and lights and mirrors in these stories were not the only Western, specialized tools introduced into colonial Africa, but they were the only equipment that regularly featured in vampire stories over a wide geographic and cultural area. These technologies aroused accusations about the forcible removal of blood not because they were foreign or even because they were associated with a dominant power; these technologies featured in these stories because they aroused the greatest anxieties.[113] But they did not arouse anxieties because they were imperfectly understood or imperfectly assimilated or because automobile lights could never become a "natural" African symbol; these were technologies that exposed other kinds of relationships. The presence of bells or cars without lights in so many personal narratives about vampires revealed the extent to which these new tools and technologies meant something terrifying to individual Africans. They were not terrifying in and of themselves but because of how they were used and by whom. In Edwardian England the stirrups became an important symbol of the abuses of gynecology and vivisection; at the same time stirrups figured in the era's pornography.[114] This is not because there was anything incomprehensible about the stirrup, but because stirrups could be used to represent domination, not mobility or sportsmanship, in a variety of contexts. In eastern Africa, the relationships revealed by the new technologies of cars and bells and lights were those of hard control: intrusive to the point of extracting blood, intensive to the point of supervising skilled labor on the job or after hours. Men and women in Uganda who translated *bazimyomwoto* as "the men who turn off the light" had a powerful, mechanical term to describe the work that extracted blood, the skilled Africans who carried it out, and the whites who supervised them. Naming the vampires after what they did to a car pronounced their work unnatural; it made it clear that these tasks were performed at night, well beyond the standards and the norms of the working day. Thus the term captured the distinctions between the skilled workers, the European overseers, and the population their job it was to abduct.[115]

But how are we to make sense of these particular arrangements of metal and electric lights and blood? Which was most horrible, the draining of blood or the use and abuse of familiar tools and trucks? Certainly the way that vehicles without lights, rubber pumps, or bells became compelling images in these stories made statements about the nature of modernity and progress,[116] but these images were always activated by employed Africans. In Kampala the bazimyomwoto "employed agents who lived among the people and had cars."[117] But was it the owners, the drivers, or the cars that took the blood? Such a question may make distinctions that these narratives studiously avoided. While my informants were crystal clear that the bazimyomwoto were humans, most described the technological aspects of human agency. They did not make a clear-cut boundary between man and machine, and if we attempt to impose such a line, we may lose sight of their questions and anxieties: If someone works with specific tools in a specific mechanized space, or even when he is taken to donate blood in a fire engine, how can he retain his masculinity, his humanity? What kind of being lives in a truck with curtained windows, and what kind of beings reproduce in the backseat of parked cars?[118]

Conclusions

Why vampires? Why did African men represent the conflicts and problematics of the new economic order in stories about public employees who suck blood? The simplest answer is perhaps best: no other idea could carry the weight of the complications of work, identities, and machines. First, it is a metaphor of colonial origin; despite official attempts to link it to "traditional" practices, banyama or bazimyomwoto emerged in the late 1910s and early 1920s.[119] Second, witchcraft accusations—which do not have the same meaning in the areas under discussion—blame misfortune on individuals; they seek to redress, or at least explain, wrongs. Vampire accusations do not have the same kind of specificity. Although individuals are named and blamed and sometimes even attacked, they were identified as agents, as part of a chain of command: they were not identified in order to get them to reverse their actions; they were identified in order to assess responsibility. Vampires were new symbols for new times.[120] And this made them uniquely well suited to represent the conflicts and ambiguities of labor, because vampiric firemen were not an established fact: many people doubted their existence, and insisted that the rumors began when Africans misconstrued European actions. The debate was not merely about whether or not colonial vampires existed but about the nature and the attributes of certain kinds of labor. The disputable character of wazimamoto was precisely its importance; such disagreements continually posed the questions, Did an identifiably separate group of skilled laborers exist? And, if they did, what was their impact on the wider society?

Notes

Research for this chapter was supported by the Division of Humanities at Rice University, the Graduate School at the University of Minnesota, the Institute for the Humanities at the University of Michigan, the American Philosophical Society, and the National Endowment for the Humanities. I would like to thank my research assistants, Odhiambo Opiyo in Siaya, Kenya, and Fred Bukulu, Remigius Kigongo, Godfrey Kigozi, and William Wagaba in Kampala, Uganda. Mark Auslander, Misty Bastian, William Beinart, Jeanne Bergman, Frederick Cooper, Susan Geiger, Gillian Feeley-Harnik, Ivan Karp, Randall Packard, Stuart Schwartz, and Ann Laura Stoler commented on earlier drafts.

1. I am using the term "vampire" with some hesitation. On the one hand, I do not want to submerge an autonomous African category—bloodsucker or blood drinker—in a European one; but on the other, I would like this work to make sense outside of Africa, and to access the confusions about gender embodied in blood accusations that is a hallmark of *Dracula* scholarship: the removal of blood by the penetration of subcutaneous fluids queries conventional ideas about penetration, orifices, and men and women. See Christopher Craft, "'Kiss Me with Those Red Lips': Gender and Inversion in Bram Stoker's *Dracula*," *Representations* 8 (1984): 107–133; Phyllis A. Roth, "Suddenly Sexual Women in Bram Stoker's *Dracula*," *Literature and Psychology* 27, no. 3 (1977): 113–121; and Stephanie Demetrakopoulos, "Feminism, Sex Role Exchanges, and Other Subliminal Fantasies in Bram Stoker's *Dracula*," *Frontiers: A Journal of Women's Studies* 11, no. 3 (1977): 104–113. Moreover, *Dracula* is a story about racial differences: vampires are not simply undead humans, but a separate group with a distinctive method of feeding and reproduction; see John Allen Stevenson, "A Vampire in the Mirror: The Sexuality of Dracula," *Proceedings of the Modern Language Association* 103, no. 2 (1988): 139–149; and Stephen D. Arata, "The Occidental Tourist: *Dracula* and the Anxiety of Reverse Colonization," *Victorian Studies* 33, no. 4 (1990): 621–645.

2. See Geoffrey Hodges, *The Carrier Corps: Military Labor in the East African Campaign* (Westport, Conn., 1986), 120–139, 206–210.

3. Frantz Fanon, *The Wretched of the Earth,* trans. Constance Farrington (New York, 1963), 56, 58.

4. Megan Vaughan, *The Story of an African Famine: Gender and Famine in Twentieth-Century Malawi* (Cambridge, 1987), vii.

5. Hortense Powdermaker, *Copper Town: Changing Africa* (New York, 1962), 62; Peter Fraenkel, *Wayaleshi* (London, 1959), 196–200; Arnold Leonard Epstein, "Unconscious Factors in the Response to Social Crisis: A Case Study from Central Africa," *Psychoanalytic Study of Society* 8 (1979): 3–39.

6. David Lan, *Guns and Rain: Guerrillas and Spirit Mediums in Zimbabwe* (London, 1985), xv–xvii.

7. Michael T. Taussig, *The Devil and Commodity Fetishism in South America* (Chapel Hill, N.C., 1980), 230.

8. See Ann Laura Stoler, "'In Cold Blood': Hierarchies of Credibility and the Politics of Colonial Narratives," *Representations* 37 (1992): 151–189.

9. See Bill Ashcroft, Gareth Griffiths, and Helen Tiffin, *The Empire Writes Back: Theory and Practice in Postcolonial Literatures* (London, 1989); Kwame Anthony Appiah, "Is the Post- in Postmodernism the Post- in Postcolonial?" *Critical Inquiry* 17, no. 2 (1991): 336–357; Ian Baucom, "Dreams of Home: Colonialism and Postmodernism," *Research in African Literatures* 22, no. 4 (1991), 5–27.

10. Frederick Cooper, "From Free Labor to Family Allowances: Labor and African Society in Colonial Discourse," *American Ethnologist* 16, no. 4 (1989): 745–765; Kristin Mann, *Marrying Well: Marriage, Status, and Social Change Among the Educated Elite in Colonial Lagos* (Cambridge, 1985); William Beinart and Colin Bundy, *Hidden Struggles in Rural South Africa* (London, 1987).

11. John Iliffe, *A Modern History of Tanganyika* (Cambridge, 1979), 314–338; Charles H. Ambler, *Kenyan Communities in the Age of Imperialism* (New Haven, 1987); Ian Goldin, "The Reconstitution of Coloured Identity in the Western Cape," in *The Politics of Race, Class, and Nationalism in Twentieth-Century South Africa*, ed. Shula Marks and Stanley Trapido, 156–181 (London, 1987); David William Cohen and E. S. Atieno Odhiambo, *Siaya: The Historical Anthropology of an African Landscape* (London, 1989), 25–35; Leroy Vail, ed., *The Creation of Tribalism in Southern Africa* (Berkeley, 1989).

12. David Arnold, "European Orphans and Vagrants in India in the Nineteenth Century," *Journal of Imperial and Commonwealth History* 7, no. 2 (1979), 104–127; Dane Kennedy, *Islands of White: Settler Society and Culture in Kenya and Southern Rhodesia, 1890–1939* (Durham, N.C., 1987); Waltraud Ernst, "The European Insane in British India, 1800–1858: A Case Study in Psychiatry and Colonial Rule," in *Imperial Medicine and Indigenous Societies,* ed. David Arnold, 27–44 (Manchester, Eng., 1988); Ann Laura Stoler, "Rethinking Colonial Categories: European Communities and the Boundaries of Rule," *Comparative Studies in Society and History* 31, no. 1 (1989): 134–161.

13. Frederick Cooper, *From Slaves to Squatters: Plantation Labor in Zanzibar and Coastal Kenya, 1890–1925* (New Haven, 1980); and *On the African Waterfront: Urban Disorder and the Transformation of Work in Colonial Mombasa* (New Haven, 1987); Louise Lennihan, "Rights in Men and Rights in Land: Slavery, Labor, and Smallholder Agriculture in Northern Nigeria," *Slavery and Abolition* 3, no. 2 (1982): 111–139; Suzanne Miers and Richard Roberts, eds., *The End of Slavery in Africa* (Madison, 1988); Dipesh Chakrabarty, "Conditions for Knowledge of Working-Class Conditions: Employers, Government, and the Jute Workers of Calcutta, 1890–1940," *Subaltern Studies* 2 (1983): 259–310.

14. Marjorie Mbilinyi, "Runaway Wives in Colonial Tanganyika: Forced Labour and Forced Marriage in Rungwe District, 1919–1961," *International Journal of the Sociology of Law* 16 (1988): 1–29; and "'This Is Unforgettable Business': Colonial State Intervention in Urban Tanzania," in Jane L. Parpart and Kathleen A. Staudt, *Women and the State in Africa* (Boulder, Colo., 1989), 111–129; Philip L. Bonner, "Family, Crime, and Political Consciousness on the East Rand, 1939–1955," *Journal of Southern African Studies* 14, no. 3 (1988): 393–420; Luise White, *The Comforts of Home: Prostitution in Colonial Nairobi* (Chicago, 1990), 65–72, 126–146, 212–217, 221–228.

15. Ranajit Guha, "The Prose of Counter-Insurgency," *Subaltern Studies* 2 (1983): 1–42; Michael T. Taussig, *Shamanism, Colonialism, and the Wild Man: A Study*

in Terror and Healing (Chicago, 1987), 2–134; Frederick Cooper, "Mau Mau and the Discourses of Decolonization," *Journal of African History* 29, no. 2 (1988): 313–320. For gendered critiques, see Lata Mani, "Contentious Traditions: The Debate on SATI in Colonial India," *Cultural Critique* 7 (1987): 119–156; and Luise White, "Separating the Men from the Boys: The Construction of Sexuality, Gender, and Terrorism in Central Kenya, 1939–59," *International Journal of African Historical Studies* 25, no. 1 (1990): 1–25.

16. Homi K. Bhabha, "Signs Taken for Wonders: Questions of Ambivalence and Authority Under a Tree Outside Delhi, May 1817," *Critical Inquiry* 12 (1985): 144–165; David Arnold, "Touching the Body: Perspectives on the Indian Plague, 1896–1900," *Subaltern Studies* 5 (1987): 55–90; Achille Mbembe, "Domaines de la nuit et autorité onirique dans les Maquis du Sud-Cameroun, 1955–1958," *Journal of African History* 32, no. 1 (1991): 89–121; and Gayatri Spivak, quoted in Henry Louis Gates, Jr., "Critical Fanonism," *Critical Inquiry* 17 (1991): 466.

17. Arnold, "European Orphans," 104–127; Randall M. Packard, "The 'Healthy Reserve' and the 'Dressed Native': Discourses on Black Health and the Language of Legitimation in South Africa," *American Ethnologist* 16, no. 4 (1989): 686–703; Ann Laura Stoler, "Carnal Knowledge and Imperial Power: Gender, Race, and Morality in Colonial Asia," in *Gender at the Crossroads of Knowledge: Feminist Anthropology in the Postmodern Era,* ed. Micaela di Leonardo, 51–101 (Berkeley, 1991).

18. Jan Vansina, *Oral Tradition* (Chicago, 1967); and Vansina, *Oral Tradition as History* (Madison, 1985); David Henige, *The Chronology of Oral Tradition: Quest for a Chimera* (Oxford, 1974); Joseph C. Miller, ed., *The African Past Speaks: Essays on Oral Tradition and History* (Folkstone, Eng., 1980); Luc de Heusch, *The Drunken King; or, The Origin of the State,* trans. Roy Willis (Bloomington, Ind., 1982); V. Y. Mudimbe, *Parables and Fables: Exegesis, Textuality, and Politics in Central Africa* (Madison, 1991), 86–138.

19. Vansina, *Oral Tradition as History,* 12–13; White, *Comforts of Home,* 21–28. In this way, the study of witchcraft or of men who turned into lions became primarily the domain of anthropologists, not historians.

20. Claire C. Robertson, "In Pursuit of Life Histories: The Problem of Bias," *Frontiers* 7, no. 2 (1983): 63–69; Susan N. G. Geiger, "Women's Life Histories: Content and Method," *Signs: Journal of Women in Culture and Society* 11, no. 2 (1986): 334–351; and "What's So Feminist About Women's Oral History," *Journal of Women's History* 2, no. 1 (1990): 169–182; Marjorie Mbilinyi, "'I'd Have Been a Man': Politics and the Labor Process in Producing Personal Narratives," and Marjorie Shostak, "'What the Wind Won't Take Away': The Genesis of *Nisa—The Life and Words of a !Kung Woman,*" in Personal Narratives Group, *Interpreting Women's Lives: Feminist Theory and Personal Narratives* (Bloomington, Ind., 1989), 204–227, 228–240.

21. Johannes Fabian, *Time and the Other: How Anthropology Makes Its Object* (New York, 1983); and James Clifford and George E. Marcus, eds., *Writing Culture: The Poetics and Politics of Ethnography* (Berkeley, 1986). In African history, the disaffection with the ethnographic object was as much a product of the researches of nationalist historiography as it was of debates in anthropology; see Steven Feierman, *Peasant Intellectuals: Anthropology and History in Tanzania* (Madison, 1990), 13–17.

22. There is a useful summary of literary debates in Gates, "Critical Fanonism," 457–470; but see Gayatri Chakrovarty Spivak, "Can the Subaltern Speak?" in *Marxism*

and the Interpretation of Culture, ed. Cary Nelson and Lawrence Grossberg, 127–157 (Urbana, Ill., 1988). For debates within oral history and anthropology, see also Vansina, *Oral Tradition as History,* 18–21; Sidney W. Mintz, "The Sensation of Moving, While Standing Still," *American Ethnologist* 16, no. 4 (1989): 786–796; and J. B. Peires, "Suicide or Genocide? Xhosa Perceptions of the Nongqawuse Catastrophe," *Radical History Review* 46, no. 7 (1990): 47–57.

23. See Mary Smith, *Baba of Karo: A Woman of the Muslim Hausa* (London, 1954; new ed., New Haven, 1981); Marjorie Shostak, *Nisa: The Life and Words of a !Kung Woman* (New York, 1983); Jean Davison with the women of Mutira, *Voices from Mutira: Lives of Rural Gikuyu Women* (Boulder, Colo., 1989); Margaret Strobel and Sarah Mirza, *Three Swahili Women: Life Histories from Mombasa, Kenya* (Bloomington, Ind., 1989); and the U.S.-produced Swahili edition, *Wanawake watatu wa Kiswahili: Hadithi za maisha kutoka Mombasa, Kenya* (Bloomington, Ind., 1991); Belinda Bozzoli with the assistance of Mmantho Nkotsoe, *Women of Phokeng: Consciousness, Life Strategy, and Migrancy in South Africa* (Portsmouth, N.H., 1991). The Swahili version of *Three Swahili Women* was published in the United States because no Kenyan publisher was interested; see Geiger, "Women's Life Histories," 182n. The life histories of women tend to proclaim their authenticity; see Domitila Barrios de Chungara and Moema Viezzer, *Let Me Speak! Testimony of Domitila, a Woman of the Bolivian Mines* (New York, 1978), while those of men are often summarized by scholars, without apology; see Hoyt Alverson, *Mind in the Heart of Darkness: Value and Self-Identity Among the Tswana of Southern Africa* (New Haven, 1978); Tim Keegan, *Facing the Storm: Portraits of Black Lives in Rural South Africa* (London, 1988); and Paul Lubeck, "Petroleum and Proletarianization: The Life History of a Muslim Nigerian Worker," *African Economic History* 18 (1989): 99–112. For a notable exception, see Allen Isaacman, ed., *The Life History of Roul Honwana: An Inside View of Colonialism to Independence, 1905–75* (Boulder, Colo., 1988).

24. Gyan Prakesh, "Writing Post-Orientalist Histories of the Third World: Perspectives from Indian Historiography," *Comparative Studies in Society and History* 32, no. 2 (1990): 383–408; see also Gates, "Critical Fanonism," 457–460.

25. Timothy Mitchell, *Colonizing Egypt* (Berkeley, 1991), 60.

26. See Feierman, *Peasant Intellectuals,* 245–264; and Jean and John L. Comaroff, "Goodly Beasts, Beastly Goods: Cattle and Commodities in a South African Context," *American Ethnologist* 17, no. 2 (1990): 195–216; Sharon Hutchinson, "The Cattle of Money and the Cattle of Girls Among the Neur, 1930–83," *American Ethnologist* 19, no. 2 (1992): 294–316.

27. See, for example, the freewheeling discussion of *Dracula* in Franco Moretti, *Signs Taken for Wonders: Essays in the Sociology of Literary Forms* (New York, 1983), 90–104; and Taussig's account of the Nakaq, the fat-extracting phantasm of the southern highlands of Peru, *Devil and Commodity Fetishism,* 238.

28. For urban women's stories, see Luise White, "Bodily Fluids and Usufruct: Controlling Property in Nairobi, 1919–39," *Canadian Journal of African Studies* 24, no. 3 (1990): 418–438.

29. Peter Hayombe, Uhunyi Village, Alego, Siaya District, Kenya, 20 August 1986; see also Menya Mauwa, Uchonga Village, Alego, Siaya District, Kenya, 19 August 1986.

30. Zebede Oyoyo, Goma Village, Yimbo, Siaya District, Kenya, 13 August 1986.

31. Anyango Mahondo, Sigoma Village, Alego, Siaya District, Kenya, 15 August 1986. Throughout the interview Mahondo insisted that my assistant, Odhiambo Opiyo, not tell me about his days as a policeman, despite the fact that I was sitting between them and Opiyo and I were conferring in English during the interview.

32. Zebede Oyoyo.

33. Rodney Needham, "Blood, Thunder, and the Mockery of Animals," *Sociologus* 14, no. 2 (1964): 136–149; Victor Turner, *The Forest of Symbols: Aspects of Ndembu Ritual* (Ithaca, N.Y., 1967), 41–42, 59–81, 249–251; de Heusch, *The Drunken King,* 168–173.

34. In Kenya in 1939 there was a spate of rumors about blankets saturated with a medicine that would make men impotent: this was a semen story, to be sure, and it involved Europeans, technology, and commodities, but it did not involve labor; *Nairobi District Annual Report,* 1939, p. 3, Kenya National Archives (KNA)/CP4/4/1.

35. George Ggingo, Kasubi, Uganda, 15 August 1990.

36. Ofwete Muriar, Uchonga Village, Alego, Siaya District, Kenya, 11 August 1986; see also Kersau Ntale Mwene, Kasubi, Uganda, 12 August 1990; Joseph Nsubuga, Kisati, Uganda, 22 August 1990; letter to the editor, *The Standard* (Tanzania), 2 February 1972, 6.

37. S. Lolila, "Firemen Are Not 'Chinja-Chinja,'" *The Standard,* 10 January 1972, 3. *Chinja-chinja* is the intensive form of the word for "slaughterer" and is sometimes used interchangeably with the local term for vampire in East Africa.

38. Letter, *The Standard,* 2 February 1972, 6.

39. Gregory Sseruwagi, Lubya, Uganda, 28 August 1990.

40. Rik Ceyssens, "Mutumbula: Mythe de l'opprime," *Cultures et développement* 7, nos. 3–4 (1975): 485–550; Mwelwa C. Musambachime, "The Impact of Rumor: The Case of Banyama (Vampire-Men) Scare in Northern Rhodesia, 1930–1964," *International Journal of African Historical Studies* 21, no. 2 (1988): 201–215.

41. Anyango Mahondo.

42. Ibid.

43. V. W. Brelsford, "The 'Banyama' Myth," *NADA* (Ministry of Internal Affairs, Salisbury, Rhodesia) 9, no. 4 (1967): 54–56: J. A. K. Leslie, pers. comm., 13 March 1990; Graham Thompson, pers. comm., 28 August 1990; Atieno Odhiambo, pers. comm., 31 December 1990.

44. Abdullah Sonsomola, Kisenyi, Uganda, 28 August 1990.

45. Peter Fraenkel, *Wayaleshi* (London, 1959), 201.

46. Samuel Mubiru, Lubya, Uganda, 28 August 1990. But according to E. E. Hutchins, district officer in Morogoro with many years experience in Tanganyika,

> The old story that certain Europeans wandered about the country seeking human blood for the purpose of making medicine was revived, I believe, some years ago in the Kiloga District, where officers of the Veterinary Department collected blood in test tubes from numbers of natives for the purpose of finding out whether yellow fever had ever been endemic in the Territory.

Morogoro District, vol. 1, part A, sheets 25–26, August 1931, film no. MF15, Tanzanian National Archives (TNA).

47. W. Arens, *The Man-Eating Myth: Anthropology and Anthropophagy* (Oxford, 1979), 12–13.

48. Michael Macoun, pers. comm., 13 March 1990.

49. Brelsford, "The 'Banyama' Myth," 54.

50. Thomas Fox-Pitt, District Commissioner, Mpika, to Provincial Commissioner, Northern Province, Kasama, 6 March 1939, National Archives of Zambia (NAZ)/SEC2/429, Native Affairs: Banyama.

51. Elspeth Huxley, *The Sorcerer's Apprentice: A Journey Through East Africa* (London, 1948), 23.

52. E. S. Atieno Odhiambo, "The Movement of Ideas: A Case Study of the Intellectual Responses to Colonialism Among the Liganua Peasants," in *Hadith 6: History and Social Change in East Africa,* ed. Bethwell A. Ogot, 172 (Nairobi, 1976).

53. John Barnes, Fort Jameson, Northern Rhodesia, to J. Clyde Mitchell, Rhodes-Livingstone Institute, Lusaka, 10 October 1948, J. C. Mitchell Papers, Rhodes House, Oxford, MSS. Afr. s. 1998/4/1.

54. Darrell Bates, *The Mango and the Palm* (London, 1962), 51–53.

55. K. D. Leaver, "The 'Transformation of Men to Meat' Story," NADform Information Sheet no. 20, Native Affairs Department, Salisbury, November 1960, p. 2, National Archives, Zimbabwe; Brelsford, "The 'Banyama' Myth," 54–55. Similar stories about pigs were commonplace in the southern Belgian Congo in the 1940s; see Ceyssens, "Mutumbula," 586–587.

56. Author's field notes, 18 August 1986.

57. N. W. Cavendish, Commissioner, Kenya Police, to Chief Secretary, Nairobi, 11 March 1939, KNA/CS/1/19/4, Fire Fighting in East Africa, 1933–46; see also the Luganda newspaper *Matalisi,* 25 March 1925, 6–7, Makarere University Library; *Uganda Herald,* 24 April 1931, 1; *Uganda Police Annual Report, 1950* (Kampala, 1951), 29–30; *Uganda Police Annual Report, 1951* (Kampala, 1952), 34; *Uganda Police Annual Report, 1952* (Kampala, 1953), 33–34; Works and Public Health Committee, 10 May 1938, KNA/PC/NBI/2/53, Municipal Nairobi Council Minutes, 1938.

58. Nichodamus Okumu Ogutu, Uhuyi Village, West Alego, Siaya District, Kenya, 28 August 1986.

59. Nairobi Fire Commission, 1926, KNA/AG4/3068; J. B. Powell, Superintendent, Nairobi Fire Brigade, Annual Report, 1935, KNA/PC/NBI/2/50, Nairobi Municipal Council Minutes, January–June 1936.

60. "'Human Vampire' Story Incites Mombasa Mob's Fire Station Attack," *East African Standard,* 21 June 1947, 3; Kenya Colony and Protectorate, *Report on Native Affairs, 1939–47* (London, 1948), 83; George to Elspeth Huxley, 20 January n.d., Elspeth Huxley Papers, Rhodes House, Oxford, RH MSS. Afr. s. 782, box 2/2, Kenya (1).

61. William H. Friedland, "Some Urban Myths of East Africa," in *Myth in Modern Africa,* ed. Allie Dubb, 94 (Lusaka, 1960).

62. In 1959 in Kampala, a man was sentenced to three years in prison for attempting to sell another man to the fire station, but the fear of the fire station and the fire brigade in and of itself never entered the oral record in Uganda. See "Three Years for Attempt to Sell Man," *Uganda Argus,* 16 February 1959, 5; "Firemen Do Not Buy People," *Tanganyika Standard,* 16 February 1959, 3.

63. Eric Mottram, *Blood on the Nash Ambassador: Investigations in American Culture* (London, 1983), 62 ff. Such concerns are articulated in popular idioms in diverse

contexts; see Barbara Allen, "'The Image on Glass': Technology, Tradition, and the Emergence of Folklore," *Western Folklore* 41 (1982), 85–103; and Caroline Walker Bynum, "Material Continuity, Personal Survival, and the Resurrection of the Body: A Scholastic Discussion in its Medieval and Modern Contexts," *History of Religions* 30, no. 1 (1990): 51–85.

64. See, for example, Jan Harold Brunvand, *The Vanishing Hitchhiker: American Urban Legends and Their Meanings* (New York, 1981), 19–46; and *The Choking Doberman* (New York, 1984), 50–68.

65. Stewart Sanderson, "The Folklore of the Motor-Car," *Folklore* 80 (1969): 241–242.

66. See Sanderson's collection of rumors about the Rolls-Royce, ibid., 246–247; and F. H. Moorhouse, "The 'Work' Ethic and 'Leisure' Activity: The Hot Rod in Post-War America," in *The Historical Meanings of Work,* ed. Patrick Joyce, 244 (Cambridge, 1987).

67. Warren James Belasco, *Americans on the Road: From Autocamp to Motel, 1910–1945* (Cambridge, Mass., 1981), 8.

68. See Mary Douglas, *Purity and Danger: An Analysis of the Concepts of Pollution and Taboo* (London, 1984), 35, 85.

69. In 1935 nine and a half hours of a Nairobi fireman's day were devoted to "station duties" and maintaining equipment, and the nightly lookout had to report "every fifteen minutes. . . . This is salutary from a disciplinary point of view, as well as keeping the guard awake"; J. B. Powell, Superintendent, Nairobi Municipal Fire Brigade AE, 1935, Nairobi Municipal Council Minutes, January–June 1936, KNA/PC/NBI2/50.

70. Daniel Sekirrata, Katwe, Uganda, 22 August 1990.

71. Dead bodies transported in vehicles were another matter, however. Corpses were purchased from hospitals and driven to Zaire. Several men "transported dead bodies in the backseat of his car. These bodies were always smartly dressed." A few others sold corpses "to Senegalese who used them to safely transport their gold in. These dead bodies were cut through the skin, opened inside, and then gold could be dumped there. If the authorities tried to arrest them, these people could claim they were taking sick relatives for treatment." Ahmed Kiziri, Katwe, Uganda, 20 August 1990; Musoke Kopliumu, Katwe, Uganda, 22 August 1990; Daniel Sekirrata, Katwe, Uganda, 22 August 1990; Gregory Sseruwagi, Lubya, Uganda, 28 August 1990.

72. Sepirya Kasule, Kisenyi, Uganda, 28 August 1990.

73. George Ggingo, Kasubi, Uganda, 15 August 1990.

74. Noah Asingo Olungu, Goma Village, Yimbo, Siaya District, Kenya, 22 August 1986.

75. Simbwa Jjuko, Lwaze, Uganda, 20 August 1990.

76. Peter Hayombe.

77. Domitila Achola, Uchonga Ukudi Village, Alego, Siaya District, Kenya, 11 August 1986; Alozius Kironde, Kasubi, Uganda, 17 August 1990.

78. Alozius Kironde, Kasubi, Uganda, 17 August 1990.

79. Margaret Mwajuma, Ndegro Uranga Village, Alego, Siaya, Kenya, 11 August 1986.

80. Brelsford, "The 'Banyama' Myth," 54–56.

81. Gregory Sseruwagi, Lubya, Uganda, 28 August 1990.

82. Anyango Mahondo.

83. See White, "Bodily Fluids," 425–431.

84. Ludmilla Jordanova, *Sexual Visions: Images of Gender in Science and Medicine Between the Eighteenth and Twentieth Centuries* (London, 1989), 92–93.

85. Washington, D.C., firefighters routinely complained that the public's ignorance of fire fighting increased the likelihood of fires while maintaining that the techniques and challenges of their work made it too esoteric to make public; see Robert McCarl, *The District of Columbia Fire Fighters' Project: A Case Study in Occupational Folklife* (Washington, D.C., 1985), 131–136.

86. Bates, *Mango and Palm;* 53–54.

87. George Ggingo; see also Mangarita Kalule, Masanafu, Uganda, 20 August 1990; Juliana Nakibuka Naloongo, Lubaga, Uganda, 21 August 1990; Joseph Nsubuge, Kisati, Uganda, 22 August 1990; Musoke Kopliumu, Katwe, Kampala, Uganda, 22 August 1990; Gregory Sseruwagi, Lubya, Uganda, 28 August 1990.

88. Karl Marx, *Capital, A Critique of Political Economy,* vol. 1 (Harmondsworth, Eng., 1976), 279–280.

89. Alec Okaro, Mahero Village, Alego, Siaya District, Kenya, 12 August 1986.

90. McCarl, *District of Columbia Fire Fighters' Project,* 39, 136–140. Apprenticeship, however, was often parodied by religious movements in colonial Zaire; see Edouard Bustin, "Government Policy Toward African Cult Movements: The Cases of Katanga," in *African Dimensions: Essays in Honor of William O. Brown,* ed. Mark Karp, 117 (Boston, 1975).

91. J. B. Powell, Superintendent, *Nairobi Municipal Fire Brigade Annual Report, 1935,* Nairobi Municipal Council Minutes, January–June 1936, KNA/PC/NBI/2/50.

92. Anyango Mahondo.

93. Brelsford, "The 'Banyama' Myth," 55.

94. Jack Santino, "'Flew the Ocean in a Plane': An Investigation of Airline Occupation Narrative," *Journal of the Folklore Institute* 15, no. 3 (1978): 202–207.

95. A miner quoted in June Nash, "The Devil in Bolivia's Nationalized Tin Mines," *Science and Society* 36, no. 2 (1972): 227; for another interpretation, see Taussig, *Devil and Commodity Fetishism,* 207–213.

96. Jeff Guy, "Technology, Ethnicity, and Ideology: Basotho Miners and Shaft Sinking on the South African Gold Mines," *Journal of Southern African Studies* 14, no. 2 (1988): 260–269.

97. Alec Okaro.

98. Sepirya Kasule. In Buhaya, just across the border in Tanzania, in the 1980s it was said that anyone who opened a door that warned "hatari umeme!" (danger electricity!) would die at once, and his body would be tossed in a pit in back. See Brad Weiss, "Electric Vampires: Haya Rumors of Wealth" (Paper presented at American Ethnological Society, Memphis, March 1992).

99. Guy, "Technology, Ethnicity, and Ideology," 269, gives a particularly graphic example of a point that has been made both by Antonio Gramsci ("The history of industrialism has always been a continuing struggle . . . against the element of 'animality' in man") and in studies of antivivisection movements; see Antonio Gramsci, *Selections from the Prison Notebooks,* ed. and trans. Quintin Hoare and Geoffrey Nowell

Smith, 297–298 (New York, 1971); Coral Lansbury, *The Old Brown Dog: Women, Workers, and Vivisection in Edwardian England* (Madison, 1985), 83–119; and Susan Sperling, *Animal Liberators: Research and Morality* (Berkeley, 1990), 141–143.

100. Quoted in Lloyd William Swantz, "The Role of Medicine Men Among the Zaramo of Dar es Salaam" (Ph.D. dissertation, University of Dar es Salaam, 1972), 336.

101. John Higginson, "Steam Without a Piston Box: Strikes and Popular Unrest in Katanga, 1943–1945," *International Journal of African Historical Studies* 21, no. 1 (1988): 101–102.

102. Timotheo Omondo, Goma Village, Yimbo, Siaya District, Kenya, 22 August 1986.

103. Anyango Mahondo.

104. This point comes from two articles by Jack Santino: "Miles of Smiles, Years of Struggle: The Negotiation of Black Occupational Identity Through the Personal Experience Narrative," *Journal of American Folklore* 96, no. 382 (1983): 394–412; and "Occupational Ghostlore: Social Context and the Expression of Belief," *Journal of American Folklore* 101, no. 400 (1988): 207–218.

105. In the classic sense, misfortune is something that requires an explanation, such as why a granary in Azande country collapsed on specific people; see E. E. Evans-Pritchard, *Witchcraft, Oracles, and Magic Among the Azande* (Oxford, 1976), 22–23. Vampire accusations do not explain disappearances or deaths; indeed, the fact that someone had disappeared was offered as "proof" that the firemen did kidnap people; see above.

106. Nyakida Omolo, Kabura, West Alego, Siaya District, Kenya, 19 August 1986.

107. F. H. Moorhouse, "The Marxist Theory of the Labour Aristocracy," *Social History* 3, no. 1 (1978): 64–66.

108. Daniel R. Headrick, *The Tools of Empire: Technology and European Imperialism in the Nineteenth Century* (Oxford, 1981); and Michael Adas, *Machines as the Measures of Men: Science, Technology, and Ideologies of Western Dominance* (Ithaca, N.Y., 1989).

109. See Ivan Karp, "Other Cultures in Museum Perspective," in Karp and Steven D. Levine, *Exhibiting Cultures: The Poetics and Politics of Museum Displays* (Washington, D.C., 1991), 373–385.

110. *Mutende* (Lusaka) no. 38 (1936), NAZ/SEC2/429, Native Affairs: Banyama; Eustace Njbovu, Kapani, Luangwa, Zambia, 22 July 1990.

111. Ceyssens, "Mutumbula," 491.

112. Quoted in Swantz, "Medicine Men," 336.

113. Gary Allen Fine, "The Kentucky Fried Rat: Legends and Modern Society," *Journal of the Folklore Institute* 17, nos. 2–3 (1980): 237; Allen, "'Image on Glass,'" 103; Bynum, "Material Continuity," 64.

114. Lansbury, *Old Brown Dog*, 99–111.

115. Moretti, *Signs Taken for Wonders*, makes a similar point about horror literature, particularly *Frankenstein* and *Dracula:* both represent the extremes of a society, he argues; "The literature of terror is born *precisely out of the terror of a split society,* and out of the desire to heal it" (p. 83).

116. See Jordanova, *Sexual Visions*, 111.

117. Samuel Mubiru.

118. *Embalasassa,* the mythical "poisonous reptiles that politicians never wanted to talk about publicly," were said to be sent by Milton Obote during his first regime to kill the Baganda people; they could also breed in machines. "Somewhere . . . near Kaziba market [on the Tanzanian border] there was something made out of an old army tank that the villagers broke into only to discover *embalasassa* eggs inside''; Jonah Waswa Kigozi, Katwe, Uganda, 16 August 1990; Alozius Matovu, Kasubi, Uganda, 17 August 1990; see also W. B. Banage, W. N. Byarugaba, and J. D. Goodman, "The *Embalasassa (Riopa fernandi):* A Story of Real and Mythical Zoology,'' *Uganda Journal* 36 (1972): 67–72.

119. Timotheo Omondo; E. E. Hutchins, District Officer, Morogoro, vol. I, pt. A, sheets 25–26, August 1931, film MF 15, TNA. D. Willis, Provincial Commissioner, Kasama, "Report on Banyama,'' 24 March 1931, NAZ/ZA1/9/62/6/1; Geoffrey Howe, Provincial Commissioner, Northern Province, Kasama, "Confidential Memo to All DCs, Northern Province,'' 24 April 1944, NAZ/SEC2/429, Native Affairs: Banyama.

120. See Moretti, *Signs Taken for Wonders,* 90–104; and Gabor Klaniczay, *The Uses of the Supernatural: The Transformation of Popular Religion in Medieval and Early Modern Europe,* trans. Susan Singerman (Princeton, N.J., 1990), 168–238.

Notes on Contributors

Homi Bhabha is the author of articles and collections on colonial and postcolonial literature, including *The Location of Culture* (1994). He teaches in the English Department of the University of Chicago.

Dipesh Chakrabarty is now Professor of History at the University of Chicago after having taught at the University of Melbourne. His publications include *Rethinking Working-Class History: Bengal 1890–1940* (1989).

Fanny Colonna is at the Centre National de Recherche Scientifique in Paris and author, most recently, of *Les versets de l'invincibilité: Permanence et changements religieux dans l'Algérie contemporaine* (1995).

John L. Comaroff is Professor of Anthropology at the University of Chicago and author with Jean Comaroff of *Of Revelation and Revolution: Christianity, Colonialism, and Consciousness in South Africa* (1991).

Frederick Cooper is Professor of History and in the Residential College at the University of Michigan. His most recent book is *Decolonization and African Society: The Labor Question in French and British Africa* (1996).

Anna Davin's *Growing Up Poor: Home, School and Street in London, 1870–1914* was published in 1996.

Nancy Rose Hunt is Assistant Professor of History at the University of Arizona. Her book, *A Colonial Lexicon: Hygiene and Birth Work in Upper Zaire,* will be published by Duke University Press.

461

Uday S. Mehta is Professor of Political Science at the University of Chicago. His book *The Anxiety of Freedom: Imagination and Individuality in Locke's Political Thought* was published in 1992.

Ann Stoler is Professor of Anthropology and of History at the University of Michigan and author, most recently, of *Race and the Education of Desire: Foucault's History of Sexuality and the Colonial Order of Things* (1995).

Susan Thorne is Assistant Professor of History at Duke University. She is completing a book entitled "Protestant Ethics and the Spirit of Imperialism: Evangelical Missions and the Making of an Imperial Culture in Nineteenth-Century Britain."

Luise White is author of *The Comforts of Home: Prostitution in Colonial Nairobi* (1990).

Lora Wildenthal is Assistant Professor of History at Pitzer College. She is completing a book on women and the colonization movement in Germany.

Gwendolyn Wright is Professor of Architecture and History at Columbia University. She is the author of *The Politics of Design in French Colonial Urbanism* (1991).

Index

Abolitionism. *See* Antislavery
Africa: anticolonial movements in, 268, 407–409, 411–416, 429n. 1; capitalism in, 164, 175–176, 182; competing colonialisms in, 5, 178–186, 188–193, 193n. 7; education in, 346–370; indigenous elites in, 352–353, 409–410; invention of, 4, 11–12, 166, 175, 191, 406; decolonization of, 406–435; labor in, 5, 29, 163–164, 180, 182, 183, 185, 248–249, 289, 297, 299–300, 406–435, 437, 439–440, 444–445, 448; missionaries in, 163–197, 291, 446; modernity of, 8, 181–183, 322–345, 408; race in, 185, 263–264, 266, 268–270, 273–277, 280–281, 293–297, 366n. 4, 437, 448; regulation of marriage in, 263–264, 267–273; regulation of reproductive practices in, 297, 308, 312n. 30, 431–432n.25; tensions of colonial rule in, 9–10, 163–166, 175, 178–193, 267–273, 409–416; tribe in, 4, 10, 11, 185, 410, 430n. 9. *See also* Breastfeeding; Education; France, colonies of; Germany, colonies of; Great Britain, colonies of; Missionaries
Afrikaners, 179, 180–181, 183–191, 268
Algeria, 7, 346–370
Alterity. *See* Difference
Anarchism, 64–65
Anderson, Benedict, 13, 22, 28, 154–155, 203, 223
Anglicanism. *See* England, Anglicanism in

Anthropology: colonialism and, 14–15, 38n. 9, 327; of colonialism, 5–6, 15, 38n. 9, 165, 192; development and, 17; feminism and, 38n. 11; political economy and, 16
Anticolonial movement, 2, 8, 34, 36, 333, 406–408, 411–416, 420–429. *See also* Nation; Nationalism
Antislavery, 2, 25, 30–31, 171, 175, 248–249, 252
Architecture. *See* Cities, architecture in; Modernism
Archives. *See* Knowledge, archives and
Ariès, Philippe, 374
Arnold, Matthew, 169, 184
Asad, Talal, 15

Bakhtin, Mikhail, 322
Balandier, George, 15
Balibar, Etienne, 199
Bandyopadhyay, Bhabanicharan, 384–392
Barthes, Roland, 400
Beidelman, Thomas, 176
Belgium, 288, 289–290
Belgium, colonies of, 287–321. *See also* Africa; Breastfeeding
Bengal, 373–405
Bentham, Jeremy, 71, 72
Berman, Bruce, 19–20
Beveridge Report, 129
Bhabha, Homi, 34
Biopower, 199. *See also* Eugenics; Motherhood; Population; Race; Racism

463

Compositor: Braun-Brumfield, Inc.
Text: Times Roman
Display: Helvetica
Printer: Braun-Brumfield, Inc.
Binder: Braun-Brumfield, Inc.